The Mystique of Transmission

Wendi L. Adamek

The Mystique of Transmission

ON AN EARLY CHAN HISTORY AND ITS CONTEXTS

Lidai fabao ji
Li-Tai Fa-Pao Chi

Columbia University Press
New York

Columbia University Press
Publishers Since 1893
New York Chichester, West Sussex

Columbia University Press and the author express appreciation to Barnard College, the Chiang Ching-kuo Foundation, and University Seminars at Columbia University for subvention grants that assisted in the publication of this book.

Library of Congress Cataloging-in-Publication Data
Adamek, Wendi Leigh.
The Mystique of transmission : on an early Chan history and its contexts /
Wendi L. Adamek.
p. cm.
Includes bibliographical references and index.
ISBN 13: 978-0-231-13664-8 (alk. paper) — ISBN 13: 978-0-231-51002-8 (e-book)
ISBN 10: 0-231-13664-1 (alk. paper) — ISBN 10: 0-231-51002-0 (e-book)
1. Zen Buddhism. I. Title. II. Title: On an early Chan history and its contexts.
BQ9265.4.A33 2006
294.3′927—dc22
2006026588

∞

Columbia University Press books are printed on
permanent and durable acid-free paper.

Printed in the United States of America

c 10 9 8 7 6 5 4 3 2 1

For the Venerable Wuzhu 無住

Contents

Acknowledgments

Working on a long-term project is an excellent exercise in interdependence, as one becomes aware that one's work is composed entirely of gifts and debts. However, this does not mean that one can dispense with the standard caveat: Nothing is mine alone but the mistakes, for which I take full responsibility.

As this is a dissertation-based project, my appreciations extend back to many teachers, mentors, and friends, but for the sake of brevity I will mention only those who contributed directly to this project. I am thankful to have studied, albeit too briefly, with the late Michel Strickmann. To Carl Bielefeldt and Bernard Faure I owe more than I can possibly express. My long graduate career gave me the privilege of getting to know them and their families, and I would also like to thank Dominique Choël-Faure for her warmth, good humor, and good advice. To Bernard I owe the guru-gift, for his work and example have shown me the value of life "at the crossroads." I have also been grateful for the fellowship and feedback of fellow students from Stanford and other institutions through the years, especially Helen Baroni, Michael Como, Franco Gatti, David Gardiner, Hank Glassman, Akemi Iwamoto, John Kieschnick, Max Moerman, Elizabeth Morrison, James Robson, and Jonathan Silk. I am especially grateful to Elizabeth Morrison for her careful reading of early drafts of this work.

During my three years of research in Kyoto, I received guidance and assistance from nearly everyone I met, as I was so clearly in need of it. My stay in Kyoto was made possible by the sponsorship of Professor Katsumi Mimaki of Kyoto University, whose erudition, warmth, and humor are a pleasure to recall. I would like to express special thanks to Professor

Yanagida Seizan for offering the hospitality of the International Research Institute for Zen Buddhism at Hanazono College, giving me many valuable research materials, and providing the research assistantship that made it possible for me to extend my stay in Japan. Professor Yanagida's seminars, as well as his awe-inspiring published work on early Chan, are part of the foundations of this project. I am also grateful to Professor Koga Hidehiko for allowing me to attend his seminar on the *Lidai fabao ji* at Hanazono College. Much appreciation is due to Urs App, who during his tenure as Professor Yanagida's assistant at the International Research Institute created many superlative electronic research tools for Chan/Zen scholars. My work also owes a great deal to weekly visits to my tutor Chizuko Inui, whose guidance is behind many Kyoto research projects. As I spent several years occupying a desk at the School of East Asian Studies of the Italian Institute of Kyoto, I cannot adequately express the extent of my gratitude to the former director of the school, the late Antonino Forte, for his generous hospitality and friendship. Dr. Michael Cooper, former editor of *Monumenta Nipponica,* has contributed many years of pep talks, good cheer, and excellent correspondence. I would also like to convey my respectful thanks to the late Morinaga Soko Rōshi of Daishū-in temple in Kyoto, Ursula Jarand and Daijō Minick of Daishū-in West in California, and the Venerable Chongmok of Haein-sa in Korea, for their encouragement and support.

Friends in the field have generously contributed time and energy to help this work along. I am grateful for Koichi Shinohara's helpful feedback during the dissertation stage of this project. Janine Sawada has been a staunch friend and an insightful reader of multiple drafts. My dear friend Anne Dutton helped me track down references when I was far from a library. Frederick Smith has been a loyal companion and champion through the many trials and tribulations of the completion process. Stephen Teiser and John McRae provided deeply appreciated suggestions and corrections for the final drafts of the book. I would also like to thank Barnard College colleagues Elizabeth Castelli, Celia Deutsch, Jack Hawley, and Dorothy Ko for their camaraderie and advice.

I have benefited greatly from time spent at the Zhongguo gudaishi yanjiu zhongxin (Institute for the Study of Ancient Chinese History) at Peking University, and my grateful thanks go to Professor Rong Xinjiang of the History Department for his hospitality and inspiring scholarship. I am also much indebted to Professor Shen Ruiwen of the Archaeology Department, and to the History Department graduate and postgraduate students Wang Jing, Su Hang, and Ji Aimin, for their generous assistance with this and other research efforts.

I would like to gratefully acknowledge Stanford University, the Foreign Language and Area Studies program, the Fulbright Program, the Bukkyū

Dendū Kyūkai (Society for the Preservation of Buddhism), the Jacob K. Javits Foundation, the University of Iowa, the Chiang Ching-kuo Foundation, and Barnard College, for the fellowships and grants that made this project possible. The editors at Columbia University Press and I would like to express our appreciation to Barnard College, the Chiang Ching-kuo Foundation, and University Seminars at Columbia University for generous subvention grants. Portions of this book were presented to the University Seminar on Buddhist Studies, and I benefited greatly from discussions of my work with colleagues at Barnard and at the Buddhist Studies Seminar. I extend grateful thanks to Wendy Lochner and the editors at Columbia University Press, and I would also like to acknowledge helpful editorial feedback received in the process of publishing portions of this work in *History of Religions* (© 2000 by The University of Chicago. All rights reserved), *Chan Buddhism in Ritual Context,* edited by Bernard Faure (2003), and *The Zen Canon,* edited by Steven Heine and Dale S. Wright (2004).

To all my relatives and closest friends—without you this work could never have come into being or made its way to completion, *me ke aloha pumehana*. I especially thank Margery Strass for her care and support in providing a quiet haven during the dissertation-writing stage, and Cynthia King for her excellent good sense and humor. And finally, much love and aloha to my brother, Brad Fitkin, and my sister, Lisa Fitkin, and their families, and to my mother and stepfather, Janet and George Allan, for their unfailing patience and wisdom.

PART 1

The Mystique of Transmission

CHAPTER 1

Authority and Authenticity

A word of praise is comparable to bestowing a princely robe;
a word of blame is as severe as capital punishment.
—Kong Yingda 孔穎達, *Chunqiu zhengyi*[1]

FABRICATIONS

Even among hagiographers the *Lidai fabao ji* 曆代法寶記 (Record of the Dharma-Jewel Through the Generations) has been called a fabric of self-promoting fictions. The text was discredited soon after it was written in the late eighth century, and it still provokes disparaging comments even now. The sharpest contemporary criticism is found in the *Beishan lu* 北山錄 (Record of North Mountain), completed in 806 by Shenqing 神清 (d. 814), a former adherent of the Jingzhong 淨眾 school.[2] According to a more recent assessment by the Chan historian John McRae, among texts of early Chan that indulge in "patent fabrications and questionable attributions," the *Lidai fabao ji* "is undoubtedly the most egregious of all."[3]

The *Lidai fabao ji* was long considered lost, and it was resurrected from among the manuscripts discovered in 1900 in the hidden library at the Mogao 莫高 caves near the Silk Road oasis of Dunhuang 敦煌. Until then, it was remembered only as a fraudulent history by a collateral branch of Chan, the Bao Tang 保唐 (Protect the Tang Dynasty) school of Jiannan 劍南 (Sichuan).[4] In this study I argue that the fabrications in the *Lidai fabao ji* are not simply inaccurate Chan history but faithfully reflect a temporary crisis in the meaning of spiritual transmission. Modern scholarship in Asia and the West has done much to distinguish fact from fiction in the accounts of Chan schools of the Tang. However, current scholarly practice also asks us to acknowledge that a quest for "facts" often reveals more about its own context than that of the apparent subject, while the fault-lines of fiction may admit echoes from the past that have been expunged from more authoritative works.

The *Lidai fabao ji* fabrication most frequently singled out for criticism is the story that the founder of their school, the Chan master Wuzhu 無住 (714–774), was in possession of the key Chan talisman, the robe of the "first patriarch" Bodhidharma (d. c. 530?). Later we trace the genealogy of works claiming that this robe was given to the sixth patriarch, Huineng 慧能 (638–713), by the fifth patriarch, Hongren 弘忍 (602–675). Only in *Lidai fabao ji* is it claimed that the robe was then given by the empress Wu Zetian 武則天 (r. 684–705) to a master in the lineage claimed by the Bao Tang school.[5] However, the *Lidai fabao ji* comes to an end after Wuzhu's death scene without having cleared up the mystery of the subsequent fate of Bodhidharma's robe and Wuzhu's Dharma.

One of the aims of the present study is to contextualize the Bao Tang transmission claim and thereby reinvest it with some of the vigor of its original presumption. In the course of investigating the background of this story, I examine the various characters and historical events that are implicated in the *Lidai fabao ji,* whose authors attempted to establish the place of the Bao Tang school within a chronicle of the history of Buddhism in China. My investigation involves tracing a number of different paths to a point of convergence in the late eighth century, when "Bodhidharma's robe" briefly became so hotly contested an item as to provoke tales of murder and intrigue.

It is clear that the *Lidai fabao ji*'s multifaceted and unorthodox (or pre-orthodox) account of Chan transmission was deployed as part of a strategy to claim authority—but what kind of authority? Whose standards of legitimacy were recognized by the author or authors of the text? I believe that these questions do not have a single answer, that the *Lidai fabao ji* reveals a number of conflicting forces at work. We can see the growing influence of the newly formulated Chan genealogical discourse, but we also discern doctrinal quandaries and succession anxieties unique to the Bao Tang.

In order to capture the polemical spirit of our inquiry, I quote an aggrieved comment written in the twentieth century, though it could well have been voiced in the ninth:

> If the true patriarchal power lay only in the robe, then the Empress Wu, as well as Chih-hsien, T'ang Ho-shang, and Wu-shiang [*sic*] must all have been patriarchs. Further, would Hui-neng have given up his robe, and consequently his power, at the mere request of Empress Wu? It is obvious that the patriarchal succession involves more than the simple handing down of a robe. Hui-neng was a Patriarch without the robe; even with it, Empress Wu was not.[6]

I include this dissertation-writer's protest because it illustrates one of the more intriguing aspects of eighth-century Chan robe-rhetoric, namely, its enduring appeal. Eighth-century beliefs about the meaning of the robe are not so very different from current beliefs, among Asians and Westerners alike, about the role of personal effects or contact relics in establishing the legitimacy of the Dalai Lama's sovereignty. Widespread cultural acceptance of the power of talismanic objects helped the early Chan movement to establish the authority of its patriarchs, but at times these and other representations of authority threatened to overshadow those who laid claim to them.

The *Lidai fabao ji* authors were not the only ones entangled in this dilemma. Any criticism of the *Lidai fabao ji* version of succession inevitably raises the inconvenient question: Where did true patriarchal power lie? The doctrinal, ideological and historical aspects of this question cannot be addressed separately, for each implicates the others. Doctrinally, the reconciliation of inherent Buddha-nature with temporal transmission of spiritual authority is as slippery as the reconciliation of the theory of anātman (no-self) with the theory of karma (the morally charged momentum of past action that shapes the actor). Spiritual continuity and individual spiritual accomplishment were both contested in "Southern School" Chan, and in the process the values associated with these aspects were transformed.

Among Chan schools of the late eighth century, the rhetoric of genealogy, which laid claim to a unique spiritual continuity, was given increasing authority. At the same time, the role of hagiographic accounts of heroic spiritual discipline was diminished. Transmission of the letter of the Law, of the moral, ritual, and exegetical traditions, had conferred the authoritative stamp of continuity in the early centuries of Buddhism's involvement in China, but during the brief transitional period that this study attempts to delineate the vehicle of transmission became as difficult to pin down as Nāgasena's carriage.[7] The stories surrounding transmission of the patriarchal robe in the *Lidai fabao ji* highlight the instability of received Buddhist criteria determining standards of authority and morality. The symbols and paradigms deployed in these stories attempt to resolve contradictions that were problematic for the nascent Chan school. Contradictions explored in the *Lidai fabao ji* include the prestige of spiritual virtuosity versus the immediacy of the practice of nonconceptualization, and the ordained community's necessary identification with defined rituals and precepts versus the apophatic deconstruction and antinomianism inherent in advanced Mahāyāna teachings like Madhyamaka (Middle Path).

At this juncture I should note that use of the seemingly innocent term "Chan school" is fraught with controversy. Thanks to careful research into Tang sources in recent decades, it has become clear that the image of the late Tang as the "golden age" of Chan is a retrospective illusion heightened by the sectarian biases of later Japanese scholars. Therefore, it has become naive to use the term "sect" or "school" in connection with Tang Chan. Nevertheless, however atypical they may have been, it is clear that the *Lidai fabao ji* authors claimed allegiance to Chan as a distinct school or vehicle of Buddhism, not just as a practice specialization or trend. Wuzhu's eulogy refers to him as a "disciple of the Chan teachings" (*Chanmen menren* 禅門門人). Bodhidharma is characterized as one who was "in the lineage of the Chan Dharma" (*zongtu Chanfa* 宗徒禅法), and the text refers to "Great Chan nature" (*da Chan xing* 大禅性).[8] One of my aims in this study is to show how the *Lidai fabao ji* authors attempted to establish an identity on the basis of the "formless" practice unique to their teacher, whom they considered the only legitimate heir of the Southern School teaching of no-thought.

ON THE BACKGROUND OF THE *LIDAI FABAO JI*

The *Lidai fabao ji* was probably composed sometime between 774 and 780 at the Bao Tang monastery in Yizhou 益州 by an anonymous disciple or disciples of the above-mentioned Bao Tang founder, Chan Master Wuzhu. Wuzhu claimed Dharma descent from the charismatic Korean Chan master Wuxiang 無相 (Kor. Musang) (684–762), who was known as the founder of another Sichuan Chan school, the Jingzhong school of Chengdu 成都. Unlike the Jingzhong school and its temple, the Bao Tang lineage and site cannot be traced beyond the generation of Wuzhu's immediate disciples. However, the *Lidai fabao ji* is preserved in a surprisingly large number of manuscripts and fragments from the Dunhuang materials.[9] Moreover, a number of other Dunhuang texts quote from or show the influence of the *Lidai fabao ji*.[10]

Except in one instance there is no way to know how the text survived until the early eleventh century, when the cave-temple cache was sealed.[11] The large number of texts and fragments of *Lidai fabao ji* in the Dunhuang cache, and evidence of its dispersion into Turfan and Tibet, shows that it was not a negligible work. Moreover, Tang historian Rong Xinjiang 榮新江 has effectively challenged the theory, promulgated by Sir Aurel Stein and later scholars, that the Dunhuang deposit was a repository of "sacred waste." Instead, he argues that the cache held the library collection of Sanjie 三界 Monastery, which included valuable texts and paintings collected and repaired by the monk Daozhen 道真 until late in the tenth century.[12] Among the apocrypha and Chan works popular in ninth and tenth-century Dunhuang, the *Lidai fabao ji* appears to have been considered worthy of frequent reproduction, and its subsequent disappearance becomes all the more puzzling. However, this disappearance means that the *Lidai fabao ji* provides us with a rare opportunity to shed light on the historical contingencies that shaped sectarian identity. The fact that the Bao Tang school was so short-lived and its remains hermetically sealed makes it a more accurate reflection of the Buddhist world of the eighth and ninth centuries, the "golden age" of Chan, than the authoritative accounts that were produced in the tenth through twelfth centuries. And, as we shall see, some of the *Lidai fabao ji* fabrications and innovations found their way into canonical versions of Chan history, though the text itself was forgotten.

The *Lidai fabao ji* is one of a handful of eighth-century texts invested in the notion of a lineage of patriarchs stemming from Bodhidharma.[13] Each of these texts had unique variations that were absorbed or superseded by the official Chan genealogical history, the *Jingde chuandeng lu* 景德傳燈錄 (Record of the Transmission of the Lamp Compiled in the Jingde Era) compiled in 1004.[14] The lore of the Chan patriarchy was reworked in numerous iterations over the course of several centuries, such that most traces of the stories' original contexts were erased or submerged. The historicity of the biographies and lineages of renowned Chan masters has been undermined not only by Dunhuang finds, but also by scholarly recognition that Chan classics on the Tang masters are largely products of the Song dynasty (960–1279), when Chan was a prestigious religious and cultural institution that enjoyed the privilege of canonizing a romanticized view of its origins.[15]

Examination of the Dunhuang cache and subsequent reexamination of epigraphical materials have given scholars glimpses of a few of the unpolished missing links, like the *Lidai fabao ji,* that nevertheless contributed to the highly allusive style of Song Chan literature.[16] Dunhuang materials have also broadened our knowledge of Tang economics, administration, music, art, and popular Buddhist practices, and these aspects are only beginning to be integrated into Chan studies. In the search for the face of Chan "before its parents were born" (to borrow a *kōan* phrase), family resemblance is not always apparent. Scholars have sifted the available biographies, commentaries, and inscriptions to find early traces of the monks and doctrinal issues that were later iconized in Chan traditional histories, but if one looks at other kinds of material then other kinds of connections appear. The rejuvenation of archaeological work in China will continue to reveal new aspects of religious practice in the many cultural and political microclimates of the early centuries of Buddhist activity, and a deeper view of these worlds will no doubt influence our understanding of the genesis of Chan. In considering past reassessments of Chan history, one must also try to take into account the metamorphoses that Asian and Western historiographical practices have undergone in the turbulent ideological battles of the past half-century, though it is not within the scope of this study to delineate the vicissitudes of these modes of discourse.[17]

The *Lidai fabao ji* retains many traces of the ideological battles from which it emerged, and this contributes to its interest for scholars today. Directly and indirectly, the *Lidai fabao ji* relies on numerous sources, and it clearly shows seams where the various passages are patched together. Themes and texts associated with disparate modes of Buddhist discourse are juxtaposed within the *Lidai fabao ji*, and I suggest that this in part reflects a broader social and religious transition.

The shift was signaled most dramatically by the 755 rebellion of the general An Lushan 安祿山 against the Tang ruling clans, but is discernible even before this critical turning point. Warring agendas in the *Lidai fabao ji* can be seen as a reflection in microcosm of a more extensive crisis of faith in the religious and secular structures of authority inherited from the early Tang. During the century preceding the An Lushan rebellion, Buddhist monastic establishments clustered in and around the two Tang capitals of Chang'an and Luoyang had grown into a collective force to be reckoned with. The power of the Buddhist network was negotiated through relations of sometimes strained interdependence with the imperial court, in a milieu of rivalry with court Daoism, as successive emperors struggled to co-opt or control its increasingly pervasive influence. Arguably the most ambitious ruler in this regard, the empress Wu Zetian created a network of monasteries to promulgate Buddhist teachings in support of her reign, fashioned a new ideology of imperial legitimation that had strong Buddhist utopian elements, and continually invited exemplary monks to court. After Empress Wu, the next ruler to have a significant impact on institutional Buddhism was Emperor Xuanzong 玄宗 (r. 712–756), whose reign effectively ended with the An Lushan rebellion. Even though the Tang forces subsequently rallied, the war effort resulted in the strengthening of the peripheries at the expense of the center.[18]

Politically as well as culturally, the eighth century saw a great deal of oscillation between the time-honored and the experimental. For example, the examination system promoted by Wu Zetian and carried on by her successors allowed nonhereditary officials to make inroads into the labyrinth of privilege previously negotiated by the imperial household, Buddhist or Daoist monastic institutions, and the aristocratic clans. While the numbers thus admitted into the bureaucracy may have been relatively small, the growing population of highly educated exam candidates concentrated in Chang'an had a significant impact on literati culture. There was a tendency toward secularization of social values within this increasingly competitive bureaucratic class.

More concretely, with the disintegration of periphery-center tribute relations, decrease in central control of the military, and greater freedom for interprovince commerce, the midlevel provincial officials and military governors became increasingly independent. Before the end of the dynasty in 907 there were several attempts to reinforce imperial authority, but some provincial centers, such as Chengdu, the birthplace of the *Lidai fabao ji,* became nearly autonomous. These factors contributed to create a milieu in which received genres and cultural paradigms were seen as inadequate or decadent,[19] and the *Lidai fabao ji* authors' contentious representations of spiritual authenticity and authority reflect the wider cultural arena of contested practices.

The shifting of the balance of power from center to peripheries also weakened the influence of the Buddhist monastic complexes of the capitals that were heavily implicated in imperial politics. Declining resources for these older institutions coupled with new opportunities for patronage in the provinces clearly contributed to the development of the so-called Southern School of Chan to which the Bao Tang school claimed allegiance. The birth of the "Southern School" can be traced to the polemics of the Chan master Shenhui 神會 (684–758), who in 730 began a series of campaigns against the successors of the Chan master Shenxiu 神秀 (d. 706), a monk who had been highly revered by Empress Wu and the Chang'an/Luoyang establishment.[20] Shenhui was responsible for fashioning the representations and ideologies that were to change what it meant to be a "Chan Master." Claiming to represent the teachings of an obscure monk named Huineng, Shenhui advocated direct and "sudden" realization of the truth of one's own Buddha-nature and contended that Shenxiu's "Northern School" followers were "gradualists," who fostered the delusion that awakening was a condition to be achieved, rather than one's inherent reality. Discussion of "sudden awakening" (*dunwu* 頓悟) in Chinese Buddhist texts predates the appropriation of this soteriology as the hallmark "Southern School" doctrine, but the appropriation was lastingly effective. Likewise, Buddhist references to "no-thought" (*wunian* 無念) predate the Southern School polemic, but in that rhetorical context it came to refer to the nonconceptual realization of the nonseparation of practice and enlightenment, and the nonreification of practice. This was said to rectify the mistaken Northern School practice of *linian* 離念 (transcending thought) that reified the extinguishing of thought.

Implicated in Shenhui's campaign was the centuries-old struggle over Buddhist elitism, an elitism that was nurtured by imperial and popular enchantment with the mystique of the adept who gained numinous power through asceticism, devotional ritual, and scriptural recitation. Although Shenhui himself did not go so far as to disavow any form of Buddhist activity whatsoever, he and subsequent Chan masters became increasingly attentive to the contradiction involved in teaching and practicing (inherently gradualist endeavors) according to the orthodoxy of the "sudden."

This tension is integral to the hybrid nature of the *Lidai fabao ji*. Although the text has features associated with "Northern School" groups that continued to evolve throughout the eighth century, it is heavily influenced by Shenhui's "Southern School" ideology. Conspicuously, it is the only text to take Shenhui's doctrine to a certain logical extreme by advocating iconoclastic and antinomian approaches to practice.

Wuzhu's mode of expression in his Dharma talks also shows affinity with eighth-century treatises related to the Niutou 牛頭 (Oxhead) lineage of Chan. Like Shenhui's "Southern School," Niutou followers were influenced by Shenxiu's legacy but began to develop a separate identity in the first part of the eighth century. The Niutou lineage was said to have arisen from a transmission from the fourth Chan patriarch, Daoxin 道信 (580–651?), and it was doctrinally grounded in the Madhyamaka *Sanlun* 三論 (Three Treatises) exegetical school. Soteriological points in common found in Niutou-related treatises and Wuzhu's sermons include deconstruction of reified notions of practice and moral precepts, and emphasis on nonconceptual practice/realization. They also share a style of discourse that Buddhist historian Robert Sharf characterizes as "sinitic" *prajñāpāramitā* (perfection of wisdom) dialectic—apophatic dialogues and effusions replete with paradox and flavored with Daoist mystical poesis. Sharf argues that relationships among the late eighth-century texts that display this style indicate a "shared literary culture" rather than distinct textual influence or doctrinal transmission.[21]

From the eighth through thirteenth centuries, Chan doctrinal issues were bound up with the development of specialized literary and artistic forms. In "Southern School" Chan texts, sūtra commentary, discursive explanation, and the traditional didactic style of question-and-answer were eliminated or molded into new genres. In the Song, it became standard to compile *yulu* 語錄 (discourse records), consisting of a distinguished master's sermons, poetry, and interactions with his disciples. Chan also developed a genre of sectarian hagiography distinct from the inclusive typologically arranged biographical collections of the *gaoseng zhuan* 高僧傳 (biographies of eminent monks) genre. Beginning with the *Zutang ji* 祖堂集 (Anthology of the Patriarchal Hall) of 952, Chan monks began to produce large collections of biographies arranged as a family trees, later designated *chuandeng lu* 傳燈錄 (lamp transmission records). Undergirding these collections was the Chan school's claim to inheritance of perfect mind-to-mind transmission from master to disciple through the generations from Śākyamuni and the Buddhas of the past. The *yulu* and *chuandeng lu* genres thus exemplify the complementarity and tension between the uniqueness and immediacy of the master-disciple encounter and the genealogy of perfect replication of the Dharma.

The *Lidai fabao ji* is prototypical of both Chan genres but has a narrower scope. The first part of the text includes a series of biographies arranged in the linear exclusive format that was the precursor to the many-branched genealogies of the *chuandeng lu* genre. The second part consists of dialogues between Wuzhu and various interlocutors and includes a *zhenzan* 真讚 (portrait eulogy) written as a memorial for the master. Through the *Lidai fabao ji* we may thus gain glimpses of an earlier stage of the sensibilities that shaped Song dynasty Chan's distinctive literary styles and its images of exemplary practice, which were in turn the styles and images adopted by Japanese monks who founded the Zen schools of the Kamakura period (1185–1333). The *Lidai fabao ji* does not, however, help to establish any firmer historical basis for the eighth-century Chan masters who figured prominently in the Song *gongan* 公案 (public cases), which currently enjoy widespread cultural recognition in their Japanese form, *kōan.* These short Chan anecdotes were culled from *yulu* and *chuandeng lu,* layered with verse and prose commentaries, and developed into a curriculum of monastic study in medieval Japan.

Due in part to a late twentieth-century Western fascination with *kōan* literature, Chan writings are often presented, in both popular and scholarly works, as bare renderings of the spontaneous expression of realized self-presence. I hope to counterbalance such perennialism by approaching the *Lidai fabao ji* in its historical particularity and analyzing its underlying contradictions, but I have no desire to thereby reduce it to a quaint relic or discount the significance of its soteriology. One need not assume that evidence of mundane concerns invalidates the spiritual claims of the unknown author or authors. To become entangled in such distinctions merely replicates the ideological hypostasis of the tradition while attempting to unsettle it; by taking issue with the fabrications of the Chan histories one joins in the reification of a separate and unwritten transmission of Chan.[22]

However, the time- and place-bound paradoxes of eighth-century Chan that may be termed a "crisis in transmission" do exemplify a perennial Buddhist dilemma. The dilemma of transmission arises from the necessary instability of the transmission of a specific yet unclosed canon of teachings (Dharma) by an ordained community (Saṅgha) that is predicated upon the ultimacy of the individual's experience of truth (Buddha/bodhi). Amid the "Three Jewels" there must always already be tension between continuity and insight.

The insoluble challenge that "Southern School" Chan presented to itself—how to teach and maintain a heritage within an orthodoxy that validated absolute immediacy—is but one form of this dilemma. As Weber has argued, contradictions within a religious system in fact serve to perpetuate it, as the tradition sustains the challenge of generating meaningful solutions to the problem of itself.[23] The essentially unresolvable nature of the foundational contradiction (how is it possible to mediate or teach immediacy?) could not be directly articulated but was expressed through secondary issues, and Chan evolved through the channeling of creative energies toward both ideal and ideological ends, necessarily intimately related. In this exploration of the *Lidai fabao ji,* my aim is to clarify the functioning of the transmission of authority in medieval Chinese Buddhism such that neither realization nor realpolitik is reduced one to the terms of the other.

AN OVERVIEW

The *Lidai fabao ji* authors practiced the kind of multiple vision required by the Chinese historiographical method of assembling a collection of often contradictory authoritative sources in order to support a new position. Like the *Lidai fabao ji* authors, I have also compiled and adapted numerous sources; inspired by the work of many scholars, I have tried to accumulate something of a "thick description" of the functioning of the authority of transmission in Buddhist China. I cannot offer an entirely new vision or an expansion of frontiers, but rather a journey through familiar territory with a long-lost text in hand.

In this study I focus for the most part on such matters as ideology, hagiography, and praxis, while purely doctrinal exposition and questions of doctrinal affiliation become ancillary. However, one cannot afford to reject a legacy weighted with doctrinal studies and simply reify "practice" in its place. Acknowledging a great debt to scholars of Buddhism past and present, I have drawn on a rich inheritance while pursuing the interest in cultural and social issues that is characteristic of my own milieu. By following the *Lidai fabao ji* authors' teleological narrative of their own spiritual legacy through the course of Chinese Buddhist history, I hope to elucidate both soteriological issues and social forces that shaped the development of a distinct Chan discourse.

In part 1, I explore the multiple contexts of the *Lidai fabao ji,* revisiting various issues and episodes in Buddhist and Chinese history from the fourth through the eighth centuries. Part 2 is an annotated translation of the entire *Lidai fabao ji,* which is the first published Western-language translation of the text.[24] Though I quote numerous passages from the *Lidai fabao ji* in part 1, these are but a few of the highlights of this multifaceted and intriguing work. Therefore, I invite readers to draw their own inferences by consulting the translation provided in part 2, which includes the Chinese text of the manuscript on which I based my translation (S. 516).

The reader should also refer to part 2 for full annotations; in order to avoid redundancy, the *Lidai fabao ji* passages quoted in part 1 have minimal notes.

Following the present introductory chapter, part 1 continues with chapter 2, "Transmission and Translation," which begins with a summary of the aims and contents of the *Lidai fabao ji*. I then discuss the opening episode of the text, the legend of Emperor Ming of the Han. The bulk of the chapter concerns fourth-century figures who are referred to in the *Lidai fabao ji* and who had a formative impact on the world of medieval Chinese Buddhism. In discussing these figures, I focus on issues that resonate with the concerns of the *Lidai fabao ji* authors. The chapter closes with a fourth-century episode that is taken up in the Tang historical record, illustrating salient Chinese ideals regarding a person invested with authority.

Chapter 3, "Transmission and Lay Practice," begins with a brief discussion of the criteria of authenticity in Indian Buddhism in order to elucidate the reasons why full ordination remained the most important criterion of authority to transmit the Dharma. This is followed by a section on key practices in which the laity participated, centering on bodhisattva precepts texts and Dharmakṣema's role in disseminating them in China. I then turn to an investigation of Chinese apocrypha in which we see the confluence of visualization practice, bodhisattva precepts, and repentance practices.

In Chapter 4, "Material Buddhism and the Dharma Kings," I discuss phases of interaction between ideologies of Buddhist utopia and ideologies of Buddhist end-time, in relation to the development of Chan notions of patriarchy. The chapter opens with a discussion of the Northern Wei dynasty as a paradigmatic example of the kind of "spiritual materialism" that fed fears of the decline of the Dharma. In the second part of the chapter, I examine five different ritual and cultic solutions to anxiety over *moshi* 末世 (the final age) from the period of disunity to the early Tang, and I discuss the relationship between eschatology and incipient Chan themes.

Chapter 5, "Robes and Patriarchs," concerns well-known materials and debates that have been identified as formative for Chan discourse. I first discuss the *Lidai fabao ji* authors' version of the introduction of Chan to China in light of other scholars' presentations of seventh-century prototype lineages. This is followed by a consideration of Shenhui's ideology of patriarchy and his promotion of Huineng, as reflected in the *Lidai fabao ji* version of patriarchal succession. In the final sections, I survey attitudes toward Buddhism manifested in the eras of Empress Wu Zetian and Emperor Xuanzong and discuss the relationship between changes in the political climate and the development of Chan.

In Chapter 6, "Wuzhu and His Others," I link aspects of Buddhist practice in the latter half of the eighth century with the unique features of the *Lidai fabao ji*. Picking up the thread of the bodhisattva precepts once again, I look at the evolution of the practice of holding large assemblies for mass reception of the bodhisattva precepts, which became important venues for Chan masters to disseminate teachings. The *Lidai fabao ji* describes both Wuxiang and Wuzhu addressing such assemblies, and against this backdrop I investigate *Lidai fabao ji* claims about the robe transmission from Wuxiang to Wuzhu and analyze the symbolism of motifs in their biographies. The last three sections take up three special characteristics of the *Lidai fabao ji:* antinomianism, the inclusion of women, and rivalry with Daoists.

Chapter 7, "The Legacy of the *Lidai fabao ji,*" is in two parts. The first and longest section is devoted to the contexts and functions of the *zhenzan* included at the end of the *Lidai fabao ji*. I explore various aspects of this unique piece, including the development of ritual uses of Buddhist monk portraiture and the aesthetics of the portrait-eulogy genre. In the second section, I follow post–*Lidai fabao ji* traces of Wuzhu and Wuxiang in Sichuan, Korea, and Tibet. My concluding remarks are a reflection on the construction and deployment of multiple collective identities in the *Lidai fabao ji*.

Broadly speaking, there are three general themes or topics of inquiry engaged throughout this study. The first topic, as the title suggests, is transmission; the *Lidai fabao ji* and this study are both multifaceted and yet incomplete views of medieval Chinese Buddhist transmission. As noted above, it is difficult to formulate a sufficient definition of Buddhist transmission, for the vehicles and the contents of transmission are mutually permeable and mutually transforming, necessarily involving continual renegotiation. Working with this instability, I highlight the rhetorical strategies and practices that effected transmission of authority, rather than transmission of teachings. Investing individuals with the authority to perform as leaders of the Buddhist community meant confirming in them the potential to fulfill multiple roles, including teacher, ritual officiant, miracle worker, and monastic administrator. Importantly, those invested with authority validated the participation of lay and ordained devotees and actualized the efficacy of offerings and community devotional activities and projects.

I also focus on transmission of the formal aspects of Buddhist authority, that is, transmission of the precepts, schedules, postures, rituals, and dress that marked the monk in fourth- through eighth-century China. Among these formal aspects, transmission of the precepts and the monk's robe are especially germane. Both of these are traditionally linked to the preservation and continuity of the Buddhist teachings, and thus the changing symbolic functions of precepts ceremonies and monastic robes serve as tokens of new directions taken in the eighth century.

The means of transmitting forms of practice were relatively consensual, negotiable, and variable in the Chinese Buddhist tradition. Southern

School notions such as the "precepts of formlessness" and the patriarchal robe represent an attempt to monopolize orthodox transmission, but instead contributed to its indeterminacy. Among the disputing voices, the Bao Tang school was certainly notable for its views on both rules and robes. Aside from their unique account of the fate of Bodhidarma's robe, its followers were best known for their application of the statement that "nonrecollection is precepts [practice]" (*wuyi shi jie* 無憶是戒). The Bao Tang attitude did not extend to deliberate transgression, but Wuzhu consistently tried to undermine those who wanted to hold onto specific practices and reify them as "keeping the precepts." In principle this antinomianism was not radical, having antecedents in Shenhui's sermons and in the liturgical texts of the "Northern School," but the Bao Tang appear to have gone further than most in attempting to put this aspect of nonattachment into practice. In order to delineate the evolution of precepts into the formless or nonconceptual precepts, I have looked at precepts teachings in influential texts from the fifth to the eighth centuries.

As the terms "antinomian" and "formless" are used throughout this study, some definitional clarification is in order. Though the term "antinomianism" (Greek: *anti,* "against"; *nomos,* "law") carries some unwanted resonances, it is a convenient way to refer to the general notion of liberation from moral precepts due to fidelity to a transcendent order or higher teaching. Not inappropriately, it also has sectarian polemical connotations.[25] "Formless" refers to an antinomian and apophatic approach to forms of religious practice like precepts, liturgies, and rituals of repentance. There is no single term that is used consistently in the *Lidai fabao ji* to render this notion, though there are many apophatic formulations applied to precepts and religious rituals. Examples include *yi wunian wei jie* 以無念為戒 (take no-thought as the precepts) and *jiexing ru xukong* 戒性如虛空 (the nature of the precepts is like emptiness).[26] Wuzhu frequently stresses that the precepts are fully realized in nonconceptualization.

The second major theme of this study involves the challenge of writing a history about a Chinese sectarian text that presents itself as a history, the challenge of simultaneous creation and deconstruction of historical narrative. There are a number of diachronic narrative structures through which one may analyze the *Lidai fabao ji,* and I highlight the following: (1) the lineage of masters as it appears in the text, (2) the roles played by rulers or imperial representatives, and (3) the chronology of the sources and different styles of discourse used in the text. Among these, the first, lineage, was clearly the most important for the *Lidai fabao ji* authors. The second, the succession of imperial eras, does not always reflect the actual rhythm of cultural metamorphoses, but the *Lidai fabao ji* authors themselves were clearly interested in including marks of imperial attention, whether positive or negative, in their account of the Dharma "through the generations." Regarding sources and voices, I have tried to shed light on the *Lidai fabao ji* authors' milieu by giving consideration to the rationale behind the arrangements of quotations in the text, and wherever possible I have commented on textual filiations and other uses of the *Lidai fabao ji* sources.

The third general topic is inquiry into the political aspects of the transmission of forms of practice and versions of history. Specifically, I examine the relationship between the means of authority exercised by the imperial system and the means of authority exercised by the Buddhist clergy and explore the strategies employed in key areas of tension. Examining such issues as the periodic outbreak of the "bowing" controversy, I view the interaction between state and Saṅgha as a struggle to establish a mutually beneficial relationship in Chinese terms, rather than a clash between an indigenous political philosophy and a "foreign" religion.

CHAPTER 2

Transmission and Translation

By insisting that its leaders no longer beget children, the Catholic Church in the West made plain that it enjoyed a supernatural guarantee of continuity that no ancient city could claim. If they were to be respected as leaders of a "holy" institution, bishops and priests had to remain anomalous creatures. . . . They administered the palpable wealth of their churches as if they were men without possessions.

—Peter Brown, *The Body and Society*

THE CHALLENGE OF CONTINUITY

In this chapter we look at some of the various means of guaranteeing continuity in the early period of the establishment of Buddhist practice and the Buddhist Saṅgha in China. Taking up episodes and topics that the *Lidai fabao ji* authors used in their presentation of the introduction of Buddhism to China, I discuss issues of continuity and community in the context of the legend of Emperor Ming of the Han and the transmission activities of Daoan, Buddhabhadra, and Huiyuan. The early history of Buddhism in China has been relatively well studied; scholars, whether Chinese, Japanese, or Western, have been understandably fascinated with the many dramatic episodes from the era of the "Chinese transformation of Buddhism" or "Buddhist conquest of China."[1] Examining the background of the episodes included in the *Lidai fabao ji,* I focus on continuities and new developments in the empowerment of the Buddhist clergy as a special separate class within Chinese society.

In this chapter we consider the nature of the Buddhist monk as an "anomalous creature," classified in terms of the specialized mode of reproduction of his species.[2] In China, what were the means by which the continuity of Dharma and Saṅgha were formalized? It is essential to maintain a sense of the context (the Chinese polity) "at work within the place" (the Saṅgha) just as Brown sees "the ancient city" at work within the Catholic Church.[3] One could say that these questions exist in "tangled hierarchy," for while individual realization and independent verification of absolute truth is integral to the self-definition of the Dharma and Saṅgha, so too are the culturally contingent forms taken by the Dharma and Saṅgha integral to individual realization.[4]

In Mahāyāna (Greater Vehicle) philosophy,[5] realization of the absolute or ultimate level of truth—of nonduality and emptiness—also confirms the conventional level, the provisionally valid experience of temporal causality and the use of many forms of *upāya* (skillful means). This doctrine of "Two Truths" does not solve the chicken-and-egg dilemma peculiar to our own context of contested rationalism (which comes first, Dharma qua truth or Dharma qua teaching of truth?), but it has often been used as a framework able to include a multiplicity of teachings and forms of practice. At the practical level, the early Buddhist community faced the dilemma of guaranteeing the unadulterated transmission of the Dharma within the context of provisional collective authority well before the abstract dilemma of the Two Truths was formulated, a topic we touch on in chapter 3. The historical Buddha was said to have taught for forty-five years but to have declined to designate a single successor as a conduit of his teachings: "After my decease, may each of you be your own island, your own refuge; have no other refuge."[6] In Buddhist tradition the "original teachings" are presented not as the Buddha's intentional bequest but as the result of the collective retentive efforts of the Buddha's immediate disciples—and the teachings as we know them are the products of a process something like the multiplication of provisional islands of consensus.

When we grapple with eighth-century Chan notions of mind-transmission, continuity becomes ever more problematic. As we see in chapter 6, the *Lidai fabao ji* includes claims to inheritance of the unaltered direct transmission of Śākyamuni Buddha along with claims that Wuzhu's reception of the transmission was superior to that of other patriarchs in his lineage, and I submit that this was an appropriate reflection of a crisis of authority besetting Buddhist and imperial institutions during the eighth century. In times when the "Three Jewels" of Buddha, Dharma, and Saṅgha adapted to new circumstances, they became even more subject to the contingencies of collective and dispersive imagination.[7]

The Saṅgha itself is of course a product of collective and dispersive imagination, harking back to the utopia of the Buddha's vision that monks should perpetually wander alone or in small groups to disseminate the Dharma, gathering together only for the rites of confession and for the rainy season retreat. This is illustrated in the oft-recurring metaphor of the monk as a vessel of the Dharma, a container and dispenser of something that he has received and also made uniquely his own. The Buddhist monk's inheritance is thus paradoxical, a fixed fluidity and a solitary solidarity. In order to be enabled to live "as if they were men without possessions," it was necessary that the monk's self-possession be both unique and transferable. Buddhist "transmission of authority" depends on this paradoxical adaptability: the unique and perfect vessel of the Dharma is the means by which uniqueness is adapted to ever-changing conditions in new and unimaginable lands.

SUMMARY OF THE CONTENTS OF THE *LIDAI FABAO JI*

The *Lidai fabao ji* could be called a history of origins, beginning with a legendary account of the introduction of Buddhism to China and ending with the record of the Bao Tang school founder, Wuzhu. As the title indicates, the *Lidai fabao ji* is meant to be a record "through successive generations." Key moments in Chinese Buddhist history are emphasized as if they were turnings of the Dharma wheel that culminate in Wuzhu's teachings. Narrative choices, scriptural quotations, and occasional narrator commentary all repeatedly orient one back to Sichuan in the eighth century even as one is brought steadily forward from Emperor Ming's court in the first century. In the course of this study I comment on a number of passages from the *Lidai fabao ji;* one may consult my appended translation to locate these passages in their original contexts, but let me here give an overview of the structure and sequence of the text.

The *Lidai fabao ji* comprises seventeen pages of the *Taishō* edition of the Buddhist canon, or approximately twenty-five thousand Chinese characters.[8] It begins with a list of thirty-seven titles that the authors claim as sources. The narrative opens with a version of the legend of the dream of Emperor Ming of the Han and his subsequent embassy to bring Buddhist scriptures and monks to China. This is followed by a description of a contest of magical powers between Buddhists and Daoists, a brief account of Śākyamuni Buddha, and a quotation from a work in the genre of Buddhist rebuttal to the third-century Daoist *Huahu jing* 化胡經 (Scripture of Conversion of the Barbarians). A second version of the legend of Emperor Ming ensues. The narrative shifts to a quasi-historical anecdote involving the famous Jin dynasty monk Huiyuan 慧遠 (334–417). Then, quotations from two well-known sūtras are followed by a quotation from a putative fifth-century "translation" of a work (probably a Chinese compilation) chronicling the transmission from the Buddha up until the twenty-third generation in India and Kashmir. A passage from this work is altered and supplemented by the *Lidai fabao ji* authors in order to bring the transmission up to the twenty-ninth generation, to "Bodhidharmatrāta," founder of the Chan lineage claimed by the Bao Tang school. The authors then dispute a rival claim made in an early eighth-century Chan text, the *Lengqie shizi ji* 楞伽師資記 (Record of the Masters and Disciples of the

Laṅkā[vatāra-sūtra]).[9] This is followed by polemics over the origins of the *Laṅkā* transmission.

For all its diversity, the rather disjointed introductory section summarized above comprises a mere tenth of the text as a whole. The *Laṅkā* transmission discussion forms a segue for a more orderly but no less lively section, the biographies of the six successive Chan patriarchs: Bodhidharmatrāta 菩提達摩多羅, more commonly known as Bodhidharma (d. c. 530), Huike 慧可 (487–593), Sengcan 僧璨 (d.u.), Daoxin 道信 (580–651?), Hongren 弘忍 (602–675), and Huineng 慧能 (638–713).[10] The text then jumps abruptly back to the fourth century with a passage on the monk Daoan 道安 (312–385), followed by a long series of quotations from Indian sūtras and apocryphal Chinese scriptures. The biography of Huineng preceding the scriptural quotations includes an account of the transmission of the robe and the Dharma from Hongren to Huineng, but immediately following the quotations we revisit the Hongren-Huineng robe-transmission episode. It is repeated in greater detail and the *Lidai fabao ji* authors embellish an episode in which the southern scholar-monk Yinzong 印宗 (627–713) ordains Huineng and becomes his disciple.

Next follows the infamous robe-transmission episode set in the court of Wu Zetian, which leads to short biographies of Zhishen 智詵 (609–702) and his disciple Chuji 處寂 (669–736). The genealogical implications are complicated by the fact that although Zhishen is actually a disciple of Hongren, he receives Huineng's robe of transmission from the empress and passes it on to Chuji. The biography of Chuji's disciple, the Korean monk Wuxiang 無相 (684–762), is given in some detail, including quotations from his Dharma sermons. This is followed by passages purporting to record dialogues between the above-mentioned Southern School advocate Shenhui and various interlocutors. These passages are certainly based on extant works related to Shenhui, but the *Lidai fabao ji* authors interpolate a spurious commentary on Sichuan Chan figures into Shenhui's discourses. These sections from Bodhidharma to Shenhui constitute approximately another 30 percent of the whole.

The remaining 60 percent of the text is devoted to the Bao Tang founder Wuzhu 無住 (714–774). He is introduced giving a dramatic Dharma sermon, followed by an extended account of his early years and wanderings, his encounter with Wuxiang, the robe transmission from Wuxiang, and his ultimate recognition as the legitimate heir after Wuxiang's death. The rest of the text is taken up by sermons and dialogues with disciples and visitors on various topics. The *Lidai fabao ji* concludes with a portrait-eulogy for Wuzhu and Wuzhu's death scene.

In a manner quite common in Tang dynasty historical and exegetical literature, perhaps a quarter of the *Lidai fabao ji* is composed of freely altered quotations from a multiplicity of other works, usually—but not always—

attributed. Source materials from different times and places, changes in writing style, and strikingly innovative passages are loosely held together by the author-compilers' arguments for formless practice as a necessary corollary to the Southern School doctrine of no-thought.

EMPEROR MING OF THE HAN

The introductory sections of the *Lidai fabao ji* include two versions of the legend of the introduction of Buddhism to China by Emperor Ming 明 of the Han 漢 (r. 57–75), as follows:

> The *Hanfa neizhuan* 漢法內傳 (Inner Commentary on the Dharma in the Han) [says]: Emperor Ming of the Later Han in the third year of the Yongping era (60 C.E.) one night dreamt he saw a golden man sixteen feet high, with a nimbus around his neck and back, flying about the palace. The next morning he asked his court officials, "What sort of auspicious sign is this?"
>
> The Grand Astrologer Fu Yi 傅毅 addressed the emperor, saying, "In the West there is a great Holy One called the Buddha. It was his image [that you saw]." Emperor Ming asked, "How do you know this?" The Grand Astrologer Fu Yi replied, "In the *Zhoushu yiji* 周書異記 it says; 'The Buddha was born in the *jiayin* year (958 B.C.E.) of the reign of King Zhao 昭, and passed into extinction in the *renshen* year (878 B.C.E.) of King Mu 穆. A thousand years after [his extinction] his teachings will spread to the Han (China).' Now that time has come."
>
> Emperor Ming dispatched the Gentleman of the Interior Cai Yin 蔡愔 and the Erudite Qin Jing 秦景 and others as envoys to India. [There] they made requests, and the Buddhist image they obtained was a statue of a bodhisattva, the scripture they obtained was the *Scripture in Forty-two Sections,*[11] and the Dharma masters they obtained were Kāśyapamātaṅga 迦葉摩騰 and Dharmaratna 竺法蘭. [When they arrived,] Emperor Ming invited them to ascend to the audience hall and made offerings to them. Consequently [the emperor] established the White Horse Monastery (Baima si 白馬寺) west of Luoyang city.[12]
>
> * * *
>
> The *Mouzi* 牟子 says, "Long ago, Emperor Xiaoming of the Han dreamt one night of a divine person. His body radiated light and he flew about in front of the palace. [The emperor] experienced an inner joy and his heart was deeply gladdened. The next day he told [his dream] and asked his ministers, 'What was it?' There was a man of penetration, Fu Yi, who said, 'I have heard that in India there was a man who attained the Way who is called

> Buddha. He can levitate and is able to fly, and his body radiates light. It was probably his spirit.' Realizing that this was the case, [the emperor] dispatched the emissary Zhang Qian 張騫, the Gentleman of the Palace Guard Qin 秦, the Erudite disciple Wang Zun 王尊 and others, twelve persons. In the Great Yuezhi 月支 [kingdom] they copied and brought back the Buddhist *Scripture in Forty-two Sections,* [and it was] placed in the fourteenth stone chamber of the Orchid Pavilion. Then the emperor had a Buddhist monastery erected outside the Xiyong 西雍 gate of Luoyang city."[13]

Employing a common mythopoetic device, the legend of Emperor Ming's dream explains the introduction of new knowledge with reference to its prior introduction. The story that has the symbolic value of being an account of the origins of Buddhism in China is in fact an account of its elevation to significance, its moment of appearance to the imperial gaze. In both sources quoted in the *Lidai fabao ji,* the minister Fu Yi is instantly able to recognize the figure in the dream as the Buddha. In the first, he specifies an obscure classic of antiquity as the source of his knowledge and "quotes" a passage that refers to the Buddha. In the second, Fu Yi is a *tongren* 通人, a man of penetrating or thorough knowledge, who has already heard of the Buddha. In both passages he plays the role of someone who knows of matters beyond the usual run of erudition. The minister has the key to the emperor's dream, but only the emperor has the power to actualize the prescience of that dream by bringing Buddhism bodily into his realm. Thus, the paradigmatic ideal Buddhist ruler, disseminating the faith through his support of monks and their wonder-working and scripture-translating activities, is made into the "founding father" of Buddhism in China.

After the figure in his dream has been identified, the emperor immediately sends men to India to obtain images, monks, and scriptures. The emperor could have simply ordered an image fashioned according to his dream, but the "inner joy" he experienced inspires him to seek the authenticity of the source. The images, monks, and *Scripture in Forty-two Sections* (which was probably compiled in China in the fourth century) represent authenticity, but the catalytic effect of the image of the Buddha appearing in an emperor's dream depends on its complete otherness. Personal visionary experience of the Buddha is here independent of the Saṅgha and the Dharma, and yet it is not enough. The emperor has had an iconographically correct dream, but he does not have access to its power and is not a Buddhist until images, scripture, and monks arrive from India and he is enabled to "take refuge" through their mediation.

Between the two versions of the dream, there is a dramatic passage quoted from the same source as the first version, the *Hanfa neizhuan.* A contingent of Daoists comes to the palace soon after the Indian monks arrive, and they insist that a contest of magical powers be staged in order to prove their superiority over the minions of the "barbarian divinity." The emperor agrees, and in the contest that is subsequently staged at the White Horse Monastery, the Daoists suffer a spectacular defeat.

This contest is discussed further in chapter 6, in the context of a more extended discussion of the treatment of Daoism in the *Lidai fabao ji*. Here, suffice it to say that Daoism was a force to be reckoned with in Sichuan during the time of the Bao Tang, and this probably spurred the *Lidai fabao ji* authors to feature a contest with Daoists as a prominent part of their opening presentation. Notably, the outcome of the contest hinges on the efficacy of the talismans, scriptures, and supranormal powers of the respective parties. Such devices of popular literature recur frequently in the *Lidai fabao ji,* for Wuzhu's iconoclastic rhetoric does not prevent the authors from relying on Bodhidharma's talismanic robe, various scriptural fusillades, and displays of extraordinary powers in order to mark turning points in the plot.

After the defeat of the Daoists, the superiority of the Buddhists is spectacularly demonstrated. The Buddha-relic radiates light, Kāśyapamātaṅga levitates and recites a verse, the Emperor "permitted the children and the concubines of nobles of the fifth rank and above to become renunciants," and "the entire realm took refuge in Buddhism."[14] When the *Hanfa neizhuan* was compiled, its authors were embroiled in struggles against Daoist opponents in order to win this imperial sanction. An emperor who allowed members of his inner circle to be Buddhists would thereby legitimate a new order of dependency and an alternative "host" within the networks of imperial and clan authority.

It is only after the synecdochic conversion of China through the person of the emperor that the latter asks for concrete information about the new deity he has embraced. This scene showcases a motif that few Buddhist hagiographers could resist, one that the *Lidai fabao ji* authors found especially compelling—the motif of an emperor or high official paying homage to and deferring to the authority of monks. The emperor does not ask about the Buddha's teachings but about his birthplace, family, and dates, the three elements that constitute the core of a Chinese biography.[15] An unmistakable implication of the monk's replies is that the position of Emperor of China is reduced to insignificance if compared to the cosmological scale of the Buddha's birthplace and genealogy.

DAOAN AND TRANSMISSION OF FORMS

The most pressing problem for the Bao Tang was defending the legitimacy of "Southern School" no-thought as the only practice, particularly as it extended to reinterpretation of ritual and precepts. Following the trail of this dominant concern, the *Lidai fabao ji* authors skipped abruptly from Emperor Ming to an episode featuring the monk Huiyuan 慧遠 (334–416) and introduced Huiyuan's teacher Daoan 道安 (312–385) later in the narrative. As we will see, the roles they are made to play in the *Lidai fabao ji* are not entirely consistent with the endeavors for which they are best remembered. Buddhabhadra 佛馱跋陀羅 (359–429), the other monk we take a look at, is refracted by the *Lidai fabao ji* authors into two fictitious characters.

In examining early representations of these figures I focus on the issue of "form," particularly the formal aspects of the traditional "three trainings" (*sanxue* 三學) of *śīla* (moral discipline), samādhi (spiritual concentration), and prajñā (wisdom). Correct form and correct translation were integrally related concerns. In our examples, concern with *śīla* is expressed in the quest to acquire and translate the Vinaya (monastic code), while traces of the desire for mastery in samādhi can be discerned in the works enumerating techniques of dhyāna (meditation). The attempt to come to grips with the elusiveness of prajñā is reflected in questions as to how to determine the soundness of one's interpretation of scripture and the efficacy of one's practice.

There was much at stake in this matter of getting the forms right. In the *Gaoseng zhuan* 高僧傳 (Biographies of Eminent Monks), there are often implicit or explicit connections drawn between a monk's fidelity to moral discipline and his experience of supramundane visions and powers. For example, it is said that not long before his death Daoan received a mysterious visitor who taught him the details of the proper bathing rituals and then vouchsafed him a marvelous vision of Tuṣita heaven where he was assured of rebirth.[16] Buddhabhadra, it is said, was such a model of rectitude that he became the target of jealousy; he had a true vision of "five ships setting out from his native country," but other monks accused him of breaking the Vinaya prohibition against pretending to supernormal powers for personal aggrandizement.[17] In Huiyuan's biography, his integrity and propriety invests him with the authority to give asylum to enemies of violent rulers.[18]

The Monastic Code

To provide background for the subsequent discussion of each monk's approach to the practice of discipline, I devote a short section to a review of early Chinese reception of the precepts and the monastic code, the Vinaya.[19] Throughout Buddhist history, the notion of merit gained by making offerings to the Saṅgha motivated devotees of all levels of society, lay and ordained, to support monks and nuns, construct temples, cast and carve votive images, and copy scriptures, and so on. As Buddhism entered

China, faith in the efficacy of "merit" was strongly linked to perception of the Buddhist monk as one who had powers produced by his adherence to a specific body of precepts, his practice of techniques of meditation, and his mastery of scriptures. There are references to third- and fourth-century translations of monastic regulations and ritual procedures, but these references are from later works. Therefore, it is difficult to determine how the monastic code was construed and used prior to the rash of Vinaya translations in the early fifth century. Some form of *prātimokṣa,* the formula for fortnightly recitation of rules and confession of transgressions, was probably transmitted orally by the first foreign monks active toward the end of the Han dynasty, but the earliest descriptions of Chinese translations of the Vinaya and the formal transmission of the precepts are in the *Chu sanzang ji ji* 出三藏記集 (Collection of Notes on the Translation of the Tripiṭaka) and the *Gaoseng zhuan* 高僧傳 (Biographies of Eminent Monks).

Sengyou 僧祐 (445–518), compiler of the *Chu sanzang ji ji,* gives a detailed account of the Chinese reception of four out of the five Vinayas.[20] The *Chu sanzang ji ji* also includes Dharmaraksa's 曇無蘭 and Daoan's fourth-century prefaces for precepts texts,[21] but Hirakawa Akira points out that the existence of prefaces does not mean that the texts they refer to were complete or that they were comprehensible. He cites as examples the number of poorly translated "ordination" texts among the early Dunhuang manuscripts, which would not have been reliable guides for proper ordination.[22] Tsukamoto Zenryu identifies a Dunhuang manuscript entitled *Shisong biqiu jieben* 十誦比丘戒本 (The Essential Sarvāstivāda Precepts for Monks) as the oldest extant Chinese precepts text, and he surmises that it is a copy of a portion of Puṇyatara's 弗若多羅 incomplete initial translation of the *Sarvāstivāda Vinaya*. The verso colophon of the manuscript avers that in 406 in Dunhuang, the precepts were administered to the monk Deyou 德祐 according to proper form.[23]

Huijiao 慧皎 (d. 554), compiler of the *Gaoseng zhuan,* inaccurately claims that all five Vinayas had been transmitted.[24] In his biography of Dharmakāla 曇柯迦羅 (active c. 249–254), he claims that before Dharmakāla translated and transmitted a *prātimokṣa* text, there were no correctly ordained Chinese monks; ordination consisted of simply taking the tonsure, and monks used Chinese ritual forms for the fortnightly ritual of confession. Dharmakāla was said to have decided that the entire Vinaya was too involved for his disciples and to have introduced a text of the essentials of the *Mahāsāṅghika prātimokṣa.*[25] Huijiao also mentions a translation of a *karmavācana* (procedural) text for the ordination ceremony itself, but the extant texts of that nature are later translations.[26]

Whatever the actual state of the code, in popular imagination strictly observing the precepts and mastering a panoply of meditation techniques were intrinsic to the mystique of the numinously adept monk, one who was detached from the world and yet uniquely empowered to affect both the natural and the political spheres. This is a lastingly influential paradigm that persists to this day, a paradigm that was shaped by the role that Western monks like Fotudeng 佛圖澄 (d. 348) were believed to have played during the violent upheavals in the north during the fourth century. Fotudeng's *Gaoseng zhuan* biography dwells on his magical displays, his powers of prediction of the outcome of battles, and his unshakable calm in his dealings with his violent royal patrons. These are presented as skillful means that he deploys in his compassionate effort to civilize the ruling clans and shield the Saṅgha and the populace from the worst effects of continual warfare.[27] At the same time, Fotudeng was also credited with an extensive knowledge of the various Vinayas.[28]

Fotudeng's Chinese student Daoan 道安 (312–385) had, through his students, a great impact on the shape of Buddhist monasticism in both the north and south in the fifth century.[29] Fotudeng's death was closely followed in 349 by that of his patron, the Later Zhao 後趙 ruler Shi Hu 石虎. Escaping the disturbances ensuing from the breakdown of the Zhao court at Ye 鄴, Daoan and his fellow students were widely dispersed. Daoan himself crisscrossed the central and northern regions for sixteen years, accumulating disciples along the way. He and his students finally retreated south to Xiangyang 襄陽 in 365, during the warfare that accompanied the Former Qin 前秦 reunification of central China.

In Xiangyang Daoan won the support of several wealthy donors, and in writings concerning the monastery that he established, Tanqi si 檀溪寺, we have the first documented traces of daily life at a flourishing monastery in China. Daoan, as head of a settled community of several hundred monks, had to grapple with problems of organization and rules of conduct in the absence of any complete Vinaya translation. Similarly disturbed by Chinese monks' scanty knowledge of monastic rules, the famous pilgrim Faxian 法顯 set out in 399 on his harrowing fifteen year journey to India and back.[30] Daoan chose instead to make known his desire to obtain Vinaya texts, and in the meantime he devised his own code based on what scriptural sources he could muster, a code that was said to have been widely adopted.

A glowing impression of his efforts is conveyed in a letter attributed to the contemporary literatus Xi Zuochi 習鑿齒 (d. 390). This letter is reproduced in two early Buddhist works in sections devoted to Daoan and may be suspected of having undergone partisan editing. Suspect or not, it is a testimony to the kind of Buddhism for which Daoan was remembered:

> He is no ordinary Gentleman of the Tao! Teachers and disciples number several hundred; indefatigable in fasting and in elucidating, they do not have

> the arts and crafts of metamorphosis and transformations with which they can befool the ears and eyes of the common folk; neither do they have any awe-inspiring gravity and great power with which they can keep in line irregularities of egregious petty folk. And yet, nevertheless, teachers and disciples, decent, decorous, themselves are mutually respectful and reverential towards each other. That so many could be calm and composed, sober and steady: this has really never been seen by me before.[31]

A description of the code responsible for such impressive results is given in the *Gaoseng zhuan* biography of Daoan, which is the source for the truncated version of this code given in the *Lidai fabao ji*. At first glance it is not apparent what function Daoan serves in the *Lidai fabao ji* narrative, for the following passage about him is an anachronism in the midst of an otherwise genealogical account of the transmission of Bodhidharma's robe.

> In the three hundred years after the Buddhist teachings came east, there was no formal standard at all. Later, around the time of Shi Le 石勒 of the Jin 晉, Fotudeng's disciple Dharma Master Daoan was at Xiangyang 襄陽. Fujian 苻堅 of the Qin 秦 heard of Daoan's fame from afar, and so he dispatched retainers to attack Xiangyang and capture Dharma Master Daoan. The Qin emperor often honored and met with him, and the sons of the nobility of Chang'an 長安 all went to him to recite their verses. [The saying] "If students don't rely on Dharma Master Daoan, they will not be able to make sense of difficulties" refers to this; everyone recognized his intelligence. Later he also established a method of organization for discourses, and made rules for monks and nuns and a set of statutes for the Buddha-Dharma. As for the rules for taking the precepts, he classified them into three sets: the first concerns circulating with incense and determining seating, the second concerns the regular six periods of repetition of the *vandana*, and the third concerns the monthly *uposatha* confession of transgressions. Formal (*shixiang* 事相) deportment, the prayers and hymns used in services, etc., originated with this Dharma Master Daoan.[32]

Though this passage cites the standard praises of Daoan, it soon becomes clear that he is to serve as an exemplar of deluded "phenomenal" practice.[33] The *Lidai fabao ji* authors laconically comment that a Sichuanese contemporary recently produced a popular liturgical text, thereby indirectly making the point that devotional practices reflect their own eras and milieus and should not be reified as timeless truths. Daoan thus marks the introduction of the main concern of the *Lidai fabao ji* authors, for they then embark on a long series of quotations from the *Laṅkāvatāra-sūtra* and other works in order to criticize attachment to the forms of teachings and practice. Under this hermeneutic, codes of behavior and meditation techniques become intechangeable, for any attention to formal particularity is considered equally futile, and even damning: "The *Laṅkāvatāra-sūtra* says . . . 'If you depend on inferior Dharma then inferior Dharma arises. If you depend on phenomena then the Dharma will be ruined.' Moreover it says, 'If you follow after words and grasp meanings then you build on dharmas, and because of that construction, when you die you fall into Hell.' "[34]

Yet Daoan himself was clear that codes of behavior must be understood as fundamentally nondual, and in spite of the *Lidai fabao ji* authors' selective editing of his biography he was no mere schoolmaster in Buddhist garb. Daoan writes in a commentary: "Therefore, in observing the precepts there is neither precept nor transgression, in practicing mental concentration there is neither concentration nor disturbance, and in dwelling in wisdom there is neither wisdom nor ignorance."[35]

Daoan's abiding interest in practical and moral codes as the foundation of the teachings of nonduality can be seen in a letter he wrote to an unknown colleague in Liangzhou 梁州 (Gansu). Stating the urgent need for a complete Vinaya, Daoan wrote: "The great work of conversion will be deficient so long as the rules for the four groups of the community (monks, nuns, male and female lay devotees) are incomplete. The *Prajñāpāramitā* scriptures depend on 'good sons and daughters' as the main teachings. Thus, initiating the fundamental 'hundred practices' of conduct set forth in the precepts is like a tree taking root."[36] In "tangled hierarchy," observance of the rules is fundamentally nondual while at the same time the Dharma is grounded in monastic rule—which Daoan envisioned as having achieved closure and sufficiency in some form not yet available in China. There was as yet no need to worry about the embarrassment of riches constituted by the voluminous sectarian variations of the Vinaya.

Techniques of Dhyāna

In the same section, the *Lidai fabao ji* authors also criticize the type of dhyāna associated with Daoan's milieu. The dhyāna techniques disparaged in the *Lidai fabao ji* are reminiscent of the techniques found in early translations of dhyāna scriptures; for some of these we have prefaces attributed to Daoan.[37] The *Lidai fabao ji* authors assert: "The various Hīnayāna dhyānas and the various samādhi gates are not the tenets of the school of the Patriarchal Master [Bodhi]dharma; examples of their names are as follows: white bones contemplation (*vidagdhaka-saṃjñā*), counting breaths contemplation, nine visualizations contemplation, five cessations of the mind contemplation, sun contemplation, moon contemplation, tower contemplation, pond contemplation, Buddha contemplation."[38]

In order to establish a basic sense of what was understood as dhyāna in the fourth and fifth centuries, it is helpful to review Tang Yongtong's classic taxonomy of early dhyāna practices.[39] Tang's classification is based on the traditional rubric of *śīla*, samādhi, and prajñā introduced at the beginning of this section. Tang weighs meditation, discipline, and asceticism on the "practice" side of a scale whose other side is "wisdom," or the theoretical aspect. Relying on translation attributions recorded in early Buddhist catalogues, Tang traces four currents in the transmission of dhyāna. The first is *nian anban* 念安般, a sobriquet for mindfulness technique derived from An Shigao's 安世高 Han translation, the *Anban shouyi jing* 安般守意經.[40] This and related works represent early Buddhist contemplative exercises aimed at the cessation of mental activity in progressive stages. The second is *bujing guan* 不淨觀 (contemplating impurity), the classic Indian meditations on corpses and the impurity of the body, practiced as an antidote to attachment to form. The third is *nianfo* 念佛 (recollection of the Buddha), introduced in the second century through Lokakṣema's 支婁迦讖 translation of the *Banzhou sanmei jing* 般舟三昧經 (*Pratyutpanna-samādhi-sūtra*).[41] This sūtra advocates visualizing the Buddhas of the ten directions and claims that one attains birth in a Buddha land through contemplation of the characteristics of the Buddha. It was a seminal work for both the Maitreya and Amitābha devotional cults and is discussed further in chapter 3. The fourth is *shoulengyan sanmei* 首楞嚴三昧, derived from the *Śūraṅgamasamādhi-sūtra* translated by Kumārajīva.[42] The *Śūraṅgamasamādhi-sūtra* claims to comprehend all practices and, at the same time, to represent a dhyāna attainable only by a bodhisattva of the highest level; it was also prized for its treatment of *abhijñā* (supernormal powers), though in theory these powers are not the highest goal.[43]

Tang Yongtong's four types of dhyāna are presented in order of the chronology of the major translations of the scriptures associated with them. The progression is also clearly a *panjiao* 判教 or "classification of the teachings" teleology, in which the *śūraṅgamasamādhi* represents the most advanced level of meditation. Tang's hierarchization scheme reflects fifth-century Two Truths hermeneutics like those found in the scripture prefaces of Sengyou's *Chu sanzang ji ji*, in that the highest level is a unity of wisdom and practice, while dhyāna represents the intermediacy and multiplicity of the practice aspect. In catalogues of early translations, the first three types of dhyāna—mindfulness, contemplation of impurity, and Buddha-visualizations—are each represented in multiple texts devoted to that type or to a particular manifestation of it, as well as appearing in compendia that include all three and permutations thereof. Dhyāna techniques lent themselves to specialization and systematization and apparently infinite proliferation.

The *Lidai fabao ji* authors targeted such dhyāna techniques for censure, in conformity with the "Southern School" position that no-thought was both a quantum leap and a return to the original truth of practice.[44] However, the notion of an "ultimate" understanding of dhyāna was not unfamiliar in the fourth century. Even if imperfectly deployed in the philosophical sphere, Kumārajīva's translations of *Prajñāpāramitā* scriptures and Madhyamaka school treatises provided a basis for use of the Two Truths hermeneutic as a means of organizing and grasping the proliferation of discourse and practice. Examination of fourth-century sūtra prefaces reveals that the tug of war between nondual deconstruction of practice and syncretic conglomeration of practices was well under way before the polarizations of the eighth century.[45]

Moreover, notions of practice as spontaneous function without fixed form had deep roots in indigenous Chinese discourse. As is well known, prior to the work of Kumārajīva and his disciples, Chinese exegetes tended to interpret Buddhist emptiness (śūnyatā) as fundamental nonbeing (*benwu* 本無), a basic concept in the metaphysics promulgated by Wang Bi 王弼 (226–249) and his heirs. Drawing from Daoist classics such as the *Daode jing* 道德經, the *Zhuangzi* 莊子, and the *Yijing* 易經, this metaphysical discourse was broadly known as *xuanxue* 玄學, "abstruse learning." Consider, for example, these lines from the *Anban shouyi jing* preface written by Xie Fu 謝敷, a fourth-century proponent of *xuanxue:* "One does not exit being to enter nonbeing. Unchanging tranquility is thus not 'exhausting conditions by taking refuge in the void.' . . . It is not that the outer is belied by purifying the inner, one does not depend on dhyāna to achieve wisdom. For this reason, what we call *avaivartika* (nonretrogression) does not mean following the progression of the four dhyānas."[46]

Xie Fu's admonition takes issue with mistaken notions of both Daoist transcendence (entering nonbeing, purifying the inner) and Buddhist meditation. Daoist and Buddhist terms are used to point to their own ultimate lack of significance, and therefore ultimate reconciliation. As is further explored in chapter 6, the treatment of Daoism in the *Lidai fabao ji* reflects a milieu of sophisticated cross-borrowing and criticism among eighth-century Buddhists and philosophical Daoists that had its roots in fourth-century *xuanxue*. Chinese Buddhist exegetes of Daoan's day already had a fertile mix of discourses with which to discuss the techniques and meanings of meditation practice. As seen in the following section, Daoan was deeply concerned about the effect that this mixing of discourses had on the transmission of the Buddhist teachings.

Translation of the Sūtras

We now turn to a consideration of the contribution for which Daoan is best known in the annals of the transmission of the Dharma. As noted in the *Lidai fabao ji* passage above, Daoan spent the latter part of his life as a valued advisor in the court of the Former Qin 前秦 ruler Fu Jian 苻堅 (r. 351–385). Fu Jian may have had other strategically compelling reasons to advance on Xiangyang besides obtaining the services of Daoan, but this particular move in his campaign to overcome the Eastern Jin 東晉 had important consequences in the history of Buddhism. The dispersion of the Xiangyang community spawned several lastingly vital communities, including Huiyuan's at Mt. Lu 廬 in the south.

Fu Jian's troops took Daoan back north to the Qin court at Chang'an in 379, and the monk began a new stage of his career at the age of sixty-seven. The Buddhist sources are eloquent in their descriptions of Daoan's prestige and influence, and the account in the *Jin shu* 晉書 (Jin History) also attests to Fu Jian's esteem of Daoan.[47] One can only speculate about the contrasts between life as the abbot of a monastery located on a former private estate and life as a prominent figure at a court whose ruler was engaged in an attempt to reunify the Han empire. Although the Qin was to fragment in 385, the year of Daoan's death, the translation atelier that Daoan established in Chang'an survived to become the nucleus of Kumārajīva's activities.

In connection with the translation efforts at Chang'an, Daoan became the first Chinese monk known to have attempted a systematic discussion of the problems involved in translating scripture into Chinese. His discussion of the "five deviations from the original and three difficulties" (*wu shiben san buyi* 五失本三不易) form part of his preface to a new *Prajñāpāramitā* translation, written in 382. While Daoan's "five deviations" seem matter-of-fact and technical, his "three difficulties" bear down upon a soteriological problem, the implications of translation for transmission of the Dharma:

> The holy ones must be in accord with the times, and the customs of the times change. However, cutting away the polish from the ancient language in order to suit the present period, this is the first difficulty. Heaven sets apart ignorance and wisdom, the holy one cannot act as a stairway. Thus, wishing to take subtle words from the eminence of a thousand years, and convey them in terms of latter-day customs devolved from the age of the hundred generations of kings, this is the second difficulty. Ānanda brought forth the scriptures when the Buddha had not been long gone; then the honored Mahākāśyapa had the five hundred arhats with supernormal powers by turns consider [Ānanda's words] carefully and write them down. This was a thousand years ago, and yet we rely on recent ideas to take their mea-

> sure. Those arhats were so very cautious, and these men of saṁsāra are so very complacent—isn't this just the presumption of those who are ignorant of the Dharma? This is the third difficulty.[48]

Daoan suggests that supranormal powers are necessary for anyone who would be an editor of the Dharma. The task as it is presented here is not one of simple transcription; rather, it requires personal verification deriving from affinity with the Buddha, such that latter-day "men of saṁsāra" cannot hope to approach the original arhats. Given this sensibility, one might see Daoan's translation concerns and his concern with dhyāna and the precepts as all of one piece. The particularity of practices that cannot be reconciled with present custom serves as a sign that the holy ones have not lowered themselves, become stairways to ignorance, and distorted the Dharma. This is reflected in various matters of praxis, such as Daoan's rejection of *geyi* 格義, the matching of Buddhist concepts with terms from Chinese metaphysics,[49] and his proposition that all Chinese monks take the Buddha's clan name, Śākya (Shi 釋), as their own.[50] Daoan argues not for adaptation to Chinese norms but rather for the creation of difference, for adherence to a particular Buddhist law as the only means to transmit the Buddhist letter.

At the same time, an important aspect of his legend of uncanny erudition was his reputation for mastery in Chinese classics and antiquities, and the standards of scholarship that he applied to cataloguing Buddhist texts were derived from secular bibliographic methods.[51] The distinction that he articulated and instituted for the Buddhist clergy was founded on notions of mastery very similar to those of the Han elite: mastery of the body through detailed codes of behavior and ritual dress, and mastery of a sanctioned corpus of texts. This similarity in principle, and Daoan's exacting attention to formal difference, proved a highly effective combination that was taken up and furthered by his student Huiyuan.

The traditions concerning Daoan raise two very important questions for fourth- and fifth-century Buddhists in China: How does a "translated" Buddhism work? And, in an undertone—does it work? A variety of claims were made in these and subsequent centuries as to the locus of a guarantee or verification that what was being disseminated was in fact the true Dharma, and a variety of fallback positions were argued. One may see frequent oscillation between appeals to correct form and appeals to visionary experience as sources of authority in early Chinese Buddhist biographies. The sources of legitimacy evoked were, on the one hand, institutional, hermeneutical, and ritual standards, and, on the other hand, the final testimony tended to be the spiritual sign, subtle or otherwise. These formal and ineffable standards were mutually dependent, signs and criteria that each referred to the other. Formal exactitude was the external mark of the mysterious, but spiritual effects were also external manifestations demonstrating that form had been rightly internalized. Consider, for example, the *Gaoseng zhuan* story of Daoan's dream:

> An (Daoan) frequently annotated the sūtras, but he feared that [his interpretations] did not harmonize with the principles [of the sacred texts], so he then pronounced the following vow (*praṇidhāna*), "If what I have explained is not very far from the principles, may I behold an auspicious sign!" He then dreamed that he saw an Indian man of the Way who had white hair and long eyebrows, and who spoke to An, saying, "The annotations made to the sūtras by you, Sir, are quite in harmony with the principles [of the sacred texts]. As for me, I have not yet attained nirvāṇa and I live in the Western Regions. I will aid you in diffusing [the doctrine]. From time to time you may make me an offering of food." Afterward when the *Sarvāstivāda-Vinaya* arrived, the Reverend Yuan (Huiyuan) then recognized that he about whom the *Upādhyāya* (i.e., Daoan) had dreamed was the [arhat] Piṇḍola. Thence they established a seat to make food offerings to him, and everywhere this became the rule.[52]

Here Daoan's concern about his exegesis is allayed by a scripturally verifiable dream, which in turn becomes the basis of modification of Chinese monastic ritual. Nor is this the only instance in Daoan's biography of spiritual validation conveyed by Piṇḍola. The arhat whom the Buddha criticized for shameful display of *abhijñā* (powers) and gluttony may seem an odd associate for the fourth century's paradigmatic disciplinarian and exegete, but both left an imprint on monastic practice. Daoan's disciple Huiyuan instituted monastic food offerings for the arhat in exile, and Piṇḍola served as guarantor and guide for earnest monks, eventually becoming the patron saint of the monastery refectory and bathroom.[53] The wandering arhat was an intermediary for the future Buddha Maitreya, who was considered an advisor for exegetes and meditators and to whom Daoan and his disciples regularly repeated their vows to be reborn in Maitreya's Tuṣita heaven. The result of these vows is confirmed by Piṇḍola who, disguised as a monk, pays Daoan a visit before his death. The arhat reveals that Daoan is assured of rebirth in Tuṣita and instructs him in the correct procedure for taking a bath.[54]

BUDDHABHADRA AND TRANSMISSION OF LINEAGE

As reflected in the *Lidai fabao ji* passage, Daoan became a kind of patron saint of monastic regulations, and in him was vested not only the responsibility for a number of specific monastic practices but also the authority to testify that, given the requisite discipline, authentic Dharma could be transmitted. A "holy response" signifying that one had gotten it right was highly appreciated, but was unfortunately subject to the dangers of misrepresentation and overproduction. To guard against this danger, there had to be signs of temporal and causal conditions of transmission working in tandem with signs of the transcendent, and this concern, amounting at times to an obsession, was a key factor in the development of the notion of spiritual lineage.

As noted, the spiritual lineage of the Chan patriarchs is the organizing principle of the first part of the *Lidai fabao ji*. The authors give a detailed account of the spiritual antecedents of the Bao Tang founder Wuzhu, in which we can discern tension between the regard for lineage and the desire to affirm Wuzhu's uniqueness. The *Lidai fabao ji* authors' distorted reflection of Buddhabhadra's link to a line of Indian masters thus introduces a motif that is taken up in subsequent sections devoted to different aspects of the *Lidai fabao ji* authors' complex presentation of lineage.

The earliest forms of Buddhist genealogy in China were formulated on the basis of transmission of texts. Daoan, in this as in other spheres, is credited with setting a precedent that would have deep and far-reaching implications. His biography claims: "From the Han and the Wei up to the Jin, there had been a gradual increase in the arrival of the scriptures, yet the names of the men who transmitted the sūtras were not stated. . . . An (i.e., Daoan) then collected and brought together the names and the titles and indicated the times and the men."[55]

In the fifth century we begin to see examples of lists of names included with Vinaya and dhyāna-related texts as records of transmission. Stories of the early generations of transmission from the Buddha are included in the two extant Aśoka texts and in certain Vinayas, but more recent transmissions were also represented in the lists appended to Chinese translations of Vinaya and meditation texts. These lists constitute claims for authority based on the translators' pedigrees.[56]

For dhyāna transmission, the earliest lineages found in a Chinese work, the *Chu sanzang ji ji*, are associated with the Kashmiri Sarvāstivāda tradition of the master Dharmatrāta. The *Chu sanzang ji ji* includes four variant lineages beginning with either Mahākāśyapa or Ánanda, and ending with Dharmatrāta and his disciples. Two of these *Chu sanzang ji ji* lists appear in prefaces to the so-called *Damoduoluo chan jing* 達摩多羅禪經 (*The Dhyāna-Scripture of Dharmatrāta*) translated by Buddhabhadra 佛馱跋陀羅 (359–429).[57] These prefaces are by Daoan's student Huiyuan, and Buddhabhadra's student Huiguan 慧觀 (d. c. 440). The *Damoduoluo chan jing* itself includes Buddhabhadra's preface with a different version of his lineage.[58]

Buddhabhadra presented and commented on the *Damoduoluo chan jing* while staying at Huiyuan's monastery on Mt. Lu in south China, after having left Chang'an with his close disciples, including Huiguan, under unfavorable circumstances.[59] The prefaces by Huiyuan and Huiguan afford fascinating glimpses of notions of lineage transmission in the early fifth century. They are also apologia for Dharma transmission, and McRae argues that conceptual similarities suggest that the two prefaces both originated from notes made from Buddhabhadra's lectures *in situ,* even though the lists of names included in the text itself and in the two prefaces differ from one another.[60] The prefaces' common claim that spiritual genealogy goes beyond mere serial oral reduplication of the teachings was to influence the subsequent development of transmission theory. The preface by Huiyuan reveals a certain reification and mystification of transmission itself, and also reveals some of the contradictions that emerge with such reification.

> The principle is obscured by repeated broadcasting and the Way is darkened in letters. Thus it was that Ānanda inherited the Buddha's oral message in all its particulars. If it happens that there is no such person [to receive it] one must conceal the mysterious storehouse. How is it that the mind is an unchanging compass when its transformations go in all directions? Mere repetition does not determine likeness, one must wait for evocation before responding. . . . The Tathāgata had not long entered nirvāṇa when Ānanda transmitted [the Dharma] to his fellow disciple Madhyāntika. Madhyāntika transmitted it to Śāṇavāsa. These three responses entirely delivered what was wanted, and profoundly tallied with the ancient original. This achievement lies outside words and is not delineated in the scriptures.[61]

Huiyuan then goes on to recount a traditional version of the decline of the Dharma, namely, that Upagupta was not quite up to the level of the Buddha's immediate disciples and Upagupta's disciples preserved only the essentials. After the five-part division into the different schools of Vinaya, the true transmission went underground, functioning to save ordinary beings like "hidden footsteps leaving no trace." However, the vulnerability of the "ancient scriptures" to external vicissitude gave rise to fears for the continuance of the teachings, and so select representatives from each school transmitted meditation scriptures to reinforce the Dharma. Huiyuan argues that diversity is a mark of the fullness of the Dharma, not its degeneration, and those who convey the endless variations of its skillful means are not known in worldly terms. They are not defined by sectarian divisions, but neither do they put forth anything that is outside the Dharma manifested within those sectarian divisions.[62]

In this passage, transmission is a verb rather than a reified object, and it is only intermittently identified with specific vessels. For Huiyuan, transmission of the Dharma is that which ultimately resolves into itself any contradiction between esoteric transmission and its putative raison d'être, exoteric dissemination, between the Buddha's original teachings and skillful means, and between the nonsectarian closure of the Dharma and the ongoing proliferation of lineages and divergent traditions. The intimate discord between the transmission, interpretation, and individual experience of truth is held in suspension within one vessel, the mind, whose "transformations go in all directions."

We recall Daoan's exhortation that one must face one's inadequacies and yet muster all one's powers in order not to lower Dharma standards by accommodation to the times. For Huiyuan, in contrast, Dharma and adaptation are coterminous. Yet Huiyuan and Daoan agree that something was lost in the transmission after the first generations. Moreover, even though Huiyuan declares that the Way is "darkened in letters" and the original transmission is not contained in the scriptures, the Dharma is said to be in serious danger if the ancient scriptures are lost. Huiyuan is caught in (and perhaps enjoys thus capturing) a paradox that was to become ever more familiar in Chan writings after Shenhui. This is the paradox of orthodox transmission outside the scriptures, of the Dharma as an ineffable power that is all-encompassing and endlessly adaptable and yet must be vigilantly guarded from the threat of annihilation by heterogeneous forces. Daoan, by contrast, had written of transmission simply as a sacred trust, empowering yet only as effective as its human trustees.

Although the passages on Daoan and Huiyuan are not linked in the *Lidai fabao ji*, the authors obliquely trace the fissure between Daoan's religious sensibilities and those of his disciple Huiyuan, for they ingeniously contrive to introduce the sudden doctrine of Bodhidharma to Huiyuan's Mt. Lu in a lively scramble of misidentifications and archetypes.

> At one point, [Bodhidharmatrāta] ascertained that the beings of the land of the Han (China) were possessed of the Great Chan nature. So he dispatched two of his disciples, Buddha 佛陀 and Yaśas 耶舍, to go to the land of the Qin[63] and explain the teaching of immediate awakening. When the worthies of the Qin first heard, they were doubtful and none would believe. [The disciples] were cast out and driven to the Donglin 東林 monastery on Mt. Lu 廬.
>
> At that time, Dharma Master Lord Yuan (Huiyuan) was there, and he asked them, "Worthies, what Dharma have you brought, that you were thus cast out?" Thereupon, the two Brahmins put out their hands and said to Lord Yuan, "The hand changes to a fist and the fist changes to a hand. Does this happen quickly or not?" Lord Yuan responded, "Very quickly." The two Brahmins said, "This is not quick. Defilement is none other than bodhi.

> *This* is quick." Lord Yuan was deeply impressed, and thereupon realized that bodhi and defilement are one and the same. Then he asked, "In this other country, from whom did you learn this Dharma?" The two Brahmins replied, "From our teacher Dharmatrāta." Lord Yuan [was moved to] a faith profound indeed.
>
> [The two disciples] translated the *Chanmen jing* 禪門經 (Scripture of the Chan Teachings) in one fascicle, which completely elucidates the Greater and Lesser Vehicles and the Chan Dharma. Those who transmitted the Dharma in the Western Kingdoms are also all included in the preface to the *Chan jing.* When the two Brahmins had completed the translation, they both passed into extinction on the same day and were buried on Mt. Lu, where their stūpa even now remains.[64]

The story of "Buddha" and "Yaśas" fleeing Chang'an to take refuge with Huiyuan on Mt. Lu, there to translate a Chan/dhyāna scripture, is obviously reminiscent of Buddhabhadra's biography, and their names clearly evoke Buddhabhadra's contemporary Buddhayaṣas 佛陀耶舍.[65] The *Gaoseng zhuan* biographies of Buddhabhadra and Buddhayaṣas would have been available in the eighth-century Buddhist world, so one suspects that the *Lidai fabao ji* authors wanted to entertain readers with verisimilitude, in a manner more akin to *chuanqi* 傳奇 ("transmitting marvels" fiction) than to *liezhuan* 列傳 (official "arrayed" biography). Through use of Buddhabhadra's biographical elements and the name of Buddhabhadra's Dharma ancestor Dharmatrāta, Buddhabhadra's lineage is yoked to a newly created referent, the Chan founding patriarch "Bodhidharmatrāta." There is a kind of vaudeville-team choreography about the Chan-in-unison of Buddha and Yaśas, who also die on the same day and share a stūpa.[66] They are tropes, akin to "divine twins,"[67] and the text that they translate is also a figurative work representing several conflicting contexts. The *Chanmen jing* is an apocryphal scripture related to the nascent Chan trend, while the *Chan jing* quoted by Shenhui quoted by the *Lidai fabao ji* is the dhyāna-sūtra of Dharmatrāta, the *Damoduoluo chan jing.*[68]

For Shenhui and the *Lidai fabao ji* authors, Buddhabhadra/Dharmatrāta's dhyāna-sūtra was an important repository of lineage, hence the claim that "those who transmitted the Dharma from the Western Kingdoms are also all included in the preface to the *Chan jing.*" However, the Dharma that the *Damoduoluo chan jing* contains is precisely the kind that is caricatured in the *Lidai fabao ji* passage on visualizations of bones, the sun, the moon, Buddhas, and the like.[69] The *Damoduoluo chan jing* employs variations on mindfulness and contemplation of impurity as organizational markers for what would otherwise seem to be endless lines of undifferentiated meditations on meditations in verse. In the final section, Buddha-visualization occupies the ultimate level, playing the same role as the *śūraṅgamasamādhi* in Tang Yongtong's taxonomy, marking a qualitative shift from the particular to the panoptic, and, not incidentally, from Hīnayāna to Mahāyāna phraseology.

Yet Buddha-visualization was also anathema to the *Lidai fabao ji* authors, and immediately following their disparagement of Hīnayāna dhyāna they quote the "real" (apocryphal) *Chanmen jing:* "The Buddha said, 'In seated meditation one sees emptiness, there are no things. If one sees the Buddha with thirty-two characteristics, of variegated radiance, soaring in the air and manifesting transformations at will, then this is all one's own mind tumbling over and over, bound up in a demon's net. In empty nirvāṇa, you see that such things are empty delusions.'"[70] However, by quoting the *Chanmen jing* the *Lidai fabao ji* authors escape from one net only to fall into another, for that text is likely to have been a product of the "Northern School."[71] Although it purports to convey "sudden teaching," it advocates seated dhyāna and tranquil extinction and is thus attuned to notions of contemplation that were labeled by Shenhui as characteristic of Shenxiu and his followers. And indeed, in the *Lidai fabao ji* the *Chanmen jing* is in its turn rendered inert by a spate of quotes, including one from another Chan-related apocryphon, the *Vajrasamādhi-sūtra:* "[The Buddha said,] 'I do not enter samādhi and do not abide in seated meditation. [When there is] no-birth and no-practice, neither activity nor meditation, this is birthless meditation.'"[72]

Although the section of the *Lidai fabao ji* in which these quotations are assembled at first glance looks like an indiscriminate collection of passages from dhyāna texts, Mahāyāna sūtras, and apocryphal works of various stamps, there is clearly a teleology at work. It is teleology with an apocalyptic edge, for the penultimate quotations are dire predictions of the threat posed by monks who establish a false Dharma.[73] Seemingly standard admonitions against precept-breaking are used as a segue to introduce Shenhui's ideology of transmission of the robe as token of the true Dharma, always imperiled by false, reified notions of practice and false monks. However, as seen above in Huiyuan's preface to the *Damoduoluo chan jing,* though reification of the power of transmission may have assuaged anxiety that the Dharma, like all things, is composite and subject to decay, it also created a host of other complications. Not the least of these complications was the problem of how to verify the path of transmission that, in Huiyuan's foreshadowing of Shenhui, "lies outside words and is not delineated in the scriptures."

Let us consider Huiyuan's fears for the integrity of the Dharma in light of circumstances described in Buddhabhadra's biography. Buddhabhadra was enabled to lecture to Huiyuan at Mt. Lu thanks to his having become persona non grata at Chang'an. His removal, with disciples, was attributed to the jealousy of those who resented Buddhabhadra's implicit criticism of their master, the great translator Kumārajīva 鳩摩羅什 (344–413). Buddhabhadra apparently affronted other monks by his more-austere-than-thou observance of the precepts, and was known for his rigorous if "Hīnayānist" standards of dhyāna.[74]

The involvement of monks and nuns in the unstable world of Six Dynasties (265–589) politics presented opportunities and dangers for the Saṅgha, especially for those in the capitals. The extant literature attests to a sense of the fragility of the earthly thread of the Dharma, a fluctuating geography that included not only India as the semimythical source of the teachings, but also the Central Asian countries of birth and places of training of many of the Western monks. Chang'an court Buddhism as it appears in the *Gaoseng zhuan* was a multicultural affair with undercurrents of tension, where political and soteriological concerns both reinforced and threatened one another. There are numerous examples of monks asked to use their powers to serve the those in power, and also examples of impious rulers who come to grief. These portrayals of the political benefits of piety rest upon the contradictory proposition that rulers place faith both in the monk's otherworldly neutrality and in his loyalty to his patron.

In the world reflected in the *Gaoseng zhuan,* monks were at risk in many senses; they were subjected, like Kumārajīva, to the violent tempers and temptations of ruling elites, and were also, like Buddhabhadra, persecuted by the intrigue and slander of fellow monks. Huiyuan claimed in the *Damoduoluo chan jing* preface that transmission of the true Dharma is quietly carried on by an elect who are not known in the world, and this assurance itself points to uneasy recognition of ever-present danger. Those most successful in spreading the Dharma were also those most exposed to corrupting influences, and the popular hagiographical topos of the uncompromising monk reflects the complicated political realities negotiated by Kumārajīva and others of the clergy who lived in luxurious surroundings and associated freely with the powerful at court.[75]

A similar dilemma was at work in the hugely popular merit-gaining activity of scripture translation. On the one hand, sūtra recitation from memory in Sanskrit was a prized feature of the Western monks' miracle-working repertoire, and the words of the Buddha's "face-covering tongue" in their original purity evoked the potent otherness of the foreign religion. On the other hand, translation into Chinese was a "skillful means" and an expression of Buddhism's many-tongued universality, not dependent on any canonical language. The Dharma was transmitted to China and was therefore destined to be Chinese; the sūtras urged their own dissemination for the benefit of all beings and promised great rewards of merit to those who assisted in this propagation.

Daoan, beset with fears that the Dharma was being lost in translation, appealed to Maitreya and was reassured in a dream. Huiyuan expressed distrust of words and warned that "mere repetition does not determine likeness, one must wait for evocation before responding." In the *Gaoseng zhuan* description of the large-scale state-sponsored translation project of Kumārajīva and Emperor Yao Xing 姚興 (r. 393–416), there was clearly much pride in the imperial and human resources that were devoted to improving the technical and literary sophistication of the translations, and yet the story of Kumārajīva's death also raises questions about the power of the transmitted word.[76] Kumārajīva was unable to stave off death with his own recitations of dhāraṇī (talismanic Sanskrit verbal formulae), and he ordered "a disciple from a foreign land to recite them in their native efficacy." This too failed, and he delivered a deathbed speech in which he expressed his regrets and hopes for the Dharma, ending with this vow: "If what I have transmitted is without error, when my body is cremated, may my tongue be unconsumed by the fire." And after the fire died down, his tongue alone remained.[77]

Like Huiyuan's preface, this final word implies that the technical skill of accurate reproduction brings no particular benefit. The words work only when Kumārajīva makes a vow on behalf of the Dharma, responding to death with a gift rather than seeking to postpone it. It is also telling that this tongue-relic vouching for the Dharma defied Chinese symbolism of state and sanctity, in which the "uncooked" signifies barbarity, and only through being "cooked" in the sacrificial vessel of imperial influence does something become civilized and refined.

HUIYUAN'S TRANSMISSION OF SPACE AND PLACE

The following *Lidai fabao ji* passage featuring Huiyuan is sandwiched in between the account of Emperor Ming of the Han and a verse in praise of Buddhism that is attributed to the Saṅgha's model patron, Emperor Wu 武 of the Liang 梁 (r. 502–549). The *Lidai fabao ji* authors apparently linked these passages in order to demonstrate the homage that exemplary benevolent rulers paid to the Saṅgha, thus prefiguring later passages emphasizing the deference with which the imperial minister Du Hongjian 杜鴻漸 (709–769) treated Wuzhu. Here we see Huiyuan remonstrating with the emperor of the short-lived Chu 楚 dynasty, Huan Xuan 桓玄 (369–404). Huan Xuan was the virtual ruler of the Eastern Jin territories from 397 to 404, but he was deposed and killed six months after he proclaimed his own dynasty.

> The *Jinshu* 晉書 (Jin History) says, "At the time of Emperor Huan of the Jin, [the emperor] wanted to cut back the Buddha-Dharma, and so he sum-

> moned Dharma Master Yuan (Huiyuan) of Mt. Lu. The emperor said, 'We have observed recently that the monks and nuns are not sincere in their practice of the precepts, and there have been many transgressions. We wish to weed out [the Saṅgha]. Shall we at once carry out this culling process?' Gentleman Yuan responded, 'The jade that is extracted from Mt. Kun 崑 is covered with dirt and grit. The Li 麗 River is rich with gold, yet it is also full of gravel. Your Majesty must respect the Dharma and value its representatives; you must not scorn its representatives or treat the Dharma with contempt.' The Jin emperor then issued a general amnesty."[78]

This passage serves as an example of an ideal resolution to the conflict between the Saṅgha's ideology of self-governance and the regulatory bent of the Confucian-Legalist state. In spite of Buddhists' repeated appeals to precedent in various petitions in support of Saṅgha autonomy, the records of the government, especially in the Tang, indicate the evolution of increasingly comprehensive regulations for controlling the clergy—though in different reigns and regions there was a great deal of variation in the degree to which these were enforced. In the *Lidai fabao ji,* the story of Huan Xuan and Huiyuan functions as the turning point of a dialectic. Chronologically and symbolically, it is in between the legendary first Chinese Buddhist emperor, Emperor Ming of the Han, and the historic first Chinese Buddhist emperor, Emperor Wu of the Liang. Huan Xuan's volte-face is dramatically placed in this representation of church-court relations, but the historical record is more ambiguous.

The status of the Saṅgha vis-à-vis imperial authority was an issue that became implicated in the power struggles among the great clans of the Eastern Jin court at Jiankang 建康 during the latter half of the fourth century. A debate was fought over whether the clergy should be required to bow before the emperor, and though the Saṅgha won this early battle, it was to lose the war in the eighth century. The bowing controversy was the subject of Huiyuan's famous treatise of 404 and the basis of his lasting reputation as the paradigmatic "defender of the Dharma."

The controversy may be said to have started with the attempt to curb the autonomy of the Saṅgha in 340, when the imperial regent Yu Bing 庾冰 (296–344)[79] of the newly powerful Yu clan petitioned to limit Saṅgha privileges that had been established under the protection of Wang Dao 王導 (276–339) of the previously ascendant Wang clan. Significantly, all the documents relating to the debate are generated from and remain within the state apparatus. The memorials and countermemorials, in which the names of monks do not appear, are submitted by lay officials associated with one or another of the factions involved, and the outcome was mediated by officials of the Ministry of Rites (*liguan* 禮官) and the Chancellery (*menxia* 門下).[80]

The main argument of Yu Bing's faction was that monks should not be allowed to get above their essential station as subjects of the state, and that if they were allowed special privileges this would undermine the five relationships,[81] the foundation of social stability:

> Yet they (i.e., the clergy), on account of the unintelligibility of their doctrines, use their deceptive costume to override the law, flaunting the arrogant manners of their alien usage, and stand upright before the [Lord of] Ten Thousand Chariots (i.e. the emperor)—this is something which I cannot accept.[82] . . . It is not that the Lord of Ten Thousand Chariots loves to be honored, nor that the common people of the empire love to be lowly. But if high and low are not set forth, the ruler's guidance is ineffective, and it is not [united as] one. If it is [divided in] two, then chaos results.[83]

The pro-Saṅgha faction countered that the monks, in observing their own order of discipline, supported rather than detracted from imperial authority. There was a slightly threatening suggestion of possible ill-effects if the Saṅgha were thwarted: "Allowing the custom of cultivating good to be abandoned in this sainted age, and letting common customs become the norm, must certainly cause it (i.e., the age) to be overshadowed by dread. It is because of this that your servants venture to feel uneasy."[84] The defenders argued that the strict discipline of the monastic code cultivates decorum and submission, but left it to be inferred that the proper recipients of that submission belong to an order other than the political. Both parties claimed a right to undivided loyalty, for the respect due to the Buddha, Dharma, and Saṅgha stressed by the Buddhist faction theoretically included the respect due to the ordained by all the nonordained, including even the emperor himself. However, it was not until Huiyuan that this point was made explicit.

The arguments in the debate of 340 remained secular and pragmatic, and the subjects of dispute were principles of governance and allegiance, not ontological claims. The detractors made some disparaging remarks about the vague origins and otherworldly orientation of Buddhism, but they also said it did not matter if Buddhism was practiced privately, as long as it did not run counter to the established practices of the public sphere. The defenders also limited their arguments to practical matters, citing the beneficial influence of the monks on behalf of the ruler and the good example that they set for the people. It remained for Huiyuan to articulate a more distinctively Buddhist position.

Huiyuan's apologia, his letters and his famous treatise arguing for clerical exemption from bowing to rulers,[85] were responses to the policies of Huan Xuan, the military dictator who appears in the *Lidai fabao ji* as "the Jin emperor." Huan Xuan was far from being an oppressor of Buddhism;

the "anticlerical" actions that he initiated arose from a judicious respect for the power and usefulness of the clergy. He had occasion in his own rise to power to make use of the influence that members of the Saṅgha exercised at court, but after he was established, it is understandable that he would want to prevent others from following his example.[86] The regulatory measures Huan Xuan attempted to impose on the Saṅgha were directed at the loose cannon in Jiankang, but do not seem to have been prompted by anti-Buddhist sentiment in principle. The biographies of Huiyuan and two other monks feature episodes in which Huan Xuan attempted to persuade them to give up the reclusive life in order to serve as his official advisors.[87] This is inconsistent with letters in which he insisted that monks and nuns should either abide by the rules constituting their special status and remain sequestered or return to lay life, but he does seem to have respected Huiyuan and valued his advice. Prior to reopening the issue of whether monks should bow to the ruler, he may have attempted a registration of monks in the region of the capital, and Huiyuan's biography attests to Huan Xuan's interest in weeding out spurious members of the clergy.[88] Apparent contradictions in his image could also be attributable to the different aims of the *Gaoseng zhuan* and the dynastic histories.

However, the frequency of the scene in which a ruler or official unsuccessfully attempts to invite or retain a monk (a favorite of the *Lidai fabao ji* authors) should not lead us to disregard the delicate paradox involved. The Saṅgha's access to the ruling elite depended upon this blank refusal, however seldom it was exercised, because the personal prestige accruing to their patrons rested on the premise of the clergy's freedom to leave. Official desire to draw clearer lines between the political and religious spheres dovetailed with the Saṅgha's desire not to let its own spheres of interest and disinterestedness appear too blurred, yet conflicts arose over who had the right to draw the lines. This is what we find in the *Gaoseng zhuan* episode that superficially resembles the *Lidai fabao ji* account of Huan Xuan's attempted selection of the Saṅgha. Here, in contrast to the *Lidai fabao ji* version, we see Huiyuan reinforcing Huan Xuan's efforts such that the Saṅgha, through Huiyuan as its representative, becomes responsible for its own selection:

> Shortly afterwards Huan Xuan wanted to select the Saṅgha, and so he instructed the magistrates under his jurisdiction as follows: "Those among the śramaṇa who are able to recite the scriptures, or who excel in explaining their meaning and principles, and those who are obedient and correct in observing the Rules, are worthy to propagate the great Doctrine. All those who deviate from these (standards) shall be secularized. Only Mt. Lu is a place where the virtue of the Way dwells—it will be exempted from investigation and selection."

> Huiyuan sent a letter to Huan Xuan: "It is already a long time since the Buddhist doctrine has become degenerated and mixed with impure elements. Whenever I come across (such things), indignation fills my bosom. I was always afraid that fate would take an unfavorable turn, and that false and true would be lost together. But now I see (that you will) purify those of the Way, and this instruction surely agrees with my innermost intentions. If the (clear) Ching river is separated from the (muddy) Wei, then pure and impure will come into different situations. . . . Once this is done, the result will be that those who gloss over their falsity will be cut off from the great open road (of the Saṅgha), and those that cherish the truth will be freed from the evil of incurring the criticism of the laity. The Way and the world will mutually prosper, and the Triple Gem will be restored to its former glory." Subsequently he enlarged the scope of Huan Xuan's regulations, and Huan Xuan followed his advice.[89]

The metaphors in the *Lidai fabao ji* passage and in this account have precisely the opposite significance—in the *Lidai fabao ji* the Saṅgha is sacrosanct regardless of the inevitable dross mixed in with its treasures, while in the *Gaoseng zhuan* muddied waters threaten the very existence of the Saṅgha. In Huiyuan's biography, this letter to Huan Xuan precedes the account of Huan Xuan's renewal of the dispute over homage to the ruler. As we will see, in that final interchange Huan Xuan capitulated, but Huiyuan's clear statements about the need for the autonomy of the clergy are presented within the context of his sympathy for Huan Xuan's concerns and a mutually respectful relationship between monk and ruler.

Once again the *Lidai fabao ji* authors molded different aspects of a complex situation into a shape that reflected their own issues, and in this case the issue was the Bao Tang community's vulnerability to the kind of selection that Huan Xuan—and a number of Tang emperors—had proposed. The Tang founder Gaozu 高祖 (618–626) had fired the opening salvo with an edict known as the *Shatai Fo Dao zhao* 沙汰佛道詔 (Edict to Sift Out Buddhism and Daoism), in which criticism of Buddhism predominates. He employed the same metaphor of jade and stones that was later used with the opposite intent in the *Lidai fabao ji:*

> During the time that We have borne up the imperial canopy of Heaven, We have prospered the teaching of the Dharma, have been intent upon its benefit and cared about its protection. We wish to cause jade and stones to be separated, and fragrant and fetid plants to be distinguished. [In order that] the subtle Way long endure, the field of merit be forever established, and the originally pure source be upheld, [the Saṅgha] should comply with the sifting-out of its gravel.[90]

Emperor Gaozu was unable to implement his proposed regulation of the Saṅgha due to his son's successful bid to seize the throne. Taizong 太宗 (626–649) rescinded his father's edicts, but he too, after his reign stabilized, tried to bring the Order to order. In 637 he implemented a code of regulations for Daoist and Buddhist clergy, the *Dao seng ge* 道僧格, but toward the end of his life his increasing reliance on the impressive Buddhist pilgrim Xuanzang 玄奘 (602–664) caused him to reverse his own policies restricting ordination.[91] And so it went, with successive Tang emperors trying various means to control and yet co-opt the power of Buddhism. As discussed in chapter 5, Emperor Xuanzong officially settled the bowing issue in the ruler's favor. The emperor Dezong 德宗 (779–805), during whose reign the *Lidai fabao ji* was composed, joined the ranks of his ancestors who began their reigns by taking a stand against Buddhist encroachment, only to be baffled in their attempts to come to terms with Buddhist influence. Yet the reforms proposed early in Dezong's reign could have hit close to home for the Bao Tang school.

In 778 Li Shuming 李叔明, a military governor in Jiannan 劍南, submitted a memorial that the monasteries under his jurisdiction (which would have included the Bao Tang) be regulated for economic reasons. According to the *Tang shu* 唐書 (Tang History), he proposed that officially registered monasteries be limited to a fixed number of monks, and advocated that "All [remaining in monasteries] should be carefully selected practitioners of the Way, the rest must return to their initial [lay condition]. Unregistered hermitages and chapels are all to be destroyed."[92] The petition as it is included in the *Tang Huiyao* 唐會要 is even more critical, and includes this pointed barb: "Moreover, those who leave home these days are all of the low-grade 'no-consciousness' (*wushi* 無識) type. Even if their practice of the precepts was noble and pure, they are of no use to rulers whatsoever."[93] Though no names are mentioned, it is possible that the governor had in mind the "no-thought" creed of the Chan school, and may even have heard of Wuzhu's followers. Li Shuming's petition briefly gained momentum in official channels and an empire-wide selection was mooted. However, possibly to the relief of those remaining at the Bao Tang monastery, Emperor Dezong was distracted by insurgent military governors from 781 to 786, and in the course of this struggle he became a more devout Buddhist.[94]

The Bao Tang school members came by their appearance of laxity honestly, eschewing traditional Buddhist practice as a matter of principle, but their only hope for widespread acceptance of their antiformalism was in reforming the terms of the Saṅgha's accountability to its patrons, official and private. Huiyuan's precedent was a mixed blessing, for although Huiyuan's autonomy and Huan Xuan's submission were heartening, the values at the heart of Huiyuan's well-known treatise in defense of not-bowing could never be construed as supportive of Bao Tang notions of formlessness. Let us take a closer look at the kind of Saṅgha that Huiyuan actually defended.

Huiyuan's famous treatise was the final word in an exchange that began with Huan Xuan's official proposal in 402 to require the clergy to pay obeisance to the ruler. Documentation for the debate chiefly consists of letters between Huan Xuan and his trusted collaborator Wang Mi 王謐 (360–407), the grandson of the great statesman and Buddhist patron Wang Dao mentioned above. This initial exchange was followed by a round of letters between Huan Xuan and Huiyuan.[95] As is evident in the summary below, both parties display a much deeper familiarity with Buddhist doctrine and practice than had been evident in the debate of 340. One of the recurring arguments made in defense of the Saṅgha was the importance of the rituals that separated the Buddhist from the secular sphere.

The exchange of letters between Huan Xuan and Wang Mi contain the opening salvos of the debate over significance of ritual. Huan Xuan argues that because monks, like all beings, rely on the life-sustaining emanation of the ruler's benevolence, "How then could they receive his virtuous power yet neglect his rites, be blessed by his favor but abstain from reverence?"[96] Wang Mi replies, "Although the śramaṇas' inner intentions are deeply fixed upon reverence, they do not [express this] by the forms of bowing in their rites, for their traces overfill the borders of countries, and transcend that which is within [physical] dimensions."[97] Huan Xuan counters with the just observation that the clergy bow to their teachers, so why should they refuse what is simply good manners in the case of the emperor?[98] Wang Mi first argues for the complete alterity of Saṅgha practice, and then inconsistently falls back on a Confucianistic appeal to the claims of seniority.[99]

The results of this exchange were equivocal, for in 402 Huan Xuan promulgated a decree requiring monks to pay homage, but in 403 he submitted all the documents, together with a request for his opinion, to Huiyuan. Huiyuan's reply forms the kernel of his treatise written early in 404, the *Shamen bu jing wangzhe lun* 沙門不敬王者論 (Treatise on [Reasons Why] *Śramaṇa* Do Not Bow to Rulers).[100] However, in the intervening period Huan Xuan's mind and his fortunes changed dramatically. Although he replied dismissively to Huiyuan's initial appeal, one of his first acts as emperor of the newly created Chu 楚 dynasty was to proclaim the Saṅgha exempt from acts of reverence to the ruler. Three months later, when Huiyuan was presumably at work on his treatise, Huan Xuan's forces were defeated by Liu Yu's 劉裕 loyalist Jin armies, and Huan Xuan himself was killed in June 404. Liu Yu, upon his restoration of the Jin (to which he himself was to deliver the final blow in 420, founding the Liu Song

劉宋 dynasty), did not reverse Huan Xuan's final permissive policy toward the Saṅgha.

Huiyuan's treatise revolves around a point made in his earlier letter to Huan Xuan, in which he claims that the Saṅgha is in effect a separate principality realized through its ritual distinctness:

> Even in the absence of the Way, one absolutely must preserve its ritual. If the ritual is preserved, the Dharma can be disseminated, and if the Dharma can be disseminated the Way can be sought. This is the great Dharma, identical and unchanging from ancient times to the present. Furthermore, the *kaṣāya* (monk's robe) is not court attire, nor is the *pātra* (alms-bowl) a vessel of the imperial audience chambers. Military and civil are different in appearance, western barbarians and Chinese do not mix. That persons who shave their heads and mutilate their bodies should heedlessly sully the rites of China—this seems like the commingling of different species, which is something I find quite unsettling.[101]

Here the monk's robe and shaved head is not merely a uniform of affiliation, but permeates deeply into "national" and even physical and racial levels of identity. Though antithetical, the Bao Tang followers' neglect of proper rites regarding tonsure and robes was no less motivated by piety and purity, for it was meant to remove the adventitious accumulation of forms that clouded an "identical and unchanging" Dharma. Unfortunately, there is no way of knowing whether it was deliberation or carelessness that led the *Lidai fabao ji* authors to separate Huiyuan from his principles and make him into an advocate of commingling, of gritty jade and graveled gold.

In the treatise itself, Huiyuan argues even more forcefully for separation of the spheres of Saṅgha versus laity and Dharma versus civil law, a separation that was indispensable to any claim for the preeminence of the Buddhist sphere. And, in contrast to the appeals to utility and Chinese historical antecedent diffidently offered by lay Buddhist apologetes in 340 and again in 402, Huiyuan forthrightly states that the power of the Way is greater than that of any temporal ruler.

However, the final section of Huiyuan's treatise is especially germane to the question of the significance of form. After a long disquisition on the immutability of subtle responsive spirit as the source of all differentiations, in a language and logic imbued with the sensibilities of metaphysical Daoism, the treatise is declared to be completed. Then, some "retired guests" who have read the treatise come in by moonlight for a chat in the Dharma hall. They raise a question—why should a monk or nun who has just embarked upon the Way (or, by unspoken extension, those unfaithful to it), whose hidden virtue and future emancipation are in no way manifest, be favored and fed? The "host" replies by drawing an analogy between the clergy and those officials who are supplied with provisions and rewarded with carriage and clothing for conveying the ruler's mandate to distant barbaric regions.[102] He concludes:

> What is meant by the name "śramaṇa"? It means one who is able to disperse the dim dusk of beclouded common persons, to clear the dark road that is beyond change. . . . If so, then the merit of [providing] transport and the benefit of supplying the means of existence do not repay even [the monk's] intention to take the first vow. How much the less then, are [these benefits] able to answer the labor of the three works (i.e., purity of body, speech, and mind)? Such a person, though his body is still conditioned, has feelings not lodged in the near-at-hand. If one looks at the offerings of the four things (i.e., food, clothing, bedding, and medicine), they are as but a mosquito passing before one. A mere drop of favor, is it worth mentioning?[103]

This was a clear statement of the Saṅgha's challenge to the Confucian system of reciprocal obligation. It claimed a right to the patronage of the spheres of family and state and offered in return only a testimony of a territory beyond the reach of those spheres. The fifth century was to be the dawning of the age of the Saṅgha as an alternative economic power in China, and it can be argued that this was made possible in part by the success of Huiyuan and his epigones in securing a separate ritual sphere.

Huiyuan was not the first to assert for monks the rights of extrality on the basis of disinterestedness,[104] but his biography draws attention to the degree to which he himself was allowed political impunity due to widespread perception of his political neutrality.[105] In contrast to Fotudeng, Daoan, and Kumārajīva, who although highly venerated at court were virtual captives of their imperial patrons, Huiyuan, who pointedly never left his domain at Mt. Lu, developed an apolitical territory whose borders were respected by rulers. Like Daoan, he worked to provide definition and rationale for this privileged space. Like Daoan, Huiyuan's concern with monastic regulations was well documented; his biography shows him sending disciples off to the West to obtain Vinaya texts,[106] a number of his writings had to do with regulations for monks and nuns,[107] and he is credited with having gotten Dharmaruci to complete a translation of the *Sarvāstivāda Vinaya.*[108] When Huiyuan was dying, it is said, he refused fermented medicines because they are not in accordance with the Vinaya. When he was offered honey and water, he ordered the Vinaya master to read the rules to find out if such medicine was acceptable, and he died while the Vinaya was being read.[109]

Huiyuan's rectitude in death is emblematic of the kind of even light and clear mapping that Buddhism promised. Armed with nonduality and nonattachment, Buddhists claimed mastery in a different manner from the metamorphoses in which Daoists specialized. They introduced a new perspective on the legacy of Han and pre-Han culture, in which ritual, worship, cosmology, and the function of the state had largely overlapped.[110] As in Huiyuan's statement that "Heaven and Earth, though they are great because they give life to living beings, cannot cause a living being not to die," one effect of the action of the Saṅgha upon Chinese culture was to bring greater definition to the distinction between this-worldly and otherworldly.

As Bernard Faure has discussed in the context of the emergence of Chan, there is to be found throughout East Asia a deep-rooted hagiographic genre involving stories of monks who move into heterogeneous and autochthonous space and open up the universal, the birthless and deathless realm of the Dharma.[111] This shift is often marked by scenes in which a monk subdues a local deity, frequently in the form of a snake, and causes springs to gush forth or drought-relieving rain to fall, all of which we find Huiyuan doing at Mt. Lu.[112] In the diaspora after the fall of the Later Zhao, Daoan is portrayed as designating two alternative modes of dissemination, for he sends his disciple Fatai 法汰 to preach to refined gentlemen in the area of the southern capital, while Fatai's fellow-disciple Fahe 法和 is sent to cultivate tranquility amid the mountains and streams of "uncivilized" Shu (Sichuan).[113] Huiyuan, however, once he had dealt with the problems of snakes and water sources, articulated a place within the wilderness for artistic and literary refinement in a Buddhist mode.[114] This universal and ideal space was to become the monk's unique demesne. Faure writes, "In the same way that Chan hagiography was a composition of places that ultimately defined an empty or different spiritual space, the construction of monasteries created a new domain, a utopian space that was a non-space or non-lieu."[115]

This metaphysical/mountainous/monastic space developed from and into a new political niche. In his classic work on early Chinese Buddhist history, Erik Zürcher draws a connection between Buddhist place and the subsequent course of Chinese metaphysics: "The autonomy of the religious community in the Confucian state has been of momentous importance socially and intellectually; the emancipation of metaphysical thought from social and political philosophy, never realized in the circles of secular literati and politicians, took place and could only have taken place in the a-social and un-political community which the *Saṅgha* claimed to be."[116] I contend that this claim itself constituted the political aspect of the Saṅgha, an aspect not manifested in aberration, in the hypocrisy of its corrupt members, but rather in its formative appropriation of the "unpolitical" and its active propagation of the notion that metaphysics was "never realized in the secular circle."

The political turbulence of the fourth century fostered an aesthetic of reclusion, poverty, and abdication of official duty as a mark of integrity. Given the near-constant state of war and the ubiquity of interclan intrigue, neither military nor civil careers could be expected to be of long duration, and monasteries offered the perfect refuge and escape for both conscientious and unconscientious objectors to prevailing social conditions. Officials in service complained unstintingly about monasteries as refuges for criminals, conscript labor dodgers, and tax evaders, while aristocrats declining duty retired there to cultivate an ethic of detachment.[117]

The freedom that the monasteries represented was not just an alternative domain but an alternative network. The legitimation of wandering as a way of life, with the monasteries serving as way-stations, was a boon to those for whom life within the familial and social order was too taxing. Though freedom of movement was always perhaps greater than official records might lead us to believe, Buddhism provided a legitimate avenue, and the monk's robe some degree of protection, for those who wanted to remain on the move. Huan Xuan's attempted registration of the Saṅgha in 399 prompted a letter of collective protest from the monks of the capital, which argues: "But the śramaṇa dwelling in the world is like an empty boat on a large stream. His coming has no objective, and he takes his leave at his leisure. Within the four seas he has no fixed abode for himself. When the country is in disorder he moves his staff with pewter [rings] and roams alone; when the Way prospers [the monks] crowd happily together."[118]

The threats and opportunities presented by this alternative network were beginning to be recognized in economic terms as well. Buddhism appealed to those in client or vassal status as a new creditor and protector, breaking into the monopolistic and oligarchic traditional conceptions of economic and social place. In hagiographical literature, the role of the monk as subduer of local scourges was often directly linked to his being invited to take up residence in an economic position analogous to that of the local elite.[119]

As Jacques Gernet has documented, the choice of mountains for monasteries was economically astute. Tamed mountains were traditionally the prerogative of wealthy clans who commanded the labor resources necessary to make them livable and profitable, but a monastery established in the mountains could also attract a labor pool due to its tax-exempt and corvée-exempt status. Monks would first develop the mountain itself and then, through influence, donation, and purchase, could gain control of the surrounding fields and waterways. Rights to tithes of grain harvest and rights to develop mills and transport on the waterways were the pillars of wealth in medieval China. The monasteries were barred from sericulture, the other major source of wealth, due to the prohibition against harming living beings, but they received ample silk, a form of currency, through donations.[120]

The full range of this economic niche was to be developed in the Tang, and this is the backdrop against which we will see Chan master Wuzhu isolated on his mountain, proclaiming his conscientious objection to the well-fed, ritually fixated, and morally debile monks of the lowland monasteries around Chengdu. In a key scene, Wuzhu is deserted by his fellow monks because they condemn his refusal to carry out any Buddhist activity besides sitting in meditation—his behavior is held responsible for the dearth of donations to their remote temple. As discussed further in chapter 6, the Bao Tang experiment with formlessness was beset by a serious liability. Without the forms that separated clerics from laypersons and Buddhist space from ordinary space, there was no rationale for a monastery at all, and nothing that would attract economic support. This may be the reason that a certain quotation appears three times in different parts of the *Lidai fabao ji*. Made up of phrases from the *Siyifantian suowen jing* 思益梵天所問經 (*Viśeṣacintibrahmaparipṛcchā-sūtra*), it takes up the issue of donation:

> "Who repays the Buddha's kindness? One who practices according to the Dharma. Who consumes offerings? One who is not involved in worldly affairs. Who is worthy of offerings? In the Dharma there is nothing that is taken."[121] If one is able to practice in this way, one naturally has offerings from Heaven's kitchen.[122]

The extreme simplicity of this formula may be the key to its appeal for the authors. The Bao Tang followers could legitimately claim to be less involved in worldly affairs than most, and they could certainly endorse any form of the principle of emptiness, such as "nothing is taken." The crux of the matter is "practice according to the Dharma." Wuzhu taught that his practice was truly in accordance with the Dharma, in contrast to the debased practice of other monastics, and in this quotation one discerns a classic spiritual gambit at work. If formlessness really is the true practice of the Dharma, then the Bao Tang should be rewarded and "naturally have offerings." Forms and boundaries, such as those shaped by Daoan and Huiyuan, were a kind of hard currency of Dharma practice that entitled the monk to say of offerings, "a mere drop of favor, is it worth mentioning?" But the Bao Tang show themselves to be more like the gambler Kumārajīva, staking their Dharma on a sign from Heaven's kitchen.

THE MYSTIQUE OF LEGITIMACY

Before leaving the fourth century, I would like to highlight one additional aspect of Huiyuan's cultural milieu that is pertinent to further discussion of the ideologies of legitimate authority. In the Eastern Jin, the émigré court developed what historian Michael Rogers calls a "mystique of legitimacy," a spirit of imperturbability that was supposed to justify the mandate of the reigning Sima 司馬 dynasty and its clients in spite of the loss of the heartland.[123] This mystique developed around the notion that the essential realm was embodied in cultural and dynastic integrity and not in any particular territory. As Rogers characterizes it, the mystique of legitimacy was " a concept of a single legitimate strand of spiritual and cultural continuity which remained inalienable and indivisible, however straitened the political circumstances of the regime invested with it."[124]

Reclaiming the north was not a realistic prospect for the Eastern Jin rulers; instead, it was necessary to instill faith in the moral superiority of acquiescence. The superior virtue of disinterestedness over mere physical force, and the *wuwei* 無為 (nonactivity) strategy of allowing one's enemies to overreach themselves, had been core themes in Chinese political philosophy since the Warring States period (475–221 B.C.E.). These qualities are exemplified in the *Jin shu* 晉書 (Jin History) story of the rise and fall of the above-mentioned Former Qin ruler Fu Jian 苻堅 (r. 351–385), one of the enemies of the Eastern Jin.

Although the *Jin shu* was compiled in the early Tang and its lessons about the tragedy of megalomania were embroidered with the hope that they might convey a warning to Emperor Taizong 太宗 (r. 626–649), Rogers argues that there remains in it a core of authentic Jin sensibility.[125] The portion of the *Jin shu* that chronicles Fu Jian's rise and fall is a mythopoetic history in which the *wuwei* spirit of the Jin regent Xie An 謝安 (320–385) triumphs over Fu Jian's superior forces at the legendary Fei River battle, where Fu Jian's bid to reunite China was said to have been broken.

The "mystique of legitimacy" is incarnated in Xie An's natural integrity and casual refinement, in contrast to the hubris and ignorance surrounding Fu Jian in spite of his earnest efforts. One of the voices of reason attempting to aid the doomed ruler is none other than Daoan, who preaches a political strategy of non-action. Fu Jian asks him about the success of his southward "jaunt" to attack the Eastern Jin, and Daoan urges him to desist, recommending the superior effects of true *wuwei* rule:

> Why should you inflict hardship on your person in fast riding and make yourself mouth-weary in [exercising] universal domination, be combed by the wind and bathed by the rain, suffer the dust, and camp in the wilds?

> . . . If your civilizing virtue is sufficient to embrace the distant, you will be able, without troubling an inch of weapon, to bring the Hundred Yue into submission while you are seated on your throne.[126]

Civilizing virtue was not the sole criterion for possession of the mandate, however. The true ruler had in his keeping two essential tokens, the state-transmitting seal and the liturgical music of the Western Jin. The seal, a jade talisman that the Han founder was said to have taken from the vanquished Qin, had purportedly been recovered by the Sima in 352.[127] The music, however, had fallen into the hands of Fu Jian. The key victory of the Fei River battle was said to have been the recovery of a troupe of musicians who still preserved their sacred trust, and with the return of the musicians to the imperial ancestral temple in Jiankang, the balance of dynastic legitimacy was shown to have been reestablished with the Jin.[128]

From antiquity, the term "rites and music" (*liyue* 禮樂) has been a standard reference to statecraft and civilization, for music was seen as having the power to harmonize the human and natural worlds.[129] The notion that the ruler's virtue made him responsive to the will of Heaven was a political ideology attributed to the Western Zhou (1050–771 B.C.E.), and resonance and response based on musical principles were deeply significant concepts in Han practical philosophy and cosmology. The power of music was not produced merely by trained musicians and noble instruments; it had to be activated through the response of the ruler.[130] Huiyuan's notion of Dharma transmission reflects this aspect of the *weltanschauung:* "Mere repetition does not determine likeness, one must wait for evocation before responding."

There are striking parallels between the romance of Jin statecraft and the Chan romance of transmission, which is also not dissimilar to Huiyuan's romance of transmission. The opposition between the characters of Xie An and Fu Jian is analogous to the opposition between the effortless nobility of the legitimate Dharma heir (such as Huineng) and anxious exertions of the lesser contender (such as Shenxiu). The motif of the state music resonating to the virtue of the legitimate ruler is analogous to the motif of the talismanic robe of verification and those whose inner response enables them to activate the Dharma. In chapters 5 and 6, I trace the development of the mystique of legitimacy in Chinese Buddhism and delineate the various factors that contributed to the Chan version of "a single legitimate strand of spiritual and cultural continuity which remained inalienable and indivisible." The Chan patriarchy may never leave the land of myth, but it was never separate from a complex and intricately detailed historical landscape.

CONCLUSION

In this chapter, I have traced a few of the means by which the mythos and ethos of the Buddhist monk were transmitted and translated in the early period of Buddhism's Chinese incarnation. In reviewing transmission of the formal qualities of spiritual and moral discipline in the fourth century, we have seen something of the doctrinal paradoxes that attended transmission of dhyāna and touched on some of the conflicts surrounding enactment of Saṅgha codes of behavior. The distorted reflection of these issues in the *Lidai fabao ji* reveals the varying distances that separated the worlds of Daoan and Huiyuan from the world of the Bao Tang. In some matters, such as attitudes toward techniques of meditation and the ritual forms of monasticism, the Bao Tang defined itself through rejection of norms that originated in the early period. In other matters, such as the mystique of legitimacy and hidden Dharma transmission, the two worlds appear surprisingly close.

In many of the topics of this chapter, interactions between Buddhist monks and the ruling elite figure prominently. We are far from finished with rulers, but in chapter 3 I consider the development of more broadly based manifestations of lay Buddhism. The issue of the autonomy of the Saṅgha vis-à-vis secular authority had ramifications for the entire body politic, and the phenomenal growth of lay Buddhism would encompass rulers who spent lavishly for merit as well as village lay societies.

CHAPTER 3

Transmission and Lay Practice

It is the most impossible of all impossibilities that this
can be the work of the imagination.
—"The Vision Doubted," from *The Life of Saint Teresa of Ávila by Herself*

THE INTERDEPENDENCE OF LAY AND ORDAINED PRACTICE

In chapter 2 we looked at fourth-century figures who were instrumental in defining the parameters of practice for the ordained, and for heuristic purposes I grouped "practice" according to the traditional categories of *śīla,* represented by the Vinaya; *samādhi,* represented by *dhyāna* techniques; and *prajñā,* represented by translation of the scriptures. In this chapter we turn to lay practice, examining the early canonical basis of the distinction between lay and ordained and the background of the practices that became popular for the laity in fifth- and sixth-century China. I highlight two categories of practice: (1) reception of the bodhisattva precepts and (2) Buddha-visualization practices, especially those connected with repentance rituals. Though there are other rich fields of lay practice left unexplored, precepts practices and devotional visualization are most germane to Bao Tang Wuzhu's deconstruction of practice. In developing these topics, I stress the ways that lay practice and self-validating experience were acknowledged and also circumscribed. During this period, devotional practice proliferated and prompted new developments in the mediating functions of the Buddhist clergy. As bodhisattva precepts ceremonies and repentance practices increased in popularity, this gave rise to relatively unmediated forms of visualization and devotional practice that were part of the cults of Akṣobhya, Maitreya, and Amitābha. I trace a trajectory from the early Buddhist scriptures, through Mahāyāna precepts scriptures, to Chinese bodhisattva precepts scriptures, and finally to an apocryphal scripture that is permeated with concepts drawn from Chinese mythology and medicology. This trajectory from the canonical to the verge of popular practice (beyond which lie vast seas explored by only a few intrepid adventurers) is not intended to be evolutionary, but rather to afford glimpses of the many layers involved in the concepts of "lay practice" and "precepts."

How are these developments to be understood in the context of an interpretation of the *Lidai fabao ji?* Mass bodhisattva precepts ceremonies, networks of lay devotional societies, and debates over the rights and responsibilities of the ordained were all key features in the expansion of Buddhism in the eighth century. More important, these were precisely the aspects of Buddhist culture that Wuzhu attempted to subvert, with his redefinition of the precepts, his rejection of devotional and repentance practices, and his tolerance for self-tonsuring. Thus, this chapter reflects a view of the fifth and sixth centuries as seen through the inverting lens of the *Lidai fabao ji*. The *Lidai fabao ji* authors venerated Wuzhu's iconoclasm, as seen in the following passage in which Wuzhu preaches to a group of local officials who have become his lay disciples:

> The Directors asked, "Venerable, why do you not teach people to read scriptures, recollect the Buddha, and perform devotions? We, your disciples, do not understand." The Venerable said, "One validates final nirvāṇa for oneself, I also teach others like this. Do not hold onto the Tathāgata's incomplete teaching. Returning to one's own understanding, self-awakening initiates training. The Buddhas validate this person as one who has attained true samādhi."[1]

Employing a strategy that is common in Buddhist sectarian exegesis, Wuzhu's teachings are presented as a break with common practice that is at the same time a recovery of original Buddhist truth: "I also teach others like this." At the same time, this original truth is held to be personally verified experience, repeatable yet unique. We will look at corresponding strategies in earlier periods and explore texts in which the lay versus ordained relationship functions as a symbolic field for the rhetorical interplay of innovation versus continuity and inclusiveness versus exclusiveness.

In the *Lidai fabao ji* passage, the lay disciples are portrayed as somewhat misguided but perfectly respectful. The receptive, childlike lay figures in the *Lidai fabao ji* and other Buddhist hagiographical writing are clearly ideal types, and their presence points to the Buddhist clergy's acute awareness of the more active role that the laity played in defining the vectors and parameters of the Dharma. The mutual dependence of the categories "lay" and "ordained" was fundamental to the identity of premodern Buddhism, a dynamic self-differential in which changes in the character of either side necessitated renegotiation of the terms of the relationship. As Buddhism permeated Chinese culture more deeply , the socioeconomic and political operations of lay-clerical interdependency became ever more complex.[2] Buddhist monastics and laypersons were involved in a relationship that was mutually beneficial and yet thereby subject to the pressures of conflicting interests.

"Merit" (*gongde* 功德, Skt. *Puṇya*) was crucial to the functioning of this relationship and the construction of mutual benefit. Early Buddhist scriptures like the *Dakkhiṇāvibhaṅga Sutta* (The Exposition of Offerings) teach that offerings to the Buddha and to the Saṅgha gain merit for the devotee, which offsets the effects of past bad actions and helps create favorable future conditions in this life and the next.[3] In traditional Buddhism, the most meritorious act was to become a monk, and the highest reward for merit was to be reborn as a monk and attain liberation from rebirth altogether. For laypeople, the most important of the merit-gaining activities was support of the community of monks and nuns. This support took many forms, including providing facilities and supplies, sponsoring vegetarian feasts and memorial services, dedicating images and ritual implements, and providing the means for family members to become monks and nuns. In China, lay devotees could be economic clients as well as patrons, for the accumulation of resources by monasteries allowed clerics to act as lenders and landlords.

The laity gained merit, instruction, emotional-psychological support, and access to social and economic networks through ties to the Saṅgha. The clergy gained merit, right livelihood, support of the conditions for practice, and successive generations of new members from their ties with devotees. As with any other intimate relationship, there were compromises involved. A monk or nun who was in regular contact with lay devotees, particularly if they were family members, would naturally find it difficult to maintain the monastic creed of detachment.[4] However, donors were more likely to support monastics (other than family members) who were reputed to be uninvolved in worldly affairs. It was a matter of constant concern to secular authorities that the clergy could misuse their privileged positions in order to impose upon or deceive the laity; at the same time, it was recognized that Buddhism could inspire devotees to higher moral standards.

Monastics and laity alike desired access to the "charisma" of the special ordained, but this contributed to dilution and overproduction. Both sides wanted guarantees that monks and nuns were indeed "anomalous creatures" able to sanction the fortunate and succor the unfortunate, but the quest to define the corps of the spiritual elite tended to produce routinization and formalization. The relationship between lay and ordained hinged on an unstable interplay between inclusivity and exclusivity, between claims for accessible salvation and claims for special status for certain types of practitioners.[5]

Rhetoric extolling the superior virtues of the Mahāyāna (Greater Vehicle) was regularly deployed in Chinese Buddhist dialectics of inclusivity versus exclusivity. These dialectics were expressed through the medium of hagiography at least as frequently as they were argued in an exegetical or dialogical mode. Although numerous scholars have questioned the construction of stark opposition between Mahāyāna and the *śrāvaka* or Hīnayāna path, by the fifth century Chinese exegetes and compilers of apocryphal scriptures had been favorably impressed by the claims of Mahāyāna scriptures promoting the inclusiveness of the bodhisattva path. More important, Mahāyāna was held to be the soteriology of supernal aid: Not only the Buddhas and bodhisattvas but also Mahāyāna texts themselves functioned as salvific manifestations of the Dharma. At the same time, the clergy protected their exclusive right to represent this soteriology, setting themselves apart by the marks of moral discipline, meditation, and ascesis.

CRITERIA OF AUTHENTICITY OF THE DHARMA AND THE AUTHORITY OF THE ORDAINED

In this section we return to the earliest basis for the claim that the ordained—normatively, monks—had an exclusive right to represent Buddhist soteriology. Examining the terms in which this exclusivity was constructed, I review current research on the scriptural bases of the criteria of authentic transmission of the Dharma in the transition between early Buddhism and Mahāyāna. This forms the background for subsequent sections on devotional practices, where I discuss the Chinese reception and adaptation of the parameters of orthopraxy.

In a nutshell, the pertinent problem is this: Because the Dharma is held to be the nature of reality, not just the teachings of the historical Buddha, any individual could verify and augment the Dharma based on his or her own spiritual experience. In the early Saṅgha, criteria were developed whereby monks could determine the eligibility of newly heard teachings, testing them against the body of Dharma that had already passed into the oral literature and against their own experience. After the Buddha's death the Saṅgha was the only legitimate agent of the Dharma, and the Saṅgha defined itself through orthopraxy rather than orthodoxy. With the Mahāyāna teaching of emptiness and nonduality, the notion of Dharma as a specific body of teachings was deconstructed, and in theory orthopraxy was also deconstructed—the paradigmatic example of this is the *Vimalakīrtinirdeśa-sūtra*. However, no matter how far rhetorical deconstruction was carried, institutionally the bottom line held firm: Authority to determine and disseminate Dharma was the prerogative of the fully ordained monk. This comes as no great surprise, of course, but tracing the bottom line elucidates its function as a dividing line and clarifies the ground rules of the power dynamic between lay and ordained as it was played out in China.

Bao Tang experiments with orthopraxy lie at the other end of this trajectory, and for some of their Chan contemporaries the Bao Tang went too far in testing the bottom line. However, Wuzhu's dissemination of Dharma was consistent with "Southern School" orthodoxy, as shown in this example taken from his debate with a group of Dharma masters:

> He also asked the Dharma masters, "The Dharma is without verbal explanation, how does one explain the Dharma? 'One who explains the Dharma does so without explaining and without manifestation. Those who listen to the Dharma do so without hearing and without obtaining.'[6] 'That there is no Dharma that can be explained is called explaining the Dharma.'[7] 'Those who always know that the Tathāgata does not explain the Dharma are called complete hearers [of the Dharma].'[8] How do the Dharma masters explain the Dharma?" A Dharma master replied, "There are three kinds of prajñā. One is the prajñā of texts and characters, the second is the prajñā characterized by actuality, and the third is the prajñā of contemplating radiance."[9] The Venerable replied, "'Texts and characters have nothing actual and nothing on which to depend. Altogether unified in tranquil extinction, fundamentally there is nothing that moves.'[10] 'My Dharma is without actuality and without void.'[11] 'The Dharma transcends all contemplation practice.'"[12] The Dharma masters all looked at each other, unable to say a word.[13]

To capture Wuzhu's version of authentic Dharma, the *Lidai fabao ji* authors crafted a position made up of quotations from the scriptural foundations shared by many Mahāyāna schools of thought. Indeed, both Wuzhu and his interlocutors rely on this foundation for support, but the Dharma masters are made to represent conventional scriptural exegesis in contrast to Wuzhu's hermeneutics of no-Dharma. There is nothing new in this rhetorical strategy, but its practical limits had long been recognized in the exegetical tradition, and there were very good reasons—soteriological and institutional—why those limits had remained in place. In order to survey the foundations of these limits, let us go back to the era when Buddhist hermeneutical standards were taking shape.

Authority in the Early *Saṅgha*

In examining the foundations of the criteria of authenticity and orthopraxy, I am indebted to two excellent articles, "An Introduction to the Standards of Scriptural Authenticity in Indian Buddhism," by Ronald Davidson, and "Authority and Orality in the Mahāyāna," by Donald Lopez, which is in part a response to Davidson's article.[14] The two articles demonstrate the rich multivalence of the term "Dharma," which admits both written and oral reproduction and does not inherently divide scripture from analysis or distinguish between authentic reception ("penetration of meaning") and authentic teaching.

Davidson argues that certain decisions attributed to the Buddha in the early Buddhist discourses were particularly important in setting the standards of authenticity. First, the Buddha was said to have countermanded those monks who wished to fix a common language as the correct form of transmission and supported those who argued that monks should be allowed to learn the teachings in their own dialects.[15] Also crucial to early transmission was the practice of spreading recitations of the Dharma through a network of monks who had attained *arhatva* rather than solely from encounters with the Buddha himself. Monks traveled in small groups but congregated during the rainy season and for fortnightly *uposatha* to recite the precepts and confess transgressions. Recitation practices continued after the Buddha's death, and certain monks were valued as repositories of the Dharma that no single monk had heard from the Buddha in entirety.[16]

After the Buddha's death, the distinction between original and reproduction became more problematic. As Davidson says, the Saṅgha elders "were compelled to address the problem of the relationship between the Buddha and the dharma preached by him. Characteristically, the dharma was defined as that which was discovered by the Buddha, but it was neither invented by him, nor indeed was he the first of the Buddhas. Therefore, the speech of the Buddha embodied the dharma, yet the dharma went beyond the speech of the Buddha."[17]

The definition of the Dharma was expanded to include words of the Buddha preached by his disciples and the words of a person inspired by the presence of the Buddha. The teachings of the disciples of the Buddha were also sanctioned, which opened the way to include others' teachings "when significant and when endowed with doctrinal principle."[18] To determine significance and doctrinal principle, the litmus test was the ability to show the way to liberation from suffering, but soteriological efficacy could only be determined by monks.

Thus, the early Saṅgha adopted a functional rather than a formal definition of Dharma, which is consistent with the Buddha's attitude as represented in the discourses, the written forms of which are the products of the early Saṅgha. However, this inescapable horizon limiting our understanding of "what the Buddha taught" does not prevent us from recognizing that the Saṅgha, quite early in its development, claimed the capacity to move beyond the horizon of Śākyamuni Buddha himself. At the same time, the liberal notion that the soteriological function of the Dharma is not dependent on a particular form or person had to be enacted within a conservative context in order to retain its significance.

To illuminate the cultural ground on which Buddhist notions of soteriological authenticity were constructed, Lopez analyzes the famous antagonism between the Mīmāṃsakas, who claimed that the Veda is eternal, uncreated speech, and the Buddhists as represented by Śāntarakṣita, who argued that exposition of the Veda is still dependent on persons, who may be fallible and are denied the possibility of enlightenment according to Mīmāṃsā doctrine. Lopez points out rhetorical affinities between the two positions; both sides argue for the salvific power of receiving the sound of the Veda or Dharma itself, regardless of reception of meaning. However, they differ as to the source or significance of that power:

> when the Mīmāṃsakas speak of the eternal and unauthored nature of the Vedas, they are speaking of a self-identical sound, whereas when the Buddhists speak of the eternal nature of the dharmas as dependently arisen, they are speaking of a self-identical reality; it may be that what we are dealing with is an issue of form versus content.[19]

The doctrinal question of form versus content set the parameters of the practice of transmission in each tradition. The Mīmāṃsakas would train acolytes in perfect reproduction of the sound of the Vedas, while Buddhist training would emphasize personal experience of the truth of the Dharma. However, both Mīmāṃsā form and Buddhist content or function link authenticity and authority with physical qualities, though in different modes. The Buddhist monk's fitness to teach was a special kind of physical fitness, for he must embody "the five aggregates of the dharma: moral conduct, concentration, insight, liberation, and the vision of the gnosis of liberation."[20]

Toward the end of the first century after the Buddha's death, a ritual pronouncement of validity came into use whereby teachings were to be guaranteed by the words "This is the dharma, this is the Vinaya, this is the teaching of the teacher."[21] A teaching stamped with this oral seal of approval was supposed to have been validated by the "four great references to authority" (*caturmahāpadeśa,* often simply referred to as the *mahāpadeśa*) whereby a monk could consider a teaching valid if it issued from (1) the Buddha, (2) a Saṅgha of elders, (3) a group of specialists in one of the scriptural divisions, or (4) an individual specialist therein.[22] The *Mūlasarvāstivāda Vinaya,* moreover, includes guidelines about how these authorities were to judge authenticity: "one should see if it conforms to the *Sūtra* and compare it with the *Vinaya.* If in doing so, a) it conforms to the *Sūtra,* and b) is reflected in the *Vinaya,* and c) does not contradict reality (*dharmatā*), then let this be said [to that bhikṣu]: 'Truly, O Noble One, these dharmas have been spoken by the Bhagavān.'"[23]

Other versions of the criteria stressed verification of the source of a given transmission, but the third caveat introduced in the *Mūlasarvāstivāda Vinaya,* that the teaching must not contradict reality, raises interesting questions. This caveat, which could contradict the injunction given in the same text to "follow the transmitted discourses rather than individuals," points to the tension between liberal and conservative criteria. Davidson claims that the "reality" caveat indicates a liberal orientation toward personal validation of the Dharma (qua analysis of dependent origination), within a context of increasing formalization of textual authority.[24] Lopez, however, argues that this caveat does nothing to offset the conservative tendency of the "four references to authority" that only sanction "those doctrines and practices which are already accepted."[25]

Lopez argues that as reality, *dharmatā,* is held to be the source of the scriptures, they cannot contradict one another and the caveat has no functional value. However, it seems to me that in spite of this doctrinal higher ground the caveat is a tacit admission that the scriptures do contain contradictions and invite a wide range of interpretations. Thus, as Davidson maintains, monks are given at least some carefully circumscribed ground from which to claim their own enlightened (and rigorously trained) insight as authoritative. Yet, since only members of the Saṅgha are permitted to appeal to personal verification, one must raise the Katzian question, namely: How are we to take account of the mutual influence between doctrines and practices that are already accepted, and the spiritual experiences that vest the individual with the authority to interpret and transmit them?[26] In the Buddhist case, what is the relationship between the monk's experience of *dharmatā* and the shared reality of the Saṅgha as constituted by its practices?

Davidson points out that the *Mūlasarvāstivāda Vinaya* injunction to "follow discourses rather than individuals" harks back to an idealized image of the early Saṅgha depicted in a story from the *Gopakamoggallāna-sutta,* set shortly after the Buddha's death. In this story, a minister of King Ajātasattu asks Ānanda if the Buddha designated any monk as his successor, or if the community appointed any monk as leader in his place. When Ānanda replies in the negative, the minister asks him to explain the continued unity of the Saṅgha. Ānanda replies that the basis for this unity is the fact that all take refuge in the Dharma. Asked to elaborate, Ānanda says that recitation and maintenance of the rules of order, the *prātimokṣa,* represents taking refuge in the Dharma.[27] Davidson comments, "When the early tradition isolated the rules of behavior as the center of gravity, it selected group conduct over individual leadership. All the other criteria reinforce the individual's position as the functioning member of a subculture, rather than as a leader or follower. . . . The empowerment for decisions was toward a broad spectrum of the community and was grounded in monastic decorum."[28]

However, it is revealing to continue reading in the *Gopakamoggallāna-sutta* and see "the other criteria" that constitute the basis for individual leadership. The minister asks Ānanda why there are individual monks on whom the Saṅgha is willing to rely, even though they are not designated as successors. Ānanda explains that if any individual monk has the "ten qualities inspiring confidence," then the Saṅgha will honor and rely upon him. These ten qualities are (1) he is perfect in conduct according to the *prātimokṣa,* (2) he is learned in good teachings, has mastered them verbally, investigated them intellectually and penetrated them through his own insight, (3) he is content with the simple life of the *bhikṣu,* (4) he obtains the four dhyānas (absorptions, higher levels of consciousness) at will, (5) he has mastered the various supernormal powers, (6) he has the "divine ear," (7) he has insight into the minds of others, (8) he recollects his past lives, (9) he has the "divine eye," and (10) he has realized the truth for himself and "abides in the deliverance of mind and deliverance by wisdom that are taintless with the destruction of the taints."[29] This detailed set of criteria indicate that although individual leadership was limited in principle, the charisma manifested in *śīla,* samādhi, and powers was a focal point of devotion and inspiration for the Saṅgha.

Although the scriptures frequently warn against cultivating dhyānas, supernormal powers (*siddhis*), and superknowledges (*abhijñās*) as ends in themselves, here they are placed within a soteriological framework that treats them as marks of valid authority.[30] *Avadāna* tales of the disciples attest to the popular appeal of the image of the charisma or presence of the monk, a theme that also permeated Chinese Buddhist culture. In the *Lidai fabao ji* the orthodox type of authority embodied in group conduct is overturned time and again by Wuzhu's charismatic authority—despite or because of his iconoclasm, his rectitude is irreproachable, his samādhi is unsurpassable, and he is endowed with insight into the minds of others and a form of the divine eye. So we see the persistence of parallel but potentially divisive sources of authority, the collective versus the individual, even though the early Saṅgha tried to subordinate the latter to the former.

Regarding the orthodoxy of collective authority, in light of the primary Buddhist tenet of impermanence it was doctrinally appropriate that the continuity of the Dharma was to be protected by a collectivity, a body composed of "the five aggregates of the Dharma." This Dharma-body or subculture was maintained by orthopraxy, both moral and epistemological, that was supposed to be keyed to soteriological effect. Taking soteriological effect as the essential standard brought a great deal of pressure to bear on the subculture's definition of liberating behavior, and we can see the effects of this pressure in the splintering of the early Saṅgha into different subgroups, each with its own version of the Vinaya.

However, exploring the background of sectarianism in his book *Absolute Delusion, Perfect Buddhahood,* Jamie Hubbard argues that orthodoxy was more important than orthopraxy as the Saṅgha grappled with the passing of the Buddha. He cites a *sutta* in the *Aṅguttara Nikāya* asserting that literal reproduction of "sayings, psalms, catechisms, songs, solemnities, speeches, birth-stories, marvels, [and] runes" is the basis of preservation of the true Dharma.[31] This is clearly attuned to a different phase or community of preservation than is reflected in the claim that monks were permitted to learn the Dharma in their own tongues. As Hubbard himself notes, there are many voices in these texts; a succeeding *sutta* in the *Aṅguttara Nikāya* denigrates literal mastery of teachings and upholds meditation.[32] Therefore, Hubbard argues for the importance of orthodoxy as a category, rather than as a specific corpus or methodology of teachings.

Instead of trying to adjudicate between orthodoxy or orthopraxy as the defining category for the Saṅgha, I would argue that these multiple voices reveal the challenge of negotiating between the need to establish criteria of authoritative transmission of the Dharma after the Buddha had gone and the desire to maintain the independence that seems to have been a feature of the early community. Thus, in the categories of orthodoxy and orthopraxy we see a continuity of tensions or oscillations between Dharma and dhyāna, scripture and experience, form and adaptation, and community and individual.

Authority in a Mahāyāna Context

The problem of validating the soteriological efficacy of a given practice or teaching would grow more vexed with Mahāyāna texts, such that the *mahāpadeśa* (references to authority) could no longer be applied. Lopez says of the *Adhyāśayasañcodana-sūtra* interpretation of *buddhavacana,* the word of the Buddha: "unlike the four *mahāpadeśa,* the words are not judged to be the word of the Buddha based on their conformity with already accepted statements but based instead on their function: to destroy the afflictions and lead to nirvāṇa, certainly the most traditional of Buddhist aims, but in the absence of an omniscient arbiter, impossible to judge."[33]

With the development of philosophical speculation regarding the nature of the Buddha, the *buddhavacana* was no longer limited to the historical or even the cosmic Buddha, and this allowed for strong forces of both conservatism and innovation to remain in play, and in conflict. The problem of reconciling the traditional parameters of the Buddha's teachings with Mahāyāna conceptions of transmission of the Dharma gave rise to a number of creative solutions. Some sūtras maintained that the Buddha taught different levels of scripture at different periods of his life or according to the different capacities of his audience. The popular and enduring Mahāyāna classic, the *Saddharmapuṇḍarīka-sūtra* (Lotus Sūtra), maintained that "all the dharma was spoken by means of just a single sound (*ekasvara*)." The *Tathāgataguhyaka-sūtra* went even further and proposed a kind of ultimate "reception theory" according to which "the Tathāgata does not preach even a single word. All doctrines and all the scriptures simply arise in the hearing of those around the Buddha, each according to his own proclivities."[34]

This is the kind of formula represented in the *Lidai fabao ji* quotation from the *Vimalakīrtinirdeśa-sūtra,* couched as Wuzhu's preaching: "One who explains the Dharma does so without explaining and without demonstrating. Those who listen to the Dharma do so without hearing and without obtaining." What then becomes of the long-standing consensus that authority was grounded in monastic discipline, in orthopraxy? Davidson cites an ingenious solution from the *Mahāyānasūtrālaṅkāra* regarding the criteria of conforming to the Vinaya: the purpose of the Vinaya is to eliminate defilement, "and for a bodhisattva the only real defilement is conceptualization (*vikalpa*). Since the elimination of this conceptualization occurs through nonconceptual gnosis (*sarvanirvikalpajñānāśrayatvena*) arising by means of the practices found in the Mahāyāna scriptures, the Mahāyāna is validated in this *Vinaya* of nonconceptual gnosis."[35]

Nevertheless, the traditional limits endured, as Davidson notes with reference to the eighth-century monk-poet Śāntideva: "It is both ironic and telling that the difficulties of definition that surrounded the generation and codification of the sūtras throughout the history of Indian Buddhism finally caused Śāntideva to define the doctrine of the Buddha as that which had its basis in the condition of the fully ordained monk." He adds, "This is certainly very close to the consensual definition of the Buddha's teaching, which, as we have seen, held the earliest communities together."[36] This "consensual definition" is summed up in Davidson's concluding observation applied to Indian Buddhism in general, that "Orthopraxy (*prātimokṣa*) was considered the 'essence' of the tradition, not orthodoxy."[37]

Lopez, commenting on Davidson's use of Śāntideva, says, "However, a reading of Prajñākaramati's commentary suggests that Śāntideva is defining bhikṣu in a very limited and polemical sense here, as an arhat who has understood Mādhyamika emptiness."[38] Yet it seems significant that what Śāntideva meant by *bhikṣu* was indeterminate enough to invite commentary. I would suggest that the dividing line between the monk as a person who has simply gone through the ordination ritual and the monk as a person who has understood emptiness was too unstable to serve as the basis of orthodoxy. It is only the simple, formal definition, the ordination ritual, that can be made to hold firm. A key definition of nirvāṇa is that it is unconditioned and undefinable, so only in the ideal realms of exegesis and hagiography could unambiguous levels of realization be categorized, personified, and validated. As we saw in the *mahāpadeśa,* the institutional guidelines adopted by the early Saṅgha subjected individual insight to the judgment of collective seniority and scriptural expertise. As we saw in the "ten qualities inspiring confidence" in the *Gopakamoggallāna-sutta,* the attempt to provide empirical criteria with which to judge individual realization resulted in an emphasis on supramundane powers.

Lopez also engages in a Derridian reading of Buddhist writing, and his insights regarding writing are also applicable to monastic discipline. Discipline, the inscribing of Dharma through bodies, is, like writing, "a technology in the wider sense, as a more amorphous, pervasively deployed, institutional practice."[39] Like writing, monastic discipline is a means of repeating the trace, the absence that allows one to assume self-presence at the original vanishing point, the enlightenment of the Buddha. Just as Dharma, "the ancient city at the end of the ancient path,"[40] was considered something the Buddha discovered but did not create, the ancient path, *prātimokṣa,* was itself reified. The scriptures treat lay mores as contingent cultural forms that must be provisionally honored,[41] but the forms marking the conduct of the monk are treated as traces of the Buddha's enlightenment.

In the concept of lineage, speech/writing and monastic discipline come together. Commenting on the authority of lineage in Buddhist tradition, Lopez says, "The notion of origin from an uncreated truth is as much at play here as it is with the Vedas, so too the power of lineage, of hearing from the teacher what he heard from his teacher, often couched in the rhetoric of father and son, of inheritance and birthright, traced back ultimately to the Buddha."[42]

Codes of conduct and genealogies of privileged "hearing" reinforce each other in defining the identity of the Saṅgha, but they also point to its self-contradictions. Whether passed down orally or in writing, the Vinaya admits, due to its anecdotal and many-layered form, the possibility of variants, interpolations and multiple interpretations, and exposes its internal contradictions. The authority of genealogy enables this bricolage to carry the weight of the community, because the symbol of the Dharma passed from one individual to another translates the unclosed "baskets" of scripture, code, and commentary into a single sign, a reference to the word of the Buddha. The image of a monk enlightened by hearing the Dharma who transmits this repetition to his successor serves to turn cultural and personal belongings into the legacy of the Buddha. Unsupported by the *prātimokṣa,* the enlightenment of the monk could not feed and clothe and educate the community, but the mystique of a lineage of transmission, like the charisma of powers, promises a few threads of pure gold woven into the patchwork robes of Saṅgha orthopraxy.

Let me briefly recapitulate the key features of the criteria of authentic transmission of the Dharma discussed above. Elements such as (1) the reliance on consensual processes within the Saṅgha to decide what was worthy of transmission, (2) the tendency to define the Dharma based on soteriological function and content rather than form, (3) the acceptance of monks' experiences of truth as sources of Dharma, and (4) the maintenance of multiple tracks of authority (collective, individual, and genealogical)—all militate for maintaining unity not through any authoritative scripture, interpretation, or lineage of interpretation, but through orthopraxy. For the "functioning member of the subculture" this allows much room for hermeneutical diversity, but it also mandates a strict distinction in this regard between members and nonmembers.

Mahāyāna speculation is far-reaching and nondiscriminative in theory —the "Vinaya of nonconceptual gnosis" is an elegant and yet elusive reinterpretation of monastic discipline, and it is a lofty ancestor of the *Lidai fabao ji*'s slogan, the Wuxiang-Wuzhu teaching that "no-recollection is *śīla.*"[43] Doctrines like these appear to transcend the differential grouping of precepts that divided the laity and novices from the fully ordained. However, though there is recognition of this ideal in works like the *Vimalakīrtinirdeśa-sūtra,* the bottom line, as expressed by the eighth-century Mādhyamika Śāntideva, was that the doctrine is that which has its basis in the condition of the fully ordained monk.

THE ROLE OF THE BODHISATTVA PRECEPTS IN LAY DEVOTIONAL PRACTICE

The bodhisattva precepts, *bodhisattvaprātimokṣa,* were meant to supplement rather than displace the authority of Vinaya ordination, but Mahāyāna devotionalism often roamed far afield while exegetes busied themselves with the Dharma gates. In the following sections I select examples of devotional practices—bodhisattva precepts, Buddha-visualization, filial piety, merit, and repentance—and trace the lay-ordained relationship through several passages of Chinese Buddhist history. I outline the scriptural prescriptions but also raise questions about new directions: given that fully ordained monks retained the authority to determine orthopraxy, how did they accommodate apocrypha that gave the visionary experiences of the laity a measure of self-determined authenticity? How did the participation of the laity influence orthodoxies, and what roles did the Saṅgha play in new forms of lay practice that developed in fifth- and sixth-century China?

The Bodhisattva Precepts in Mahāyāna Scriptures

In the classic Mahāyāna conception of the path, receiving the *bodhisattvaprātimokṣa* was one of the early stages of the bodhisattva's career, usually the second of the ten *bhūmis* (stages). Taking vows to uphold the bodhisattva precepts became a key part of Mahāyāna rites of confession and repentance to destroy the ill effects of past deeds. While classic Mahāyāna texts on the bodhisattva path routinely criticize the precepts of the *śrāvaka* or "hearer," the ten proscriptive precepts of traditional Buddhism continued to be foundational.

We may take the schematization in the *Avataṃsaka-sūtra* as the basic blueprint for the bodhisattva precepts. In the *Avataṃsaka,* the second or "purity" stage of the bodhisattva path is grouped into three levels: (1) the ten fundamental precepts of traditional Buddhism, (2) the obverse of the ten evil acts, positive cultivation of right action, word, thought, and (3) compassion and altruistic acts towards all beings, which are further developed in succeeding stages.[44] The *Avataṃsaka* thus sets out a tripartite division of the Mahāyāna precepts, which were expressed most succinctly in the rubric of the Three Pure Precepts: avoid all evil, do all good, and save all beings. This rubric was elaborated in many subsequent texts that detailed the bodhisattva precepts.[45] The *Avataṃsaka* is in some sense a precepts text in its entirety, reinterpreting the basic acts of Buddhist practice in terms of universal compassion and the cosmological significance of the bodhisattva path, and reinforcing this path with visions of Buddhas, bodhisattvas, and divinities.

Hirakawa Akira argues for an historical development in canonical formulations of the precepts, a development that takes the fourfold Saṅgha from inclusive and simple precepts through a phase of differentiation and complexity to return again to all-inclusiveness. Hirakawa's teleology implicitly favors the inclusive Mahāyāna precepts. He traces this process from the *Āgamas,* in which the ten virtuous acts (*daśakuśalakarmapathāḥ, shishanye dao* 十善業道) were the foundation of both lay and ordained practice, to the Abhidharma texts in which the precepts for lay and ordained were differentiated by content and format, and finally to the Vinaya, which represents the furthest extent of differentiation. Hirakawa claims that the precepts of the ten virtues in the *Avataṃsaka* and the ten *pāramitās* of the *Prajñāpāramitā-sūtra* are reinterpretations of the earliest strata of precepts, the all-inclusive precepts of the *Āgamas.*[46]

Countering this sort of teleology in her recent *A Few Good Men: The Bodhisattva Path According to The Inquiry of Ugra* (*Ugraparipṛcchā*), Jan

Nattier makes a convincing case for reassessment of Mahāyāna in general and especially for its reputation for "inclusiveness."[47] She argues that the most popular Mahāyāna scriptures, such as the *Lotus, Avataṃsaka, Prajñāpāramitā,* and *Vimalakīrti,* expound what she and others call "bodhisattva universalism," but represent only one of "many Mahāyānas." She argues that this lay-inclusive bodhisattva universalism and its scriptures have eclipsed other Mahāyānas due to their importance in Japanese Buddhism, whose scholarly traditions have shaped the field of Buddhist studies. She points out that the tendency to stress the inclusivity of Mahāyāna is also due to the compatibility between this aspect of Buddhism and Western cultural values.[48]

She shows that when we examine *The Inquiry of Ugra,* a heretofore-neglected early Mahāyāna scripture, we find a very narrow notion of the bodhisattva path as the way to attain Buddhahood, an ambitious goal to which only "a few good men" will aspire. The scripture is divided into two parts, laying out practices of renunciation for both laymen and monks. For our purposes, the most important overthrown assumption is the notion that Mahāyāna doctrines were more householder-friendly. Instead, the bodhisattva in *The Inquiry of Ugra* is urged to seek full ordination, and there is a strong flavor of the misogyny and antipathy to household life that was characteristic of monastic Buddhism. Interestingly, there is no connection with cults of devotion to Buddhas, bodhisattvas, or the Mahāyāna scriptures.[49] *The Inquiry of Ugra* advocates a list of eleven basic precepts, roughly corresponding to the ten traditional precepts, but the ideal is clearly a monk who is an elite among monks, practicing a more stringent asceticism.[50]

Let us turn to a review of the history of bodhisattva precepts rituals. At least in the textual realm, the concept of the *bodhisattvaprātimokṣa* seems to have predated its activation through specific ceremonies, and there was no single orthodox source for such a ceremony. Paul Groner notes that, while the detailed Vinaya procedure for ordination of monks and nuns remained consistent as Buddhism spread, the corresponding precepts ceremonies for novices and laity were not as thoroughly described, leaving room for variations. Regarding the bodhisattva ordinations in Mahāyāna scriptures he states: "Although some of these *sūtras* were more respected than others by the monks, none of them occupied a position of such authority that it alone could serve as the major source for bodhisattva ordinations in the same way that the vinaya had served as the authority for Hīnayāna full ordination."[51]

Possibly the earliest source for a bodhisattva precepts ceremony was the *Mañjuśrīparipṛcchā,*[52] but the scripture that was most influential for the content and form of bodhisattva precepts ceremony in China was the *Bodhisattvabhūmi,* derived from a section of Asaṅga's fourth-century

Yogācārabhūmi-śāstra.[53] The precepts ceremony in the *Bodhisattvabhūmi* became the template for later apocryphal Chinese bodhisattva precepts texts. The treatise opens with an assertion of the superiority of the bodhisattva precepts over the *śrāvaka* precepts and then explicates the Three Groups of Pure Precepts (*sanju jingjie* 三聚淨戒), which correspond to the three groups seen above in the *Avataṃsaka-sūtra.* The three groups in the *Bodhisattvabhūmi* are: (1) Precepts of Restrictions (*saṃvaraśīla, luyi jie* 律儀戒) differentiated according to the religious status of the petitioner (monks and nuns observe the Vinaya precepts, and novices, candidates and laypersons each observe a different set); (2) Precepts of the Good Dharma (*kuśaladharmasaṃgrāhaka-śīla, sheshanfa jie* 攝善法戒), meritorious deeds of body, speech, and mind that cultivate the path of awakening; and (3) Precepts on Behalf of Beings (*sattvārthakrīyā-śīla, shezhongsheng jie* 攝眾生戒), which comprise eleven categories of cultivation of altruistic acts. This is followed by the ordination or precepts initiation ceremony, in which the petitioner prostrates him- or herself before the master and states his/her request to receive the precepts. He/she pays homage to the Buddhas and bodhisattvas and obtains the benefit of their merit in order to be purified. Prostrate before an image of the Buddha, he/she repeats the request to receive the precepts, and concentrates on the merit obtained thereby. He/she is asked to repeat three times that he/she is a bodhisattva, follows the path of awakening, and desires to receive the Three Groups of Pure Precepts. Then the master requests administration of the precepts from the Buddhas and bodhisattvas on behalf of the petitioner, and the ceremony is concluded. The text has a list of the categories of transgressions and the levels of confession and contrition necessary to exculpate them. Finally, it is said that in the absence of a qualified member of the clergy, one can administer the precepts to oneself according to the formula given in the text.[54]

The *Bodhisattvabhūmi* is inclusive in that the ritual is the same for all, but the proscriptive precepts serve to distinguish monks, nuns, novices, postulants, and laypersons. The text opens with denigration of the *śrāvaka* precepts, protesting that the *śrāvaka* precepts are intended solely to destroy passions, whereas according to the bodhisattva precepts one experiences passions without violating the precepts, infractions are not irremediable, and gradual cultivation is accommodated. However, these *śrāvaka* precepts are retained at the foundational level of the all-inclusive Pure Precepts.[55]

This kind of tolerant but confining embrace is characteristic of many of the "all-inclusive" *bodhisattvaprātimokṣa* schema. Such schema were very popular and yet, as Hirakawa Akira notes, would not bear detailed examination, for there are clear points of contradiction between the Vinaya and the bodhisattva ethos. For example, the Vinaya prohibits clergy from receiving precious metals and gems, but the bodhisattva precepts stipulate that a bodhisattva must accept gold if it is offered by a merit-seeking devotee.[56]

The bodhisattva precepts texts could thus sanction acceptance of a wider range of practices and persons into the Saṅgha, but still restrict access to authority to transmit the Dharma. Although provision is made for self-administration of the bodhisattva precepts, the *Bodhisattvabhūmi* stipulates that the self-ministrant must state that he/she had already received the full Vinaya precepts. In Indian precepts texts, self-administration of full Vinaya ordination does not seem to have ever been an option.[57]

It was due in part to their lax ordination procedures that the Bao Tang were shunted aside in the race to a new orthopraxy. Focusing on this touchy point, the *Lidai fabao ji* authors include a story of the insults Wuzhu received from a master specializing in the bodhisattva precepts. Three monks who are presented as a persons with some repute in the monastic community come to call, and one of them loses his temper in response to Wuzhu's questioning. Wuzhu's opponent displays poor form as well as poor emptiness:

> The Venerable knew they didn't understand, and so he asked Yijing 義淨, "Ācārya, what scriptures and treatises have you explicated?" He replied, "I have explicated the *Pusa jie* 菩薩戒 (Bodhisattva Precepts), I have lectured on it for the monks." The Venerable asked, "What is the substance of the precepts, and what is their meaning?" Yijing had no words with which to reply, and then he burst out with invective: "It is not that I don't understand, it was only in order to test you. Your sort of 'Chan'—I despise [such] 'not practicing'!" Zhumo 處默 chimed in, "I despise your dull 'not-doing,' I despise [your] stupefying 'not-practicing,' I despise [your] lazy 'not-doing,' I despise [your] slovenly 'not-entering!' "
>
> The Venerable addressed the monks, " 'The principle of suchness [*tathatā*] encompasses all wisdom.'[58] 'My unsurpassed Mahāyāna goes beyond names and words. Its meaning is [for those of] profound understanding, fools do not comprehend it.' "[59]

Moral *gongfu* is a familiar motif in traditional Chinese biography and fiction, but this portrayal of petty authority overbalancing itself is especially incisive because the question of conduct is at the heart of the encounter. The monks' inability to contain themselves shows them to be unworthy representatives even of the Vinaya, let alone the Dharmakāya. Wuzhu tells the monks, "You Ācārya shave off your hair and put on robes and say to yourselves, 'I am the Buddha's disciple,' but you are unwilling to learn the *śramaṇa* Dharma. You just say, 'slovenly doing, lazy doing, I despise dull not-entering.' This is not the *śramaṇa* lion, this is a kind of wild dog."[60]

Yijing preemptively rejects an antinomian interpretation of the bodhisattva precepts, yet, as Wuzhu points out, the specific provisions of the precepts (such as proper deportment) are nothing if not empty.

Moreover, it is possible that the *Pusa jie* meant here is Tiantai Zhiyi's 天台智顗 (538–597) commentary on the *Fanwang jing* 梵網經, the *Pusa jie jing shu* 菩薩戒經疏.[61] In East Asia, the most influential bodhisattva precepts texts were fifth-century Chinese apocrypha based on the scriptures reviewed above, and among them the *Fanwang jing* was particularly important. The *Fanwang jing* established a foundation for Chinese Buddhist practice, and, as we see in a subsequent section devoted to it and other apocrypha, it did so in part by reinterpreting the roles of lay and ordained in Chinese terms.

By contrast, *pusa jie* (*bodhisattvaprātimokṣa*) as a generic term points to a cultural domain with a fascinating and complex history. The bodhisattva precepts became a medium of visualization practices and new forms of collective practice that were inscribed in Chinese Buddhism long before Wuzhu and the Chan masters came face to face in the *Lidai fabao ji*. To put a face on the functioning of the *pusa jie*, let us examine an important figure in the history of the introduction of bodhisattva precepts texts and practices in early fifth-century China.

Dharmakṣema and Transmission of the Bodhisattva Precepts

Dharmakṣema 曇無讖 (385–433) came to China during a time of warfare and instability following the fragmentation of the Former Qin dynasty. He arrived in 412 at the Northern Liang 涼 capital of Guzang 姑臧 in the northwest[62] and translated the *Nirvāṇa-sūtra* under the sponsorship of the Northern Liang ruler Juqu Mengxun 沮渠蒙遜. According to Dharmakṣema's *Gaoseng zhuan* biography, he was murdered by his patron in 433, when he set out on a trip to the west to obtain the last part of the *Nirvāṇa-sūtra*. Mengxun's apparent motive was fear that the wonder-working monk would defect to his rivals, the rising Northern Wei 北魏.[63]

Although Dharmakṣema died before northern reunification under the Wei in 439, the style of Buddhism linked with his name was to have continued impact on the character of northern Buddhism in the latter half of the fifth century. His influence was transplanted from Liangzhou across the breadth of China, for when the Northern Wei conquered the Northern Liang in 439, the new empire-builders forced the remaining population to move to Pingcheng 平城, their capital in the northeast.[64]

The Buddhism spread by Dharmakṣema and his followers was characterized by: (1) emphasis on observance of the precepts, (2) rituals of penance and confession to gain merit, expiate past sins, and forestall retribution, (3) practices of visualization and focus on the significance of dreams and visions, and (4) recitation of *dhāraṇī*, repetition of the Buddha's name, and circumambulation of images. Episodes in Dharmakṣema's biography illustrate many of these themes and practices, and the translations attributed to him also reflect the tenor of his transmission efforts.

The key aspect of his practice/transmission appears to have been traditional Vinaya under the aegis of Mahāyāna. Dharmakṣema's translation of the *Nirvāṇa-sūtra* was important in popularizing the notion of a Mahāyāna Vinaya, and three of the other translations attributed to him in the *Gaoseng zhuan* include *bodhisattvaprātimokṣa:* the *Pusadichi jing,* the *Pusa jieben,* and the *Youposaijie jing.*[65] The last was a bodhisattva precepts text designed specifically for laypersons, and it stipulates the five lay precepts rather than the Vinaya as a prerequisite.[66] Dharmakṣema was clearly promulgating the *Bodhisattvabhūmi* ethos, with its inclusive yet differentiated precepts for clergy and laity. A story from his biography regarding his own failure to observe the precepts shows the value placed on Vinaya forms:

> Dharmakṣema departed for Kashmir carrying the first part of the *Mahāparinirvāṇa-sūtra* in ten fascicles, along with the *Bodhisattvabhūmi* and the *Bodhisattvaprātimokṣa,* and other works. In that country there were many who studied Hīnayāna and did not believe in the *Nirvāṇa-*[*sūtra*]. So he went east to Kucha and continued on to Guzang, where he stayed at a way-post. He was anxious about losing the sūtras, so he pillowed them [beneath his head] to sleep. Someone tugged at them on the ground, and Dharmakṣema started awake, attributing it to thieves. On the third night of this, he heard a voice from the air saying, "These are the repository of the Tathāgata's teachings of liberation. Why do you pillow them [beneath your head]?" Dharmakṣema was greatly ashamed, and placed them apart in a high place. In the night there was someone who [wanted to] steal them, and though he tried and tried to lift [the sūtras], in the end he couldn't do it. The next day, however, Dharmakṣema picked up the sūtras and left as if they were not at all heavy. The thief saw it, and acknowledged that this was a holy man. All came to pay their respects.[67]

Even though the Mahāyāna precepts were included under the rubric of "skillful means" and were thus accessible to more flexible notions of cultivation and sanctity, here we observe the tension between formal observance of the precepts and a situation that would seem to call for adaptation. The didactic thrust of the story, however, leaves no doubt as to which course is considered superior. This disembodied remonstrance for improper treatment of sūtras in transit harks back to the transmission anxieties of the exegete Daoan, who was worried about the soteriological implications of faulty translation. Here, too, we see soteriological and formal vigilance working in tandem. Adherence to Vinaya ritual serves as a prophylactic against the perils of both physical and linguistic mishandling, and was thus a guarantee of the continuity and efficacy of the Dharma: The Vinaya rules protect the Mahāyāna precepts.

Other anecdotes in Dharmakṣema's biography also feature extraordinary voices and visions as guarantors of continuity and correct transmission/reception. One story in particular illustrates the increasingly popular notion that the precepts were conveyed by the timeless Buddhas and bodhisattvas, with or without the mediation of a human precepts master.

> Previously, when Dharmakṣema was at Guzang, there was a monk from Zhangye 張掖 named Daojin 道進.[68] He wanted to receive the bodhisattva precepts from Dharmakṣema. Dharmakṣema said, "Repent your transgressions!" [Daojin] did so with the utmost earnestness for seven days and seven nights.[69] On the eighth day he went to see Dharmakṣema, seeking ordination. Dharmakṣema suddenly became terribly angry. Daojin then reflected, "It could only be that my karmic hindrances are not yet dispelled." So he made a concerted effort for three years, meditating and confessing. Then, when Daojin was in samādhi, he saw Śākyamuni Buddha and all the great worthies conferring the precepts upon him. That night he was staying with more than ten other people, and all miraculously dreamed just what Daojin had seen. Daojin wanted to go to Dharmakṣema and tell him. He was still several tens of paces away when Dharmakṣema started to his feet and called out, "Good, good! You have already miraculously [received] the precepts! I will act as witness for you." Then, in front of the image of the Buddha, [Dharmakṣema] explained the characteristics of the precepts for him.[70]

Here the master's transmission of the "characteristics" (*xiang* 相), or verbal and conceptual forms of the precepts, is ancillary to the disciple's samādhi experience. In the world of northern Buddhist practice of the fifth century, the testimony of visualization became extremely important both as a cause and sign of purification of karmic residue. The visionary warrant of purity was also an essential gateway to thaumaturgic powers; specifically, the efficacy of verbal *dhāraṇī* depended upon prior performance of the *uposatha*, the rites of confession and penance.[71]

Dharmakṣema is in some ways a stereotypical figure, for in his biography one can see the early and perennial Chinese Buddhist fascination with stories of the monk's ability to tap supranormal resources to subdue demons and thieves and deal with royal patrons. He is also a seminal figure, for in his biography one can see elements of what would become the basic structure of popular practice in China. This basic structure combined conferral of the bodhisattva precepts, retreats for the intensive practice of meditation, confession and repentance, and reliance on visions or signs of the Buddhas. The seeds transplanted from Dharmakṣema's community in Liangzhou proved hardy and fertile, as we see in subsequent sections on the apocryphal bodhisattva precepts texts designed for lay practitioners.

Seeing the Buddha at Mt. Lu

It is also important to get a glimpse of the ground in which these seeds were nourished—the devotional cults that helped visualization practice spread from the sphere of monastic virtuosity into the sphere of lay practice. For a salient example let us return briefly to Mt. Lu, where Huiyuan is said to have instituted a devotional society focused on Amitābha.[72] His group originated with a collective vow in 402 and was probably influenced by the Tusita cult of his master, Daoan. The participants were monks and educated laymen who took a vow to help each other practice *śīla* and samādhi and attain rebirth in Sukhāvati. Huiyuan stressed the practice of the samādhi of reflecting on the Buddha (*nianfo sanmei* 念佛三昧, *Buddhānusmṛtisamādhi*), which was to enable the practitioner to view Amitābha and obtain his direct guidance.[73]

The community's practice was much influenced by the *Banzhou sanmei jing* 般舟三昧經, a visualization sūtra that advocates ceaseless walking or circumambulation for seven days, or thirty days, in order to achieve a samādhi in which one comes face to face with one or all of the Buddhas.[74] The sūtra claimed that visions of the Buddha are not gained through supranormal powers or after death, but are the result of Amitābha's *adhiṣṭhāna* (*weishenli* 威神力), his bestowal of "grace" due to the power of his accumulated merit. The practitioner hears and accepts the Dharma from Amitābha and then emerges from samādhi to tell others about it. At the same time, the *Banzhou sanmei jing* teaches that mind is the source of all things; everything, including the Buddhas, is an appearance:

> One reflects [*nian* 念] thus: From what place did the Buddhas come? To what place am "I" going to go? One reflects for oneself that the Buddhas come from nowhere, and that "I" also go nowhere. One reflects for oneself on the triple world, of desire, form, and formlessness. This triple world comes into being from intention and nothing more. What I reflect on, I then see. The mind makes the Buddhas; the mind sees itself. The mind is the Buddhas; the mind is the Tathāgata. The mind is my body; the mind sees the Buddha. The mind does not of itself know mind. The mind does not of itself see mind.[75]

The *Banzhou sanmei jing* message that vision of the emptiness of the Buddhas is vouchsafed by the power of the Buddhas was also couched in more iconoclastic terms. Many passages urge the practitioners to practice tirelessly until the splendid vision of the Buddhas is realized. In one passage, however, the Buddha draws an analogy between visualizing Buddhas and dreaming of famous courtesans:

> It is as if there is a man who hears that in the land Vaiśālī there is a harlot named Sumanā, another who hears that there is one named Āmrapāli, and another who hears that there is one named Upapannā. At the time, each man thinks about them. Although they have never seen these three women, hearing of them agitates their lust. In a dream, each goes to one of them. At the time, all three men are in Rājagṛha, but they are at the same time reflecting [on a harlot]. Each goes in a dream to a harlot's place, where he stays with her. Once awake, each reflects on his own.[76]

For Huiyuan, this combination of consecrated visualization and daring deconstruction seems to have been a source of inspiration mixed with unease. In a celebrated exchange of letters with Kumārajīva, Huiyuan addresses doubts raised by the scripture's frequent use of the analogy of dreams to explicate visions of the Buddhas. He argues that if the Buddhas seen through the *Banzhou sanmei jing* practice of *Buddhānusmṛtisamādhi* are like dreams, then they are subjective illusions, but if they are really external responses, then they are not like dreams. Even if one sees visions as the result of supranormal powers, such visions are not absolute truth and are not the intended purpose of samādhi, so how can they lead to understanding? The *Banzhou sanmei jing* stipulates three conditions for attaining samādhi: the power of the Buddha, the power of the Buddha's samādhi, and the practitioner's roots of merit, his maintenance of the precepts. Huiyuan objects that, even if the Buddhas are seen in samādhi, how one can really know whether they are based in subjective conception? And if the Buddhas are experienced outside samādhi, then they are indeed dream apparitions. The experience is not merely interior, and it cannot be the same as dreams. Is the Dharma of the *Buddhānusmṛtisamādhi* Dharma as such or not?[77]

Huiyuan astutely presents the problems posed by opening the Dharma gate of visualization to all comers, "each reflecting on his own." Beneath the question of subjectivity lurks the problem of authority and the adjudication of the criteria of authentic practice. If, for lay devotees, practice of the precepts and acts of merit became ancillary to samādhi experience of the Buddha's teaching, this could undermine the privileged status of the ordained as the vehicles of Dharma transmission. However, as we will see, there are indications that the members of lay societies expected a stricter moral standard from one another than they did from the clergy, and this included deference to the ordained regardless of attainments or worthiness.

The *Banzhou sanmei jing* does validate lay practice, for it prescribes the same procedures for all (monks, nuns, laymen, and laywomen) who seek a vision of the Buddhas. It was also apparently the basis for a nonextant treatise by Huiyuan on the practice of samādhi while remaining "in the family."[78] However, the *Banzhou sanmei jing* interpretation of the five precepts for "lay bodhisattvas" could hardly be considered compatible with family life:

> The Buddha declared to Bhadrapāla, "A white-robed bodhisattva who, [cultivating the Path at home and] having heard of this *samādhi,* wishes to learn and to keep it, is to keep to the Five Prohibitions, purely and firmly dwelling within them. . . . He cannot have affection for wife and children, he cannot take thought for sons or daughters, he cannot take thought for goods or chattels. His constant thought is of the wish to reject wife and children, in his behavior to become a *śramaṇa,* ever to keep the Eightfold Fast, and that always in a Buddhist monastery.[79]

This is reminiscent of the elitist *Inquiry of Ugra* and a rather different ideal from the image associated with Vimalakīrti, the best-known "white-robed bodhisattva" in Buddhist literature. The Buddhist ideal of renunciation of family life was a frequent subject for bitter complaint by Confucian elites, and Vimalakīrti served as sign of the possibility of reconciliation of the householder's and renunciant's life. Vimalakīrti's popularity in China is reflected in the frequency with which he is depicted in the paintings of the Dunhuang Mogao caves and is also reflected in a later Chinese work devoted to a homegrown lay paradigm, Layman Pang.[80] Wuzhu was apparently sympathetic to this ideal; in chapter 6 we see him heaping scathing criticism on a group of laymen for thinking that the "wish to reject wife and children" is an exemplary form of practice.

Yet precisely because Vimalakīrti is so exceptional—a Buddha in disguise, he teaches the Dharma to gamblers and prostitutes and intimidates even the bodhisattvas—the *Vimalakīrtinirdeśa-sūtra* does not challenge the institutions of clerical authority. The *Banzhou sanmei jing,* however, preaches a monkish standard of purity for laymen who wish to see the Buddha for themselves. The model for practice that it articulated proved to be a compelling one in the Chinese context; in Buddhist prescriptive texts written in China, we begin to see various means of appropriating śramaṇa standards of behavior in order to have direct access to the powers of the Buddhas and bodhisattvas.

Lay Practice in Apocryphal Bodhisattva Precepts Texts

Here we make a break with Indian canonical versions of the bodhisattva precepts and visualization scriptures and turn to guidelines for practice that were composed in China. In the following apocryphal bodhisattva precepts texts, we see prescriptions for standards of behavior for both lay and ordained that are inflected with Chinese concerns. We also see the articulation of means to verify signs of authentic vision, the favor of the Buddhas and bodhisattvas, and merit. These texts could be used as maps for practice with or without clerical guidance.

A number of new scriptures appeared during the decades following the Northern Wei persecution (444–452). While some were indeed translations, many were "indigenous scriptures" or apocrypha, compilations that may have elaborated on earlier translations of authentically Indian scriptures but introduced new features that made them more relevant to the Chinese milieu. Once these nebulous texts had gained sufficient importance, they acquired translation and transmission histories.[81] Here we look at two apocrypha in which lay-precepts ordination and repentance play a central role, paying particular attention to the forms of authority and degrees of inclusivity and exclusivity mandated by the texts.

The fifth century saw a tremendous increase in the popularity of ceremonies for confessing transgressions and taking the bodhisattva precepts. Kyoko Tokuno, quoting a study by Ono Hōdo in which he found that nearly three-quarters of the two hundred Mahāyāna precepts scriptures (including apocrypha) that he examined dated from the Six Dynasties period, concludes: "This statistic is a concrete barometer of the importance of moral issues within fifth-century Buddhism."[82] However, it is difficult to separate "moral issues" and self-interest, nor, indeed, must they be antithetical. Bodhisattva precepts rituals were undertaken by both lay and ordained devotees in order to produce and dedicate merit, in the hope of obtaining favorable future conditions for themselves and their loved ones.

Among the most popular of the apocryphal bodhisattva precepts texts were the *Fanwang jing* 梵網經 (*Brahmajāla-sūtra;* Scripture of Brahma's Net);[83] and the *[Pusa] yingluo [benye] jing* [菩薩]瓔珞[本業]經 (Scripture of the [Original Acts That Serve as] Necklaces [for the Bodhisattvas]).[84] These closely related texts drew from the *Nirvāṇa-sūtra, Bodhisattva-bhūmi,* and *Upāsakaśīla-sūtra* translations discussed previously, but they also share characteristics that distinguish them from earlier Mahāyāna precepts texts.

The *Fanwang jing* became the best-known and most commonly used precepts text in East Asia and eventually supplanted the Vinaya as the basis of monastic ordination in the Tendai sect in Japan. It introduced the practice of filial piety into its schema of precepts, it gave rulers a significant role, and it promised worldly peace and prosperity as well as liberation. As Paul Groner points out, increased access to the complete Vinaya translations of the early fifth century would have brought the alien qualities of Buddhist practice and ideology more sharply into focus.[85] Anyone who had imbibed the Chinese cultural compound of reverence for ruler and parents, Confucian notions of service to the state and the family, and "Daoist" notions of spiritual hygiene would have been put off by the Vinaya stories dwelling on abandonment of family and social obligations and the repulsiveness of the body.

The *Fanwang jing* attempted to mitigate these incompatibilities between Buddhist precepts and Chinese mores. The substantial section detailing its ten major and forty-eight minor precepts proved so popular that it circulated as an independent text by the end of the fifth century.[86] Filial piety is introduced in the section preceding the precepts: "When Śākyamuni Buddha sat under the bodhi tree and attained supreme enlightenment, that was when he first enjoined the *bodhisattvaprātimokṣa* and filial submission toward parents, teachers, clergy, and the Three Jewels. Filial submission is the Dharma of the ultimate path. Filial piety is called *śīla,* also called restraint."[87]

It is noteworthy that this accommodation to Chinese principles condoned the Confucian obligations of laypersons and extended the notion of filiality to include submission to the clergy, but did not force Confucian obligations on clerics. Countering the praise of filial piety in the introductory section, the fortieth minor precept says that those who have left home should not pay obeisance to rulers or parents or honor kin and spirits; they are only obliged to understand the words of the Dharma master.[88]

The *Fanwang jing* creates explicit precepts out of the kind of negative reciprocity defended by Huiyuan and the leading clerics of the southern regimes. By "negative reciprocity" I mean the mirror-image negation of Confucian principles: The clergy were not to pay homage to parents or rulers, but they were also (theoretically) not allowed to seek benefit from the system of patronage sustained by Confucian notions of reciprocity. The twenty-sixth through twenty-eighth minor precepts develop this theme at length, prohibiting the clergy from accepting personal gifts and invitations from the laity, and prohibiting the laity from offering such personal favors.[89] The thirty-sixth minor precept recommends that a monk or nun should make vows that call down an imaginative array of fiery torments should he or she accept gifts in violation of the precepts.[90]

In practice, of course, there was a fine line between accepting individual benefit and accepting universal benefit on behalf of the Three Jewels. This danger is implicitly acknowledged in the eloquent warning of the forty-eighth and final precept, admonishing that the most reprehensible abuses of the Dharma are those stemming from within the Saṅgha. Clergy who would preach the precepts to gain favors or who would implicate monks, nuns, or lay disciples in "enfettering" behavior are responsible for degrading the Buddhist teachings to the level of prisoners and slaves.[91]

Groner argues that "the contents of the *Fan-wang* precepts also suggest that the compilers hoped to compose a set of precepts that would join monks, nuns, and lay believers in a common organization."[92] The *Fanwang jing* certainly inveighs against secular class distinctions, and the thirty-eighth minor precept includes a leveling measure encompassing both clergy and laity: "Those who were ordained first should be seated first, and those who were ordained later should sit below them. It does not matter whether one is young, old, a monk, nun, king, prince, or even a eunuch or a slave."[93] However, final authority was vested in the clergy, and I cannot find support in the *Fanwang jing* for Groner's claim that "Lay believers might confer the precepts on others."[94] Rather, the forty-first minor precept says that "a bodhisattva" can instruct a neophyte, but when someone wants to receive the precepts he or she should request the attendance of the recognized preceptors, the Upādhyāya (*heshang* 和上) and Ācārya (*asheli* 阿闍梨).[95]

The fortieth minor precept, which includes the injunction against obeisance to parents or rulers, also exemplifies the oscillation between inclusive and exclusive tendencies. It begins by stating that everyone without distinction may receive the precepts, and then it stresses the importance of distinctly colored *kaṣāya,* the symbolism of which is expanded to refer to all the accouterments of the practitioner, even bedding. The thrust of the passage at first seems to be that all who take precepts are to be distinguished from those who do not, but the final line introduces ambiguity about who is being distinguished from whom—whether "monk" (*biqiu* 比丘) stands for all precepts recipients, or whether fully ordained monks are being distinguished from bodhisattva precepts recipients:

> When a disciple of the Buddha would allow people to receive the precepts, he/she cannot be selective. All kings and princes, great ministers and public officials, monks and nuns, laymen and laywomen, male adulterers and female adulterers, the emperors of the eighteen Brāhmalokas and the six desire-realms, those of no sex and hermaphrodites, eunuchs, male and female slaves, and absolutely any demon and spirit can receive the precepts. One must teach about the *kaṣāya* that is worn on the body, all use dull colors in conformity with the Way. All [must] dye every dyed cloth with blue, yellow, red, black or purple colors, even bedding is completely in dull colors. Any cloth worn on the body is of dyed colors. [Contrasting with] any clothing worn by the peoples of [other] domains and the Middle

Kingdom, the [clothing of] monks must be differentiated from such worldly clothing.[96]

In principle, following this precept would mark all devotees of the *Fanwang jing* alike, whether monk or hermaphrodite (who were not eligible for ordination according to the Vinaya). Groner, however, surmises that application of the *Fanwang jing*'s all-inclusive principles was probably limited: "And while members of the Buddhist Order and lay believers were sometimes ordained at the same time, there is little indication that they actually practiced together."[97] According to his assessment of the attitudes of later Chinese commentators, it seems that most opted to maintain some system distinguishing precepts for laity, novices, and clergy and that the bodhisattva precepts served as a kind of capping "Mahāyānization" of the process, seldom taken as solely sufficient.[98] In spite of its standard denigration of "*śrāvaka* precepts" this is in keeping with the spirit of the *Fanwang jing*, for its key value is noblesse oblige and its tacit message is that fully ordained clergy are the most obligated, and the most noble.

Though it drew from the *Fanwang jing*, the *Yingluo jing* sanctioned use of the bodhisattva precepts alone and also sanctioned administration of the precepts by lay believers—spouses and family members could even confer them on each other.[99] A fifth-century apocryphon, the *Yingluo jing* was based on a third-century translation of the *Pusa benye jing* 菩薩本業經 (Scripture of the Original Acts of the Bodhisattva), which was the earliest translation to outline the ten stage bodhisattva path.[100] Interestingly, the *Yingluo jing* is included in the list of sources at the beginning of the *Lidai fabao ji*, but the *Fanwang jing* is not. The *Yingluo jing* is notable for emphasizing the "ten beliefs" (*shixin* 十信) that precede the forty-two-stage bodhisattva path, allowing for multiple lifetimes spent on mastery of the ten basic precepts and initial vows. While progress is to be measured by one's success in keeping these precepts, provisions were made for lapses on the part of the "bodhisattva in intention."[101]

However, taking a significant step toward the telescoped path of early Chan, the *Yingluo jing* placed more weight than the *Avataṃsaka* on the notion that all stages of progress are already encompassed in the initial inclination. As Stephen Bokenkamp, who discusses the incorporation of the bodhisattva path into Daoist scriptures, says: "The *Ying-lo ching*, though concerned primarily with those on the initial stages of the path and itself guilty of helping to lengthen the bodhisattva path with its ten stages of belief, dares to raise the notion of "sudden enlightenment' (*tun-chüeh*) and gradual enlightenment (*chien-chüeh*), concluding that 'there are no gradually enlightened world-honored ones, but only suddenly-enlightened Tathāgatas.'"[102]

Like the *Fanwang jing*, the *Yingluo jing* encouraged laypeople to partake in practices previously reserved for the ordained. Both works formalized procedures for receiving the precepts by confession and repentance that were validated by the penitent's reception of visionary signs, without requiring mediation by the clergy. Repentance and reception of the precepts was one of the most accessible means of gaining merit in order to sweeten karmic retribution, and the incorporation of self-administered vows into many of the apocryphal bodhisattva precepts texts suggests that the practice became widespread. Groner notes that, although in the *Yingluo jing* self-administration was ranked lower than precepts conferred by a qualified teacher, the description of the former is more detailed, from which he infers its popularity.[103]

As discussed above, emphasis on the testimony of visualization for self-administered vows was a feature of the Dharmakṣema-influenced Buddhism imported from Liangzhou.[104] Dharmakṣema's sources for the practice, the *Yogācārabhūmi* and *Bodhisattvabhūmi*, allowed for monks and nuns, but not laypeople, to receive bodhisattva precepts without a master. The petitioner was to repeat formulae of confessions and vows before Buddhist images and ask the Buddhas and bodhisattvas to confer the precepts, and only if he/she received a "good sign" was he/she assured of having obtained the precepts. These texts did not elaborate on how to go about obtaining a sign, although in the *Bodhisattvabhūmi* "a cool wind" is specified as acceptable.[105]

In the twenty-third minor precept of the *Fanwang jing*, the protocol for visionary authentication is more detailed. As in the *Bodhisattvabhūmi*, reception of the precepts is validated by a sign (*haoxiang* 好相), but the *Fanwang jing* also says that if an ordained teacher confers the precepts then a sign is unnecessary. In contrast to the *Bodhisattvabhūmi*, the *Fanwang jing* protocol does not require the self-ministrant to state that he or she is already fully ordained, but it also does not go as far as another apocryphon that explicitly allows for self-conferral of full ordination.[106] The *Fanwang jing* maintains the bottom line, but the authority of ordination and authentic transmission are, more clearly than ever, signs within a system of signs:

> Once one obtains a good sign then one has succeeded in receiving the precepts before images of the Buddhas and bodhisattvas. If one does not obtain a good sign, then although one has [self-]administered the precepts before the image of a Buddha, one has not obtained the precepts. If one receives the precepts directly from a Dharma master who has previously received the bodhisattva precepts, then one need not see a good sign. Why? Because the Dharma masters confer [the precepts] from master to master, there is no need for good signs, and so when one receives the precepts be-

fore a Dharma master, one has indeed obtained the precepts. It is because one produces the most heartfelt respect that one succeeds in obtaining the precepts.[107]

The reception of a good sign obviates the need for the clergy, and the presence of properly invested clergy obviates the need for a good sign. This underscores their mutual signification and substitution—regardless of the merits of the monk as an individual, once invested with the role of Dharma master, he is a good sign. The good sign is vouchsafed by the images of the Buddhas and bodhisattvas and by the transmission of the precepts from one master to another. Thus we have another level of substitution in which both Buddhist images and the lineage of transmission of the precepts masters embody the Dharma and are empowered to reproduce the good signs of themselves. The Chinese principle of sympathetic resonance is clearly at work here, binding these substitutions and reproductions in tangled hierarchies. In succeeding texts we explore further manifestations of the principle of resonance and further attempts to rationalize and stabilize the hierarchies among these signs.

The strength and extent of the resonances linking the bodhisattva precepts, images, repentance, and good signs are reinforced in the *Guan Puxianpusa xingfa jing* 觀普賢菩薩行法經 (Scripture of the Methods of Contemplation of the Bodhisattva Samantabhadra).[108] In the ritual for self-administered bodhisattva precepts prescribed in this text, the petitioner appeals to the omniscience, wisdom, and mercy of Śākyamuni, Mañjuśri, and Maitreya. The petitioner then asks that Śākyamuni serve as his or her Upādhyāya (Preceptor, *heshang* 和上), Mañjuśri as [Karma]-ācārya (Master [of karma], *[jiemo]asheli* [羯磨]阿闍梨), and Maitreya as Anuśāsanī-ācārya (Guarantor, *jiaoshoushi* 教授師).[109] It is said to be not absolutely necessary that these vows be taken before an image in order to obtain the good signs confirming possession of the precepts. As Kuo Li-ying points out, here we find the officiants of Vinaya ordination ritual transposed into a Mahāyāna context of visualization and contemplation.[110]

Once more, visionary blending of Buddha images and precepts masters points to their mutual signification, the "form that is emptiness" that would serve, a few centuries later, to convey the formless nonconceptual precepts. The *Guan Puxianpusa xingfa jing* also included practices for contemplation of emptiness as the basis of the precepts. Groner says of this text:

> The crucial point in the ceremony was devoted to the candidate's realization of the supreme truth of nonsubstantiality, not to the conferral of the precepts. Once the candidate had understood that all is nonsubstantial, he would no longer have any desires that would lead to violations of the pre-

cepts. This view is similar to some of the statements in the *Liuzu tanjing* 六祖壇經 (hereafter *Platform Sūtra*), though no direct connection between the two texts can be demonstrated.[111]

Whether or not actual influence between these works can be traced, we should note the conceptual proximity between face-to-face encounters with the Buddhas and bodhisattvas offered in the bodhisattva precepts texts, and the mind-to-mind encounters of Chan. "This very image is the Buddha" became "this very body is the Buddha" and "this very teacher is the Buddha." In the *Lidai fabao ji,* however, Wuzhu's teachings depend on a different application of the Prajñāpāramitā hermeneutic. In the *Guan Puxianpusa xingfa jing,* contemplation of the emptiness of the rites of repentance and the bodhisattva precepts reinforces rather than obviates their efficacy, while for Wuzhu it was more important to preach that all forms of practice were forms of delusion: "When the Venerable took his seat, he usually taught the precepts to all those studying the Way. Fearing that they would get attached to verbal explanation, from time to time he would quote the crabs in the paddy-field and ask about it, but the assembly didn't understand."[112] Displaying the "Southern School" preoccupation with the pitfall of reified practice, this anecdote is but one manifestation of Wuzhu's attempt to undermine spiritual attachments. Nevertheless, his paddy-crab precepts remain part of a time-honored ritual structure in which teachings on the precepts are the preface to all other Dharma.

Transgression and Illness in the *Tiwei jing*

While visualization texts opened the gate of emptiness to the practitioner's self-authentication, in practice this freedom was usually circumscribed by some form of moral accounting system. In this final section we turn to the complex moral accounting system in the *Tiwei [Boli]jing* 提謂[波利]經 (Scripture of Trapuṣa [and Ballika]), perhaps the most thinly disguised of the Northern Wei apocrypha.[113] The *Tiwei jing* provides a window into a world of popular practice focused on interpretation of negative signs, especially illness.

The *Tiwei jing* remains at the nearer edge of a territory explored by Michel Strickmann in *Chinese Magical Medicine,* a work that allows us glimpses of the vast array of medical and apotropaic practices mixing Buddhist magical techniques with Daoist medicology. This is a "territory" that is very difficult to define, for it encompasses visualization practice, schemes of salvation, demonology, physiology, cosmology, and much more. The protean and fertile nature of popular practice merits more careful attention for its own sake, but in the context of this study I have focused on the adaptation of popular Chinese beliefs and practices that would become part of the foundation on which Chan orthodoxy and orthopraxy are built. As discussed in chapter 6, the foundation of the Southern School doctrines espoused by the Bao Tang is quite literally the bodhisattva precepts-ritual platform, and both the *Lidai fabao ji* and the *Platform Sūtra* convey the message that one need not be ordained in order to attain the highest fruits of practice. In more general terms, it appears that at least on the prescriptive level (bracketing the question of actual practice), East Asian forms of Buddhism tended to embrace the laity-inclusive aspects of Mahāyāna. I would argue that this tendency was linked to the Chinese renegotiation of the relationship between lay and ordained in order to accommodate what were considered superior cultural values (such as filial piety) and orders of knowledge (such as morally inflected medicology and cosmology).

As was the case with the *Fanwang jing* and *Yingluo jing*, the familiar *Nirvāṇa-sūtra*, *Yogācārabhūmi*, and *Bodhisattvabhūmi* were clearly sources for the *Tiwei jing* compiler. Other likely Buddhist sources include two early fifth-century indigenous compilations elaborating on the five precepts and a fourth-century southern treatise on essential teachings for the laity. The framing pretext was possibly inspired by Dharmakṣema's lay precepts text, the *Upāsakaśīla-sūtra*,[114] in which the merchant Trapuṣa is mentioned as a recipient of the Buddha's teaching on the Three Refuges.[115]

The *Tiwei jing* is most notable, however, for its assimilation of indigenous Chinese sources and concepts. The five basic Buddhist precepts are overlaid with Han Chinese notions of correspondence between the directions, planets, mountains, mythic emperors, elements, and organs of the body. It is striking how much of the text is taken up with precisely correlating diseases with transgressions; for example, taking life is associated with diseases of the liver and a bluish-yellow complexion.[116] The text also stresses filial piety and loyalty and equates the Buddhist precepts with the five practical virtues of a Han classic, the *Xiao jing* 孝經 (Classic of Filial Piety), as well as evoking the five secular-legalist punishments for transgressions. One of the versions includes an appendix enumerating 250 rules of deportment, clearly intended as a lay counterpart to the Vinaya rules for monks. The Daoist-Confucian blend of Ge Hong's 葛洪 (283–343) *Baopu zi* 抱朴子 (The Master Who Embraces Simplicity) was a direct source for the *Tiwei jing* version of the belief that celestial account-keeping regarding one's good and bad actions determines one's life-span.[117] And, as is still the case even today, any schema that links sin and illness and prescribes group repentance rituals also harkens back, with dangerous undertones, to the confessional practices of the millenarian Taiping rebels of the Han.

In the *Tiwei jing,* rituals of repentance played a crucial role in eliminating demerit. The basic formula for confession and petition is similar to that of the precepts texts discussed above, but there is also a lengthy litany of confession for every terrible sin that the petitioner has committed in past lives. Keeping the precepts was promised to increase the protective spirits who guard against the evil forces that cause disease.[118] Hence, failure to keep the precepts is revealed by disease:

> [Conversely,] those who fail to keep one precept will have five demerits and five good spirits will leave them, while violating five precepts brings twenty-five demerits and twenty-five good spirits will leave them. All gods and good spirits will be grieved and unhappy, the commissioner of fate will reduce their life-span, and all evil ghost-spirits will encamp before the gates and doors [of their bodies.] Accordingly, they will become debilitated and diseased. . . . Those worldly, ordinary people who do not understand the dharma say that they serve the Buddha; but contrary to [their claims] they also become debilitated and die.[119]

Association with a preceptor or a "good friend" was of inestimable value in negotiating this difficult accounting, because receiving the precepts from a truly qualified person effected the removal of demerits. The criteria for the locus of this true efficacy are, perhaps necessarily, inconsistent. As the soteriology of the *Tiwei jing* rests on health as a confirmation of virtue, the presence of robust physical health should override any other standard of intercessional efficacy, but this could clearly lead to absurd contradictions and is not proposed in the text. Vinaya rules debarred the physically and mentally disabled from full ordination, but for the *Tiwei jing* the fitness warranted by ordination did not alone guarantee the power to remove the effects of others' sins. The efficacious preceptor was said to be one who mastered the precepts in his (and presumably her) own life and complied with secular law, begging the question of what is meant by mastery of precepts. The fully ordained could be unfit and lay persons could be qualified, allowing collective and consensual assessment of worth to weigh more heavily than the formal distinction between lay and ordained. Significantly, however, even a dissolute monk was to be treated with all the proper ritual marks of respect as a representative of the Saṅgha, while a layperson, however worthy, was not.[120]

> Besides, oh *upāsaka,* even if there were no *śramaṇas* in this country, if men and women enjoy doing good and enjoy [observing] the precepts, then the *upāsaka* precepts will be complete. [As long as] they understand [proper] conduct and deportment, they are the possessors of wisdom and thought-

> fulness, and the possessors of authority who fittingly understand the salvation of others. Those who are completely equipped with all the above [qualities] can themselves confer the precepts on others. But only the Buddhas and the *bhikṣusaṅgha,* who can teach and convert the ten directions, can accept the worship of the laity. It is not fitting even for an elder to accept worship [simply because of his status].[121]

What is remarkable here is the degree of bifurcation between efficacy and formal legitimacy. Although the existence of worthless monks was frequently lamented both within and without the Saṅgha, until this time transmission of teachings had remained the prerogative of fully ordained monks. The phrase "the possessors of authority who fittingly understand the salvation of others" could be read as a license for laypersons to teach others, but it is difficult to assess how far this license went in practice or how it effected the organization and practices of lay Buddhists in the Northern Wei. The *Tiwei jing* itself prescribes retreats for particular observance of the precepts according to the yin/yang-based calendar of the Buddho-Chinese celestial officials who were supposed to be keeping an account of one's actions.[122] Daoxuan 道宣 (596–667), however, speaks of contemporary *Tiwei* cultists of a lay association (*yiyi* 義邑) who observed a semblance of the fortnightly *uposatha* of the ordained, "wearing robes and holding bowls."[123]

The *Tiwei jing* provided the means for the practitioner to diagnose his own spiritual condition and to gather with others to engage in the group cure of confession and repentance. By the eighth century this was a widespread practice for both lay and ordained, but Chan texts influenced by the "Southern School" ideology pointedly engaged in reinterpretations of confession and repentance. The best-known example is from the *Platform Sūtra:* "Good friends, what is repentance (*chanhui* 懺悔)? 'Seeking forgiveness' (*chan*) is, for one's whole life, to not-do (*bu zuo* 不作). 'Repentance' (*hui*) is to know the wrongs and evil deeds you have done in the past were never separate from mind. It is useless to verbally [confess] before the Buddhas. In this teaching of mine, by not-doing to forever cease [wrongdoing] is called repentance."[124]

"Not-doing" refers to not doing evil, a shorthand for the first of the three groups of pure precepts. Here it is reinterpreted in the sense of no-thought, to be free of action in the midst of action, in order to accord with the subitist stress on nonduality. Wuzhu is even more directly critical of the practice of repentance in several episodes in the *Lidai fabao ji.* However, in Chan texts the attempt to undermine deeply rooted popular belief in the link between illness and transgression was carried out through the use of symbolism and anecdote as well as through discursive hermeneutics. In the *Lidai fabao ji* and later Chan texts, the third Chan patriarch Sengcan 僧璨 (d.u.) becomes a symbol of the subitist cure that is offered in place of confession:

> When he first encountered Great Master Ke, [Seng]can appeared to have palsy, and they met in the midst of a crowd. Great Master Ke asked, "Where are you from? Why are you here?" Sengcan replied, "Because I want to serve the Venerable." Great Master Ke said, "For you, a person afflicted with palsy, what good is it to meet with me?" Can replied, "Although my body is afflicted, between the mind of the afflicted and the Venerable's mind, there is not any difference."[125] Great Master Ke realized that Can was no ordinary man and therefore entrusted the Dharma and the *kāṣāya* robe of verification to Sengcan.[126]

In theory, this is about as far from the soteriological scheme of the *Tiwei jing* as one can come. The one who is chosen to be the sole legitimate vessel of the Dharma is one whose physical unfitness signifies a heavy karmic burden, suffering from an illness that would mark him as ineligible for ordination according to the Vinaya. This encounter between Huike and Sengcan has a structure identical to the famous *Platform Sūtra* story of Hongren's encounter with Huineng.[127] In the latter encounter, Hongren voices the customary antipathy to "barbarians," and in this encounter Huike voices popular prejudice against the afflicted. As further discussed in chapter 5, the motif of Sengcan's illness continued to function as a good inversion of the "good sign" in the definitive Chan transmission record, the *Jingde chuandeng lu* 景德傳燈錄 (Record of the Transmission of the Lamp Compiled in the Jingde Era). In the *Jingde chuandeng lu* the point is driven home, and the one physically unfit for the Saṅgha becomes the quintessence of the Saṅgha: "The Great Master deeply appreciated his capacity, and had him tonsured. He said, 'This is our jewel! He should be called Sengcan (Saṅgha-gem).'"[128]

CONCLUSION

In this chapter we traced a spectrum from orthopraxy, as represented by the authority of the fully ordained monk, to the relatively uncharted territory of popular practice. In the process, we touched on the canonical bases for the authority of the ordained and canonical sources for the bodhisattva precepts. Moving on to practices in early Buddhist communities in China, we looked at visualization practices for lay and ordained in Dharmakṣema's community in Liangzhou and in Huiyuan's community at Mt. Lu. We then turned to apocryphal bodhisattva precepts scriptures and an indigenous scripture heavily imbued with Chinese cosmology and medicology. As noted, this spectrum is not intended to represent a chronological evolution (or devolution) from orthodox monastic practice to popular lay practice; rather, it is a representation of the different levels on which the lay-ordained relationship functioned in various prescriptive texts and contexts. At the same time, I hope to have shown that the latitude for accommodation of lay social practices and Chinese cultural practices was greater in the apocrypha.

It is also important to take note of the compound of associated practices within which the bodhisattva precepts functioned. In examples from Dharmakṣema's and Huiyuan's communities, we find many of the key elements that would come to be standardized in later systems of practice, such as Tiantai and Northern School Chan. Drawn from the bodhisattva precepts scriptures and from visualization scriptures such as the *Jin guangming jing* and the *Banzhou sanmei jing*, these associated practices revolved around conferral of the bodhisattva precepts, formulas for confession and repentance, short periods of intensive repentance, meditation, circumambulation practice, and reliance on visions and signs to confirm the efficacy of one's practice. In this context, achieving a vision of the Buddhas, successfully removing one's karmic hindrances through confession and repentance, and receiving assurance of salvation from an authoritative source (whether monk or visionary Buddha) were linked and mutually reinforcing. Notably, Huiyuan raised questions about relying on something as subjective as visionary experience. In the *Lidai fabao ji*, seeking visions of the Buddha and bodhisattvas and practicing confession and repentance are repeatedly targeted as deluded practices.

However, there are also significant areas of continuity between the Bao Tang practices and these fourth- and fifth-century practices centered on the bodhisattva precepts. This is especially apparent when we turn to the apocryphal bodhisattva precepts scriptures. In subsequent chapters we see the continued usefulness of the models for practice provided in the apocryphal scriptures, models that validated self-perpetuation of the lay group while paying the coin of respect formally due to the ordained Saṅgha. The schema of practice in the apocryphal scriptures created the structures and criteria of distinction that lay groups needed in order to legitimate their own identities and yet work in tandem with the authoritative institutions of the ordained. Through Dunhuang administrative and devotional materials, we see that lay groups functioned as mutual-aid societies. Through eulogies and incidental writings, we get glimpses of how like-minded lay literati associated in loosely defined coteries of appreciation for a particular Buddhist master or location. The early apocrypha gave a measure of legitimacy to the self-renewing and self-validating functions of various types of lay organizations by allowing them to receive their own visionary confirmation, hold their own confessionals, confer precepts on one another, and sometimes also to teach one another. In this regard, the members of the Bao Tang, by relying on each other rather than on the reciprocities mandated by formal status distinctions, and by practicing according to their own criteria of authenticity and their own definitions of the precepts, functioned as a group that bears more resemblance to a lay society than to a monastic sect.

CHAPTER 4

Material Buddhism and the Dharma Kings

Dr. Grantly, if he admits the Queen's supremacy in things spiritual, only admits it as being due to the quasi priesthood conveyed in the consecrating qualities of her coronation; and he regards things temporal as being by their nature subject to those which are spiritual. Mr. Slope's ideas of sacerdotal rule are of quite a different class. He cares nothing, one way or the other, for the Queen's supremacy; these to his ears are empty words, meaning nothing. . . . Let him be supreme who can. The temporal king, judge, or gaoler, can work but on the body. The spiritual master, if he have the necessary gifts, and can duly use them, has a wider field of empire.

—Anthony Trollope, *Barchester Towers*

THE DANGERS OF EMPIRE

In the fifth and sixth centuries, the practice of making offerings to gain merit gathered momentum among clergy and laity alike, and this was closely linked to widespread interest in stories of karmic retribution and theories of the decline of the Dharma. In chapter 3, we looked at some of the figures, practices, and texts involved in the dissemination of Buddhist devotionalism, and in this chapter we explore a few of the currents in this rising tide of piety. In the first section, I introduce the motif of the threat of spiritual materialism through a brief chronicle of the Northern Wei dynasty. In the second section, entitled "Empires of Signs," I explore five different textual and ritual responses to the fear of corruption of the Saṅgha that was intrinsic to Chinese *famie* 法滅 (decline of the Dharma) or *moshi* 末世 (final age) eschatology, better known by the later Japanese designation *mappō* 末法 (Chin. *mofa*).[1] We examine the mystique of transmission in the *Fu fazang zhuan*, the paradigms of practice developed by Tiantai Zhiyi, signs of the end-time in the *Renwang jing*, the extremes of the "universal" soteriology of the Sanjie (Three Levels) school, and Daoxuan's visions. In the period from the Northern Wei to the beginning of the Tang, criticism of Buddhism's wealth and political power moved closer to the center of Buddhist discourse. In each of the topics covered in this chapter we see different approaches to a mounting sense of crisis, and from among the inspirational, exegetical, and ritual remedies that were attempted, I highlight the aspects that contributed to the development of Chan and have counterparts in Bao Tang soteriology.

THE NORTHERN WEI AND SPIRITUAL MATERIALISM

The Northern Wei is here treated as a study in the enthusiasms of a particular Buddhist "age of innocence," a short period when practical, propitiatory, and lavishly material Buddhism was adopted unreservedly.[2] Textual and artistic remains from the Northern Wei afford us the opportunity to trace a relationship between state and Saṅgha from hazy beginnings, through persecution and triumphant resurgence, to a precipitous end; the destruction of the Northern Wei would continue to be an object lesson throughout Chinese Buddhist history. As we will see in chapter 5, the development of Chan was quickened in part by reactions against the material Buddhism of the empress Wu Zetian, and there are certain resonances between Buddhist Luoyang at the end of the Northern Wei and at the height of Wu Zetian's power.

By the time of the Bao Tang, the denunciation of spiritual materialism was a well-worn theme in both Buddhist and non-Buddhist discourse, and Wuzhu turns to this topic in his talk to a group of lay donors:

> [The Venerable said,] "In the Prajñāpāramitā, one does not see the one who repays the kindness nor does one see the one who does the kindness. I, Wuzhu, practice unconditioned compassion, practice desireless compassion, practice not-grasping compassion, and practice causeless compassion. It is neither that nor this, I do not practice upper, middle, and lower Dharma, do not practice 'conditioned and unconditioned' or 'real and unreal' Dharma. It is not for the sake of increase and not for the sake of decrease, there is no great good fortune and no small good fortune. With nothing that is received, one yet receives all that is received. In the uncompleted Buddha-Dharma, there is also no end to receiving. 'If you want to confess and repent, sit properly and contemplate the characteristic of actuality.'[3] No-thought is thus the characteristic of actuality, thought is thus empty delusion. Confessing and repenting and intoning prayers, all this is empty delusion."[4]

Wuzhu caricatures doctrinal labels and implies that these distinctions are bound up with the materialistic concerns of both the monasteries and their merit-seeking clients. Then he links materialistic concerns with the practices of confession and repentance, disparaging both. As discussed in chapter 3, the bodhisattva precepts, merit-gaining, and repentance practices were at the heart of Buddhist practice, the wellspring that allowed the monasteries to flourish. Wuzhu's juxtapositions prompt the listener to infer that the abstruse doctrinal distinctions and systems debated by exegetes are compromised by the fountain of anxious and greedy popular piety that nourishes them. Critical reminders like Wuzhu's were as integral to the functioning of the Saṅgha as the flow of pious donations itself. The principles of austerity ("the bhikṣu must not handle gold and silver") and of the generation of wealth (the bhikṣu must accept all that is given") are both part of the soteriological set-up that has effectively reproduced the Saṅgha in a wide array of places and times.

Turning to the history of the Northern Wei and the powerful partnership that developed between Saṅgha and state, we gain a sense of the tremendous force of the dynamo of Buddhist wealth, a force that is enjoying a resurgence even now, against which Wuzhu's apophatic dictums seem feather-light. The dramatic circumstances of the rise and fall of the Northern Wei made it the paradigmatic northern dynasty of the period. In chapter 2 we saw that Tang historians were fascinated by the lessons of Fujian's hubristic earnestness and the fall of the Qin; similarly, the Northern Wei provided much material for the didactic biography of a dynasty. However, while Buddhism played only a small ancillary role in the drama of the Qin, the postmortem chroniclers of the Northern Wei explicitly linked its fate with the vicissitudes of its Buddhism. This attitude is conveyed in two key sources for the period, Wei Shou's 魏收 (506–572) *Shilao zhi* 釋老志 (Treatise on Buddhism and Daoism) written in the early part of the Northern Qi 北齊 (550–577),[5] and Yang Xuanzhi's 楊衒之 *Luoyang qielan ji* 洛陽伽藍記 (A Record of Buddhist Monasteries in Luoyang) completed in 547.[6]

The Wei was formed when the armies led by Tuoba Gui 拓跋珪, posthumously known as the founding emperor Taizu 太祖, swept through present-day Shanxi and Hebei during the latter part of the fourth century.[7] Wei Shou notes that the Wei founder at first merely reciprocated the signs of respect shown him by the Buddhist clergy of the conquered territories. However, the reputation of the monk Faguo 法果 caught the emperor's attention, and Faguo was invited to court and honored by both Taizu and his successor. In contrast to the struggle for clerical autonomy carried out by monks in the south, Faguo cast the emperor as the progenitor of Buddhist authority, thereby removing the basis of conflict: "Fa-kuo would say to the others, 'He who propagates the teaching of the Buddha is the lord of men. I am not doing obeisance to the Emperor, I am merely worshipping the Buddha.'"[8]

Cordial relations between court and clergy lasted until late in the reign of the third Wei emperor, Taiwu 太武 (r. 424–452). As is well known, Taiwu launched the first violent persecution of Buddhism in China, purportedly instigated by the reformist Daoist master Kou Qianzhi 寇謙之 and the powerful minister Cui Hao 崔浩 (381–450). In the years leading up to the persecution, Kou Qianzhi and Cui Hao nearly succeeded in making the Wei court into what Richard Mather terms a "Daoist theocracy."[9] They also proscribed local cults; ironically, the Northern Wei might not have become such a thoroughly Buddhist state without the focusing effect of the persecution and its aftermath. It is also possible that the extent of the persecution was exaggerated by later Buddhist chroniclers in order to dramatize the ensuing reversal of fortunes, for the deepest impression left by the persecution was the swiftness and completeness with which punishment fell upon the persecutors.[10]

After the persecution there was a determined effort to recast all the Wei emperors, including Taiwu, not only as Buddhist patrons but as Buddhist authorities, and even as Buddhas. Through the latter half of the fifth century, Buddhism served as the primary unifying force for the state. The ending of the persecution unleashed a deluge of Buddhist piety, encompassing all levels of society and diverse ethnic groups. This is attested by Wei Shou and later chroniclers, by the proliferation of indigenous scriptures (including a number of bodhisattva precepts texts), by the numerous Northern Wei Buddhist stele and votive images, and by the awe-inspiring cave-temples at Yungang 雲岡.

The monk Tanyao 曇曜 (d. c. 485) was especially instrumental in the postpersecution Buddhist revival. He was appointed to the highest clerical office, and in this capacity he persuaded the emperor to institute a kind of joint venture between the government and the Saṅgha:

> T'an-yao petitioned that the households of P'ing-ch'i 平齊 and those of the people who could yearly convey sixty "hu" of grain and present them to the clerical officials constitute Saṃgha-households, and their grain be designated Saṃgha-grain, to be used in lean years to relieve the famine-stricken people. He also requested that those of the people who committed grave crimes, as well as the public slaves, be constituted Buddha-households, to serve the temples as sweepers and sprinklers, and also manage the fields and transport the grain. Kao-tsung 高宗 granted all these requests. Thereafter Saṃgha-households and Saṃgha-grain and temple-households were to be found everywhere in the prefectures and garrisons.[11]

Tanyao also urged the emperor to undertake the building of the cave temples at Yungang, and he oversaw the construction.[12] The huge caves are testimony to the melding of state cult and popular Buddhism, and the congregation of individual donor niches also tells of the appropriation of state cult by popular Buddhism. Yungang's towering, benevolent Tathāgata-rulers and its repeated figures of Śākyamuni and Maitreya manifest the imperial predilection for images of continuity and authority.

Connections between iconography and practice at the caves of Yungang, Dunhuang, Longmen, and other sites are the subject of a growing body of scholarly literature, which is beyond the scope of this study to present.[13] However, I briefly summarize James Caswell's discussion of various theories on the periodization of construction at Yungang, as his work sheds light on patronage and practice in the Northern Wei. In the first phase of development of the Yungang caves, roughly 460–467, we see constructions that were imperially sponsored and political in purpose, in which there is discernible unity of purpose and stylistic continuity. Monumental Buddha images dominate the space of these caves, which are not designed for entry. Work on additional caves began after imperial construction ceased, and the relatively remote site at Yungang became the focus of religious activities of the wealthy laity, the clergy, and religious associations. In the later phase of construction, there is more stylistic and organizational variety, and the caves have open spaces suitable for practices such as circumambulation.[14] Moreover, the second phase included two levels of patronage. Wealthy donors provided for the excavation of new caves and the main images and designs, while devotees with limited resources crowded the available spaces with minor niches and images.[15]

Unfortunately, merit-making excesses began to overburden the Northern Wei economic system. As the pace of military expansion slowed, state-building energies merged ever more powerfully with the energies of the Buddhist clergy and lay believers, and the imperial family and the aristocracy vied with one another to build palaces and temples. As the mania for durable records of merit caused real wealth to pour into the Saṅgha, it also created the aura of prestige and power that further fed the fetishism. This tendency for Buddhism to swell into a dangerous bubble in the Chinese economy was to be a recurring problem, but the bonding of Buddhist and state operations rendered the Northern Wei particularly vulnerable. Due in part to the tax-free Buddha- and Saṅgha-households, the Northern Wei economic base was gradually weakening as the resources diverted into the construction of monuments increased, thus overburdening the architecture of the entire polity.[16]

Wei Shou's record shows continued alternation between the reverent and the regulatory in imperial edicts regarding the Saṅgha. In 493 two significant events occurred: the promulgation of a Clerical Code (*sengzhi* 僧制) in forty-seven articles, and the removal of the capital from Pingcheng 平城 in the north to the old Chinese capital of Luoyang.[17] The latter event seems to have had more impact on the Saṅgha than the former. The capital was moved for political and symbolic reasons by the Sinophile Emperor Xiaowen 孝文 (r. 471–499), and it ushered in a "golden age" for Buddhism. The shift to Luoyang brought with it more conscious appropriation of Chinese culture and administrative norms, and, building over the buried ruins of the Han imperial city, the new aristocracy sought and found talismans that they hoped would contribute to their own mystique of legitimacy. The *Luoyang qielan ji* is full of stories of discoveries of Buddhist statues and other remnants of the old city. At the same time that the newly Sinified were trying to connect with the Chinese past, Buddhism represented a tradition old enough to rival the Chinese layers of history, and powerful enough to pacify the disturbed ghosts and force them, or bribe them with merit, to sanction the new inheritors.

Buddhism also served as a unifying creed amid the disparate peoples and regional cultures gathered in the capital. Luoyang, the greatest northern Buddhist center and the eastern terminus of the Silk Route, absorbed the full impact of the "second wave" of Mahāyāna, the latest trend in Yogācāra philosophy, which made its way south only gradually. The Wei court sponsored new Yogācāra translations, Bodhiruci's 菩提流支 (d. 527) lectures, and the sūtra-seeking Indian mission of Song Yun 宋雲 and the monk Huisheng 惠生.[18]

Yet disaffection multiplied along with the temples. The last part of Wei Shou's *Shilao zhi* becomes a record of edicts and memorials cast like twigs into the path of a flood of clerical abuses. One such memorial states:

> Yet the Wei-na (monastic overseer) General Sêng-hsien 僧暹 and Sêng-p'in 僧頻 on the one hand violate an established decree, on the other turn their backs on the clerical laws. Selfish in thought, reckless in feeling, they memorialize for compulsory services, causing crying anguish to fill the roadways. Those who have abandoned their children, killed, strangled themselves, and drowned are more than fifty persons. Is this what is meant by honoring saintly wisdom and merciful guidance? Nay, it profoundly misses Your Majesty's intent in taking the Refuges.[19]

One might surmise that the outrage was all the sharper because more was expected of the Saṅgha-overlords than of the usual worldly kind. In spite of the manifest abuses, the mystique of the holy, wonder-working monk remained powerful, as attested by the *Xu gaoseng zhuan* biographies of Northern Wei monks. This recalls Peter Brown's discussion of the social function of the paradigm of the holy man in the early Christian church, which was developing half a world away during the same period as Buddhism's ascent in China. Brown writes of the role of the holy man in eastern Mediterranean societies of the fourth and fifth centuries: "The position of the holy men in Syria is a paradigm of the need of eastern Christians to consider as 'holy' ascetic figures on whom they could place their hopes for a 'holy,' that is for an idealized, patronage, in a world overshadowed by the 'unholy,' that is, by an only too real, patronage. This aspect of East Roman social and spiritual life is well summed up by Thomas Hobbes in chapter ten of his Leviathan: 'Reputation of power is power: because it draweth with it the adherence of those who need protection.'"[20] Brown then asks how "East Romans framed their expectations of the holy, and how they combined these in such a way not only to facilitate the exercise of 'reputation of power' but, tacitly, to delimit this same exercise."[21] He delicately and vividly evokes Late Antique expectations of the holy in several of his works, but one of his main theses is that the delimitation of the holy was calibrated to the contrasts between the desert and village and, in turn, between village and town. The holy man was seen to derive his powers from his ability to live the antithesis of human life in the desert or to move among the people but remain marked as an outsider. "The holy, therefore, was at its most holy when least connected with that conflict of human interests which it was constantly called upon to palliate."[22]

Stories such as a *Luoyang qielan ji* tale of the consignment of lecturers and monastic officials to Hell indicates very similar calibration and delimitation at work.[23] In memorials and stories attempting to separate false from true clergy one can discern a high level of skepticism and resentment toward worldly monastics, but one can also discern the persistence of high expectations. The cloud of mystery that had once set apart all the ordained began to recede to the lonelier peaks of spiritual athleticism. On the ground, however, the second decade of the sixth century saw increasingly frequent rebellions that were fueled in part by anger toward ordinary "altar rats of the Law" who grew fat on Saṅgha-grain.[24] One particularly violent episode was the so-called Mahāyāna rebellion of 515, whose leader Faqing 法慶, fashioning his ideology from scraps of Buddhist doctrine, fomented an eschatological mission to slaughter the clergy and other "devils."[25]

The Empress Dowager Ling 靈太后 was an ardent supporter of Buddhism and the founding patroness of the magnificent Yongning 永寧 monastery, constructed in 516. Apparently, however, she believed that the wrong element was threatening to ruin the tone of her religion, for in the following year she promulgated a decree limiting the clergy and prohibiting "private ordination" (*sidu* 私度): "From now on, if there be one person privately ordained, all concerned shall be considered to have disobeyed an Imperial edict. . . . The person privately ordained shall be assigned to hard labor in his respective province."[26] The decree specifically objected to monks and nuns who ordained slaves as their disciples and thereby raised the social degree of their personal attendants and prevented them from being claimed by the state.[27]

Seeking merit, the Wei aristocracy raised the clergy to levels of political and economic power rivaling their own and then attempted to control admission to the eminence that they had created. When one reads the description of Yongning monastery in the *Luoyang qielan ji,* one understands that the clergy lived in splendid surroundings comparable to the palaces of the aristocracy. The conflagration of Yongning monastery in 534 was later seen as an unmistakable omen of the impending fall of the dynasty, heralding a new regime and remaining in imperial memory as a sign of the increasing power of a Buddhist mandate in uneasy alliance with that of Heaven.[28] In hindsight, the faults of the Northern Wei were pitilessly exposed with the ruins of Luoyang, and it seemed clear that Buddhist piety had overstepped the bounds of Buddhist principles.

As discussed in chapter 5, the famous story of Bodhidharma's terse assessment of "no merit" in response to the good works of Emperor Wu 武 (r. 502–549) of the Liang 梁 was an eighth-century creation. However, its criticism of dependency on illusory spiritual wealth has echoes of Bodhidharma's "actual" milieu, in which merit-making began to be shadowed by the possibility of karmic retribution for spiritual greed. Gazing at the carvings of Yungang, or the Northern Wei statues now scattered across the globe in various museums, it is difficult to imagine the passions and fears that contributed to their creation. When one views the "archaic smile" of a Northern Wei Buddha, it seems the very embodiment of the teaching that "there is no great good fortune and no small good fortune."

EMPIRES OF SIGNS

In chapter 5, I argue that the need to clarify the stream of true Dharma transmission within the flood of mere ordination was one of the formative tensions that shaped the early Chan school. For the remainder of this chapter we look at five different kinds of responses to the same tension: (1) an early chronicle of Indian Dharma transmission that was probably compiled in China, (2) Zhiyi's systematization of doctrines and practices, (3) the state-protecting rituals of the *Renwang jing,* (4) Xinxing's inexhaustible treasury, and (5) Daoxuan's visionary ordination ritual. Against the background of sixth- and seventh-century attempts to unite or definitively divide the Saṅgha, the challenge that "Southern School" ideology presented to the Buddhist establishment may be seen as yet another sharp skirmish in the ongoing struggle to claim watertight transmission of the true Dharma.

Though I hope to avoid reducing the selected topics to the status of merely dependent or reactive positionings, in each of these soteriological programs we can discern traces of a polemical context and the seeds of sectarianism. I argue that these seeds germinated from the increasing desire to clarify a workable pan-Buddhist identity and hierarchy in response to the patronage and pressures of the imperial "other." This "other" was of course itself continually engaged in self-definition and was itself composed of conflicting elements (such as the inner court versus the apparatus of the state).

In histories of relations between sacerdotal and temporal spheres of authority, it frequently appears that the benefit each side gains from the other depends on maintaining an agonistic edge to the relationship. In other words, the value of the ideological currency that clerical and lay elites derive from each other is made greater insofar as they avoid hierarchical stasis but maintain a serious struggle for domination. Yet how are we to separate religious and mundane when we consider political function in medieval China? The interchange among Confucian, Daoist, and Buddhist factors in the ongoing construction of the Chinese imperial state is an inexhaustible subject, beyond the scope of the present study. Nevertheless, one cannot claim that the imperium, however deeply sacralized, was a religious order in the same manner as the Saṅgha. For our purposes, it is the undeniable exchange of pressure and resistance between one "side" and the other that helps us to distinguish them and to identify sensitive points in the body politic, where the religious authority enacted by the imperium and the political authority enacted from within the Saṅgha meet.

Confucian scholars have frequently argued that the normative Confucian-Legalist style of governance developed in the Han was a political philosophy, not a religion. The practical business of government was nevertheless a highly ritualized affair, and for the Confucian official careful attention to etiquette, maintenance of parents and ancestors, civil service, and noblesse oblige were in effect a religious vocation. Moreover, at the heart of the Chinese polity lay the imperial cult with its calendar of sacrifices honoring ancestors and patron deities. Although the imperial cult at times included Buddhist deities in its pantheon, the "mystique of legitimacy" it conferred had its source in Confucian-Legalist theories of the mandate of the Sage-ruler. Notions of the nature and function of the Sage-ruler were drawn from a wide range of texts, including "Daoist" classics, such as the *Yijing*, the *Daode jing*, and the *Zhuangzi*.[29] Han state-cult icons carried much weight even in apparently Buddhist-oriented regimes; for example, though the Northern Wei court was imbued with Buddhist devotionalism, Emperor Xiaowen also instituted the first official Confucian temple.

On the Buddhist side, the emphasis on *upāya*, the desirable ability to adapt the teachings to the capacities of the listeners, provided a basis for the multitiered presentations of the teachings known as *panjiao* 判教 (classification of the teachings). This exegetical scaffolding contained many levels on which the Buddhist clergy could relate to and compete with homologous aspects of non-Buddhist society. As we have seen, Buddhist clerics' flexible relationship with political power was not always smooth, yet without a strong civil and military service maintaining order and borders and the kind of economy that could generate expenditure for merit, Buddhist monasteries could not thrive. For Buddhists, conversion of those in power was clearly the most effective means of spreading the Dharma, but the involvement of leading clerics in the social and political life of the court made the Saṅgha vulnerable to accusations of corruption from both Buddhists and non-Buddhists. For rulers, the Triple Jewel served as an alluring mirror, a mysterious "other" and a potentially dangerous rival for the favor of the masses, and a reservoir of spiritual wealth that could also become a tempting hoard of real wealth in times of fiscal crisis.

This tension shapes the "decline of the Dharma" discourse that runs throughout the examples discussed below, all of which reflect the Saṅgha's tug-of-war between self-accusation and persecution complex. This can be seen in the two major currents of Indian "decline" eschatology identified by Jan Nattier: (1) variations on *Saṃyutta Nikāya*-based periodization schemes of true and semblance teachings, which came to be associated with the claim that the Buddhist order causes its own decline;[30] and (2) narratives drawing from the Kauśāmbi prophesy, in which end-time is marked by the reign of cleric-killing evil kings.[31] In China, however, these motifs began to be used to support claims that the final age had arrived or was about to arrive. Saṅgha-directed criticisms linked to the first motif are clearly implicated in the growing sectarianism of the seventh century, as clerical efforts were devoted to defensive denials and preemptive self-critical strategies.

Signs of decline due to external causes were not lacking. Buddhists in recent memory had seen the rise and fall of the Northern Wei as well as the Northern Zhou persecution of Buddhism from 574 to 577. Moreover, the constant warfare and regime changes that plagued North China in the sixth century gave new life to indigenous eschatologies. During the Han, theorists and strategists mapped out a complex system of correspondences between cosmological, political, physical, and moral phenomena, and debated the relationship between these phenomena and underlying principles. Central to these debates was concern with the cycles of the Mandate of Heaven (*tianming* 天命) that gave legitimacy to the ruler and the regime, and both imperial and opposition forces in the Han evoked signs and anomalies as evidence of the right to govern. At the end of the Han these theories were incorporated into Daoist messianic movements, and the mixture of what one might call political phenomenology and Daoist theology proved to be potent and volatile throughout the period of north-south division and into the Sui. One must keep in mind that the Buddhist eschatologies discussed in this chapter developed in a milieu of simmering popular messianic sentiment, punctuated by periodic uprisings.[32]

However, in Buddhist texts claims that attributed decline to external causes (implying the ruler's lack of virtue) tended to be muted, as this was dangerously associated with subversive prophetic apocrypha and the outbreak of popular uprisings. In the following sections we see different emphases laid on the twin motifs of external and internal corruption: in the *Fu fazang zhuan* the chronicle of the special monks who preserve the Dharma comes to a tragic end due to a murderous ruler, Zhiyi is deeply concerned with reform of the Saṅgha, the *Renwang jing* includes praise and blame for both clerics and rulers and extols the benefits of cooperation, Xinxing stresses that all are equally and hopelessly corrupt, and Daoxuan exhorts the monk to clean up his act (both moral and ritual) in light of the coming apocalypse.

THE *FU FAZANG ZHUAN*

The *Fu fazang [yinyuan] zhuan* 付法藏[因緣]傳 (Account of the [Avādana] of the Transmission of the Dharma Treasury)[33] has traditionally been linked to the postpersecution anxieties of the Northern Wei clergy. However, in the remaining traces of the Northern Wei what is most noticeable about the postpersecution clergy is not their anxiety but their populist piety and energy; it was only later that the apocalyptic mood would become palpable. For this and other reasons, the *Fu fazang zhuan* is more likely to have been a sixth-century work attuned to "final age" pessimism, as control of the north was disputed by a series of short-lived successors to the Northern Wei.

It is clear that the *Fu fazang zhuan* appeals to different instincts of preservation and transmission than the inclusive tendencies apparent in the fifth-century bodhisattva precepts texts. While the apocryphal precepts texts were concerned to clarify practices that would define potentially limitless Buddhist communities, the *Fu fazang zhuan* upholds a very narrow definition of true Dharma—identified as a single line of transmission from master to disciple, beginning with Śākyamuni and ending with the murder of the twenty-third patriarch, Siṃha Bhikṣu 師子比丘, in Kashmir.[34] It is a major source for the version of the patriarchal lineage that is found in the *Lidai fabao ji* and later Chan texts, but the *Lidai fabao ji* authors or some unknown predecessor had to rework the final biography in the *Fu fazang zhuan* in order to justify the claim to an unbroken lineage that continued onward to Bodhidharma and the Chinese patriarchs.[35]

The origins of the *Fu fazang zhuan* are obscure. In the *Chu sanzang ji ji* it is listed as a translation completed in 472 by Tanyao and the Indian monk Kiṅkara 吉迦夜.[36] In its notice on the *Fu fazang zhuan*, the *Lidai sanbao ji* 歷代三寶記 (Record of the Three Jewels Through the Generations) cites the inclusion of the text in an earlier catalogue by Bodhiruci 菩提流支,[37] and it claims that after the persecution Tanyao sequestered himself with a group of monks and worked on retranslating sūtras, including the *Fu fazang zhuan*, in order to restore scriptures that had been lost in the persecution.[38]

The *Baolin zhuan* 寶林傳 (Transmission of the Baolin [Temple]), compiled in 801 by Zhiju 智炬, contains an account of the origins of the text that would become an accepted pretext both for relying on the *Fu fazang zhuan* and for dismissing its shortcomings. A disciple of Huineng's is said to have informed an assembly that Tanyao escaped the persecution with the single record of the patriarchy that was in the imperial storehouse, but it was lost during his years in the mountains. Tanyao kept it in his memory, and when Buddhism was restored he gathered other monks and together they produced the *Fu fazang zhuan*. However, their reconstruction of the patriarchal lineage was faulty and incomplete.[39]

In his *Chuanfa zhengzong lun* 傳法正宗論 (Treatise of the True Doctrine of Transmission of the Dharma), the Song dynasty Chan scholar Qisong 契嵩 (1007–1072) draws from the *Baolin zhuan* for this and other accounts of the Indian patriarchs.[40] Given that the eighth century saw the advent of a passion for the unbroken Chan lineage, a passion that by the eleventh century had become canonical, both Zhiju and Qisong had reason to want to discredit the veracity of the *Fu fazang zhuan*. The *Fu fazang zhuan* ends dramatically with the severance of the direct line of transmission from the Buddha, with the murder of Siṁha Bhikṣu. Qisong waxes rather indignant over the idea that a patriarch would not be able to foresee his own death and transmit the Dharma forthwith.[41] In the stories of transmission Qisong uses as examples, he emphasizes the predestined quality of the patriarchal succession even more prominently than do his immediate sources, the *Baolin zhuan* and *Jingde chuandeng lu*.

Henri Maspéro raises the question of whether the present *Fu fazang zhuan* is the same as the text in fifth-century catalogues. His analysis of notices in sixth-century catalogues shows that it is possible there were two versions of the *Fu fazang zhuan*, and he favors the hypothesis that the *Fu fazang zhuan* is a sixth-century Chinese compilation that may have existed simultaneously with an earlier authentic translation.[42] However, the earliest quotations of the text as we know it date from the seventh century and are all in texts linked to Daoxuan or the *Dharmaguptaka Vinaya*.[43] Daoxuan was considered the founding patriarch of the Dharmagupta Vinaya school, so this connection with the *Fu fazang zhuan* merits further investigation.

The extant *Fu fazang zhuan* seems to be a pastiche of translated Indian texts, relying heavily on the *Aśokarāja-sūtra* and including material from the *Sarvāstivāda Vinaya* and individual biographies.[44] There is some conceptual similarity between the *Fu fazang zhuan* and the *Mohemoye jing* 摩訶摩耶經 (*Mahāmāyā-sūtra*, Scripture of [the Buddha's Mother] Mahāmāyā), translated in the south between 479 and 502. In this work, the Buddha predicts the appearance of seven masters at hundred-year intervals, corresponding to the five periods of the true Dharma. After them, Aśvaghoṣa and Nāgārjuna extend the Dharma in the spirit of previous generations, but the Dharma is thereafter in decline.[45]

Carvings and inscriptions in the Dazhusheng 大住聖 cave at Baoshan 寶山 (Henan) provide clear evidence of a late sixth-century *Fu fazang zhuan* containing the same patriarchal names and origins (with minor variations) as the present text. Inside the cave on the south wall there is a magnificent floor-to-ceiling carving of the *Fu fazang zhuan* figures, represented as twenty-four patriarchs facing one another in pairs with their names and origins inscribed beneath them. Dated 589, the year of the Sui 隋 unification of China, the dedicatory inscription for the cave identifies the images in Dazhusheng cave and thus provides us with an example of the kind of devotional program in which the *Fu fazang zhuan* was placed.[46]

The cave was founded by Lingyu 靈裕 (518–605), a disciple of Daoping 道憑, who was the disciple of the Northern Wei master Huiguang 慧光, one of the masters of Dilun 地論 exegesis.[47] Lingyu may have been a teacher of Xinxing 信行 (540–594), the founder of the Sanjie 三階 (Three Levels) movement. Dilun/Sanjie elements in the inscription and the surviving carvings include the reference to the thirty-five Buddhas[48] and the seven Buddhas of the past; Xinxing used both these sets of Buddhas in his eschatological teaching that the present age was the final age of the Dharma. The dedicatory inscription is as follows:

> In the ninth year of the Kaihuang 開皇 era of the Great Sui, a jiyou 己酉 year (589), [we] reverently constructed [this] cave, accomplished one thousand six hundred and twenty-four images, world-honored, [and] accomplished nine hundred [days of work. (?) The images are as follows:] Vairocana, world-honored, one niche; Amitābha, world-honored, one niche; Maitreya, world-honored, one niche; the thirty-five Buddhas, world-honored, thirty-five niches; the seven Buddhas, world-honored, seven niches; and the Dharma-transmitting Holy Great Dharma Masters, twenty-four men. The "Praise of the Three Jewels" gāthā says: "The samādhi and prajñā of the Tathāgata is limitless, his supramundane powers are great and subtle and difficult to conceive. His major and minor marks brightly illumine the world-net, thus he bids the Three Worlds all take refuge in the Dharma-Jewel, pure as the void. The 'good home' is profound and inexhaustible; not born and not extinguished, not departing and not coming home [yet] extinguishing and separating from defilements, it is difficult to conceive. The sea of merit of the (character illegible—images?) of the group of Holy Ones extirpates all defilements, [so that] *śīla* and samādhi are pure and flawless."[49]

The "Dharma-transmitting Holy Great Dharma Masters" are thus included in the eternal and incorruptible nature of the Three Jewels. At the same time, the images chosen also evoke temporality—the seven Buddhas of past ages, the future Buddha Maitreya, and the fragile bridge of Dharma Masters. Simple carved inscriptions attached to the images of the twenty-four patriarchs inside the cave state that the good works of Siṁha Bhikṣu in Kashmir were severed, but the implications for the present age of the

Dharma are not spelled out. Other early uses of the *Fu fazang zhuan* also emphasize the long continuity of Dharma transmission rather than its termination; in the next section we look at one such use of the *Fu fazang zhuan* in early Tiantai writings.

When we look for signs of the development of an unbroken patriarchal sequence, we find that the archaeological record again provides earlier evidence than does the textual. At Longmen, in addition to the Wu Zetian–era representations and inscriptions of twenty-five patriarchs based on the *Fu fazang zhuan,* there are bas-relief images of twenty-nine patriarchs in the Kanjing 看經 temple cave, which is dated 732.[50] However, the earliest textual reference to twenty-nine Chan patriarchs (without listing them) is in an epitaph written in 754 by Li Hua 李華 (d. c. 766) for the Tiantai master Xuanlang 玄朗 (673–754).[51] Interestingly, this account of the Chinese Chan patriarchs blends Northern School, Southern School, and Oxhead School figures, a point discussed further in chapter 5.

Various factions of the nascent Chan school produced several different lists of Indian and Chinese patriarchs, which all drew from the *Fu fazang zhuan* and Buddhabhadra's preface to his translation of the *Damoduoluo chan jing* (*Dhyāna-sūtra of Dharmatrāta*), discussed in chapter 3.[52] Buddhabhadra's preface included the standard five successors in the four generations after the Buddha, plus three masters from the Kashmiri Sarvāstivāda lineage. Huiyuan's and Huiguan's prefaces to the same work include slightly different versions of this pedigree.[53] Furthermore, Sengyou compiled a record of the lineages of transmission of the Sarvāstivāda Vinaya that includes two long variant lists of fifty-three and fifty-four names, and there is some overlap between the *Fu fazang zhuan* list and Sengyou's Sarvāstivāda list.[54]

Demiéville discusses an intriguing mythos linking the Kashmiri Sarvāstivāda masters with the future Buddhas, connected also with traditions of the rebirth of Sarvāstivāda masters in Tuṣita. In Daoan's preface to the *Zun Poxumi pusa suoji lun* 尊婆須蜜菩薩所集論, Vasumitra is said to be the next future Buddha after Maitreya (the fifth Buddha of this age), to be reborn eventually as Siṃha Tathāgata (the sixth). Vasumitra/Siṃha Tathāgata was said to have gone to Tuṣita in samādhi and visited the other future Buddhas: Maitreya, and the two Sarvāstivāda masters Maitreyaśrī (the seventh, Pradyota Tathāgata) and Saṅgharakṣa (the eighth, the Buddha Muni).[55] One might thus surmise that the *Fu fazang zhuan* legend of the martyrdom of Siṁha Bhikṣu may owe something to the Kashmiri tradition of the future Buddha Siṃha Tathāgata.

Tanaka Ryōshō has demonstrated that the Faxiang 法相 Yogācāra school used a twenty-eight patriarch scheme in the *Fuzhu fazang zhuan lue chao* 付囑法藏傳略抄, whose provenance can be dated to 766 based on internal evidence.[56] In this text, the *Fu fazang zhuan* lineage is augmented by the masters from Buddhabhadra's preface, but Yogācāra influences are revealed in the placement of Asaṅga and Vasubandhu as the twenty-sixth and twenty-seventh patriarchs immediately prior to Bodhidharma, thus disregarding chronology even more flagrantly than the Chan texts. Sometime in the late Tang or Five Dynasties, this text was included in an esoteric compilation and edited to reflect the concerns of the lineage of Amoghavajra; among other changes, the fourth Chinese patriarch became Xinxing, the Sanjie movement founder, rather than Daoxin. Interestingly, the twenty-eighth patriarch became Bodhisattva Bodhidharma-Guanyin 菩提達摩觀音菩薩.[57] This substitution is but one example of the intermingling of esoteric, apocalyptic, and Chan currents in ninth- and tenth-century Chinese Buddhism.[58]

Thus, the *Lidai fabao ji* authors were neither the first nor the last to make creative use of various transmission schemes in order to overcome the unsatisfactory ending of the *Fu fazang zhuan*. However, the *Lidai fabao ji* is the earliest extant text that directly responds to the obvious insufficiency of Shenhui's notion of "unbroken transmission." In Shenhui's list in the *Putidamou nanzong ding shifei lun* 菩提達摩南宗定是非論 (Treatise Determining the True and False About the Southern School of Bodhidharma), the gap between the standard first five Indian "patriarchs" and the Chinese patriarchs is bridged by names derived from the Sarvāstivāda lineage: (6) Śubhamitra 須婆蜜多, which probably results from a mistaken inversion of the first two characters in the name Vasumitra 婆須蜜 from Buddhabhadra's list,[59] and (7) Saṅgharakṣa 僧迦羅叉, who is the figure between Vasumitra and Dharmatrāta 達摩多羅 in Buddhabhadra's list.[60] Shenhui replaced Dharmatrāta with (8) Bodhidharma, but the *Lidai fabao ji* authors tried to retain both, coming up with the name "Bodhidharmatrāta 菩提達摩多羅."[61] The *Lidai fabao ji* uses the entire *Fu fazang zhuan* list and interpolates the names Śaṇavāsa and Upagupta in between Siṁha Bhikṣu and "Śubhamitra," making for a total of twenty-nine Indian patriarchs. Śaṇavāsa 舍那婆斯 and Upagupta 優婆掘 are the fourth and fifth figures in the *Aśokarāja-sūtra* account of the initial transmissions, but the *Lidai fabao ji* authors distinguish the traditional fourth and fifth Indian patriarchs Śaṇavāsa 商那和修 and Upagupta 優波掬多 from the newly minted twenty-fifth and twenty-sixth Śaṇavāsa 舍那婆斯 and Upagupta 優婆掘 by using alternative transliterations.

Therefore, the complete *Lidai fabao ji* list is as follows: (1) Mahākāśyapa 摩訶迦葉, (2) Ānanda 阿難, (3) Madhyāntika 末田地, (4) Śaṇavāsa 商那和修, (5) Upagupta 優波掬多, (6) Dhṛtaka 提多迦, (7) Miccaka 彌遮迦, (8) Buddhanandi 佛陀難提, (9) Buddhamitra 佛陀蜜多, (10) Pārśva Bhikṣu 脅比丘, (11) Puṇyayaśas 富那耶奢, (12) Aśvaghoṣa 馬鳴, (13) Kapimala 毘羅長老, (14) Nāgārjuna 龍樹, (15) Kāṇadeva 迦那提婆, (16) Rāhula 羅侯羅, (17) Saṅghānandi 僧迦那提, (18) Saṅghāyaśas 僧迦那舍, (19) Kumārata 鳩摩

羅馱, (20) Jayata 闍夜多, (21) Vasubandhu 婆修槃陀, (22) Manora 摩拏羅, (23) Haklena[yaśa] 鶴勒那, (24) Siṁha Bhikṣu 師子比丘, (25) Śaṇavāsa 舍那婆斯, (26) Upagupta 優婆掘, (27) Śubhamitra 須婆蜜多, (28) Saṅgharakṣa 僧迦羅叉, and (29) Bodhidharmatrāta 菩提達摩多羅.[62]

However, it is the *Baolin zhuan* list of twenty-eight Indian patriarchs that was to become the standard version. Its author duplicated most of the *Lidai fabao ji* list but eliminated Madhyāntika and substituted three different names from Sengyou's Sarvāstivāda list after Siṁha Bhikṣu, ending with Bodhidharma.[63] Thus, the *Lidai fabao ji* list was one of the sources for the version of the Chan lineage that was to become canonical in the Song. In the final analysis, the *Lidai fabao ji* authors appear to have drawn from Shenhui's ideology and his list, Buddhabhadra's tradition linking the Indian and Kashmiri masters, and the *Fu fazang zhuan* list without its ideology.

What can be said about the ideology of the *Fu fazang zhuan?* With the aid of certain rhetorical flourishes, the text plays on "decline of the Dharma" sensibilities in order to make an appeal for greater effort in the present. For example, there is an episode in the *Aśokarāja-sūtra* in which Ānanda's words are disregarded by a younger monk because his teacher has told him that Ānanda is senile. This is followed by Ānanda's reflection that although no one alive now has the authority to rebuke that monk's teacher, nevertheless "by the power of the Buddha, the Dharma will abide for one thousand years." Ānanda then follows his departed co-disciples into nirvāṇa.[64] However, in the *Fu fazang zhuan* version Ānanda is not so complacent. He embarks upon extended lamentations over how the world will be sunk in misery for countless eons and dwells on the corruption of all things, ending like a tragedian with the query, "Why should I long linger in present [circumstances]?"[65]

Following the narrative of Siṁha Bhikṣu's death, the *Fu fazang zhuan*'s final exhortations urge that the Dharma must be maintained and protected ever more diligently, precisely because the world has gone dark with the ending of the lineage of the Buddha's disciples. The universal efficacy of the Buddha-Dharma and the importance of revering the Saṅgha are evoked in such stories as that of an elephant whose blood-lust is tamed by the chanting of the monks from a nearby monastery.[66]

The sensibilities that shaped the *Fu fazang zhuan* could thus conceive the continuity of the Dharma, though weakened, through preservation of the formal practices and traditional roles of the Saṅgha. As discussed in the context of Buddhist criteria of authority, this reflects a long-standing tendency to rely on orthopraxy rather than orthodoxy as the basis for continued viability of the Dharma. In marked contrast, eighth-century Chan sectarians' increasing ideological dependence on lineage as the source of continuity made the *Fu fazang zhuan* account difficult either to ignore or to accept unaltered. The story of how the peerless lineage was saved from extinction begged to be told, just as traditional Buddhism's wanton extinction of fully realized arhats had begged for the resuscitating doctrine of the bodhisattva path. The *Lidai fabao ji* authors' oft-cited freedom with sources qualified them well for the task. They appropriated the *Fu fazang zhuan* lineage and included the story of the martyrdom of Siṁha Bhikṣu, but claimed that transmission was accomplished before the patriarch's death:

> When Siṁha Bhikṣu had transmitted [the Dharma] to Śaṇavāsa, then he went from Central India to Kashmir. The king there was named Mihirakula.[67] This king did not believe in the Buddha-Dharma. He destroyed stūpas, demolished monasteries, slaughtered sentient beings, and honored the two heretics Momanni 末曼尼 (Mani) and Mishihe 彌師訶 (Messiah, i.e., Jesus).[68] At that time Siṁha Bhikṣu purposely came to convert this kingdom, and the pathless king with his own hands took up a sharp double-edged sword and swore an oath: "If you are a Holy One, the [other] masters must suffer punishment." Siṁha Bhikṣu then manifested a form whereby his body bled white milk. Momanni and Mishihe were executed, and like ordinary men their blood spattered the ground. The king was inspired to take refuge in the Buddha, and he ordered the disciple of Siṁha Bhikṣu (the Dharma had already been transmitted to Śaṇavāsa) to enter South India to preach extensively and liberate beings. The king then sought out and captured the disciples of the heretics Moman and Mishihe. When he had captured them, he set up stocks at court and suspended them by their necks, and the people of the entire country shot arrows at them. The king of Kashmir ordered that if there were [followers] of these creeds in any of the kingdoms, they should be driven from the kingdom. Therefore, the Buddha-Dharma of Siṁha Bhikṣu flourished again.[69]

The *Fu fazang zhuan* does not mention the heretic masters, the conversion of the king, or the subsequent mission to liberate beings and slaughter heretics. The martyrdom is summary and graphic; the king beheads Siṁha Bhikṣu, and the story ends thus: "In his head there was no blood, only milk flowed out. The persons who had transmitted the Dharma one to the other were in this manner severed."[70] In contrast, the *Lidai fabao ji* authors appear to have been somewhat anxious to make their main point, repeating that the transmission had already passed to Śaṇavāsa.

I would like to underscore the appeal of the *Fu fazang zhuan,* with or without emendation, to those who were engaged in spreading the Dharma in the sixth through eighth centuries. We have touched on the fifth-century proliferation of different prescriptions for transmission of the bodhisattva precepts, which developed increasingly apotropaic and visionary tendencies. The bodhisattva precepts acted as a seal of the Dharma and thus became the vehicle for homegrown forms of practice, diluting the need for clear Indian scriptural precedent or the mediation of the ordained. As I argued in chapter 3, discourse surrounding the bodhisattva precepts encompassed self-validation, validation by the ordained, and validation by the Buddhas and bodhisattvas within a system of homologous signs that could be made to supersede, supplement, and defer to one another. Though Chan and Pure Land sectarians developed sophisticated, mutually differential hermeneutics that attempted to determine a hierarchy between effort and grace, it can be argued that most East Asian Buddhists continued to seek assurance from both. The *Fu fazang zhuan* responds to this pursuit in an oracular manner—it is both reassuring and frightening. On the one hand, the transmission of the "holy ones" is evidence of the temporal extension of the Buddha's power; on the other hand, the fragility of that transmission calls for even greater exertion and faith from devotees.

The underlying message of the *Fu fazang zhuan* is that the true current of transmission runs in a narrow and hidden channel, encompassing the paradox of its destructible human vessels and its perpetual pure nourishment, a stream of milk running in the veins of the preordained. Consider the following episode from the *Fu fazang zhuan* account of the sixteenth master, Saṅghanandi 僧伽難提:

> Once there was an arhat who had cast aside the heavy burden [of karmic residue] and fulfilled all meritorious virtues. Saṅghanandi wanted to test him, so he expounded a gāthā and questioned him: "'Born among the wheel-turning kind, not a Buddha, not an arhat, not receiving a subsequent existence, and also not a *pratyekabuddha.*'[71] Bhadanta, you must examine and investigate well—what sort of thing is like that of which I have spoken?"
>
> Then the arhat entered samādhi. He examined and meditated deeply but was unable to comprehend. So he used his spiritual power to divide his body, flew to Tuṣita Heaven and reached Maitreya's place. He fully laid out the matter as above, and asked [Maitreya] to resolve his doubts. Maitreya told the arhat, "In the world one takes a lump of clay and puts it on a wheel. Working it by hand, it becomes an earthen vessel. Such an earthen vessel [is] like the holy ones, how could it have a subsequent [existence]? At that, the arhat understood. He returned to Jambudvīpa and expounded this matter. Saṅghanandi said, "Bhadanta, this must be understanding [reached] after Maitreya Bodhisattva expounded it for you. Wisdom like this is [merely] the transformations of spiritual powers. To save the many beings, one cannot be [so] limited."[72]

This places the "holy ones" who transmit the Dharma in a special category, and this is precisely the special category appropriated in the Chan master rhetoric of the eighth century. Like the "holy one," the Chan Master is an earthen vessel, an ordinary man who is a teacher of Dharma without being an arhat or Buddha, shaped by circumstances but not bound by karma—an anomalous creature. This ambiguous quality is exemplified by the manner of Saṅghanandi's death; it is said that Saṅghanandi "desired to abandon his body," and so he grasped the branch of a tree and died standing upright. His disciples wanted to lay his body on a cremation pyre, but it was absolutely immovable even with the help of large white elephants. Finally they burned him where he stood, and although his body was consumed the tree was unhurt. While the Tuṣita-traveling arhat has superficial powers of transformation, Saṅghanandi leaves no trace but the unborn: "[Saṅghanandi's] spiritual power was exhausted [with physical death], but still [there remained] the characteristic of the unchanging."[73] Here again are elements that would become important in the Chan patriarchal ethos: the devaluation of merely expedient spiritual powers, the perpetuity of the "wheel-turning" transmission of the Dharma, and the play upon the notion of Dharma as both function and essence, impermanent vessel and empty container. Moreover, the third Chan Patriarch Sengcan is given the same upright death as his half-namesake Saṅghanandi, holding fast to the branch of a tree.[74]

Whatever its origins, the *Fu fazang zhuan* mystique of the transmission of the "holy ones" was an appealing, if procrustean, solution to the blooming confusion that confronted clerics as Buddhism continued to seed and grow. It is commonly recognized that sixth-century clerics were much occupied with the challenge of reconciling contradictions in the vast array of scriptures that had become available to them, giving rise to various systematizing efforts. However, while studies of Chinese Buddhism that demonstrate "fifth-century proliferation and sixth-century systematization" or "sixth-century blending of the trends of southern exegesis and northern practice" are useful up to a certain point, broad characterizations cannot capture the complex interplay of such factors as periodic diaspora from urban centers of Buddhism destroyed by war, competitive interaction with indigenous local traditions, and the disturbing side of Buddhism's success. These factors necessitated continual renegotiation of the relative identities of lay and ordained, inclusive and exclusive Dharma transmission, and state and Saṅgha. Chinese apocrypha played a key role in addressing perplexing issues, and it is notable that one of the features shared by the *Fu fazang zhuan* and the Chinese bodhisattva precepts texts is the attempt to address the problem of unworthy monks without allowing the ordained to be subjected to outside judgment.

As we saw in chapter 2, the need to protect clerical autonomy and yet regulate the Saṅgha for its own good presented difficulties even when Buddhism was just beginning to be established in China, and these difficulties could only assume the proportions of a crisis as the Saṅgha underwent a period of phenomenal expansion and bewildering diversification. For clergy who called for the reestablishment of the integrity of the Saṅgha, retreat to the fortress of strict observance of the "śrāvaka" Vinaya was an expedient but unsatisfactory fallback position. It was unsatisfactory because of "Hīnayāna" associations and also because of the frustrating difficulties of regulating such a miscellaneous, populous, and amorphous body as the Saṅgha had become. Under the circumstances, it was necessary to find better means to separate the rich taste of the crème de la crème of Dharma transmission from the expensive tastes of its privileged clergy.

THE LEGACY OF TIANTAI ZHIYI

Tiantai Zhiyi 天台智顗 (538–597), surely one of the most influential Chinese Buddhist monks in history, was a multifaceted master who responded skillfully to the challenges presented by the reunification of north and south under the Sui 隋 dynasty (589–618).[75] The Sui elites were largely descended from the Northern Wei, via the equally short-lived Western Wei (535–557) and Northern Zhou (556–581) dynasties. The Sui inherited both the northern style of administration, wherein military clans with hereditary ranks controlled a centrally administered polity, and the southern style of multiple political units consisting of landed literati clans and their clients. Attempting to assimilate both kinds of elites, Sui administration combined a hierarchical military organization and a civil-service bureaucracy, and it bequeathed this structure and the resulting tension to the Tang, which was also established by a clan of northern origins. The corresponding tension in the Saṅgha might best be exemplified by the contrast between the intense concentration of temples in the northern imperial capitals and the dispersed monastic estates of the south that, like Huiyuan's Mt. Lu, managed to maintain relative autonomy.

The two Sui emperors endorsed Buddhism, in part to strengthen ties between north and south, and tried to manage the Saṅgha by keeping it dependent on the court. In *Making and Remaking History: A Study of Tiantai Sectarian Historiography,* Chen Jinhua argues that the ties between Zhiyi's circle and the Sui rulers were not nearly so close as they are often made out to be: "Coming from a bureaucratic family in Jingzhou, Zhiyi had many family members and relatives in the elite society of the Southern dynasties including the Liang and Chen [the former rulers]. . . . Partly out of his affection for the old dynasty and partly in fear of political persecution from the Sui rulers, Zhiyi tried to distance himself from the new dynasty."[76]

However, Emperor Wen (r. 581–604) persisted in his patronage of Zhiyi and his group, partly in an effort to placate the southern elites. Contrary to the common view that Zhiyi's disciples were also specially favored by the Sui emperors, Chen persuasively argues that "Tiantai's honeymoon with the Sui leaders was already long over before the Sui came to an end in 616."[77] Zhiyi's disciple Guanding 灌頂 (561–632) was in disfavor with Emperor Yang, and Guanding's disciples in the Tang covered this by fabricating evidence for his connections with the second Sui ruler. This corrects the usual notion that Zhiyi's followers were under a cloud in the early Tang due to their close ties with the Sui court.[78]

Zhiyi's monumental *Mohe zhiguan* 摩訶止觀 (Great Calming and Insight) is a systematization and reconciliation of different strata of Buddhist doctrine and practice that has been compared to the imperial reunification effort. The work is founded on Zhiyi's doctrine of the Three Truths, the two truths of the Provisional (*jia* 假) and Empty (*kong* 空) reconciled in the truth of the Middle (*zhong* 中). The "Middle," the simultaneous distinction and identity of the absolutely empty and relatively real, is the principle or Buddha-nature inherent in all things, immanent in a single instant of thought. The reconciliation of śūnyatā and *upāya* is the structural support of Zhiyi's system, most notably his *panjiao* ("classification of the teachings"), in which the fourth and highest of the Buddha's teachings is the "sudden and perfect," identified with the Truth of the Middle and the simultaneous realization of calming (*zhi* 止, *śamatha*) and insight (*guan* 觀, *vipaśyanā*). The highest level is represented by the teaching of the One Vehicle in the *Lotus Sūtra.*[79]

The *Mohe zhiguan* is based on Zhiyi's lectures as recorded and edited by Guanding. After Zhiyi's death, Guanding wrote several versions of a preface for the *Mohe zhiguan,* and in the final version he created the foundation of the lineage and transmission ideology of what would become the Tiantai school.[80] In this preface, he summarizes the *Fu fazang zhuan* account of the Indian patriarchs and refers to them as those who "received prediction from the golden mouth" of the Buddha.[81] The chain of golden links leads toward but is not made to stretch as far as the lineage of Zhiyi in China.

In her article "In the Beginning . . . Guanding 灌頂 (561–632) and the Creation of Early Tiantai," Linda Penkower discusses the distinctions between the "western" and "eastern" parts of the lineage Guanding articulates in his preface. The western line (from the *Fu fazang zhuan*) moves forward from Śākyamuni, and the eastern line moves backward from Zhiyi to his master Huisi 慧思 (515–577) and Huisi's master, Huiwen 慧文 (fl. mid-sixth century). However, there is no attempt to craft a "string of pearls" linking the two lines. Instead, Nāgārjuna, the thirteenth patriarch in the western line, is evoked as the "high ancestral teacher" (*gaozushi* 高祖師). Nāgārjuna becomes a spiritual ancestor because Huiwen's insights into the *Dazhidu lun* 大智度論,[82] then believed to be a work by Nāgārjuna, are the source of the special method of cultivation passed down to Huisi and explicated in Zhiyi's *Mohe zhiguan*.[83]

This is an elegant solution to the problem of validating both the continuity of transmitted teachings and the discontinuity of individual insight. Diachrony is represented in the western and eastern lineages, which are at the same time parallel and synchronous, enabling transhistorical relationships. While Huiwen was said to be directly linked to Nāgārjuna through his intensive study of the *Dazhidu lun*, the mythos of Zhiyi's access to the original teachings was made even more dramatic. In Guanding's biography of Zhiyi, Huisi is said to have claimed karmic connection with Zhiyi due to their having listened to the Buddha preach the *Lotus Sūtra* together in a past life.[84] At the same time, Guanding also refers to the *Lotus Sūtra*'s assurance that Śākyamuni is constantly preaching the *Lotus* in his Saṃbhogakāya manifestation on Vulture Peak.[85] Zhiyi's enlightenment experience through meditative study of the *Lotus Sūtra* is thus linked to both the past and the presence of direct transmission from the Buddha, and Penkower argues that this synthesis of Guanding's would become an important paradigm for the Tiantai school.[86]

At the end of this chapter, we turn to an exploration of Daoxuan's visionary ordination platform, and there we see a different kind of effort designed to access the parallel universe of ever-present original Dharma, through the creation of a special physical and temporal space. Penkower comments on the significance of the question of such access for Guanding, "Thus Guanding prefaces his lineage account with a powerful series of quotations that claims for Zhiyi what the Buddha has claimed for himself, namely, that his authority is sufficient unto itself and does not rely on what he has learned from a teacher."[87] In his preface, Guanding evokes the teachings of the Buddha as truth that needs no medium, no teacher, asking rhetorically, "Do they shine of themselves with the truth of heaven [or do they need to be dyed] like the blue of the indigo plant?"[88]

Recognition of both aspects of authority, the authority of self-realization and the authority of textual interpretation, reflects the structure of the *Mohe zhiguan* itself, which stresses the balance and reconciliation of meditative stabilization and active insight. For Zhiyi, the "Truth of the Middle" was an historical and a psychological as well as an absolute truth. Imbalance, overreliance on either meditation (shining of itself) or textual study (indigo dye), was not only ineffective practice, but it was also a threat to the continuity of the Saṅgha. Daniel Stevenson discusses Zhiyi's excoriation of two personifications of the degradation of the Dharma, the intellectually arrogant and unenlightened Dharma master and the ignorant and vision-crazed Dhyāna master. Stevenson says that for Zhiyi "both figures were endowed with a tangible historicity," and Zhiyi attributed the Northern Zhou persecution to their excesses. Yet Zhiyi does not identify these offenders with specific individuals, and Stevenson argues that this allowed them to remain powerful paradigms embodying both lessons from the past and dangers in the present.[89] Zhiyi mapped a middle ground that rose above these failed paradigms, and scholars have drawn connections between his doctrinal structure and the reunification of northern Dhyāna and southern Dharma that was facilitated by the Sui during his lifetime.[90] Zhiyi drew on existing cultural stereotypes, but he also brought them into sharper focus.

The structural dialectic of differentiation and reconciliation between Buddha and Dharma, *zhi* and *guan*, or Dhyāna Master and Dharma Master was also applied to Saṅgha and *śīla*. In his *Shi chan poluomi cidi famen* 釋禪波羅蜜次第法門, a work on meditation practice, Zhiyi articulates three mutually reinforcing and hierarchical acts in the confession ritual. These three are (1) acknowledging one's sins according to the Vinaya, (2) seeking miraculous signs attesting to the removal of karmic burdens, as when receiving the bodhisattva precepts, and (3) meditating on the empty nature of sins.[91] The first level was the tacitly accepted "Hīnayāna" foundation of the standard bodhisattva path. Zhiyi's second level, the seeking of signs, was a key element in many apocryphal bodhisattva precepts texts, as discussed in chapter 3.[92] Within the ordered yet flexible logic of Zhiyi's system, the third level was manifested in the two expedient levels, just as they were also to be realized as interdependent and empty. However, the third level would become a point of departure for Chan rhetoric.

In Zhiyi's system, the array of doctrines and contemplative and devotional practices are subordinated to their own interdependence. Inevitably, subsequent reformers were tempted to claim the highest middle ground either in Zhiyi's terms or in critical responses to them. In his article "The Concept of One-Practice Samādhi in Early Chan," Bernard Faure discusses how exclusive notions of practice in the Chan and Pure Land sects were developed in part through a process of reduction of the Tiantai model, and he also notes that Shenhui's sudden teaching was especially radical in leveling Zhiyi's edifice to its "sudden" pinnacle.[93]

In "Southern School" Chan ideology, the complexity of Zhiyi's system was sacrificed in favor of its dramatic climaxes. Similarly, Guanding's twofold and dual-directional genealogy, embodying the presence and the past of the Buddha's teachings, was appropriated by early architects of the patriarchal lineage, forged into a continuous chain, and thereby lost some of its flexibility. And at least in the discourse to which the *Lidai fabao ji* authors were attuned, practice also lost quite a lot of its diversity. Rather than reconciling absolute and contingent in the performance of confession, meditation, and analysis, one was to see the nature and not-perform. Ironically, one of the few remaining expedients was contestation, such that depreciating all that belonged to the expedient levels was taken to be an expression of the highest level. For the Bao Tang, the meaning of the empty nature of sins was to be manifested through rejection of marked conduct or the seeking of visionary signs. However, Chan followers would in time grow more subtle, and demonstrations of ironic or playful indifference masked these traces of the hostile takeover of Zhiyi's empire of signs.

THE *RENWANG JING*

The *Renwang [banruopoluomi] jing* 仁王[般若波羅蜜]經 ([*Prajñāpāramitā*] Scripture of Humane Kings) is addressed to "humane king" bodhisattvas who are enjoined to practice the initial "ten stages of belief" (*shixin* 十信) of the bodhisattva path and to carry out the prescribed ritual.[94] This fifth-century apocryphon was doctrinally and politically important for Zhiyi and his followers. Both the *Mohe zhiguan* and the *Renwang jing* address the soteriological and political dilemmas created by the growing power of the Saṅgha,[95] and Zhiyi and his disciples produced commentaries on the *Renwang jing* for the benefit of the Sui rulers.[96] Zhiyi also used the *Renwang jing* as support for his doctrine of the Three Truths, citing the *Renwang jing* rubric of true, conventional, and absolute truths.[97] The reflexive relationship between difference and identity in Zhiyi's *panjiao* mirrors the reflexive political soteriology of the *Renwang jing*, in which the mark of the humane king is his willing subordination to great bodhisattvas (monks), although humane kings are themselves always-already great bodhisattvas, who manifest reverence to monks for the sake of all beings.[98]

The *Renwang jing* emphasizes faith and ritual as appropriate practices for the final age of the Dharma (rendered as *famo* 法末).[99] In *Once Upon a Future Time*, Jan Nattier argues that belief in the advent of the final age of the Dharma was triggered as much by anxiety over internal laxity of the Saṅgha as by external persecution; she characterizes the *Renwang jing* as the only example of a scripture "which blames the demise of the Dharma not on non-Buddhist intruders but on the overregulation of the sangha by the state."[100] Charles Orzech, in *Politics and Transcendent Wisdom: The Scripture for Humane Kings in the Creation of Chinese Buddhism*, emphasizes the more optimistic side of the *Renwang jing*: "In fifth-century North China this display of Buddhist bodies (monks, statues, texts, and so on) promoted by flamboyant royal patronage functioned as a sign that the temporal decay of Buddhism had been halted and that the clock had been turned back to the period of the Correct Teaching (*cheng-fa*)."[101]

These contesting views on the motivation of the unknown author reflect the ambiguous nature of the text. Orzech argues that the key to the text is the tangled hierarchy between state and Saṅgha: the Saṅgha is corrupted by its co-option by the state, yet it is the "humane king" who will establish the new age of Correct Dharma (*zhengfa* 正法) in which monks are properly revered as state protectors. Therefore, "The Buddhist body became a canvas for conflicting notions of cosmology, soteriology, polity. At one extreme the body was described as 'crumbling, diseased, wounded,' and at the other 'like a priceless jewel of lapis lazuli.'"[102]

According to the *Renwang jing*, the well-being of the state is contingent on protection of the Dharma and Saṅgha. The premise of the text is that an indispensable ritual for state protection was originally prescribed by the Buddha to King Prasenajit and other Great Kings:

> At that time the Buddha told the Great Kings, "All of you listen well. I will now correctly explain the method for protecting the state. You ought to receive and keep this Perfection of Wisdom [scripture]. When disorder, ruination, bandits, conflagration, and thieves come and are about to crush the state, you must invite one hundred Buddha-images, one hundred bodhisattva-images, one hundred arhat-images and an assembly of one hundred monks. The four great assemblies and the seven assemblies shall gather together to listen; invite a hundred Dharma masters to expound the Perfection of Wisdom [scripture]. In front of one hundred lion thrones light one hundred lamps, burn one hundred blends of incense, and [scatter] one hundred kinds of colorful flowers as offerings to the Triple Jewel. Offer the three robes and various things to the Dharma masters. Eat a small meal in the middle of the day and again at another time. Great Kings, twice daily have this scripture expounded and recited."[103]

Like many Mahāyāna scriptures, the *Renwang jing* is prefaced with a description of a magnificent assembly in which the figures on stage are both altar-images and audience. In this apocryphal scripture the Buddha speaks from the most familiar of such settings, Vulture's Peak, in order to instruct the Great Kings in the proper production of ritual stage and script. By following these instructions, human audience/actors are enabled to ascend the stage of the scripture itself. Moreover, the instructions about meals reveal that the rite is a purification retreat in which the laity share for a certain period of time in monastic practices. As we shall see, East Mountain and Southern School platform ordination assemblies of the seventh and eighth centuries were also lay purification retreats, and making offerings in a ritually utopian space was a crucial aspect of the participant's practice.

In the *Renwang jing* the Buddha preaches that the scripture is to be disseminated in order to mitigate the evils of the final age of the Dharma, which are described at length. Orzech points out that the *Renwang jing* solution to *mofa* is quite unusual in that the scripture assigns to worldly kings, rather than to the future Buddha, the responsibility for reversing the course of end-time and establishing a new age.[104] In the midst of its warnings of crisis and imminent chaos, the *Renwang jing* holds out the promise that rulers are able to restore balance and prosperity by accomplishing a rectification of signs. Orzech explains the pun involved in naming the secular rulers "humane kings" (*renwang* 仁王) and the monks "kings of forbearance" (*renwang* 忍王). This pun is not mere wordplay, but involves complex analogies. *Ren* 仁 is one of the primary Confucian virtues just as *ren* 忍 (*kṣanti*) is one of the primary pāramitās. True kings are the saviors of worldly realms just as bodhisattvas are the kings of salvific realms. The two are woven together in the same continuum, the same mārga, and, as discussed above, are dynamically interdependent in the same manner as conventional and absolute truth.[105]

The scripture enumerates the signs that announce the age of the end of the Dharma, and the trope of the white robe is one of the key signs of the degradation of the Saṅgha: "White-robed [lay people will occupy the] lofty seats [reserved for clergy], while *bhikṣus* will stand on the ground. . . . You should know that at that time the extinction of the Teaching will not be long [off]."[106] Evoking inversion and usurpation, this is also a reference to popular *mofa* eschatology in which monastic robes themselves turn white, signaling loss of the efficacy of the Saṅgha. Orzech points out that *mofa* and *Prajñāpāramitā* doctrines are linked, for eschatology and transcendent wisdom both pivot on the unreliability of conventional signs and referents. The *Renwang jing* plays on this "crisis of referentiality" to dramatize the fearfulness of a time when outward signs of authority to transmit the Dharma, such as the monk's robe, can no longer to be trusted as evidence of worthiness.[107]

There is a certain contradiction inherent in the admonitions of the *Renwang jing*. The ruler is repeatedly warned against subjecting the clergy to secular authority, yet he is also held responsible for failing to oppose false monks who would themselves undermine the separate status of the Saṅgha: "And evil monks seeking fame and profit will not rely on my Teaching, and they will go before the kings of states and will themselves utter transgressions and evil, becoming the cause of the destruction of the Teaching. These kings will not distinguish [between the good and evil monks], and trusting and accepting these sayings they will perversely establish regulation [of monastic communities rather than] rely on the Buddhist prohibitions."[108]

This puts the ruler in an impossible position—how is he to exercise his discernment between good and evil monks and yet not subject the Saṅgha to any regulation? Such impossible positions frequently conceal and reveal ideological mechanisms. The position of ruler is marked as belonging to the order of provisional truth and the inevitable structural contradictions of expedients. The paradox in which he is bound accentuates the contrasting lack of obstruction of the ultimate level, represented by the monk.

This hierarchy is masked by the utopian truth of the "middle," in which ruler and monk are identically great bodhisattvas.

The tension between different spheres of power and between reverence and regulation can be seen in other Buddhist projects of the Sui rulers, under whom the *Renwang jing* first won the status of authentic scripture. The *Zhongjing mulu* 眾經目錄 (Catalogue of Scriptures), the catalogue in which the *Renwang jing* is legitimated, is itself marked with this tension; many apocrypha were marked for destruction yet many others, equally dubious, were condoned.[109] Prophecy was held to be an indication of spuriousness, yet although the *Renwang jing* includes apocalyptic prophecy the *Zhongjing mulu* assigns to it the status of a translation by Kumārajīva.[110] It is possible that the *Renwang jing* had much in common with the banned eschatological apocrypha that we know only from censorious references in the *Zhongjing mulu* and other Buddhist catalogues.

Buddhist and Daoist apocrypha inspired a number of messianic uprisings of the late fifth and early sixth centuries and exposed the persistence of a compound that was potentially lethal to rulers and monks alike. These utopian and messianic movements drew from the same spring as the mystical, Daoist-Legalist ideology of the Sage-Ruler. This cryptic source of power was eulogized in works such as the *Guan zi* 管子 and *Huainan zi* 淮南子 and was handled with great delicacy, like political plutonium, in Han commentarial literature. Messianic undercurrents had repeatedly disturbed Chinese polities ever since the Taiping rebellions of the Han, but in the fifth century Buddhist elements began to find their way into the mix. Zürcher points out that Buddhist orthodox teachings on the periodization of the Dharma or the advent of Maitreya were non-eschatological and were not labeled subversive until it began to be whispered that the current situation was the prelude to the apocalypse: "Any statements to the effect that the *mofa* period was at hand automatically implied a condemnation of the establishment, both ecclesiastical and political."[111] Notably, it is said that Zhiyi's teacher Huisi was persecuted by fellow monks for declaring that "*mofa* is now."[112]

However, the value of the *Renwang jing* as a blueprint for Buddhist political soteriology apparently outweighed its potential dangers. Its humane kings were homologous to Chinese Sage-Rulers, and, as Orzech argues, its cosmology was sophisticated enough to appeal to Chinese masters of statecraft: "Thus, the cosmology of the scripture was no mere ornamental flourish, nor is the scripture a crude attempt to curry royal favor. Rather, it is a sophisticated application of Buddhist notions of cosmology and authority to create a new Buddhism for new historical circumstances. This process of adapting Buddhist notions of authority to Chinese needs was expressed in a distinctly Chinese manner."[113] Moreover, the very opulence of the rite on which its efficacy depends was perhaps deemed a sufficient safety catch, limiting its use to those who could command the resources of a state.

In the subsequent Chinese incarnation of the *Renwang jing*, the ritual and its political deployment became even more elaborate. The *Renwang jing* was revived as part of the state cult during Bao Tang Wuzhu's lifetime. It was "retranslated" and promoted by Bukong 不空 (Amoghavajra, 705–774), the revered monk who specialized in Chinese Esoteric Buddhism (Zhenyan 真言) and served three Tang emperors. Bukong's version incorporates Zhenyan rites and dhāraṇī, and these rites were performed at court in 765 in an attempt to repulse the encroaching Tibetans.

In the esoteric version, the master assumes the wrathful manifestation of the Buddha in order to subdue the invaders and then confers on them an *abhiṣeka* (royal consecration) initiation, the culmination of the bodhisattva path.[114] This ritual subjugation and salvation of the other takes place within the sacred space and time created through replication of the offering of King Prasenajit. Continuity with the time/space of the original offering is assured in the prescription, but this efficacious continuity depends on the ruler's willingness to interpret threats to the state as signs of *mofa*. In other words, this requires the ruler to endorse the idea that the condition of the body politic is a symptom of the state of the Dharma-body.

The *Renwang jing* had an unusual degree of success in making subordination of state to Saṅgha palatable to rulers not only in China but also in Korea and Japan, and this was due, I would argue, to its skillful means of sublimation. Three Truths soteriology provided a useful ideological mediation of the violent processes of the state, which was continually engaged in constructing itself through representations of identity and difference, purity and danger. The "truth of the middle" allows for a homology between humane king bodhisattvas and monk-kings of forbearance that bootstraps the sacrificer-bodhisattva as well as the enemy other into ideal kingship. However, the power of the rite to give assurance to the "humane king" who makes the offering depends on his willing subordination to the monk.

René Girard's theories regarding the fear of the contagion of violence at the origins of culture are illuminating in this regard. He argues that victory in war or personal feuds brings with it fear of reprisal, which is even more acute if the victor has extended the added insult of clemency to the vanquished. Therefore, the victor seeks to sublimate the danger of his position through sacrifice of a substitute.[115] The *Renwang jing* provides a space for sacrifice and ritual humility, through which the ruler is enabled to transfer the responsibility for both violence and forbearance to the ultimate level, where both wrathful and compassionate manifestations have their source. In the *Renwang jing* ritual, the esoteric master assumes this responsibility and places himself into the breach in the barrier against the contagion of violence, sanctioning the actions of the king as an agent of the Dharma. The utopian impossibility of enemies as unobstructed mutual universal monarchs is mediated by the provisional ultimacy of the sign of the monk, without whom the apocalypse would ensue.

Let us recall that western Sichuan was one of the theaters of the Sino-Tibetan war, and the movement of troops forms the backdrop for the *Lidai fabao ji* episode that establishes Wuzhu's possession of the talismanic patriarchal robe.[116] It is likely that the Bao Tang followers were aware of the ascendancy of Esoteric Buddhism at court, and the aforementioned *Lidai fabao ji* passage featuring the victory of the seventh patriarch over an Indian master with esoteric powers may have been a cautious criticism of Bukong's style of Buddhism.[117] Wuzhu, of military background himself, is first recognized as a master by officers in the border encampments, and it is through them that he is made known to his own "humane king" counterpart, the eunuch and military imperial minister Du Hongjian. Outside the pages of the *Lidai fabao ji,* however, Du is better known for having been devoted to Esoteric Buddhist masters, including Bukong.[118]

Though Wuzhu was established in a temple named "Bao Tang," we do not find any claim in the *Lidai fabao ji* that Wuzhu or no-thought "protects the Tang." Such a claim would, of course, be incompatible with Wuzhu's iconoclasm. However, Wuzhu is repeatedly shown contesting other textual and ritual sites of apotropaic power. For example, Wuzhu mocks those who make pilgrimage to Mt. Wutai, at a time when Bukong was involving the state in massive expenditure at this site in order to glorify China as the domain of the bodhisattva Manjuśrī.[119] Though their explicit message is the universalistic teaching of intrinsic Buddha-nature, the *Lidai fabao ji* authors, like Shenhui, were acutely sensitive to the problem of pretenders to the crown of the true Dharma.

In fact, the *Lidai fabao ji* authors make Shenhui proclaim their Dharma-king by insinuating a new dialogue into the scene of the debate between Shenhui and Dharma Master Yuan: "Dharma Master Yuan asked, 'Who has got this *kāṣāya* robe?' Hui replied, 'Someone has got it. In due course it should be apparent. When this person expounds on the Dharma, the true Dharma (*zhengfa* 正法) will flow forth, and false Dharmas will perish of themselves. In order to further the great work of the Buddha-Dharma, he is hidden and has not yet come out.' "[120]

Whether opportunistically or not, in claiming exclusive transmission of *zhengfa* the Bao Tang were in tune with messianic undertones that had been in play in Chinese political ideology for over a millennium and had latterly been performed in conformity with Buddhist notions of time. Within this system of signs it is Wuzhu, in the hidden manner of the Daoist Sage-Ruler, who becomes the power holding *mofa* in abeyance.

THE SANJIE (THREE LEVELS) MOVEMENT

The rise and decline of the Sanjie 三階 (Three Levels) movement is a fascinating example of an alternative trajectory for *mofa/zhengfa* ideology and exhibits pertinent contrasts with the emerging Chan alternative. This brief overview of the Sanjie movement is drawn from Jamie Hubbard's compelling recent work *Absolute Delusion, Perfect Buddhahood: The Rise and Fall of a Chinese Heresy,* with a view to the light it sheds on "decline" discourse and sectarianism. Hubbard argues that, although Sanjie texts and practices were targeted in five imperial proscriptions between 600 and 725, its doctrines were not exceptional, and it shared many features with other movements of that era.[121] At the same time, Sanjie soteriology remains startling for the ways it anticipated powerful sectarian vehicles like Chan and the Pure Land movement and for the ways it drew on common doctrines and exaggerated them or used them with a fresh syntax.

The career of the Sanjie founder, Xinxing 信行 (540–594), itself raises interesting questions about the substance and locus of authority of a monastic vocation. Xinxing discarded the full monastic precepts after some years as a monk, but he continued to maintain a life-style that was in many ways more rigorous than the monastic norm.[122] There is no hint of antinomianism or antiformalism in his abandonment of clerical status, and he and his most dedicated lay and ordained followers adhered to the same demanding regimen. This was characterized by the common practices of meditation, repentance retreats (*fangdeng chanfa* 方等懺法), and the six daily periods of worship, as well as extreme austerities (*dhūta, toutuo* 頭陀) such as begging for food and fasting. The Sanjie program was notable for a special emphasis on the practice of "universal respect" and universal giving.[123]

Interestingly, the Sanjie repertoire of meditation practices includes a subitist-type "markless samādhi" (*wuxiang sanmei guan* 無相三昧觀), in which sin and virtue are understood to be ultimately nondual. However, as in Zhiyi's system, these higher levels are upheld by a system of concrete contemplations, including contemplations of impurity and contemplations of Buddha images. In Sanjie monasteries, the higher levels were also upheld by the participation of all members in the six periods of worship (*liushi li* 六時禮), three during the day and three at night.[124]

As we will see, Wuzhu's abandonment of the six periods of worship is presented in the *Lidai fabao ji* as a radical departure that provoked charges of laxity, and yet he also imposed extreme austerities on himself and his followers. Moreover, though Wuzhu endorsed the subitist rhetorical rejection of devotional and confessional practice, this was possible, as Bernard Faure and others have argued, because the Chan patriarchs themselves became sites of refuge. For Sanjie followers, the devotional focus for the six periods of worship was probably the "Seven Roster Buddhanāma" (*Qijie foming* 七階佛名), which was both a liturgical and contemplative practice.[125] The configuration of Buddhas in the "Seven Roster Buddhanāma" rite matches the devotional program of the Baoshan cave constructed by the Dilun master Lingyu and, as noted above, this program included the earliest-known representation of the lineage of Indian patriarchs from the *Fu fazang zhuan*.

I do not think that these foreshadowings of the Chan blend of sudden doctrine and icons of supercharged linear transmission are indicative of direct "influence." However, I do think there is a significant structural similarity that can be discerned in bodhisattva-precepts apocrypha like the *Yingluo jing* and the *Renwang jing*, in early Tiantai, and in the Sanjie movement. In these systems, as later in Chan, subitism (synchronic) and linear transmission (diachronic) are yoked together and incorporated into clearly defined soteriological programs. Moreover, we see this structural pattern emerging from a more diffuse matrix of repentance and contemplation practices referencing fears of "decline." In the following chapters we explore the means by which Chan ideology transforms subitism from a syntactical and differential marker ("perfect") into a polemical one, and how it transforms icons of continuity into flesh-and-bone paradigms. Here, however, let us look more closely at the particular features of Sanjie soteriology and the contrasts and similarities it exhibits with Bao Tang soteriology.

Xinxing's particular inflection of "decline" discourse is instructive. Although the diminished capacity of beings in the final age (*moshi*) was the foundation of his soteriology, he did not refer to periodization of the decline of the power of the Dharma itself (*mofa*). Hubbard characterizes this as Xinxing's concern with the existential rather than the eschatological aspect of the ideology of decline. The sparsely populated first and second levels of Xinxing's "Three Levels" belong to those with the capacity for the teachings of the One Vehicle (Ekayāna bodhisattvas) and the Three Vehicles (ordinary monastics), respectively, and these two levels were loosely linked to periodizations of the Dharma after the Buddha's death. However, the majority of beings are characterized as belonging to the "third level," marked by attachment to false views. Significantly, it was the tendency to bias and dispute, rather than precept-breaking, that Xinxing saw as most problematic. He proposed to remedy this with the "universal Dharma" (*pufa* 普法) that included all teachings, even perverse views; acceptance of this all-inclusive teaching was an expression of the third-level disciple's acknowledgement of his/her inability to distinguish between true and false Dharma.[126] While Xinxing emphasized the degenerate nature of the mass of third-level beings, he also stressed universal Buddha-nature and the universal potential to realize it. This Janus-faced pessimism/optimism is captured in the "absolute delusion, perfect Buddhahood" of Hubbard's title.

A combination of a differential groupings and a focus on innate nature is also integral to the soteriology of the *Renwang jing*, where it is expressed in terms of levels of kingship. Drawing on the *Bodhisattvabhūmi* and *Yogācārabhūmi* teachings of the two "seed-natures," acquired and innate, the *Renwang jing* presents ascending stages in the path of bodhisattva-kingship that progress from acquired seed-nature (*xi zhongxing* 習種性, Skt. *samudānīta gotra*), to innate seed-nature (*xing zhongxing* 性種性, Skt. *prakṛtitstha gotra*), to the seed-nature of the Way (*Dao zhongxing* 道種性), which is correlated with the highest kingship status, the golden *cakravartin*.[127] Orzech translates *zhongxing* as "lineage," arguing that the Indian Buddhist use of *gotra* "implies some innate and substantive distinction among beings" that has been acquired through practice.[128] This acquisition of the innate allows for the appealing possibility that the practitioner is in reality a member of an exclusive family and, at the same time, evokes Ekayāna soteriology guaranteeing membership to all. We will see that emerging Chan ideology, without explicitly evoking the context of the "final age," also emphasized the existential dilemma of beings endowed with innate Buddha-nature who are divided by innate capacities. Chan rhetoric also in effect depended on a three-tiered structure, in which the highest level was reserved for the patriarchs, elevated to the rank of manifestations of the Buddha, the middle level was occupied by disciples of Chan, and the lowest level was made up of the mass of beings ignorant of their own Buddha nature, who could change their membership status through the sudden teaching.

Hubbard argues that numerous clerics of Xinxing's milieu were working with the contradictory compound of "decline" discourse and versions of innate Buddha-nature theory, and that Xinxing "as with many others, transformed this dilemma into an opportunity for advocating new doctrinal and institutional configurations of traditional Buddhist practice."[129] The dual teaching of the recognition of universal Buddha-nature in all beings and the recognition of one's own degenerate nature became the hallmark of the Sanjie movement. This is aptly summed up in a characterization of Xinxing's teachings in the mid-seventh-century *Mingbao ji* 冥報記 (Tales of Miraculous Retribution): "The purport [of his teachings is to] encourage people [to cultivate] universal respect (*pujing* 普敬) [of others] and recognition of [one's own] evil (*ren'e* 認惡) nature, contemplate the [universal] Buddha-nature, and dispense medicine in accord with the affliction. It is a sudden teaching of the One Vehicle."[130]

In order to understand more precisely what is meant by "sudden teaching" in this context, let us examine the details of Hubbard's argument that Xinxing responded to decline discourse in an existential rather than an eschatological mode, focusing on human failings and sufferings rather than indulging in cosmological speculation or millenarian expectations.[131] Xinxing's use of tathāgatagarbha (Buddha-matrix) theory in his soteriology underscores a key dilemma in both tathāgatagarbha and Yogācāra thought. If delusion and defilement are only apparent, then the unenlightened mind and the unenlightened self is "not real" in relation to the purity and reality of intrinsic Buddha-nature or the *ālayavijñāna* (storehouse consciousness). In the famous *Laṅkā-sūtra* simile (also used in the *Lidai fabao ji*), the activities of mind are merely the appearance of waves, inseparable from the fathomless ocean.[132] This exacerbated the long-standing challenge of accounting for karmic retribution for individuals, if all activities are only adventitious appearances. Even more important, the very lack of reality of the divide between ignorance and enlightenment problematizes the notion of path and mediation (the "gradual"). As Hubbard writes of this dilemma, "All that remains is a leap, as sudden as it is ineffable, or the 'other-power' of salvific grace, as soteriologically necessary as it is necessarily external."[133] This characterization of the available options clearly points to the classic Japanese formulation of the divide between the salvific strategies of Zen and Pure Land. Hubbard notes that Xinxing's approach is comparable in some respects to emerging Chinese Pure Land soteriology, particularly with regard to the practice of "recognizing the evil of one's nature." However, I also think it is important to stress that "recognizing the evil of one's nature" is founded on the same logic as the Chan teaching of the emptiness of defilements.

Wuzhu's teachings reflect the polemical "Southern School" approach to the challenge of working with the unreal, an aggressive (and false) claim that other schools were leading people astray by teaching that defilements were real. This is reflected in the *Lidai fabao ji* passage in which Wuzhu quashes Dharma master Wuying 无盈, a representative of Yogācāra, in language reminiscent of Xinxing's exhortation to "recognize the evil of one's nature."

> The Venerable said, "The Dharma Master does not recognize host and guest. Concentrating on sense-objects, you take the flowing mind of birth and extinction itself as understanding. It is like boiling sand wishing it to become fine viands—however many kalpas [it boils], it will only become hot sand. It is only deceiving yourself and deceiving others."[134]

Wuzhu's use of Yogācāra soteriology to defeat a Yogācāra straw man draws on the same subitist logic that Xinxing used so brilliantly, in which recognition of the evil of one's nature (i.e., the ignorance of one's true nature) cannot be other than recognition of the emptiness of one's nature. This logic is most fully developed in Xinxing's interpretation of the practice of refuge in Buddha, Dharma, and Saṅgha. In the *Lidai fabao ji* passage above, Dharma Master Wuying attempts to test Wuzhu on the technical terminology of moral categorization of actions, and he ends up being dazzled by Wuzhu's mastery of the terminology and his lordly dismissal of it. The Sanjie response was a more faithful and finely contoured acknowledgment of Yogācāra and Dilun antecedents, reflecting an earlier stage in Chinese digestion of complex Buddha-nature and path theories. Deploying the rubric of the Three Jewels, several Sanjie texts elaborate on the distinctive practice of taking refuge in the "universal" Buddha, Dharma, and Saṅgha. One of the most comprehensive explications is found in the *Dui gen qixing fa* 對根起行法 (Practice That Arises in Accord with Capacity),[135] which explains that the "Refuge of the Universal Buddha" (*pufo* 普佛) means taking refuge in all Buddhas, even the false Māra Buddhas preaching wrong views. In delineating the four aspects of the "Universal Buddha," the *Dui gen qixing fa* cites the *Laṅkāvatāra-sūtra,* the *Śrīmālā-devī-sūtra,* the *Nirvāṇa-sūtra,* the *Lotus Sūtra,* the *Avataṃsaka-sūtra,* and the *Daśacakra-sūtra* in order to articulate the coinherence of the "Tathāgatagarbha Buddha" and the Buddha-nature of all beings, and the coinherence of future and already actualized realization of Buddhahood.[136]

Alluded to above, "Refuge of the Universal Dharma" (*pufa* 普法) meant taking refuge in both true and false teachings, but it is Xinxing's teaching of refuge of the "Universal Saṅgha" that is most provocative. The universal Saṅgha encompasses the Saṅgha of the third level, including monks "complete in the twelve kinds of perverted, false views."[137] However, rather than preaching elimination of the distinction between Saṅgha and laity, Xinxing taught that monks and nuns who broke the precepts were the most fitting refuge for third-level beings. The merit of giving nondiscriminately was said to far outweigh the merit accruing to conventional offerings, such that one should decline to give to clergy who keep the precepts.[138] This is inconsistent, a practice of reverse discrimination rather than nondiscrimination, but its rhetorical power was stronger than its logic.

As with the Bao Tang followers, who also argued for a nondiscriminatory concept of Saṅgha, this could have appeared as a self-serving justification for laxity but, instead, resulted in the adoption of practices more austere than the monastic norm. Both schools were also hypersensitive to issues of form and distinguished themselves from surrounding Buddhist communities on the basis of their particular orientation to form. In this regard, Sanjie and Bao Tang are like spiritual twins who chose apparently opposite paths, for the Sanjie followers developed an exacting set of forms unique to their community. They produced a manual of strict community regulations, the *Zhifa* 制法, that detailed observances keyed to hierarchical distinctions among members, complete with precise punishments for infractions. The *Zhifa* mandates that Sanjie clergy, due to their unworthiness to mix with regular clergy, should practice separately.[139] This may have been the origin of Sanjie cloisters (Sanjie yuan 三階院), perhaps the earliest example of a distinct institutional identity created by a Chinese-born school.[140] Notably, attempts to pinpoint the coalescence of Chan identity have also focused on the question of the development of community-specific regulations and separate buildings. Hubbard notes that these Sanjie cloisters may have been necessitated by special Sanjie liturgical practices, but he also argues that Xinxing's "universal" rhetoric and "decline" discourse in general reflects the beginnings of polemical separatist tendencies in the Chinese Buddhist community.[141]

Sanjie separatist tendencies may well have been given added impetus by Xinxing's best-known soteriological effort, his articulation of the "sixteen inexhaustible practices" that became the basis of the phenomenally successful Sanjie "Inexhaustible Storehouse" (*wujinzang* 無盡藏).[142] Xinxing's redefinition of this charitable merit-generating practice was grounded in the doctrine of universal respect, for devotees were enjoined to practice *dāna* (generosity) toward all beings, not just toward Buddha, Dharma, and Saṅgha.[143] Several key Mahāyāna scriptures are cited in the two Sanjie texts centered on the *wujinzang*,[144] but Hubbard argues that one of Xinxing's most important sources of inspiration was the *Xiangfa jueyi jing* 像法決疑經 (Scripture of Resolving Doubts in the Semblance Dharma), an apocryphon claiming that merit of giving to the needy far outweighs that of giving to the Three Jewels.[145] Following the lead of the *Xiangfa jueyi jing*, the Sanjie texts present a special interpretation of the notion that pious donations should cultivate two merit fields, the "field of respect" (*jingtian* 敬田) benefiting the Three Jewels and the "field of compassion" (*beitian* 悲田) benefiting the needy. In Sanjie texts, cultivating the "field of respect" meant that the donor was to give to precept-breaking clerics in preference to the precept-keeping ones, and cultivating the "field of compassion" meant that the donor was to give for the relief of all suffering beings, not discriminating between those who practice and those who do not.[146]

Xinxing's most striking use of the practice of giving, however, was his use of the notion of merit-sharing, inspired by the *Avataṃsaka-sūtra* doctrine of mutual coinherence of all beings. By giving to the *wujinzang*, even a third-level being established a karmic link with all others who have contributed to the merit field, including Ekayāna bodhisattvas of the first level. A Sanjie commentary, the *Dasheng fajie wujinzang fa shi* 大乘法界無盡藏法釋 (Commentary on the Dharma of the Inexhaustible Storehouse of the Mahāyāna Universe), asserts: "In accordance with the teaching, one only needs to give to the Inexhaustible Storehouse and by so doing he will enter into the Universal Inexhaustible Storehouse of the dharma-realm of the Dhyāna Master Hsin-hsing. Again, one not only engages in the same practices together with the Dhyāna Master Hsin-hsing, but together with all the Ekayāna bodhisattvas of the past, present, and future in all of the lands in all of the dharma-realms of the ten quarters of space—this one practice is the same."[147]

On the one hand, this practice simply deploys the foundational Buddhist economy—support of the spiritual elite in return for merit—with a characteristic Mahāyāna assurance that return on one's investment is guaranteed by the merit-store of the bodhisattva. However, the Inexhaustible Storehouse was a potent symbol of the unlimited power of the merit-field, skillfully mediating its paradoxical inclusiveness/exclusiveness. Mutual coinherence of all beings (sinful, suffering, and beneficent alike) becomes the guarantee of coinherence with a subset of beings, a special karmic family. The strict practices of the Sanjie monks and nuns made them the elites of this family, and yet even the most inadequate practitioners could partake in their merit and could in turn practice compassion as if they themselves were Ekayāna bodhisattvas. This sense of membership in a beneficial society was reinforced by various means, such as the assertion in the *Dui gen qixing fa* that giving communally, rather than individually, was the most effective practice.[148] Moreover, after Xinxing's death the practices of the Inexhaustible Storehouse became the focus of a memorial cult, as reflected in the reference above to "the dharma-realm of the Dhyāna Master Xinxing." Xinxing was placed on a par with the Ekayāna bodhisattvas, and the memorial day of his death became a spectacle of lavish giving. The Inexhaustible Storehouse associated with Xinxing at Huadu 化渡 monastery in Chang'an was said to be the most efficacious and was the most successful of the *wujinzang* cults in spite of attempts to replicate it.[149]

Finally, this brings us to the matter of the condemnation and eventual erasure of the Sanjie community. Hubbard advances a number of hypotheses about the five suppressions of Sanjie texts and practices, under Sui Wendi in 600, under Wu Zetian in 694 and 699, and under Xuanzong in 721 and 725. If the suppressions were triggered by the subversive potential of "decline" rhetoric, then why was Sanjie singled out? Hubbard points out that Daochuo's 道綽 (562–645) Pure Land teachings were similar to Xinxing's soteriology, but were not subjected to the same proscription.[150] Carrying out a detailed, case-by-case analysis of the suppressions, Hubbard concludes that each imperial proscription is attributable to a unique set of political circumstances.[151]

Hubbard's outline of the political context of each case is illuminating, and his wish to avoid the reductionism of a single, all-purpose explanation is much appreciated. However, he also includes an alternative political-economic explanation advanced by Whalen Lai, to which I would be inclined to give more weight than Hubbard does. Lai argues that "any private party presuming to feed the poor would be stealing loyalty from the sovereign and could be perceived as challenging his right to rule."[152] The Inexhaustible Storehouse was an extraordinarily effective means of amassing wealth, and its mandate included expenditure on social welfare. This meant that it could function as a rival patron or host in terms of Chinese host-client political ideology. If this powerful rival could not be co-opted (and Wu Zetian tried to set up an Inexhaustible Storehouse with utopian underpinnings, but it did not attract donations) then it had to be curtailed or eliminated. Although other Buddhist monasteries were wealthier, the Sanjie network of monasteries abrogated statelike functions: relief for the needy and redistribution of wealth.[153] Furthermore, the Sanjie ability to raise revenue quickly must have raised the specter of its potential co-optation by a political/military rival. In 721 Emperor Xuanzong ordered the dissolution of the Inexhaustible Storehouse and had its wealth distributed to other monasteries, and in 725 he prohibited Sanjie separate cloisters and banned its scriptures. However, there is evidence of the movement's continued popularity into the tenth century.[154]

Both Sanjie and Bao Tang were marked as unorthodox and ultimately banished from the family of acceptable practices, though the career of the Sanjie movement was longer and more spectacular. Aspects the two groups shared include a fondness for *dhūta,* an emphasis on universal Buddha-nature, and advocacy of practices that they themselves claimed were departures from the status quo. While official standards for monastic routines were more clearly articulated by the late eighth century, both Sanjie and Bao Tang created distinct identities through resistance to a normative institutional pattern. I would argue that the normative institutional pattern was similar in Xinxing's day and in Wuzhu's insofar as Buddhist monasteries were expected to accommodate a range of individual practices and doctrinal affiliations. Regularized monasteries enjoyed support from the laity on the basis of an understanding that the clergy fulfilled their salvific and protective functions by adhering to a fixed standard of behavior and collectively participating in the monastic liturgical schedule.

Sanjie distinctiveness, however, was grounded in Xinxing's rhetoric emphasizing the sins of beings and the power of giving, and his intensification of the demands of monastic liturgy and ritual. The popular appeal of this program gave the Sanjie movement momentum and strength enough to survive political pressures that would have destroyed a lesser sect. In contrast, Bao Tang distinction was grounded in Wuzhu's rejection of the notion of sin, the power of merit, and the need for monastic ritual, and this limited its appeal to those few who felt the impact of Wuzhu's charisma. I would thus argue that Sanjie and Bao Tang are opposites "implying each other,"[155] for both were paradigms of a breach of the acceptable limits of subitist/universalist soteriology. Such oppositions undeniably depend on the selective work of the erstwhile structuralist; nevertheless, I think that the kinship between Sanjie and Chan soteriology should be more widely recognized.

IMAGINARY CULTIC ROBES

As we will see in chapter 5, Daoxuan 道宣 (596–667) did much to contribute to the mystique of the visionary Dhyāna master in his *Xu gaoseng zhuan* 續高僧傳 (Continued Biographies of Eminent Monks). Here we have the opportunity to appreciate Daoxuan's own visionary powers as revealed in his writings on the ordination platform. The rich matrix of symbolism that Daoxuan developed to reify the power of the monk's robe and other objects of the ordination ritual foreshadows the robe mythos of eighth-century Chan. Daoxuan's writings may or may not have influenced Shenhui directly, but they appear to have shaped the clerical *imaginaire*, contributing greatly to the mystique of transmission in the final age of the Dharma.

Koichi Shinohara elucidates Daoxuan's ordination platform and its "imaginary cultic objects" in his articles "The Kasaya Robe of the Past Buddha Kasyapa in the Miraculous Instruction Given to the Vinaya Master Daoxuan (596~667)" and "Imagining the Jetavana in Medieval China: An Exploratory Discussion of Daoxuan's Jetavana Diagram Scripture." He discusses a series of visions that Daoxuan claimed to have experienced shortly before his death, visions that he experienced while constructing an ordination platform at the Jingye 淨業 temple in the Zhongnan 終南 mountains southwest of Chang'an. Daoxuan's visionary experiences, his completion of the platform, and the first ordination ceremony at the site all took place in 667, the year of his death.

The account summarized here is drawn from Shinohara's reconstruction of the version in the *Fayuan zhulin* 法苑珠林 (Jade Grove of the Dharma Garden),[156] which was completed in 668 by Daoxuan's confrère Daoshi 道世. The "miraculous instructions" passages are dispersed throughout the *Fayuan zhulin* according to topic, but they are purported to be from yet another work by Daoxuan and contain material not found in Daoxuan's extant works.[157] Daoshi, placing the material based on Daoxuan's vision among Indian scriptural quotations rather than among miracle stories, gives it the status of a revelation equal to the translated scriptures.[158]

Daoxuan was ill and was immersed in researching Buddhist texts for information on Jetavana and its ordination platform[159] when he received his first vision. In the vision, he is visited by the deity Zhang Qiong 張瓊, a son of the Vaidurya king of the Southern Heaven where the Dharma is said to be upheld with great diligence. The deity assumes an ordinary human form and treats Daoxuan with the deference of a lay devotee toward a distinguished master. Zhang predicts that Daoxuan will soon die and will be received into the Fourth Heaven, that is, Tuṣita. There he will be welcomed by Zhang's brother, who is a Buddhist scholar after Daoxuan's own heart. When Daoxuan hears that Zhang's brother has compiled a Jetavana Diagram Scripture, he is delighted and asks the visitor to describe the contents of the work to him. Zhang, in turn, admires Daoxuan's own work and praises him for upholding traditions regarding sacred sites and objects. He then begins to impart to Daoxuan his knowledge of these subjects, and Daoxuan rises from his sickbed to write it all down. Daoxuan claims that, after this first encounter, the deity came every day for several months, providing Daoxuan with material for ten fascicles, containing 3,800 items. He reassures his readers that "though the teaching was received from a god, it was still identical with what the Buddha taught."[160]

The miraculous instructions purport to be based on records of sermons by the Buddha, and each sermon follows a set pattern. The sermons take place at a great assembly called together by Śākyamuni at a particular site, and the time is also specified in relation to his enlightenment or final nirvāṇa. The sermons consist of stories about the various objects that were entrusted to Śākyamuni by former Buddhas. These objects include items of use prescribed for the renunciant by the Vinaya, such as the robe, bowl, razor, and water-sprinkler, as well as enshrined relics of the former Buddhas and enshrined scriptures. Shinohara terms the narratives "cosmic histories of cultic objects." For each object, Śākyamuni tells the assembly how the object was presented by a deity (such as a nāga or an autochthonous spirit) who told him that he or she was enjoined by the Buddhas of the past to pass it on to Śākyamuni. Each object with its attendant deity appears at a crucial moment in the course of Śākyamuni 's path to enlightenment, and it is understood that the same object was presented at parallel junctures in the careers of the previous Buddhas. After the story has been told, Śākyamuni provides for the enshrinement of the object in a stūpa so that its power will preserve the teaching during a future time when the true Dharma will be under attack.[161]

The instructions emphasize the importance of entrusting (*fuzhu* 付囑) the object to an intermediary guardian who will entrust it to the next Buddha. The following passage describes Śākyamuni 's reception of his predecessor's robe:

> The World-Honored One told Manjuśrī and the great assembly: "When I left the palace and entered the mountains to train in the Way, I put aside my priceless jeweled clothes and put on clothing made of deer skin. A Tree Deity appeared holding a *saṃghāṭi* robe in his hand, and he said to me, 'Prince Siddhārtha, your present cultivation of the Way will certainly result

> in correct awakening. In the past when Kāśyapa [Buddha] entered nirvāṇa, he entrusted this *saṃghāṭi* large robe to me. He ordered me to guard it well until you, humane one, should appear in the world. He ordered me to pass it on to Siddhārtha.' When I was about to receive the large robe, the ground moved greatly. The Tree Deity said, 'I will now open the robe and display the characteristics of the merit-field for you.' The Tree Deity opened the robe and I saw the characteristics of the merit-field, whereupon I entered the Vajrasamādhi (Adamantine concentration). The ground moved greatly once more. The Tree Deity spoke again, 'You are still a lay person, not yet fit to wear this Dharma-robe. You ought to place it on top of your head to offer it respect.'"[162]

The prince discards his robes for animal skin, which, like the monk's robe stitched from filthy rags, is a scriptural trope for deep pollution transformed into the highest purity. Both Śākyamuni's princely, worldly attire and his ascetic garb contrast with the *saṃghāṭi* robe, the one worn when expounding the Dharma. This robe has physically contained all the teachings of all the Buddhas, and thus the exposure of the merit-field (*futian* 福田) is a revelation of the matrix of the Buddha-Dharma, the Dharmakāya.[163] Although Śākyamuni is preordained to receive the robe, until he is enlightened/ordained he must wear it on his head rather than his back; thus, his relationship with various robes takes precise measure of his spiritual status.

Completing the cycle, Śākyamuni passes on the *saṃghāṭi* robe in the prescribed manner, foretelling the future. The following passage describes his last act before entering nirvāṇa:

> The Buddha told Manjuśrī and the eight divisions of the assembly, including monks, gods, and dragons: "This is Kāśyapa Buddha's *saṃghāṭi* robe made of coarse cloth and it has great power. I see with the Buddha-eye that gods, dragons, demons and spirits and even tenth-*bhūmi* bodhisattvas would be unable to move this great robe so much as a hair. Unless one is a Tathāgata one is unable to hold this robe-stūpa." The Buddha circumambulated the ordination platform three times, faced south and ascended the western stairs to the ordination platform, and facing west he turned northward until he stood facing the north. The World-Honored One threw the robe-stūpa into the air. The robe-stūpa spread light everywhere and illumined billions of lands. All the sufferings of the inferior realms of rebirth were removed by the light, and they became like heavenly trees in the land of subtle bliss. (There follows an episode in which the Buddhas of the ten directions donate their robes and Māra builds stūpas for them all, then the Buddha has Manjuśrī summoned to receive his last instructions.) . . . The Buddha told Manjuśrī and the great assembly who had gathered, "I now [enter] nirvāṇa and

> wish to entrust to you the stūpa of Kāśyapa Buddha's robe to maintain the Dharma that I hand down. After I enter nirvāṇa, bring the stūpa of Kāśyapa's robe to my ordination platform and place it at the north side for twelve years."[164]

The Buddha then predicts that during this twelve-year period a king will reign who will put faith in evil Hīnayāna monks and destroy the true Dharma, and the followers of Mahāyāna will be persecuted and murdered. Manjuśri is then to gather the martyrs' robes into the robe-stūpa and convey the survivors to safety. The Buddha instructs Manjuśri:

> Under the reign of the evil king when the correct Dharma is destroyed, you should use your supernatural power to take up the robe-stūpa and travel through that kingdom. The Mahāyāna teachings are contained within the stūpa. Those monks who upheld the precepts and were murdered by the king each had a *saṃghāṭi* robe that they received according to the Dharma, and you should place these inside the stūpa of my robe. Those monks who uphold the precepts and yet live you should use your supernatural power to place in safety at the top of Mt. Sumeru.[165]

The narratives of the *saṃghāṭi* robe and the other objects embody both synchrony and diachrony in the teachings of the past, present, and future Buddhas. As in the *Fu fazang zhuan* stories, here the Dharma is perennially imperiled yet ultimately inviolable. The notion of "diagram scripture" recurs throughout these writings, reminding the reader of the timeless patterns of destiny that work in tandem with particular histories of sacrifice and redemption. The histories of particular objects establish locations and events in the lifetime of Śākyamuni's Dharma, marking an unfinished yet finite cycle within the cosmic repeating pattern of Buddhahood.

When Śākyamuni has entered nirvāṇa the various enshrined objects are to be guarded at such potent locations as Manjuśrī's abode at Mt. Qingliang 清涼, the palace of a nāga-king, or Jetavana itself. Jetavana is evoked within different levels of the narrative, functioning as the site of some of the sermons as well as the repository of some of the enshrined objects. It is also the metalevel, the heavenly Jetavana, which is a cosmic maṇḍala or diagram of all the sites and a reliquary of all the sermon-histories.

The heavenly Jetavana centers on the ordination platform, the location of the enshrined *saṃghāṭi* robe and the ritual site of both eternal preservation of the Dharma and the recurring preservation of the Dharma through each individual's reception and maintenance of the precepts. Shinohara notes the confluences between Daoxuan's "Jetavana Diagram Scripture" and his "Ordination Platform Diagram Scripture," that is, between his last vision and his last project. He says: "In this larger context, Daoxuan's maṇḍala, explaining how the true teaching had been expounded by past, present, and future Buddhas, was also to be read as a diagram that showed how others could take part in this story through ordination."[166]

However, there was always the danger that the salvific robe might be misused. Shinohara highlights the tension between the story of the robe passed down by the Buddhas and a story found in another section of the *Fayuan zhulin,* in which the Buddha produces multiple apotropaic robes. The wealth of detail pertaining to care of the monks' robes in Daoxuan's Vinaya commentary and in the *Fayuan zhulin* may reflect Daoxuan's concern that overproduction of robes would dilute their efficacy.[167]

The ordination platform and robe are the primary sites of protection of the Dharma and are by the same token the primary sites of decay: "The Buddha told the monks, 'This *saṃghāṭi* of mine was worn by all the Buddhas of past and future to attain liberation. In the future evil monks will not uphold the [rules regarding the] three robes, and also in not keeping [other] precepts they dishonor the Dharma robe. They cause the Dharma to be quickly destroyed.'"[168]

As noted in the previous section, internal corruption of the Saṅgha was perhaps the dominant motif in "decline" eschatology, and the warning knell against false clergy sounds throughout Chinese Buddhist works of the fifth and sixth centuries. However, in Daoxuan's talismania we hear echoes of the intense contemporary rivalry with Daoists over ritual authority in the Tang state cult, and we also discern a greater willingness to rely on Chinese symbols of legitimacy.[169]

Daoxuan's work (in its several versions) retains the format and linguistic style of a translated Indian scripture, yet, with the confidence of inspiration, Daoxuan also glorifies his own Buddhist context. Though he uses the Indian notion of cyclic ages of the Dharma, the marks of Daoxuan's eschatological *mofa* are more Daoist than Indian. His divine messenger, Zhang, is the son of "the Vaidurya king of the Southern Heaven" but has thoroughly Chinese official duties. And the *saṃghāṭi* robe of the Buddhas is enshrined at the ritual platform of the heavenly Jetavana, which resembles a Chinese imperial sacrificial platform and similarly guarantees protection to all realms under its sway. In a privileged milieu imbued with foreign concepts, images, and objects, Daoxuan brought forth a vision that made the exotic familiar and also exalted the familiar, merging India and China in a Dharma-realm and ritual space with recognizable points of orientation.

For our purposes, the most striking notes in Daoxuan's miraculous instructions resonate with developments yet to come, namely, the complex of meanings that would accrue to the robe of liberation and the ordination platform in eighth-century Chan.[170] Shinohara suggests that both Daoxuan and the eighth-century "Southern School" sectarian Shenhui were tapping a "broader religious culture" fed by the stories of the *Fu fazang zhuan* and the *Aśokāvadāna.*[171] Whether attributable to direct influence or to the *weltanschauung,* there is significant resemblance between Daoxuan's notion of a special transmission between Buddhas marked by the transferal of objects, and Shenhui's emphasis on a single robe passed down by the patriarchs, which is likened to Śākyamuni's gold-embroidered robe held in trust for Maitreya at Mt. Kukkuṭapāda.[172]

However, Shinohara notes Yanagida's suggestion that a comment by Huizhong 慧忠 (d. 775) reveals rival claims to Daoxuan's legacy.[173] In the *Jingde chuandeng lu,* Huizhong is recorded as a critic of the Southern School's appropriation of the appellation "Platform Scripture," as follows:

> Recently I traveled about, and I met many of this sort. Lately they have been especially numerous. At an assembly of three hundred and fifty people, [I heard that kind of] "with my own eyes I have seen the Milky Way" bragging: "This is the Southern Doctrine." [Someone has] substituted another "Platform Scripture," added an assortment of vulgar boasts and cut away the holy meaning to delude and confuse later disciples. Have these come to be words of teaching? Bitterly indeed I mourn the doctrine![174]

Yanagida suggests that, as the *Liuzu tanjing* 六祖壇經 (Platform Scripture of the Sixth Patriarch, commonly known as the *Platform Sūtra*)[175] was probably not in existence at the time of Huizhong's lament, it is possible he was complaining that Shenhui's *Tanyu* 壇語 (Platform Address, c. 720) was upstaging Daoxuan's "Platform Scripture."[176] To a State Preceptor (*guoshi* 國師) such as Huizhong, liberties taken with Daoxuan's divinely inspired writings must have seemed grievous, yet perhaps his interest in the matter was not entirely exegetical. Huizhong and Shenhui were both considered disciples of Huineng and were thus rival candidates for the contested position of seventh patriarch. Both were closely associated with temples in Nanyang 南陽, such that both were assigned this toponym. In the biographies of Huineng's disciples in the *Jingde chuandeng lu,* Huizhong and Shenhui are side by side as the last two entries.[177]

Huizhong was invited to be an imperial preceptor by Emperor Suzong 肅宗 (r. 756–762) and was also favored by Emperor Daizong 代宗 (r. 762–779). He appears in the famous *Biyan lu* 碧巖錄 (Blue Cliff Record) kōan collection attempting unsuccessfully to enlighten these emperors, but he was not so laconic about it as Bodhidharma had been.[178] According to the *Song gaoseng zhuan,* Huizhong's espousal of "Southern School" doctrines was rather moderate: "When he discussed the sudden he left no traces; when he spoke of the 'gradual' he returned to the conventional and yet was in accord with the Way."[179] If it is true that Huizhong's criticisms were directed at Shenhui's *Tanyu,* then his reaction may tell us something about Huineng's "sudden" teaching. Chan scholars have recognized that Huineng's teachings are unrecoverable except as reflected and embellished by "Southern School" sects, including the Bao Tang. Though also a student of Huineng's, Huizhong seems attuned to a sudden teaching in which "holy meanings," such as revelations of the Buddha's sermons imparted by a deity, were not yet marked as gradual and that mark was not yet so damning. Moreover, this imaginary sudden teaching was only beginning to be overburdened with "vulgar boasts" arising from doctrinal-genealogical rivalries.

And if it is true that Huizhong was lamenting the eclipse of Daoxuan's "Platform Scripture," then this points to a process of Chan appropriation of Daoxuan's work that began with Shenhui's *Tanyu* and proceeded to the elevation of the *Platform Sūtra,* which was the first work to claim the status of scripture for the teachings of a Chinese master. Discussed in greater detail in chapter 5, references to a distinctive "formless" precepts ritual are found in both Shenhui's *Tanyu* and the *Platform Sūtra,* but Shenhui did not create the formless platform out of thin air. The various materials for this construction are perhaps unrecoverable, but Daoxuan's robe is likely to have been among them. The "Jetavana Diagram Scripture" clearly resonated with Chinese ritual and utopian sensibilities, and its combination of cyclic and heroic narrative patterns helped to intensify the mystique of Buddhist talismans of transmission.

CONCLUSION

Perhaps there is some limited tolerance left for an irony-free accolade. In any case, I venture to express deep admiration for the political, aesthetic, and spiritual power of the Yungang caves, the drama of the Dharma brought to life in the *Fu fazang zhuan,* the intellectual beauty of Zhiyi's system, the daring scope of Xinxing's soteriology, and the poetic and ritual richness of Daoxuan's vision. These creative efforts addressed and contributed to the powerful anxieties and high hopes sustaining the rapidly expanding "merit field" of Chinese Buddhist soteriology, the ground that produced the efflorescence of the High Tang.

At the same time, we must also acknowledge the ritual or talismanic functions that certain names acquired. Like Daoan and Huiyuan, the figures of Zhiyi and Daoxuan accrued mass and gravity over time and were used to bear heavy loads in subsequent sectarian campaigns. They became paradigms and "master functions," sites for specific positions within a broader discourse, through which the field of practice was concentrated and limited.[180] Also illustrative of this process, Xinxing became a representative of the limit beyond which lay territories marked as heterodoxy and excess.

Whether attributable to individual piety and genius or to the creative force of rivalry, effort and expenditure on a massive scale emerge as recurring themes in the works examined in this chapter. In the frenzy for Buddhist projects in the Northern Wei, the *Fu fazang zhuan*'s account of heroic deeds in service of the Dharma, the potlatch-scale offerings of the humane king in the *Renwang jing,* the contagion of giving envisioned by Xinxing, and the self-renewing cosmic ritual in Daoxuan's final visions, we see the craving for assurance that the champions of the Dharma will hold firm. Yet it was the overwhelming pressure of faith itself that the clergy were asked to withstand. In an era in which the Buddhist *imaginaire* fed on utopian spectacle, eschatological awe, and the fabulous productivity of merit, both the spaces and the systems of practice appear to burst at the seams with complex and rich detail, animated by the mutual resistance of fecundity and order. The ambition to expand the Buddhist empire of faith would reach its apex with Empress Wu, but even before the end of her reign we may discern an undercurrent of desire for human-sized refuges, robes, and merit-fields.

In chapter 5 we examine the rise of "Southern School" sectarianism and turn to the biographies of the Chan patriarchs. As noted above, the *Lidai fabao ji*'s "Southern School" ideology lays claim to the *zhengfa* without reference to *mofa* eschatology. The Bao Tang followed Shenhui's exhortation to have faith in the line of patriarchs, who represented a guarantee of the Dharma against the fallibility of both monastic and political authority. And in chapter 6 we see that the *Lidai fabao ji* authors were quite willing to go into detail regarding the names, circumstances, and personalities of individual rivals and supporters, both clerical and secular. While Shenhui's patriarchal ideology may appear overblown and the *Lidai fabao ji*'s account of Dharma-hall sparring may appear petty, we should also recognize in them echoes of the soteriological campaigns of the sixth and seventh centuries, spurred by belief in a cosmic-scale crisis.

CHAPTER 5
Robes and Patriarchs

Dignity, and even holiness too, sometimes, are more questions of coat and waistcoat than some people imagine.
—Charles Dickens, *Oliver Twist*

THE "CHAN" QUESTION

We turn now to issues pertaining to that much-debated entity, the Chan school. In the seventh and eighth centuries, lineage and transmission schemes became ever more varied and complex. In this chapter I continue to explore the role that court-clergy relations played in shaping Chinese Buddhist transmission discourse, here highlighting the motif of ambivalence toward imperial patronage, a prominent trope in transmission paradigms. On the one hand, eminent monks like Zhiyi and Daoxuan developed rich fields of symbolism based on the interplay of royalty and renunciation, whereby the ideal reciprocity between rulers and clerics was to be achieved without compromising either power. On the other hand, in some popular hagiographical and apocalyptic works, favored monks at court were treated as a sign of the corruption of the Saṅgha.

As noted in chapter 1, the notion of a Chan school in the late eighth century is a vexed one. In this chapter I return to the question of the sectarian identity claimed in the *Lidai fabao ji*. The Bao Tang appear to have seen themselves as members of a school that they broadly defined as "Chan" (*Chanmen* 禪門 or *Chanfa* 禪法) and more narrowly defined as Bodhidharma's lineage. Both broad and narrow conceptions can be seen in the following claim, in which the *Lidai fabao ji* authors repudiate the notion that Guṇabhadra, a mere translator, could be considered a patriarch: "All of the above were translator-Trepiṭakas and not Chan Masters. All of them transmitted the teachings of the written word. Patriarchal Master Dharma was in the lineage of the Chan Dharma (*zongtu Chanfa* 宗徒禪法). He did not bring a single word, [just] silently transmitted the mind-seal."[1]

would pose against the figure of Bodhidharma is not a rival or a double but, rather, the multitude. In the earliest accounts, Bodhidharma is one of a number of bright silhouettes posed against a background of the shadowy ranks of the lesser clergy.

The sectarian significance of the hagiographies in Daoxuan's 道宣 (596–667) *Xu gaoseng zhuan* 續高僧傳 (Continued Biographies of Eminent Monks),[4] first completed in 649, is still contested. While it is clear that he was influenced by and contributed to developments in Buddhist sectarian consciousness, the topical issues that caused him to draw boundaries and define affiliations were not always taken into account by scholars who used his work as a source for the beginnings of Chan or other schools.

During Daoxuan's lifetime, the piety of Sui Wendi, who had supported major Buddhist projects and removed all restrictions on ordination, was succeeded by the more openly self-serving patronage of his son, Emperor Yang 煬 (r. 604–617), and then by the grudging tolerance of the Tang founders. In the early Tang, educated clergy had to negotiate ground somewhere in between an imperial house inclined to favor Daoists and Confucians, and the less discriminating enthusiasm (and generosity) of lay Buddhists on all levels of society. Some, such as the monk Falin 法琳 (572–640), entered into vigorous polemics in defense of their creed.[5]

Daoxuan himself took part in one of the most illustrious episodes in the long-running "bowing" controversy. In yet another attempt to compel the clergy to pay obeisance to their parents and the emperor, in 662 the ailing emperor Gaozong 高宗 (r. 649–683) called on his ministers to debate the issue. Gaozong restricted the discussion to lay officials, and so the clergy made efforts to gain the support of influential laypersons. Daoxuan exerted himself in writing appeals, arguing that forcing the clergy to bow to the laity was equivalent to forcing them to break their vows. Using arguments similar to those we saw in the earliest manifestations of the bowing controversy, Daoxuan asserted that preventing the clergy from fulfilling their vows would alienate protective deities and precipitate decline and chaos throughout the realm. In the course of long-drawn-out proceedings, Gaozong failed to win a clear mandate of support from his ministers and finally abandoned the attempt.[6] Notably, this drama was unfolding in the midst of Gaozong's and Empress Wu's support of excavation and veneration of the Famen 法門 monastery relic, concluding with a procession in which Daoxuan also participated.[7] Both of these elaborate rituals, one of the state and the other of the temple, demonstrated the power of the clergy.

In considering the defense of Buddhist systems and traditions, one must also consider the pressure of competition among Buddhist clergy to meet the high moral and intellectual standards expected of them by their elite patrons.[8] Early in the Tang, demarcation among Buddhist "schools" with established links to fifth- and sixth-century exegetical traditions afforded political respectability, mirroring the legitimating structure of the ancestral clan, and it distinguished well-connected and serious-minded clergy from the elusive irregulars of the roads, villages, and remote monasteries. However, after the pilgrim Xuanzang 玄奘 (602?–664) returned in 645 to be greeted with imperial and popular acclaim, his new translations and his championship of new Yogācāra treatises caused competitive struggles among the exegetical camps.[9]

These tensions are reflected in the *Xu gaoseng zhuan,* which was substantially augmented by Daoxuan near the end of his life and appears to have been supplemented even after his death.[10] The typological organizing principle inherited from Huijiao's *Gaoseng zhuan* became with Daoxuan such a finely honed instrument that he sometimes divided one monk into two, based on his assumptions about exclusive trends in practice and doctrinal affiliation.[11] The proclivities that Daoxuan differentiated had been considered mutually reinforcing in hagiographies of the Six Dynasties period, when a monk could be a master of both Vinaya and dhyāna, acts of piety and ascesis went hand in hand, and translators performed miracles. Daoxuan's rationalization of hagiographic types did not entail any devaluation of supranormal powers; on the contrary, he held that miracles are the way in which the Dharma is made manifest.[12] In the appeals he made to gain support for the Buddhist position in the above-mentioned bowing controversy of 662, Daoxuan defended the special status of the clergy with an account of miraculous events in the history of Buddhism in China.[13]

Two evident interests of Daoxuan's later years, his collections of miracle stories and his additions to the dhyāna/Chan section of the *Xu gaoseng zhuan,* have prompted Koichi Shinohara to argue that this reflects a new development in Buddhist hagiography.[14] Biographical collections of both thaumaturges and Chan masters were detached from their common origins in the typological *gaoseng zhuan* genre and began to go their separate ways. However, Daoxuan's expansion of the "dhyāna-practitioners" category of biographies has also been credited with creating awareness of a Chan trend, thus giving it substance.[15]

More elusive than the samādhi virtuosi associated with dhyāna-practice in an earlier era, the meditators praised in the *Xu gaoseng zhuan* were invested with a mystique of legitimacy and became a pool of candidates for later Chan affiliates seeking ancestry. There was as yet no Chan lineage, but Daoxuan noted master-disciple relationships, inviting those who came later to try to connect the lines between the clusters of dots. Even though the finds at Dunhuang have reoriented our understanding of early Chan, it is important to realize that many Dunhuang Chan sectarian works rely significantly on the *Xu gaoseng zhuan.* Daoxuan himself often relied on material that was produced by the disciples of the master in question.

For Daoxuan, Bodhidharma and his disciples appear to have been in a special category, though there is a range of scholarly opinion as to the nature of that category. Bodhidharma's *Xu gaoseng zhuan* biography includes a fairly elaborate discussion of his teachings and identifies his hallmark practice as "wall-contemplation" (*biguan* 壁觀), said to be an embodiment of the realization of the principle of nondual true nature, which is to be reinforced with four concrete methods or practices that actualize realization.[16] The *Xu gaoseng zhuan* thus contains a summary of the treatise that is purported to give an account of the teachings of Bodhidharma, the so-called *Erru sixing lun* 二入四行論 (Treatise on the Two Entrances and Four Practices).[17] However, Daoxuan's biographical information does not tally with the biographical information found in the Dunhuang manuscripts of Tanlin's 曇林 (c. 506–574) preface to the *Erru sixing lun*.[18] Based on textual and conceptual similarities between the *Erru sixing* and Tanlin's speciality, the *Śrīmālā-sūtra,* Jeffrey Broughton argues that Tanlin was probably the author of "Bodhidharma's" text (and not simply the compiler as is claimed in the *Lengqie shizi ji*).[19] Moreover, Broughton suggests that the real Chan ancestor in the sixth century may be a Master Yuan 緣, a possible disciple of Bodhidharma who is known only from the Dunhuang fragments that Broughton calls *Record II* and *Record III.*[20] We return to these texts shortly.

Yanagida Seizan suggests that when we trace connections, such as the link that was later forged between Bodhidharma and Song shan 嵩山, Bodhidharma's brief appearance in the *Luoyang qielan ji* at Yongning monastery, and his biographer-disciple Tanlin's clerical duties and connections at the Northern Wei court, we find patterns similar to those of the meditator-monk known as Buddha 佛陀 or Bhadra 跋陀, a mountain ascetic supported at a benevolent distance by imperial patronage.[21] The temple that Emperor Xiaowen built for Buddha/Bhadra on Song shan later became Shaolin 少林 monastery, a key site in the developing Bodhidharma legend.[22] Faure has also traced the strands of a complex web in which the names and attributes of Bodhidharma, Bodhiruci, Buddhabhadra, Buddha or Bhadra, Sengchou, and Guṇabhadra link, cross, and are transposed throughout the hagiographical and epigraphical record. Tangled in this web are variant master-disciple relationships and rival traditions of transmission of the *Laṅkāvatāra-sūtra.*[23]

In *Monks and Monarchs, Kingship and Kinship,* Chen Jinhua proposes a different view of these relationships, based on an analysis of Daoxuan's overview of six Chinese traditions of meditation practice current in his day.[24] Chen argues that Daoxuan favored the two northern meditation groups associated with Sengchou 僧稠 (480–560) and Sengshi 僧實 (476–563), who were prominent in the Northern Qi and Northern Zhou, respectively.[25] He also claims that Daoxuan was antagonistic to Bodhidharma's group. However, having reconsidered Daoxuan's assessment in this light I still find it more ambiguous than Chen represents it to be. Daoxuan characterizes Bodhidharma's teachings as difficult for all but a few, with a tendency toward antinomianism and the nihilistic aspect of Two Truths theory.[26] He also presents Sengchou and Bodhidharma as polarized paradigms: they are as if "two separate tracks for vehicles," and Sengchou's track is more easily followed.[27] It is true that Daoxuan appears to have favored Sengchou's approach, but it does not follow that Bodhidharma's disciples were therefore pariahs.

However, Chen argues that a subsequent passage is a condemnation of Bodhidharma's followers, even though no specific targets are identified and the passage appears to be a general condemnation of superficial and arrogant dhyāna practitioners.[28] In my view, Daoxuan's antipathy toward some meditation practitioners' laxness and overemphasis of immanence appears to be a warning about the pitfalls into which unlearned meditation practitioners may fall, a familiar theme that Tiantai Zhiyi also stressed. Chen points out that Daoxuan omitted Bodhidharma from his final assessment, but there is not sufficient evidence to support his theory that the spurious story of Bodhidharma's poisoning "reflects the harshness of the suppression of Bodhidharma and Huike's followers by the Sengchou-Huiguang group and the intensity of resentment that the former felt against the latter because of the confrontation between them."[29] However, Chen's research into the rich web of monastic and kinship relationships implicated in Daoxuan's assessments has the overall effect of revealing many worlds within Daoxuan's short but densely packed treatise, providing keys to the relationships found in the biographies themselves.[30]

Whatever his intentions may have been, Daoxuan's biographies of Bodhidharma and Huike and other dhyāna practitioners contributed to a romantic image that has proved perennially appealing. This is the image of a lone ascetic who sometimes joined with others in small temporary groups, seldom stayed long at any particular location, was weather-beaten but not unlearned, and occasionally suffered persecution both from monks more firmly allied with the system and from fellow-vagrants even further beyond the pale. Significantly, this ascetic could be a layperson as well as a monk.[31]

Though these biographies provide no evidence for an autonomous "Chan" school, they do contribute to a mystique of autonomy. Daoxuan's dhyāna monks are frequently required to develop toughness and endurance under adverse circumstances, and it is notable that the metaphors used emphasize a "gradual" process. For example, Bodhidharma's disciple Huike 慧可 (487–593) is likened to a potter who must rid the clay of impurities in order to produce a vessel of a strength and hardness that will not be "shattered by conditions."[32] This is quite different from the metaphor's import in the above-mentioned *Fu fazang zhuan* account of Saṅghanandi's riddle, in which the holy ones, like clay vessels, are continually turned on the wheel of the Dharma and have no subsequent existence. In the *Fu fazang zhuan* the transmission is accomplished through a series of similarly patterned vessels, and the replication of these "response-bodies" of the Dharma accentuates the tragedy of the martyrdom of Siṁha Bhikṣu. In Daoxuan's biographies, accounts of persecution serve to deepen the aura of individual destiny, and we see this device used even more lavishly by the *Lidai fabao ji* authors.

As Yanagida has argued, it is not difficult to construe a connection between the political chaos in the north and the themes of ignoring slander and abuse, dealing with hardship, and the evanescence of honor and fortune emphasized in Bodhidharma's teaching of the "four practices." With the fall of the Northern Wei in 534, many monks followed Emperor Xiaowu 孝武 (r. 532–534) and the Gao 高 clan to form the Western Wei 西魏 dynasty (535–556) at Ye 鄴 in the east. Yanagida surmises that Bodhidharma, as documented in the case of Tanlin and Huike, may have also gone to Ye after the fragmentation of the Northern Wei.[33] One might indeed imagine that the teeming "altar-rats of the Law" fleeing Luoyang were hard put to find new granaries, lending credence to the account of slander and jealousy found in the biography of Huike.[34] Yet if one is searching for circumstantial evidence, Daoxuan's own milieu was as likely a source of inspiration and material for stories of clerical rivalry.

More important, Daoxuan's circumstances would have called for the sharpening of old tools. In chapter 4, we saw Huiyuan attempting to forestall imperial curtailment of the Saṅgha by articulating and instituting his own standards for separating the worthy from the unworthy. Similarly, Daoxuan uses the time-honored trope of the uncompromising monk as a precision instrument. The distinctions that he draws may have been part of his campaign against imperial regulation and may also have included veiled criticism of the negative effects of conspicuous imperial favor such as Xuanzang received. At the same time, the doctrinal and practical bases of his evaluations are stylized and relative, not systematic. Daoxuan praises Bodhidharma for "abandoning affiliation with both blame and blessing" and contrasts him with Sengchou, who was honored by Emperor Xuan of the Northern Qi.[35] On the other hand, Daoxuan eulogizes the marks of imperial honor that both Sengchou and Sengshi received and links this imperial support with the two monks' successful transmission of the meditation tradition. Using a metaphor that would become one of the hallmarks of Chan, he extols the uninterrupted transmission that is like "one lamp [lighting] the next."[36] Again on the other hand, Sengchou is lauded for abandoning worldly honor and returning to the wilderness.[37]

Most interesting in the context of this study is the account of the monk Tanlun 曇倫 (c. 546–626), who, like Wuzhu, refused to recite sūtras or carry out devotional practices, but shut himself away and ceaselessly practiced no-thought.[38] Though Tanlun did not conform to the standards of conduct that Daoxuan himself endorsed, this did not deter Daoxuan from giving an account of the profound admiration Tanlun elicited from the famous exegete Sengcan 僧粲 (529–613), thereby tacitly endorsing Tanlun's unorthodox practice.[39]

Daoxuan's usefulness to later sectarians stems from the multiplicity of his distinctions, not their rigidity. Through a process of polarization within polarization, Daoxuan draws fine lines between various forms of cultivation and excludes only the uncultivated. Beyond the pale are the masses of nominal dhyāna practitioners, those without learning who "count robes received and food begged, [such that] calculation is taken to be the Mind-Way."[40]

Self-sacrifice in Chan Accounts of Patriarchal Transmission

In later sections of this chapter we examine the many facets of the symbolism of the robe, but in this section I focus on the relationship between the themes of self-sacrifice and conferral of the robe in the Bodhidharma-Huike transmission in the *Lidai fabao ji*.

Gifts, ranging from Huike's offering of an arm to Wuzhu's offering of bud-tea, weave patterns of relationship through the transmission stories in the *Lidai fabao ji*. However, the patterns are not as repetitive and structured as the transmission of the Dharma in the *Fu fazang zhuan* or transmission of objects in Daoxuan's Jetavana scripture. Many different kinds of self-sacrifice are offered by the *Lidai fabao ji* patriarchs, and these episodes serve to set them apart from common monks and mark them as worthy to receive and transmit the robe and Dharma. At the same time, devotional giving for the purpose of gaining merit is depreciated as empty delusion.

It was Shenhui who first put this Chan economy into practice, inscribing the robe of verification and "no merit" into his account of Bodhidharma.[41] Shenhui's well-known story of an encounter between Bodhidharma and Emperor Wu of the Liang (r. 502–549) reflects his efforts to redirect the focus of pious giving away from the goal of merit and toward the goal of "seeing the nature." As will be discussed in chapter 6, Shenhui's success in sermonizing and fund-raising from the bodhisattva precepts ordination platform was a key vehicle for "Southern School" subitism. The bodhisattva precepts ceremony venue had already undergone a process of redefinition and popularization with the "East Mountain" school prior to Shenhui, but Shenhui's acumen with symbolism and the effect of changing political circumstances gave new force to these innovations. During Shenhui's early career, lavish imperial expenditure on Buddhism was negatively associated with the reigns of Empress Wu and her sons. Though his teachings may well have disseminated widely prior to the An Lushan rebellion, his brief stint as a fund-raiser for the Tang restoration gave a boost to Shenhui's fame. It is not difficult to understand why this would appeal to those in power, for through his efforts Buddhism was made to support the imperium instead of the other way around. The claim that Bodhidharma's arrival in China was marked by a bold rejection of the efficacy of imperial expenditure on Buddhism was likely to have been received favorably by Shenhui's patrons.[42]

Let us turn to the *Lidai fabao ji* version of the famous "no merit" encounter, and take a look at the background of its symbolism.

> Emperor Wu came out of the city to welcome him personally. He had [Bodhidharma] ascend to the audience hall and asked the Venerable, "What teachings to convert beings have you brought from the other country?" Great Master Dharma replied, "I have not brought a single word." The emperor asked, "What merit have We gained in having monasteries built and people saved, scriptures copied and statues cast?" The Great Master responded, "No merit whatsoever." He replied [further], "This is contrived goodness, not true merit."[43]

Prior to this comedown, Liang Wudi had been enshrined in Buddhist lore for having emulated the extreme generosity of King Aśoka. He repeatedly "gave" himself, his family, and his royal robes to the Saṅgha to be ransomed back by his ministers. In pageants of self-abnegation, he donned white robes to offer himself up as a servant in order to raise funds for monasteries he wished to endow.[44]

The *Aśokāvadāna* was a key inspiration for Liang Wudi and a key reference point in Chinese Buddhist representations of merit. As we saw in the section on the *Fu fazang zhuan,* it was one of the sources for the notion of a lineage of the Buddha's disciples. However, in medieval Chinese Buddhism its usefulness in supporting the notion of Dharma transmission was ancillary to its usefulness as a reference to the power of relics to protect the Dharma, and the power of making offerings.[45]

The *Aśokāvadāna* theme of the tremendous productivity of the cycle of giving stands in sharp contrast to the Chan rhetoric of "no-merit." In the *Aśokāvadāna,* Aśoka's status as Cakravartin is attributed to the fact that as a little boy in a former life he put dirt into the Buddha's begging bowl as an offering. Though transgressing mundane laws of pollution, the boy's offering and vow are acknowledged by the Buddha's smile and his prediction of future kingship. The text elaborates on the great salvific powers of the Buddha's smile; it is said to emit rays of light that inspire beings in the six realms to have faith in the Dharma. These rays are then reabsorbed back into the Buddha's body, and the point at which the light reenters indicates the future state of the one upon whom he has smiled.[46] In later Chan, the merit of offering and the Buddha's smile both undergo subitist transformation. In the story of the "original" transmission that developed in the Song, the Buddha holds up a flower and the first patriarch Mahākśyapa responds with a smile, receiving mind-to-mind transmission.[47] Offering, merit, vow, and prediction all disappear into an image of the ultimate truth of presented presence.

In the well-known denouement of the *Aśokāvadāna*, King Aśoka makes his dying decree and gives the whole earth (excepting the state treasury) to the Saṅgha. Appropriately, the boy Jaya and the king he becomes both make offerings of the earth, the "given" from which exceptions are made, producing both wealth and pollution.[48] The *Aśokāvadāna* extols giving to the utmost, but the implicit counterpart to Aśoka's beggaring himself for the sake of the Saṅgha is the self-sacrifice motif in the early *Jātaka* tales, in which the Buddha as a bodhisattva in previous lives surrenders his (or its) own body for the sake of other beings. Although the doctrine of the Middle Way eschewed ascetic self-mortification, the theme of self-sacrifice was a recurrent one in *avadāna* literature, which became popular in China. Moreover, the fiery self-immolation of Bhaiṣajyaraja in the *Lotus Sūtra* was taken as the paradigmatic self-sacrifice, and a hagiographic category was devoted to monks and nuns who followed this example by making offerings of their entire bodies or their limbs.[49]

In the *Lidai fabao ji* accounts of Bodhidharma and the other patriarchs, devotional gifts are denigrated while personal gifts, offerings of the body, and physical austerities (*dhūta*) are praised. The most dramatic example of physical sacrifice in Chan lore is the famous story of the second patriarch Huike cutting off one of his arms in order to demonstrate his sincere desire to become Bodhidharma's disciple. Offering an arm was one of the practices attributed to those in the hagiographic category of "self-immolators," noted above. Stories featuring those who offered limbs or pieces of flesh, and then died due to loss of blood, form a background for Chan accounts of Huike's extraordinary feat.[50] Here is the *Lidai fabao ji* version of Huike's story:

> When he first came [with the intention] to serve the Great Master, he stood before the Great Master in the night. That night there was a heavy snowfall, and the snow rose up to [Huike's] waist, but he did not stir. The Great Master said, "He who would seek the Dharma must spare neither life nor limb." [Huike] then chopped off one of his arms, whereupon the blood flowed out as white milk. The Great Master then silently transmitted the mind-pledge, and passed on to him a *kāṣāya* (monk's) robe.[51]

Prior to its deployment as an offering of good faith, Huike's severed arm had served as a sign of distinction: in the *Xu gaoseng zhuan*, Huike and Tanlin both lose an arm to bandits, and Huike's stoicism contrasts with Tanlin's pitiful screaming. Their experience serves as a bond, and they are said to have understood and appreciated one another.[52] They are thus "symmetrical figures that imply each other," as Faure characterizes another key pair, Bodhidharma and Sengchou. Faure argues that nascent consciousness of Chan as a distinct entity can be discerned in the hagiographic processes of doubling and polarization of attributes, in the proliferation of figures who are substitutes on one level and adversaries on another.[53] In the case of Huike and Tanlin, the missing arm marks them as doubles and mutually dependent paradigmatic opposites. As the Bodhidharma lineage began to take shape and nascent consciousness became self-consciousness, the traces of Huike's fellow disciple were removed.

If we look at Huike's arm intertextually, we find subtle variations throughout the stratigraphy of Chan stories of the Bodhidharma-Huike transmission. In the *Chuan fabao ji* 傳法寶紀 (Annals of the Transmission of the Dharma-Jewel) Huike instantly cuts off his arm when Bodhidharma asks him if he could give up his life for the sake of the Dharma.[54] In the *Lengqie shizi ji* 楞伽師資記 (Record of the Masters and Disciples of the *Laṅkā[vatāra-sūtra]*), Huike's self-mutilation and subsequent lack of pain during his vigil in the snow becomes an illustration of the power of true awareness.[55] In Shenhui's version, Bodhidharma has already approved of Huike's dedication, and so the arm becomes an offering sealing their bond rather than a proof of determination or a bid for recognition. Shenhui compares Huike's story to the *Nirvāṇa-sūtra* tale of a bodhisattva selflessly throwing himself off a cliff, a topos that harks back to the *Jātaka* tales.[56] Only in the *Lidai fabao ji* does Huike bleed white milk like the Indian patriarch Siṁha Bhikṣu, and he does so again when he is executed in circumstances recalling Siṁha Bhikṣu's martyrdom. The *Lidai fabao ji* authors frequently mixed the perennial motif of miracles (a form of salvific mediation), with their subitist and "im-mediate" representations of no-thought.

The subsequent permutations of this scene are too numerous to cite, but I will trace two important further steps in the development of the standard version. Completed in 801, the *Baolin zhuan* 寶林傳 is closest to Shenhui's version: the disciple Shenguang 神光 stands outside in the snowy night appealing to Bodhidharma to emerge and teach for the sake of all beings. Bodhidharma admonishes him about the strength of will necessary to seek the Dharma, and the disciple thereupon cuts off his arm and presents it to the master. Bodhidharma is delighted with his capacity (*ke* 可) and gives him the name Huike, and then transmits the Dharma to him.[57]

Drawn from the *Baolin zhuan,* the account of Huike in the eleventh-century *Jingde chuandeng lu* 景德傳燈錄 (Record of the Transmission of the Lamp Compiled in the Jingde Era) incorporates the challenging nature of Bodhidharma's exchange with Huike and his evocation of the spirit of self-sacrifice necessary to attain the Dharma. However, the most famous exchange in the eleventh-century version is not found in the eighth century precursors examined above. The *Jingde chuandeng lu* includes a dialogue in which Huike asks Bodhidharma to pacify his mind, to which Bodhidharma replies, "Bring me your mind." Huike replies that he cannot find it anywhere, and Bodhidharma tells him that he has thus pacified his mind for him.[58]

The pattern of this encounter is derived from an eighth-century source, however, for it is similar to the *Baolin zhuan* account of the exchange between Huike and the third patriarch, Sengcan 僧璨 (d.u.). In the *Baolin zhuan* dialogue, the key term is no longer "mind" but "transgression" (*zui* 罪). Afflicted with a chronic ailment, Sengcan asks Huike to administer the rites of repentance for him, and performance of such rites for those seeking relief from illness would have been one of the accepted functions of the clergy. Huike asks him to bring his transgression, and when Sengcan is unable to do so Huike declares that he has thus administered repentance.[59] This encounter perfectly encapsulates Chan subitist iconoclasm (no-ritual) and antinomianism (no-transgression), and it too passed into the canons of Chan lore when it was reproduced and expanded in the *Jingde chuandeng lu:*

> There was a layman of over forty years of age who did not give his name. He came to pay obeisance [to Huike] and asked him, "My body is afflicted with palsy. I beg the Venerable to [effect my] repentance and relieve me of transgression." The master replied, "Bring me your transgression and I will relieve you." After a while the layman said, "I have searched for my transgression, and I can't do it." The master said, "I have relieved you of transgression altogether. You should take refuge in the Buddha, Dharma, and Saṅgha." [The layman] said, "Looking at you, Venerable, I know this is 'Saṅgha.' But I haven't yet figured out how to identify 'Buddha' and 'Dharma.'" The master said, "This mind is Buddha. This mind is Dharma. Dharma and Buddha are nondual. The jewel of the Saṅgha is also thus." [The layman] said, "Today for the first time I know that the transgression-nature is neither inside nor outside nor in between. If one's mind is thus, Buddha and Dharma are nondual!" The Great Master deeply appreciated his capacity and had him tonsured. He said, "This is our jewel! He should be called Sengcan (Saṅgha-gem)."[60]

Huike's enactment of a "formless" repentance for Sengcan severs the conceptual assumption that there is a karmic link between transgression and physical affliction and between merit and health. This conceptual fetter was sanctioned by Vinaya prohibitions against physically unfit candidates for ordination. It was also central to Chinese notions of the correspondence between one's deeds and one's health, such as we saw in the *Tiwei jing.*[61] Cutting through these conceptual barriers serves to admit the handicapped layman to the Saṅgha and thence to the patriarchy.

In the *Lidai fabao ji* account of the encounter between Huike and Sengcan, discussed at the end of chapter 3, the theme of affliction remains pivotal. However, the passage becomes a foreshadowing of the Hongren-Huineng transmission, rather than an echo of the Bodhidharma-Huike transmission. It prefigures Huineng's first encounter with Hongren, focusing on the supplicant's physical rather than ethnic disqualifications.[62] Huike's callous dismissal of Sengcan ("For you, a person afflicted with palsy, what good is it to meet with me?")[63] presents another twist in the theme of offering and the patriarchy. Unlike the *Jingde chuandeng lu* passage in which Huike's "bring me your transgression" replicates Bodhidharma's "bring me your mind," here Huike, though himself missing an arm, seems to reject the imperfect body that is offered to him. As in the parallel encounter between Huineng and Hongren, this performance has two masters. Sengcan appears to be more insightful than Huike, but Huike's apparent prejudice is a test for Sengcan to pass, less extreme than the ordeal Huike himself underwent.

Interestingly, both the "bring me your mind" and the "bring me your transgression" motifs are found in the Dunhuang text that Jeffrey Broughton calls *Record II,* in passages that purport to be Huike's answers to a disciple's questions:

> [Huike was asked] another question: "Teach me to quiet the mind." He answered, "Bring your mind here and I will quiet it for you." [The disciple] went on: "Just quiet my mind for me!" [Huike] answered, "This is like asking a craftsman to cut out a garment. Once the craftsman gets your silk, then he can set his blade to work. Without having seen the silk, how could he have cut out the pattern from space for you? Since you are unable to present your mind to me, I don't[64] know what mind I shall quiet for you. I certainly am unable to quiet space!"
>
> [The disciple] went on: "Administer confession and repentance for me." [Huike] answered, "Bring your transgressions here, and I will administer confession and repentance for you." [The disciple] went on: "Transgressions lack any characteristic of form that can be apprehended. I [don't] know what to bring!" [Huike] answered, "My administration of confession and repentance to you is over. Go to your quarters." Comment: If there is transgression one must confess and repent, but since one does not see transgression, it is unnecessary to confess and repent.[65]

The question of the existence or reality of the transgression is related to the question of collective versus individual responsibility. Michel Strickmann, in his analysis of fourth-century Mao Shan materials, discusses a document in which a son offers a "confession" to the Shangqing deity Lady Wei, praying that he be allowed to expiate the transgressions of his ailing father and brother: "A younger son here offers himself as a hostage for the recovery of his elders, including his own father. As in the prescriptive formularies, the "confession" itself is of the most general sort. Like the liturgical confessions, it is a supplication more than a declaration of repentance. Above all, it serves as a formal means for Hsü Hui to offer himself to the vengeful powers that are afflicting his father and brother, to give his life for theirs."[66] Strickmann goes on to point out that although the literatus Chi Chao (339–377) had written a catechism emphasizing the notion of individual responsibility, the principle of collective family responsibility for illness and transgression remained the dominant paradigm, and indeed continues to be seen in Chinese communities to this day.

However, it is instructive to examine the manner in which Chi Chao treats the notion of individual responsibility in his catechism, the *Fengfa yao* (The Essentials of Religion). As the complex long-term workings of karma are acknowledged to be inscrutable to the ordinary, the nature of responsibility and expiation is necessarily abstract. Strickmann summarizes: "For Ch'ih Ch'ao and his fellow-Buddhists, the fault is indeed one's own and not shared with one's family, yet it was also committed long ago, in another body and by a "self" whose identity might well be a matter for debate. Moreover, precise knowledge of the fault is given to very few, if any. Thus the most general formulae of penitence and confession will suffice to purge it, and countervailing good deeds performed in the present life will then tip the balance of merit in your favor."[67]

In the Huike and Sengcan material in the *Baolin zhuan, Record II,* and *Jingde chuandeng lu* dialogues examined above, it is the indeterminability of the transgression and the "self" who committed it that is interrogated. Huike offers his own arm and Sengcan presents his afflicted body, but both are stumped when it comes to bringing the "mind" or the transgression with which it is associated. This perfectly illustrates Wuzhu's repeated assertions that the phenomenal mind of "characteristics" (*xiang* 相) is the illusory locus of transgression and moral distinctions, and that once one transcends characteristics in no-thought one realizes that transgressions do not exist. Nevertheless, the *Lidai fabao ji* authors present the biographies of the early patriarchs in a traditional manner, showcasing performance of miracles rather than the struggle to realize no-thought and Buddha-nature.

In each successive patriarchal biography, the *Lidai fabao ji* authors further embroider the motif of the patriarchs' self-sacrifice and self-mastery. Maligned by jealous enemies, Huike goes willingly to his execution and then bleeds white milk, and both he and Sengcan pretend to be mad in order to preach the Chan Dharma in the marketplace. As noted earlier, Sengcan shows his mastery of death by choosing to die while standing and holding on to the branch of a tree. In the case of Sengcan's successor Daoxin, these themes take a humorous turn. The following incident arises due to Daoxin's refusal to comply with an invitation to court:

> In the seventeenth year of the Zhenguan era (643), Emperor Wenwu (i.e., Taizong) sent a messenger to Mt. Shuangfeng to invite Chan Master Xin to enter the imperial presence. Chan Master Xin pleaded old age and did not go. The messenger returned to the Emperor and delivered the message, "Chan Master Xin pleads old age and will not come."
>
> The messenger was sent again, to repeat the invitation. He went to Chan Master Xin's place and said, "The Emperor sends me to invite the Chan Master." The Chan Master earnestly pleaded old age and would not go, telling the messenger, "If you want my head you are welcome to behead me and take it, but I absolutely will not go." The messenger returned to the emperor and delivered the message, "He would allow his head to be cut off and taken, but his mind absolutely will not go."
>
> The Emperor again sent off the messenger, [this time] wearing a sword with which to get Chan Master Xin's head. He ordered him, "Do not harm the Venerable." The messenger arrived at the Venerable's place and said, "The Emperor orders me to get the Venerable's head. Will the Chan Master go or not?" The Venerable replied, "I absolutely will not go." The messenger said, "The Emperor orders that if the Chan Master will not come, I am to cut off his head and bring it." Great Master Xin extended his head and said, "Chop it and take it." The messenger turned the blade and bent [Daoxin's] neck. Great Master Xin sang out, "Why don't you chop, how much longer must I wait?" The messenger replied, "The Emperor ordered me not to harm the Venerable." Chan Master Xin gave a great laugh and said, "I've taught you to recognize someone who stays put."[68]

In this passage the subitist conundrum of bringing/not bringing the mind is worked into a light and lively scene reminiscent of dialogues in the earlier "pure conversation" tradition of metaphysical Daoism as well as later *gongan* dialogues. Here, however, I would like to focus briefly on Daoxin's rejection of an imperial invitation, a trope signifying detachment and superiority of character that had been deployed in Chinese literature at least since Zhuangzi's famous refusal of royal honor in favor of "dragging his tail in the mud." In this case, it reinforces a key *Lidai fabao ji* theme: devotional offering (the honor of an imperial invitation, with the wealth and prestige that such an invitation implied) is deemed inconsequential, and the gift of true value is the patriarch's willingness to be martyred in order to express the true Chan Dharma.

In the *Lidai fabao ji* we see the scale of merit repeatedly tipping away from the offering of material goods, *dāna,* toward offerings of the body and physical suffering, *dhūta.* These offerings were associated with the spheres of lay and ordained devotees, respectively, and validations of both were abundant in the Buddhist literature available in China. The treasury of scriptural praise for the *pāramitā* of lay generosity was virtually inexhaustible, and though the extremes of *dhūta* were technically heterodox (associated with the excesses of the Buddha's evil cousin Devadatta), the *Jātaka* and *avadāna* accounts and their derivatives were replete with paradigms of self-sacrifice. In spite of the necessary functions of both kinds of offering, we see the *Lidai fabao ji* consistently upholding *dhūta* over *dāna,* and in attempting to maintain this imbalance the Bao Tang appears extreme even within the Chan spectrum of values.

Conferral of the Robe in Chan Accounts of Patriarchal Transmission

Let us turn now to consideration of the transmission of the robe, the other side of the coin in the Chan economy of "no-merit." According to Guifeng Zongmi, the Bao Tang's severest critic, Wuzhu's followers were notorious for not maintaining any monastic observances and for tonsuring and conferring robes on people without requiring of them any evidence of Buddhist practice.[69] This radical de-signification of the monastic robe contrasts with the extraordinary weight given to Bodhidharma's "*kāṣāya* robe of verification" (*xin jiasha* 信袈裟) in the *Lidai fabao ji.*

In the *Lidai fabao ji,* the initial transmission of Bodhidharma's robe is shrouded in the ambivalence of redundancy. In the section on Bodhidharma, Huike receives a robe from Bodhidharma just before the latter's death. However, in the section devoted to Huike, the second patriarch receives the robe and transmission in his first encounter with Bodhidharma, just after he offers his arm: "The Great Master then silently transmitted the mind-pledge, and passed on to him a *kāṣāya* robe."[70] It is not necessary to ask "is it one robe, or two?" Instead, we should look more closely at the claim that the Dharma is transmitted directly, as a "mind-pledge" from master to disciple, while the robe serves as evidence or guarantee of this unique patriarchal transmission.

A monk's robe is a belonging that stands for renunciation of belongings, belonging to the body of the Saṅgha as a whole and, at the same time, the most personal of the objects that the monk is sanctioned to use. As we saw in Daoxuan's Jetavana narratives, the Buddha's abandonment of princely robes remained a powerful paradigm. The monk's *saṃghāṭi* robe made of bleached refuse cloth represented his autonomy from the authority of family and monarch, an autonomy that depended on the power of the Dharma to turn mundane pollution into highest purity. The motif of worldly pollution turned to purity is the basis of the economy of merit, for "filthy lucre" given to the Saṅgha is returned as an all-purpose stain remover, merit. Robes and cloth for robes were among the canonically backed currencies in the economy of merit, instituted as a traditional gift to the Saṅgha in the early Buddhist *kaṭhina* rite.

In the Bodhidharma-Huike transmission, the giving and receiving of a robe serves as confirmation that a special consecration or ordination has taken place. In the terms of the bodhisattva precepts texts discussed in chapter 3, the robe becomes a "good sign." In the precepts texts, the "good sign" constituted acknowledgment of the petitioner's confession and repentance and signified his or her successful reception of the precepts. Here, the good sign of the robe is given in confirmation of Huike's sacrificed arm and Bodhidharma's wordless mind-pledge. Thus, structurally speaking, ritual confession and reception of the precepts is homologous to Huike's arm-offering and his reception of the Chan Dharma and the robe. We recall that in the examples in the previous section, the motif of offering a severed arm or a severed head often occurred in conjunction with the motif of "bringing/not bringing the mind" or "bringing/not bringing the transgression." These motifs woven throughout the Bodhidharma-Huike-Sengcan mythos express the key subitist polemical claim that the Northern school wrongly reified transgression by its practice of mind-purification.

In the *Lidai fabao ji,* Huike serves Bodhidharma for six years after the initial transmission. Then the authors turn to an account of Bodhidharma's apparent death, elaborating on the *Chuan fabao ji* story that jealous monks from the Northern Wei court repeatedly tried to poison the patriarch.[71] The *Lidai fabao ji* identifies his enemies as the translator and exegete Bodhiruci 菩提流支 (d. 527?) and the Vinaya Master Guangtong 光統. The *Lidai fabao ji* authors might have chosen these two as representatives of the exegetical tendency, for by the eighth century they were considered representatives of the northern and southern branches of the Dilun school. Yanagida also points out that the identification of a Vinaya master as an antagonist may have had something to do with the Bao Tang feud with Vinaya masters over the matter of Wuxiang's chapel.[72]

> Now it happened that in the Wei the Trepiṭaka Bodhiruci and the Vinaya Master Guangtong put poison in some food which they offered [to Bodhidharma]. When the Great Master had finished eating he asked for a dish and vomited up a pint of snakes. Once again they offered him poisoned food. When the Great Master had taken the food and eaten it, he sat atop a massive boulder, and when the poison came out the boulder cracked. Altogether they tried to poison him six times. The Great Master informed

> his disciples, "I originally came in order to pass on the Dharma. Now that I've gotten someone, what's the good of lingering?" Then he transmitted a *kāṣāya* robe as a verification of the Dharma transmission. He said to Huike, "My destiny is this poison; you also will not escape these tribulations. In the sixth generation, the life of the Dharma heir will be as a dangling thread." He finished speaking and immediately died of the poison.[73]

Here the *kāṣāya* is clearly marked as the robe of the patriarchy, with an allusion to Huineng in the sixth generation. After this transmission scene we are given Bodhidharma's pronouncement on his disciples, the first known appearance of this oft-quoted assessment: "The one who got my marrow is Huike, the one who got my bones is Daoyu 道育, and the one who got my flesh is the nun Zongchi 摠持."[74] In versions after the *Lidai fabao ji,* we find the addition of a fourth disciple who attains either "blood" or "skin." Stuart Thompson's work on funerary ritual in modern Taiwan points to a pertinent semantic field: blood and flesh are considered to be yin, symbolizing fertility, while bones are considered to be yang, connoting lineage. Both elements are needed for continuity, and this symbolism is also found in a story of bringing a corpse back to life.[75] In the *Lidai fabao ji,* the evocation of flesh and bone is followed by a creative account of Bodhidharma's resurrection, utilizing topoi associated with Daoist stories of "liberation from the corpse."[76]

The *Lidai fabao ji* authors repeat the scene of Bodhidharma's death in their subsequent section on Huike. In this reprise, however, Huike questions Bodhidharma about the important matter of the transmission:

> Great Master Ke asked, "Venerable, about this Dharma of yours that has been passed down through the generations in your native country, and those to whom the Dharma was entrusted—please explain it again." [Bodhidharma] replied, "All the particulars are as explained in the preface to the *Chan jing.*" [Huike] further questioned the Great Master, "In the Western Kingdoms, to whom did you pass the succession, and did you also transmit the *kāṣāya* robe of verification to him, or not?" The Great Master replied, "The people of the Western Kingdoms are devout, they are not devious. My successor there is Prajñāpāramitāra, and I have passed the succession to him without transmitting the robe. In the Tang Kingdom beings have the Great Vehicle nature, [yet there are some who] falsely claim to have obtained the Way and the fruit [of enlightenment], and so I have transmitted the robe for the sake of verification of the teachings. It is like the consecration of the son of a Cakravartin (Wheel-Turning King), when he obtains the seven jewels and inherits his eminent position as King. Possession of the robe represents the true inheritance of the Dharma."[77]

Bodhidharma here compares the *kāṣāya* robe to the regalia of an universal monarch. There is a long-standing scriptural association between the consecration of a king (*abhiṣeka*) and Buddhist ordination ritual, and *abhiṣeka* is the final stage in many Mahāyāna texts, such as the *Mahāvastu,* that describe the bodhisattva path.[78] Anna Seidel pointed out that Bodhidharma's analogy would have resonated with Chinese regard for the sacred talismans that validated the reigning dynasty's mandate to rule. These sacred heirlooms were supposed to protect the dynasty until the time had come for a new cycle and a new dynastic succession.[79] In the same manner, one of the underlying implications of the story of Bodhidharma's death is that by finally consecrating Huike as his heir, Bodhidharma has passed on the Dharma along with the robe and therefore no longer has the power to pass the poison. At the same time, as noted, there is a resurrection motif. The gift of the robe is thus bound with the motif of the death-bed scene and final words, and also with the motif of conquering death, through the continuity of the patriarchy and the patriarchs' individual feats of mastery of death.

When considered from a wider perspective, the theme of the mastery of death is at the heart of the symbolic function of the robe. We may recall that in Daoxuan's Jetavana visions, the robe is a talisman within the matrix of power guaranteeing the continuity of the Dharma. For the Vinaya master Daoxuan, robe and precepts together maintain the "merit-field" through which the Dharma is continually made manifest regardless of conditions. At the same time, the universal infallible Dharma is the backdrop for human history, eschatological crisis, and individual salvation. We may recall that the Buddha's instructions to Manjuśrī included apotheosis of the martyrs: "Those monks who upheld the precepts and were murdered by the king each had a *saṃghāṭi* robe that they received according to the Dharma, and you should place these inside the stūpa of my robe. Those monks who uphold the precepts and yet live you should use your supernatural power to place in safety at the top of Mt. Sumeru."[80]

Faure considers the symbolic significance of the monastic robe in Daoxuan's Vinaya tradition and its role as a symbol of transmission in Chan to stem from two independent developments.[81] Yet the Jetavana robe and Bodhidharma's robe, both imaginary cultic objects within imagined histories, reflect a larger symbolic field in which talismanic objects serve as a sign of the virtue, and thus the legitimacy, of the person who is entrusted with them. We encountered this symbolic field previously, when we examined the empowerment conferred by legitimate "inner" possession of the state music in the romanticized account of the conflict between Fu Jian and Xie An. On the abstract level, one can see that there are homologies between the role that sacred objects play in legitimation of the authority of monks and the authority of rulers. Moreover, there are clearly processes of mutual Buddhist-imperial borrowing at work in the creation of legends about legitimating objects. Notably, the Buddha's almsbowl, another of the "imaginary cultic objects" of Daoxuan's Jetavana platform, was appropriated for the purposes of legitimation of political authority.[82]

To further extend the scope of this discussion of legitimating objects, I turn to Anna Seidel's analysis of the interdependence of Daoist and imperial talismans in "Imperial Treasures and Taoist Sacraments; Taoist Roots in the Apocrypha." Describing the interplay between the Daoist priesthood and the Chinese imperium through the Han and Six Dynasties, she argues that reflection of the imperial cult was fundamental to the constitution of "Daoism": "Their very creed was based on a revelation homologous with the manifestation of the Mandate of Heaven, their priests were empowered by sacred objects homologous with the auspicious portents legitimizing Chinese sovereignty, and their ultimate concern was identical to that of the ruler: Great Peace."[83]

Seidel argues that the mediating role Daoist priests played was crucial for the state. However, after the destruction of the Celestial Masters kingdom in Sichuan at the end of the Han and "apart from rebel movements" (an important caveat), the Daoist priesthood remained dependent on the imperium, not the other way around: "The very fact that the Taoist priest served a celestial hierarchy in which the Son of Heaven had his hallowed place, prevented Taoism from ever assuming a spiritual authority against the empire as in the medieval Christian dispute between spiritual and worldly power."[84]

Seventh- and eighth-century Buddhist sectarians thus appear to be doing something similar to what the Daoists were doing in the Han—drawing from the symbolic field of imperial continuity and proceeding as if their derivation was the true continuity. Indeed, in her article on Buddhist transmission of the robe, Seidel argues that the Southern School attempted to elevate the robe to the status of an imperial talisman, as evidenced by the fabricated imperial proclamation honoring Huineng's robe that is found in the *Caoqi dashi zhuan* 曹溪大師傳 (Biography of the Great Master of Caoqi) and the *Jingde chuandeng lu*.[85]

Prior to the eighth century, Chinese Buddhists had repeatedly tried to create a place from which to assume spiritual authority that was independent from the state, and, as we saw in previous chapters, this attempt was at the crux of numerous struggles between Saṅgha and state. At the same time, the greatest danger of a Buddhist coup d'état stemmed from the emperors and empresses themselves. However, during the political instability in the late Tang, provincial representatives of the Chan school focused their polemical attention on one another, and struggles with Daoists or other Buddhists for imperial recognition assumed secondary importance.

Ironically, these provincial sectarian Chan works were so effective at tapping the symbolic field of imperial continuity that they created a mystique of spiritual authority that persists to this day, a century after the (ostensible) demise of the imperial system.

Seidel draws attention to inconsistencies in the Chan use of imperial symbols, namely, the claims that in India the robe was not necessary as a token of Dharma inheritance and the comparison of the robe to the regalia consecrating an Indian king.[86] These inconsistencies stem from Shenhui, who asserted that Bodhidharma did not transmit the patriarchal robe in India because there was no need, but then also cited the transmission of a robe from Śākyamuni to Mahākāśyapa as a precedent:

> Master Yuan asked, "I'm not yet convinced that the Dharma is in the robe and that one can use the robe as transmission of the Dharma."
>
> Shenhui replied, "Although the Dharma is not in the robe, [Dharma] succession through the generations is represented by taking transmission of the robe as verification. It guarantees that disseminators of the Dharma have legitimacy, and it guarantees that students of the Way know the main tenets of the doctrine, without error. Śākyamuni Tathāgata's gold-embroidered *kāṣāya* robe is now at Mt. Kukkuṭapāda, and Kāśyapa even now keeps this *kāṣāya* robe, waiting for Maitreya to be born. It is proper to pass down this robe, it represents Śākyamuni Tathāgata's transmission of the robe as verification. Our sixth patriarch is also like this."[87]

Shenhui's transmission ideology is discussed at greater length in subsequent sections, but here let me highlight its distinguishing feature: For Shenhui there was only one true transmission of the Dharma, vested in one patriarch per generation. His agenda may well have been linked to personal ambitions, but it should also be viewed within the larger context discussed in chapter 4, where we reviewed several different kinds of efforts to establish doctrinal, ritual, and institutional foundations for an independent Buddhist authority. One of the most frequently cited signs of the final age of the Dharma was the multiplication of false teachings and corrupt monks, and many clerics attempted to formulate means to guarantee that a pure Dharma and Saṅgha could arise from the mire of lavish donation and elite patronage. "Bodhidharma's robe" may thus be viewed as a variation or further stage in the struggle to establish a true Dharma within the Dharma and a true Saṅgha within the Saṅgha. Naturally, this variation in its turn became obsolete; less than a generation after the *Lidai fabao ji,* the author of the *Baolin zhuan* demoted the symbolic function of the robe to that of a supplementary token.[88]

The *Lidai fabao ji* authors, however, followed Shenhui in claiming that Bodhidharma's robe is the singular guarantee of an elect who protect the Dharma in the midst of clergy who "falsely claim to have obtained the Way." However, the patriarchs in the *Lidai fabao ji* suffer more than Shenhui's patriarchs—their careers are marked by persecutions, various forms of martyrdom, and periods spent in hiding. Furthermore, while the *Lidai fabao ji* authors echo Shenhui's statement about the precedent and rationale for transmission of the robe, their statement is more strongly worded, and it occurs at the end of a long collection of scriptural quotations that emphasize *mofa* or *moshi* themes of false teachings and evil or self-deluded monks:

> This is why Śākya-Tathāgatha transmitted the gold-embroidered robe. He ordered Mahākāśyapa to wait in Mt. Kukkkuṭapāda until the World-honored Maitreya descends to be incarnated, to then hand it over to him. In this evil age, students of Chan are many. Our Patriarchal Master [Bodhi]dharma therefore transmitted a robe representing verification of his Dharma, and ordered that later students must have this [token of] inherited authorization.[89]

I would like to draw attention to the statement "in this evil age, students of Chan are many." While one could argue that the phrase should be translated as "students of dhyāna," I think that the *Lidai fabao ji* as a whole displays sufficiently strong sectarian consciousness to justify reading this as an indication that *moshi* anxiety was here brought to bear on Chan and even "Southern School" rivals, not simply false clergy. This would explain why the *Lidai fabao ji* episodes of robe-transmission are linked with the motifs of martyrdom, persecution, and secrecy. As noted, the Bao Tang seem to have regarded Wuzhu as the hidden carrier of the only transmission of *zhengfa,* passed down from the mind of one patriarch to the next.

At the same time, Bodhidharma's statement in the *Lidai fabao ji* that "the people of the Western Kingdoms are devout, they are not devious" appears to reify a separate realm where the Dharma is not threatened. In this Shangri-la, transmission of the Dharma is the self-defining function of the Dharma—the teachings of the *Prajñāpāramitā* are carried on by Bodhidharma's disciple Prajñāpāramitā, who has no rivals and no need of the robe.

A GENEALOGY OF PATRIARCHAL LINEAGES

In this section we backtrack and trace the development of the Chan patriarchal ideology that emerges full-blown with Shenhui. Thus, we cover the ground in between the two parts of the section just concluded on Bodhidharma and Huike, in between Daoxuan and the *Lidai fabao ji.* This was also a period during which imperial authority itself underwent unprecedented transformations and came under intense scrutiny, due to the rise to power of Empress Wu Zetian and the aftermath of her reign. These developments have been the subject of much scholarship in recent decades, yet in spite of the inevitable redundancy of what follows, one must traverse this well-trodden ground in order to follow the trail of the patriarchal robe and the mystique of transmission.

The seventh and early eighth centuries saw the appearance of key elements of the Chan transmission mystique. Bodhidharma and Huike became associated with a special "*Laṅkā*" (*Laṅkāvatāra–sūtra*) transmission, which was coupled with the "East Mountain" succession. The notion of patriarchal succession became more theoretically precise and more detailed, as various versions of the successions, biographies, and doctrines of the patriarchs were advanced. We see Bodhidharma's robe prefigured in the lore of the East Mountain school, and we also see overt reference to Chan patriarchal succession as a counterpart to dynastic succession.

The Biography of Fachong

An early source for the notion of a *Laṅkā* transmission from Bodhidharma to Huike is the biography of Fachong 法沖 (587–665?) in the *Xu gaoseng zhuan.*[90] This biography is one of Daoxuan's later additions to the work, and he concludes with the assumption that Fachong is still living. The biography includes accounts of miraculous powers, one of Daoxuan's favorite themes in his later years, but it is mostly taken up by an account of persons involved in transmission of the *Laṅkāvatāra–sūtra.* Among this group, Huike's descendents are said to be the most prominent. Daoxuan praises Guṇabhadra's (394–468) initial translation of the scripture and says that Bodhidharma later transmitted it as well. It is said that Huike and Huiyu 惠育 (a.k.a. Daoyu) were the two recipients of Bodhidharma's teaching on the *Laṅkā,* but Huiyu remained silent and only Huike had disciples. Among Huike's disciples who are said to have left no written works there are eight names, including a Dhyāna master Can 粲.[91] Four additional disciples are said to have produced texts on the *Laṅkā,* then there is a list of *Laṅkā* commentators who were distantly connected or unconnected with Huike, and an account of his disciple's disciples. The lists conclude with a comment in small characters: "They successively transmitted the lamp down to the present dissemination."[92] Daoxuan uses the term "transmission of the lamp" to refer to other successions as well, but for him the phrase clearly did not mean the exclusive serial transmission that it came to connote in later Chan.[93]

There is some foreshadowing of the later notion of a special "mind-to-mind" transmission, however. Throughout Fachong's biography there is a flavor of secret, esoteric transmission, and it is stressed that the essence of the *Laṅkā* transmission is wisdom that does not depend on words. There are references to people not understanding the scripture or understanding it incorrectly, and it is said that although Fachong produced a commentary, he did so reluctantly. However, he is praised for lecturing on it two hundred times and quoting from it freely. Thus, the biography displays an appreciation for both esoteric transmission from a master to select disciples and for conventional exoteric *upāyas,* such as translations, lectures, and commentaries. In support of convention, there is an episode at the end where Fachong purportedly castigates Xuanzang for not allowing anyone to lecture on old translations of the sūtras, only on new translations (i.e., Xuanzang's). Fachong tells Xuanzang that since he was ordained on the basis of the old translations, he ought to return to lay status and then become reordained on the basis of new translations. This causes Xuanzang to desist.[94]

As Faure points out, Fachong and his group appear to be distinguished from both the traditional *Laṅkā*-related Dilun school of Bodhiruci et al. and from Xuanzang's Yogācāra reformation.[95] Furthermore, Fachong's biography and the latter part of Huike's biography show similar tendencies and affiliations. Hu Shi notes that the latter half of Huike's shows evidence of having been supplemented after the initial completion of the text, so that it could have been added at the same time as Fachong's biography.[96] For example, Huike's biography first states that he left no successors and then goes on to give biographies of other figures, some of whom are clearly successors, and some of whom are also mentioned in Fachong's biography.[97] There are consistent themes in both biographies: *dhūta* practice, doctrinal conservatism, and devaluation of exegesis. Moreover, the latter part of Huike's biography contains the famous passage in which Bodhidharma gives Huike the four-*juan Laṅkā* and says: "I observe that in the land of Han there is only this scripture. The benevolent one who relies [on it] to practice will himself be able to save the world."[98] It is then said that Huike handed down this "abstruse principle" (*xuanli* 玄理). However, Huike also makes a prediction that the *Laṅkā* transmission will degenerate: "After four generations, this scripture will become [merely] nominal. How lamentable!"[99]

In the classic form of the Chan lineage, the next recipient of the transmission would be Sengcan, but the question of whether the various mentions of a Can or Sengcan in the *Xu gaoseng zhuan* can be identified with the Chan patriarch remains vexed.[100] There is, however, a *Xu gaoseng zhuan* biography for the future fourth Chan patriarch, Daoxin 道信 (580–651), that makes no mention of Bodhidharma, Huike, or the *Laṅkā* transmission.[101] As he is about to die, Daoxin is asked about his successor and replies, "Throughout my life I have entrusted [the Dharma] to many."[102]

The Epitaph for Faru

Another important document for reconstructing the development of Chan patriarchal ideology is the late seventh-century *Tang zhongyue shamen Shi Faru chanshi xingzhuang* 唐中岳沙門釋法如禪師行狀 (Epitaph for the Tang [Dynasty] Śramaṇa of the Central Peak, Dhyāna Master Shi Faru).[103] On the basis of a quotation from Huiyuan's *Chan jing* preface, the author of the piece claims that the transmission of the Buddha passed down by Ānanda, Madhyāntika, Śāṇvāsa, and further unidentified generations was then brought by Bodhidharma to China.[104] Also striking is the subsequent succession from Bodhidharma to Ke, Can, Xin, and Ren (Hongren 弘忍), with Faru 法如 (638–689) as Hongren's heir. Moreover, Hongren is designated as a "Patriarchal Master" (*zushi* 祖師).[105]

The transmission is without words, sudden, and esoteric: "In India they passed it down from one to another, from the origin it was [passed down] without the written word. Those who enter this gate transmit only mind [*yi* 意] to each other."[106] This transmission has hidden but extensive soteriological efficacy: "The many beings, in the moment it takes to bend and extend one's arm, immediately attain the fundamental mind [*xin* 心]. The Master takes the one-seal Dharma and secretly seals the minds [*yi* 意] of the many."[107]

In Faru's epitaph there is no mention of a *Laṅkā* transmission, but a eulogy written in 725 for Faru's disciple Yuangui 元珪 cites the same lineage and mentions reliance on the *Laṅkā-sūtra*. However, the mind-to-mind wordless transmission is identified as "one-practice samādhi," which had become a characteristic teaching of the East Mountain school of Daoxin and Hongren. Yuangui is said to be the seventh generation of the transmission in China, and it is said that the masters are "Dharma Lords" in successive generations.[108]

The *Chuan fabao ji*

Perhaps the most influential of the "proto-Chan" texts was the *Chuan fabao ji* 傳法寶紀 (Annals of the Transmission of the Dharma-Jewel) by Du Fei 杜朏, written c. 713.[109] It appears to be the first text to have arranged the patriarchs' biographies in a generational sequence, in the same order as the epitaph for Faru. The names of the Indian patriarchs from the *Chan jing* prefaces are followed by biographies of Bodhidharma, Huike, Sengcan, Daoxin, Hongren and Faru, with the addition of Shenxiu 神秀 (d. 706) as the final of seven successive biographies. However, Shenxiu is not presented as Faru's heir, but as a less senior heir of Hongren who defers to Faru and delays his own transmission of the Dharma for ten years.[110]

Although Shenhui of course takes issue with this latter part of the *Chuan fabao ji* lineage, he and the *Lidai fabao ji* authors drew heavily from its biographies of the first five Chinese generations. They were also influenced by its elitism and its antiscriptural, antiformalist tendencies; the *Chuan fabao ji* is cast in the same esoteric mold as the Faru epitaph, denigrating discursive teaching and emphasizing the secrecy of the Dharma transmission. Du Fei takes care to distinguish the masters from ordinary practitioners and relegates meditational-devotional practice to a lower level:

> During the lifetimes of [Hung]-jen, [Fa]-ju, and Ta-t'ung (= Shen-hsiu), the teachings were opened up to great [numbers of students] without regard to abilities. [These students] were all immediately made to recite the name of the Buddha (*nien fo-ming*). [Those who could be] made to demonstrate [the nature of] the Pure Mind in intimate [conference with the master] were thus qualified to receive transmission of the Dharma, but this [was an eventuality] to be treasured in secret by both master and disciple. [Such transmissions] were never publicly announced.[111]

The *Laṅkā* theme surfaces again, although it is no longer the content and is not yet the symbol of Dharma transmission. Du Fei quotes the *Laṅkāvatāra–sūtra* and uses the *Xu gaoseng zhuan* passage in which Bodhidharma praises the scripture and gives it to Huike. However, he criticizes Daoxuan's inclusion of Bodhidharma's "wall-contemplation" (*biguan* 壁觀) practice and the teachings of the *Erru sixing lun,* saying that these merely reflect the provisional level of Bodhidharma's transmission.[112] Du Fei also twice repeats Huike's prediction in the *Xu gaoseng zhuan* that after four generations the understanding of the *Laṅkā* will become superficial.[113] He introduces a new twist, however, with the story of Bodhidharma's poisoning.[114] This story reflects then-current notions of rivalry between different *Laṅkā* factions, and it serves to showcase the powers of Bodhidharma and his transmission. As discussed earlier, in the *Lidai fabao ji* the poisoning story is elaborated and Dilun masters are pointedly identified as the villains.

In comparing the *Chuan fabao ji* and the *Lengqie shizi ji,* Faure notes that the former is less literary in style, less concerned with doctrine, and focuses instead on the persona of the masters. He writes: "In the *Chuan fabao ji,* what distinguishes Bodhidharma from other *dhyāna* practitioners is not the superiority of his doctrine or his practice but rather the fact that he had been invested with a sacred mission, to transmit the Dharma. This radically new point of view appears to be specifically Chinese. . . .

This almost sacramental nature of the Dharma makes those who possess it exceptional beings: hence the emphasis placed by the *Chuan fabao ji* on legends about Bodhidharma and Huike."[115]

Indeed, in his preface Du Fei suggests that worship of these exceptional beings, like that rendered the Buddhas and bodhisattvas, may be a sufficient cause of enlightenment: "If it were not for the guidance of these perfect ones, it would be difficult to identify [the content of this teaching.] I believe that in the future, spiritual awakening will in some cases be based on the adoration [of former worthies]."[116]

Before turning to the *Lengqie shizi ji,* let us take a quick glance at a text related to the *Chuan fabao ji,* the *Xiande ji yu Shuangfeng shan ta ge tan xuanli shier* 先德集於雙峰山塔各談玄理十二 (Twelve Former Worthies Gather at the Stūpa on Mt. Shuangfeng and Each Discusses the Mysterious Principle).[117] The premise of this short document is that twelve masters from the past gather at Hongren's stūpa, and each speaks a verse on the theme of nondual mind and no-thought; the format thus prefigures the transmission verses of the *Baolin zhuan*. The figures are not a succession of patriarchs, but they are arranged in roughly chronological order. Two names at the head of the list, Pārśva and Aśvaghoṣa, appear in the *Lidai fabao ji* list of Indian patriarchs, as discussed in chapter 4. The names "Neng 能" and "Xiu 秀" in the list are presumably Huineng and Shenxiu, affording a glimpse of the relative harmony that prevailed before Shenhui made the two into rivals for Hongren's transmission.

The *Lengqie shizi ji*

Although the *Chuan fabao ji* sets forth the lineage of what would become known as the Dongshan 東山 or East Mountain tradition, the term itself first appears in other texts of roughly the same early eighth-century vintage.[118] The name is derived from the location of Hongren's monastery, but it was also retrospectively applied to Daoxin's teachings.[119] The *Lengqie shizi ji* 楞伽師資記 (Record of the Masters and Disciples of the *Laṅkā[vatāra-sūtra]*) is the main text in which the *Laṅkā* tradition and a distinct East Mountain tradition are linked and promoted.[120] Reference to the East Mountain teaching occurs prominently in the section on Hongren: "The sixth, the Great Master posthumously called Hongren, of Youju 幽居 monastery on Mt. Shuangfeng of Qizhou in the Tang dynasty, was the successor of Chan Master Xin. The Dharma that Ren transmitted was the subtle Dharma, and when people praised it they called it the Pure Teaching of the East Mountain."[121]

The *Lengqie shizi ji* was written by the monk Jingjue 淨覺 (c. 688–746), who incorporated within it an otherwise nonextant text by his teacher Xuanze 玄賾 (d.u.). Xuanze was one of Hongren's disciples, and Jingjue clearly regards the East Mountain teaching as his own affiliation. The lineage presented by Jingjue differs slightly from previous lists. The most conspicuous change is that the *Laṅkā* translator Guṇabhadra is the first patriarch and Bodhidharma is said to have received the transmission from him. As noted above, the *Xu gaoseng zhuan* biography of Fachong made a similar claim regarding the *Laṅkā* scriptural transmission, without implying that this went along with a special Dharma transmission. Jingjue developed his own ideology of special transmission from the patriarchs to their select disciples, but this was not yet as exclusive as Shenhui's notion of one Dharma-heir in each generation. In the *Lengqie shizi ji* the line of succession remains linear through Huike, Sengcan, Daoxin, and Hongren. However, in the biography of Shenxiu near the end of the work, Shenxiu, Laoan 老安, and Xuanze are named as the three principle heirs of Hongren. Hongren is also quoted as saying that only about ten people would transmit his teachings.[122]

There is also a passage in Jingjue's biography of Hongren in which the patriarch evaluates his ten Dharma heirs. In a lament reminiscent of Confucius' regret for Yan Hui's early death and his assessment of his ten remaining disciples, Hongren says that his best disciples have died, and gives mixed reviews of the survivors.[123] Of the ten, only Shenxiu and Laoan are commended without reservation. However, the master concludes by addressing Xuanze, the eleventh disciple, saying, "Your conjoined practice [of dhyāna and Dharma] will take good care of you. After my nirvāṇa, you and Shenxiu should make the Buddha-sun shine once again and the mind-lamp doubly illuminating."[124] Notably, Jingjue considered himself the disciple of both Xuanze and Shenxiu.

Although Huineng is included in the list of ten, he is characterized along with Faru and the Korean monk Zhide 智德 as "a person of only local distinction."[125] Furthermore, Zhishen 智詵 of Zizhou 資州, who would later be included in the *Lidai fabao ji* lineage, is very faintly praised as "having a literary nature."[126] This, in addition to the explicit point of the attack, may be why Jingjue is singled out for a special denunciation by the *Lidai fabao ji* authors:

> There was a śramaṇa of the Eastern Capital (Luoyang), Master Jingjue, who was the disciple of Chan Master Shenxiu of Yuquan 玉泉 [monastery] and compiled the *Lengqie shizi xuemo ji* 楞伽師資血脈記 (Record of the Lineage of the Masters and Disciples of the *Laṅkā[vatāra-sūtra]*) in one fascicle. He falsely alleged that the Trepiṭaka Guṇabhadra was the first patriarch. I do not know his source, but he deluded and confused later students by saying [Guṇabhadra] was the Patriarchal Master Dharma's (i.e., Bodhidharma's) master. Guṇabhadra was from the first a scripture-translating

> Trepiṭaka, a student of the Lesser Vehicle, not a Chan Master. He translated the *Laṅkā-sūtra* in four fascicles, but he did not give an explanation of the *Laṅkā-sūtra* or transmit it to the Patriarchal Master Dharma. The Patriarchal Master Dharma, from the continuous line of direct transmission of the twenty-eight generations, inherited it from Saṅgharakṣa. Later at the Shaolin Monastery on Mt. Songgao 嵩高, Great Master Huike personally asked Patriarchal Master Dharma about the succession of the direct transmission, and because there is this record [the matter] is clear. When this Master Jingjue falsely alleged that Guṇabhadra was the first patriarch he profoundly confused the study of the Dharma.[127]

The *Lidai fabao ji* authors' indignation over spurious sources is a case of the pot calling the kettle black, and Jingjue's presentation of his lineage is at least somewhat more verifiable than the *Lidai fabao ji* authors' presentation of theirs. In any case, the tradition of ten disciples of Hongren would be repeated in various Chan histories, including the *Lidai fabao ji*, but the names and ordering varied according to the affiliations of the authors. By the end of the eighth century, there was general agreement that Huineng was the sixth patriarch, and Shenxiu was relegated to the ranks of the lesser disciples.

This is the case in the *Lidai fabao ji*, where the ten disciples are listed as Huineng 慧能, Shenxiu 神秀, Zhishen 智詵, Zhide 智德, Xuanze 玄賾, Laoan 老安, Faru 法如, Huizang 慧藏, Xuanyue 玄約, and the layman Liu Zhubu 劉主簿. Huineng is set apart, and to the rest Hongren says, "Although you never left me, each of you is but one aspect (*yifang* 一方) of a Master."[128] In the context of the *Lidai fabao ji*, this appears to be an observation similar to Bodhidharma's comment that each disciple only got one part of him. As possession and division of relics was an important theme throughout Buddhist history, such statements may also reflect uneasy recognition of the inevitable dilution of charisma, akin to anxiety over the decline of the Dharma. In the *Lidai fabao ji*, Hongren's dismissive assessment is mitigated in Zhishen's favor when Hongren's disciples Shenxiu, Xuanyue, Laoan, and Xuanze are shown at a disadvantage in Wu Zetian's court, appearing to have only a conventional level of understanding in comparison to Zhishen.[129]

In the *Lengqie shizi ji*, Jingjue presents what is probably a more accurate view not only of Zhishen but also of Laoan (582–709) (a.k.a. Huian 慧安). Laoan is important because contemporaries, including Wu Zetian, considered him equal in stature to Shenxiu,[130] and he assumes particular significance in relation to the *Lidai fabao ji* because Zongmi would later assert that Wuzhu's true lineage was through a lay disciple of Laoan's.[131] Jingjue's contemporaneous presentation of the relative standing of Hongren's disciples is an invaluable counterweight to the competing post-Shenhui versions of succession.

The rival lineages eventually attained a fixed form and were canonized as history in the *Jingde chuandeng lu*. However, in tracing the theme of transmission of the robe, the most intriguing aspect of Jingjue's legacy is found not in the *Lengqie shizi ji*, but in the lay disciple Li Zhifei's 李知非 preface to Jingjue's commentary on the *Heart Sūtra*.[132] The preface mentions Jingjue's aristocratic background and notes that he studied with Shenxiu, Huian (i.e., Laoan), and Xuanze. Jingjue is designated as Xuanze's "transmission of the lamp disciple" (*chuandeng dizi* 傳燈弟子), and the masters of the *Lengqie shizi ji* lineage are named. This is followed by praise for Hongren, and then this statement: "The fine linen *kāṣāya*, water jar, begging bowl, and pewter [-ringed] staff that Great Master Ze had were all entrusted to Chan Master Jingjue."[133]

In the preface to Jingjue's commentary we find juxtaposition of the notion of a "transmission of the lamp disciple" and the motif of the master giving his personal Dharma belongings to his disciple. However, the robe that is given has more associations with Wu Zetian than with Bodhidharma, and Faure claims that for Jingjue himself it was the *Laṅkā-sūtra* and not the robe that functioned as the sacralized symbol of his heritage. Faure addresses the role of the *Laṅkā-sūtra* in his discussion of the questions raised by the chronology of Jingjue's scriptural interests. Jingjue's progression from a commentary (no longer extant) on the *Vajracchedikā-sūtra*, to the *Lengqie shizi ji*, and finally to a commentary on the *Heart Sūtra*, confounds the notion of *Prajñāpāramitā*/Madhyamaka ascendancy over the *Laṅkā*/Yogācāra exegetical trends. Shenhui's "Southern School" ideology placed the *Prajñāpāramitā* scriptures, especially the *Vajracchedikā*, over the gradualist "Northern School" *Laṅkā-sūtra*. Notably, the *Lidai fabao ji* fails to conform to this implicit *panjiao*, though otherwise so faithful to Shenhui. Although Wuzhu's sermons in the *Lidai fabao ji* are sprinkled with quotations drawn from various *Prajñāpāramitā* scriptures, the *Laṅkā-sūtra* is by far the most frequently quoted source, with and without attribution.

Taking up the question of Jingjue's scriptural allegiances, Faure rejects a hypothetical argument that Jingjue's *Prajñāpāramitā* writings were a concession to lay followers and endorses a point of view proposed by Yanagida:

> The second argument, to which I give my tentative support, holds that Jingjue's thought was deeply coherent and ultimately based on *Prajñāpāramitā* doctrine. The *Record* [i.e., the *Lengqie shizi ji*] did a great deal to bolster the identification of the Chan of the Northern School with the

> *Laṅkāvatāra-sūtra.* But, despite the reference to the *Laṅkāvatāra* in the title of the *Record,* Jingjue quotes this text much less than he did the *Prajñāpāramitā* texts. Jingjue does not seem to have had a great interest in its doctrinal content. We get the impression that for him, as for some of his predecessors, this canonical text is most important for its quasi-magical power and the authority it confers on its possessors. Its transmission is a measure of orthodoxy, a little like that, at the same period, of the Daoist talismanic texts.[134]

The argument that the *Laṅkā* had a talismanic function for Jingjue rests largely on Jingjue's choice of title and first patriarch. These emblematic choices are significant, but within the *Lengqie shizi ji* as a whole the *Laṅkā* is one of a number of threads of transmission. Faure's most compelling arguments show that Jingjue was attempting to negotiate among and reconcile a number of conflicting trends in doctrine and practice. The complexity of *Laṅkā* affiliations emerging from the *Xu gaoseng zhuan* biographies reflects the tension between the Dharma and dhyāna tendencies that Zhiyi also addressed and tried to balance. Historically situated in between Zhiyi's massive system and the Southern School's talismanic phrase "a special transmission outside the scriptures," Jingjue weaves a transmission discourse that is less consistent but was perhaps closer to an actual practice milieu than either. In a passage that Jingjue quotes from Xuanze's *Lengqie renfa zhi,* Shenxiu represents his transmission in the following manner:

> The Great Sage Empress Zetian asked Dhyāna Master Shenxiu: "Whose doctrinal tenet is the Dharma you transmit?" He answered, "I have been favored with the Qizhou East Mountain teachings." [She] asked, "Upon what scriptural patent do you rely?" [He] replied, "I rely upon the one-practice samādhi of the *Wenshu shuo banruo jing* 文殊說般若經 (The Scripture of Mañjuśrī Expounding on the *Prajñā[pāramitā]*)."[135] Zetian said: "If one would speak of cultivation the Way, nothing surpasses the East Mountain teachings."[136]

Earlier in the *Lengqie shizi ji,* the one-practice samādhi of the *Wenshu shou banruo jing* is identified with Daoxin's teachings.[137] Thus, the passage above achieves a synthesis of the East Mountain tradition, Hongren, Daoxin, one-practice samādhi, and the ineffable transmission associated with the *Prajñāpāramitā* tradition, all sheltering under the umbrella of the *Laṅkā.* Not named in any of the transmission passages in the *Lengqie shizi ji,* the *Laṅkā* serves not only as a tradition-sanctioned appeal to a single Indian scriptural authority but also evokes the distant mythical context of the sūtra itself, a place where all Dharmas may be included without conflict. It is also noteworthy that the "East Mountain" seal is impressed on this ideal harmony by the empress herself.

One-practice samādhi and dhyāna are prominent themes throughout the *Lengqie shizi ji,* which warns against reducing dhyāna to any one teaching or practice. Hongren is quoted as saying that what he verifies in his students is none other than the vision of the Dharmakāya: "It is also said: 'The void has neither center nor border, the Buddhas' bodies are also thus.' My sanctioning (*yinke* 印可) of your clear vision of the Buddha-nature is exactly this."[138]

This is followed by another quotation from Hongren, in which the vision of the Dharmakāya is brought home to the individual monk sitting in the meditation hall:

> He also said, "At the same time that you are in the monastery sitting in dhyāna, is your body also sitting in dhyāna beneath the trees of the mountain groves? Are earth, wood, tiles, and stones also able to sit in dhyāna? Are earth, wood, tiles, and stones also able to see forms and hear sounds, wear a robe and hold an alms-bowl? The *Laṅkā-sūtra* reference to the objective (*viṣaya*) Dharmakāya is precisely this."[139]

The tenor of this passage echoes the *Nirvāṇa-sūtra,* resonates with the later story of Huairang's demonstration to Mazu that sitting in meditation to make a Buddha is like polishing a tile to make a mirror, and is amplified in Dōgen's writings.[140] This juxtaposition between "sanctioning" the vision of Buddha-nature and probing the nonsource of the vision points to a tension that would emerge more clearly with the subitist orthodoxy of the "Southern School." The uncontained and all-encompassing Dharmakāya is/not realized in a monk in a robe sitting in a monastery, but as soon as the question of sanctioning this realization arises, then mind, body (gender), robe, and institutional context suddenly become as distinct and obdurate as earth, wood, tiles, and stones. Justification for the objective "means" of monastery and meditating monk was only to be found within the "gradualist" confines of Two Truths soteriology.

In Jingjue's time the problem of validating and maintaining a "special transmission" that was not dependent on a particular set of scriptures or an orthopraxy was just beginning to become apparent. He was able to articulate the various tendencies that would go into the formation of a new doctrinal compound, which he unified under the label of the "Southern School" of *Laṅkā-sūtra* exegesis, and in doing so he made its internal contradictions more obvious. Faure argues that this was both prescient and self-defeating:

> Thus, several major themes in the *Record* would give birth to doctrines held by branches of Chan violently opposed to each other. Was Jingjue unaware of these latent contradictions, or was he trying to reconcile them by an appropriate synthesis? The second hypothesis seems closer to the truth. But Jingjue, in his desire to establish a school, underestimated the strength of the centrifugal forces at work in his doctrine and could achieve only a superficial compromise. This weakness mars the *Record* seriously, and explains in part its rapid descent into oblivion.[141]

Jingjue's inclusive version of the "Southern School" was superseded by Shenhui's polemical one. In Shenhui's version, the tension between objective (provisional) and "special" (immediate) means of teaching and transmission was resolved in the manner of the *Chuan fabao ji,* by obscuring it in a thick atmosphere of patriarchal mystique. Out of this atmosphere there arose in turn Northern and Southern, *mozhao* 默照 (silent illumination) and *kanhua* 看話 (examining sayings), and kōans and "just sitting."

Inscriptions for "Northern School" Monks

Before proceeding to discussion of Shenhui's "Southern School" polemic, I would like to touch on the role played by memorial inscriptions in shaping the conception of patriarchal transmission. In the early decades of the eighth century, there were a number of inscriptions written for monks who would later be designated "Northern School," that is, Shenxiu and his heirs. In these inscriptions, the subject was linked to a special lineal transmission from Bodhidharma and this lineage portrayed in highly exalted terms.[142] Let us take a look at the exaltation of transmission and lineage in two inscriptions, one for Shenxiu and one for his disciple.

The *Jingzhou Yuquansi Datong chanshi beiming bing xu* 荊州玉泉寺大通禪師碑銘并序 (Stele Inscription for Chan Master Datong [Shenxiu] of Yuquan Monastery in Jingzhou, with preface) was written by the eminent literatus Zhang Yue 張說 (667–730).[143] In it, the pedigree of the East Mountain transmission is listed in what would become the standard form: Bodhidharma, Huike, Sengcan, Daoxin, and Hongren, and only Shenxiu is designated as Hongren's heir. There is a hint of mystery in the passage regarding Hongren's transmission to Shenxiu, which recalls the esotericism of the *Chuan fabao ji* and prefigures the transmission in the *Platform Sūtra.* Hongren praises Shenxiu and invites him to share his seat, and after having been thus elevated to equality with his master, Shenxiu departs in tears and is "sequestered in secrecy."[144] There is also reference to mind-transmission (*yichuan* 意傳), described as follows: "Powerfully maintaining virtue, for ten thousand kalpas [the Tathāgatas] have long handed down the Dharma-seal, in one moment they suddenly confer the Dharmakāya."[145] This phrase captures the ideal complementarity between the temporal esoteric transmission of the patriarchs, and the "sudden and perfect" awakening that it conveys. Significantly, Shenxiu's transmission is also linked to the *Laṅkā:* "He upheld the *Laṅkā*, transmitting it as the mind-essence. 'To go beyond this—there is no longer anyone who knows.'"[146]

Inscriptions written for Shenxiu's disciple Puji 普寂 (651–739) were implicated in Shenhui's denunciations of Puji and Shenxiu. In an oft-quoted epitaph written by the imperial prince Li Yong 李邕 in 742, Puji was put on a par with the reigning emperor Xuanzong.[147] Another inscription for Puji, the *Diqizu Dazhao heshang jimie ri zhai zanwen* 第七祖大照和尚寂滅日齋讚文 (Funeral Eulogy for the Seventh Patriarch, the Venerable Dazhao), draws a similar parallel:

> Only Heaven is great, and Yao alone corresponded to it. Only the Buddha is saintly, and Chan [teachings] alone succeed to it. Therefore in the West in India [the masters] handed down the trust, five suns illuminating the early days, and in the East in China [the masters] transmitted the lamp, seven patriarchs brightening imperial fortunes. Our seventh patriarch, State Preceptor of three courts, the Venerable Dazhao, has departed from the two extremes, transcended all *bhūmis,* attained the compassion of the Tathāgatas, and entered into the super-knowledge of the Buddhas.[148]

What appears to be *lèse majesté* may instead reflect the long-standing eulogistic tradition of taking the imperial lineage as the paradigm of honor, so that the parallel placement of the subject's lineage becomes a sincere form of flattery. However, these eulogists' willingness to insert Dharma lineages in places formerly reserved for aristocratic lineages appears to have set off a train of both imitations and reactions in Buddhist circles. Even before Shenhui's denunciation, two Tiantai nuns were said to have repudiated Puji's claims to spiritual authority, and it was said that even Puji's disciple Yixing 一行 (683–727) supported them.[149] In time, Puji was chiefly remembered as the object of Shenhui's most virulent diatribes and colorful accusations.[150]

In the next section, we examine Shenhui's claims in more detail and ask how Shenhui's patriarchal ideology, no less hubristic than that expressed in Puji's epitaphs, was able to supersede its originating "other." Faure underscores the key role that scapegoating played and continues to play in the creation of a Chan/Zen identity: "By assigning the role of scapegoat to the Northern School, which thus became the emblematic figure of heterodoxy, one could succeed in limiting in time and space those deviationist risks (intellectualism, quietism, secularization, etc.) to which Chan is constantly exposed. . . . This exorcism has permitted the maintenance to our own time of the myth of an idealized, 'pure' Chan, a doctrine uncontaminated by its relationship to history, a school from which any power connections would be, if not completely rejected, at least subordinated to the search for a transcendent truth."[151]

Faure argues that prior to Shenhui's scapegoating of Shenxiu and his heirs a different kind of Chan identity had been emerging, one that was characterized by eclecticism rather than "purist" sectarianism. Both Faure and McRae have demonstrated that many of the teachings associated with the "Southern School," including its trademark subitism, were anticipated in the far-ranging doctrines found in "Northern School" works.[152] Faure shows that the lives and works of Shenxiu and his disciples were enriched by Tiantai, Pure Land, Vinaya and Tantric influences.[153] However, he asserts, as the "will to orthodoxy" gained force these interdependent doctrinal currents separated into schools: "The establishment of patriarchal lineages within every school in the eighth century tended to conceal any lateral relations among the various patterns of thought. In theory, only vertical relationships remained, those between master and disciple. Although there are reasons for their existence, this primacy given to genealogy and the tree-shaped schemas it imposes do not permit us to see the rhizomes, the tangled web of influences actually at work beneath the surface."[154]

Faure maintains that, contrary to Chan sectarian mythology, Shenxiu's heirs were not irrevocably stigmatized by Shenxiu's association with Wu Zetian and were not vanquished by Shenhui. Many withdrew to various mountains and declined to become embroiled. Rather than to dishonor and defeat, Faure attributes the waning influence of Shenxiu's remaining heirs at court to the change of generations and issues. Xuanzong was more attuned to Yixing's practical esoteric Buddhism than to the intellectual heritage of Yixing's master Puji. Moreover, the officials who supported Shenxiu and his heirs were supplanted by a younger set of successful examinees and by the resurgent aristocratic faction.[155] In spite of "Southern School" dominance of late eighth-century Chan discourse, Shenxiu's heirs continued to flourish, particularly at Nanyue, and lent their subtle influence to a number of sectarian branches, including the Bao Tang.

SHENHUI'S RHETORIC

In this section I summarize Shenhui's key teachings and his impact and then turn to the *Lidai fabao ji* authors' representation of him. Through a fantastic manipulation of the "imaginary cultic history" of Bodhidharma's robe, the *Lidai fabao ji* authors managed to include Huineng in their transmission narrative. There was no similar attempt to claim Shenhui in Wuzhu's lineage, but he stands out as the only nonlineage master whose words and deeds are featured. This tribute to Shenhui is ambiguous at best, as we will see.

Although Shenhui began his campaign against the "Northern School" in 730, the most famous scene of Shenhui's revelations about Hongren's heirs was the *wuzhe dahui* 無遮大會 (unrestricted great assembly) of 732 at the Dayun 大雲 monastery in Huatai 滑臺. As recorded by his disciple Dugu Pei 獨孤沛, the work entitled *Putidamou nanzong ding shifei lun* 菩提達摩南宗定是非論 (Treatise Determining the True and False about the Southern School of Bodhidharma; hereafter, *Ding shifei lun*) purports to contain Shenhui's answers to questions at Huatai and on previous occasions.[156]

Shenhui asserted that Buddhist history had been misrepresented, and his contending version undercut the spiritual legitimacy of Shenxiu and his heirs. He fused historical and doctrinal claims into an exclusive notion of patriarchal succession in which only one patriarch in each generation received mind-to-mind transmission of the true Dharma from the previous patriarch, all the way back to Śākyamuni's transmission to Mahākāśyapa. According to Shenhui, in China this unique transmission and Bodhidharma's robe of verification had been passed from Huike, Sengcan, Daoxin, and Hongren to the "sixth patriarch," Huineng. Shenhui also claimed to be Huineng's disciple. In fashioning his own version of the lineage and biographies of the ancestral patriarchs of the Chan school, Shenhui drew from the *Chuan fabao ji* and the *Lengqie shizi ji*.

In 753 Shenhui was temporarily banished from the capital by order of Emperor Xuanzong. This has generally been attributed to vengeful motives on the part of "Northern School" followers, but the problem may have been the size of Shenhui's audiences rather than their views. In any case, his exile was hardly onerous. He was given a private audience with the emperor prior to his relocation, and he was then sent to four provincial monasteries over the course of several years. McRae writes of this period: "Far from being a 'banishment,' the impression given by the description of Shenhui's movements is that of an imperially sponsored regional lecture tour."[157] Of course, we must keep in mind that one of the main sources of this impression is Shenhui's fifth-generation heir Zongmi, who would have wanted to present the matter in the best possible light.

Shenhui was restored to imperial favor after the An Lushan rebellion of 755, when his success in attracting large audiences to the ordination platform was seen as an asset rather than a threat. While in theory the implications of Shenhui's teachings undercut the boundary between lay and ordained, ordination remained a social privilege affording exemption from conscription and taxation. It was also an expensive privilege, and after the rebellion sales of ordination certificates became a means by which the Tang could raise short-term revenue for the war effort against the rebel forces. Shenhui's contributions were recognized by Emperor Suzong 肅宗 (r. 756–762), though, if we accept the Longmen stele inscription date of 758 for Shenhui's death, then his fund-raising career was rather brief.[158]

This inscription (dated 765) refers to Shenhui as the seventh patriarch and Huineng's heir, but contending lineages were already in the making. Shenhui's legacy is a topic of ongoing discussion in Chan studies, but it seems clear that Shenhui's doctrinal and genealogical claims became influential only to be modified and superseded.[159]

When Shenhui denounced "Northern School" practice as dualistic striving to purify oneself of adventitious defilements, he drew from and simplified Yogācāra, Tiantai, and *tathāgatagarbha* doctrines. He claimed that "purity Chan" was counterproductive insofar as it focused attention on the distinction between wisdom and delusion, since this distinction was itself the only delusion. His charge that Shenxiu and his heirs advocated such a notion of practice has been effectively challenged.[160] The tenets of sudden awakening and realization of Buddha-nature were not new, but Shenhui set these rubrics in a context of imminent crisis, in which both the historical fate of the Dharma and the personal awakening of the listener were implicated. This is the context of the "sudden teaching" (*dunjiao* 頓教) referred to in the title of Shenhui's *Platform Address*.[161]

The scapegoating of the Northern School helped fuel the sense of urgency. In the records of Shenhui's debates and in the *Lidai fabao ji* record of Wuzhu's debates, doctrinal arguments and ad hominem attacks go hand in hand. The image of Shenhui as a pugnacious adversary was apparently still current at the time the *Lidai fabao ji* was written, as shown in the following passage:

> When the Venerable Hui (i.e., Shenhui) was in Jing 荊 subprefecture, there were men of the Western Kingdoms, the Bhadra (Elder) Kaśya, Anshuti, and about twenty others, who went up to the place where the Venerable was expounding on the Dharma and asked, "The First Patriarch's *kāṣāya* robe of verification—has the Venerable got it or not?" [Shenhui] replied, "It is not at my place." He then asked the Bhadra and the others, "Where have you come from?" Kaśya replied, "We have come from Jiannan." [Shenhui] asked, "Do you know Chan Master Kim?" Kaśya replied, "We are all the Venerable Kim's disciples." The Venerable Hui asked, "Explain how Chan Master Kim teaches people to study the Way." Kaśya replied, "'When a bit of ignorance emerges, a bit of nirvāṇa sinks, when a bit of prajñā emerges, a bit of ignorance sinks. When there is thought it is like the face of a mirror.'"
>
> The Venerable Hui shouted at him, "Don't speak such empty prattle! Your name is Kaśya, a Brāhmanical sort of name, [so one would think that] surely you had some intelligence, but you are nothing but a bed-wetting Brāhman!"[162]

The *Lidai fabao ji* authors caricature Shenhui's belligerent manner and the censorious quality of his nondual doctrine. Moreover, stealing Shenhui's own robe rodomontade, they imply that his attitude was due to a secret sore spot—he claimed to be Huineng's heir, but he did not have *the* robe. The *Lidai fabao ji* authors' ungrateful handling of the progenitor of their discourse is a good example of the effect of Shenhui's rhetoric, which set off a kind of "cultural revolution" in Buddhist soteriology. McRae describes the effect as follows:

> In combination with his doctrine of subitism, the very heat of Shen-hui's criticism of gradualism had a rhetorical impact of the highest significance: by publicly criticizing one faction's meditation teachings he made all the members of the growing Ch'an school more aware of the external expression—the packaging, if you will—of their ideas and modes of practice. After Shen-hui, Ch'an masters learned to protect themselves from criticism by avoiding dualist formulations. . . . This imposition of the avoidance of dualistic formulations, which I call the rule of rhetorical purity, was one of Shenhui's most important areas of impact on Chinese Ch'an.[163]

This "rule of rhetorical purity" structures an increasingly complex game of "doing things with words" in Chan worlds/works, where every encounter was a chance to play Vimalakīrti. Probing the deeper ramifications of this orthodoxy, Faure has explored the complicated effects of the denial or inversion of conventional means that followed in the wake of what he calls the "rhetoric of immediacy." His deconstruction of the paradoxes of this rhetoric is founded on the recognition that the distinctive Chan idiom depends on the denial of intermediate stages and mediating functions of practice. In other words, Chan rhetoric of the "sudden" attempts to preclude provisional truth and gradual practice. Faure argues that this resulted in various forms of the "return of the repressed" in which the Chan master, rather than Buddhas and bodhisattvas, became the focus of sometimes bizarre forms of devotion, representation, and propitiation. He maintains that the "rhetoric of immediacy" was a further extension of the denial of hierarchy and multiplicity already intrinsic to Buddhist discourse:

> One may reinterpret from this point of view the Chan discourse on nonduality, "returning to the principle," as a makeshift response to the actual situation provoked by the epistemological cut initiated by the doctrine of the Buddha-nature and leading to the theory of the twofold truth. In theory, the two truths are affirmed only to be negated by the Middle Way, which consists in seizing them simultaneously while acknowledging their hierarchy. In practice, however, and more precisely in Chan practice, conventional truth tends to be negated for the sake of ultimate truth.[164]

The *Lidai fabao ji* is one of the first works after Shenhui to deploy this epistemological cut in the service of sectarianism. Wuzhu's sermons depend on negation of the conventional in two ways: first, through criticism of conventional practices and forms and, second, through constant recourse to apophasis. As noted in chapter 4, Wuzhu tells his lay supporters that the conventional practices of confession, repentance, and prayer are delusory. He continues this lecture in a Shenhui-like manner, exhorting his listeners to realize their true natures:

> How about if you *dānapati* (lay donors) root out the source of delusory views and awaken to your unborn substance? . . . If one experiences the twin illumination of the Two Truths, then one truly sees the Buddha. If you *dānapati* would only rely on this Dharma this instant without delay, then even if the border is closed and we are kept far apart, we will always see each other without any alienation. If you dare disregard this meaning, you will be swept along by sense-defilements, anxieties and strife will be produced, and the stain of arrogance will be unlimited. Then, though we might often be face to face, it is as difficult to meet as the states of Chu and Yue.[165]

Wuzhu's rhetoric illustrates what Faure calls "seizing the Two Truths simultaneously," but he also vividly evokes the suffering connected with mundane states of mind and recommends the practice of meditation as a means, something that the rule of rhetorical purity would eventually purge. More significantly, he offers himself as a refuge. This *upāya* is accomplished by the rhetoric of immediacy itself—in the sun of wisdom, the twin illumination of the Two Truths, there is no separation between Wuzhu and his *dānapati.*

At the same time, in creating the historical background for Wuzhu's teachings, the *Lidai fabao ji* authors reveal their concerns about the contradictions inherent in the rhetoric of immediacy. They make Shenhui speak for the dilemma created by his own rhetoric—why and how does one preach a truth that is intrinsic to each member of the audience? In later Chan literature, nearly every Chan master proves his mettle by sporting with this paradox (why *did* Bodhidharma come from the West?), but here it is still relatively fresh. The *Lidai fabao ji* authors' approach is characteristically direct, yet wary. Their section on Shenhui begins with a description of his popular sermons, and Shenhui is made to speak his ultimate truth in Two Truths terms. On the one hand, he speaks of "realizing for oneself," but the *Lidai fabao ji* authors also make him take responsibility for the other hand, teaching followers how to do it. Shenhui opens up an immanent and ambiguous space for the mediations of moral discipline and meditation, and for the mediating act of expressing the sudden:

> The Venerable Shenhui of Heze monastery in the Eastern Capital [Luoyang] would set up an [ordination] platform every month and expound on the

> Dharma for people, knocking down "Purity Chan" and upholding "Tathāgata Chan." He upheld direct experience and verbal explanation—regarding precepts, meditation, and wisdom, he did not knock down verbal explanation. He said, "Just as I am speaking now is none other than *śīla* (moral discipline), just as I am speaking now is none other than samādhi (meditation), just as I am speaking now is none other than prajñā (wisdom)." He expounded the Dharma of no-thought and upheld seeing the nature.[166]

Prajñā is and is not mediated by Shenhui's speaking—but what if this aporia is spoken by a member of the audience? The *Lidai fabao ji* justifies the act of speaking for nonduality, at least for the Chan master, and this passage does echo the teachings in Shenhui's *Platform Address*.[167] However, the *Lidai fabao ji* authors frequently set up other masters for a fall, and the series of episodes that follow show Shenhui at a disadvantage. Shenhui is made to yield the figurative high seat of the Southern School to Wuzhu, saying, "There is yet someone who will explain it [fully], I really cannot presume to explain it."[168]

Moreover, in a passage alluded to in chapter 4, the *Lidai fabao ji* authors further dramatize Wuzhu's advent by transfiguring a portion of the *Ding shifei lun*. The *Lidai fabao ji* passage centers on the argument between Shenhui and Chongyuan about Cunda, the lay follower who served the Buddha his last meal. At first the *Lidai fabao ji* appears to reproduce the *Ding shifei lun* passage, introducing Cunda with a quote from the *Nirvāṇa-sūtra:* "Homage to Cunda, homage to Cunda, his body was that of an ordinary mortal, his mind was the same as the Buddha's mind."[169] However, after this the two versions diverge. The *Ding shifei lun* passage is as follows:

> Dharma Master Chongyuan asked, "Have you seen (*jian* 見) the Buddha-nature? His Reverence (i.e., Shenhui) answered, "I have seen it." Dharma Master Chongyuan asked, "Did you see it inferentially (*biliang* 比量), or did you see it directly (*xianliang* 現量)?" His Reverence answered, "I saw it inferentially." [The Dharma Master] also rebuked, "What is comparison (*bi* 比), and what is estimation (*liang* 量)?" His Reverence answered, "That which is called 'comparison' is comparison to Cunda. That which is called 'estimation' is equivalence to Cunda." Dharma Master Chongyuan said, "Did you definitely see it?" His Reverence answered, "I definitely saw it." Dharma Master Chongyuan asked, "In what fashion did you see it?" His Reverence answered, "In no [describable] fashion." Dharma Master Chongyuan was silent and did not speak. His Reverence saw that the other was silent, did not understand what he had said, and was not going to ask anything more.[170]

And this is the version in the *Lidai fabao ji:*

Dharma Master Yuan then asked, "Has the Venerable Hui perceived (*jian* 見) Buddha-nature or not?" Hui (i.e., Shenhui) replied, "I have perceived it." [Yuan] asked, "In what way do you perceive, is it by the eyes that you have perceived, or by the ears or the nose, etc., that you have perceived?" Hui replied, "Perceiving is not so quantifiable, perceiving is simply perceiving." [Yuan] asked, "Do you perceive the same as Cunda, or not?" Hui replied, "I perceive by inference (*biliang jian* 比量見). Comparison (*bi* 比) means 'comparable to Cunda,' estimation/knowing (*liang* 量) is 'equivalent to Cunda.' I dare not make a final conclusion."

He was further questioned by Dharma Master Yuan, "Chan Master, has the First Patriarch's *kāṣāya* robe been transmitted or not?" Hui replied, "It has been transmitted. When it is not transmitted, the Dharma will be broken off." [Yuan] asked, "Has the Chan Master got it or not?" [Shenhui] replied, "It is not at my place." Dharma Master Yuan asked, "Who has got this *kāṣāya* robe?" Hui replied, "Someone has got it. In due course it should be apparent. When this person expounds on the Dharma, the true Dharma (*zhengfa* 正法) will flow forth, and false Dharmas will perish of themselves. In order to further the great work of the Buddha-Dharma, he is hidden and has not yet come out."[171]

While in the *Ding shifei lun* Shenhui is shown repeatedly baffling Chongyuan with his profundity and quick responses, in the *Lidai fabao ji* Shenhui submits to an interrogation and ends by giving a prophetic endorsement of Wuzhu. There is no need to belabor the motives for such different portrayals, but the question remains—why Cunda?[172]

Both "Northern" and "Southern" Chan monks were very fond of evoking the lay paragon Vimalakīrti, who used nonduality to cut both ways. Instead, Shenhui claimed fraternity with the layperson who gave the Buddha his last and fatal meal. Shenhui drew this example of Buddha-nature from the *Nirvāṇa-sūtra,* in which Cunda's role is praised—he is said to be a Buddha with a human body. McRae discusses the symbolism of Shenhui's use of Cunda as a model, arguing that there is an implied homology between Shenhui himself as Cunda and Huineng as the Buddha. Even more significantly, this identification allowed Shenhui to claim spiritual authority commensurate with the enlightenment of a Buddha, while at the same time claiming to be an ordinary human being without the powers of a Buddha-body.[173]

The figure of the lay devotee who kills the Buddha with his offering is oddly evocative of the Saṅgha perpetually in danger of being killed by kindness, done in by its great wealth and accessibility. The figure of Cunda also embodies the interplay of erasure and doubling—the one responsible for the Buddha's death is identical to the Buddha. And in the context of Chan inversion of symbols, one without the physical characteristics of a

Buddha is the true Buddha. These doublings and inversions are also seen in the *Lidai fabao ji* authors' complex handling of the possibly nonexistent relationship between Wuzhu and Wuxiang. Wuzhu is said to be nearly identical to Wuxiang in appearance, to have understood him immediately, and, at the same time, is said to eclipse Wuxiang.

Cunda's multivalent position also recalls Linji's 臨濟 famous injunction, "If you meet the Buddha, kill the Buddha," pointing to the unreality of reified notions of the Buddha, the immediate destruction of such delusions in the face of Buddha-nature, and the lack of any Buddha that can be killed. The notion of the sudden transmission of the Dharma from one patriarch to the next is founded on the same deconstruction as "killing the Buddha"—all the apparent elements of the interchange are subject to the operations of Mādhyamika-style dialectic, both/neither existing, nor transmitting/killing, dependent on each other in relative identity and/not self-identity.[174] This is also reflected in the twin motifs of mutual recognition and violent conflict between master and disciple that is played out in encounter dialogue literature such as the *Linji lu* 臨濟錄 (The Record of Linji).

Shenhui's parables and polemics cannot be reduced either to elegant abstractions about identity and difference or to stark one-upmanship, but neither can they be differentiated from these extremes. The following exchange on the Middle Path from the "Miscellaneous Dialogues" is a good illustration of the subitist doctrine of mutual coinherence of extremes brought to life in an antagonistic encounter:

> Dharma Master Jian of Mount Lu asked, "What is the meaning of the Middle Path?" Answer: "It is the extremes." Question: "I just asked you about the meaning of the Middle Path. Why do you answer that it is the extremes?" Answer: "The Middle Path you just mentioned is necessarily dependent on the meaning of the extremes. Without depending on the meaning of the extremes one cannot posit the Middle Path."[175]

Shenhui makes his point about the interdependence and therefore lack of inherent identity of the concepts of path and progress, but this could apply as well to the "no place" in between the two extremes he taught—immediate Buddha-nature of and for everyone, and strictly serial identical patriarchal transmission. Shenhui preached his message of the single line of true transmission from the ordination platform, and the drama of the patriarchal robe was set against ceremonies of mass tonsuring and the donning of temporary robes. The audience—lay and ordained, intrinsic Buddhas and renewable bodhisattvas—were excluded from and supported by this exclusive transmission as they crowded the ordination assemblies of Chan masters.

Depictions of mass ordination from wall murals at Dunhuang and Yulin create harmonious composition out of hierarchical interrelated clusters—the central image of Maitreya flanked by bodhisattvas and arhats, the groups of women and men awaiting tonsure, the woman at the Buddha's right hand and the man at his left undergoing tonsure while monks hold up robes for them, and the rows of folded robes and mendicants' vessels.[176] We may imagine this detailed and crowded visionary setting as the context at work within Shenhui's Middle Path, where the exclusive/inclusive contradiction inherent in the bodhisattva precepts engendered the extremes of patriarchal transmission and the formless precepts.

INCONCEIVABLE ROBES IN THE *VAJRASAMĀDHI-SŪTRA* AND THE *PLATFORM SŪTRA*

One of Shenhui's key influences appears to have been the *Vajrasamādhi-sūtra.*[177] This late seventh-century apocryphon points toward the signature subitism of eighth-century Chan and also reinterprets or questions traditional symbols of Buddhist authority. In one such passage the features of ordinary monasticism, including the monk's robe, are held to be unnecessary for liberation:

> Although he does not go forth into homelessness (*pravrajita*) he is no longer part of the household. For this reason, while he does not wear the dharma-robes and neither observes all the Prātimokṣa precepts [monk's disciplinary rules] nor participates in the Poṣada [fortnightly religious observance], he does not engage in personal licentiousness in his own mind and obtains the fruition of sainthood. . . . Taeryŏk Bodhisattva remarked, "This is inconceivable! Even though such a person has not gone forth into homelessness, he cannot but have gone forth. Why is this? He has entered the domicile of nirvāṇa, where he dons the robe of the tathāgatas and sits on the bodhi-seat (*bodhimaṇḍa*). Such a person should be worshipped respectfully even by śramaṇas."[178]

The figure who wears the "robe of the tathāgatas" is not an exception who proves the rule like Vimalakīrti, but neither is he an ordinary monk. Huineng, the archetypal Chan patriarch, is the embodiment of one who "cannot but have gone forth," for he is an illiterate who receives the robe and the Dharma while a layman in the monastery. As McRae says, "Huineng has no capabilities or characteristics other than his enlightened mind; he represents nothing but enlightened potentiality."[179] For the purposes of the Chan ideology of the patriarchy, the key claim in the *Vajrasamādhi-sūtra* is that the one wearing the "robe of the tathāgatas" is one to whom monks in ordinary Dharma-robes should pay homage.[180]

In both Shenhui's writings and the *Lidai fabao ji,* Huineng is not ordained until after he has received transmission from Hongren and then only when begged to do so by an eminent monk who wishes to become his disciple. This loosening of the link between ordination and status as a realized person is exaggerated even further in the *Lidai fabao ji,* and Zongmi faulted the Bao Tang precisely for tonsuring and conferring robes on people without requiring of them any evidence of Buddhist practice. The *Lidai fabao ji* authors and Zongmi were perhaps the most explicit of the disputants over the implications of Shenhui's writings, but they articulated a tension that was far more comprehensive.

On the one hand, the growing significance attached to lay retreats for bodhisattva precepts ordination meant that, as Huineng says in the *Platform Sūtra,* "if you wish to practice, it is all right to do so as laymen; you don't have to be in a temple."[181] The account of Layman Pang, whose entire family was able to manifest deep realization in everyday encounters, is a paradigmatic example of idealization of the ones who "cannot but have gone forth" and the monastery without walls. On the other hand, as institutional means of marking legitimacy were challenged, authoritative transmission and transmission of authority became more problematic, and this intensified the competition between competing ideologies.

Shenhui's account of the transmission of the patriarchal robe emerged as one of the successful ideologies, in part through the vehicle of the *Platform Sūtra,* a text that did not endorse Shenhui's patriarchal status. Regarding the relationship between Shenhui and the *Platform Sūtra,* Yanagida Seizan has offered different theories over the years, initially arguing that although the *Platform Sūtra* has obvious affinities with Shenhui's writings, it is actually the product of a member or members of the Niutou 牛頭 school lineage who reworked Shenhui's symbolic and rhetorical framework and used it to promote a more sophisticated doctrine and lineage.[182] He later surmised that it was written by a third generation legitimate successor to Huineng as a direct challenge to Shenhui's claim to Huineng's doctrine and lineage.[183] More recently, Yanagida has stated that, whatever the origins of the *Platform Sūtra,* there are no traces of Huineng's doctrine and lineage that can be separated from Shenhui's writings.[184]

The earliest extant versions of the *Platform Sūtra* are roughly contemporaneous with the *Lidai fabao ji,*[185] but the *Lidai fabao ji* account relies on Shenhui more heavily. Below, corresponding passages from the *Platform Sūtra* and the *Lidai fabao ji* illustrate the relative similarity of their accounts of Huineng's inheritance of the robe and their subsequent divergence. In the *Platform Sūtra,* Huineng tells his story from the platform of a bodhisattva precepts ordination assembly as a prelude to his sermon.

> At midnight the Fifth Patriarch called me into the hall and expounded the *Diamond Sūtra* to me. Hearing it but once, I was immediately awakened, and that night I received the Dharma. None of the others knew anything about it. Then he transmitted to me the Dharma of Sudden Enlightenment and the robe, saying: "I make you the Sixth Patriarch. The robe is the proof and is to be handed down from generation to generation. My Dharma must be transmitted from mind to mind. You must make people awaken to themselves. . . . If you stay here there are people who will harm you. You must leave at once."[186]

The corresponding passage from the *Lidai fabao ji* is as follows:

> In the night he was covertly summoned to [Hongren's] room, and when they had spoken together for three days and three nights, [Hongren] entrusted the Dharma and *kāṣāya* robe to him [and said], "You are the Great Master of this world, and thus I command you to depart quickly."[187]

At the end of the *Platform Sūtra,* when Huineng is on the point of death and has been asked who will inherit the robe and the Dharma, he says:

> The robe may not be handed down. In case you do not trust in me, I shall recite the verses of the preceding five patriarchs, composed when they transmitted the robe and the Dharma. If you depend on the meaning of the verse of the first patriarch, Bodhidharma, then there is no need to hand down the robe.[188]

While this is the end of the line for the robe in the *Platform Sūtra,* in the *Lidai fabao ji* it is just the beginning. When Huineng leaves Caoqi to go back to Xinzhou 新州, where his reliquary stūpa has been prepared, the Caoqi monks ask him about the succession:

> "Do not ask. After this, hardships will arise in great profusion. How often have I faced death on account of this robe? At Master Xin's (i.e. Daoxin's) place it was stolen three times, at Master Ren's (i.e. Hongren's) place it was stolen three times, and now at my place it has been stolen six times. But at last no one will steal this robe of mine, for a woman has taken it away. So don't ask me any more."[189]

The woman is Empress Wu Zetian, who is to give the robe to Zhishen 智詵 (609–702), Wuzhu's great-grandfather in the Dharma. To understand the significance of the line "a woman has taken it away,"[190] we must grapple with complex legacy of Wu Zetian. As we saw in chapter 4, within the context of *mofa* symbolism monks' robes became indices of corruption or purity. I would suggest that the mystique of the "robe of the tathāgatas" and Shenhui's/Huineng's patriarchal robe reflects the need to counter the "dilution of the charisma" of the Buddhist monk. As the number of the ordained grew, and as Buddhist institutions became part of the social and economic fabric of the polity, there was a certain disenchantment that went along with the need for regularization and rationalization of Buddhist practices. In the next section, we look at this disenchantment in relation to Wu Zetian's attempt to fashion a new order of Buddhist elites.

ROBES PURPLE AND GOLD

As introduced at the outset of this study, the *Lidai fabao ji*'s most frequently disputed claim involves the fate of Bodhidharma's robe. The *Lidai fabao ji* authors averred that in 692 Bodhidharma's robe was sent by its legitimate trustee, Huineng, to the court of Empress Wu Zetian 武則天 (r. 684–705). The empress was said to have later bestowed it on Zhishen 智詵 (609–702), who was thus claimed to be the seventh patriarch in the lineage of the Bao Tang school. The *Lidai fabao ji* authors further claim that Zhishen passed the robe to Chuji 處寂 (669–736), who passed it to Wuxiang, who passed it finally to Wuzhu. The genealogical implications are complicated by the fact that Zhishen was actually Huineng's fellow-disciple. Just as the Bao Tang followers took Shenhui's doctrine to its logical extreme by advocating radically antinomian "formless" practice, so too they tried, by the device of Empress Wu's mediation, to extend the life of Shenhui's robe beyond the sixth generation.[191] Let us turn to an examination of the passage in the *Lidai fabao ji* that develops this claim.

According to the *Lidai fabao ji* authors, Zhishen was invited to Empress Wu's court, where he encountered the challenge of an Indian Trepiṭaka with magical powers. Reading Zhishen's mind, the Trepiṭaka detects that the Chan master is pining for home and taunts him about attachment. The Trepiṭaka boasts that he can identify anything that Zhishen can bring to mind and Zhishen amiably agrees. Zhishen then defeats the Indian master in an exchange reminiscent of the meeting between Huzi and a shaman as related in the *Zhuangzi*.[192] Zhishen's success brings him to the attention of the empress, with whom he engages in a kind of encounter dialogue:

> [Empress Wu] Zetian saw that the Trepiṭaka had taken refuge in Chan Master Shen. Zetian submitted a question to all the *bhadanta:* "Do the Venerables have desires, or not? Shenxiu 神秀, Xuanyue 玄約, Laoan 老安 and Xuanze 玄賾 all said, "We have no desires." Zetian asked Chan Master Shen, "Does the Venerable have desires, or not?" Chan Master Shen, fearing that he would not be allowed to return home, complied with the will of Zetian and replied, "I have desires." Zetian responded, "How can the Vener-

> able have desires?" Shen replied, "That which is born has desire. That which is not born has no desire." At these words, Zetian was awakened.[193]

When Zhishen insists on leaving, the empress gives him Huineng's robe and other gifts, including an embroidered image of Maitreya. It is significant that bestowal of the robe takes place in the context of a Dharma transmission, just as in prior robe-transmission episodes. Here, however, the transmission is characterized by several kinds of inversion. First, the transmission of the sudden teaching, the identity of Buddha-nature and ordinary function that is beyond words, finds its voice as affirmation of the codependence of desire and no-desire. Second, it is the bestower who is awakened by the recipient. Third, a worldly ruler stands in for the Dharma-ruler, Huineng, who is still alive at the time and is subsequently informed by the empress of the fate of his robe. Finally, the bestower is a woman and an emperor, a *lusus naturae*—who, perhaps not incidentally, was known for her sexual appetites and for having had her lover ordained and later murdered.

The empress was also the patroness of such widely revered and impeccable monks as the Huayan founder Fazang 法藏 (643–712) and the "Northern School" Chan masters Shenxiu and Laoan, named in the *Lidai fabao ji* passage as two of the monks invited to court.[194] As noted in the previous section, references to the empress bestowing robes on Hongren's heirs are scattered throughout the hagiographical literature. Interestingly, there is an account in the *Song gaoseng zhuan* biography of Wuxiang 無相 (684–762) in which the empress bestows a robe not on Zhishen but on his disciple Chuji, who passes it on to Wuxiang. It is not claimed that the robe Wu Zetian bestows is Huineng's, but it becomes the symbol of Chuji's transmission.[195] In what was probably a deliberate attempt to counter the *Lidai fabao ji* story, in the *Caoqi dashi zhuan* it is said that Emperor Suzong had Huineng's robe brought to court in Chang'an and subsequently had it returned to Caoqi after dreaming that he was to do so.[196]

Accounts of the empress conferring robes on monks at court are also included in the official histories, which are critical of her reign. It is said that in 690 Empress Wu set a precedent by bestowing purple *kāṣāya* robes upon a group of monks, including her alleged lover Huaiyi 懷義, as a mark of special favor. The earliest source for the event is the *Tang shu* 唐書 (Tang History):

> Huaiyi, Faming and others made the *Dayun jing*, in which was displayed a series of signs [concerning the Heavenly] Mandate and in which it was said that Zetian was Maitreya who had descended to be born and act as head of the Jambudvīpa. . . . Huaiyi, Faming and others, nine people, were all enfeoffed dukes of a subprefecture and were given different objects: all were given the purple *kāṣāya* and a "silver bag for the tortoise."[197]

This investiture enfolds Chinese patents of nobility within and around a gesture born of Indian Buddhist mythology. Princely robe, imperial talisman, and fief were the Chinese symbols and substance of enfranchisement, granting permission to enter into the ritual arena constituted by the interplay of ancestral merit, heavenly sanction, and material privilege. The conferral of a robe signified imperial favor but was not one of the talismans of imperial legitimacy.[198] However, in Maitreya mythology transfer of the *kāṣāya* robe evokes the vast cycles of succession from Buddha to Buddha. Meritorious gifts from the ruler to the community of monks also recalls the Cakravartin "wheel-turning king" mythology of ideal confluence between world monarch and world salvation, an ideology we saw promoted in the *Renwang jing*. Wu Zetian's gesture thus reflects the intricate interplay of signs characteristic of her reign. Her efforts were directed toward fashioning a dynastic identity in the time-honored manner, through the relationship of names (such as the Zhou 周) and symbols (such as the tortoise) intended to evoke harmonious reverberations in the sanctioned terms of Han-derived cosmology.

On the other hand, she and her trusted advisors among the Buddhist clergy strove to build a new kind of empire, not through expansion of borders but by investing the entire realm in a rich (and expensive) overlay of institutional Buddhism. Other Chinese rulers before her, notably Liang Wudi and Sui Wendi, had been taken with variations on the theme of the ruler as bodhisattva who reigns for the benefit of sentient beings. Wu Zetian's state ideology was also replete with complex Cakravartin and bodhisattva symbolism.[199] However, as evidenced in the passage from the *Tang shu* quoted above, she is remembered in official history as the one who dared to take up the mantle of Maitreya, the future Buddha.

In *Political Propaganda and Ideology in China at the End of the Seventh Century*, sinologist Antonino Forte presents a more nuanced picture. He shows that the subtle manipulation of Maitreya symbolism stemmed from Wu Zetian's cadre of monk advisors, who can be credited at least provisionally for their sincere belief in the advent of a utopian Buddhist realm inaugurated by their empress. Their commentary to the *Dayun jing* 大雲經 (*Mahāmegha-sūtra*) does claim that Wu Zetian is Maitreya—softened by a note that *maitreya* merely means one who is compassionate or benevolent.[200] Forte puts forth the interesting argument that the monks responsible for this commentary were playing on the popular appeal of Maitreya, but were also wary of the subversive aspects of millenarian Maitreyism. In other words, they were attempting to win popular support and yet avoid becoming overly involved with the kind of messianic Maitreyism advocated in the banned apocrypha of the Sui, which might raise expectations too high and trigger a full-scale uprising.[201] In concrete political terms, they were trying to shift the balance of power from the aristocracy to the military and civil bureaucracy.[202] This is seen, for example, in the commentator's quotation from the so-called *Guangwu ming* 廣武銘 (Inscription Magnifying [Empress] Wu): "'All the people will be happy: it will be learned that civilians and soldiers will develop.' [Commentary:] Here it is made clear that the 'hundred offices' of the civil and military administration will be extended from now on."[203] These efforts of the empress's advisors can be said to have had mixed results, for in spite of the dynastic reversion back to the Tang neither the uprising nor the shift in balance were avoided.

Wu Zetian's legacy is a complex subject, but it is the lasting association between the empress and messianic Maitreyism, spoken of with distaste in official sources, that is our concern here. Later Buddhists, including the influential Zanning 贊寧 (919–1001), took pains to disparage the activities of the monks who supported the empress.[204] However, there must have been others for whom in retrospect her reign seemed as it was advertised—the advent of a Buddhist utopia where monks were enfranchised as the aristocracy.

The *Lidai fabao ji* authors seem to have been susceptible to this nostalgia insofar as their lineage claim hinges on Wu Zetian's power to bestow Huineng's robe, and by implication the patriarchy, on Zhishen. At the same time, the authors appear to have been sensitive to the fact that their Shenhui-derived doctrine and practice were based on the repudiation of monks whom Wu Zetian had sponsored. The *Lidai fabao ji* account of Zhishen's sojourn at court and his defeat of the Trepiṭaka is designed to showcase the empress's acknowledgment of the superiority of the doctrine of no-thought over the old-fashioned magic of her former favorites.

Although Wu Zetian thus plays an important role in the *Lidai fabao ji* saga, this role remains an ambivalent one. On the one hand, the *Lidai fabao ji* claim rests on Wu Zetian's authority to stand in for Huineng and transmit the "robe of verification," and thus the Dharma, to its next legitimate representative. On the other hand, the *Lidai fabao ji* authors represent her as a somewhat overzealous devotee who has taken it upon herself to act as intermediary. As an intermediary, in terms of the early Buddhist myths of transmission her role is more like that of Mahākāśyapa than Maitreya.

According to Buddhist lore, Mahākāśyapa has sealed himself up in order to await Maitreya's advent and, in some versions, to convey the Buddha's robe to him. Let us take a closer look at some of the variations on this theme. There are many versions of the legend that Śākyamuni gave his robe to his chief disciple Mahākāśyapa, or exchanged robes with him, in order that Mahākāśyapa might appear with the Buddha's robe when Maitreya becomes the next Buddha.[205] As we have seen, the motif of transmission of objects from Buddha to Buddha is evoked in Daoxuan's "Jetavana Diagram Scripture," wherein the *saṃghāṭī* robe is said to await Maitreya's advent in a stūpa on the Jetavana ordination platform. There is also a version in one of the *Lidai fabao ji* sources, the *Fu fazang zhuan*. In the *Fu fazang zhuan* account, which is derived from the *Aśokāvadāna,* as Mahākāśyapa prepares to enter nirvāṇa on Mount Kukkuṭapāda he dons the Buddha's robe and takes up his bowl, uttering this prayer: "Now I put on this body the robe of refuse rags of the Buddha and [hold] the bowl that he himself once held. Until the coming of Maitreya let it not decay, so that his disciples may all see my body and bring forth an utter loathing of evil."[206] In this version the robe is a symbol of the Dharma's power to counter the corruptions of impurity, physical decay, and vice, and it is not a talisman of transmission.

In the *Da Tang xiyu ji* 大唐西域記 (The Tang Dynasty Account of the Western Regions), Xuanzang relates a version of the Buddha-Mahākāśyapa conferral that offers richer material for the developing Chan mythology of transmission.[207] Due to the presence of a distinctive identifying feature, a gold-embroidered *kāṣāya,* it appears likely that Xuanzang's version was a source for Shenhui's representation of transmission. Furthermore, it may also have been a source for a pattern favored in the *Lidai fabao ji,* whereby an intermediary passes the robe as a symbol of authority between two links in a chain that are not in direct contact. This pattern is repeated twice in the *Lidai fabao ji:* the transmission of the robe from Huineng to Zhishen via Empress Wu prefigures the transmission of robe and Dharma from Wuxiang to Wuzhu via a servant of Wuxiang's.

In Xuanzang's version the Buddha, about to enter nirvāṇa, entrusts his gold-embroidered *kāṣāya* to his disciple Mahākāśyapa and, at the same time, publicly invests him as leader of the community and successor to the transmission of the true Dharma. The Buddha then predicts that twenty years after the first assembly when Mahākāśyapa is on the point of entering nirvāṇa, he will enter Mount Kukkuṭapāda and stand holding Śākyamuni 's robe in his arms. The mountain will enclose him and he will thus await Maitreya. When the future Buddha comes, the mountain will open of itself and Mahākāśyapa will transmit the robe to Maitreya in view of the assembled crowd, and thereafter he will ascend into the air and self-combust, entering nirvāṇa.[208]

Besides its significance as a symbol of transferred authority, the other distinctive quality of the robe in Xuanzang's version is that it is a gold-embroidered *kāṣāya.* The gold-embroidered robe is traditionally held to be a gift from the Buddha's aunt Mahāprajāpatī, the first Buddhist nun and also the woman who raised him after his mother died. The Buddha's royal aunt and foster-mother is an ambiguous figure, for her ordination is most famously associated with the Buddha's prediction that women's admission to the order will cause the Dharma to last only five hundred instead of one thousand years.[209]

Xuanzang's identification of the entrusted robe conflicts with a separate set of Indian sūtra stories concerning Mahāprajāpatī's gift. Jonathan Silk, in his dissertation on the *Mahāratnakūṭa* tradition, says of these stories: "I know of no version in which Śākyamuni himself actually accepts the proffered robes."[210] However, both Shenhui and the *Lidai fabao ji* authors refer to the robe entrusted to Mahākāśyapa as "gold-embroidered."[211] Given the fact that Mahāprajāpatī's admission to the Saṅgha is strongly linked to the theme of the decline of the Dharma, it is ironic that Shenhui cites conferral of the gold-embroidered robe as the precedent for the power of the transmission of Bodhidharma's robe to guard against decline of the Dharma.

The recurring motif in the stories of Mahāprajāpatī's gift is the Buddha's refusal, but Silk notes variants in which "Mahāprajāpatī wanders into the assembly looking for a monk to accept the robes, and all refuse—except Maitreya." Maitreya is said to have once been Śākyamuni 's disciple Ajita, a novice who received cloth or a robe that had been intended as a gift to the Buddha from his aunt.[212] Silk comments: "This version, of course, which omits Mahākāśyapa completely, provides a direct link between Śākyamuni and Maitreya."[213] For our purposes, the main interest of the story lies in the fact that the link is not direct; the robe is conveyed to Maitreya through the mediation of Mahāprajāpatī.

Although the *Lidai fabao ji* account of the empress conveying Bodhidharma's robe between patriarchs makes her a kind of interregnum regent homologous to Mahākāśyapa, her bestowal of princely robes also inadvertently recalls the premature decline of Śākyamuni's Dharma that is associated with Mahāprajāpatī. It was not the sort of symbolism the empress would have welcomed—the motif of fated decline would have resonated uncomfortably with Chinese notions of history in which certain fatal flaws could bring about the premature end of a life, a clan, or a dynasty. Nevertheless, in the complex web of associations involved in the abovementioned *Dayun jing* ideology, Mahāprajāpati appears, perhaps an unwelcome shadow, in the company of Wu Zetian's opposites and doubles. Mahāprajāpatī is the "matriarch" of the order of nuns and as such takes her place in a trinity heading the great assembly described at the opening of the *Dayun jing*.[214] She is beside Mahākāśyapa who represents the order of monks and the "Great Cloud Matrix" Bodhisattva (*Dayun mizang* 大雲密藏) who represents the bodhisattvas. In the *Dayun jing* this bodhisattva is the Buddha's interlocutor, and he also serves as a foil for the Devī who-would-be-queen whom the commentary identifies as the empress.

The *Dayun jing* prophecy that the Devī Jingguang 淨光 would become a female Buddhist ruler was one of the central supports of Wu Zetian's ideology. In a passage from the *Dayun jing* that is included in the commentary, the Buddha praises Devī Jingguang—which causes her to feel "ashamed in her heart"—and then he foretells her future conditions: "Excellent! Excellent! Shame is the good Dharma robe of the many beings. . . . On my appearing in the world you have once more listened to the profound and good [Dharma]. When you abandon this Devī-form you shall, with the body of a woman, rule over the territory of a country and obtain one quarter of the places governed by a Cakravartin king."[215]

In the *Zhengming jing* 證明經 (Attestation Scripture),[216] an apocryphal scripture also used to support Wu Zetian's reign, there is an apocalyptic vision of the birth of a Buddhist kingdom in China in which the bodhisattva Samantabhadra has the role of avenging angel and protective midwife. In one passage Samantabhadra is called Mahāprajāpatī (in transcription), because Mahāprajāpatī's name was translated into Chinese as Dasheng zhu 大生主 (Great Lord of Beings), an epithet of Samantabhadra.[217] This sūtra was quoted in the commentary to the *Dayun jing* to encourage people to connect the utopian realm prophesied by Samantabhadra with the reign of Wu Zetian.

Perhaps fittingly, while weaving a mantle of scriptural prophecy to bestow upon their empress, the cadre of monks captured not only a blushing Devī but also the more ambiguous shades of a willful Mahāprajāpatī and a punitive Samantabhadra. Although in the *Dayun jing* the Buddha praises "shame" as the Dharma robe of all beings, it is hubris for which Wu Zetian is most consistently remembered by Chinese historians. Thus, the precedent she established of bestowing robes on monks became a dubious honor, resonant with the story of Mahāprajāpatī. Although Buddhist literature abounds with words of praise and evocations of merit for those who give food, clothing, bedding, and medicine for the use of the Saṅgha, there was ambivalence toward laypersons who gave costly and personal gifts to individual monks.

In this light, we might cast a glance at the empress's ill-starred *mingtang* 明堂 (Luminous Hall) project. Antonino Forte's study of Wu Zetian's *mingtang* elucidates the history and ideological significance of this imperial ritual structure, arguing that the empress's grandiose conception, if it had succeeded, would have spatially and symbolically established Buddhism's dominance over Confucianism and Daoism in the main ritual edifice of the state cult.[218] He also suggests that the popular will to realize this vision was fanned into flame by the utopian appeal of the empress's ideology as disseminated in the *Dayun jing* commentary and the *Zhengming jing*.[219]

However, the huge *tiantang* 天堂 (Celestial Hall) tower that was to have been the Buddhist centerpiece of the complex was destroyed first by wind and then by fire before it could be completed. The final disaster, like the burning of Yongning monastery near the end of the Northern Wei, appeared to vindicate those who condemned the dynasty's Buddhist orientation. The timing of the fire was almost too symbolic, for it occurred just a day after an inaugural Pañcavārṣika (*wuzhe dahui* 無遮大會, unrestricted great assembly) was held in the *mingtang*. The Pañcavārṣika was an important Buddhist ritual feast symbolically uniting all classes of devotees, a feast that "when run by Buddhist kings, essentially represented the unity between subjects and kings."[220]

Though Wu Zetian's reign would continue for more than a decade longer, Forte claims that the mood of cooperative fervor was destroyed, and the Buddhist establishment moved quickly to dissociate itself from the disaster.[221] Immediately after the fire, numerous critics pressed for abandonment of the project. In the official Liu Chengqing's 劉承慶 memorial to the empress, he argues: "To limit oneself to venerating that 'teaching' is the essential thing! Why does one need a 'purple palace,' in order to realize enlightenment?"[222]

Bernard Faure has argued that the shift from doctrinal eclecticism toward sectarianism and the "will to orthodoxy" began under Wu Zetian's reign. The empress and the new elite who had been empowered by her began to seek a more respectable yet not hidebound Buddhist partnership, which they found in Shenxiu and his followers.[223] However, Wu Zetian's attempt to raise the social and ritual importance of the Saṅgha was soon succeeded by attempts to reign in and regulate the clergy. There is much to suggest that the mood of reform was also felt within the Saṅgha, and Shenhui's campaigns against Shenxiu and his heirs can be seen in this light. In his sermon at the *wuzhe dahui* at the Huatai Dayun monastery, former site of dissemination of the *Dayun jing* ideology, Shenhui redefined "the essential thing" and gave a further push to sectarianism.

Under Empress Wu the monk's robe had become a mantle of worldly power, which was one of the signs of the corruption of the final age of the Dharma. As noted, Liang Wudi donned monk's robes and then had his minister ransom him and his divested royal raiment back from the monastery, establishing an "inexhaustible" and independent financial base for the Saṅgha. In contrast, Wu Zetian's edifice and her lavish gifts reached toward monarchical assumption of the power to confer legitimacy on monks. Thus, the *Vajrasamādhi-sūtra* invocation of an immaterial "robe of the tathāgatas" may have resonated with a current of feeling against the empress's presumption.

THE REFORMS OF EMPEROR XUANZONG

The question of the distinction between material Buddhism and formlessness became even more vexed during the era of Shenhui's activities, the reign of Emperor Xuanzong 玄宗 (r. 712–756). Xuanzong was notably ambivalent about Buddhism, well aware of its role in the renegade reign of Wu Zetian and the attempted coup of the Taiping Princess 太平公主 (d. 713), but he supported the clergy in a clearly defined and limited capacity. During the reign of Xuanzong we see the first signs of a different kind of imperial attitude toward Buddhism.[224] This attitude differs from earlier attempts to control Buddhism by outright persecution, differs from the massive scale of Wu Zetian's co-optation, and differs again from imperial policy that suffered Buddhism to flourish as a kind of side bet alongside the dominant Confucian ritual and archival concerns. With Xuanzong, we see attempts to persuade the loose network of Buddhist institutions to enforce critical standards that were arguably of benefit to the network itself.

Xuanzong's decrees proscribed marketplace proselytization, curbed irregular ordination and temple building, prohibited merchants from casting images and copying scriptures for profit, and strictly limited fraternization between lay and ordained.[225] These measures contributed to greater monastic control and yet, at the same time, "routinized the charisma" such that the center shifted towards decorum and ritual, an atmosphere in which Daoist priests and Esoteric specialists thrived. It is noteworthy that after centuries of clerical protest against repeated imperial attempts to require monks and nuns to pay obeisance to the emperor and their parents, there is no record of clerical resistance to Xuanzong's 733 decree to that effect.[226]

This is certainly not to claim that no emperor before Xuanzong had ever managed to control monks. However, previous policies had aimed primarily to curb Buddhism from without, whereas eighth-century edicts seem more successfully designed to set centralized administrative standards to work within the monastic network, instituting restrictions that could not be interpreted as being inimical to monastic vows. For example, in 724 Xuanzong issued an edict instituting an examination system for the clergy and ordered that those who could not memorize and recite the requisite amount of scripture be laicized. The decree further stipulated that skill in meditation would not be an acceptable substitute.[227] At the same time, Xuanzong is also well known for his predilection for masters of esoteric Buddhism and their thaumaturgic powers. Outside the sphere of these favorites, however, the ordinary monk was beginning to be regularized, acquiring worldly status that put him on a par with an official, but steadily losing the otherworldly mystique that allowed him to look benevolently down on the emperor.

The sites where authority in the Dharma are enacted—such as speech, writing, discipline, and genealogy—supplement and resist one another, and the Saṅgha depends on this resistance in order to maintain both diversity and continuity. By the time of the Bao Tang, the relationship among these sites of authority had become the subject of intense debate among different Buddhist groups and between Buddhist and imperial authorities. During Xuanzong's era, the state tried to appropriate the authority to judge the standards of discipline of the clergy and assigned values to certain kinds of speech and writing and certain genealogies. Thus, it is no coincidence that this era also saw the development of various ideologies meant to convey the Saṅgha beyond the limits of provisional orthopraxy, as all formal means of legitimation were being subjected to usurpation by an outside authority, the state.

Shenhui's robe-rhetoric was one such attempt to establish a special status for an elite among the clergy and legitimacy for a "separate transmission." In an insightful article, John Jorgensen draws connections between Shenhui's notions of patriarchal succession and the complex issues surrounding Tang imperial succession that were current in Shenhui's day. Jorgensen discusses Zongmi's commentary correlating Chan patriarchal succession and Chinese ancestral rites, in which a founder and six linear descendents are necessary in order to establish the ancestral temple of a clan or dynasty. In the aftermath of Empress Wu's interregnum, there were disputes over the sequence of the tablets in the Tang ancestral temple, and Jorgensen demonstrates that Shenhui's rhetoric echoed or perhaps even inspired "Southern Learning" (*nanxue* 南學) factionalists at court who were moving toward unequivocal ritual erasure of her reign.[228] Jorgensen says:

> If Tsung-mi correctly interpreted the ideas of Shen-hui, then Shen-hui is making a two-pronged attack on Northern Ch'an by associating it with the Empress Wu. Firstly he alleges that Northern Ch'an was an illegitimate succession like that of Empress Wu who reigned while Emperors Chung-tsung and Jui-tsung were still alive, with two masters per generation, or two suns in the sky. Secondly there was guilt by association with the perverted "materialistic" Buddhism of her times, a perversion that was probably due to a woman being on the throne.
>
> There was another political dimension to Shen-hui's emphasis on the sixth generation. Yanagida Seizan has suggested that a comparison was being made by Shen-hui with the lineage of the T'ang house itself. If Empress Wu is eliminated as being illegitimate, ruling while two former emperors were still alive, this would make Hsüan-tsung the sixth emperor.[229]

It was precisely during Shenhui's generation that fixing the identity of a sixth patriarch or a sixth Tang emperor became a crucial issue, for this would determine the composition of the foundational ancestral phalanx. Bodhidharma's robe is, therefore, the talisman of the restored dynasty of the "Southern School," of which Shenhui intended himself to be the crowning seventh patriarch. According to Shenhui,

> The robe serves as verification of the Dharma and the Dharma is the robe lineage [*yizong* 衣宗]. Robe and Dharma are transferred from one [patriarch] to another and are handed down without alteration. Without the robe

> one does not spread forth the Dharma, without the Dharma one does not receive the robe. . . . To know empty quietude is to fully realize the Dharma-body, and to be truly liberated.[230]

Empress Wu's luxurious robes and Emperor Xuanzong's uniforms both threatened to bind the spiritual to the political realm, and Shenhui took up Bodhidharma's empty robe in order to establish the Chan patriarchs in the Dharmakāya realm, where they reigned supreme.[231] The *Lidai fabao ji* is more faithful to Shenhui's doctrine, practice, and rhetoric than any of its rivals for "Southern School" legitimacy. Yet, in letting Bodhidharma's robe pass through Wu Zetian's hands, it allows the primary symbol of that legitimacy to pass through the milieu that was the focus of Shenhui's most vehement attack.

Perhaps the *Lidai fabao ji* authors were inadvertently correct in acknowledging the pivotal role that the empress's mixed blessing played in the formation of the "Southern School." In tandem with her lavish support of the Saṅgha, her ideological projects set the realm reverberating with the apocalyptic tones and imagery of immanence. Her Dharma realm was two-tiered, at once temporal and metaphysical. Shenhui's sudden teaching was immanent in two mutually contradictory yet interdependent absolutes, for it was realized exclusively in its patriarchal bearers and inclusively in each individual devotee. The danger was that the ordinary devotee might fail to see the difference and point out the nakedness of Buddha-nature in both the patriarch and his pupils.

Let us consider a passage from the above-mentioned *Zhengming jing*, in which homage to the empress's new mandate, like that rendered the invisible robe of the tathāgatas, serves to distinguish the ordinary from the discerning who alone are able to see the "luminous king of the Dharma":

> Then in the Sahā [world] there will not be the five kinds of people. All corruption will be cured, and all will be given the names of Bodhisattvas. . . . The countries will be Buddhist countries, the regions will be Buddhist regions, the commanderies will be Buddhist commanderies, the districts will be Buddhist districts, the villages will be Buddhist villages, the neighborhoods will be Buddhist neighborhoods. All will assemble in the Transformation City . . . and they will be able to see this Luminous King. . . . If there are distrustful people they will not be able to see this Dharma.[232]

Wu Zetian's attempt to build a utopian "Transformation City" out of precious metals, wood, stone, and symbolism disturbingly blurred the line between visible and invisible Buddhist realms. Shenhui's concept of the patriarchy was an attempt to redraw that line, and his patriarchal robe was a self-contained tathāgata realm with a monarchy separate from both secular and ordinary institutional Buddhist authority. His success is attested by the number of rivals who tried to lay claim to this new territory.

The *Lidai fabao ji* authors seem to have evoked the empress as a source of legitimacy separate from the Chan infighting alluded to in the lament over frequent thefts of the robe. Yet perhaps this was not such a retrogression as it might seem. At the end of chapter 6, we take a look at the intriguing passage in the *Lidai fabao ji* concerning Wuzhu's female disciple Liaojianxing 了見性 (Completely Seeing the [Buddha] Nature), who receives one of the most detailed treatments of any of the ordained disciples.[233] In this passage, it is said that Liaojianxing became a nun simply by donning robes and tonsuring herself.[234] Self-tonsuring, especially by women, was probably not unknown, but the extent of this practice may be impossible to gauge. However, in the context of the *Lidai fabao ji* it is a perfect enactment of Wuzhu's teachings.

There is no other record of Liaojianxing, and we can only speculate as to why neither she nor any other disciple was named as Wuzhu's successor. Was it because his closest disciples were laypersons and women, or was it because his radical interpretation of sudden practice was incompatible with any form, including that of transmission? If the latter, then why is so much of the *Lidai fabao ji* invested in establishing a claim to legitimacy in these conventional and fabricated terms? Perhaps the story of the empress, who used imperial rhetoric to establish a position not recognized by the imperial system, struck a sympathetic chord among Wuzhu's disciples. By including Wu Zetian, briefly and fictitiously, in its chronicle of Chan succession, the *Lidai fabao ji* authors allow us a tantalizing glimpse of uncertainties hidden beneath the reflective surface of historical verisimilitude. In chapter 6 we turn to the Bao Tang lineage and teachings, and we will see that, whatever the ambitions and fears of Wuzhu's followers may have been, they were soon lost in the gathering momentum of "Southern School" orthodoxy.

CHAPTER 6
Wuzhu and His Others

If there is a karmic cause it will penetrate a thousand li; if there is no cause, then even people facing each other will not recognize one another.[1]

—The Venerable Wuzhu

THE SECOND PART OF THE *LIDAI FABAO JI*

Wuzhu takes center stage in this chapter, and the history of Buddhism in China becomes the backdrop for his dramatic entrance. Wuzhu's lines claim the absence of the actor—"In meditation there is neither exiting nor entering"[2]—and the *Lidai fabao ji* celebrates his unique character. In this chapter we see how key transmission themes play out in Wuzhu's story. Beginning with the development of the Chan ordination platform and formless precepts, I explore the various ways that the ordination platform influenced Bao Tang identity. I then turn to transmission of Huineng's robe and the relationship between Wuzhu and other key characters in the *Lidai fabao ji*. Next, taking up Wuzhu's teachings and his dialogues with a series of interlocutors, I highlight three distinctive features of the *Lidai fabao ji:* its signature antinomianism, its inclusion of women, and its anti-Daoist tendencies.

To sum up where we have been and where we are going, one could say that we have been following a Buddhism modeled on diachronic dynastic phases through the first part of the *Lidai fabao ji,* whereas we now enter into the synchronic kinship concerns of the second part.[3] The diachronic representation of Buddhist transmission is expressed through emblems of inherited legitimacy, such as scriptures, rituals, and talismanic objects. As we have seen, Southern School ideology is replete with royal or imperial references, and the succession of biographies of the Chan masters and the story of the robe are at once dynastic histories and historical romances.[4]

Exploring the second part of the *Lidai fabao ji,* we look at paradigmatic representations of the Bao Tang through stories of their heroes and heroines, followers and foes. Kinship concerns are also genealogical and diachronic, of course, but here I focus on how the Bao Tang representation of the past serves to validate existing hierarchies, clarify family values, and demonstrate the effectiveness of Wuzhu's patriarchy.[5] Metaphors like kingship and kinship, or trunk and branches, describe the genealogical principle that began to structure Chan hagiographical works in the eighth century, leading to the highly developed "transmission of the lamp" genre in the Song.

A NOTE ABOUT STYLE

In the *Lidai fabao ji,* the shift from Dharma kings to Dharma kin is signaled by a shift in style as well as context. The first part of the *Lidai fabao ji* is largely a pastiche of earlier material or imitations of traditional Buddhist scholarship. I refer to the sources discussed in previous chapters, such as the legend of Emperor Ming, the modified *Xu Gaoseng zhuan* biographies, the knots of sūtra quotations, and material from the East Mountain School and from Shenhui.

In the second part of the *Lidai fabao ji,* the use of other Buddhist material is largely confined to Wuzhu's quotations from sūtras. The impressive effect with which Wuzhu deploys his quotations reveals the *Lidai fabao ji* authors' reverence for treasures from the storehouse of Buddhist lore. The quotations have a talismanic function; they are not always clearly related to the topic at hand, but they are always followed by an account of the respectful awe that they induce in the succession of Wuzhu's interlocutors. Moreover, they are imbedded in other modes of discourse characteristic of Wuzhu—telegraphic, almost hypnotic, *wunian* phrases, ostentatious displays of doctrinal terminology, and earthy, piquant stories. We see examples of all these elements in the following sections.

In the late Tang, both Chan literature and secular fiction developed in new directions, and the second part of the *Lidai fabao ji* reflects these trends. As with Tang *chuanqi* 傳奇 (transmitted marvels) fiction, what were once preparatory sketches and notes in the margins of official literature became the features of a new genre. In both Chan lore and *chuanqi,* interactions in ordinary settings were used to establish the relative spiritual or moral standing of the characters.

It is significant that the adoption of a sparser and more colloquial mode in Chan literature coincided with similar stylistic experiments formulated and practiced by late Tang literati such as Han Yü 韓愈 (768–824) and his followers, proponents of the *guwen* 古文(ancient writing) movement. In his prose Han Yü favored the archaic to the point of severity, but he and other writers of the late Tang also began to include colloquial elements in their poetry and fiction. Though Han Yü is famous for criticizing the emperor for his worship of a Buddhist relic, the sensibilities that prompted Han Yü's memorial had much in common with Chan discourse on formless practice. In particular, Han Yü's critique of lavish expenditure, credulous superstition, and undignified public spectacle shares a kind of "Protestant" minimalist attitude with the Bao Tang critique of liturgy, pilgrimage, and devotionalism.[6] There were aspects of Chan that Han Yü found sympathetic, as Charles Hartman notes: "Although Han Yü did not share the Ch'an school's need for an historical face-to-face transmission lineage, he did share their partiality for face-to-face oral transmission of a teaching method."[7] Naturalness in dialogue, portrayal of ordinary settings and everyday events, and the valorization of spontaneous directness in art, literature, and teaching method—all these qualities were appreciated by literati and monastics alike. The authorial voice that carries the *Lidai fabao ji* narrative from one island of borrowed material to the next is direct and colloquial to the point of rusticity, making it unlikely that the style was adopted in conscious imitation of cutting-edge literary trends. Nevertheless, there is a pungency in some of the anecdotes about Wuzhu that anticipates the more studied immediacy of refined Song *yulu*.

Like Han Yü, Chan writers were at pains to present innovation as excavation, to establish reform on ancient foundations. Indeed, Song dynasty Chan genres, such as *yulu* 語錄 (discourse record), *chuandeng lu* 傳燈錄 (lamp transmission record), and *gongan* 公案 (public case), graft new material onto old roots.[8] In format, *yulu* clearly had antecedents in pre-Han classics like the *Lunyu* and the *Zhuangzi*. In style and content they are reminiscent of the products of third- and fourth-century *qingtan* 清談 (pure conversation) circles, such as the *Shishuo xinyu* 世說新語 (A New Account of Tales of the World).[9] However, *yulu* were also influenced by the tastes of the Song Daoxue 道學 or "Neo-Confucian" literati, who rejected ornate commentarial prose in favor of a spare and direct, yet elegant, style. Song Chan masters were part of an intellectual milieu that favored skillful use of language and deftly rendered personal immediacy, associated with the moral qualities of penetrating understanding and sincerity.

Chan genres are unique, yet complement and refer to one another in a familiar manner, and Chan eccentricities depended on a bedrock of traditional Buddhist practices and institutions. Just as accounts of the bizarre (*zhiguai* 志怪) complemented official didactic "arrayed" biographies (*liezhuan* 列傳) and the brevity and wit of *qingtan* 清談 (pure conversation) were related to the more formal dialogical treatises of the third and fourth centuries, so too did the Chan school's turning words, scatological references, and shouts depend on daily recitation of the sūtras.[10] The appeal of the *Lidai fabao ji* is that the sūtras and the scatology are not yet divided into separate genres.

MASS PRECEPTS CEREMONIES AND FORMLESS PRECEPTS

Wuzhu's sermons often include criticisms of those who are fixated on the precepts, and one of the deplored features of Bao Tang antinomianism was their disregard for official ordination of their monks and nuns. At the same time, Wuzhu's teachings as recorded in the *Lidai fabao ji* show distinct affinities with a preaching style that evolved on the platform for conferring the bodhisattva precepts. In chapter 3 we looked at the evolution of Chinese bodhisattva precepts texts, and in this section I show how conferral of the bodhisattva precepts was a key vehicle for the spread of Chan subitism. Also noted in chapter 3, we find that when Wuzhu taught the precepts he often "quoted the paddy-crabs" in order to gently mock the devotees' desire to receive verbal formulae. He was also perhaps mocking the concessions he made to that desire: "When the Venerable took his seat, he usually taught the precepts to all those studying the Way."[11]

Mass precepts ceremonies enjoyed a boom after the An Lushan rebellion and continued to be a popular practice in the late eighth and early ninth centuries.[12] This is reflected in Chan texts of the period—the *Platform Sūtra* is set on the platform of a precepts assembly, and in the *Lidai fabao ji* the crucial meeting between Wuzhu and Wuxiang takes place at a precepts retreat. Eighth-century precepts ceremony manuals, which were based on the apocryphal bodhisattva precepts texts, include scripts of the responses and vows that the petitioner was to make when receiving the precepts. From Dunhuang colophons of texts dedicated on the occasion of receiving the precepts, we know that the preceptors would generally have lectured on a well-known scripture for the assembly.

In his article "The Ordination Ritual in the Platform *Sūtra* Within the Context of the East Asian Buddhist Vinaya Tradition," Paul Groner traces the evolution of specialized sixth- to eighth-century bodhisattva precepts manuals that were based on the bodhisattva precepts texts, an evolution in which the Tiantai school played a key role. Groner speculates about a trend that one might characterize as "professionalization" of bodhisattva ordination rituals: "Ceremonies based on the *Mo-ho-seng-ch'i lü* (T. 1425, *Mahāsaṅghikavinaya*) were designed to obtain good luck in marriage, birth, on long journeys and for use in funeral ceremonies and at dedications of new buildings. The bodhisattva precepts were probably used in a similar fashion."[13]

Sengyou's *Chu sanzang ji ji* lists a number of texts recorded on the occasion of reception of the bodhisattva precepts by imperial or aristocratic devotees during the Six Dynasties period, none of which are extant.[14] An important text of this type is included in Daoxuan's *Guang Hongming ji*, entitled *Sui Yangdi yu Tiantai shan Yi chanshi suo shou pusajie wen* 隋煬帝於天台山顗禪師所受菩薩戒文 (Text of Emperor Yang of the Sui's Reception of the Bodhisattva Precepts from Dhyāna Master Yi of Mt. Tiantai). Zhiyi was the master of ceremonies and Śākyamuni and Mañjuśrī were evoked as preceptors. Zhiyi's would-be patron, who was not yet emperor at the time of the ceremony, is quoted as saying "no matter what powers the divine masters possess, they need human masters to propagate the doctrine."[15] In hindsight, the future parricide's recommendation of human agency is rather chilling, but Zhiyi's power to propagate the doctrine did indeed prove lasting. His *Mohe zhiguan* would long remain a key source for the structure and procedures of ritual repentance and meditation assemblies.[16]

Groner compares the antecedents and format of Tiantai and Chan bodhisattva ordinations, noting the comparative simplicity of the ordination ceremonies found in Shenhui's platform sermon and in the *Platform Sūtra*. The manuals generally do not distinguish between lay and monastic recipients, and some of them expand on the provisions for individual practice such as found in the *Fanwang jing*. The influential *Fanwang jing*-based ordination manual of the Tiantai renovator and ninth patriarch Zhanran 湛然 (711–782) is instructive in this regard. It included "self-ordination" aspects, such as taking the Buddhas and bodhisattvas as officiants of the ceremony and the notion that taking the refuges caused arising of the essence of the precepts (*jieti* 戒體) in the participant.[17] Zhanran claimed that "Although my manual does not follow (the ordination procedure of) any particular school, it does not differ from the Buddha's teachings."[18]

There was a trend toward interiorization and self-validation of the precepts in the Tiantai school as well as the Northern and Southern schools of Chan. However, in contrast to the Tiantai precepts manuals, in the *Platform Sūtra* the preliminary period of purification and meditation is not explicitly prescribed, and no "sign" from the Buddhas and bodhisattvas is required.[19] That "innate precepts" were necessarily linked to formal precepts had been a scriptural theme from the inception of the notion of the bodhisattva precepts, found in the *Nirvāṇa-sūtra* and the *Bodhisattvabhūmi* as well as in apocrypha like the *Fanwang jing*.[20] The Bao Tang school would go even further to open the Dharma gates within, breaking down the remains of the barrier that had been maintained between inner and outer precepts.

There are indications of the existence of a Chan ordination ceremony stemming from the East Mountain tradition. The nonextant *Pusa jiefa*

菩薩戒法 (Method for the Bodhisattva Precepts), attributed to Daoxin, may have been the basis for the precepts ceremony in both the Northern School *Dasheng wusheng fangbian men* 大乘無生方便門 (The Expedient Means of [Attaining] Birthlessness in the Mahāyāna)[21] and in the *Platform Sūtra*.

The *Dasheng wusheng fangbian men* required the candidate to vow that he or she is able to uphold certain practices; Yanagida suggests that it may have been "intended to control an expanding order."[22] The text opens with a precepts ceremony that scripts audience response:

> Next request the Buddhas of the ten directions to be your preceptors.
>
> Next request Buddhas and bodhisattvas of the three periods of time [to be your witnesses (?)].
>
> Next I will ask about the five capabilities. First, can you reject all bad associates from now until the time of your enlightenment? *I can.*
>
> Second, can you become close to spiritual compatriots? *I can.*
>
> Third, can you maintain the precepts without transgression even in the face of death? *I can.*
>
> Fourth, can you read the Mahāyāna scriptures and inquire of their profound meaning? *I can.*
>
> Fifth, can you [strive] to the extent of your own power to save sentient beings from their suffering? *I can.*
>
> Next, each must say his own name and repent his transgressions, saying:
>
> *I now profoundly repent with all my heart all the karma of body, speech, and mind, and the ten evil transgressions [committed by me] during the past, future, and present. I hope that my transgressions will be eradicated, never to occur again. . . .*
>
> To maintain the Bodhisattva Precepts is to maintain the precepts of the mind, because the Buddha nature is the "nature of the precepts" (*jiexing*). To activate (*qi*) the mind for the briefest instant is to go counter to the Buddha-nature, to break the Bodhisattva Precepts. *(This [subject] is to be explained thrice.)*[23]

Of the many noteworthy points of this liturgy, the most germane is that the traditional forms for taking the bodhisattva precepts are retained—taking the Buddhas and bodhisattvas as preceptors, repeating the precepts, and uttering a formula of repentance—along with ritualistically repeated explanations that the true nature of one's own mind is the same as the nature of the precepts. The two levels of truth of the precepts are thus maintained within the ordination ceremony itself.

Taking another step away from the conventional precepts platform, let us consider Shenhui's *Tanyu* (Platform Address).[24] The setting of the address is clearly one of the ordination gatherings for which Shenhui was so famous. At the beginning of the *Tanyu* there is a collective ceremony of homage and confession of sins, which is too lengthy to include here.[25] The repentance of transgressions proceeds according to numerical groupings of the four, five, seven, and ten transgressions, which are not described. In fact, these groupings are all based on the essential lay precepts, and so their contents are largely redundant. Shenhui's address stresses maintenance of conventional precepts:

> You must each maintain [mental and physical] abstinence. If you do not maintain this abstinence, you will ultimately never be able to generate all the good dharmas. If you are going to seek the unsurpassable *bodhi* you must first maintain this abstinence, only after doing which will you gain entry [into *bodhi*]. If you do not maintain this abstinence, you won't even be able to get the body of a mangy fox [in your next life], so how could you possibly acquire the meritorious *dharmakāya* of a Tathāgata? . . . You must depend on conditioned morality and conditioned wisdom to manifest the unconditioned [morality and unconditioned] wisdom.[26]

One cannot help but be reminded of revival-tent exhortation when reading Shenhui's *Tanyu*. At the same time, his free handling of the scriptures also recalls the elegant reconstructions of doctrine through "contemplative interpretation" (*guanxin shi* 觀心釋) that are found in works attributed to the East Mountain school, particularly in the works of Shenxiu. "Contemplative interpretation" refers to the East Mountain hermeneutic that transfigured orthodox scriptural doctrines from transcendent abstractions into interiorized contemplative analogues. As noted, both Faure and McRae have shown that the distinction between "Northern" and "Southern" was not as clear as it has been represented to be, but in Shenhui's address the cool cloister breath of contemplative interpretation is indisputably quickened, if not evaporated: "Now, friends, now that you have been able to come to this place of enlightenment (*daochang* 道場, *bodhimaṇḍa*), you can each and every one generate the unsurpassable *bodhicitta* and seek the unsurpassable Dharma of bodhi!"[27]

Reconstruction of practices according to contemplative interpretation became, in Southern School contexts, reconstruction according to formlessness or no-thought. The *Platform Sūtra* begins by linking the *Prajñāpāramitā* and transmission of the formless precepts (*wuxiang jie* 無相戒): "The Master Hui-neng ascended the high seat at the lecture hall of the Ta-fan temple and expounded the Dharma of the Great Perfection of Wisdom, and transmitted the precepts of formlessness. At that time over ten thousand monks, nuns, and lay followers sat before him."[28] In the sermon that follows Huineng's story of his reception of the robe and Dharma, all the elements of the typical bodhisattva precepts ceremony are reinterpreted as formless: taking refuge in the three bodies of the Buddha (representing the three groups of pure precepts), the four vows, repentance, and taking refuge in the Triple Jewel.[29] The following is the refuge in the three bodies of the Buddha:

> Good friends, you must all with your own bodies receive the precepts of formlessness and recite in unison what I am about to say. It will make you see the threefold body of the Buddha in your own selves. "I take refuge in the pure *Dharmakāya* Buddha in my own physical body. I take refuge in the ten thousand hundred billion *Nirmāṇakāya* Buddhas in my own physical body. I take refuge in the future perfect *Saṃbhogakāya* Buddha in my own physical body." (Recite the above three times.)[30]

At the end of the ceremony, the non-duality of good and evil is emphasized: "The ten thousand things are all in self-nature. Although you see all men and non-men, evil and good, evil things and good things, you must not throw them aside, nor must you cling to them, nor must you be stained by them, but you must regard them as being like the empty sky."[31] Groner explicates this potentially antinomian teaching in terms of its continuity with the Northern School *Dasheng wusheng fangbian men*, and with interpretations of the precepts in found in canonical exegetical works and the *Prajñāpāramitā* scriptures:

> In a similar manner, in the ordination in the *Dasheng wusheng men*, the precepts of the mind (*xinjie*) are conferred and the ceremony concludes with a discussion of meditation. The precepts thus seem to be similar to "precepts that arise with or accompany meditation" (*dinggong jie*). This concept, called *dhyānaja-saṃvara*, found in *abhidharma* sources such as the *Abhidharmakośa*, was based on the view that a person in deep trances associated with the form-realm would not violate any of the precepts associated with the desire-realm. However, when the practitioner emerged from the trance, he might then violate the precepts again. . . . In the *Platform Sūtra*, however, no static form of trance is advocated: rather, no-thought is established. When no-thought is present, then the precepts and wisdom are manifested. . . .
>
> In the *Platform Sūtra*, the explanation of *Mahaprajñāpāramitā* at the end of the ceremony corresponds to the explanation of the precepts found in other ceremonies. However, this explanation is unlike that found in most other manuals insofar as the non-substantiality of good and bad are stressed. If these basic concepts are non-substantial, then the precepts themselves are formless, that is, without characteristics. Such a concept is

> not new: according to the *Pañcaviṃśatisāhasrikā,* "The bodhisattva should fulfill the perfection of wisdom by basing himself on the non-existence of sin and good action."[32]

Though the notion of the formless precepts as the nature of one's own mind had a basis in scripture, as well as links with practices in the Tiantai school and the East Mountain group, this does not appear to have detracted from the cachet of the ultraradical that permeates the *Tanyu,* the *Platform Sūtra,* and the *Lidai fabao ji.* I would suggest that the atmosphere of the mass ordination assembly is the common context for the self-conscious antinomianism in all three texts. It was precisely within the well-defined time and space of such an assembly, in a ritual context, that the precepts of formlessness could be iterated. Even within this context, however, Shenhui was careful to stress the importance of conventional precepts. The uniqueness of the Bao Tang disciples is that they were willing to let the formless precepts go beyond the boundaries of public ritual and into the temple, there to inform the daily practice of monks and nuns.

As we see in the next section, Wuzhu arrives at Wuxiang's place, the Jingzhong 淨眾 monastery in Chengdu, in the midst of a three-day ordination assembly. In his *Yuanjue jing dashu chao* 圓覺經大疏鈔 (Subcommentary to the Scripture of Perfect Enlightenment), Zongmi 宗密 (780–841) provides a detailed description of the Jingzhong ceremonies:

> Their ceremony (*yishi* 儀式) for (dharma) transmission (*chuanshou* 傳授) is, in general, similar to the procedures (*fangbian* 方便) for receiving the full precepts (*juzujie* 具足戒) currently followed at the official (ordination) platforms (*guantan* 官壇) in this country. That is to say, one or two months in advance, they first fix a time [for holding the ceremony] and send out a circular inviting monks, nuns, and laymen and laywomen to assemble. They establish a "Mahāyāna" (*fangdeng* 方等)[33] ritual site (*daochang* 道場). The worship and repentance services (*lichan* 禮懺) go on for three or five seven-day periods, after which they give the dharma (*shoufa* 授法). This takes place entirely at night, in order to cut off contact with the outside [world] and avoid noise and confusion. The dharma having been given, [the ordinands] are ordered immediately to sit in meditation (*zuochan* 坐禪) and practice mindfulness of breathing (*xinian* 息念). Everyone, even those who cannot remain for long—such as persons who have come from a great distance and those belonging to the classes of nuns and laity—must remain for one or two seven-day periods of sitting meditation before dispersing in accord with [their individual] circumstances. As in the case with the rules (*fa* 法) for mounting the platform (*lintan* 臨壇) [explained in] the vinaya tradition, it is necessary for those in the assembly [who are planning to "mount the platform" for full ordination] to present their ordination licenses (*you-*

> *zhuang* 由狀). The government office grants ordination certificates (*wendie* 文牒); this is called "establishing a connection" (*kaiyuan* 開緣).[34]

In the *Lidai fabao ji,* this elaborate ceremony is the stage setting for Wuxiang's exclusive message to Wuzhu to leave the monastery and go into the mountains: "Every day in the midst of the great assembly the Venerable Kim would intone in a loud voice, 'Why do you not go into the mountains, what good is it to linger?'"[35] When Wuzhu obeys, he goes off to engage in practice that has none of the institutional forms of a regular monastery, for which he is criticized by the Jingzhong monks.[36]

The first occurrence of a sermon by Wuzhu is in the *Lidai fabao ji* section following the one on Shenhui and preceding the long section on Wuzhu's early years, his wanderings, his meeting with Wuxiang, and his long-delayed confirmation as the keeper of the robe. This sermon is clearly meant to be envisioned in the context of a large assembly:

> Whenever the Venerable Wuzhu of the Dali 大曆 [era] Bao Tang monastery in Chengdu subprefecture in Jiannan addressed students of the Way of the four assemblies, [he would say], "Whether a multitude or a single person, regardless of the time, if you have doubts you may confide your questions to me. I am occupying the seat and explaining the Dharma [so that you] directly see your own natures. Regard direct mind as the *bodhimaṇḍa* (*daochang* 道場). Regard aspiration to practice as the *bodhimaṇḍa.* Regard the profound mind as the *bodhimaṇḍa.* Regard the unstained as the *bodhimaṇḍa.* Regard not-grasping as the *bodhimaṇḍa.* Regard not-rejecting as the *bodhimaṇḍa.* Regard nonaction as expedient means. Regard the vast as expedient means. Regard equanimity as expedient means. Regard transcendence of characteristics as the fire and regard liberation as the incense. Regard nonobstruction as repentance. Regard no-thought as the precepts, nonaction and nothing to attain as meditation, and nonduality as wisdom. Do not regard the constructed ritual arena as the *bodhimaṇḍa.*"[37]

Wuzhu's sermon is not dissimilar in tone to Shenhui's in the *Tanyu* or Huineng's in the *Platform Sūtra.* Moreover, Wuzhu's explication of the *bodhimaṇḍa,* the sacred place of practice, is modeled after a section in the *Vimalakīrtinirdeśa-sūtra:* "The mind that aspires to bodhi is the place of practice, for it is without error or misconception. Almsgiving is the place of practice, because it hopes for no reward. Observance of the precepts is the place of practice, because it brings fulfillment of the vows."[38]

The *Vimalakīrti* passage deconstructs the notion of a specific place of practice by interpreting observance of the precepts and cultivation of the perfections as the *bodhimaṇḍa.* Elsewhere in the sūtra the meaning of practices like almsgiving and observance of the precepts are themselves interpreted in terms of nonduality. Wuzhu's *wunian* reinterpretation of the phenomenal aspects of Buddhist practice—establishing a place of practice, taking refuge, offering incense, repentance, and practicing the precepts, meditation, and wisdom—was thus a further step along an established path. However, the injunction "Do not regard the constructed ritual arena as the *bodhimaṇḍa*" is a clear indication of the direction that the Bao Tang school would take. Although Wuzhu's sermon echoes the sermons given in the context of ordination ceremonies by Shenhui and Wuxiang, the Bao Tang doctrinal stance precluded such Buddhist formalities as ceremonies for mass reception of the precepts.

Nevertheless, the *Lidai fabao ji* does grant us glimpses of the audience, and the assembly's influence may be felt in Wuzhu's resistance to their dependence on forms, rituals, and precepts. In the following sections, the drama of Wuzhu's secret transmission from Wuxiang and his isolated mountain practice is at the same time a public drama, though we cannot know whether these stories ever entertained an assembly.[39] Without the image of the assembly, however, the image of Wuzhu all alone in the mountains is meaningless.

TRANSMISSION FROM WUXIANG TO WUZHU

There is a certain discordance between the *Lidai fabao ji* authors' claim that Wuzhu's was a superior transmission of the doctrine of no-thought, and their reliance on mind-to-mind transmission as the ultimate source of authority. The account of what passes between Wuxiang and Wuzhu reflects the tension between an ideology of exceptional realization and an ideology of complete transmission. In each transmission the complete identity between master and disciple is stressed, yet, as we will see, the *Lidai fabao ji* authors also take pains to argue that Zhishen 智詵 (609–702), his disciple Chuji 處寂 (669–736), and even Wuxiang 無相 (684–762) did not preach the ultimate teaching.

Interestingly, both Zongmi and the *Lidai fabao ji* authors themselves indicate that Wuzhu's first significant discipleship was under a lay student of Laoan's named Chen Chuzhang 陳楚璋.[40] The *Lidai fabao ji* states: "[Wuzhu] chanced to meet the white-robed layman Chen Chuzhang, whose origins are unknown. People then called him an incarnation of Vimalakīrti. He expounded the Dharma of the sudden teaching. From the moment that he met the Venerable [Wuzhu] he privately sealed their mutual understanding, and silently transmitted the mind-Dharma."[41] The *Lidai fabao ji* claims that Wuzhu then practiced as a layman for "three to five years" and was finally prevailed on to take the tonsure by master Zizai

自在 of Taiyuan 太原. Thereafter he began the peregrinations that would lead him eventually to Wuxiang and the true Dharma transmission.[42]

The following *Lidai fabao ji* passage establishes identity between Wuxiang and Wuzhu through the trope of mysterious resemblance, with reference to the doctrine of the "transformation body" (*huashen* 化身), manifestations that the Buddhas and bodhisattvas take in order to teach beings:

> It happened that there was a merchant [named] Cao Gui 曹[玉 + 褁] who came to pay his respects [to Wuzhu] and asked, "Has the Venerable ever been to Jiannan? Do you know the Venerable Kim?" [Wuzhu] answered, "I don't know him." Gui said, "Your features are exactly like those of the Venerable Kim. You [both] have a mole above the bridge of your nose, and the shape of your face so resembles that of the Venerable in our locale that one could even say there is no difference. It must be a transformation-body (*huashen* 化身)."
>
> The Venerable asked Cao Gui, "So the layman has come from Jiannan. [Tell me], what doctrine does that Venerable preach? Cao Gui replied, "No-recollection, no-thought, and do not forget."[43] (Cao Gui then relates an incident in which Wuxiang tried to get him to apply these teachings in his own life, but he did not understand Wuxiang's point.) . . . When the Venerable heard this teaching he understood clearly, and from afar he met the Venerable Kim face-to-face.[44]

Along with this encapsulation of Wuxiang's Dharma, a kind of *panjiao* 判教 (classification of the teachings) of the Bao Tang school is also established. Zhishen and Chuji's transmissions are relegated to a lower level:

> [Wuxiang] also would say, "These three phrases of mine are teachings that were originally transmitted by the Patriarchal Master [Bodhi]dharma. I do not say that this is what was taught by the Venerable Shen (i.e., Zhishen) or the Venerable Tang 唐 (i.e., Chuji)."[45] He also said, "It has been permitted that the disciple has understanding surpassing that of his masters. Because the Venerables Shen and Tang did not expound the ultimate teaching, I have by a winding course inherited the robe of verification."
>
> The Venerable Kim thus did not draw from areas in which the Venerables Shen and Tang had expounded. Whenever he taught the precepts from the high seat he said directly, "These three phrases of mine that were transmitted by the Patriarchal Master [Bodhi]dharma are the gates of completely maintaining [the practice]. The nonarising of thought is the gate of *śīla*, the nonarising of thought is the gate of samādhi, the nonarising of thought [is] the gate of prajñā. No-thought is thus the complete fulfillment of *śīla*,

samādhi, and prajñā; it is the gate through which all the Buddhas of the past, present, and future, [countless as] the Ganges sands, have entered. It is not possible that there could be any other gates."[46]

The question of the correct version of the "three phrases" was implicated in the *Lidai fabao ji* authors' claim that Wuzhu held the only true transmission from Wuxiang; one should note that Wuxiang is made to attribute the origins of the three phrases to Bodhidharma. According to the *Lidai fabao ji,* Bodhidharma/Wuxiang's three phrases were "no-recollection, no-thought, and do not be deluded" (*wuyi wunian mowang* 無憶無念莫妄), which were correlated with the traditional "three trainings" of moral discipline, meditation, and wisdom: "No-recollection is *śīla,* no-thought is samādhi, and 'do not be deluded' is prajñā."[47] The *Lidai fabao ji* alludes to the contested nature of the term *mowang* and insists that the version Wuzhu taught was the correct one; the Jingzhong school apparently maintained that Wuxiang had taught the homophonous *mowang* 莫忘, "do not forget." Zongmi concurred with the Jingzhong school version, and he described Wuxiang's teaching as follows:

The "three phrases" are: no-recollection, no-thought, and "do not forget." The idea is: do not recall past *visayas* (domains); do not anticipate future glorious events; always be yoked to these insights, never darkening, never erring. This is called "do not forget." Sometimes [the three topics run]: no remembering of external *visayas,* no thinking of internal mind, dried up with nothing to rely on. *Śīla,* samādhi, and prajñā correspond respectively to the three phrases.[48]

Zongmi asserted that the Bao Tang usage *mowang* 莫妄 (do not be deluded) was Wuzhu's idea and not the original:

[The Bao Tang] also transmit the Venerable Kim's three-phrase oral teaching, but they change the character for "forget" to the character for "delusion." They say that all the fellow students have misconstrued the former master's oral tenets. Their characterization of the meaning is that no-recollection and no-thought are reality, and that recollecting thoughts is delusion; recollecting thoughts is not allowed. Therefore they say "do not be deluded."[49]

The Bao Tang interpretation was clearly influenced by Shenhui, for *wang* 妄 is the basis of Shenhui's interpretation of *śīla,* samādhi, and prajñā in the *Tanyu:*

Friends, the necessity of undertaking the three trainings has from the beginning distinguished the Buddhist teachings. What are the three trainings?

They are *śīla*, samādhi, and prajñā. That the deluded mind does not arise is called *śīla*, that there is no deluded mind is called samādhi, and knowing that the mind is without delusion is called prajñā. These are called the three trainings.[50]

According to the *Lidai fabao ji* authors' classification, Wuxiang's teaching in general was more advanced than Shenhui's, but it did not match Wuzhu's teaching that *śīla*, samādhi and prajñā were effortlessly manifested in no-thought. As in the passage above, the *Lidai fabao ji* authors also take pains to imply that Wuzhu is the one who has fully manifested the transmission of Bodhidharma that he received through the medium of a line of worthy but lesser masters.

Shenhui's teachings are admitted into the implicit *Lidai fabao ji* "classification of the teachings," but with qualifications. Shenhui is not included in the Bao Tang lineage, but a passage on his life and teachings is placed in between the section on Wuxiang and the beginning of the account of Wuzhu. Most important, an ambivalent assessment of Wuxiang's teachings is put into Shenhui's mouth, perhaps because it was considered a pre-established site of hazardous judgments: "Kim of Yizhou 益州 is a Chan Master, but he also did not manage to expound the ultimate teaching. Although he did not expound the ultimate teaching, the Buddha-Dharma is only at his place."[51]

In the *Lidai fabao ji*, the mysterious resemblance and unspoken understanding between Wuxiang and Wuzhu is much more significant than the transmission of the "three phrases," and immediate nonverbal transmission is of course at the heart of the Chan "mystique of transmission." The scene in which Wuzhu and Wuxiang meet is a compelling one, with at least as much dramatic merit as the better-known *Platform Sūtra* story of the meeting between Huineng and Hongren.

In the first month of the second year of the Qianyuan 乾元 era (759), [Wuzhu] reached Jingzhong 淨眾 (Pure Assembly) monastery in Chengdu subprefecture. When he first arrived he met Master Anqian 安乾, who led him in to see the Venerable Kim. When the Venerable Kim saw him he was extremely pleased. The Venerable Kim delegated Master Anqian to act as host, and he arranged for Wuzhu to stay in a cloister below the bell-tower. This was during a bodhisattva precepts [retreat], and that night [Wuzhu] followed the crowd and received the precepts. It lasted only three days and three nights.

Every day in the midst of the great assembly the Venerable Kim would intone in a loud voice, "Why do you not go into the mountains, what good is it to linger?" His attendant disciples considered this strange, [and said,] "The Venerable Kim has never said anything like this before. Why would he suddenly come out with these words?" But the Venerable Wuzhu quietly entered the mountains.[52]

Wuxiang and Wuzhu's subsequent long-distance relationship can be seen as a device to explain away the fact that Wuzhu was never Wuxiang's disciple. At the same time, it is a powerful means of expressing the formless teaching, not bound by physical presence or monastic formalities. We should also consider the motif of the long-distance relationship in light of the tension between the exclusive soteriology of mind-to-mind transmission and the inclusive soteriology of innate Buddha-nature. This tension is symbolically erased in the hagiographic motif of immediate recognition between master and disciple. The trope of sympathetic resonance between protagonists who are fated to meet is not exclusive to Chan or to Buddhism, but it was useful in solving one of the dilemmas of subitism. Any time spent studying with the master before receiving Dharma transmission would admit the taint of the gradual, implying that Buddha-nature is something learned. Huike spends years with Bodhidharma after receiving the initial transmission in the snow. Huineng spends nine months at Hongren's place, but they have only one encounter before Huineng receives transmission. The immediate affinity and resonance at the center of the *Lidai fabao ji* transmission story represents an extreme example of this hagiographic motif—Wuzhu and Wuxiang meet face to face only once.[53]

Though Wuzhu does not see Wuxiang again after the initial encounter, he is shown to be intimately connected with Wuxiang and aware of events at the distant Jingzhong monastery. In the scene that immediately follows the passage above, Wuzhu on his mountain-top answers a question that other monks are asking Wuxiang in his hall miles away. Wuzhu's answer is a challenge to the monastic community, and the scene presents a striking image of his mind-to-mind identity with Wuxiang.

> [Later] the Venerable Kim longed for him [and said,] "Why doesn't he come?" Preceptor Kong 空 and Preceptor Qin 秦 wanted to be able to recognize [Wuzhu, and so they said,] "We fear that one day we might chance to meet but not know who he is."
>
> [From the mountains] the Venerable [Wuzhu] faced toward them with a keen glance and exclaimed, "Although I am here, the Venerable Kim and I see each other constantly. Even if we wish not to know each other, we are face to face [though separated by] a thousand *li*. With my regards, I will preach a parable for you."[54]

Wuzhu then relates a scriptural episode, to be discussed in greater detail in the final section of this chapter, in which all the disciples flock to see the Buddha when he returns from preaching to his mother in Heaven.

A nun resorts to magical powers to be first in line to greet the Buddha, but it turns out that the disciple Subhuti, who was meditating in his cell miles away, was really "the first." The Buddha tells the nun, "Subhuti is in a stone cell continuously in samādhi, and so he was first, being able to see my Dharma-body. You came rushing to see my form-body, and so you are last." Wuzhu then concludes this lecture-from-afar to the Jingzhong monks by saying: "The Buddha has given a clear mandate, and that is why I do not go [to see the Venerable Kim]."[55]

Later in the *Lidai fabao ji,* two fragments apparently garnered from Wuzhu's Dharma-talks allude to the theme of distance and immediate presence (the first was used as the epigraph for this chapter):

> The Venerable always said, "If there is a karmic cause it will penetrate a thousand li; if there is no cause, then even people facing each other will not recognize one another." . . . He also quoted Brahmacarya Wang's 王梵志 poem, "The eye of wisdom is close to the mind of emptiness, not the holes that open into your skull. You don't recognize what [the person] facing you says, it doesn't matter that your mother's surname is respectable."[56]

Wuzhu's teachings thus reinforce his claim that he and Wuxiang are "face to face though separated by a thousand *li.*" Brahmacarya Wang's poem, like the parable of the Buddha and Subhuti, plays on the immediate and unfathomable recognition of emptiness/self/connection with the other. One wonders whether Wuzhu considered his relationship with Wuxiang to be like "the eye of wisdom close to the mind of emptiness," and it is clear that he (or the *Lidai fabao ji* authors) considered Wuxiang's other disciples to lack the insight necessary for true recognition.

Returning to the story of the long-distance transmission, Wuzhu's challenge from afar to the monks of Jingzhong monastery leads up to the story of how he received of the patents of legitimacy, the robe and Wuxiang's prediction confirming the future of the transmission. According to the *Lidai fabao ji,* the robe and the message were supposed to have been conveyed to Wuzhu by an intermediary. There are two divergent versions of this transmission; the first precedes Wuxiang's death scene, and the second, more elaborate account occurs in the long passage on Wuzhu. Let us look at the first account, said to have taken place four days before Wuxiang's death:

> On the fifteenth day of the fifth month of the first year of the Baoying 寶應 era (762), [Wuxiang] suddenly thought of Chan Master Wuzhu of the Baiyai 白崖 mountains and [thought], "I am ill. Surely [Wuzhu] will come to see me." Time and again he asked his attendants, "Why hasn't Chan Master Wuzhu come? I am growing old." He secretly sent the laborer Dong Xuan

> 董璿, [saying], "Take my robe of verification and seventeen other items of clothing, and secretly deliver them to Chan Master Wuzhu. He must protect himself well. It is not yet time for him to come out of the mountains, he should wait three to five more years, and when he hears that there is peace throughout the land then he can come out." [Thus] the transmission was settled from afar.[57]

The second version claims that at some time during the period when Wuzhu was sequestered in the mountains (759–766), he told the lay disciple Dong Xuan that he should go to Wuxiang to receive the precepts. Wuzhu sent him off with a gift of tea for Wuxiang, and when he went to Chengdu and presented the tea to Wuxiang, Dong Xuan lied and said he was a personal disciple of Wuzhu's.[58] In the following scene, Dong Xuan is about to return to the mountains and Wuxiang gives him Huineng's robe and other articles to give to Wuzhu:

> On the fifteenth day, [Dong Xuan] went to see the Venerable Kim. He said, "I wish to return to the Baiyai mountains, I am at your command." That time [Wuxiang] sent away his personal attendant disciples, [saying,] "You must all leave the hall." Then he summoned Dong Xuan to enter; Xuan obeyed and entered the hall kneeling, with his palms joined. The Venerable Kim brought out a *kāṣāya* robe, [the one that] the rarest few among men have had in their keeping. He revealed it [and said,] "This was given to the Venerable Shen by Empress [Wu] Zetian. The Venerable Shen gave it to the Venerable Tang, the Venerable Tang gave it to me, and I transmit it to Chan Master Wuzhu. This robe has long been cherished, don't let anyone know of it." When he finished speaking he became choked with sobbing [and said,] "This robe has been passed from legitimate heir to legitimate heir, one must make utmost effort, utmost effort!" Then he took from his own person his *kāṣāya*, under and outer robes, and sitting cloth. Altogether there were seventeen things. [He said,] "I am getting on in years. You take these things and convey them secretly to Chan Master Wuzhu, and transmit my words: 'Take good care of yourself, and make utmost effort, utmost effort! It is not yet time to leave the mountains. Wait three to five years longer, and only leave when a person of consequence welcomes you.'" At that he dispatched Dong Xuan, [saying,] "Go quickly, and do not let anyone learn of this." When he had seen Dong Xuan go, the Venerable Kim said to himself, "These things will get there late, but they will get through in the end."[59]

Later, when his disciples ask him about the robe, he says, "My Dharma has gone to the place of nonabiding (*wuzhu*). The robe is hanging from the top of a tree, no one has got it."[60] Still later it is revealed that the robe made it to Wuzhu only after further complications. Some army officers who have met Wuzhu in the mountains tell this story to the imperial minister Du Hongjian:

> We saw that this Chan Master looked exactly like the Venerable Kim. When we first saw him it was as if he were a transformation body of the Venerable Kim. We ventured to question him and remained for some time, and we learned that the Venerable Kim's robe and bowl had previously been dispatched to him via a messenger. [The messenger] hid them for two years and did not deliver them, and then sold them to a monk. When the monk obtained the robe, that night a spirit appeared who told him to send it back to its original owner, [saying] "If you do not return it, you are most certainly throwing away your life." The buyer exchanged it, giving an account of what had happened. After that [the messenger] couldn't sell it, and restored it to the original Chan Master's place. As soon as we heard that the robe our previous searching had not discovered was now in the immediate vicinity, we asked to make obeisance. Without reservations, [Wuzhu] carried the robe out aloft and revealed it to all the army officers and soldiers, so we know it is at that place.[61]

The *Lidai fabao ji*'s subsequent rebuttal of the story that Wuzhu actually stole the robe is the only remaining evidence that there was such a story in circulation. It occurs in the context of an attempt by some Vinaya masters to appropriate Wuxiang's lineage for themselves. They have Wuxiang's cloister and meditation hall in the Jingzhong monastery turned into a Vinaya cloister and hall, they produce another robe and claim it is Wuxiang's. In the following scene, they try to discourage the local gentry from following Du Hongjian's lead in supporting Wuzhu:

> Vinaya Master Yingyao 英耀 replied, "To rely on this Chan Master Wuzhu would be unwise. Inviting this monk would be profoundly disadvantageous to the clergy as a whole." The minister [Yan 嚴] asked, "Why would it be disadvantageous for the clergy?" [Yingyao] replied, "There is a craftsman on the Min 汶 river who is an inlay-artisan of average skill. He got a *kāṣāya* [as payment] that had an estimated value of twenty thousand cash. The craftsman's robe was taken away by that Chan Master and was never returned. [Wuzhu] claimed, 'This was bestowed on me by the Venerable Kim.' [Moreover], he does not practice the forms of worship and recitation. Based on this evidence, it would be disadvantageous for the clergy [were he to be invited]."
>
> The vice-director [Cui 崔] said to the Vinaya masters, "Previously, when I was with the cavalry in the western mountains, I learned the whole situa-

tion. Why do you Vinaya masters resort to slander?" So saying, he left his seat. [The faces of] the malicious clique drained of color, they were utterly at a loss. Their evil deed was thus thwarted.[62]

Here the charge of theft is coupled with the charge of departing from orthopraxy, departing from the forms of worship. The Vinaya masters' accusations are cast as puerile lies, but they also represent orthodox reactions against the challenge that Bao Tang nonconformity presented to the clergy as a body. In contrast, Wuzhu's self-possession in the face of these challenges and difficulties is meant to prove that he truly merits the transmission of the robe. In terms of the mystique of legitimacy, he is shown possessing not only the talisman but also the inner worth to call forth the mysterious response. But what is it that he possesses?

Let us look at the *Lidai fabao ji* claim that Wuzhu was Wuxiang's true successor in light of other claims about Wuxiang's heirs. Much of the contemporaneous information about the Jingzhong and Bao Tang schools comes from Zongmi, and Zongmi's interest in these lineages was partly due to his own lineage concerns. In fact, Zongmi himself may have more properly belonged to Wuxiang's lineage than that of the "seventh patriarch" Shenhui, for Hu Shi and other scholars have contended that Zongmi's connection with Shenhui's line was tenuous at best.[63]

According to the *Song gaoseng zhuan*, Wuxiang's acknowledged Dharma successor was Jingzhong Shenhui 淨眾神會 (720–794), who became abbot of the Jingzhong monastery after his death.[64] Jingzhong Shenhui's successor was Zhang Weizhong 張惟忠, also known as Nanyin 南印 (d. 821), and Nanyin was Zongmi's "grandfather" in the Dharma. However, Nanyin may also have studied with the legendary Southern School champion Shenhui (i.e., Heze Shenhui 荷澤神會), and he or his followers may have used the name Weizhong in order to be associated with Heze Shenhui's disciple of that name (whose dates were 705–782).[65] This may be the source of the confusion over Zongmi's claim to be Shenhui's successor through Nanyin/Weizhong, and Peter Gregory argues that if deliberate falsification occurred, it originated with Nanyin and not Zongmi. Gregory proposes a subsect of the Jingzhong, the "Shengshou 聖壽" (after Nanyin's temple in Chengdu) in order to capture the flavor that Heze Shenhui may have in fact imparted to Zongmi through Nanyin, even if the latter was not Heze Shenhui's recognized Dharma-heir.[66] Gregory says: "Even though Nan-yin's teaching seems to have been nothing more than an extension of Ching-chung Ch'an, in claiming a direct filiation with Ho-tse Shen-hui his tradition asserted its institutional independence."[67]

As the notion of "*zong* 宗" encompassed both formal lineage and essential doctrine, and as Zongmi used it in both senses, Gregory, in company with other scholars, cautions against taking an overly legalistic view of claims of affiliation in eighth- and ninth-century Chan writings. Thus, Gregory argues, the fact that Zongmi's Chan lineage stemmed from Wuxiang through Jingzhong Shenhui while he considered himself to be an heir of Heze Shenhui was not problematic: "The particular tsung to which a teacher belonged was not merely a matter of lineal filiation but also had to do with the source of inspiration to which his tradition turned. It was the essential teaching emphasized within a given tradition that defined it as a tsung as much as the lineal filiation of a succession of teachers. A tsung was, as it were, the 'progenitive idea' around which a tradition crystallized."[68]

Scholars of Chinese Buddhism are indebted to T. Griffith Foulk for an understanding of how watertight Chan lineages, schools, transmission protocols, and mythologies created in the Song claimed anchorage in the murky depths of the Tang, and how inconvenient baggage was cast overboard in the process.[69] It is easy to see why the *Lidai fabao ji*'s conflicting accounts of the Bao Tang lineage would have been considered too cumbersome to keep afloat. Shenhui was clearly a "progenitive idea" for the Bao Tang, but he was not claimed in their lineage. At the same time, the *Lidai fabao ji* authors undercut the essential teachings of the lineal filiation (Zhishen-Chuji-Wuxiang) that they took such pains to claim. Moreover, by the showing of the *Lidai fabao ji* itself, Wuxiang's prestige was a rich legacy coveted by several competing factions.

Prestige is a volatile market, tempting to speculators. Gregory, noting that "changing trends within the Chinese Buddhist world" influenced the formation of *zong,* says: "That factors directly related to a teacher's own self-interest were often involved in such matters does not mean that there was anything inherently 'dishonest' about it. It was simply a matter of putting one's best foot forward."[70] However, Zongmi's and especially Shenqing's indignant repudiation of the fancy footwork of the *Lidai fabao ji* authors shows that dishonesty about lineage was an issue for them. The *Lidai fabao ji*'s own elaborate stories draw attention to the stakes involved in deception. If the formation of eighth- and ninth-century *zong* simply involved demonstrating consistency with one's claimed intellectual and spiritual antecedents, then the *Ding shifei lun, Platform Sūtra, Lidai fabao ji, Caoqi dashi zhuan, Baolin zhuan, Beishan lu,* and so on, would not have been so concerned with disputing claims to legitimate transmission and lineage.

Throughout this study I have repeatedly returned to the question of how patronage and economic aspects may have influenced sectarian formation and dissension. However, I do not by any means consider these to be conclusive factors in the formation of sectarian identity. If the Bao Tang community had merely wanted warm robes and regular meals, it would have been easier for them to change their tune rather than go such lengths to defend an unpalatable application of Shenhui's thought. The coverings in which the *Lidai fabao ji* authors attempt to hide and give shape to their spiritual/communal identity underlines the self-contradictory nature of such an identity. The *Lidai fabao ji* presents us with an especially revealing account of the tension that any spiritual community faces, the tension between invoking and challenging what is already sanctioned.

LOCATING WUZHU

In this section I attempt to elucidate the delicate balance of affiliations claimed by the Bao Tang by presenting these affiliations within patterns of ideological opposition. I take four of the *Lidai fabao ji* figures—Zhishen, Shenhui, Wuxiang, and Wuzhu—as representatives of the range within which the tension between formal and formless transmission of authority oscillated. So far, I have discussed the *Lidai fabao ji* passages on the first three figures in terms of the roles that they play in the *Lidai fabao ji* narrative regarding the patriarchal robe. In this section I sketch their paradigmatic functions in order to "locate" Wuzhu within and beyond this set of relationships. Placing Zhishen, Shenhui, Wuxiang, and Wuzhu along a historical and doctrinal spectrum is primarily a heuristic device, but I hope that it is more suggested by the *Lidai fabao ji* than imposed on it. A diachronic progression from "old order" forms to "new order" formlessness is consistent with the text's thrust toward Wuzhu's teachings and, at the same time, displays the synchronic range of virtuosity within which Wuzhu is presented as anomalous and incomparable.

Zhishen, associated with the old Buddhist order of the capitals, represents one extreme that defines the Bao Tang school, and Wuzhu of the new Chan of the provinces embodies the other. Shenhui and Wuxiang can be said to occupy intermediate positions. By "old order" I mean the Buddhist establishments subject to the centralizing force of the Tang imperium and aristocratic elites. The "new order" drew support from the increasingly autonomous forces of the provincial military and administrative elites who patronized a variety of forms of popular Buddhism, including the assemblies of the emerging Southern School-based sects. There are traditional dates dividing the old from the new—for the political order it is the An Lushan rebellion of 755, and for the Buddhist order it is Shenhui's challenge of 732.

Zhishen, as we recall, is said to have conveyed Huineng's robe from the court of Empress Wu to its new destiny in Jiannan. Zhishen thus links the power of the new Southern School with the old prestige of the era of Hongren's heirs at Wu Zetian's court. In the *Lidai fabao ji* court scene, Zhishen's demonstration and verbal teaching of no-thought shows him to be superior to any of Hongren's other disciples, but his Dharma and that of his heir Chuji are still considered by the *Lidai fabao ji* authors to be inferior to Wuxiang's and Wuzhu's.

Shenhui, whose influence was associated with the period of post-rebellion Tang restoration, is presented as somewhere in between old and new. Shenhui enshrined the old order, making a patriarchal icon out of the East Mountain figure Hongren, in order to put him in service of the new order represented by Huineng, who was perhaps largely Shenhui's creation. Shenhui/Huineng's doctrines of formlessness and no-thought were the doctrinal patents of Southern School legitimacy, yet in the *Lidai fabao ji* Shenhui is made to endorse Wuzhu's superior ability to teach it. And although Shenhui became the official seventh patriarch, his own Heze 荷澤 school lasted hardly longer than the Bao Tang.

Wuxiang was born a prince in Silla, a kingdom on the Korean peninsula with tributary relations with the Tang. As a Chan master in Chengdu he was known for extreme asceticism and magical powers, as reflected in his biography in the *Song gaoseng zhuan.*[71] Devaluation of magical powers was part of the Chan rhetorical arsenal, but the *Lidai fabao ji* authors could not resist showcasing the uncanny in the relationship between Wuzhu and Wuxiang. Wuzhu is shown to partake of Wuxiang's thaumaturgic qualities by his ability to survive without food and his ability to know what is going on at Wuxiang's temple many miles away. Having seen Wuzhu only once, Wuxiang later gives him the robe and Dharma transmission.

Wuzhu is of low-ranking military origins, and his decision to leave the army and pursue the Way leads him to crisscross north China. As noted, it is claimed that he first received the Dharma of the sudden teaching and mind-transmission from the layman Chen Chuzang. Subsequently, while still a layman, he is said to have practiced with three of Huineng's Dharma heirs, including Shenhui, and to have taken the tonsure under one of them, Master Zizai, in 749. It is during a sojourn at Mt. Helan in Ningxia prefecture from 751 to 753 that the merchant Cao Gui comes to visit him and tells him that he looks exactly like the Venerable Kim of Jiannan. This prompts Wuzhu to leave Mt. Helan and gradually make his way south to Sichuan, finally arriving at Jingzhong monastery in 759. When Wuzhu arrives in the midst of a precepts assembly that has gathered to hear Wuxiang, he understands the mysterious command directed to him and passes beyond the normal circuit of monkish activities to isolate himself in the mountains.[72]

The independence and privations of Wuzhu's mountain are contrasted with the order, elegance, and decadence of the Jingzhong monastic establishment near Chengdu. In the mountains Wuzhu practices an asceticism more radical than Wuxiang's. It is there we see him preaching, for the first time, a formless practice more absolute than his fellow monks can stomach. In a passage that is discussed further below, Wuzhu's way is repudiated by a fellow monk:

> As Master Daoyi's 道逸 views did not go along with [Wuzhu's] fundamental intent, he took leave of the Venerable and left Mt. Tiancang 天蒼. Arriving at Jingzhong monastery in Yizhou, he met with Preceptor Kong and the others and said, "Chan Master Wuzhu in the mountains doesn't practice worship or recitation, he just sits in vacuity [*kongxianzuo* 空閑坐]. Hekong 何空 and the others heard this with manifold amazement, [exclaiming] "How could this be the Buddha-Dharma?" They took Master Daoyi to see the Venerable Kim.
>
> Before Daoyi had finished making obeisances, Hekong and the others informed the Venerable Kim, "Chan master Wuzhu of Mt. Tiancang just sits in vacuity. He is not willing to worship and recite, and neither will he teach his fellow inmates to worship and recite. What is this? How could this be the Buddha-Dharma!"
>
> The Venerable Kim exploded at Hekong, Daoyi, and the others, "You get out! When I was at the stage of learning, I wouldn't get around to eating, I just sat in vacuity. I didn't even make an effort to shit or piss. You lot don't realize that when I was at Mt. Tiangu 天谷, I didn't worship or recite, either. All my fellow-students got angry with me and left the mountain. No one sent provisions and I had only smelted earth (*liantu* 練土) as food. But even then I didn't even make an effort to leave the mountain, and I devoted myself to sitting in idleness. When Abbot Meng 孟 heard from my fellow-students that I was sitting in idleness, he immediately went to the Venerable Tang to slander me. When the Venerable Tang heard I was sitting in idleness he was overjoyed. Meanwhile I was at Mt. Tiangu and knew nothing of the slander. Hearing that the Venerable Tang was gravely ill, I came from Mt. Tiangu to Dechun Monastery in Zizhou. Abbot Meng saw me coming and would not let me enter the monastery. [But] the Venerable Tang heard that I had come and sent someone to summon me to appear before his hall. I had not yet completed my obeisance when the Venerable Tang asked me, 'At Mt. Tiangu, how do you occupy yourself?' I replied, 'I don't do a thing. I am just immersed and oblivious.' The Venerable Tang retorted, 'You are oblivious, I am also oblivious!' The Venerable Tang knew, the others had no inkling." [73]

Here we see a homology established—Wuzhu's "sitting in vacuity" in the mountains and his wordless bond with Wuxiang parallels Wuxiang's early practice and his relationship with his master Chuji. The trope of mysterious resemblance is reinforced, and the replication of the Dharma from one generation to the next is shown to be impervious to the intrigues of the unworthy. At the same time, as we have seen, the *Lidai fabao ji* is careful to make the point (through Shenhui) that Wuzhu's Dharma is superior to Wuxiang's. These oppositions—north versus south, monastery versus mountain, prince versus commoner, hierarchy versus mutual recognition, effort versus vacancy—are made meaningful through the time- and space-defying connections and sympathetic resonance between the counterpoised figures.

In presenting these pairs and oppositions, I would like to draw an analogy between these intratextual structural dynamics and Faure's analysis of Chan's intertextual structural dynamics:

> The differentiation produces a dissemination, a setting in motion of various paradigmatic pairs that can no longer be assigned to precise and unchanging sectarian positions. Once again, it is important to consider these various examples of "differential Chan" merely as ideal types and to avoid reifying the divisions into groups. Chan is, and always was, an "imagined community." The notions of distinction on the social level and of *differénce* on the philosophical level may help us to account for this constant production of gaps (*écarts*).[74]

On the social level of distinction,[75] the *Lidai fabao ji* authors advanced their claims for the ultimacy of the Bao Tang school by borrowing symbols of prestige from both the old and new orders of Buddhism, and oscillated between the widest possible paradigmatic poles. Attempting to distinguish themselves within the society of Southern School Chan, the authors exposed their social insecurity by the variety and inconsistency of their postures. In order to raise (or split) this social insecurity to the philosophical level of *differénce,* we must look to the putative source, Wuzhu. As noted, the various orders of the text—teleology, mediated oppositions, duplicity (recurrence of doubles and of fabrication), and hierarchies established through doctrinal polemics—all converge in Wuzhu. The disparate sources, styles, and forces of the text center on this figure for whom few other traces remain. Jacques Derrida's comments provide a means to draw attention to the forces that bind and pit the text against itself:

> And as always, coherence in contradiction expresses the force of a desire. The concept of centered structure is in fact the concept of a play based on a fundamental ground, a play constituted on the basis of a fundamental immobility and a reassuring certitude, which itself is beyond the reach of play. And on the basis of this certitude anxiety can be mastered, for anxiety is invariably the result of a certain mode of being implicated in the game, of being caught by the game, of being as it were at stake in the game from the outset.[76]

Wuzhu is the "fundamental immobility and reassuring certitude" that reveals the force of the *Lidai fabao ji* authors' desire to be in the game and also their anxiety about it. This anxiety is not merely the social insecurity of those on the margins of a group, but reflects the philosophical impossibilities that are intrinsic to Prajñāpāramitā doctrine and Southern School subitism. These impossibilities would provide scope for endless play in subsequent Chan texts, as proponents worked to find means to teach the immediate, uphold both the precepts and the sudden principle of no-defilement, and convey realization of fundamental nature as no-nature. In the words of Wuzhu's signature phrase, "At the time of true no-thought, no-thought itself is not."[77]

By implicating the *Lidai fabao ji* authors in such games, my intention is not to critique their performance on either the social or philosophical levels, but to highlight their strategies for the mastery of anxiety on both levels. Nor do I intend to imply that Wuzhu was a mere textual paradigm and not a "real person." Rather, I wish to draw attention to the manner in which Wuzhu 無住, nonabiding, becomes an apt occupant of the text's tension- and anxiety-mastering unoccupied center. In the manner of the analysis of the Bodhidharma-Sengchou and Huike-Tanlin relationships in chapter 5, by thinking of the Bao Tang masters as pairs, or quartets, we approach the aspect of Wuzhu that is, in Derrida's words, "not a fixed locus but a function, a sort of nonlocus in which an infinite number of sign-substitutions came into play."[78] Wuzhu, palpably an individual, also functions as the center and virtual space from which the *Lidai fabao ji* authors made their case—their "public case" (*gongan* 公安)—for the importance of this particular rendering of the "sudden." Wuzhu becomes the manifestation of the True Dharma of the Southern School and the embodiment of formless practice. And as the text unfolds, each of Wuzhu's devoted converts and vanquished opponents (there are no neutral parties) function as responsive "good signs" confirming this True Dharma. We now turn to Wuzhu's encounters with these disciples and would-be detractors.

ANTINOMIANISM IN THE MONASTERY

Wuzhu's antinomianism is firmly grounded in the "no-ground" of subitism, the assertion that moral and formal distinctions belong to the delusory mind that is transcended in no-thought. This view is repeated throughout the *Lidai fabao ji*, but some of his strongest statements are found in the context of a rather one-sided dialogue with a group of Vinaya masters who come to call. He opens his discussion by questioning them about the meaning of "host and guest," and then proceeds to critique the Vinaya:

> The significance of the Vinaya is to regulate and subdue, and the precepts are not blue, yellow, red or white. Not color/desire (*se* 色) and not mind, this is the substance of precepts, this is the fundamental nature of beings, fundamentally complete, fundamentally pure. When deluded thoughts are

> produced, then one "turns away from awakening and adheres to dust,"[79] and this is precisely "violating the Vinaya precepts." When deluded thoughts are not produced, then one turns away from dust and adheres to awakening, and this is precisely "fulfilling the Vinaya precepts." When thoughts are not produced, this is precisely *Vinayottara;* when thoughts are not produced, this is precisely *Vinayaviniścaya.* When thoughts are not produced, this is precisely destroying all mind-consciousnesses. "If one has views of upholding the precepts then one violates the precepts. Whether 'precepts' or 'not precepts,' the two views are a single characteristic. One who is able to know this is a great Master of the Way."[80] "One sees that the *bhikṣus* who commit grave offenses do not fall into Hell, and sees that those who practice purity do not enter nirvāṇa. If you abide in views like these, this is impartial seeing."[81]

Views like these can be found in a number of eighth-century texts, including Shenhui's works, the arguments of Moheyan 摩訶衍 in the *Dunwu dasheng zhenglijue* 頓悟大乘正理決 (Verification of Sudden Awakening in the Mahāyāna), the *Zhujing yaochao* 諸經要抄 (Digest of Scriptures), and the Dunhuang texts and fragments that Jeffrey Broughton has dubbed "The Bodhidharma Anthology."[82] In *Record II* and *Record III* of the latter collection, we find numerous passages that are analogous to statements in the *Lidai fabao ji,* as, for example, the following:

> Another question: "If you bind mind to bring karma into being, how can it be cut off?" Answer: "Since there is no mind, it is unnecessary to cut it off. This mind has neither a locus of arising nor a locus of extinguishing, because false thoughts give rise to dharmas. The sūtra says: 'The sins of karmic obstacles do not come from the south, the west, or the north, or from the four corners, or from above or below. They all arise from perverted views.' There is no need to doubt this. The bodhisattva, examining the Dharma of all the Buddhas of the past, seeks [the sins of karmic obstacles] in the ten directions but cannot apprehend any of them."[83]

And in the *Zhujing yaochao,* we find the following comment on the meaning of "real precepts" (*zhenjie* 真戒):

> All beings fundamentally of themselves have Buddha-nature. One who upholds the "real precepts" is someone who recognizes the mind and sees the nature. At the time of seeing the nature, conceptualizations are not produced. When discriminations do not arise, this is [the completion of] non-outflow training (i.e., attaining *arhatva*). Entering the non-precepts is not self and not other, not stained and not pure, without "I," without others, without thought, without discrimination, without host (lord), without ruler, without guest (vassal), without *xibai* 惜百 and without anything that is

> compulsory. Desires are forever at rest and equivalent to emptiness. Just like insensate things, body and mind themselves are not. Precepts and transgressions are nondual. One who is capable of knowing this is someone who [practices] the real precepts.[84]

Antinomian statements like these should be seen within the larger context of Chinese elaborations on apophatic Prajñāpāramitā discourse. Deconstruction of moral distinctions and the precepts serves as a particularly dramatic means to introduce the student to the disorienting paradoxes of nonduality, and the *Vimalakīrti-sūtra* was a paradigm for this kind of *upāya.* Statements comparable to Wuzhu's "no-thought is the precepts" were not intended to rationalize lax practices, although in chapter 3 we heard from the trio of scolding critics who voice such accusations in the *Lidai fabao ji.* Rather, focus on the precepts serves to highlight the shocking otherness of true nature's lack of reference to conventional distinctions.

However, until the Bao Tang no Chan school actually abandoned daily monastic and devotional routines, thereby ceasing to contribute to the circulation of merit. This attitude presented a dilemma even within the context of the Southern School, for possession of the true transmission was still a soteriological trust fund, a source of support that was intended to be passed down through the generations. Wuzhu's teachings and debates in the second half of the *Lidai fabao ji* revolve around the themes of formless practice and no-thought, and the same apophatic phrases are repeated frequently within a series of structurally similar stories of Wuzhu's encounters with would-be challengers and followers. At the same time, the encounters include attempts to demonstrate why and how practitioners of no-thought should continue to receive donations.

Leading these encounters is the lengthy and dramatic narrative in which Wuzhu is invited down from the mountains by the imperial minister Du Hongjian 杜鴻漸 (709–769), the "person of consequence" alluded to in Wuxiang's message to Wuzhu.[85] The story of Wuzhu's meeting with the minister could be considered the centerpiece of the *Lidai fabao ji.* Du was sent to Sichuan in 766 in order to put down an uprising by the cavalry officer Cui Gan 崔旰, who had been highly effective in keeping the Tibetans at bay. Du was able to quell the uprising by accusing Cui of cowardice, but after Du returned to Chang'an in 767 Cui consolidated his power in the area around Chengdu.[86] The *Lidai fabao ji* authors make no mention of this conflict, and both men are shown taking refuge with Wuzhu. However, Du, with a reputation as a devout Buddhist, was clearly considered to be the primary patron.

As the *Lidai fabao ji* narrative unfolds, Du's efforts to discover the true fate of the robe lead him at length to Wuzhu, and he then invites Wuzhu to be his guest and arranges a grand ceremonial procession for Wuzhu's descent from the mountains. Wuzhu is accommodated in the Konghui 空惠 monastery when he arrives in Chengdu, and there Du comes to see him for the first time.

> (Various officials of Du Hongjian's entourage) came first to tell the Venerable, "The Lord Minister is coming to present himself to the Venerable." [Wuzhu] replied, "If he's coming then it's up to him." The Lackeys told the Venerable, "A Minister of State is a very important person, you ought to go out and welcome him." The Venerable said, "It would not be appropriate to welcome him. 'Welcoming' is human feelings. 'Not welcoming' is the Buddha-Dharma."
>
> The Lackeys wanted to say more, but [at the moment] the Lord Minister entered the cloister and saw that the Venerable's demeanor was unmoving, majestically composed. The Lord Minister bowed at the lower level, made obeisance with palms joined, and politely inquired after [Wuzhu's] "rising and resting" (i.e., his health and comfort). None of the Directors and Attendant-Censors had ever seen such a thing.[87]

As discussed in chapter 2, Buddhist refusal to conform to secular protocol was a long-standing issue. The image of a monk declining to show respect to officials was common enough, but here we may note that the symbolic refusal has shifted from "not-bowing" to "not-rising."[88] Either way, the claim to be exempt from ordinary etiquette was based on the rationale that the Buddhist clergy observed a higher discipline. However, as the Bao Tang eschewed normative Buddhist practice, they could not have made the traditional claim to be exempt from normative secular practice. It was certainly unclear why they should be supported by lay patrons, and it is the latter point that is taken up in several places in the *Lidai fabao ji*.

The independent attitude of the Bao Tang followers seems to have been more than symbolic, and the following passages stress acceptance of the consequences of independence. In a scene from the period of his seclusion in the mountains, Wuzhu is deserted by his fellow monks because his refusal to carry out any recognizably Buddhist activity besides sitting in meditation is, it is implied, responsible for the dearth of donations to their remote temple:

> Master Daoyi, [Wuzhu's] fellow inmate [at the mountain hermitage], practiced chanting [scripture], worship, and recitation [of the Buddha's name], while the Venerable [Wuzhu] completely cut through thinking and ceased all anxiety, and entered into the field of self-validating [enlightenment]. Daoyi, accompanied by all the minor masters who were their fellow-inmates, said to the Venerable, "I, together with all our fellow inmates, want

you to join us in the six daily periods of worship and repentance. We humbly beg the Venerable to listen and accede." The Venerable said to Daoyi and the others, "Because here we are altogether cut off from provisions, people carry them on foot deep into the mountains. You can't rely on legalistic practice—you want to get ravings by rote, but this is not the Buddha-Dharma at all." The Venerable quoted the *Śūraṅgama-sūtra*, " 'The raving mind is not at rest. At rest, it is bodhi. Peerless pure bright mind fundamentally pervades the Dharmadhātu.'[89] No-thought is none other than seeing the Buddha. The presence of thought is none other than birth-and-death. If you want to practice worship and recitation, then leave the mountains. On the plains there are gracious and easeful temple-quarters, and you are free to go. If you want to stay with me, you must utterly devote yourself to no-thought. If you can, then you are free to stay. If you cannot, then you must go down."[90]

Daoyi does leave the mountain to go down to the Jingzhong monastery and bear tales of Wuzhu to Wuxiang, as previously discussed. As we saw, Wuxiang is portrayed as being delighted rather than dismayed by reports of Wuzhu's behavior. He says that he too suffered hunger due to his independent attitude and recalls that he had only "smelted earth" (*liantu* 練土) to eat.[91] Whether intentionally or not, the notion of eating earth evokes the Buddhist motif of honeyed earth, as well as Daoist alchemical practices. This is an apt symbol of distance from the scheduled meals of communal monastic life and freedom from the stains of material wealth.

The *Lidai fabao ji* authors defended their own standards for distinguishing the true "Dharma-Jewel" from the dust of material wealth, and distinguishing those who were worthy of offerings from those who were not. Bao Tang survival depended on wider acceptance of these standards, yet they must have been aware that their manifesto, the *Lidai fabao ji*, would draw more critical attention to the group. It is possible that even sympathizers might have been hard put to explain the basis of the Bao Tang claim for support as Buddhist clergy.

In the following passages, Wuzhu defends the Bao Tang attitude toward the relationship between precepts and patronage to three different audiences: an eminent Chan master from the capital, the group of visiting Vinaya masters alluded to above, and a group of lay supporters. The first passage features his exchange with Chan Master Tiwu:

[Chan Master] Tiwu 體無 knew that the Venerable was the Venerable Kim's disciple, but his words were malicious: "I wish to observe that the people of Jiannan do not arouse the [true] mind. The Chan masters [hereabouts] strike people and call it not-striking, berate people and call it not-berating, and when they receive donations they say 'not-received.' I am deeply perplexed by these matters."

The Venerable replied, "Practicing Prajñāpāramitā one does not see the one who is awarded favor and does not see the one who extends favor. It is because already there is nothing to receive that one receives all one receives. The not-yet-complete Buddha-Dharma is also endlessly received. From the time when I first put forth the mind up until the present, I have never received a single hair in donations."

When Tiwu heard this he looked around at the officials and said, "The Chan Master speaks with a big voice."

The Venerable asked Tiwu, "So the Ācārya (*sheli* 闍梨) verbally recognizes a Chan Master! Why would one arousing the mind strike people, arousing the mind berate people, and arousing the mind receive donations?"

Tiwu knew himself that he had lost doctrinal [ground].[92]

Wuzhu catches his opponent in this exchange by pointing out that the distinction between abusing people and receiving offerings from them only arises in the mind of duality. Later we see him turning the tables, for in his dialogue with the Vinaya masters he implies that their exacting attention to form is due to greed for worldly benefits:

> These days Vinaya masters preach about [sense] "contact" and preach about "purity," preach about "upholding" and preach about "violating." They make forms [*zuo xiang* 作相] for receiving the precepts, they make forms for decorum, and even for eating food—everything is made into forms. . . . Nowadays Vinaya masters are only motivated by fame and benefits. Like cats stalking mice, they take mincing steps and creep along, seeing "true" and seeing "false" with their self-styled precepts practice. This is really the extinction of the Buddha-Dharma, it is not the practice of the śramaṇa.[93]

Wuzhu here highlights the hypocrisy of the monastic system itself. Not confining himself to the standard criticism of false monks, Wuzhu points out that ostentatious forms of rectitude enabled the monks to continue consuming the rewards of their proper decorum. However, in order to gain support for the Bao Tang way, it was not sufficient to defend it against fellow-clerics' accusations of laxity or to mount a counteroffensive critiquing current monastic practice. It was even more crucial to convert lay supporters to the Bao Tang point of view. As previously noted, Wuzhu tells his lay supporters that "Confessing and repenting and intoning prayers, all this is empty delusion." This sermon to the laity occupies an important place in the *Lidai fabao ji*, for it is the last of Wuzhu's discourses to be included in the text. Wuzhu continues and concludes as follows:

> "Who repays the Buddha's kindness? One who practices according to the Dharma. Who is worthy to receive offerings? One who is not involved in

> worldly affairs. Who consumes offerings? In the Dharma there is nothing that is taken."[94] . . . How about if you *dānapati* root out the source of delusory views and awaken to your unborn substance? Like the roiling of thick clouds and the sun of bright wisdom, the veil of karma will suddenly roll back. Expel delusory conceptualization by emptying the mind, tranquilly not moving.[95]

Even though Wuzhu is shown interpreting precepts and patronage in terms of no-thought in all three passages, occasionally even using the same phrases, there are nevertheless differences in style and content to accommodate the different audiences. With the Chan master he engages in Dharma-debate, with the Vinaya masters he speaks of the emptiness of the notions of Hell and nirvāṇa, and with the laity he preaches against dependence on notions of good fortune, repentance, and prayers. However, he does give the lay followers a modicum of formal advice. He tells them to "empty the mind," and earlier in the lecture he advises them, "if you want to confess and repent, sit properly and contemplate the characteristic of actuality,"[96] which is a phrase from the type of contemplation scripture that he criticizes in other contexts. He also quotes from a scripture popular in Chan circles, the *Viśeṣacintibrahmaparipṛcchā-sūtra,* in order to make claims for the rights of those who are detached from the world to be supported by the laity.

As noted, Zongmi confirmed and depreciated the unconventional Bao Tang manner of practicing and receiving offerings. The following passage is from his *Yuanjue jing dashu chao,* in which he describes Bao Tang doctrine and practice:

> Even though the Dharma idea of [Wuzhu's] instruction was just about the same as that of Kim's [Jingzhong] school, [Wuzhu's] teaching of ritual was completely different. The difference lies in the fact that [Wuzhu's school] practices none of the phenomenal marks (*shixiang* 事相) of Buddhism. Having cut their hair and donned robes, they do not receive the precepts. When it comes to doing obeisance and confession, turning and reading [the scriptures], making paintings of Buddha figures, copying sūtras, they revile all such things as delusions (*abhūtaparikalpa, wangxiang* 妄想). In the cloister where they dwell they set up no Buddhist artifacts (*foshi* 佛事). This is why [I say the Bao Tang idea is] "bound by neither teaching nor praxes" (*jiaoxing buju* 教行不拘). As to "extinguishing consciousness" (*mieshi* 滅識), this is the path that the Bao Tang practices. The meaning is: all samsaric wheel-turning is caused by the arising of mind (*qixin* 起心). Arising of mind is the unreal (*wang* 妄). They do not discuss good and bad; nonarising is the real. [Their practice] shows no resemblance whatsoever to practice in terms of phenomenal marks. They take discrimination (*vi-*

> *kalpa, fenbie* 分別) as the enemy and non-discrimination (*avikalpa, wu-fenbie* 無分別) as the wondrous path. . . . Moreover, their idea in reviling all the marks of the teachings (*jiaoxiang* 教相) lies in extinguishing consciousness and [manifesting] the completely real. Therefore, in their dwellings they do not discuss food and clothing, but leave it to people to send offerings. If sent, then they have warm clothing and food enough to eat. If not sent, then they leave matters to hunger and cold. They do not seek to convert, nor do they beg for food. If someone enters their cloister, it does not matter whether he is highborn or lowly, in no case do they welcome him—they do not even stand up. As to singing hymns and praises, making offerings, reprimanding abuses, in all such things they leave it to the other. Indeed, because the purport of their thesis speaks of non-discrimination, their gate of practice has neither right nor wrong. They just value no-mind (*wuxin* 無心) as the wondrous ultimate. Therefore, I have called it "extinguishing consciousness."[97]

The term *mieshi* (extinguishing consciousness) was Zongmi's way of expressing the problem with the Bao Tang interpretation of Shenhui's *wunian* (無念, no-thought).[98] For Zongmi, Bao Tang antinomianism was similar to the laissez-faire spontaneity advocated by another Sichuan Chan school, the Hongzhou 洪州 line of Mazu 馬祖 (709–788). Zongmi argued that the "sudden enlightenment" (*dunwu* 頓悟) experience of direct perception of one's own true nature should be the basis of subsequent "gradual cultivation" (*jianxiu* 漸修) and integration of insight. He claimed that the Hongzhou followers' emphasis on all activity as the expression of true nature did not accommodate the necessarily transformative aspects of direct experience and gradual cultivation. Peter Gregory characterizes his views as follows: "This means, for Tsung-mi, that followers of the Hung-chou line have no clear assurance that their insight is true and, accordingly, their practice of 'simply allowing the mind to act spontaneously' can become a rationalization for deluded activity."[99]

Gregory suggests that Zongmi's knowledge of actual Bao Tang practices heightened his awareness of the potential for antinomianism inherent in Southern School Chan doctrines and even, perhaps, in Huayan doctrines: "The Hua-yen teaching of *shih-shih wu ai* 事事無礙 thus refers to the intricate web of interconnections that obtain among phenomenal appearances. They are that which—in the context of his criticism of the Hung-chou line of Ch'an—he refers to as the functioning-in-accord-with-conditions, merely the ever-changing images reflected on the surface of the mind, nothing more than the epiphenomena (*mo* 末) of the intrinsically enlightened true mind."[100]

However, I suggest that Bao Tang practice was perhaps closer to a sudden enlightenment-gradual cultivation model than Zongmi would allow, and the *Lidai fabao ji* authors were as wary of reifying mere function as he was. Wuzhu's "just sitting in vacuity" is not spontaneous function; in the earthy words of the *Lidai fabao ji*'s Wuxiang, it is forgetting to eat and shit and piss. The incantations of *wunian* repeated over and over again throughout Wuzhu's Dharma-talks are like dhāraṇī of direct sudden experience. For the Bao Tang, antiformalism became a kind of gradual cultivation, which Zongmi may be justified in seeing as nihilistic, a negative attachment to form. However, as attested by Zongmi's own words, the Bao Tang inversion of institutional norms did not promote carefree spontaneity; rather, it was a school of hard training in relinquishing expectations and becoming inured to the fluctuations of abundance and privation.

WOMEN IN THE *LIDAI FABAO JI*

Bao Tang anti-institutionalism may have appealed to a group of practitioners who would otherwise have been at the bottom of the fourfold assembly: female lay practitioners. Dispensing with the ritual and institutional forms that maintained a clear distinction between lay and ordained, the Bao Tang school also seems to have blurred the line between female lay practitioners and nuns, as well as the line between female and male disciples.

Below I outline some of the main features of Buddhist notions of gender, but first let me introduce a key motif in the *Lidai fabao ji* treatment of gender, namely, formlessness as lack of physical form (*xing* 形) rather than the lack of forms of practice (*xiang* 相). Let us return to Wuzhu's sermon-from-afar to the Jingzhong monks. As we recall, he used a scriptural anecdote in order to illustrate his point that mind-to-mind identity in Buddha-nature preempts the issue of who is first and last to see the Buddha. The following is the passage summarized earlier:

> At that time [when the Buddha was about to descend to Jambudvīpa after preaching to his mother in Trāyastriṃśa Heaven], the *bhikṣuṇī* Utpalavarṇa (Lianhuase 蓮華色), being determined to expunge the evil reputation [of her sex], desired to be the first to greet the Buddha. All the kings of great kingdoms and the eight divisions of nāgas and divinities had completely encircled [the Buddha] in circumambulations, and there was no path through. [The nun] transformed herself into the thousand sons of a Great Cakravartin King and surrounded [the company], and the nāgas, divinities, and kings opened a path. Utpalavarṇā Bhikṣuṇī then returned to her original form, and when she had circumambulated the World-Honored One, she joined her palms and spoke a gāthā: "I am the first to greet the Buddha, I am the first to make obeisance to the Buddha." Having spoken the gāthā,

> she made obeisance and stood up. At that, the World-Honored One told the *bhikṣunī,* "In this company, you are last." The bhikṣunī said to the World-Honored One, "In this company there are no arhats, why do you say I am last?" The World-Honored One told the *bhikṣunī,* "Subhuti is in a stone cell continuously in samādhi, and so he was first, being able to see my Dharma-body. You came rushing to see my form-body, and so you are last."[101]

In the version recorded by Faxian, it is simply stated that the nun used her powers to transform into a Cakravartin and was the first to greet the Buddha.[102] Nancy Falk notes that there are both positive and negative versions of the same story in the scriptures, and argues that sociopolitical factors contributed to the gradual increase of misogynist elements in Buddhist literature.[103] However, one could view the negative version in the *Lidai fabao ji* as an inadvertent precedent for an entirely different message: A woman does not have to change herself into the thousand sons of a Cakravartin in order to see the Buddha, just as Wuzhu does not have to be in Chengdu to be with Wuxiang.

Notably, in a passage in *Record III* of the so-called *Bodhidharma Anthology,* we find a nun making a similar point with reference to "seeing the Buddha." This is one of several cases in which we find parallels between the *Bodhidharma Anthology* texts and the *Lidai fabao ji*.[104] The passage in question is as follows:

> The nun Yuanji 圓寂 says: "All dharmas are nonreacting. They are intrinsically liberated. Why? When the eye sees forms, there are none that it does not see. Even when the mind consciousness knows, there is nothing that it does not know and nothing that it knows. At the time of delusion there is no understanding; at the time of understanding there is no delusion. During a dream there is no awakening; at the time of awakening there is no dream. Therefore, the sūtra says: 'The great assembly, having seen Akṣobhya Buddha, no longer saw that Buddha. Ānanda! No dharma associates with the eye and ear organs to create a reaction. Why? Dharmas do not see dharmas. Dharmas do not know dharmas.' Also, the sūtra says: 'The non-production of consciousness due to forms is called not seeing forms.'"[105]

Here a nun is featured as a spokesperson for the ultimate truth of formlessness, the lack of all characteristics, including sight, in "seeing the Buddha." Moreover, in the *Jingde chuandeng lu* the nun Zongchi 惣持 is given the following signature teaching: "According to present understanding, they rejoiced in seeing the Land of Akṣobhya Buddha. Having seen it once, they did not see it again."[106] As mentioned in chapter 5, the *Lidai fabao ji* is the source for the provocative and ambivalent phrase attributed to Bodhidharma, in which the first patriarch names this nun as one of his disciples: "The one who got my marrow is Huike, the one who got my bones is Daoyu, and the one who got my flesh is the nun Zongchi."[107] Thus, we find an intriguing juxtaposition between the proclamations of nuns and the motifs of seeing/not seeing the Buddha, of physicality and formlessness, in each of these texts. Implicit in each is the notion that gender is meaningless when even seeing is/not.

Though there is much scriptural precedent for affirming the lack of gender and other distinctions in nonduality, a Bao Tang follower sitting in vacuity had some reason to hope that "the evil reputation of her sex" and her low place in the assembly could be forgotten on both the conventional and the ultimate levels. In the *Lidai fabao ji* passages on Wuzhu's female disciples that we examine below, we see these disciples taking Wuzhu's formless practice in a new direction. First, however, let us look at some of the basic elements of Buddhist representations of gender.

Two of the best-known Mahāyāna scriptural precedents deploying representations of gender are found in the *Lotus Sūtra* and the *Vimalakīrti-sūtra.* In the *Lotus Sūtra* passage, the dragon king's daughter's ability to achieve enlightenment in spite of her sex and youth proves the efficacy of the Buddha-vehicle promoted by the *Lotus*. However, she has to turn into a male in order to teach as a Buddha.[108] In the *Vimalakīrti-sūtra,* however, the Buddha's disciple Śāriputra is changed into a woman by a goddess who is trying to teach him about nonduality. Although he is unable to change back into a man and must rely on her powers before he is restored to "himself," he remains resistant to her lesson. He asks her when she will attain full enlightenment, and she replies that she will do so when Śāriputra returns to the state of an ordinary unenlightened man. Śāriputra replies that it is unthinkable that an arhat like himself could return to the state of an ordinary man. The goddess then says that attaining full enlightenment is likewise unthinkable, for there is nothing to be attained.[109]

In both these scriptural passages, the issue of gender is in service of larger didactic points, albeit ambivalent ones—in the first, even a little dragon girl can turn into a complete but therefore male Buddha, and in the second a goddess turns a man into a woman in order to help him overcome the dualistic notions that keep him from complete enlightenment. Both are gems of Mahāyāna literature, but they do not address the problems that beset real-life female Buddhist practitioners. Though it is beyond the scope of this study to develop a history of female practitioners of Buddhism, I sketch in some of the relevant background here.[110]

The paradigmatic first Buddhist nun is the Buddha's aunt and foster mother, Mahāprajāpatī Gotamī, discussed in chapter 5. One might say that the Buddha himself contributed to the conditions that led her to persist in her efforts to establish an order of nuns in the face of his opposition. Her elder male clan members, including her husband, had died, but the son and nephews on whom she might have relied instead had followed the Buddha into homelessness. Many of her followers were female members of the Buddha's former household or the former wives of men who had become Buddhist monks.

As is well known, the Buddha several times refused Ānanda's pleas on behalf of the nuns before finally allowing the order to be formed. However, he stipulated eight special rules that would subordinate the nuns to monks and even to male novices, and this in turn led to significantly more rules in the prātimokṣa required for a nun's ordination. These special rules maintained an institutional and ritual imbalance between the two Saṅghas. Monks could instruct nuns, but not the other way around. An assembly of monks could ordain further monks, but a nun's ordination required both senior nuns and monks. As related in the sixth-century *Biqiuni zhuan* 比丘尼傳 (Biographies of Nuns), this created difficulties for the first Chinese female aspirants to ordination, for there were no senior Indian nuns in China.[111]

However, these special rules designed to maintain propriety were not sufficient to protect the Dharma from the ill consequences of Ānanda's excessive compassion. The Buddha was said to have declared that, due to the presence of women in the Saṅgha, his Dharma would go into decline far earlier than it would otherwise have done. In notable contrast to the female-friendly tone of the *Lidai fabao ji*, the *Baolin zhuan* account of Dharma transmission opens with this ominous prediction.[112]

While the presence of women within the Saṅgha was thus a source of tension and ambivalence, much of the Saṅgha's day-to-day existence depended on the support of pious laywomen. In early Buddhist literature, the paradigmatic laywoman Viṣaka is more lavishly praised than the nuns, and she was allowed a freedom to associate with the Buddha and senior monks that the nuns were not.[113] Lay devotional practice and support of the Saṅgha were seen as the proper sphere of women's practice, a distinction related to the brāhmaṇical meaning of Dharma as the individual's social role. Women who renounce householder life transgress against Dharma, but males do not. As Nancy Falk has argued, the pertinent questions are not why the nun's order was so restricted and why it declined earlier than the monk's order in India, but why it was established at all, and how it survived as long as it did, given the strength of the cultural norms it was resisting?[114]

In contrast, Chinese Confucian cultural norms were explicitly inimical to males who left family life, but female renunciation was generally tolerated so long as it did not transgress codes of propriety. The Chinese nuns' Saṅgha managed to survive and even flourish, despite its institutional and economic dependency on the monks' Saṅgha. Yet there is no collection of biographies of Chinese nuns after the sixth-century *Biqiuni zhuan;* information on Tang nuns is drawn from scattered inscriptions, tales of the miraculous, and depictions in cave-temples.[115] The *Lidai fabao ji* not only provides us with brief but significant reflections on women's practice in the Tang, but is the first text to feature Chan nuns. Given the Bao Tang penchant for ostentatiously inverting norms, we might suspect that the inclusion of women in the *Lidai fabao ji* fulfills a familiar didactic and symbolic function, similar to the gender inversions in the scriptures and in later Chan *gongan* literature. However, let us examine the relevant *Lidai fabao ji* episodes more closely.

Wuzhu apparently felt that it was more acceptable to bring dependents to the monastery than to abandon them. This is a further extension of the ramifications of subitism voiced in the *Platform Sūtra:* "Good friends, if you wish to practice, it is all right to do so as laymen; you don't have to be in a temple."[116] In the context of the doctrine of realizing one's own Buddha nature "all at once," without delay and without mediation, the privilege of delay and mediation afforded by a well-supported monastery was theoretically unnecessary.

In the *Lidai fabao ji,* Wuzhu sharply criticizes a group of old laymen for wanting to leave their families and become Wuzhu's disciples:

> There were some old men who told the Venerable, "We, your disciples, have wives and children, and young male and female household dependents. We wish to give them up entirely and submit to the Venerable and study the Way." The Venerable said, "The Way does not have any particular form that can be cultivated, the Dharma does not have any particular form that can be validated. Just unrestricted no-recollection and no-thought, at all times everything is the Way." He asked the old men, "Do you get it?" The old men were silent and did not answer, because they didn't understand. The Venerable expounded a gāthā: "Your wife is an earless shackle, your young are rattling manacles. You are a worthless slave, you have reached old age and cannot escape."[117]

Wuzhu throws the laymen's own thinking back in their faces, mocking their fettered state to show them that they are bound by ignorance and not by family life. In contrast, a monk who was evidently one of Wuzhu's earliest and closest followers brought his mother with him into the cloister:

> There was also Master Fayuan 法縁 of Longyou 隴右, whose secular surname was Lü 魯. From afar he heard of the Venerable and, bringing his mother along with him, he arrived at the Baiyai mountains and made obeisance to the Venerable.[118] (There follows an account of their dialogue, in which Wuzhu shows Fayuan that his previous reliance on commentaries

rather than the sūtras themselves has misled him. Wuzhu concludes with one of his paeans to no-thought.)

[Wuzhu said,] "'Someone who sees 'I' through form and seeks 'I' through sounds is taking a false path, and is unable to see the Tathāgata.'[119] The words of this scripture are none other than this mind. Seeing the nature is the Way of becoming a Buddha. No-thought is thus seeing the nature, no-thought is no-defilements. No-thought is thus no-self, no-thought is thus no-other. No-thought is thus no-Buddha, no-thought is no-beings. At the time of true no-thought, no-thought itself is not." When Master Fayuan heard this, he joined his palms and said to the Venerable, "I am exceedingly glad that I have been able to meet the Venerable. Fayuan and his aged relative (i.e., my mother and I) humbly beg you to compassionately accept us." And so they stayed in the mountains and never left [the Venerable's] side.[120]

In addition to these teachings on the nonduality of seeing/not seeing and "leaving" or "bringing," there are a number of brief but striking inclusions of women in the *Lidai fabao ji* version of Chan history. First, there is the above-noted introduction of a nun among Bodhidharma's disciples. Also, as discussed in chapter 5, Empress Wu Zetian has a decisive role in the *Lidai fabao ji* saga of the patriarchy, and she is portrayed in an unusually sympathetic manner.

Furthermore, in the biography of Wuxiang, it is said that his sister's example motivated him to become a monk, a story found only in the *Lidai fabao ji:*

Chan Master Wuxiang of the Jingzhong monastery in Chengdu City Prefecture in Jiannan had the lay surname Kim and was from a clan of Silla princes, his family went back for generations East-of-the-Sea (i.e., Korea). Formerly, when he was in his homeland, he had a younger sister. When she first heard of her betrothal ceremony, she picked up a knife, slashed her face, and vowed her determination to "return to the true." The Venerable [Wuxiang] saw this and cried, "Girls are pliant and weak, yet she knows the meaning of sticking to chastity. Fellows are hard and strong—how can I be so lacking in spirit?" He thereupon took the tonsure and left his kin, crossed the sea westward and arrived in the Kingdom of Tang.[121]

Finally, and most significantly, there is the passage on the female disciples of Wuzhu, which I quote in full:

The wife and daughter of Administrator Murong 慕容 of Qingzhou 慶州 were determined to seek the Mahāyāna. Accompanied by the entire family, young and old, they came to pay obeisance to the Venerable [Wuzhu].

> The Venerable asked the wife, "Where did you come from?"
>
> She replied, "Your disciple heard from afar that the Venerable had great compassion, so we came to pay obeisance."
>
> The Venerable then expounded various essentials of the Dharma for them. When the daughter had heard his talk, she knelt on one knee with her palms joined and explained to the Venerable, "Your disciple is a woman with the three obstructions and five difficulties, and a body that is not free. That is why I have come now to submit to the Venerable, I am determined to cut off the source of birth and death. I humbly beg the Venerable to point out the essentials of the Dharma."
>
> The Venerable said, "If you are capable of such [resolution], then you are a great heroic male (*dazhangfu er* 大丈夫兒), why are you 'a woman'?" The Venerable expounded the essentials of the Dharma for her: "No-thought is thus no 'male,' no-thought is thus no 'female.' No-thought is thus no-obstruction, no-thought is thus no-hindrance. No-thought is thus no-birth, no-thought is thus no-death. At the time of true no-thought, no-thought itself is not. This is none other than cutting off the source of birth and death."
>
> When the daughter heard his talk, her eyes did not blink and she stood absolutely still. In an instant, the Venerable knew that this woman had a resolute mind. He gave her the Dharma name Changjingjin 常精進 (Ever-Pure Progress), and her mother was named Zhengbianzhi 正遍知 (Right Knowledge). They took the tonsure and practiced, and became leaders among nuns.[122]

I would like to draw particular attention to the second female disciple featured in this section. One might note that the bestowal of her name, Liaojianxing 了見性 (Completely Seeing the Nature), once again plays on the motif of seeing the Buddha/nature and transcending female form:

> Later, they brought a younger female cousin with the surname Wei 韋, who was the grand-daughter of Grand Councilor Su 蘇. She was quick-witted and clever, extensively learned and knowledgeable, and when asked a question she was never without an answer. She came to pay obeisance to the Venerable, and the Venerable saw that she was obdurate and determined on chastity (*zhicao* 志操), and so he expounded the Dharma for her: "This Dharma is not caused and conditioned, it has neither false nor not-false, and has neither truth nor not-truth. 'Transcending all characteristics is thus all Dharmas.' 'The Dharma is beyond eye, ear, nose, tongue, body, and mind, the Dharma transcends all contemplation practices.'[123] No-thought is thus no-practice, no-thought is thus no-contemplation. No-thought is thus no-body, no-thought is thus no-mind. No-thought is thus no-nobility,

no-thought is thus no-lowliness. No-thought is thus no-high, no-thought is thus no-low. At the time of true no-thought, no-thought itself is not."

When the woman heard his talk, she joined her palms together and told the Venerable, "Your disciple is a woman whose obstructions from transgressions are very weighty, but now that I have heard the Dharma, stain and obstruction are completely eliminated." So saying she wept grievously, a rain of tears. She then requested a Dharma name, and she was named Liaojianxing. When she had been named, she tonsured herself and donned robes (*zi luofa piyi* 自落髮披衣), and became a leader among nuns.

"Who repays the Buddha's kindness? One who practices according to the Dharma. Who consumes offerings? One who is not involved in worldly affairs. Who is worthy of offerings? In the Dharma there is nothing that is taken."[124] If one is able to practice in this way, one naturally has offerings from Heaven's kitchen.[125]

The quotation immediately following the account of Liaojianxing is a favorite one in the *Lidai fabao ji,* occurring three times: first in the collection of sūtra quotations, here, and again in the sermon to the laymen. In this passage, the quotation leads a collection of choice teachings and quotations recorded from Wuzhu's sermons. The question "who is worthy of offerings?" is clearly one of the underlying issues of the *Lidai fabao ji,* and its burning importance for the Bao Tang community is implicit in the account of Liaojianxing's vocation. Is a self-tonsured disciple who practices no-thought, whether nun or monk, less worthy of offerings than a fully ordained monk who practices recitation of scriptures and a daily schedule of devotions?

Praise of the worthiness of these two women is more specific than anything said of the male disciples in the *Lidai fabao ji*—with the notable exception of Master Fayuan, the one who brought his mother to the monastery. Is this heuristic inversion or condescension, or does it reflect extraordinary circumstances?

Among the accounts of Wuzhu's disciples, the three that stand out are the stories of Changjingjin, Liaojianxing, and Master Fayuan. These accounts include information about family background, and they also include less formulaic dialogue and more personal and emotional shadings. Changjingjin, Liaojianxing, and Master Fayuan emerge as the heros, the *dazhangfu* among Wuzhu's followers, and perhaps as the *er* among his followers, his "sons." Let us consider the epithet Wuzhu uses more closely.

In "Lin-chi (Rinzai) Ch'an and Gender: The Rhetoric of Equality and the Rhetoric of Heroism," Miriam Levering discusses similar epithets of masculine heroism that were used to praise the enlightenment of a female Chan lay practitioner in the Song.[126] Levering hears a note of insincerity in the fulsome praise that the Chan master Dahui heaped on his female lay devotee Lady Qinguo. In her conclusions, Levering argues: "The rhetoric of equality cannot stand up against the rhetoric of masculine heroism, when the latter is supported by gender distinctions so 'real' to the culture, and remain unambiguous. In this sermon Ta-hui says, 'You see her as a woman, but she is a *ta-chang-fu,* a great hero.' This is as unambiguous a statement of equality as this rhetoric can yield. But it is not so different from the formulation several times repeated elsewhere in Ta-hui's records, 'Even though you are a woman, you have the will of a *ta-chang-fu,*' a formulation that shows the androcentric character of Chinese Buddhism in general and of Ch'an in particular."[127]

In Chan in general and the Bao Tang school in particular, inversion of norms became normative. Aside from the handful of feisty old women who crop up in the *gongan* collections, the most pointed example is Layman Pang's daughter, who bests a visiting master in Dharma-combat and upstages her father by preceding him in a magisterial death.[128] Representations of male heroism applied to women were used to exemplify the nondual, and the pointedness of the application reinforces the duality. Just as the power of the tumultuous Chan encounter dialogues depends on the bland regularities of monastic life, so too the force of the image of a female *dazhangfu* depends on androcentrism. Yet does this preclude a shift of balance? What if a woman applied the term *dazhangfu* to herself? What if the static rhetoric of nonduality turns performative, bringing itself to life like the "painted dragon" bringing rain?

In a recent article, "Voices of Dissent: Women in Early Chan and Tiantai," Bernard Faure argues that the case of two Tiantai nuns, sisters who criticized Shenxiu's disciple Puji 普寂 (651–739), presents us with a unique example of women actively challenging the male status quo. While recognizing the sectarian agendas and hagiographical elements of the inscription valorizing the Tiantai nuns, Faure maintains that the inscription stands as a unique testament of individual feminine agency, an active challenge of the patriarchal religious and political order. Briefly, the story is that the two nuns deprecate Puji's awareness, and when Puji demands that they be censored, his disciple Yixing 一行 (683–727), sent as imperial representative of Puji's interests, ends by being impressed by them. This results in their being honored by Emperor Xuanzong. Faure argues that this episode stands in contradistinction to other types of material that only apparently valorize women, while in fact reinforcing the patriarchal norm. He includes the *Lidai fabao ji* passage on Changjingjin and Liaojianxing as an example of portrayals of women that reinforce the status quo.[129]

In response, I suggest that Faure's singling out of the Tiantai nuns is based on a specific notion of power as a property of the individual—yet in this case, it is the double. He deploys one of his fundamental theses regarding the hagiographic construction of magical powers as the basis of Buddhist social and political power:

> The hagiographical topos is clear when the author implies that the two sister's true master, the strange nun named Konggu, was actually a manifestation of the Bodhisattva Samantabhadra—in female form. This emphasis on the nuns' powers should perhaps also be understood against the background of their disagreement with Puji. Significantly, Puji's popularity derived in large part from the psychic powers that were attributed to him. . . . Thus, the attribution of psychic powers was essential in establishing the credentials of a Buddhist master. The same was apparently true in the case of the nuns.[130]

Rather than focusing on powers and the symbolic confrontation between "individuals" as the basis of social and political validation, let us consider the function of doubling in this story. The sisters are as if twins, and are not given individual identities. Their ability to challenge the dominant order cannot be separated from their special charismatic status as anomalous creatures, double prodigies who are secretly taught by a bodhisattva-in-disguise. Notably, the *Biqiuni zhuan* also features a pair of special sisters, who mysteriously disappear and then reappear with miraculous skills, having been tonsured and instructed by a bodhisattva-like nun in the Pure Land.[131] Like Western "divine twins," these paired nuns serve a paradigmatic function and are in this respect analogous to other well-known canonical anomalies, such as the Nāga princess in the *Lotus Sūtra* and the goddess in the *Vimilakīrti*. The Tiantai nuns are *lusus naturae,* duly investigated by the imperial representative, the famous Master Yixing, and subsequently given imperial recognition.[132]

In making the case for the active agency of the voices of Changjingjin and Liaojianxing, I argue that it is not their dissent that makes them powerful. Rather, it is the power of their devotion that makes its mark. In light of the passages discussed above, I advance a hypothesis that is no doubt transferential, but worth considering nonetheless: What if Changjingjin and Liaojianxing wrote the *Lidai fabao ji,* or had a hand in compiling it? Everywhere else in the *Lidai fabao ji* literary and intellectual skills are devalued, but in the passage on Liaojianxing these attributes are praised in a manner that may betray an element of anxious self-justification. As summarized above, female figures play small but significant roles in the *Lidai fabao ji* history of Chan, roles that we do not see in any other sectarian history of this period. The kind of figure validated by the sum of these stories is telling: that of a young girl who refuses marriage (Wuxiang's sister), a nun who surfaces inexplicably amid the better-known male disciples of a famous master (Bodhidharma's disciple Zongchi), and a powerful woman who secretly holds the true Dharma robe in trust. The pair of well-connected and well-educated young women who became Wuzhu's disciples could conceivably have seen themselves in these roles.

I would like to add to these suggestions an argument based on intuition, considering the cause worthwhile enough to risk baiting the unforgiving demon of gender caricatures. Intimately familiar with the text and its moods as I have had to be, I was gradually influenced by the sense that the method and tone of the *Lidai fabao ji* author or main compiler was not like that of near-contemporary monks, such as Shenhui, Zongmi, the erudite and acerbic Shenqing, or the unknown author of the *Platform Sūtra*. Of course, this might simply mark it as the product of someone who had not received a monastic education. However, I find that the tone of the *Lidai fabao ji* betrays the kind of exclusive commitment to the master and to the Bao Tang group that would be conceivable in an educated layperson who had decided to bind her or his fate to that of an unorthodox community, with no hope of any other future or recognized place within the monastic system.

This hypothesis could also cast a different light on the most dramatic episode of the *Lidai fabao ji*, the story of Wuzhu's and Wuxiang's secret bond outside the relationships of the official monastic network and regular discipleship. Their connection is imbued with an intimacy that goes beyond its apparent model, the structurally similar story of Huineng and Hongren. Wuzhu not only gains instantaneous understanding the first time he hears Wuxiang's teachings repeated, but he also speaks to and understands Wuxiang across the physical distance that separates them. Moreover, in a possibly transferential play on the topos of the master-disciple relationship, the master Wuxiang, like a mother or a woman bound to the inner quarters, is said to long for his disciple Wuzhu to come and visit him.

I am not suggesting that Bao Tang antinomianism included disregarding the rule of chastity, though that might improve sales of this book. In fact, the high tone of devotion in the *Lidai fabao ji* precludes the mundane, while at the same time allowing glimpses of the Bao Tang as a small and close-knit family. In between the repetitive passages that represent Wuzhu's Dharma talks, we obtain glimpses of interactions between Wuzhu and his disciples that reveal the wit, self-importance, and occasional ill humor of a living master rather than a living Buddha. These brief glimmers betray a more personal quality than the patriarchal antics and outbursts in didactic *yulu* and *gongan* anecdotes.

I waver between the probability that Changjingjin and Liaojianxing really are painted dragons and the possibility that these painted dragons are real, gazing at the image of Wuzhu they created. One can imagine the particular interest that Wuzhu's antinomianism might have had for female Buddhist practitioners. Liaojianxing's account is the only disciple story in the *Lidai fabao ji* that features self-tonsuring: She cuts her own hair, dons robes, and becomes a nun immediately. This was a subitism that could have no value in the ideological battle for Chan legitimacy, but it was a logical consequence of the sudden teaching—any practitioner could become a nun at her own desire.[133]

DAOISTS IN THE DHARMA HALL

In this final section, I turn to what is perhaps the most singular of the various polemics that animate the *Lidai fabao ji*, namely its markedly anti-Daoist flavor. Even though distinctions among the schools and traditions of Chinese "religion" have been questioned and problematized in every conceivable manner, the boundary between Buddhism and Daoism makes itself felt, one may recognize a tangible resistance when crossing it. However, neither can one ignore the minefield in which this elusive boundary is situated. The study of Buddhist-Daoist interactions involves such hotly contested issues as whether it is misleading to speak of Buddhism, Daoism, and Confucianism as "religions," whether one can speak of "syncretism" among these traditions, whether it is possible to draw distinctions between "elite" and "popular" religion, how the relationship between belief and practice should be conceived, and the ways in which the history of interaction between Asia and the West has influenced the construction of such categories.[134]

In order to bring into sharper focus the puzzles of "elite" versus "popular" and belief versus practice in the context of Buddhist-Daoist interaction, let us take a look at Henrik Sørensen's arguments in his recent review of Michel Strickmann's *Chinese Magical Medicine:*

> As I understand it, Strickmann saw the practices and beliefs relating to the realm of the dead, and the demonic in particular, as the primary point of coalescence between Daoism and Buddhism in their more popular forms during the medieval period in China. While there can be no doubt that this holds true as far as the more general aspects of Daoist and Buddhist practices and beliefs go, and as such may be used as a gateway to understanding the overall concerns governing the ritual behavior of these two creeds as well as their mutual points of coalescence, we should also acknowledge that their underlying beliefs and doctrines often differed greatly, frequently even to the point of contradiction if not downright confrontation. In other words, even though Buddhism and Daoism both made use of process magic, their respective raison d'être for doing so, as well as the contexts in which such

> use took place, may not necessarily have converged on the same world-views. In his penchant for understanding the common ground of Buddhist and Daoist practitioners—a ground that in many ways does appear to have been one of shared values and patterns of belief—Strickmann seems to have overlooked the fact that it is mainly in the area of popular beliefs and practices that this would seem to hold true. As soon as we focus our attention away from the sphere of popular religion, the picture changes dramatically. In fact, we will often find that the concerns and purposes guiding ritual proceedings often have entirely different foci in Daoism and Buddhism respectively. The reasons for this are many, but most evidently they hinge on the obvious fact that the soteriological processes of the two religions have radically different objectives. The Daoists strive for immortality, bodily purity and cosmic order, while the Buddhists seek enlightenment, transcendental wisdom, and on the more popular level, a fortunate rebirth.[135]

Works like Strickmann's address the unbalanced picture of Chinese religion that has resulted from scholarly biases, both Asian and Western, favoring studies of discrete "Buddhist" or "Daoist" doctrine and exegesis. Sørensen's point is well taken, however: neither can one ignore levels of cultural production in which Buddhism and Daoism present themselves as distinct and even antagonistic entities. In the present context, the point I would like to take up is the notion that elite beliefs and purposive soteriological processes are "underlying," essential, and normative in relation to the epiphenomena of popular practice, or "the myriad practices that deal with the fulfillment of material and health-related concerns" as Sørensen subsequently characterizes them. In examining the *Lidai fabao ji* approach to Daoism, we focus on two passages: one in which "popular" concern with "process magic" is featured, and the other in which "elite" issues, such as transcendence and metaphysics, are featured. We traverse common ground as well as common heights, but there is no indication that the *Lidai fabao ji* authors themselves distinguished between these levels. Both passages are polemical, pitting Buddhist magic against Daoist magic and Wuzhu's doctrines against Daoist doctrines, but I endeavor to show that Wuzhu's doctrines were not really so different from those of literati Daoists of his day.

In this and other contexts, the *Lidai fabao ji* confounds attempts to define its level of discourse. By including colloquialism and naturalistic dialogue its authors, whether knowingly or not, participated in cutting-edge literary trends. Yet affinities with popular tales are revealed when the authors stage showy scenes with elites like the imperial minister Du Hongjian and his retinue. It is within the context of an elite audience that both battles against Daoists are carried out—the mythical magic contest is performed before Emperor Ming of the Han and his court, and the metaphysical debate takes place in Wuzhu's Dharma hall. However, by setting himself against practices oriented toward "the fulfillment of material and health-related concerns," Wuzhu displays an equitable willingness to alienate Buddhists and Daoists, gentry and folk alike. Yet syncretism, usually associated with popular religion, appears in the most literate and elegant portion of the *Lidai fabao ji*—the eulogy for Wuzhu featured in chapter 7 is written by a lay disciple of Wuzhu's who is also sympathetic to the syncretic "unity of the three teachings" approach to Buddhist-Daoist-Confucian relations.

One could continue to pit the *Lidai fabao ji* against categorizations and against itself, but let us stop there. The purpose of these oscillations has not been to determine the degree of correspondence between the *Lidai fabao ji*'s elitism and its antagonism to Daoism, or to determine whether the underlying objective of this antagonism was soteriological or strategic. Rather, I hope to have indicated something of the nature of the minefield alluded to above, before venturing into it.

The *Lidai fabao ji* representation of Daoism is unquestionably polemical, but in looking at what was not taken up in this polemic, we may get a sense of the ways that Daoist thought was actually at work around and within the *Lidai fabao ji*. Two "real" potential competitors are dimly reflected in the Daoist straw men constructed in the *Lidai fabao ji*, but the authors' failure to address these rivals directly is revealing. These competitors were (1) Sichuanese local cults, and (2) the sophisticated visionary dialectics of eighth century *chongxuan* 重玄 (twofold mystery) exegesis and *neiguan* 內觀 (inner contemplation) practice. I first briefly discuss Sichuanese local cults and the ways in which the *Lidai fabao ji* authors express antagonism to Daoist ritual, magic, and sacred sites. Then I turn to a more extended discussion of eighth century Daoist trends, in the context of an episode focused on Wuzhu's encounter with a group of Daoists.

Contesting Local Powers

Local shrines dedicated to miracle-working sites, deities, images, and saints flourished in Sichuan, which was a cradle of early Daoism. As is well known, in the second century Daoist messianic groups formed utopian societies in Shu 蜀(Sichuan), known as the Wudoumi dao 五斗米道 (Way of Five Pecks of Rice) and the Tianshi dao 天師道 (Way of the Celestial Masters). Led by Zhang Daoling 張道陵 and expanded by his grandson Zhang Lu 張魯, the latter group established a "kingdom" in Sichuan that survived the fall of the Han, allying itself first with the new Wei dynasty and then with the subsequent Jin dynasty. The Tianshi dao tradition went south with the remnants of the Jin in the early fourth century, having lost its base as an independent political and social entity in Sichuan.[136]

Daoism remained an important facet of Sichuanese religion and culture. Chengdu is the site of one of the most important Daoist temples, the Qingyang gong 青羊宮, which commemorates the "Green Ram Market" where Laozi returned to complete the instruction of his disciple Yin Xi 尹喜 one thousand days after having transmitted the *Daode jing*. Among Buddhist clerics, Shu was known as an important battleground for the Dharma, and various accounts of the "protectors of the Dharma" celebrate the monks who opposed the Daoists entrenched in this area.[137] The revival of support for Daoism under Emperor Xuanzong gave an added boost to local Daoist activities in the eighth century. Daoist cults in Sichuan were nurtured by both imperial and popular attention to miracles and omens, and the iconography of surviving cave shrines and carved images (some of which I have visited) show Buddhist-Daoist syncretic tendencies.[138]

The *Lidai fabao ji* authors' antagonism to Daoist ritual and magic is made clear in the opening story of Emperor Ming of the Han, discussed in chapter 2. As we may recall, the first *Lidai fabao ji* account of Emperor Ming of the Han is based on the *Hanfa neizhuan* 漢法內傳 (Inner Commentary on the Dharma in the Han).[139] The *Hanfa neizhuan* stems from Buddhist-Daoist polemics of the third century, and it was proscribed in the eighth century by Emperor Xuanzong because of its anti-Daoist content.

The *Hanfa neizhuan* account of a magic contest between the newly arrived Indian monks and a disgruntled and jealous contingent of Daoists is prominently featured in the *Lidai fabao ji:*

> On the first day of the first month of the fourteenth year of the Yongping 永平 era (71 C.E.), Daoists from Mt. Huo 霍 of the Five Marchmounts and Mt. Bailu 白鹿, Chu Shanxin 褚善信 and Fei Shucai 費叔才 and six hundred and ninety others, submitted a memorial:
>
> > "We, your servants, have heard that the Ultimate is without form, empty and spontaneous. From remotest antiquity it has been venerated by all alike, and this has not changed in the reigns of a hundred rulers. Yet Your Majesty has given up the root for the branches and has sought teachings in the Western Regions. You have been converted by the preachings of a barbarian divinity and neglect China. We, your servants, are sagacious men, and have read extensively in the classics. We beg that You allow us to compare [our Way with that of the Buddhists]. If there is a victor, we desire that You abolish the one that is specious and false. We know that they will not prove our equals, and will abide by Your Majesty's decision."
>
> The emperor said, "Very well." He ordered that those in charge should see to the preparation of implements. Together with the inner and outer palace officials, civil and military, of the fifth rank and above, on the fifteenth at dawn all were assembled at the White Horse monastery. Outside the gate

> of the monastery the Daoists set up three altars and opened twenty-four pickets. Outside the southern gate of the monastery the emperor placed a relic [of the Buddha] as well as Buddhist scriptures and images, and he set up a pavilion adorned with the seven precious gems. Chu Shanxin and Fei Shucai and the others placed Daoist scriptures, treatises, and talismans on the altars. Then they set fire to them to verify their efficacy and, lamenting and wailing, they incanted: "A Barbarian divinity disturbs our China, we beg the Highest Celestial Venerables to enlighten all beings to the difference between true and false." But as soon as the Daoist scriptures, treatises and talismans were put in the fire they were instantly burnt to ashes. The Daoists were greatly surprised. Those who formerly ascended to Heaven now could not; those who formerly rendered themselves invisible now could not; those who formerly entered fire and water now dared not; those who formerly cast spells and those who did divinations could not get any response. Of all their various abilities there was not one that was efficacious. Chu Shanxin, Fei Shucai, and the others took it to heart so much that they died.[140]

After the Daoists are vanquished, the relic of the Buddha spontaneously produces marvelous light and the Indian monks effortlessly demonstrate superior powers. Daoist sacred ritual is degraded to the level of ineffective magical technique, while the powers of the Buddhist monks, relics, and texts are as if direct manifestations from the Buddha. The powers of local sites, the Daoist sacred mountains, are also implicated in the defeat, while the forces of the Buddha are proved universally effective.

These are, of course, tropes that one could find in various forms in tales of the miraculous. Notably, in Sichuan a century after the *Lidai fabao ji,* Du Guangting 杜光庭 (850–933) would compile two works featuring tales of the miraculous (and superior) powers of Daoist divinities, scriptures and rituals. A number of these miracles were purported to have taken place in eighth-century Sichuan, and early versions of these stories may have been part of local lore known to the *Lidai fabao ji* authors.[141]

The fact that they were situated in the middle of Daoist territory and under the rule of emperors who claimed ancestral ties with Laozi may explain why the *Lidai fabao ji* authors reached back to pre-Tang sources for support. The authors reinforced their opening episode with a series of quotations that reflect Buddhist strategic maneuvers of the fourth and fifth centuries. The first of these quotations is from the apocryphal *Qingjing faxing jing* 清淨法行經 (Scripture of the Pure Practice of the Dharma):

> To the northeast of India is the kingdom of China. Few of the people are devout, and evildoers are legion. For the present, I will dispatch three holy disciples, all bodhisattvas, to appear there and make conversions. Mahākā-

> śyapa will there be styled Laozi. Kumara (Guanjing tongzi 光淨童子) will there be called Confucius. Sumedha (Mingyue rutong 明月儒童) will there be called Yanhui 顏回.[142]

This recasting of Laozi, Confucius, and Yanhui as Buddhist figures was part of a genre of Buddhist counterattack against the infamous third-century Daoist *Huahu jing* 化胡經 (Scripture of Conversion of the Barbarians), which claimed that Buddhism was a punitive creed imposed on foreigners by Laozi after he left China.[143]

The *Qingjing faxing jing* passage is followed by a different version of the story of Emperor Ming of the Han taken from the *Mouzi lihuo lun* 牟子理惑論 (Mouzi's Treatise Settling Doubts),[144] in which the beneficial results of the emperor's merit-making activities are emphasized. The subsequent passage features Huiyuan successfully preventing Emperor Huan Xuan from purging the Saṅgha. As noted in chapter 2, Huan Xuan was known for his interest in Daoist-oriented "abstruse learning," so this episode may also have a hint of Buddhist-Daoist confrontation about it. The episode is capped with a poem attributed to Emperor Wu of the Liang, in which he praises Buddhism's superiority to Daoism and Confucianism.[145] Tanaka Ryōshō notes that, among Dunhuang Chan texts, the *Lidai fabao ji* stands out for its frequent evocations of Six Dynasties Buddhist-Daoist polemics.[146] Within the context of Tang imperial support of Daoism, the use of these texts and stories might even be considered politically provocative, though not as risky as would have been the case during Xuanzong's reign.

These venerable accounts of defeated Daoists and pro-Buddhist rulers represent the initial campaign in a two-part attack. Wuzhu's face-to-face engagement with Daoists over points of Daoist philosophy represents the second campaign, which comes near the end of the *Lidai fabao ji*. This engagement could be characterized as "militant syncretism" designed to subsume the antagonist. We see Wuzhu lecturing authoritatively on the *Yijing*, the *Daode jing*, and the *Zhuangzi*, arguing the nearly silent Daoists into admiring submission.

Wuzhu's Discourse with Daoists

It is significant that a generation before the *Lidai fabao ji* was written, Emperor Xuanzong's policies had greatly enhanced the prestige of Daoism. The emperor invited Daoist scholars to court, instituted new Daoist official positions, and established an empire-wide system of Daoist temples and academies of Daoist studies. He also mandated Daoist ritual services for the benefit of the state and made the *Daode jing* into one of the paramount texts of the official exam system.[147] As Victor Xiong has demonstrated,

Xuanzong also had a personal interest in Daoist ritual and alchemy.[148] Imperial involvement gave a higher status to Daoist thought and practices and boosted literati interest in Daoism. Reaching a high pitch during the Tianbao 天寶 era (742–756), these activities represented, according to Timothy Barrett, an "attempt to create an alternative to the traditional Confucian conception of monarchy."[149] Xuanzong's investment in Daoism was also meant to annul Empress Wu Zetian's attempt to establish Buddhist ascendancy over Confucianism and Daoism as the main ideological and ritual edifice of the state cult. Emperors Suzong 肅宗 (r. 756–762) and Daizong 代宗 (r. 762–779) continued to support Daoism, albeit on a less-extensive scale, and Daizong was more favorable to Buddhism. By the time of the writing of the *Lidai fabao ji*, the influence of state-appointed Daoists was already waning, but Chengdu and its environs had strong Daoist roots that would continue to bring forth new shoots.[150]

In his dialogue with a group of Daoist guests, Wuzhu is presented as a master of Daoist texts who exposes his interlocutors' lack of insight into their own classics. However, Wuzhu's quotations are of the most basic and familiar kind, and it is possible that his interpretations owed more to Daoist contemporaries than was acknowledged. The world of late eighth-century Daoist thought and practice was far more complex than the *Lidai fabao ji* authors admit, for mainstream Daoist traditions had developed sophisticated offshoots that drew from earlier *xuanxue* 玄學 traditions as well as from Buddhism. These newer developments are not directly addressed in Wuzhu's dialogue, although the Bao Tang followers may have included literati who were cognizant of these trends or who had studied Daoist texts in the era of Xuanzong's promulgations. Sun Huan, the follower who authored the portrait-eulogy for Wuzhu discussed in chapter 7, appears to have had such a background.

Here I compare Wuzhu's handling of Daoist thought with eighth-century Daoist trends that have been provisionally designated as *chongxuan* 重玄 (twofold mystery) and *neiguan* 內觀 (interior meditation). These terms refer not to Daoist sects but, rather, to related modes of exegesis and practice found in a handful of Tang Daoist texts. These texts reveal skillful appropriation and adaptation of Buddhist concepts and practices, and engagement with some of the same soteriological issues that shaped Chan. Wuzhu's manner of interpreting Daoist texts could indicate a familiarity with this subtle flavor of Daoism; if so, he was participating in a long Buddhist-Daoist tradition of borrowing and counter-borrowing.

Wuzhu's discussion with the Daoists opens in a typical fashion, showing the Chan master receiving visitors in his Dharma hall.

> Another time [Wuzhu was visited by] scores of Daoist priests and scores of recluses, and also twenty Dharma masters, Vinaya masters, and Trea-

tise masters. They were all "collars and sleeves" (leading figures) in Jiannan. The Venerable asked the Daoists, "'The Way that can be spoken/trodden is not the constant Way, the names that can be named are not the constant names.'[151] Is this not what Laojun (Laozi) taught?" The Daoist answered, "It is." The Venerable said, "Do you, Honored Masters, understand the meaning or not?" The Daoists were silent and did not reply.

The Venerable further asked [about the meaning of]: "'To undertake learning one increases day by day, to undertake the Way one decreases day by day. Decreasing it and further decreasing it, one finally arrives at non-doing. In non-doing, there is nothing that is not done.'"[152]

Wuzhu's well-known quotations from the *Daode jing* were also seminal for *chongxuan* exegesis. The term *chongxuan* is based on a famous phrase in the first section of the *Daodejing: xuan zhi you xuan* 玄之又玄, "render it mysterious and again mysterious." Robert Sharf delves into the question of *chongxuan* in *Coming to Terms with Chinese Buddhism,* his study of a late eighth-century Buddhist text permeated with Daoist concepts and terms.[153] The term *chongxuan* was used by the above-mentioned tenth-century Daoist scholar Du Guangting to categorize a style of exegesis practiced by a handful of early Tang Daoist literati, but Sharf argues that it was never a self-conscious school or sect. While contesting recent scholarly attempts to identify a *chongxuan* "school," Sharf concedes that there are discernible "doctrinal and rhetorical affinities" among the Daoist texts included under that rubric.[154] However, he points out that the term was also used in a large number of seventh- and eighth-century Buddhist texts and that the use of *chongxuan* in a dialectical sense appears to have first arisen in a Buddhist context.[155]

Many of the Daoist literati who favored this style of discourse were active in the court-sponsored Buddhist-Daoist debates of the early Tang; it is notable that Li Rong 李榮 (fl. mid-seventh century), one of the most influential of the *chongxuan* exegetes and debaters, was originally from Sichuan.[156] These Daoist literati used Mādhyamika-style dialectics to interpret the *Daode jing* and other early texts, creating Daoism-inflected expositions of Two Truths theory and *Prajñāpāramitā* thought. For example, the *Daode jing* phrase quoted by Wuzhu, "decreasing it and further decreasing it,"[157] was taken by *chongxuan* literati to be expressive of the successive abandonment of the concept of being, then nonbeing, and further abandonment of the concept of abandonment, in an infinite analytic/contemplative recursus that is indebted to Nāgārjuna's tetralemma and the *Prajñāpāramitā* notion of the "emptiness of emptiness."[158] Discourse on "*you* 有" (being) and "*wu* 無" (nonbeing) had been the foundation of the Daoist *xuanxue* metaphysical school of Wang Bi 王弼 (226–249) et al., a discourse in which original nonbeing is understood as giving rise to being. However, under the influence of Madhyamaka texts as introduced by Kumārajīva and his heirs, *xuanxue* emphasis also shifted from ontology and cosmology toward epistemology, and this was one of the roots of Tang *chongxuan* hermeneutics.

The new style of contemplative exegesis or exegetical contemplation did not abandon the patterns and principles of the old metaphysics. In the manner of the Daoist yin-yang symbol in which each of the two aspects nurtures the seed of its opposite, *chongxuan* thought stressed the complementarity and harmony of dialectical phases. According to Isabelle Robinet, *chongxuan* dialectics posited *wu*, the transcendence or absence of the concept of being and nonbeing, as the premise of a "two-fold synthesis." *Zhenwu* 真無 (true nonbeing) was formulated as the absence of the duality of being and nonbeing, therefore presupposing being, while *miaoyou* 妙有 (wondrous or subtle being) represented the interdependence of nonbeing and being, therefore presupposing nonbeing. The practice of this twofold synthesis was expressed as "double forgetting" (*jianwang* 兼忘), the continuous transcendence of reified dualities and transcendence of that transcendence.[159]

Just such doubling or emptying of emptiness is alluded to in Wuzhu's explication of his opening quotations from the *Daode jing:*

> The Way is fundamental nature. Reaching the Way cuts off words, deluded thoughts are not produced, and this is precisely "decreasing it." When one contemplates the Mind King, one parts with everything altogether, and this is "further decreasing it." [Regarding] "One finally arrives at nondoing"—when one experiences the emptiness of the nature in nirvāṇa, this Dharma is at this time seen. "In nondoing, there is nothing that is not done"—this means not abiding in nondoing. Practicing nonarising, one does not make nonarising into evidence. Practicing in emptiness, one does not make emptiness into evidence, and this is the meaning of "nothing that is not done."[160]

Wuzhu echoes the notion of "double forgetting" when he stresses "not abiding in nondoing" and letting go of the reflex to make emptiness into "evidence" (*zheng* 證), i.e., to reify it. Despite Wuzhu's claim of Buddhist superiority, both Chan and *chongxuan* soteriologies were occupied with circumventing reification and dependence on verbal formulae. It is noteworthy that Wuzhu makes a reference to the "Mind King" in this context, as the piece known as the *Xinwang ming* 心王銘 (Inscription on the Mind King) is one of a handful of late eighth-century Chan texts that show affinities with *chongxuan* Daoism. In the following verse from the *Xinwang ming,* we find some of the trademarks of this shared discourse in the references to spontaneity, "neither being nor nonbeing," and transcending both morality and emptiness:

> Illuminating the mind, the adept awakens to this mysterious sound. Body and mind-nature are subtle function without alteration; thus the sage rests his mind in spontaneity (*zizai* 自在). Not put into words, the Mind King is emptiness without substance-nature. It is able to cause the form-body to do wrong or do right; not being and not nonbeing, its hidden manifestations are not determined. The mind-nature transcends emptiness, it can be a common man or a saint.[161]

The Daoist tradition that associated such transcending of transcendence with "forgetting" may also have had other implications for Wuzhu. As noted, Zongmi's interpretation of Wuxiang's signature phrase "do not forget" (*mowang* 莫忘) was: "do not recall past visayas (domains); do not anticipate future glorious events; always be yoked to these insights, never darkening, never erring." However, it is tempting to wonder whether Wuxiang's injunction could have been aimed, instead, at Daoist or more generally "quietist" notions of forgetting oneself in seated meditation. Reference to meditation or mystical experience as "forgetting" harks back to Zhuangzi's "sitting and forgetting" (*zuowang* 坐忘),[162] and is evoked in the title of an important *chongxuan*-style text, Sima Chengzhen's 司馬承禎 (646–735) *Zuowang lun* 坐忘論 (Essay on Sitting and Forgetting).[163] If Wuxiang had such associations in mind, this could shed a different light on Wuzhu's insistence that Wuxiang had taught "do not be deluded" (*mowang* 莫妄) instead. Might Wuzhu have felt an uneasy recognition of the similarity between Daoist "sitting and forgetting" and his own "sitting in vacuity" (*kongxianzuo* 空閑坐)? Is it possible that he recognized an affinity between Daoist double-forgetting and his own "when there is true no-thought, no thought itself is not"?[164]

Analogous notions are also found in the *chongxuan*-related eighth-century texts that expound on a form of practice that Isabelle Robinet has provisionally classed as *neiguan*. Though texts associated with this trend might include visualizations, its distinguishing characteristic was the elevation of objectless, nonconceptual meditation to the highest level. For example, the practices in the *Neiguan jing* 內觀經 (Scripture of Interior Meditation)[165] are largely consistent with the visualizations of the mainstream Shangqing 上清 (Highest Clarity) and Lingbao 靈寶 (Numinous Treasure) traditions, involving contemplation of gods of the body and cosmological analogies, and formation of the perfected embryo. Buddhist influence, however, is seen in the practice focused on *xin,* heart/mind. *Xin* is both the originally pure spirit (*shen* 神) and the physical heart, which is troubled by emotions, the concept of self, and desire. The *Neiguan jing* advocates emptying the heart and spirit, which then allows it to function as the Dao without obstruction. However, this is not a Daoist form of subitism, even though the text holds that the original spirit is pure and that self-willed practice is counterproductive. The text ends with an admonition from Laozi that he too had to work to attain the Dao, upholding the deliberate and consistent gradualism that Robinet says is characteristic of the Daoist tradition through the centuries.[166]

Buddhist Tiantai school soteriology contributed to *neiguan*-style discourse on objectless concentration and insight. In the seventh-century *Dingguan jing* 定觀經 (Scripture of Concentration and Meditation)[167] there is a clearly marked path of ascent through five stages of meditative stabilization and seven steps of progressive transcendence. The *ding* (concentration) and *guan* (meditation, insight) of the title correspond to the Tiantai rubric of the complementary aspects of practice, calming (*zhi* 止, *śamatha*) and insight (*guan* 觀, *vipaśyanā*). As used in the *neiguan* tradition, *ding* is stable concentration, corresponding with yin and Earth, and *guan* (or *hui* 慧) is the active play of insight and illumination, corresponding with yang and Heaven. The two aspects of practice are ideally balanced, like yin and yang, and practice of a set of precepts helps the adept to maintain this balance. Related to the *Dingguan jing* in structure and soteriology, the above-mentioned *Zuowang lun* expounds on the subtle emptying of the spirit that is neither application nor extinguishing of awareness.[168]

When Wuzhu interprets the *Yijing* for his Daoist audience, he likewise emphasizes nonconceptualization that is not mere passive stillness but rather a naturally virtuous responsiveness:

> The Venerable then expounded for them: "The *Yijing* says, 'Nonconceiving and nondoing, tranquil and unmoving; stimulated, the [response] that follows pervades all.'[169] What is the meaning of this?" The recluses dared not reply.
>
> The Venerable explained further, "In the *Yijing,* 'Not transforming, not changing' is the fundamental nature of beings. 'Nonconceiving, nondoing, tranquil and unmoving' is the fundamental nature of beings. If one does not transform and does not change, does not conceptualize and does not imagine, this is the practice of benevolence, righteousness, propriety, wisdom, and faith. These days scholars do not see fundamental nature, they do not recognize host and guest. They concentrate on sense-objects and take this as scholarly inquiry, a great mistake. Confucius explained nonconceiving and nondoing, [he had] great discernment."[170]

In keeping with his assertion that the Buddhist precepts are completely fulfilled in no-thought, Wuzhu assures his audience that the traditional Confucian virtues (as articulated by Mencius) are fulfilled in the nonconceptual realization of Dao/fundamental nature. Wuzhu identifies antinomian subitism in the cultural bedrock of Confucius' *Yijing* commentary and chides his audience for having lost touch with this original insight.

However, the *Benji jing* 本際經 (Scripture of the Genesis Point), one of the Daoist texts promoted by Emperor Xuanzong, also has an antinomian aspect. It teaches that on the higher level one understands the nonobtaining (*wude* 無得) precepts, which cannot be upheld or transgressed, and understands that "leaving home" means leaving behind the precepts and observances one has previously maintained.[171] Nevertheless, the antinomianism of the *Benji jing* is closer to conventional Two Truths doctrine than to subitist Chan, as prior diligence in the precepts is held to be the foundation of the higher level.

As I have shown in previous chapters, the notion of fulfillment of the precepts in nonconceptualization presented such serious challenges to cultural and institutional structures that it was usually circumscribed or qualified wherever it appeared. This was no less an issue in the Daoist trends we are exploring. When his guests ask him to further explain the lines he has quoted from the *Yijing* commentary, Wuzhu addresses the important issue of moral accountability according to subitist soteriology:

> The recluses asked the Venerable, "'Stimulated (*gan* 感), the [response] that follows pervades all'—what does this mean?" The Venerable replied, "If the Brahmaloka is not sought, the Brahmaloka is reached of itself; if karmic reward is not sought, karmic reward is reached of itself.[172] The defilements are completely exhausted, the seeds [in the *ālayavijñāna,* storehouse consciousness] are also removed, and Brāhma, Indra, the nāgas and devas are all moved to do reverence. For this reason, when the Tathāgata entered a town to eat, all the grasses and trees bowed their heads, and all the mountains and rivers leaned toward the Buddha. How much more so the many beings? This is 'stimulated, the [response] that follows pervades all.'"[173]

Wuzhu harnesses the Daoist notion of the spontaneous and all-pervasive action of the Dao to support the Chan claim that karmic obstructions naturally vanish in the moment of insight into emptiness. He adroitly links this to an image of the Buddha that reflects Chinese notions of the Sage, who by his unmoved moving stimulates all things to follow. The nature and character of the Sage-ruler was a central concern in the Chinese classics of the Zhou and Han periods, and the *Yijing* and its commentaries were fundamental to this political-philosophical discourse.[174] Discourse on the Sage-ruler was interwoven with notions of *ganying* 感應 (stimulus-response or sympathetic resonance) and *gantong* 感通 (supramundane powers), and these were by no means obsolete topics in eighth-century exegetical debate.

Sharf devotes a chapter of *Coming to Terms with Chinese Buddhism* to the relationship between eighth-century *chongxuan* thought and Chinese notions of sympathetic resonance. Han metaphysical theories of *ganying* were embedded in the system of the "five phases" (*wuxing* 五行), whereby things affect one another through patterns and cycles of categorical affinities. Interpretations based on yin-yang and the five phases rendered what appeared to be supernatural occurrences (for example, rain in response to sacrifice or an omen prefiguring death) apprehensible as natural processes of mutual influence between corollaries. This was illustrated by the "sympathetic" tone made by an instrument spontaneously sounding in response when another like instrument was struck or plucked.[175] Thus, from the *Wenyan* 文言 commentary to the *Yijing:* "Things with the same tonality resonate together. . . . The sage bestirs himself, and all creatures look to him."[176] This notion of the ideal Sage-ruler as a resonator is rooted in ancient sacrificial practice, in which the ruler acts as the pivot between Heaven and Earth and maintains harmonious correspondences through his carefully calibrated ritual behavior and offerings. Emphasis on ritual, *li* 禮, is thus the purposive or coercive aspect of *ganying* theory, in contrast to the *wuwei* aspect stressing spontaneity and natural response.[177]

In his own commentary on the *Yijing,* Wuzhu extols the spontaneity and immediacy of the function of the Dharma and Buddha. In the *wuwei* practice of no-thought (not-seeking), the practitioner's karmic residues are all-at-once removed, and he/she becomes like the Sage/Buddha whom all creatures reverence. Wuzhu was not the first to offer such a synthesis of Sage-ruler, Buddha, and liberation from karmic consequences. Sharf cites several fourth- and fifth-century examples of the Sage ideal transposed into a Buddhist context; most noteworthy is the monk Zhidun's 支遁 (314–366) memorial to the throne, in which he assures the ruler that the practice of *wuwei* will save him from the karmic effects of exercising state functions, such as the execution of criminals.[178]

Taken together, when we review the manner in which Wuzhu's interpretations resonate with *chongxuan* and *neiguan* concepts, it seems highly likely that he or his followers were familiar with some aspect of this protean Daoist-Buddhist-Daoist discourse. In order to define the Buddhist-Daoist boundary, the *Lidai fabao ji* authors rely on a "heteroglossia" that they share with their putative opponents.[179] Each attempt to consume and transcend the other deepens the mutual entanglement, generating analogous yet mutually differential semantic fields. We see this mutually evocative differentiation in the rubrics of nonconceptual contemplation ("decreasing and further decreasing," "emptying," and "double-forgetting"), *wunian/wuwei* as realization of the precepts/cardinal virtues, and the Buddha/Sage as a pivot of sympathetic resonance and spontaneous response.

The Buddhist and Daoist texts that contributed to this rhetorical context tended to freely incorporate and manipulate each other's terms and allusions while maintaining a particular soteriological or devotional framework. Wuzhu takes a less subtle approach, and flatly asserts that harmony among the teachings is possible only if the superiority of the Buddhist teachings is acknowledged. He sternly rebuffs the Daoists' hopeful attempt to meet on common ground:

> When the Daoists had heard his talk, they joined their palms and asked the Venerable, "If one explains it like this, then this means 'Buddhism and Daoism are not two.'" The Venerable said, "Not so. Zhuangzi and Laozi covered nondoing and no-characteristics, the one, purity, and spontaneity. The Buddha is not like this, he taught that both causation and spontaneity are idle theories."[180]

Wuzhu takes up the labels "causation" or "causes and conditions" (*yinyuan* 因緣) and "spontaneity" or "naturalness" (*ziran* 自然) to represent the polar errors of gradualism and naturalism (i.e., the Daoist metaphysics of the spontaneous generation and unfolding of the Dao). The Buddha is made to represent subitist transcendence of these false views. Wuzhu's use of this polarity recalls passages from Shenhui's "Miscellaneous Dialogues," in which Shenhui is challenged to draw a distinction between Daoism and Buddhism:

> QUESTION: "If ignorance is natural, then how is this different from the 'naturalness' of the non-Buddhists?"
>
> ANSWER: "It is identical with the naturalness of the [philosophical] Daoists (*daojia* 道家), but the understanding of it is different."
>
> QUESTION: "How is it different?"
>
> ANSWER: "Within the teachings of Buddhism the Buddha-nature and ignorance are both natural. Why? Because all the myriad dharmas all depend on the power of the Buddha-nature. Therefore, all the dharmas all belong to the natural. With the naturalness of the Daoists, 'the Way generates the one, the one generates the two, the two generate the three, and the three generate the myriad things.'[181] From the one on down, the myriad things are all 'natural.' Consequently, the understandings are not identical."[182]

Shenhui's rejection of Buddhist-Daoist identity is milder than Wuzhu's, but he too insists that the Daoist view is limited. He takes up the standard Buddhist claim that philosophical Daoism is based on a dualistic devolutionary ontology (nonbeing spontaneously generates being, a lesser order). He contrasts this with the nondual subitist view that phenomena and spontaneous self-realization are not separate, that ignorance and wisdom are coinherent in the "birthless" nature of reality. In the above dialogue he equates the teachings of Buddhism with the correct view, but in a subsequent dialogue he also accuses fellow-Buddhists of missing the point:

> Administrative Aide Ma then asked, "The monks who respond to the imperial court from throughout the land only speak of causes and conditions and do not speak of naturalness. The Daoist priests from throughout the land only speak of naturalness, without speaking of causes and conditions."
>
> Answer: "That the monks posit causes and conditions without positing naturalness is the monks' stupid error. That the priests just posit naturalness without positing causes and conditions is the priests' stupid error."
>
> The Administrative Aide said, "I can understand the causes and conditions of the Buddhists, but what would their naturalness be? I can understand the Daoists' naturalness, but what would their causes and conditions be?"
>
> Answer: "The naturalness of the Buddhists is the fundamental nature of sentient beings. Furthermore, a sūtra says, 'Sentient beings have a natural wisdom, a teacherless wisdom, which is called natural.' The Daoist priests' causes and conditions are that 'The Dao gives birth to the one, the one gives birth to the two, the two gives birth to the three, and from the three are born the myriad things.' They are born dependent on the Dao. If there were no Dao, the myriad things would not be born. What I refer to as 'myriad things' all belong to causes and conditions."[183]

Thus, gradualist Buddhists who reify karmic conditions miss the spontaneous realization of Buddha-nature. Shenhui appears to imply that Daoists, by contrast, recognize the temporal causation of the Dao but do not recognize it as the immediate and inherent wisdom of all beings. When we look at the tenor of *chongxuan* and *neiguan* texts, it is clear that this imputation would not have applied to Shenhui's literati Daoist contemporaries.

Regardless of whether Wuzhu and the *Lidai fabao ji* authors were influenced by Shenhui's views, they were obviously willing to take the offensive much more forcefully. Wuzhu concludes his lecture to his guests by asserting an ineradicable divide between Buddhism and Daoism:

> Zhuangzi's, Laozi's, and Confucius' teachings are to be lumped together with those of the Śrāvakas. The Buddha rebuked the Śrāvakas, [saying they were] as if blind, as if deaf. "Stream-entrants, once-returners, nonreturners, and arhats are all saints, yet their minds are completely deluded."[184] The Buddha thus does not sink into the crowd, but transcends all. The Dharma is without stain or purity, the Dharma is without form or feature, the Dharma is without restless disturbance, the Dharma is without a location, the Dharma is without grasping or discarding. Therefore it transcends Confucius, Zhuangzi, and Laozi. "The Buddha is always in the world, yet is not stained by worldly dharmas. Due to not separating 'the world' [from the ultimate], we do reverence without having anything to contemplate."[185] What Confucius and Laozi taught all had something attached. All of it is the sphere of Śrāvakas, the two vehicles.[186]

Wuzhu equates Daoists and Confucians with practitioners of the lesser vehicles, asserting that they are attached to the dualisms inherent in notions of purification and transcendence, and he emphasizes the superiority of Buddhist nonduality and Chan formless practice. However, as we have seen, the thrust of *chongxuan* "double forgetting" is in complete accord with the nonterritory that Wuzhu claims belongs to the Buddhists. Moreover, his evocation of "doing reverence without having anything to contemplate" is in accord with the *neiguan* practice of objectless contemplation and reverence of the Dao as one's own mind.

It is said that at the end of Wuzhu's discourse all the Daoists converted to Buddhism and became Wuzhu's disciples. Viewed from the perspective of *chongxuan* discourse, however, it would be difficult to identify the boundary crossed in such a conversion. Wuzhu's final claim for Buddhist superiority is built on a foundation of eggshells, fragments in which the derivation of one discourse from the other is difficult to determine. As we will see in chapter 7, the portrait-eulogy for Wuzhu includes allusions to the *Daode jing*, the *Zhuangzi*, and the *Lunyu*, and these allusions are treated in a manner indicating that the eulogist found no incompatibility between these texts and Wuzhu's doctrines. Thus, in spite of the polemical tenor of the contests with Daoists featured in the main part of the *Lidai fabao ji*, it is "harmony among the teachings" that gets the final word.

CHAPTER 7

The Legacy of the *Lidai fabao ji*

"That's the great thing," Isabel solemnly pondered; "that's the supreme good fortune: to be in a better position for appreciating people than they are for appreciating you."

—Henry James, *The Portrait of a Lady*

BLAME AND praise centered on Chan's antinomian qualities have had a long history and have been used for quite disparate purposes. Jesuits encountering Chan in the eighteenth century repudiated it as antinomian and quietistic, and this animus seems to have been a reflection of their distaste for such tendencies in European rivals.[1] By contrast, Japanese sectarians in general and D. T. Suzuki in particular have celebrated Chan/Zen spontaneity and iconoclasm. As a corrective, scholars like Bernard Faure, T. Griffith Foulk, and Robert Sharf have devoted careful effort to show that Chan's iconoclastic, anti-institutional, antinomian, and subitist rhetoric went hand in hand with the development of distinctive Chan iconographies, ritual and institutional settings, disciplines, and esotericism.

However, if we take seriously the claims in the *Lidai fabao ji* itself and the criticisms that Zongmi directed against the Bao Tang, then we can say that here was one group that seems to have interpreted the precepts in a way that could indeed be called antinomian and advocated a practice of *wunian* that could indeed be called quietist ("sitting in vacuity"). What I have attempted to portray is how this moment arrived, and now I turn to the question of how it passed away.

To return to a point made at the outset of this study, I am not interested in defending the Bao Tang interpretation of formlessness, for attempts to establish criteria by which to judge Chan authenticity are ineluctably bound up with the local concerns of those who would establish such criteria. However, I recognize that the assortment of approaches adopted in this study are no more firmly founded than is the traditional Buddhist scholar's quest for authenticity. Throughout, I have tried to maintain a due regard for the intertextual and also reader-referential nature of meanings (such as authenticity and legitimacy). At the same time, I have not excluded the notion that the rhetoric and representations of the *Lidai fabao ji* tell us meaningful things about a group of people who lived in a temple in Chengdu in the late eighth century. The intertextualities shaping the *Lidai fabao ji* and our readings of it are inseparable from the events and personalities it represents, but the nature of that relationship is indeterminable. Nevertheless, impossible as it may be to define, this relationship—between representations and "realities," or between intertextual and embodied representations—cannot be ignored.

In this study I have highlighted points of tension in order to try to discern the forces that left impressions on texts and persons, including the texts and persons that have made "Chan" a contemporary contested topic of study. Both the textual icons and the personalities were shaped by the differential interdependence between adaptation and continuity, lay and ordained, rival ideologies, and formlessness/forms. So far, we have looked into the tangled histories of certain key forms—bodhisattva precepts, the final age, the patriarchal robe, and the formless precepts—and seen something of the resonances among rival representations. Layer by layer, polemical pressures created a history of Dharma transmission, and the forms of practice, lineages, stories, and talismans that were transmitted were like fossils through which we see traces of individual lives as well as the stratigraphy of generative conflict.

In this chapter I focus on one of the most remarkable fossils in the *Lidai fabao ji,* the eulogy praising what was probably the funeral portrait of Wuzhu. Through this portrait-eulogy evoking Wuzhu's image, his persona, we may probe the issue of Chan iconoclasm, follow the development of a distinctive Chan genre, and examine the polemical uses of this genre. In the concluding section of this chapter and this study, I discuss further developments after the *Lidai fabao ji,* tracing tributes and challenges to the legacy of Wuxiang and Wuzhu in Sichuan, Korea, and Tibet. Finally, I offer some closing reflections regarding the legacy of the formless practice of the Bao Tang school.

THE PORTRAIT-EULOGY FOR WUZHU

Exploring the antecedents of the *Lidai fabao ji* portrait-eulogy and its functions, I first give an overview of different types of portraits and images of Buddhist masters. I then compare the *Lidai fabao ji* eulogy with selected examples of other eighth-century eulogies and discuss the development of the portrait-eulogy genre in a Chan context. Finally, I examine the convergence of conflicting soteriological paradigms in the (imagined) portrait in light of assertions made in the eulogy. We will pay particular attention to the creative tension between the emerging Chan orthodoxy of formlessness, and the artistic, literary, and ritual forms that were appropriated to express this formlessness.

Priestly Portraiture

Preceding the account of Wuzhu's death and the close of the *Lidai fabao ji*, there is a lengthy composition in a style that differs from that of the rest of the text. This piece is identified as a *zhenzan* 真讚 (portrait-eulogy), and it evokes Wuzhu through the portrait of him that the Bao Tang disciples apparently had painted immediately after his death.

How might one imagine this portrait? References to commemorative portraits of monks appear in works as early as the sixth century, but the practice of making portraits of Buddhist masters appears to have increased in the latter half of the eighth century. Dunhuang specialist Jiang Boqin 姜伯勤 contends that from the ninth century onward, the development of portrait arts was closely tied to commemorative practices in Buddhist monasteries. There are records of monks who were known as skilled portrait-painters, and monks also contributed to the development of the genre of "appreciations" (*zan* 讚) for both portraits and Buddhist images. Portraits of eminent monks and prominent lay figures were used in funeral rituals and were also sometimes displayed in monasteries while the subject was still alive.[2]

In the eighth century, portraits may have been implicated in Shenhui's polemical claims; he denounced Puji for setting up a Hall of Seven Patriarchs (*qizu tang* 七祖堂) without including Huineng.[3] In their article entitled "On the Ritual Use of Ch'an Portraiture in Medieval China," T. Griffith Foulk and Robert Sharf surmise that the hall in question contained spirit tablets and possibly images of the patriarchs. Other references to the placement of portraits in portrait-halls (*zhentang* 真堂 or *yingtang* 影堂) in the eighth and ninth centuries indicate that they were patterned after ancestral shrines and that there was a connection between the arrangement of the portraits or tablets in the hall and the configuration of biographies in the Chan sectarian histories.[4] By the time of the *Chanyuan qinggui* 禪苑清規 (Rules of Purity for Chan Monasteries) of 1103, there is an elaborate funeral protocol for Chan abbots in which the abbot's portrait becomes the focus for mourning devotions open to the public, in contrast to the devotions of close disciples who keep vigil over the body. After the funeral, the portrait was enshrined in the portrait-hall and received regular offerings and devotions appropriate to a powerful icon.[5]

In the Tang, a variety of memorial media were used to represent deceased monks and nuns: painted scrolls and murals, statues of clay, lacquer, and stone, and images and inscriptions engraved on tablets. In the eighth and ninth centuries, clay mixed with the ashes of the deceased was a favored medium in which to capture the likeness of an individual revered monk. Attested by inscriptions and niches at Dunhuang, and references in the mid-ninth century *Sita ji* 寺塔記 (Record of Temples and Stūpas), these individual images were often placed in a separate niche or memorial chapel.[6] The *Song gaoseng zhuan* features a striking story about a clay-and-relics portrait statue of Wuxiang, to which we return below.[7]

The earliest extant examples of portrait paintings of Chinese monks are preserved in Japan. These are the paintings of the so-called five patriarchs of the Zhenyan 真言 (Esoteric) school, brought back from China by the Japanese monk Kūkai 空海 (774–835) and now held in the Tōji 東寺 temple treasury in Kyoto. This group includes portraits of Wuzhu's contemporary Bukong (Amoghavajra) and Bukong's Dharma "family."[8] As these portraits are the closest contemporary examples remaining, we cannot help but turn to them for suggestions as to how Wuzhu's portrait might have looked. The portraits are by the artist Li Zhen 李真, who was active in the late eighth century. The portrait of Bukong is the only original that is still well-preserved. In it we see the master kneeling on a small platform with his hands raised in obeisance. He is fully shaven and his face is seen in a three-quarter view. He has a rather large nose; Bukong was said to be from south India, and it is difficult to say whether this was an actual feature or an exaggeration typical in portrayals of foreigners.[9]

Although the painting of Bukong is from the same period as the lost portrait of Wuzhu, there are no clues in the eulogy as to the format and size of Wuzhu's portrait or of the posture in which he was portrayed. Nevertheless, Wuzhu's portrait probably resembled the Zhenyan patriarchs' portraits more than it resembled the typical Chan or Zen priest portrait familiar from a number of thirteenth- to sixteenth-century examples, one of which we consider below.

Wuzhu's portrait was presumably painted in color on silk, but there is an impressive example of the early use of monochrome ink on paper to produce the image of a monk, found in the Stein collection of Dunhuang painting scrolls.[10] Based on stylistic features, it has been dated to the late ninth or early tenth century, and it displays the artist's confident use of line alone to produce a finished image. The monk is shown seated on a mat on the ground with his wallet and rosary hanging on a tree behind him, his water jar beside him, and his shoes placed in front of him on the mat. These objects correspond to the accoutrements painted on the walls behind the Dunhuang niches that once held portrait statues. Given Wuzhu's penchant for meditation alfresco it might not be inappropriate to imagine him in this manner, seated in meditation posture under a tree. Although Helmut Brinker calls the open-air portrait "the most informal kind of Zen Buddhist imagery," this may be more true of Song examples modeled after idealized images of gentlemen in relaxed postures amid natural scenes.[11] The Dunhuang drawing reflects the more formal iconography of reliquary statues in painted niches, and it may also have evoked images of the Arhats in wilderness settings, discussed further below. There is evidence that there was a demand for copies of portraits of revered monks, and it is possible that this line drawing is a copy of a more elaborate portrait mural or even a statue.[12] Jiang Boqin argues that this drawing was intended as a finished portrait, and he cites a portrait-eulogy by the monk-poet Jiaoran 皎然 (b. 720?, a.k.a. Qing Zhou 清晝) in order to demonstrate how the drawing accords with Jiaoran's description of the ideal portrait:

> The painting is in accord with principle, it sounds the depths of feeling and comprehends discriminating awareness. The two bodies (i.e., painting and subject) are not different, the [close correspondence between them, as if of] "eyebrows and lashes" is just perfect. What does he want to say, what is he thinking of doing? Sitting alone on the bed, his implements of the Way have long accompanied him—the water pitcher he holds could be poured, and the rosary turns as if it's moving. A clear breeze blows his plain garments, as if straightening his majestic demeanor.[13]

Praise for the quality of presence in the painting draws attention to the unfathomable surfacing between subject and artist. As early as the *Zhuangzi* (albeit in one of the "outer chapters") we encounter the notion that the ability to capture the spirit of the subject in a portrait was reflected in the unconventional behavior of the painter. Note that this unconventionality was portrayed not as flamboyance, but obliviousness to forms of etiquette:

> When Prince Yuan of Song was about to have a portrait painted, all the official painters came, bowed, and at the royal command stood waiting, licking their brushes and mixing their ink. Half of them were outside the room. One official came late. He sauntered in without hurrying himself, bowed at the royal command, and would not remain standing. Thereupon he was given lodging. The prince sent a man to see what he did. He took off his clothes and squatted down bare-backed. The ruler said, 'He will do. He is a true painter.' "[14]

It is beyond the scope of the present study to delve into the role of the artist, but this sketch of the "true painter" raises the question of modes of production and the related question of style.[15] According to seventeenth-century arbiters of aesthetics, "professional" religious paintings were to be considered stylistically and genealogically distinct from amateur or "literati" paintings, and the Chan terminology of "Northern School" and

"Southern School" was marshaled to make this distinction. However, it is likely that in the Tang and Song the same artist could have employed a variety of styles. In the Song, professionals produced and sold monochrome ink-on-paper originals and copies of paintings on typical literati and "Chan" themes (Bodhidharma, Hanshan and Shide, gibbons, landscapes, etc.), and amateurs also produced color-on-silk, iconographically correct depictions of Buddhas and bodhisattvas like those commissioned by donors from professional artists.[16] Nevertheless, Chinese aesthetic canons inherited from the Ming have given pride of place to the brush unconstrained by necessity or overmuch color.

Traditions of Chinese painting associate a broken-contour, spontaneous brush style developed in tenth-century Chengdu with the artist Shi Ke 石恪, who was said to have influenced the use of experimental brushwork styles for Chan subjects.[17] Thus, we might well contemplate the famous paired paintings "Two Patriarchs Harmonizing the Mind" (*Erzu tiaoxin* 二祖調心), considered representative of the *yipin* 逸品 (untrammeled brush) style. The paintings are from a thirteenth-century handscroll copy, including what is purported to be a copy of the signatory inscription by Shi Ke in 963. The subjects are clearly related to the popular Song "four sleepers" theme, in which the Chan eccentric friends Shide 拾得, Hanshan 寒山, and Fenggan 豐干 are shown snoozing in a heap with Fenggan's tiger.[18] However, these masterful ink-blots invite a host of free-associations. Because Wuxiang, in popular legend, came to be linked with a tiger companion, and the *Lidai fabao ji* describes Wuzhu and Wuxiang sharing a rapport and a fondness for "sitting in vacuity" even though separated, for me these paintings have become unintentional evocations of the estranged but empathetic Bao Tang master and disciple—they are dreaming, perhaps, of each other.

We might also consider the influence of the popular images of the Buddha's important disciples, the Sixteen (or Eighteen) Arhats (Lohan 羅漢). These apparently highly individualistic "portraits" reflect a long tradition of depicting foreigners with exaggerated facial features. Though Song Chan master portraits show figures clearly meant to look Chinese, in the Lohan images individualized "foreign" features are emphasized to the point of caricature, playing on the mystique of the otherness and uncanny powers of the Buddha's disciples. Arhats and Chan patriarchs are explicitly juxtaposed in the magnificent "Long Roll" or "Dali Scroll" of Buddhist images important to the state cult of an independent kingdom in Yunnan that was known successively as Nanzhao 南詔 (728–898), Dali 大理 (937–1004) and Hou Li 後理 (1096–1253). Dated c. 1175, the scroll is 51 feet long and includes a depiction of the emperor who had the painting made, sixteen Arhats, sixteen Chan patriarchs, scenes of the *Maitreya Sūtra* and the vows of Bhaiṣajyaguru, numerous forms of Avalokiteśvara, "wrathful" protector deities, and the sixteen kings of the *Renwang jing* 仁王經 (Scripture of Humane Kings).[19] The Arhats "count down" in more or less standard iconographic order to Piṇḍola, followed by an image of Śākyamuni, from whom the Chan patriarchs "count up" in chronological order from Kāśyapa and Ānanda, then the six patriarchs in China followed by Shenhui (all designated "Great Master") and the monk Zhang Weizhong 張惟忠.[20]

This last figure provides a link with Sichuan Chan. As noted in chapter 6, Zhang Weizhong, also known as Nanyin, was a successor of Jingzhong Shenhui, though he may also have studied with our better-known "seventh patriarch" Heze Shenhui. Jingzhong Shenhui, unlike Bao Tang Wuzhu, was acknowledged by posterity as Wuxiang's successor. Zhang Weizhong's presence in the scroll reflects the connection between Jingzhong Shenhui and the Military Governor of Jiannan West, Wei Gao 韋皋 (d. 805), the architect of an alliance between the Nanzhao kingdom and the Tang.[21] The final six figures in the group of patriarchs are all presumably Yunnan notables, two of whom are known from other sources.[22] The scroll is thus a good illustration of how collateral local traditions were grafted onto the "trunk" of the lineal six Chan patriarchs.[23]

In his annotation to Helen Chapin's pioneering work on the "Long Roll," art historian Alexander Soper states his conviction that those portions of the scroll that were not clearly copied from Song models were probably copied from Tang models, long since lost.[24] Regardless of whether they were stylistically similar, there is one feature that the portraits of the Chan patriarchs of the "Long Roll" share with the portrait of Wuzhu: The images themselves are clearly meant to be powerful. The Chan patriarchs appear among other images of protector figures, especially the various forms of Avalokiteśvara. The "Long Roll" is in fact a visual roll-call of guardians of the state, from the emperor who commissioned the work at the beginning of the scroll, to the wrathful deities and sixteen great kings at the end.[25]

By the Song dynasty, portraits of Chan abbots could be commissioned by disciples, and, according to Dōgen, were sometimes fraudulently retailed in Japan as proof of authentic Dharma transmission.[26] The finishing touch was given to these commissioned portraits by the subjects themselves, and self-inscribed "portrait-eulogies" survive in great numbers. Stylistic distinctions between funerary portraits and these personalized effects remain to be explored.

We may take the superb portrait of Wuzhun Shifan 無準師範 (1178–1249) as a prime example of the Chan priest portrait genre, known as *dingxiang* 頂相 or *zhenxiang* 真相 (Jap. *chinzō*). Wuzhun Shifan's elegant, polished portrait was painted in ink and color on silk, presumably by a professional. In 1238, Master Wuzhun gave this portrait to his Japanese disciple Enni 圓爾 (1202–1280), who took it to Japan, where it now resides in the Tōfukuji collection in Kyoto. Wuzhun is portrayed on the occasion when he was summoned to court and gave a Dharma talk for the Southern Song Emperor Lizong 理宗 in 1233, when he received an honorary title and the gold-embroidered *kaśaya* he is wearing in the portrait.[27] Typically, in such portraits the master is in full monastic robes seated in lotus posture in a chair, with his shoes neatly placed on a footstool before him and his right hand holding an implement such as a whisk or staff, and he may be shown with hair and a beard.[28]

In a final appearance of the Chan master portrait, let us consider an anonymous Ming painting in which the gentleman-connoisseur is the subject, and the priest has become the objet d'art. From a seventeenth-century series depicting the "four accomplishments of the gentleman"—zither, chess, calligraphy, and painting—the scroll on "painting" shows a cluster of gentlemen appreciating a Chan master's portrait.[29] In this "portrait" the master is shown seated on a chair, and facing him is a gentleman layman, presumably a disciple appreciating the master's discourse. From behind the painted painting peeks the pretty face of the boy attendant who is apparently holding up the scroll with a stick. The scroll is displayed against a background of collector's rocks and miniature trees, a secular counterpart to the stylized natural settings painted in portrait-statue niches at Dunhuang.

By commissioning a portrait of their master, the Bao Tang followers were participating in a respected form of memorialization, but Chan priest portraiture was not yet the social mannerism or even tongue-in-cheek practice that it eventually became. Furthermore, from the examples above one can see that the nature of "Chan painting" is rather difficult to define. "Chan painting" included formal memorial portraits, and it also included paintings on Chan subjects executed in "spontaneous" styles by both professionals and nonprofessionals, all of which were treasured and collected in both religious and secular milieux. The contrasting types of images (formal and spontaneous) exemplify a complementarity we also see in the styles of portrait-eulogies considered in the next section. Chan genres do not so much describe as create "spontaneous" encounters by setting up ritual boundaries for them. If we can appreciate the authentic work of scripted spontaneity, then we can also appreciate that the work is successful only if it coveys its own unreliability.[30] The repeated breakdown of received form became a necessary part of Chan continuity and viability, thanks in no small part to artistic, literary, and doctrinal experimentation in ninth-century Sichuan.

Portrait-Eulogies

As noted in chapter 1, the *Lidai fabao ji* is a pastiche of textual formats that anticipated the genres of mature Chan: the Chan sectarian account of Buddhist history (with an emphasis on "schools" and affiliations), the *chuandeng lu* or "transmission of the lamp" genealogy of biographies of Chan patriarchs, and the *yulu* or "discourse records" of a master's sermons and his dialogues with disciples and visitors. Focusing here on the *zhenzan* genre, let us take a look at correspondences between the *Lidai fabao ji* portrait-eulogy and other eighth-century examples of memorial appreciations, and then compare these with the style of the Chan *zhenzan* of the Song dynasty.

As noted, the portrait-eulogy immediately precedes the scene of Wuzhu's death, which is portrayed in the standard manner of Buddhist hagiography. The eulogy is entitled "Portrait-eulogy, with preface, composed for a disciple of the Chan teachings of sudden awakening in the Mahāyāna," and the preface to the eulogy begins with identification of the author, "the recluse Sun Huan 孫寰."[31] The preface to the eulogy praises Wuzhu's teachings and gives the reasons for having a portrait made, and the eulogy itself praises the Dharma and the portrait. The piece echoes Wuzhu's sermons as given in other sections of the *Lidai fabao ji,* but is written in a more polished style than that of the person or persons who wrote the rest of the text. In the preface Wuzhu is referred to as "our teacher," so the writer identifies himself as a Bao Tang follower. Sun Huan is otherwise unknown, but he seems to have been a retired scholar and lay disciple with a Daoist background. It is possible that the preface and eulogy are earlier than the rest of the text, if they were in fact written immediately after Wuzhu's death.

This *zhenzan* is written in a style similar to that of *beiming* 碑銘, epitaphs or memorial inscriptions. Reconstruction of the history of Chan owes a great deal to surviving *beiming;* as we saw in chapter 5, Shenhui's attack on the "Northern School" focused on claims made in epitaphs for Shenxiu and his disciples, especially Puji. Chan histories are also founded on spurious or very belated *beiming* for Chan patriarchs; the *Baolin zhuan* includes an impressive collection of these.

Sun Huan's style in the *Lidai fabao ji* portrait-eulogy is more akin to eighth-century *beiming* for Chan masters than it is to the eccentric, yet also formulaic, Song Chan *zhenzan* that we will examine below. Like Puji's memorialist, Sun Huan places his subject within the exalted lineage of the Chan patriarchy:

> The highest vehicle of the Dharma is neither principle nor phenomena. The many gates of the good teaching all return to nonduality. [Mahā]kāśyapa attained it, and it spread westward to Buddha-regions; [Bodhi]dharma received it, and it flowed eastward to the land of the Han. These are matters spanning over one thousand years, the holy ones for thirty-four generations have passed it from legitimate heir to legitimate heir, from one

generation to the next. The Dharma they obtained tallies with the Dao's source, the robe they transmitted clearly shows true and false. Our teacher secretly received it and graciously displayed it, opening the secret mysterious gates of the Buddhas and revealing the complete meaning of the Mahāyāna.[32]

In his eulogy, Sun Huan makes a strong claim for Wuzhu's singular authority. Regardless of whether the eulogy was originally written to stand alone, in the context in which it is preserved the battle over this claim to authority has already been clarified—or obscured—in preceding narratives. In the eulogy the central concern of the *Lidai fabao ji* is alluded to, namely, Wuzhu's contested possession of the true Dharma transmission and Bodhidharma's robe, but neither in the *Lidai fabao ji* nor in the eulogy is there any hint about Wuzhu's Dharma successor.

As with *beiming,* the conventions of the *zhenzan* genre were adapted to fit Buddhist concerns. The earliest known reference to a eulogy for a monk's portrait is in the sixth-century *Gaoseng zhuan* entry for Kang Senghui 康僧會 (d. 280): "Therefore, his portrait was drawn, and it has been passed down to this day. Sun Chao 孫綽 composed the eulogy (*zan* 贊) [inscribed on the portrait]."[33] A number of Tang *zhenzan* for ordained and lay Buddhist subjects are extant, and the Dunhuang materials include a rich trove of late Tang and Five Dynasties examples. Let us look at what may be the earliest of the Dunhuang *zhenzan,* probably written within a few decades of the *Lidai fabao ji* eulogy, entitled *Gu qian shimen dufalu jingzhao Du heshang xie zhenzan* 故前釋門都法律京兆杜和尚寫真讃 (Portrait-Eulogy for the Late Buddhist Head Preceptor, Venerable Du of the Capital).[34]

Five hundred successive births, and in one ascent he becomes a sage-worthy. When very young he studied the Way, and all mouths praised him. He criticized treatises, kept the Vinaya, and was most able in the practice of meditation. Because he maintained chastity, he was enrolled in the ranks of eminent monks. He is like Luoshe 羅什 of old, or the Moteng 摩騰 of his day.[35] The three carts are all traces, all return to the one vehicle. The pearls of the precepts are constantly bright, his pure conduct is like clear ice. A thousand [surrounding] layers of dark rooms rely on one bright light; aiding the Buddha in preaching and converting, he is the "legs and arms" (assistant) of the Dharma-King. The pond skimmed [of weeds] is tranquil and hidden, the depths remain frozen (unmoving). [Since he has] abandoned the evil world and returned to purity, who will further the Buddhist teachings? An unlucky sign (*buxiang ruiying* 不詳瑞應)—the branches of the twin trees snapped. This morning the [corresponding] manifestation (*xiang* 像) was revealed, as those of the Vinaya announced the death of their prince. The followers weep together, "What can we rely on?" He takes leave of this corrupt age, the Pure Land has summoned him to be received. Now that he has returned to ultimate joy, the triple world is without illumination. The fragrant wind leads the way, a thousand monks run quickly [to pay last respects.] He is in the first assembly of the dragon flower[36] and barefoot he ascends ahead. The poem:

> His [karmic] endowment contained true wisdom, when very young he had already tired of worldly glories. He did not seek vermilion and purple honors, and adamantly refused the imperial court. He took the tonsure and purified the sense-spheres, wore black and walked as far as the sea. He has already saved all beings; he has reached nirvāṇa and entered the lotus.[37]

It is notable that the portrait itself is not mentioned; the only *xiang* 像 here refers to the monk's death as the appearance or manifestation heralded by the ominous sign, itself a reference to the Buddha's *parinirvāṇa* under paired trees. Many *zhenzan* praise the artist for capturing living qualities of the subject, and some allude to a personal relationship with the subject; we see both of these qualities in the *Lidai fabao ji* eulogy. In contrast, the *zhenzan* for the Venerable Du gives an impression of formality and even impersonality. Perhaps his death was sudden, and the monk Zhizhao 智照 (d.u.), who appears to have been prominent at Dunhuang in his day, was requested to write the eulogy for the funeral ceremony while the portrait was still in preparation.

Let us take a look at the salient contrasts presented by the following secular *zhenzan,* also from the latter part of the eighth century. This is the *Shangshu youcheng Xu gong xie zhentuzan bing xu* 尚書右承徐公寫真圖贊并序 (Portrait-Eulogy, with Preface, for the Right Assistant Director of the Department of State Affairs, Gentleman Xu), by Dugu Ji 獨孤及 (725–777).[38]

> The Attendant Censor Gentleman Han 韓 reaches purity; through the excellence of his study of the arts and his painting, he is everywhere renowned. In the third month of the *xinchou* 辛丑 year (761), he was at Yuzhang 豫章[39] in the office of Examiner of Wastefulness in Princely Affairs, and he resided with the former[40] Right Assistant Director of the Department of State Affairs, Gentleman Xu, in the Pure Rooms (*jingshi* 淨室) of Huiming 慧命 monastery. [Gentleman Han] once spent a day of leisure tearing plain [silk or paper] and scattering [ink] from the brush, and painted Gentleman Xu's portrait. It was hung in that gentleman's sitting-nook, and his beautiful eyes and square mouth, his harmonious disposition and refined bones (i.e., intrinsic nature) are [portrayed] without the least divergence, as if discerning his form in a mirror. Some of those coming in from the outside want to kneel reverently and fold their hands, bow down and pay obeisance, not knowing

it is a painting. The exclamations of all the gentlemen[41] are not sufficient, so I frame words to eulogize its beauty, aspiring to carry on singing [its praises] to later [generations]. Thus I eulogize:

The master artist conveys his conception, natural graces are made complete; although he borrows the essence of the brush, he is in truth engaging the spirit. He spontaneously accomplishes the image, as suddenly as parting the fog. Looking reverently at his spirit-[brush] tip is like spying into an armory [of fine weapons]. [Gentleman Xu] is genially eminent, proudly standing forth alone, [like] the highest lone pine, the white egret on the empty bank. His look of not having transgressed is because of having been able to criticize himself. Who knows its transformations? It is also in brush and silk.

In contrast to the Zhizhao's *zhenzan* for the Venerable Du, which was clearly designed for memorialization of a personage, Dugu Ji's magnificent yet intimate eulogy focuses on the artist and the qualities of the portrait and is only secondarily concerned with the merits of the subject. The Venerable Du's eulogy was composed for his funeral, while Gentleman Xu's portrait was informally produced as an expression of friendship and was displayed in his room while he was still alive.[42] Zhizhao's piece presents a shiny surface of moral rectitude, but Dugu Ji emphasizes the blending of aesthetic, spiritual, and personal qualities, making only a faint reference to moral shadings. In Sun Huan's *Lidai fabao ji* eulogy we see elements of all these qualities: formal (even generic) memorialization of the subject's character, praise of the artist's achievement insofar as it imparts the living qualities of the subject, and allusion to personal relationship.

What we might call the "aesthetic of immediacy" in Sun Huan's and Dugu Ji's eulogies resonates with the nostalgia expressed by Zhang Yanyuan 張彥遠 (815?-875?) in his *Lidai minghua ji* 歷代名畫記 (Record of Famous Paintings Through the Ages): "Ancient paintings could pass down the semblance [of the subject] and its inner nature, seeking to depict it with what is beyond semblance; this is very difficult to explain to an ordinary person. Present-day paintings achieve semblance, but they don't produce *qiyun* 氣韻 (spirit-vitality-tone). If they sought to depict it with *qiyun,* then the semblance would be there in its midst."[43] Sun Huan enshrines this *qiyun,* this presence or immediacy, within a virtuoso glorification of Wuzhu's teachings; we return to this point in the subsequent discussion of the significance of the "response body" (*yingshen* 應身).

Song Chan Portrait-Eulogies

Foulk and Sharf point out that *zhenzan* became a standard feature included at the end of Song Chan *yulu* (discourse records), but the first example that they mention dates from the eleventh century.[44] The *Lidai fabao ji* appears to be the earliest Chan work in which we find biography, discourse records, and portrait-eulogy conjoined. By the eleventh century it was not unknown to have hundreds of portrait-eulogies collected at the end of the discourse record of a famous Chan master.[45] These eulogies were incorporated into the *yulu* from the autograph inscriptions that the master in question had written on various portraits of himself, thus differing from the *Lidai fabao ji* eulogy written by a disciple.

The Song practice may have been an echo of the model of transmission found in the ninth-century *Baolin zhuan,* in which each master transmits his Dharma through a gāthā that he has composed. However, contrary to a widespread misapprehension, portraits were not used as proof of Dharma transmission. Instead, Foulk and Sharf assert, the written inscription by the master on the portrait was meant to establish a connection between the master, the image, and the recipient, "enlivening the portrait just as relics were used to enliven sculptural effigies of Buddhist saints."[46]

In this regard, we might consider Helmut Brinker's discussion of the aesthetics of re-creation as articulated in Song literati circles:

> Already traditional Chinese art theories call signatures on ancient masterpieces of writing or painting "seals of the mind," *xinyin* 心印. These theories emphasize the possibility to enter into virtually mystic contact not only with the work, but with its creator, by meditative empathy and the aesthetic act of re-creating, *rushen* 入神, "to penetrate the spirit," in such a way that the viewer and the viewed object would fuse into one. This intense experience of "complete absorption" was also called *shenhui* 神會, "spiritual communion," by the literati of the eleventh and twelfth centuries.[47]

Although this passage is worded somewhat ambiguously, the supporting examples show that these "traditional" art theories reflect rather than anticipate Chan sensibilities. Nevertheless, the currency of such an aesthetic in the Song underscores the appropriateness of the auto-inscription as a Chan medium of expression. How better to enact the Chan axiom "not one, not two?" In fact, the inscribed Chan abbot portrait seems to have been only a little more exclusive than the autographed photo of a movie star. In the section on priests' portraits, we glanced at the "typical" Chan priest portrait given by Wuzhun Shifan to Enni in 1238; the auto-inscription is a good example of the social uses of the genre. Diplomatic and witty, it flatters the guest and disparages the host by means of elegant literary allusions.[48]

It also became a trope for Chan masters to complain in their portrait inscriptions about the practice of having portraits made and being requested to write portrait inscriptions. In these complaints, the characteristic Chan fine line is applied with greater or lesser degrees of skill. In a gāthā by Gaofeng Yuanmiao 高峰原妙 (1238–1295) that was inscribed on a portrait given to his disciple Zhongfeng Mingben 中峰明本 (1263–1323), we can appreciate the light handling of the complementarity between the impossibility of representing emptiness and the assertion of representation-as-emptiness: "My face is inconceivable, even Buddhas and patriarchs cannot have a glimpse. I allow this no-good son alone to have a peep at half of my nose."[49]

Whether mystic, politic, or ironic, the language of the Song auto-inscription portrait-eulogy differed greatly from the panegyric mode employed by the *Lidai fabao ji* eulogist Sun Huan. The Song inscriptions often reflected the Chan "encounter dialogue" language of vivid put-downs and flagrant eccentricity. Consider this example from the discourse record of the master Yangqi Fanghui 楊岐方會 (992–1049): "A mouth like a beggar's open sack; a nose like a shit ladle in the garden! This gentleman troubled himself, applying his talented brush to the completion [of this portrait]."[50]

Though the language of Sun Huan's *zhenzan* clearly reflects the conventions of Tang eulogistic genres and bears little resemblance to Song Chan auto-*zhenzan*, his piece does reflect a developing sensibility of immanence-in-representation. In the excerpt below, the evocation of Wuzhu's gaze emphasizes the lively, scintillating qualities of the image; it is as if produced by the brush of Wu Daozi 吳道子 (fl. 710–760), the legendary Tang artist said to have produced, in miraculous bursts of spontaneous brushwork, paintings with mysterious effect on the beholder and the power to come to life.[51]

> Accordingly we summoned the fine artist, secretly he made the painting. [The artist] brandished his brush and produced the characteristics, and gazing at the majestic response-body (*yingshen* 應身) transcending characteristics and emptied of words, we see the expansive vessel of the Dharma. His attainments are like Heaven's gifts, his bones (i.e., intrinsic qualities) are not like those of this world. How silently mysterious and fine! [The portrait] seems to be truly breathing, the face quivers and wants to speak, the eyes dance and are about to see. "I look up and it is ever loftier, I venerate and it is ever more dear."[52]

Having evoked this life-like "response-body," let us turn to a consideration of its function in the *Lidai fabao ji* and in the economy of charisma of late eighth-century Chan.

The Response-Body

The portrait of Wuzhu does not appear to have functioned for the Bao Tang followers in the same way as the later Chan abbot portraits of the Song. Wuzhu's portrait is treated as unique, not one portrait among many commissioned by disciples during the master's lifetime, and not as a mortuary image included in a lineage hall of patriarchs.[53] This tempers previously held notions of Chan portraiture such as stated by Helmut Brinker in *Zen Masters of Meditation in Images and Writings:* "As one might suspect, the portrait group rather than the single portrait is the oldest category in the development of Zen Buddhist portrait painting."[54] There are references in Song dynasty works to Chan patriarchal portrait series made in the eighth and ninth centuries. However, in the *Lidai fabao ji* eulogy, Wuzhu's portrait is approached as if it were an individual relic, empowered like a portrait-statue, rather than the central piece in a genealogical set. Though the eulogy makes claims about Wuzhu's lineage, the portrait is a unique site of direct contact with Wuzhu's Dharma: "Those who gaze at the portrait are able to destroy evil, those who rely on the Dharma are able to attain the mystery."[55]

The ancestral portraits of abbots of later Chan practice hovered somewhere on the borderline between sacralized signifiers of the notion of the "living Buddha" and analogues to household ancestral spirits or local deities, settling toward the latter plane as time went on.[56] The portrait of Wuzhu seems to have resided in the realm of the special sacred relic, perhaps standing in for that mysteriously absent "contact relic," the disputed robe. However, it is not claimed that the portrait is a seal of transmission.

Sun Huan's repeated reference to the secrecy of the process may reflect the notion, alluded to in both Zhang Yanyuan's critique and Dugu Ji's *zhenzan,* above, that the artist aimed to capture or engage the numinous essence of the subject's intrinsic nature. Many of the Dunhuang *zhenzan* specify that the portrait was done while the subject was still alive, and in some cases it is clear that the painter was summoned when death seemed imminent.[57] In later Song Chan monasteries, the aura of the numinous was institutionalized. Foulk and Sharf tell us: "Song monastic rules stipulated that as an abbot approached death, his portrait was to be painted, since a portrait of the deceased was necessary for the upcoming funeral rites. . . . Song biographical chronicles confirm that portraits were indeed produced just prior to or, if need be, soon after an abbot's death."[58]

Among the Dunhuang manuscripts there is an interesting monastic memo regarding an upcoming funerary procession, affording us some notion of the manner in which the portrait of a deceased eminent monk was used in funerary ritual. The funeral protocol in the *Chanyuan qinggui* of 1103, noted above, prescribes the following for a Chan abbot's procession: "prepare the portable shrines for the portrait and the incense, as well as the music, the flowers, and the banners."[59] The Dunhuang memo, P. 2856, dated 895, bears out many of the features described in the *Chanyuan qinggui*. Thus, we catch a glimpse of the antecedents of funerary portrait ritual, which the Chan school made more elaborate in order to transfer its abbots through the liminal postmortem period into their new abode in the portrait hall.

> Funeral Arrangements Notice: The Venerable "Monastic Controller" (Sengtong 僧統) has died, and the funeral will be on the fourteenth day of this month. We have prepared the ordering of the procession according to funeral ritual, in the following divisions. The spirit-carriage (i.e., carrying the coffin) will be attended by the entire —*pan* ■潘 Association, the Vinaya Master Ciyin 慈音, and the Vinaya [Master] Xiqing 喜慶. The incense sedan chair will be attended by the Qinqing 親情 Association,[60] the Vinaya Master Cihui 慈惠, and the Vinaya Master Qingguo 慶果. The portrait[61] sedan chair will be attended by the disciples, the Vinaya Master Qingxiu 慶休, and the Vinaya Master Zhigang 智剛. The bell-carriage will be attended by Zhang Su— 張速■, Li Titi 李體體, and Zhu Shende 朱神德 of the Middle Regiment. The drum-carriage will be attended by Shi Xingzi 史興子 and Zhang Xingsheng 張興晟 of the Western Regiment. The Nine Ranks of Future Birth sedan-chair [will be attended by] a representative from each of the monasteries and convents. The living-image[62] sedan-chair will be attended by [members of] this monastery. The paper pennants will be continuous along the way, colored [*mo*] *na* [摩] 納 (linen) [will be used to pay?] Vinaya Master Xiji 喜寂 [to officiate as?] Daoji 道濟. There will be two large banners, one of a dragon and one of a lotus. There will be a pair of pennants each from Jingtu 淨土 [monastery] and Kaiyuan 開元 [monastery]. The foregoing who have been asked to be involved in these capacities [should keep in mind that] the destined funeral day fast approaches, you cannot be lax, it is urgent that you live according to the Dharma, you cannot do anything contrary to [an attitude of] reverence.
>
> The eleventh day of the third month of the second year of the Qianning 乾寧 era (895). [Endorsed by:] Monastic Administrator, Chief Monastic Registrar, Chief Monastic Registrar Xianzhao 賢照, Monastic Administrator, Monastic Administrator.[63]

In the Chan abbot funerary protocol set forth in the *Chanyuan qinggui*, prior to the funeral the disciples are sequestered with the body, and in the procession they follow immediately behind the coffin with the first group. Before the funeral procession, the portrait was to be placed in the public portion of the Dharma Hall to receive the obeisance of lay mourners, and it is not clear where it was carried in the procession.[64] In the Dunhuang memo, we see a lay society accompanying the body, while the sedan-chair carrying the portrait is attended by the deceased's disciples.

Sociologist Nancy Jay argues persuasively that in many cultures we find a connection between restrictions on the persons and manner of participating in sacrificial ritual and the need to maintain a patrilineage.[65] Several provocative studies analyze the ways in which Buddhist mortuary practices were adapted to reflect Chinese patriarchal sacrificial rituals.[66] Here I focus on a single aspect; by highlighting the ritual placement of the deceased's disciples at the funeral, we see that in both the *Chanyuan qinggui* and the Dunhuang memo P. 2856, the relationship between the corpse and its painted substitute is mediated by oppositions between private and public and between monastic disciples and lay devotees. In both texts we see the group of disciples and the group of lay devotees interposed between the hidden body and the displayed portrait, but they are assigned to different posts. The fact that the disciples are made custodians of the portrait in the Dunhuang document suggests, using Jay's logic of sacrificial definition of lineage, that the portrait is intended to serve as a future site of offerings and that the deceased's disciples are identified through their involvement with this site.

An alternative possibility is that the portrait was intended to be destroyed. Rong Xinjiang has suggested that portraits might have been burned, either accompanying the body or substituting for it. This would account for the absence of portraits of monks in the Dunhuang cache, though many portrait-eulogies and devotional paintings remain.[67] One may also surmise that the immolation of a portrait could refer to a more dramatic cultic form of sacrifice: Alan Cole points out that later Chan cremation ritual appropriated the vocabulary of fiery self-immolation, after the manner of the ritual suicides inspired by the image of the cosmic self-offering of Bhaiṣajyarāja in the *Lotus Sūtra*.[68] The fate of the Dunhuang portraits remains an intriguing mystery; what is clear from P. 2856 is that both the external order and the internal state of mind of the participants was a serious matter. The relationships enacted through the funeral had ramifications for the entire community, involving the monasteries, the lay societies, and even the military in a cooperative effort.

In both the *Chanyuan qinggui* and the Dunhuang memo, the portrait of the high-ranking monk plays a key role in the performance of continuity, lineage, and community. In the *Lidai fabao ji* eulogy, the portrait of Wuzhu, regardless of whether it figured in a funeral ritual, becomes the sole reference to the continuity of Wuzhu's teachings and his assembly of disciples. The eulogy ends with a chill breath of the "decline of the Dharma" sensibility that wafts through the work as a whole: "Without our master, this Dharma will sink."[69] At the same time, the preface claims that his portrait has magical and soteriological effect. This claim is all the more striking because much of the *Lidai fabao ji* has to do with the drama of patriarchal transmission and the story of Wuzhu's inheritance of the true Dharma and Bodhidharma's robe. Yet at the scene of Wuzhu's death no Dharma heir is named and the robe is conspicuously absent. Instead, the manifestation of Wuzhu's Dharma becomes this singular painted likeness.

Bernard Faure writes of the power ascribed to the *śarīra* (relics) and mummies of Chan masters: "They symbolize (or effect) sudden awakening; the ultimate realization or "transformation" of the saint; a reincorporation into a higher, absolute, ontological plane; but they also achieve mediation for the worshipers by channeling the saint's power and bringing it down to earth. To the extent that this transformative power, ritually activated, allows the practitioner to achieve a spiritual breakthrough, the relics have a soteriological function."[70] Faure claims that relics and images mediate both conceptually and soteriologically, symbolizing (or effecting) and channeling the experience of direct encounter with the master, saint, or Buddha. In the *Lidai fabao ji* the emphasis is placed on direct effect, and Wuzhu's portrait is itself a "response-body (*yingshen* 應身) transcending characteristics and emptied of words." Not incidentally, *yingshen* is a term that is sometimes used to translate Nirmānakaya (the "teaching" manifestations of the Buddha) and sometimes used to translate Saṃbhogakāya (the "reward" manifestations), a point that is discussed further below.

First, however, I would like make a broader comparison between this "response-body" and the South Asian notion of *darśan.* Reginald Ray defines *darśan* as follows: "The receiving of *darśan* (*darśana;* P., *dassana*), a physical-spiritual seeing and being seen, whereby the devotee may participate in the Buddha's enlightened charisma. . . . The Buddha presents himself to be seen by the suppliant, and the suppliant responds by opening himself—in the imagery of the text, opening his eyes wide—and taking in the spiritual energy of the Buddha."[71] Ray, however, adopts and only slightly adapts a "two-tiered" perspective wherein the *darśan* of relics and images are considered cheap imitations consumed by lay devotees who are unable to meditate in the forest or sit at the feet of a master. On the contrary, Gregory Schopen's work with the dedicatory inscriptions at early Buddhist stūpas (reliquary mounds or edifices) and cave-temple sites has shown that monks and nuns sought contact with and guarded access to the *darśan* of relics more fervently than did the lay devotees, and perhaps more fervently than they guarded access to living monks.[72]

It is difficult to represent the manner in which relics or images function soteriologically, how they provide "physical-spiritual seeing and being-seen." Perhaps this is not because it is impossible to imaginatively "fuse horizons," but because it is difficult to fuse genres of representation. In the *Lidai fabao ji* portrait-eulogy, memorialization and presence are "not one, not two." Sun Huan tells us that when Wuzhu's disciples looked at his portrait it reminded them of what they had lost; at the same time, it directly met the needs of the individual devotee. Within the constraints of representations current in the religious studies, steering a wobbly course between the Scylla and Charybdis of Cartesian and post-Cartesian forms of hegemonist discourse, the subject, the devotee, is "not us, not other." On one hand, we may say that the image or the relic, even more than the living teacher, provides an unlimited field for the votary's projections; the image provides the zenith of the solipsistic orbital through which he or she fuels the content and the force of his or her own transformative experience.

On the other hand, it is necessary to continue to question "Western" faith in the geometry of the closed loop. For example, in *Coming to Terms with Chinese Buddhism,* Robert Sharf discusses the difficulty of interpreting the term *ganfo* 感佛 (affect the Buddha) among Chinese exegetes, whose interpretations do not resolve its meaning according to the distinction between epistemology and ontology that is assumed in Western Cartesian discourse. However, Sharf argues, our encounter with a sphere of discourse that does not draw a rigorous distinction between subjective experience and objective moving (or being moved by) something outside of oneself should not lead us to assume that medieval Chinese exegetes lacked awareness of the possibility of subjective error, but should make us aware that there is an alternative conception of the relationship between epistemology and ontology at work.[73]

Let us return from the horizons to the ground and look at an example of an image with powers that are more tangible and thus easier to place in the distance. It is common in East Asian hagiographies and temple records to find stories of the power of images to provide aid and work miracles, such as the *Song gaoseng zhuan* story of the image of Wuxiang. In his biography it is said that a clay image mixed with his ashes performed a miracle during the restoration of Buddhism after the persecution of the Huichang 會昌 era (841–846). Wuxiang's former seat, the Jingzhong monastery, was destroyed, but its bell had been saved and was to be moved back to the reconstructed temple. When the bell was returned to its old home with miraculous ease, it was found that the image of Wuxiang was covered with sweat, thus proving that its power had aided in the bell's quick return.[74]

Faure points out that it is ironic that a master named Wuxiang 無相 "formless" or "no-characteristics" should then become a form-icon.[75] However, it may be appropriate that the Dharma of a master named Wuzhu, nonabiding, should be considered to abide in his portrait. As noted, one of the recurrent themes in the autograph inscriptions of Song Chan abbots is the idea that the true form of no-form is representation. The representation signs that it is impossible to render the true image, the *zhenxiang* or portrait of the awakening, and at the same time the image functions as emptiness functions, as the multifaceted transformations of *upāya*, or skillful means. Foulk and Sharf write: "According to the ritual logic of Sung Buddhist monasteries, the icon of the Buddha, the living person of the abbot, and the abbot's portrait were largely interchangeable. It would seem that the body of the living abbot, like his portrait, had come to be regarded as the 'simulacrum' (*xiang* 像) of Buddhahood."[76]

The notion that the abbot and his image are equally similacra, virtual Buddhas, has roots in ninth-century references to Chan masters as a "living Buddhas." The concept of the "living Buddha" may be said to amalgamate the traditional concept of the sage with the teaching of intrinsic Buddha nature. The *Platform Sūtra* teaching that the true self is the Trikāya, the Three Bodies of the Buddha, expresses a similar synthesis of devotionalism and the realization of the virtual as ultimate truth.[77]

Sharf emphasizes the importance of understanding the matrix of indigenous thought within which Chinese theories of the nature of the Buddha were engendered, and he regards an understanding of the notion of *ganying* 感應, sympathetic resonance, to be crucial to any meaningful explication of eighth-century Trikāya and Buddha-Nature theory. He reflects on the use of the terms *yingshen* and *huashen* 化身 (transformation-body) in Chinese Buddhist discourse, and shows that by the eighth century notions of *yingshen* and *huashen* were integral to a lively and complex debate on the nature of the Buddha, in which there was little consensus and no clear derivation from Indian sources. Indeed, this serves as an example of his contention that Chinese Buddhism is more like foreclosure than "conquest" by an alien discourse. Even as Buddhism became naturalized in Chinese terms, Indian Buddhist texts and concepts continued to carry great prestige (as is evident in the *Lidai fabao ji*). However, Sharf argues, Chinese patterns of thought and Chinese cosmological principles were always-already at work in the processes of interpreting and representing "Indian" concepts. Thus, while Chinese *yingshen* and *huashen* may have been associated with Indian Trikāya theory, they functioned according to the principles of *ganying*.[78]

As discussed in the section on Wuzhu's dialogue with the Daoists in chapter 6, Buddhists began to make use of the Han notion of *ganying* early in the process of representing the nature and powers of the Buddhas and bodhisattvas. It was natural that Buddhas, bodhisattvas, and monks would be represented as responding to suffering beings in the spontaneous manner of the sage harmonizing all things. However, controversial consequences of the principle of "like responding to like" also manifested early. Responding to the *ganying* theories of opponents in the previous generation, Sanlun exegete Junzheng 均正 (d.u.) takes up a vexing question: if all beings have Buddha-nature, and Buddhas resonate with like kinds, why can't everyone see the Buddha?" Junzheng uses the metaphor of the indeterminable identity of mirror and image in his response: "For if you say they are identical, then given a mirror there must always be an image, irrespective of whether or not the mirror is clean. Yet if you say they are different, then how would you go about separating them? . . . Therefore, when the mirror is clean, the image appears. The purity of the mirror is like a stimulus, and the appearance of the mirror is like the response."[79]

The indeterminable identity of "original face" and spontaneous reflection/response would continue to kindle debate, giving rise to numerous exegetical and metaphorical formulations. When we examine the *Lidai fabao ji* authors' use of the *yingshen* and *huashen* terminology, we also discern an amalgamation of elements that refer to the different soteriological inflections given to "seeing (recollecting) the Buddha" and "being the Buddha." In chapter 6, we looked at a passage in which the merchant Cao Gui says that Wuzhu and Wuxiang are so alike in appearance that they must be manifestations of a transformation-body.[80] In that passage, the two are said to have moles in the center of their foreheads, which is the place of the *ūrṇā,* the curl of hair that is one of the marks of a Buddha. The close physical resemblance also shows that Wuzhu and Wuxiang belong to the same family of phenomena, which explains their mutual resonance, like musical instruments, even when apart. This quality is vividly evoked in other *Lidai fabao ji* passages about Wuzhu and Wuxiang, always in conjunction with the note of destiny and the preordained nature of their connection. Moreover, the sound of the teaching of "no-thought" becomes the medium through which Wuzhu meets Wuxiang "face to face," immediately.

Similarly, the *Lidai fabao ji* eulogy's characterization of Wuzhu's portrait as a "response-body transcending characteristics and emptied of words" at once evokes a votive image, a site of power that is nevertheless a natural phenomenon, Buddha-nature, and the practice of no-thought. We may also consider this an early example of the soteriological and ritual logic of representation as the "form" of emptiness that would later become institutionalized in Song Chan monastic practice. Then again, it may be neither so sophisticated nor so empty.

An Iconoclastic Icon

Wuzhu tended to focus on monastic etiquette and scriptural recitation as the prime examples of delusive formal practice, but his deconstruction of such activities as daily devotions, confession, and repentance would have implied that devotion to images was also meaningless. In the following passage he criticizes the popular practice of pilgrimage to Wutai shan 五臺山, disparaging the pilgrims' delusory identification of the bodhisattva Mañjuśrī with a particular site:

> Another time, some masters and monks of Jiannan wanted to go to [Wu]tai shan to pay obeisance, and they took their leave of the Venerable. The Venerable asked, "Worthies, where are you going?" The monks replied, "To pay our respects to Mañjuśrī." The Venerable said, "Worthies, the Buddha is in body and mind, Mañjuśrī is not far. When deluded thoughts are not produced, this is none other than 'seeing the Buddha.' Why take the trouble to go so far?" The masters and monks wanted to leave. The Venerable expounded a gāthā for them: "Lost children restlessly dashing like waves, circling the mountain and paying obeisance to a pile of earth. Mañjuśrī is right here, you are climbing the Buddha's back to search for Amitābha."[81]

Iconoclastic commentary on the worship of images and sacred sites became a favorite Chan rhetorical theme, as such practices presented a perfect opportunity to drive home the point that Buddha-nature could not be reified. Wuzhu's dialogue prefigures Linji's better-known sermon on the same theme:

> There are some types of students who go off to Mt. Wu-t'ai looking for Manjushri. They're wrong from the very start! Manjushri isn't on Mt. Wu-t'ai. Would you like to get to know Manjushri? You here in front of my eyes, carrying out your activities, from first to last never changing, wherever you go never doubting—this is the living Manjushri![82]

As noted in chapter 6, Wuzhu also redefined the construction of a sacred space for receiving the precepts, interpreting this space in terms of the no-dimension of no-thought: "Regard direct mind as the *bodhimaṇḍa*. . . . Regard no-thought as the precepts, nonaction and nothing to attain as meditation, and nonduality as wisdom. Do not regard the constructed ritual arena as the *bodhimaṇḍa*."[83] The thrust of both the pilgrimage and *bodhimaṇḍa* passages is that it is delusory to locate the Buddha and Dharma outside one's true nature, the Buddha-body of emptiness.[84] Naturally, then, one might wonder why the Bao Tang followers saw nothing amiss in attributing the power of Wuzhu's Dharma to an external image.

That Wuzhu's disciples did not balk at iconization of their teacher's iconoclasm is perhaps a manifestation of the recovery or revenge of the conventional level that Faure claims was the inevitable "other power" at work within Chan ideology: "Chan/Zen monks were in fact trying to limit the proliferation of sacred symbols and to reserve for themselves the privilege of the possession of selected symbols or icons such as *śarīra* and mummies. Their iconoclasm was therefore a relative one, although the most radical among them, carried away by the rhetoric of immediacy, attempted to deny any symbolic mediation."[85]

Regardless of whether Wuzhu's followers intended to make a didactic "no-point" in attributing the power of his Dharma to a votive image, it is significant that the Bao Tang school, with a reputation as being "the most radical among them," may have influenced the form of Chan literary-funerary ritual more than they influenced the shape of formless practice. As noted, regular offerings and devotions to images of patriarchal masters became a part of the Song Chan monastic code. Taking an unintentional step in this direction, Wuzhu weaned his followers from devotional practices centered on Buddhist images only to became a focus of devotion himself, and this was both the logical and the paradoxical consequence of the doctrine of intrinsic Buddha-nature. In the subsequent development of Chan, the antinomianism and iconoclasm became ever more antic and literary. For example, would Wuzhu's teachings have been better served if his disciples' response to his death had been recorded in the following manner?

> When Ziming died, the monks sent a letter to the master, gathered the assembly together, hung the [master's] portrait and grieved. . . . [When the memorial offerings were set out, Yangqi] went before the portrait, clenched both hands into fists and rested them on top of his head, took his sitting cloth and folded it once, drew a circle [in the air] and burnt incense. He then withdrew three steps and prostrated himself in the manner of a woman (*zuo nuren bai* 作女人拜).[86]

Somehow, the fervent eulogy in the *Lidai fabao ji* seems less formal. Nevertheless, Sun Huan's *zhenzan* and this Song example both emphasize the contrast between the performance and the pro forma, reflecting the paradox of separation and surfaces intrinsic to transformative devotion. In both eulogies, engaging the representations and necessary excess of devotionalism becomes the act of devotion. It is clear that paradoxes and ironies that were unintentional in the *Lidai fabao ji* had become all too familiar in the Song, but we cannot therefore assume that the Bao Tang followers were naive and Song Chan monks such as Yangqi Fanghui were cynical.

The elements of the *Lidai fabao ji* that were incorporated into the mainstream of Chan underwent a trimming process in which the eccentric qualities, particularly the antinomianism, were excised. In this process Wuzhu's portrait was also lost. That there is no surviving painting is, of course, no surprise—few Tang paintings of any kind remain. However, through the conventional language of Sun Huan's *zhenzan* we may still attune ourselves to the resonances that bound together the image of the master, the eulogist, and the Bao Tang community. The mysterious portrait balances on the same crux that characterizes the *Lidai fabao ji* as a whole, because those responsible for creating it treated it both conventionally and absolutely, both gradually and suddenly, as an icon and as a representation of iconoclasm. It combined many qualities and abided in none—it was at once a memorial portrait, a sacred relic, a response-body, representation as the true face of the Dharma, and the lasting image of a unique and ephemeral group of devotees. Wuzhu became for his followers the form of the formless practice he taught, and whether this was the revenge of suppressed devotionalism or a demonstration of his disciples' true understanding of the emptiness of reverence, we must leave it for Mañjuśrī, the bodhisattva of wisdom, to decide.

DEVELOPMENTS AFTER THE *LIDAI FABAO JI*

Before concluding, let us survey some of the traces of Wuxiang and Wuzhu found in texts postdating the *Lidai fabao ji*. In the following sections, I discuss (1) later allusions to the Bao Tang and the Jingzhong schools, (2) evidence of Wuxiang's and Wuzhu's teachings in Tibet, and (3) connections between the Bao Tang and the Hongzhou schools.

Later References to the Bao Tang and Jingzhong Schools

We do not know how long the Bao Tang school survived as an independent Chan line, for few clues remain. It is likely that the *Caoqi dashi zhuan* and *Baolin zhuan* were composed in part to refute the claims of the *Lidai fabao ji*. Apart from Zongmi's comments, the most significant reactions came from the former Jingzhong follower Shenqing 神清 of Huiyi 慧義 monastery in Zizhou 梓州. In 806 he produced the *Beishan lu* 北山錄 (Record of North Mountain), in which he condemned both the *Lidai fabao ji* and *Baolin zhuan* without mentioning them by name. Like Zongmi, Shenqing felt precepts and study were essential to Chan practice, and he advocated "unity of the three teachings."

In the course of presenting his own history of the transmission of Buddhism to China, Shenqing launches his critique of the *Lidai fabao ji* and the *Baolin zhuan*. He uses the language of a legal case, and his judgments are based on moral arguments and analyses of factual errors. Shenqing wanted to show the complementarity of Confucian Daoist and Buddhist practices, and from his point of view morality and historiography were linked. He vociferated against the fabrications in the *Lidai fabao ji* and the *Baolin zhuan*, arguing that such falsifications indicated that the Dharma practice of the perpetrators was seriously flawed. For Shenqing, exemplary moral character was the key expression of practice and this moral character included Confucian virtues and observances, Buddhist precepts and meditation, and Daoist purification and concentration of energy. One of his objections to the dramatic "perils of the patriarchs" style of hagiography favored by the *Lidai fabao ji* and the *Baolin zhuan* was that it was damaging to the Dharma to portray masters as "only human" and not as Holy Ones (*shengren* 聖人). It is notable that he voices this objection at a time when teachings such as Mazu's "everyday mind is Buddha mind" were beginning to spread.

Let us turn to the passages in the *Beishan lu* that contain the most pointed criticisms of the *Lidai fabao ji* and the *Baolin zhuan*. Shenqing's style is highly erudite, allusive, and circuitous, and the following account has been considerably abridged and streamlined. The pertinent passages are found in the sixth fascicle, which begins with an exposition on Confucian filial piety and mourning ritual and goes on to stress the importance of the Buddhist precepts. Somewhat abruptly, Shenqing embarks on a discussion of the transmission of Buddhism to China in the period of disunity, saying that the Western monks all taught the methods of dhyāna/Chan (*chanfa* 禪法). He cites stories of the miracles performed by monks skilled in meditation, including Bhadra and Sengchou. He then turns to Bodhidharma and Huike, relating the story that a thief cut off Huike's arm, and he associates Huike's ability to transcend pain with the Yogācāra insights of the *Laṅkāvatāra-sūtra*.[87]

Setting the stage for subsequent criticism of those who tell tall tales about the patriarchs, Shenqing uses musical metaphors to describe the correspondence between practice and actions, saying that no one who has attained the virtue and wisdom of the Way says stupid things. He then praises the Jingzhong school, allowing the reader to infer that this school sets a standard of excellence in conduct that others (i.e., the Bao Tang and Hongzhou) do not attain: "I formerly contemplated the Chan teachings of the Jingzhong school. They are elevated but not excessive, extensive but not pretentious. They never use marvels to frighten the laity. One can truly say that they are worthy and mild gentlemen."[88]

He then complains generally about self-indulgent braggarts, and this is followed by his first specific objection to the *Lidai fabao ji*. Shenqing protests against the four supplementary patriarchs who have been added to the *Fu fazang zhuan* account of the Indian patriarchs, and we are able to identify his intended target because he uses the *Lidai fabao ji* version of the name of the twenty-fifth patriarch (Śaṇavāsa 舍那婆斯), rather than the *Baolin zhuan* version (Basiasita 婆舍斯多). He also protests the use of the name Dharmatrāta 菩提達摩多羅 instead of Bodhidharma 菩提達磨. However, Shenqing's Northern Song commentator Huibao 慧寶 demonstrates in this and other instances that he is unaware of the *Lidai fabao ji*, because he identifies Shenqing's source as the *Baolin zhuan*.[89]

Shenqing dares to question the very notion of a line of Indian patriarchs, on the grounds that the list includes śrāvakas like Kāśyapa and Ānanda, whom he doubts could have transmitted the "Buddha-mind seal" (*foxin yin* 佛心印).[90] However, he ventures still further, mounting a critique of the ideology of transmission itself. This critique is introduced through an unidentified "quotation" that is structurally similar to passages in the *Aśokavadāna* and the *Aśokarāja-sūtra,* but it is probably his own ingenious alteration of a passage from the *Baolin zhuan:*

> Of old, Śaṇavāsa 商那和脩 (i.e., the fourth patriarch) said to Upagupta 優波鞠多 (the fifth), 'The samādhi of the Buddha is unknown to pratyekabuddhas, the samādhi of pratyekabuddhas is unknown to śrāvakas. The samādhi of the great śrāvakas is unknown to the rest of the śrāvakas. My samādhi is also unknown to you. Samādhi is like this. After my nirvāṇa there will still be the seventy-seven thousand original scriptures, the ten thousand Abhidharmas, and the eighty thousand pure Vinayas. After our nirvāṇas, that is why those who transmit the Dharma will only transmit the words. Those who inherit the Dharma substantiate the words and see the mind, and this is obtaining the Dharma.[91]

Similar passages in the *Aśokavadāna* and the *Aśokarāja-sūtra* illustrate the devolution of both meditative skills and insight in successive generations.[92] In the *Baolin zhuan,* the import is quite different—Śaṇavāsa says that the samādhi of the Buddha is unknown to the bodhisattvas, *et cetera,* in order to illustrate the notion that samādhis *qua* states of mind are not knowable by another. However, the point that Śaṇavāsa wishes to impress on Upagupta is that "this samādhi," ultimate wisdom and compassion, is the universal experience of all the patriarchs who transmit the Dharma.[93] Thus, by modifying this particular passage Shenqing stages an attack on the ideology of lineal patriarchal transmission, implying that *anyone* who substantiates the Dharma is a Dharma-heir. He goes on to cite examples, including the wheelwright story from the *Zhuangzi,* to illustrate the point that even though skills may be transmitted, inner mastery is not transferable. One wonders if he is perhaps referring to his own experiences as he concludes:

> Thus there is long study without result, and there is manifesting the mind and producing evidence. Or else there is subtle flow and solitary attainment. A person of talent does not [necessarily] realize the value of inner understanding. This is not necessarily interactively taught. Although now the teachings are all "Chan," few know the Buddha. Is Chan alone the whole family?[94]

Shenqing then enters into his next indictment of false stories of the patriarchs. He cites the *Lidai fabao ji* story that Bodhidharma's two disciples were driven to Mt. Lu by the people of the Qin, and the story that Bodhidharma first came to the Liang and then went north to the Wei.[95] In his character as the prosecutor (*jizhe* 譏者), Shenqing informs us that "the case is lost at this point." He inveighs against the devolution of Chan into base sectarianism and then proceeds to demolish the *Lidai fabao ji* story on the basis of its chronology. He claims that the twenty-fourth patriarch, Siṁha Bhikṣu, lived during the Qi 齊 (479–501). If Bodhidharma's disciples were driven out in the Later Qin 秦 (385–417), then this would mean that Bodhidharma significantly preceded Siṁha Bhikṣu. As the Song Buddhist scholar Qisong 契嵩 later points out, Shenqing's argument depends on an unprovable assertion regarding Siṁha Bhikṣu's dates.[96] However, Shenqing does indirectly expose another anachronism in the *Lidai fabao ji:* Bodhidharma's disciples arrive in China about a century before he does. However, at a time when Bodhidharma's Methuselan life-span was an article of faith, this does not appear to have been seen as a serious problem.

Shenqing next takes up the *Lidai fabao ji* story that Bodhidharma was poisoned six times by Bodhiruci and Guangtong.[97] He strenuously objects to the notion that a master like Bodhidharma could be harmed against his will and laments that such slander will be harmful for posterity. One of Shenqing's recurrent themes is the imperviousness and imperturbability of the character of the sage or holy man, and he says, "Of old one who had the Way was placid and without extremes. Crowds followed him, tigers didn't seize him and birds of prey didn't attack him, much less people. Suppose [such a person] met with poison six times—if he ate it knowingly, why would he seek to kill himself? If he ate it unwittingly, who could say that he had the Way?"[98]

After further denunciation of the authors of such tales, Shenqing pauses for a moment of Confucian self-examination, with allusions to the *Analects:* "Who can say that they [have the authority to] blame, and moreover to try the case? I am also human (*ren* 人). If one cannot successfully judge one's own humanity (*ren* 仁), how can one successfully judge the humanity of an evil person? Therefore, the superior person (*junzi* 君子) internalizes reciprocity and uses himself to measure others."[99]

Shenqing thus attempts to present himself an example of the person who does not rush to denounce others, but turns first to self-criticism. He then returns to his main theme, condemnation of the tales of jealous competition found in various unidentified accounts of Bodhidharma, Huike, and the sixth patriarch. He cites contrasting examples of true sagely behavior and argues that because suffering is due to karmic residue sages do not blame their sufferings on others.[100]

Turning to "lies about transmission," Shenqing takes a passing swipe at the notion of a robe of transmission: "The one who attains the Way loses the self, and to lose the self is to lose the myriad things—how could a robe remain?"[101] He then embarks on an extended critique of iconoclasm and antinomianism, and it is quite clear that he had the Bao Tang in mind:

> Another account says that the source of fault and merit is only the mind, and that is all. [According to these people] extinguishing of the mind is nonactivity (*wuwei* 無為), and the Way resides in no-phenomena (*wushi* 無事). They don't do rituals or liturgy, nor do they lecture or recite the scriptures, and they claim this is true nonactivity. They don't request the precepts or guard against transgressions, and they claim this is true transcendence of characteristics. They teach that when there is the mind of practicing [the Dharma] or when there is something that one knows [about the Dharma] then this is the Dharma of the śrāvakas. Therefore, [they think that] only when the arrangement of [Buddhist] images is discarded and the methods of scriptural [study] are abandoned can one call it the sudden teaching. [They say that] if anything is expounded one should consult one's own feelings, and in approaching texts one should consider and decide [for oneself]—why depend on exegesis and commentary?[102]

Shenqing "the prosecutor" then comments on the approach he has described:

> One who [realizes] nonactivity is fused with the void and anchored in tranquility. There is no good that he does not do. Improperly taking ritual, recitation, copying [of scripture], and carving [of images] as obstacles—there we see "activity" (*youwei* 有為), not "nonactivity" (*wuwei* 無為). As for "transcending characteristics"—when illumination penetrates the mind of desires, there are no characteristics that can be obtained. Nonobtaining is then obtaining; abandoning attachment is called transcendence [of characteristics]. However, if one considers not receiving the precepts and giving up maintaining them as transcendence of characteristics, this is assuredly grasping at characteristics. How is this "transcendence of characteristics"?[103]

Zongmi would later assume a tone of relative objectivity in his assessment of the Bao Tang, but his "descriptions" are very similar to Shenqing's objections here. Shenqing cites the practice of "extinguishing of the mind" (*xinmie* 心滅) as characteristic of the group in question, and this is, of course, reminiscent of Zongmi's claim that the Bao Tang practiced "extinguishing consciousness" (*mieshi* 滅識). In the passages in which *xinmie* and related concepts appear in the *Lidai fabao ji* (*mieshi* is not used), one can understand why Wuzhu would be accused of equating the practice of no-thought, *wunian*, with extinguishing the mind. After all, one of the subtitles of the *Lidai fabao ji* is "destroying all mind [consciousnesses]."[104] This appearance of nihilism is largely due to the manner in which Wuzhu associates "mind" with the mind of sense-consciousnesses and characteristics. For example, *xinmie* appears in a quotation that is used several times: "*Xinsheng ji zhongzhongfa sheng, xinmie ji zhongzhongfa mie* 心生即種種法生，心滅即種種法滅. When the mind is produced then the various dharmas are produced, when the mind is extinguished then the various dharmas are extinguished."[105]

However, taken in context, "mind" can be seen to be the mind of delusion or birth-and-death, and Wuzhu asserts that true *wunian* is the realization that phenomena—most significantly, the karmic burden of past sins—come into being and are extinguished along with the delusory mind that identifies with thoughts. On the other side of the coin, Wuzhu also frequently emphasizes that all the precepts and the meaning of all the scriptures are realized in true *wunian*. While these are antinomian views expressed in an apophatic manner ("at the time of true no-thought, no-thought itself is not"), it is difficult to determine the degree to which they are dualistic or nihilistic.

Notably, part of Wuzhu's dialogue with his patron Du Hongjian centers on the question of the manner in which the enlightened mind is conscious of phenomenon. Du questions Wuzhu as to how he perceives a tree in front of the courtyard and hears a crow calling.[106] The doctrinal issue in question had been raised in Shenhui's *Tanyu:* "One who experiences no-thought is still fully seeing, hearing, perceiving, and knowing; but this unceasing emptiness and tranquility is precisely the practice of *śīla,* samādhi and prajñā."[107] While Shenhui teaches the practical point that no-thought does not mean trying to shut down the normal personality factors of sensation, perception, and conceptualization, Wuzhu's responses to Du seem rather dualistic. First he claims the power of supramundane vision, and then he asserts that mundane and ultimate seeing should be distinguished. Ironically, Du's responses are more in accord with later Chan than Wuzhu's, for he appears to play with Wuzhu, giving him the opportunity to claim supramundane seeing and then turning the tables on him by asking about mundane seeing. Wuzhu's retreat to the ultimate level and his use of a series of scriptural quotations would not have been considered impressive in the context of the later *gongan* cases, but he earnestly avoids advocating either "ordinary mind" or "extinguishing mind":

> The Venerable replied, "This seeing, hearing, perceiving, and knowing [that you are getting at] is worldly seeing, hearing, perceiving, and knowing. The *Vimalakīrti-sūtra* says, 'If you go about seeing, hearing, perceiving, and knowing, then this is seeing, hearing, perceiving, and knowing. The Dharma transcends seeing, hearing, perceiving, and knowing.'[108] No-thought is thus no-seeing, no-thought is thus no-knowing. It is because beings have thought that one provisionally teaches no-thought, but at the time of true no-thought, no-thought itself is not." He went on to quote the *Vajrasamādhi-sūtra,* "The Most Honored Greatly Enlightened One ex-

pounded the Dharma of producing no-thought. [Regarding] the mind of no-thought and non-production, the mind is constantly producing and never extinguished."[109]

Wuzhu's (or the *Lidai fabao ji* authors') dependence on scriptural quotations may be one reason why the dialogue appears so differently in later versions in the *Jingde chuandeng lu* and in the *Fozu lidai tongzai* 佛祖歷代通裁 (Comprehensive Register of the Buddhas and Patriarchs through the Ages).[110] In these versions Du is reduced to a mere foil for Wuzhu's discourse, and the discourse is closer to Song notions of classic Chan teaching. The *Jingde chuandeng lu* version (upon which the *Fozu lidai tongzai* account is based) is as follows:

> Just then a crow called from the tree in the courtyard. The lord (Du Hongjian) asked, "Do you, master, hear it or not?" [Wuzhu] said, "I hear it." The crow left, and the lord asked again, "Do you hear it or not?" [Wuzhu] said, "I hear it." The lord said, "The crow is gone and there is no sound, how can you say that you hear it?" The master then addressed the assembly, "A Buddha in the world is difficult to meet and the true Dharma is difficult to hear. With each and every truth you listen to, hearing is without hearing and does not impede the nature of hearing. Originally it is not born, does it ever happen that it is extinguished? When there is sound it is the defilement of sound produced of itself. When there is no sound it is the defilement of sound extinguished of itself. But this hearing-nature does not follow sound's production and does not follow sound's extinction. If you awaken to this hearing-nature then you escape the karmic transmission of the defilement of sound. Then you know that hearing is without production or extinction, hearing is without going or coming."[111]

This dialogue comprises the bulk of the notice on Wuzhu in both later sources. Thus, the question of whether Wuzhu advocated "extinguishing consciousness" continued to reverberate in these distant echoes of his teachings. The *Jingde chuandeng lu* passage reflects (and refines) aspects of Wuzhu's teachings as found in the *Lidai fabao ji*. Though Daoyuan 道原, the *Jingde chuandeng lu* compiler, does not quote directly from the text, it seems likely that he had access to some version of the *Lidai fabao ji* that contained more than just the Du Hongjian encounter. Most significantly, Daoyuan does not appear to endorse Shenqing's or Zongmi's negative assessment of Wuzhu's teachings. He conveys Wuzhu's repeated subitist assertions that the fundamental nature of the mind/senses cannot be extinguished or defiled and that apparent karmic entanglement disappears with this realization.

Moreover, contrary to Shenqing's final accusation, nowhere in the *Lidai fabao ji* is a hermeneutic of "consulting ones' own feelings" recommended.

In their critiques of the Bao Tang approach, both Shenqing and Zongmi ignore Wuzhu's claim that *wunian* perfects rather than precludes study of the scriptures and practice of the precepts. Both critics focus on Bao Tang abandonment of recognized forms of practice as a form of antipractice and, therefore, as grasping and manipulative (*youwei* 有為). Wuzhu's repeated teachings that one should not depend on forms was pointedly instantiated in Bao Tang "not-doing," but in his sermons this abandonment of form is embedded in the nonduality of *wunian*, that is, in doing/not-doing, neither doing nor not-doing, and both doing and not-doing.

Whatever his reasons for doing so, Shenqing at least appears to have read the *Lidai fabao ji* carefully, which we cannot assert with confidence in the case of Zongmi. Indeed, Shenqing provides the only concrete evidence that the *Lidai fabao ji* was ever taken seriously by fellow-clergy in Sichuan. As we will see in the following inscription, an aura of respect still adhered to Wuzhu's name a generation after his death. However, the *Lidai fabao ji* itself was fated to be seen but not named; it was copied and borrowed from, but it was not directly quoted or referred to as were the *Platform Sūtra*, the *Baolin zhuan*, and other eighth-century Chan texts.

Another important ninth century source is the *Tang Zizhou Huiyi jingshe nanchanyuan sizhengtang beiming* 唐梓州慧義精舍南禪院四證堂碑銘 (Stele Inscription for the Four Exemplars Hall of the Southern Chan Cloister of Huiyi Monastery in Zizhou, Tang Dynasty) by the celebrated poet and literatus Li Shangyin 李商隱 (813–858).[112] In 851 Li Shangyin went to Sichuan as private secretary to Liu Zhongying 柳仲郢.[113] When Lord Liu had the "Four Exemplars Hall" built in 853 (only seven years after the ending of the Huichang-era Buddhist persecution), Li Shangyin composed the inscription. The "four exemplars" are listed as Yizhou Jing[zhong] Wuxiang 益州靜無相,[114] Bao Tang Wuzhu, Hongzhou Daoyi 洪州道一 (Mazu), and Xitang Zhizang 西堂智藏 (Mazu's disciple).[115] Neither Wuzhu nor Zhizang receive as much attention as their masters in later records, though Zhizang seems to have been considered a leading Chan figure in the south. Yanagida argues that at the time the hall was built these four must have been considered the most important Chan masters to have hailed from Sichuan.[116] Though there appears to have been no protest of this public pairing of Wuxiang and Wuzhu, Shenqing's relics must have been rattling in his reliquary, for Huiyi monastery had been his home-temple.

Li Shangyin's piece is densely packed with allusions to classics, commentaries, and poetry, with relatively few allusions to Buddhist sources. There is no new information on Wuxiang or Wuzhu, and there is nothing that proves Li had read the *Lidai fabao ji* itself. There are, however, references and motifs that may indicate familiarity with stories from the *Lidai fabao ji* or other sources that had become part of Sichuanese lore about the two monks. Let us make a quick survey of these references.

In his preface, Li says that portraits of the four exemplars were made on the walls of the shrine and were models of "transformation-bodies" (*huashen*).[117] There are also obscure allusions to the blessings associated with the *kāṣāya* robe (8141c). Li makes several references to transmission accompanied by talismans—"mind to mind receiving the seal" and "crown to crown transmitting the pearl" (8141b), a reference to possession of the "robe of verification" (8141d–8142a), and an allusion to a story in the *Jin shu* of the transmission of a sword signifying succession (8142a). The latter may be meant to affirm the validity of Wuzhu's dubious claim to the robe of verification. Much is made of both Wuxiang's and Wuzhu's sojourns in the wilds with little to eat, and there is a reference to Wuxiang eating earth (8141c). Wuxiang's putative patron Zhangqiu Jianqiong 章仇兼瓊 is mentioned (8141c).[118] Allusion is made to the conflict between Du Hongjian and Cui Gan, but it is implied that they harmonized in their devotion to Buddhism and, we infer, to Wuzhu (8142a). The Jingzhong and Bao Tang are paired as illustrious names in Sichuan (8142a).

Thereafter the traces of Wuzhu and his school become faint and far-between. As noted above, Wuzhu was given short notices in the *Jingde chuandeng lu* and the *Fozu lidai tongzai.* Two minor references to the Bao Tang are found in the *Song gaoseng zhuan,* though only one of these clearly points to Wuzhu's school. This is the biography of the Tang monk Huanxi 歡喜, who cannot be identified with any of the monks mentioned in the *Lidai fabao ji:*

> It is not known from whence he came. His nature was one of unfettered compassionate mercy and kindness; no one ever saw him get angry. This is why he was called so (i.e., "Happiness"). In the course of traveling about he went to the capital (Chang'an). Both noble and lowly invited him to stay and were seldom refused. He spoke little and the traces of his deeds were difficult to measure. The emperor Dezong heard of him and honored him. In the twelfth year of the Xingyuan 興元 era (796?),[119] a precepts platform to ordain monks was established at Yongtai 永泰 temple by imperial decree. At that time, Xi separated from the Bao Tang Chan school, and received the precepts by imperial order. The black-robed ranks (i.e., monks) honored him. On the nineteenth day of the sixth month of the same year, he died at that temple.[120]

Huanxi's induction into the orthodox clergy is applauded and so, by implication, is his disassociation from the Bao Tang. This is in keeping with the fact that Zanning included a notice for Wuxiang but not Wuzhu in the *Song gaoseng zhuan.* The other *Song gaoseng zhuan* reference is to a "Bao Tang Chan Master Man 滿,"[121] but there is nothing to indicate that this master had anything to do with Wuzhu's school. Datong 大同, the subject of the biography, enters the Buddhist order when he becomes

Master Man's disciple. As Datong is said to have died in 914 at the age of ninety-six, we can surmise that his ordination could have taken place some time in the middle of the ninth century. Thus, it is quite possible that another Bao Tang temple is meant, for after the Huichang-era Buddhist persecution ended in 846 a number of temples were given new patriotic names, including Bao Tang.[122] However, Datong does seem to have shared Wuzhu's tastes: "Secluded at Mt. Touzi 投子 he knotted thatch (to make a dwelling), and settled in tranquility to seek his purpose."[123]

The later traces of Wuxiang's Jingzhong school are scarcely more abundant. Following the persecution of Buddhism in the mid-ninth century, the reconstructed Jingzhong school and temple devoted to Wuxiang developed a syncretic and popular character. Evidence of the development of a cult devoted to Wuxiang is found in Wuxiang's biography in the *Song gaoseng zhuan*[124] and in the above-noted inscription by Li Shangyin. Wuxiang was an object of devotion for his countrymen as well; in a stele for the Korean monk Nanggong 朗空, it is said that in 875 he went on foot to Chengdu to pay his respects at Wuxiang's memorial hall at Jingzhong temple.[125]

One of the popular practices associated with Wuxiang was his special style of vocal *nianfo* 念佛. In the *Lidai fabao ji* it is said that Wuxiang had a particular method of chanting *nianfo* at the beginning of his precepts assemblies:

> The Venerable Kim, every twelfth and first month, administered the "receiving of conditions" for countless numbers of people of the four assemblies. The *bodhimaṇḍa* sanctuary was magnificently arranged, and [Wuxiang] occupied the high seat to expound the Dharma. He would first lead a vocal recollection of the Buddha. As the recitation ended at the end of an exhalation and the cessation of sound, he would expound, "No-recollection, no-thought, and 'do not be deluded': no-recollection is *śīla,* no-thought is samādhi, and 'do not be deluded' is prajñā. These three phrases are the gates of perfectly maintaining [the precepts]."[126]

We may note that Wuxiang's use of a putative "Pure Land" signature practice, vocal *nianfo,* was not criticized even by the pugnaciously antiliturgical *Lidai fabao ji* authors. Though they claimed an identity based on the sudden teaching and targeted certain classes of opponents such as Vinaya masters and Daoists, this lack of concern over the boundary between Pure Land and Chan is further evidence that these were not yet considered oppositional identities.

There may have been a close connection between Wuxiang's style of chanting and that of the monk Fazhao 法照 (d. 820?). Fazhao was a disciple of the Pure Land devotee Chengyuan 承遠 (712–802), who was a disciple of Wuxiang's master Chuji, and Fazhao developed a special method of chanting that was linked with visualization of Amitābha.[127] The Jingzhong monastery was primarily associated with Pure Land practices in the ninth century, so Wuxiang's legacy contributed to both Pure Land and Chan developments.

As noted, the *Song gaoseng zhuan* states that Wuxiang's Dharma heir Jingzhong Shenhui 淨眾神會 (720–794) became abbot of Jingzhong monastery after Wuxiang's death. Jingzhong Shenhui's patron Wei Gao 韋皋, the military governor of Jiannan West from 785 until his death in 805, was even more powerful in Chengdu than Wuzhu's patron Du Hongjian had been.[128] Wei Gao seems to have been a devout believer in *nianfo* practice; Gregory relates the following anecdote about him:

> A curious testament to his piety has survived in an epitaph he wrote for a stūpa containing the relics of a parrot. Apparently a certain Mr. Pei had trained this remarkable bird to recite the Buddha's name, as a result of which it attained Buddhahood. After it died its body was cremated, and more than ten relics were found. Hearing of this, the monk Huiguan had the relics enshrined, and Wei Gao wrote his commemoration in 803.[129]

Had Wuzhu lived to hear about this, one can only imagine what his comments might have been; perhaps he would have quoted the paddy-crabs.

Tibetan Traces

Tibet also had a role to play in the fate of the *Lidai fabao ji*. The rise and fall of the Tibetan Yarlung dynasty influenced the course of events in Sichuan, as Sichuan was the Tang staging area for military campaigns against the Nanzhao kingdom (Yunnan) and the Tibetans. Nanzhao allied itself with Tibet against the Tang from 749 until 793, and Tang campaigns into Yunnan in the early 750s led to disastrous troop losses. This greatly contributed to the weakening of the military that made the Tang so vulnerable when An Lushan rebelled.[130] One may speculate that if Wuzhu had remained in the military, and if he had not been ordained in 749, it is quite possible that he would have been sent into Yunnan in the early 750s—and it is likely that the *Lidai fabao ji* would not have been written.

The cavalry officers who led Du Hongjian to Wuzhu were part of the Tang campaign against the Tibetans in northwestern Sichuan. Tang-era Sino-Tibetan hostilities lasted from 737 until the 860s, when the empire created by the Yarlung dynasty collapsed.[131] The rapidly expanding Tibetan empire was a serious threat; the Tibetan army occupied Chang'an in 763, and Dunhuang was part of Tibetan territory from 786 to 848. In the period between the composition of the *Lidai fabao ji* and its entombment in Dunhuang in the eleventh century, there was a complex pattern of military, commercial, and religious interaction, interspersed with periods of isolation, among the cultural centers of western Sichuan, Nanzhao, Tibet, and Gansu. This interaction is attested by the Tibetan manuscripts in the Dunhuang cache, and at least four Tibetan Dunhuang manuscripts include elements of the *Lidai fabao ji* versions of the biographies of the Chan patriarchs.[132]

One of the most interesting of the intersections between Tibet and the world of the *Lidai fabao ji* concerns a Tibetan account of Wuxiang. According to the *Sba-bzhed* (The Testament of Ba), the Tibetan envoy Ba Sangshi[133] met Wuxiang ("Kim Heshang") in Sichuan and received a prophecy from him.[134]

> On the road along which the five emissaries were traveling to Tibet was a rock out-cropping around which no one could move. Whoever saw it died in landslides. The powerful Kim Hwa-shang of the city of Eg-chu,[135] who was able to harness a tiger,[136] and who was clairvoyant, entered into meditation for three days at the order of his preceptor.[137] In this way he shattered the rock and then built a temple in the tamed space that was left. He also then had that region put under plow. Separating [some of the fields] as temple-lands, he came back to Eg-chu, whereupon the Tibetan emissaries received a meditation transmission [from him]. When they asked for prognostications about what would then happen, asking whether the Buddha's doctrine would be established in Tibet, or if the life-threatening demons of Tibet might not act up if the Buddha's scriptures were proclaimed, and whether or not the Tsenpo (emperor) and his son were at ease, the Hwa-shang investigated [these matters] clairvoyantly.[138]

"Kim Heshang" is then said to have correctly predicted to the emissaries that the Tibetan emperor Trhi Detsuktsen had died in their absence and that evil ministers had destroyed the Buddhist temple that he had established. Furthermore, they were told that if the prince survived he would convert to Buddhism—and this prince did indeed become the great Buddhist ruler Trhi Songdetsen (r. 755–797).[139] According to the chronicle, Buddhism was suppressed by pro-Bon ministers until 761, after which Ba Sangshi brought out the three Chinese Dharma texts he had received from Wuxiang and had subsequently hidden until conditions became favorable. He translated these texts into Tibetan and became the abbot of Samye monastery; Jeffrey Broughton speculates that he was regarded as a master in Wuxiang's lineage.[140]

Broughton also gives an account of another intriguing claim made in the *Sba-bzhed,* namely, that the chronicle's author Salnan (Gsal-snaṅ) made a journey to China in search of the Dharma and was instructed by Wuxiang. This story includes the rather far-fetched claim that the Chinese emperor summoned Wuxiang to court in order to instruct Salnan in the Dharma. Furthermore, Salnan's putative journey would have begun sometime after 763, and according to the *Lidai fabao ji* Wuxiang died in 762. However, following arguments made by Obata Hironobu, Broughton suggests that it was not Wuxiang but Wuzhu whom Salnan encountered in Sichuan, even though Wuzhu's name is not mentioned in the chronicle.[141]

In addition to these stories in the *Sba-bzhed* and fragments of accounts of the masters of the Bao Tang lineage, it also seems that some form of Wuxiang's and Wuzhu's teachings flowed westward. These traces are discernible in the texts that contain the slender remains of the Chan movement in Tibet.[142] As is well known, the fate of Chan in Tibet was said to have been decided in a debate at the Samye monastery near Lhasa in c. 792–797. The debate was said to have been carried out between the Chinese Chan master Moheyan 摩訶衍 and the Indian Mādhyamika master Kamalaśīla, and the latter won the endorsement of Emperor Trhi Songdetsen. The two figures were considered representatives of the sudden versus gradual approaches to practice, but the "positions" of Moheyan and Kamalaśīla are probably renderings of a more extended controversy that was not limited to one event or debate.[143]

The Dunhuang text entitled *Dunwu dasheng zhenglijue* 頓悟大乘正理決 (Verification of Sudden Awakening in the Mahāyāna) gives an account of Moheyan's arguments.[144] Obata Hironobu characterizes the *Dunwu dasheng zhenglijue* as a unique synthesis that includes concepts reflective of Moheyan's Northern School teachers, Shenhui, and Wuzhu. It does not, however, show any traces of the Southern School polemic against the Northern School. Obata contends that although Moheyan places emphasis on the apparently "Northern School" practice of *kanxin* 看心 (viewing the mind), in fact his interpretation of this practice is more in keeping with the subitism of Shenhui's "*jianxing chengfo* 見性成佛 (see the nature and become a Buddha)." Moreover, Obata argues that although the *Dunwu dasheng zhenglijue* includes elements of Shenhui's thought, Moheyan's interpretation of "no-thought" appears to be primarily based on Wuzhu's teachings as given in the *Lidai fabao ji*. The most pointed example of this is the close correspondence between Moheyan's interpretation of no-thought (*bu si zhe yi bu si* 不思者亦不思 "one is not even thinking that one is not thinking") and Wuzhu's signature phrase "At the time of true no-thought, no-thought itself is not."[145]

Moheyan's subitism is also notably antinomian, and this is said to be the reason that Trhi Songdetsen decided in favor of "gradualist" Indian Mahāyāna teachings. Moheyan draws an analogy between the practice of complete nonconceptualization and nonexamination (*busi buguan* 不思不觀) and the eighth-level bodhisattva's achievement of nonexamination, in which he or she transcends all practices and achieves nonproduction of dharmas (and thus nonproduction of good or bad karma). There follows an extended discussion as to whether the practice of the six perfections (pāramitās) and the other rubrics of the Dharma are necessary. Moheyan maintains a line of argumentation based on ultimate truth: in "nonexamination" there are no longer any false notions, and the question of the necessity or nonnecessity of practice does not arise.[146] In this discussion the "six perfections" represent practice as such. However, the Two Truths logic that Moheyan uses is similar to the logic that Shenhui, Wuxiang, and Wuzhu use in their antinomian interpretations of *śīla,* samādhi, and prajñā, as encapsulated in their varying versions of a three-phrase formula discussed above. As we recall, Wuzhu asserts: "No-thought is thus the complete fulfillment of *śīla,* samādhi, and prajñā."[147]

Nevertheless, Moheyan takes a more "gradualist" line when he repeatedly admits the necessity of cultivation for those who are not able to practice nonexamination.[148] In fact, the extant *Dunwu dasheng zhenglijue* closes with the reassurance that practitioners who cultivate morality and good deeds will all become Buddhas.[149] Luis Gómez argues that the surviving Tibetan fragments of Moheyan's responses show that his attitude toward practice may have been more nuanced than the iconoclastic position presented in the polemical *Dunwu dasheng zhenglijue.* Gómez suggests that Moheyan's position in the Tibetan texts is similar to Zongmi's in positing "sudden enlightenment followed by gradual cultivation," but he also points out inconsistencies between Moheyan's extreme subitist nondualism and his concessions to ordinary practice.[150]

These concessions were apparently not enough to win imperial endorsement of Moheyan's teachings. Nevertheless, though Chan was virtually suppressed in Tibet, a few Tibetan works showing Chan influences remain. For our purposes, the most important of these is the Dunhuang manuscript Pelliot Tibetan (P. Tib.) 116, which is actually a collection of excerpts from Chinese Chan texts and other works related to Chan topics.[151] Passages showing direct and indirect connections with Wuxiang and Wuzhu are found in various sections of this work. For example, there are two quotations attributed to a master called Kim-hun-shen-shi, who may or may not be Wuxiang. In style they do not strikingly resemble Wuxiang's teachings as represented in the *Lidai fabao ji,* but the basic Chan themes are recognizable: if there is awareness of fundamental nondual mind then there is no objectification of true nature ("the genuine") and the afflictions do not arise, and this liberation is found in the practice of nonconceptualization.[152] Furthermore, P. Tib. 116 also contains the first part of Wuzhu's sermon on regarding the mind as the *bodhimaṇḍa.*[153] Finally, P. Tib. 116 includes a work entitled *Sudden Awakening to the Fundamental Reality* that displays a family resemblance to the *Dunwu dasheng zhenglijue* and the *Lidai fabao ji.*[154] The text is cast in the form of questions posed by the disciple Yem and answered by his master Unimpeded Wisdom,[155] and it shows the blending of Northern School meditation technique and the *Lidai fabao ji* style of Southern School subitism that we see in Moheyan's teachings. There are also signs of antinomian formless practice; one of the responses of Chan Master Unimpeded Wisdom sounds as if it could have come directly from Wuzhu's mouth: "What's the use of you giving me gifts, of making vows, and of bowing and burning incense?"[156]

Possible threads of connection between eighth- and ninth-century Sichuan Chan and the post-eleventh century Dzogchen and Nyingma schools have become the subject of both scholarly and unscholarly speculation, but the complexity of this issue takes it beyond the scope of the present study. Interestingly, however, Matthew Kapstein suggests that tracking later appearances of the *Vajrasamādhi-sūtra* may be one reliable method of tracing the persistence of traditions of Sichuan Chan in Tibet. He argues that the subitism in the *Vajrasamādhi* was rendered acceptable by the work's supposed canonical status, while direct references to Chan works and figures became politically incorrect.[157] Two subitist apocrypha that are frequently quoted in the *Lidai fabao ji*, the *Vajrasamādhi* and the *Śūraṅgama,* made it into the earliest surviving Tibetan canonical catalogue compiled in c. 812.[158] It is possible that these scriptures became more widely known in Tibet through the medium of quotations in the *Lidai fabao ji*—if so, this would be yet another way in which the *Lidai fabao ji* acted as a carrier for elements of Chan that continued to function in a later tradition in a different form.

Sichuan Chan and the Hongzhou School

The Hongzhou 洪州 was the Chan school that best survived the Buddhist persecution of the Huichang era. Mazu Daoyi 馬祖道一 (709–788), the progenitor of the Hongzhou lineage, became the common patriarch of the Linji 臨濟 and Guiyang 溈仰 schools, two of the "Five Houses" of Song Chan. As the Linji lineage was and remains one of the most important of the Chan/Zen traditions, the question of Mazu's antecedents is not an insignificant matter. Zongmi asserts that Mazu was at one time Wuxiang's disciple; Mazu was also a native of Sichuan, and there is some controversy over whether Mazu was more influenced by Wuxiang or by his acknowledged master, Huairang 懷讓 (677–744).[159] The biographies of Korean monks included in the mid-tenth century *Zutang ji* 祖堂集 (Anthology from the Patriarchal Hall) show evidence that Korean monks believed Mazu's lineage to have stemmed from Wuxiang.[160] Discussion of this controversy becomes more complex when one is attuned to nationalist or sectarian perspectives among the twentieth-century scholars (Chinese, Korean, and Japanese) who have written about it.[161]

The paradigm of Mazu as presented in his biography and the style of his "recorded sayings" reflects, as does the *Lidai fabao ji*, the need to find an appropriate form for the sudden teaching. However, the Mazu material mediates between conventional and radical approaches that are less extreme than Wuzhu's, but are also more clearly and confidently on the side of the new. Mazu was known for his emphasis on immanence and spontaneous function, such that Buddha nature is fully manifest in everyday activities like eating, sleeping, and wearing clothes. This had an antinomian aspect, as Zongmi points out in his characterization of the Hongzhou teaching: "This means that one should not rouse the mind to cut off bad or practice good. One does not even cultivate the path. The path is mind."[162] As discussed in chapter 6, according to Zongmi the Bao Tang and the Hongzhou schools were both guilty of misinterpreting the sudden teaching.

There are some differences of opinion over the degree to which Hongzhou antinomianism and iconoclasm were put into practice. Jeffrey Broughton argues that Pei Xiu 裴休 (787?–860), a lay disciple of Zongmi's who became an admirer of the Hongzhou approach, corroborates Zongmi's characterization of Hongzhou practices from the standpoint of a defender rather than a detractor.[163] Mario Poceski, by contrast, argues that because the early Hongzhou texts show no evidence of having been precursors of the Song encounter-dialogue style of eccentric pedagogy, therefore the Hongzhou school was not as radical as it has been made out to be.[164]

No matter how we imagine the Dharma-hall behavior of Mazu and his disciples, it is clear that taking immanence rather than formlessness as a soteriological foundation meant that the Hongzhou approach was more flexible than the Bao Tang approach. Unlike the Bao Tang denial of formal precepts and practices, the notion of "everyday function" neither privileged nor precluded monastic ordination, and it facilitated the adaptation of existing monastic institutions. The choice of immanence as the foundation of orthopraxy allowed reclamation of the conventional, whereas Wuzhu's absolutism was bound to fall back to dualism on the symbolic level, due to its investment in the inversion of symbols.

In this context, it is not insignificant that the development of a Chan monastic code is associated by tradition with Mazu's line. Mazu's disciple Baizhang 百丈 (749–814) was said to be the founder of the first independent Chan monastery and the first Chan monastic code, the *Baizhang qinggui* 百丈清規 (Baizhang's Pure Rules). In Baizhang's biography in the *Song gaoseng zhuan*, it is said that he decided to draw from both the Vinaya and bodhisattva precepts texts in order to create regulations for a separate monastic institution that would not follow the Vinaya.[165] Although the existence of such a text is doubtful, it was claimed to be the basis of the authoritative *Chanyuan qinggui* 禪苑清規 (Rules of Purity for Chan Monasteries) of 1103.[166]

Regardless of whether Baizhang can be credited with creating some form of distinctive Chan monasticism, it appears that both Mazu and Zongmi contributed to the development of a more inclusive yet distinctive notion of authentic Chan transmission. Hongzhou immanence provided the foundation for a new "Middle Way" in between the Vinaya and bodhisattva precepts, on the one hand, and the formless precepts, on the other. Zongmi's project to reconcile Chan and study of the scriptures, sudden enlightenment and gradual practice, and to create a map of the known Chan teachings, provided a model for more subtle means of negotiating lineages and identities.

Another contemporaneous work that contributed to the evolution of a more inclusive notion of Chan lineage is the aforementioned *Baolin zhuan*.[167] It is unfortunately incomplete, but its extant sections prove it to be related to the *Lidai fabao ji* in style and content. As noted in chapter 5, rather than emphasizing a talismanic patriarchal robe the *Baolin zhuan* instituted the notion of transmission verses, and these verses were included in later biographies even after their use as seals of transmission was abandoned (if they were ever in fact instantiated). Moreover, the *Baolin zhuan* includes an account of branching lineages, and this inclusive tendency would reach full flower with the Song *chuandeng lu* genre.[168]

This is not to claim that these texts were free of sectarian biases and agendas, but the competition among Chan lineages was increasingly subordinated to the representation of the Chan school as a powerful clan consisting of many families. This is exemplified in the *Jingde chuandeng lu,* which became the authoritative account of eighth- and ninth-century Chan transmission. It represents a coalition among the main Chan "houses" and the absorption of the patriarchal lineages into a many-limbed genealogy. Thus the tensions inherent in the "kingship" or linear master-disciple model of early Chan were resolved into a more traditional "kinship" model. Transmission was vested in the rhizomatic structure of a widespread "gnostic community" rather than in its actualization in an anointed series of charismatic individuals.

CONCLUSION

The many elements discussed in this chapter—making icons out of Chan masters, the blending of Chan and Pure Land practices, connections with Korea and Tibet, the rise of the Hongzhou lineage, and the development of Chan genealogies—all contributed to the unique character of Sichuan Chan Buddhism. Sichuan Chan became an important source for the styles, traditions, and practices of mainstream Chan in the Song dynasty. Therefore, these regional developments would leave their imprint on Chinese society as a whole during the era of Chan Buddhism's greatest political and cultural influence. The imprint of the Bao Tang school on Sichuan Chan is not negligible. What, in the end, is the transmission of the Bao Tang?

The huge repository of Chan lore owes much to Wuzhu's disciples, one or several of whom created the written portrait of the master whose spirit lives on in the *Lidai fabao ji*. The *Lidai fabao ji* modified received genres or introduced new stylistic features in ways that would shape the standard genres of Song Chan literature—*chuandeng lu, yulu,* and *zhenzan.* Furthermore, the *Lidai fabao ji* version of the Indian line of patriarchs was the source for the version that became official. Many anecdotes that have their origins in the *Lidai fabao ji* found their way into the official annals of Chan, yet the *Lidai fabao ji* itself was repudiated and all but forgotten.

The doctrine of formlessness was nothing new, yet the Bao Tang remain unique. In order to discern both the derivative and the innovative aspects of the Bao Tang, one must look at them in the context of sacred performance, the participant-audience of the ordination assembly. In the traditional Vinaya context, senior monks function as preceptors and confirm ordination. In the "bodhisattva precepts" context, the practitioner could take the Buddhas and bodhisattvas as preceptors and could take his or her own visionary reception of a "good sign" as confirmation. The visualization ritual was geared toward purification rather than attaining clerical status, yet nevertheless undermined the exclusivity of clerical privilege. In the context of Chan, Chan masters as living Buddha functioned as preceptors, and, because of a combination of political circumstances and doctrinal evolution, the Chan formless precepts were preached in a context in which people became members of the clergy by buying ordination certificates. In the *Lidai fabao ji,* we have the example of a female practitioner tonsuring herself and becoming a nun, functioning all-at-once as the preceptor, the essence of the precepts, and the audience-recipient.

The precepts were the heart of the roles of the monk and the nun, the empowerment that "painted the eyes" of the icon. The Chan teaching of the formless precepts expressed what had been true all along, that there was no abiding identity to the role of a member of the Saṅgha. In the sudden teaching, one becomes a Buddha because one is a Buddha—so far so good, but how does one become a monk or nun? In traditional Buddhism, one became a monk or nun by vowing to act like one, but in Chan, what is that acting "like"? There is a kind of Catch-22 at work here—one can bring life to the role only by practicing, rehearsing, and getting it right, but one can get it right only by living it fully all at once. In Chan, the art of the role, empowered by ritual, became the living source of likeness.

> On the third day of the sixth month of the ninth year of the Dali era (774), [the Venerable] told his disciples, "Bring me a fresh clean robe, I wish to

> bathe." When he had bathed and put on the robe, he asked his disciples, "Is it the time of abstinence (i.e., noon) yet?" They answered, "Yes." He bound all his disciples to a promise: "If you are filial obedient children you will not disobey my teachings. I am at the point of the great practice. After I am gone you are not to knit your brows [in distress], you are not to act like worldly and untrained persons. Those who weep, wear mourning garments, and knit their brows shall not be called my disciples. Weeping is precisely the way of the world, the Buddha-Dharma is not thus. 'Transcending all characteristics; this is precisely seeing the Buddha.'"[169]
>
> When he finished speaking, he passed away while remaining in a seated position. The Great Master's springs and autumns amounted to sixty-one.[170]

When Wuzhu tells his followers to act like followers of the Buddha-Dharma, not "worldly and untrained persons," he assumes the grand time-honored role of the Buddha at his *parinirvāṇa,* who also admonished his followers not to weep. This is a scriptural and hagiographic trope, yet it is a trope in service of the irreplaceable and unrepeatable; it signals not that Wuzhu is the Buddha, but that Wuzhu is being portrayed enacting the role of the Buddha for the last time and forever, with local, topical, and personal verisimilitude. The notion of "internalization" of a role is post-Cartesian; in the world of the *Lidai fabao ji,* there is no abiding internal psyche that is the source of the role, no reified experience that confirms the reality of "being." The stereotypical portrayal of Wuzhu's death is like the final ritual of painting the eyes on a sacred image; the art and the role, empowered by rite and trope, becomes a living source of power.

Ritual studies show us that the elaboration of ritual is serendipitous and, at the same time, keeps within certain bounds that are extremely difficult to define. In this regard we might return briefly to the two versions of Wuxiang's three phrases—no-recollection, no-thought, and do not forget. Wuzhu's elaboration "do not be deluded" creates a likeness of his master by changing his master, whom he may never have met. The replication-in-alteration of the master role became in time a highly ritualized system of allusions.

In Donald Sutton's study of contemporary ritual performers in Taiwan, he examines the evolution of the troupe's ritual performance forms over a period of time. After describing the performance and its contexts, he reiterates the questions that have informed the study and proposes some of his answers:

> If officialdom does not standardize in post-Qing Taiwan, what does? Why does change keep within fixed bounds, even when in myth, iconographic interpretation, ritual, and choreography, innovation and fluidity are the rule?

> What, in other words, keeps innovation consistent with the underlying logic of the Jiajiang described above? The deliberate traditionalism of local religion, asserting old ways in spite of modernity, is only part of the answer; after all, participating alongside the Jiajiang at festivals are comic troupes that show heavy influence from modern commercial and industrial values. . . . What is specifically traditionalist about the Jiajiang is that they are not just performers before the gods but also escorts and exorcisers on their behalf. As divine agents they must keep their actions and appearance ritualized in order to convey the requisite weight and importance. To persuade, ritual has to remind us of what we already know in our bones.[171]

He goes on to say that the agent of both standardization and innovation in creating the "requisite weight and importance" of the ritual performance is plural. In other words, it is a relationship: the relationship between the community temple, the troupe leader as performance master and purveyor of ritual services, and the festival marketplace for performances.[172] I would suggest that late eighth-century Chan standardization and innovation developed out of an analogous relationship among the established local religious institutions, the Chan master and his troupe of disciples, and the marketplace for religious performance, especially mass ordination ritual performance. This is not meant to be reductive; as Sutton says, ritual reminds us of what we already know in our bones. (And what is that?) The performance master reminds us not to forget no-recollection and no-thought, and "at the time of true no-thought, no-thought itself is not." The performance connects the gods to the costumes and masks of the actors, the Dharma to the portrait, the flesh to bones.

Wuzhu's robe is a costume for being possessed by the patriarchs and by the transmission of no-thought. Shenhui imbued the robe with mind-to-mind transmission so that the two are as emptiness and form, nondual. The *Lidai fabao ji* authors reintroduced a seam between robe and Dharma by having Bodhidharma say that the robe is like a dynastic talisman, but only where there are false monks is such an external symbol needed. This seam allows one to see the internal pressures of Southern School ideology more clearly. That is, it allows one to see the tension between the unmediated identity of self-nature/Dharma and the continued need to negotiate the relationship among the community temple, the Chan master and his troupe, and the religious marketplace.

The *Lidai fabao ji*'s imperfect seams give us a different view of the "Golden Age" of Chan, for in it we can see the stitches binding different levels of discourse, and the unmatched edges between the ultimate, mythical, local, and political patches of Bodhidharma's costume are more clearly revealed. Must these gaps expose a lack of integrity, or anyway a lack of sophistication, a vulgarization of Daoxuan's Jetavana opera and

Shenhui's pageant of the patriarchy? The Bao Tang may certainly be seen as engaged in Buddhist business as usual, wearing a cloak of disinterestedness in order to attract secular elites, the consumers in the religious marketplace, and then turning patronage to advantage in factional rivalries with other performance troupes. However, Wuzhu truly went into this marketplace with empty hands, offering no sin and repentance, no merit, and no-thought.

At this distance it becomes impossible to distinguish transparent rhetoric from formless practice, but it is also impossible to know what is thereby hidden, and what is revealed. If indeed the Bao Tang practiced no-thought to the extent of dispensing with the costumes, masks, and script, so that their own separate status as clergy all but disappeared, this should win them a special place in the history of Buddhist monasticism. Bao Tang antinomianism was lost in the mainstream of Chan. Repudiated, it nevertheless imparted a subtle pervasive flavor, and perhaps a warning about the necessary limits of the ultimate teaching. Wuzhu and his robe would seem to be not-recollected, only to reappear in surprising guises.

To belabor a favorite metaphor one last time, the *Lidai fabao ji* has much in common with the emperor's new clothes—it reveals vanity and courage, the ridiculous and the radical, the deluded and denuded. The unthinkable became the costume of wisdom, and unlike other robes of the gods this one could not be removed. The *Lidai fabao ji* shows that it is impossible to separate jade from grit, robe from patriarch, and the Triple Jewel from flesh and bone. Perhaps the ultimate fate of Bodhidharma's robe is that Wuzhu is wearing it in his portrait.

PART 2

Annotated Translation of the *Lidai fabao ji*

RECORD OF THE DHARMA-JEWEL
THROUGH THE GENERATIONS

THIS TRANSLATION based on S. 516, with P. 2125 as the alternate text for portions illegible in S. 516. While at Hanazono College in Kyoto from 1991 to 1993, I attended Koga Hidehiko's 古賀英彦 seminar on the *Lidai fabao ji*, and he argued convincingly that, except for its missing front portion, S. 516 was the best of the remaining manuscripts. I have also compared S. 516 and P. 2125 character by character, and S. 516 requires less editorial adjustment than P. 2125. While this may be an indication that S. 516 is therefore an edited and less "original" text, for the most part the differences between the two texts concern stylistic polish rather than altered meaning. If S. 516 is indeed a text that has come under an editor's brush, I am willing to take advantage of his (or her) attention to such matters. Characters in boldface are emendations or missing sections taken from P. 2125. Text titles are underlined. Notes include identification of all interlinear additions or other indications of attempted corrections to the text. I have reproduced the sometimes nonstandard characters as closely as possible, noting places where use of cognates has been necessary. In the manuscript, repetition of characters (such as 種種) is indicated by a characteristic "ditto" mark, but for the sake of clarity I have chosen to repeat the characters.

Throughout, I have consulted Yanagida Seizan's Japanese translation of P. 2125, with emendations, in *Shoki no zenshi II*. I have tried to be as consistent as possible, but at times the same term is translated differently according to variations in context. Most of the annotations below are based on Yanagida's annotations, and in cases where I cite his opinions or have not myself consulted the original sources I refer the reader to his notes in *Shoki no zenshi II,* indicated by attribution to "Yanagida 1976a." The division of the text into sections follows Yanagida's sections, which follow logical divisions in the narrative. Corresponding *Taishō* page and line numbers are given for each section, but the *Taishō* text T. 51 (2075), based largely on P. 2125, has a number of errors.

The translation is followed by an appendix describing the texts cited as sources in the *Lidai fabao ji*. The first time I cite a scripture I give both the Chinese and Sanskrit titles (and appendix number, if applicable) and thereafter refer to it using the Sanskrit title alone. In identifying quotations I do not usually include the text of the original source in the notes, but I note whether the *Lidai fabao ji* version deviates from the original, and I include the text if the deviation significantly alters the meaning. There are many repeated quotations and phrases in the *Lidai fabao ji;* the note for the first use of a quotation is the most detailed, and thereafter I note only the original source and the other occurrences of the phrase in the *Lidai fabao ji.*

SECTION 1

Sources and the Legend of Emperor Ming of the Han

(T. 51. 179A1–179C4)[1]

曆代法寶記。[2] 亦名師資血脈傳。亦名定是非摧邪顯正破壞一切心傳。亦名最上乘頓悟法門。

Record of the Dharma-Jewel Through the Generations. Also called: *The Transmission of the Masters and Disciples of the [True] Lineage.* Also called: *The Transmission Determining True and False, Annihilating Wrong and Displaying Right, and Destroying All Mind [Consciousnesses].*[3] Also called: *The Supreme Vehicle, the Dharma-Gate of Sudden Awakening.*[4]

案本行経云、雑[5]阿含経、普曜経云、應瑞経[6]、文殊師利涅槃経、清浄法行経、无垢光轉女身経、決定毘尼経、大佛頂経、金剛三昧経、法句経、佛蔵経、纓絡経、華嚴経、大般若経、禪門経、涅槃経、楞伽経、思益経、法華経、維摩経、藥師経、金剛般若經、藥師経[7]、付法蔵経、道教西昇経、釋法琳傳、釋虚實記、開元釋教目、周書異記、漢法内傳、尹喜内傳、牟子、列子、苻子、呉書、并古録、及楊楞伽鄴都故事等。

Based on the authority of the *Abhiniṣkramaṇa-sūtra* (Scripture of the Initial Steps on the Path), *Saṃyuktāgama-sūtra* (Miscellaneous Discourses), *Lalitavistara-sūtra* (Scripture of the Unfolding of the Divine Play [of the Buddha]), *Kumārakuśalaphalanidāna-sūtra* (Scripture of Auspicious Signs), *Manjuśrīparinirvāṇa-sūtra* (Scripture of the Final Nirvāṇa of Manjuśrī), *Qingjing faxing jing* (Scripture of the Practice of the Pure Dharma), *Strīvivartavyākaraṇa-sūtra* (Scripture of the Unstained Radiant Transformation of the Female Body), *Vinayaviniścaya-Upālipariprcchā-sūtra* (Scripture of the Inquiry of Upāli Regarding Determination of the Vinaya), *Śūraṃgama-sūtra* (Scripture of the Crown of the Buddha's Head), *Vajrasamādhi-sūtra* (Scripture of Adamantine Concentration), "*Dhammapada*" (Verses on Dharma), *Buddhapiṭakaduḥśīlanirgraha-sūtra* (Scripture in Which the Admonitions of the Buddha-Treasury Are Understood), *Yingluo jing* (Gem-Necklace Scripture), *Avataṃsaka-sūtra* (Flower-Garland Scripture), *Mahāprajñāpāramitā-sūtra* (Scripture of the Great Perfection of Wisdom), *Chanmen jing* (Scripture of the Chan Teachings), *Mahāparinirvāṇa-sūtra* (Scripture of the Great Final Nirvāṇa), *Laṇkāvatāra-sūtra* (Scripture of the Appearance of the Dharma in Laṇkā), *Viśeṣacintabrahmaparipṛcchā-sūtra* (Scripture of the Inquiry of the Deity of Thinking), *Saddharmapuṇḍarīka-sūtra* (Scripture of the Lotus of the True Dharma), *Vimalakīrtinirdeśa-sūtra* (Scripture on the Expositions of Vimalakīrti), *Bhaiṣajyaguruvaiḍūryaprabhāsapūrvapraṇidhānaviśeṣavistara-sūtra* (Elaboration on the Merit of the Previous Vows of the Medicine Master Who Shines Like an Emerald), *Vajracchedikā-sūtra* (Diamond Scripture), *Fu fazang jing* (Scripture of the Transmission of the Dharma Treasury), *Daojiao xisheng jing* (Scripture of the Ascension to the West of the Daoist Teachings), *Shi Falin zhuan* (Biography of Shi Falin), *Shi Xushi ji* (Record of the Monk Shi Xushi), *Kaiyuan shijiao mu* (Catalogue of Buddhism in the Kaiyuan Era), *Zhou shu yiji* (Supplement to the Zhou History), *Hanfa neizhuan* (Inner Commentary on the Dharma in the Han), *Yin Xi neizhuan* (Yin Xi's Inner Commentary), *Mouzi* (The Book of Master Mou), *Liezi* (The Book of Master Lie), *Fuzi* (The Book of Master Fu), *Wu shu* (The Wu History), *Bing gu lu, Yang Lengqie Yedu gushi* (Yang Lengqie's Stories of Ye), etc.[8]

漢法内傳「後漢明帝、永平三年、**夜夢見金人、身長一丈六尺、項背圓光、飛行殿**庭。於晨旦問朝臣、『是何**瑞應?** 』**太史傳毅奏曰**、『**西方有大聖人号**曰佛、是其像也。』明帝問、『**何以知之?** 』**太史傳毅對曰**、『周書異記曰、昭王甲**寅歳佛生、穆王壬申**[9] **歳佛滅度、一千年**後教法流於漢地。今**時是也**。』**明帝遣**郎中蔡愔、博士秦景等、使於天竺國。請得佛像菩薩形像、経四十二章、得法師二人、迦葉摩騰竺法蘭。明帝請昇殿供養、故洛陽城西創置白馬寺。

永平十四年正月一日、五岳霍山、白鹿山道士褚善信、費叔才等六百九十人等表奏、『臣聞太上無刑[10]、虚无自然。上古同遵[11]、百王不易。陛下棄本逐末、求教西域、化謂胡神所説、不参華夏。臣等多有聡恵、博渉経典。願陛下許臣等、得与比校。若有勝**者**[12] 願除虚詐。如[13] 其不如、任従重決。』帝曰、『依。』

勅有司命辦供具、并五品已上文武内外官**寮、至十五日平**旦、集於白馬寺。道士在寺門外、置三壇開廿四門。**帝在寺**南門外、置舍利及佛経像、設七寶行殿。褚善信**費叔才**等、以道経子書苻術等、置燈(?)[14] 於上。以火験之、悲涙呪曰、胡神乱我華夏、願太上天尊曉示(?)[15] 衆生得辦真偽。道経子書苻術等、見火化為煨燼。道士驚愕。先昇天者、不得昇天、先隠形者、不能隠、先入水火者、更不敢入、禁呪者、喚策者不能應。種種功能、无一可験。褚善信費寂才等、自感而死。時佛舍利五色光明、璉環如盖、遍覆大衆、光蔽日輪。摩騰法師坐臥虚空、神化自在、天雨寶花及天音楽。竺法蘭梵音讃 (言 +堇)[16]。摩騰法師説偈曰『狐非師子類、燈非日月明。池无巨海納、丘无嵩岳榮。』

明帝大悦、放五品已上公侯子女及**陰夫人等出**家。道士六百人投佛出家。法蘭誦<u>出家功徳経</u>及<u>佛本生</u>等経。明帝大喜、挙國歸依佛教。

明帝問二師、『佛号法王、何為不生於漢國? 』迦葉摩騰法師對曰、『迦毘羅衛城者、百億日月之中心、三千大千世界之主。一切龍神有福之者、皆生彼國。法王所以生於天竺國。』明帝又問法師、『佛種族是誰? 何時生、何時滅? 』摩騰法師答曰、『佛是千代金輪王孫、浄飯王子、姓瞿曇氏、亦名釋種。癸丑歳七月十五日、従兜率天宮降下、摩耶夫人託胎。甲寅之歳四月八日、於毘尼園、摩耶夫人右脇而誕。又五百釋種五百白馬、乾渉車匿等供佛四月八日同時生。壬申之歳二月八日、踰城出家、癸未之歳二月十五日、入般涅槃。佛雖不生漢於地[17]、一千年後或五[18] 百年後、衆生有縁、先令聖弟子於彼行化。』」

The *Hanfa neizhuan* (Inner Commentary on the Dharma in the Han)[19] [says]: Emperor Ming of the Later Han in the third year of the Yongping era (60 C.E.) one night dreamt he saw a golden man thirteen feet high, with a nimbus around his neck and back, flying about the palace. The next morning he asked his court officials, "What sort of auspicious sign is this?"

The Grand Astrologer Fu Yi[20] addressed the emperor, saying, "In the West there is a great Holy One called the Buddha. It was his image [that you saw]." Emperor Ming asked, "How do you know this?" The Grand Astrologer Fu Yi replied, "In the *Zhou shu yiji* it says; 'The Buddha was born in the *jiayin* year (958 B.C.E.) of the reign of King Zhao, and passed into extinction in the *renshen* year (878 B.C.E.) of King Mu.[21] A thousand years after [his extinction] his teachings will spread to the Han (China).' Now that time has come."

Emperor Ming dispatched the Gentleman of the Interior Cai Yin and the Erudite Qin Jing and others as envoys to India.[22] [There] they made requests, and the Buddhist image they obtained was a statue of a bodhisattva, the scripture they obtained was the *Scripture in Forty-two Sections,*[23] and the two Dharma masters they obtained were Kāśyapamātaṇga and Dharmaratna.[24] [When they arrived,] Emperor Ming invited them to ascend to the audience hall and made offerings to them.[25] Consequently [the emperor] established the White Horse Monastery west of Luoyang city.[26]

On the first day of the first month of the fourteenth year of the Yongping era (71 C.E.), Daoists from Mt. Huo of the Five Marchmounts and Mt. Bailu,[27] Chu Shanxin and Fei Shucai[28] and six hundred and ninety others, submitted a memorial:

> We, your servants, have heard that the Ultimate[29] is without form, empty and spontaneous. From remotest antiquity it has been venerated by all alike, and this has not changed in the reigns of a hundred rulers. Yet Your Majesty has given up the root for the branches and has sought teachings in the Western Regions. You have been converted by the preachings of a barbarian divinity and neglect China. We, your servants, are sagacious men, and have read extensively in the classics. We beg that You allow us to compare [our Way with that of the Buddhists]. If there is a victor, we desire that You abolish the one that is specious and false. We know that they will not prove our equals, and will abide by Your Majesty's decision.

The emperor said, "Very well." He ordered that those in charge should see to the preparation of implements. Together with the inner and outer palace officials, civil and military, of the fifth rank and above, on the fifteenth at dawn all were assembled at the White Horse Monastery.

Outside the gate of the monastery the Daoists set up three altars and opened twenty-four pickets.[30] Outside the southern gate of the monastery the emperor placed a relic [of the Buddha] as well as Buddhist scriptures and images, and he set up a pavilion adorned with the seven precious gems.[31] Chu Shanxin and Fei Shucai and the others placed Daoist scriptures, treatises, and talismans on the altars. Then they set fire to them to verify their efficacy and, lamenting and wailing, they incanted: "A Barbarian divinity disturbs our China, we beg the Highest Celestial Venerables[32] to enlighten all beings to the difference between true and false." But as soon as the Daoist scriptures, treatises, and talismans were put in the fire they were instantly burned to ashes. The Daoists were greatly surprised. Those who formerly ascended to Heaven now could not; those who formerly rendered themselves invisible now could not; those who formerly entered fire and water now dared not; those who formerly cast spells and those who did divinations could not get any response. Of all their various abilities there was not one that was efficacious. Chu Shanxin, Fei Shucai, and the others took it to heart so much that they died.

Then the Buddha-relic radiated five-colored light, and linked jewels like a canopy covered the entire assembly, outshining the disk of the sun. The Dharma Master [Kāśyapa]mātaṇga assumed seated and reclining postures in empty space and manifested supra-mundane transformations at will. The heavens rained precious flowers and [there was] celestial music. Dharmaratna chanted hymns in the "brahmanical voice,"[33] and [Kāśyapa]mātaṇga spoke the following gāthā:

> A fox is not in the same class with a lion,
> a lamp is not as brilliant as the sun and moon.
> A pond is not so capacious as the vast ocean,
> and a hillock is not so lofty as Mt. Song.

Emperor Ming was greatly pleased, and permitted the children and the concubines of nobles of the fifth rank and above to become renunciants, and six hundred Daoists submitted to the Buddha and became renunciants. Dharmaratna chanted the *Sūtra of the Merit of Renunciation,*[34] the *Abhiniṣkramaṇa-sūtra,*[35] and other scriptures. Emperor Ming was overjoyed, and the entire realm took refuge in Buddhism.

Emperor Ming asked the two masters, "The Buddha is called the King of the Dharma. Why was he not born in China?"

The Dharma Master Kāśyapamātaṇga replied, "The city of Kapilavastu is the center of a hundred thousand suns and moons, it is the sovereign of the trichilio-megachiliocosms. All nāgas, gods, and those who are fortunate are born there, and that is why the King of the Dharma was born in India."

Emperor Ming further questioned the Dharma Master, "What was the Buddha's clan? When was he born and when did he die?" The Dharma Master [Kāśyapa]mātaṇga replied, "The Buddha was the descendent of a thousand generations of Golden Cakravartins and the son of King Śuddhodana. His surname was Gautama, also called the Śākya clan. On the fifteenth day of the seventh month of the *guichou* year (957 B.C.E.) he descended from his palace in Tuṣita Heaven and was incarnated in the womb of the Lady Māyā. On the eighth day of the fourth month of the *jiayin* year (958 B.C.E.), in Lumbini Park, Lady Māyā gave birth to him from her right side. Five hundred men of the Śākya clan, five hundred white horses, and Kaṇṭhaka and Chandaka[36] were born with the Buddha at the same time on the eighth day of the fourth month. On the eighth day of the second month of the *renshen* year (940 B.C.E.) he left the city and became a renunciant, and on the fifteenth day of the second month of the *guiwei* year[37] he entered *parinirvāṇa.* Although the Buddha was not born in the land of the Han, [it was predestined that] one thousand years later, or five hundred years later, [when] the beings' conditions [were suitable], he would first have his holy disciples go there and make conversions."[38]

SECTION 2

Buddhism in China (T. 51. 179C4–180A2)

案清浄法行経云、「天竺國東北真丹國。人民多不信敬、造罪者甚衆、吾我[39]今先遣聖弟子三人悉是菩薩、於彼示現行化。摩訶迦葉彼稱老子、光浄童子彼号仲尼明月儒童彼名顔迴。講論五経詩書礼楽、威儀法則、以漸誘化、後然[40]佛経當往。」

牟子云、「昔漢孝明皇帝夜夢見神人身有日光、飛在殿前、意中欣然也心甚悦之。明日傳問群臣、『此為何？』有通人傳毅曰、『臣聞天竺有徳道者号日佛。軽挙能飛、身有日光、殆将其神。』於是上悟、遣使張騫羽林郎中秦、博士弟子王尊等一十二人、大月支写取佛経四十二章、在蘭臺石室第十四。即時洛陽城西雍門外起佛寺、其壁畫朝廷千乗萬騎繞騎十三匝。又於南宮清涼臺及開陽門上作佛像形[41]。明帝在時、知命无常、先造寿陵、陵曰顕節、亦於其上作佛[42]圖像、於未滅時、國豊民寧、遠残暮夷慕義、咸来歸徳、願為臣妾者、以為億数。故謚曰明也。自是之後、京城左右及諸州縣處處各有佛寺、學者由此而滋。」

晋書云、「晉桓帝時、欲删除佛法、召盧山遠法師。帝問曰、『朕比来見僧尼、戒行不純、多有毀犯。朕欲删除揀擇、事今可否。』遠公答曰、『崑山出玉、上雑塵砂、麗水豊金、猶饒瓦礫。陛下只得敬法重人、不可軽人慢 法。』晉[43]帝大赦之。」

蕭梁武帝會三教云、「小時學周礼、弱冠窮六経、中復觀道書、有名與無名、晩年開釋卷、猶日映衆星。」

The *Qingjing faxing jing* (Scripture of the Pure Practice of the Dharma)[44] says: "To the northeast of India is the kingdom of China. Few of the people are devout, and evil-doers are legion. For the present, I will dispatch three holy disciples, all bodhisattvas, to appear there and make conversions. Mahākśyapa will there be styled Laozi. Kumara will there be called Confucius.[45] Sumedha will there be called Yanhui.[46] They will expound on the five classics: the *Classic of Poetry, Classic of Documents, Classic of Rites,* and the *Classic of Music.*[47] By setting august standards they will gradually bring about a transformation [in the people]. Only after that will the Buddhist scriptures proceed [to China].

The *Mouzi*[48] says, "Long ago, Emperor Xiaoming of the Han dreamt one night of a divine person. His body radiated light and he flew about in front of the palace. [The emperor] experienced an inner joy and his heart was deeply gladdened. The next day he told [his dream] and asked his ministers, 'What was this?' There was a man of penetration, Fu Yi, who said, 'I have heard that in India there was a man who attained the Way who is called Buddha. He can levitate and is able to fly, and his body radiates light. It was probably his spirit.' Realizing that this was the case, [the emperor] dispatched the emissary Zhang Qian, the Gentleman of the Palace

Guard Qin,[49] the Erudite disciple Wang Zun and others, twelve persons.[50] In the Great Yuezhi [kingdom][51] they copied and brought back the Buddhist *Scripture in Forty-two Sections,* [and it was] placed in the fourteenth stone chamber of the Orchid Pavilion.[52] Then the emperor had a Buddhist monastery erected outside of the Xiyong gate of Luoyang city. He had a court painted on the walls with one thousand chariots and ten thousand cavalrymen encircling it thirteen deep [to welcome the Buddha]. He also had images of the Buddha made for the Qingliang Pavilion of the Southern Palace, and above the Kaiyang Gate. The time came when Emperor Ming knew his life was impermanent, and he prepared his tomb. The tomb was called 'Displaying Temperance' and he also had Buddhist images made for the top of it. While he was alive the country was prosperous and the people were at peace. Distant barbarian tribes emulated righteousness and all came to 'return to virtue.' Those who desired to be his subjects numbered in the hundreds of thousands. This was why he was posthumously styled 'Ming' (Brilliant). From that time on there were Buddhist monasteries in the vicinity of the capital as well in all the counties and districts, and the students [of Buddhism] accordingly multiplied."

The *Jinshu* (Jin History) says, "At the time of Emperor Huan (Huan Xuan 桓玄, 369–404) of the Jin, [the emperor] wanted to cut back the Buddha-Dharma, and so he summoned Dharma Master Yuan (Huiyuan 慧遠, 334–416) of Mt. Lu. The emperor said, 'We have observed recently that the monks and nuns are not sincere in their practice of the precepts, and there have been many transgressions. We wish to weed out [the Saṅgha]. Shall We at once carry out this culling process?' Lord Yuan responded, 'The jade that is extracted from Mt. Kun is covered with dirt and grit. The Li River is rich with gold, yet it is also full of gravel. Your Majesty must respect the Dharma and value its representatives; you must not scorn its representatives or treat the Dharma with contempt.' The Jin emperor then issued a general amnesty."[53]

Emperor Wu of the Xiao Liang (r. 502–549) [wrote the poem] *Hui sanjiao* (Encountering the Three Teachings),[54] which says, "When I was a child I studied the *Zhou Li* (Rites of Zhou). When I was a youth (not yet capped), I thoroughly investigated the six classics. In my middle years I repeatedly examined Daoist books and the 'named and nameless.' In my later years I have opened the Buddhist scrolls and it is like the sun outshining the myriad stars."

SECTION 3
Transmission from India to China (the *Fu fazang zhuan*)
(T. 51. 180A2–180C2)

按花厳経云、「一切諸佛退位、或作菩薩、或作聲聞、或作轉輪聖王、或作魔王、或作國王大臣、居士長者、綵女百官、或作大力鬼神、山神河神、江神海神、主日神主月神、晝神夜神、主火神主水神、一切苗稼神、樹神及諸外道。作種種方便、助我釋迦如来化道[55]衆生。」

按大般若経陀羅尼品云、「尒時舍利子白佛言、『世尊如是般若波羅蜜多、甚深経典、佛般涅槃後、何方興盛。』佛言『舍利子、如是般若波羅蜜多、甚深経[56]典、我涅槃後、従北方至東北方、漸當興盛、彼方多[57]有安住大乘諸苾芻、苾芻[苾芻][58]尼、烏波索迦、烏波斯迦、能依如是甚深般若波羅蜜多、深信樂。』又佛告舍利子、『我涅槃後、後時後分後五百歳、如是甚深般若波羅蜜多、於東北方大作佛事。』」

按付法藏経云、釋迦如来滅度後、法眼付囑摩訶迦葉、迦葉付囑阿難、阿難付囑末田地、末田地付囑商那和脩、商那和脩付囑優波掬多、優波掬多付囑提多迦、提多迦付囑弥遮加、弥遮加付囑佛陀難提、佛陀難提付囑佛陀蜜多、佛陀蜜多付囑脇比丘、　脇比丘[59]付囑富那耶奢、富那耶奢付囑馬鳴、馬鳴付囑毘羅長老、毘羅長老付囑龍樹、龍樹付囑迦那提婆、迦那提婆付囑羅 [目+候]、羅 [目+候]付囑僧迦那提、僧迦那提付囑僧迦耶舍、僧迦耶舍付囑鳩摩羅馱、鳩摩羅馱付囑闍夜多、闍夜多付囑婆脩槃陀、婆脩槃陀付囑摩拏羅、摩拏羅付囑鶴勒那、鶴勒那付囑師子比丘、師子比丘付囑舍那婆斯已。故従中天竺國来向罽賓國王名弥多羅掘、其王不信佛法、毀塔壊寺、殺害衆生、奉事外道末曼尼及弥師訶等。時師子比丘故来化此國王、其王无道、自手持利釼口云[60]、「若是聖人諸師等惣須誡形。」時師子比丘示刑、身流白乳。末曼尼弥師訶等被刑死、如凡人流血灑地。其王發心歸佛、即命師子比丘弟子（師子比丘先付囑舍那婆斯已）入南天竺國、廣行教化、度脱衆生。

王即追尋外道末曼弟子、及弥師訶弟子等、得已於朝堂立架懸首、挙國人射之。罽賓國王告令諸國、若有此法、駈令出國。因師子比丘佛法再興。舍那婆斯付囑優婆掘、優婆掘付囑須婆蜜、須婆蜜付囑僧迦羅叉、僧迦羅叉付囑菩提達摩多羅。西國廿九代、除達摩多羅即廿八代也。

有東都沙門浄覺師、是玉泉神秀禅師弟子、造楞伽師資血脉記一卷、妄引宋朝求那跋陀三藏、為弟一祖。不知根由、或乱後學云、是達摩祖師之師。求那跋陀自是訳経三藏、小乘學人、不是禅師、譯出四卷楞伽経、非開受楞伽経与達摩祖師。達摩祖師[61]自廿八代首尾相傳、承僧迦羅叉、後恵可大師親於嵩山少林寺問達摩祖師承上相傳、付囑自有文記分明、彼浄覺師妄引求那跋陀、稱為弟一祖、深乱學法。[62]

法華経云、「不許親近三藏小乘學人。」求那跋陀三藏譯出四卷楞伽経、名阿跋陀寳楞伽経。魏朝菩提流支三藏譯出十卷、名入楞伽経。唐朝則天時、實叉難陀譯出七卷名入楞伽経。已上盡是譯経三藏、不是禅師、並傳文字教法。達摩祖師宗徒禅法、不将一字教来、黙傳心印。

The *Avataṃsaka-sūtra* says: "All Buddhas abdicate their status [as Buddhas]; some become bodhisattvas, some become śrāvakas, some become Cakravartins, some become demon kings, some become princes of kingdoms or great ministers, or lay elders, or palace women and officials, some become powerful ghosts and spirits, or mountain spirits or stream spirits, or river spirits or sea spirits, or spirits that rule the sun or spirits that rule the moon, or morning spirits or evening spirits, or spirits that rule fire or spirits that rule water, or all the spirits of sprouting and ripe grain, or spirits of the trees, and they even become non-Buddhists. They perform various kinds of expedient means in order to assist our Śākyamuni Tathāgata to convert and guide all sentient beings."[63]

The *Dharāṇī* section of the *Mahāprajñāpāramitā-sūtra* says: "At that time, Śāriputra addressed the Buddha, saying, 'World Honored One, after you enter into nirvāṇa, how will this most profound scripture, the *Prajñāpāramitā,* flourish and prosper?' The Buddha said, 'Śāriputra, after I enter into nirvāṇa, this most profound [scripture], the *Prajñāpāramitā,* will go from the north to the northeast where it will gradually flourish and prosper. In that place will be many *bhikṣus, bhikṣuṇīs, upāsakas,* and *upāsikās* grounded in the Greater Vehicle who will be able to rely on this most profound [scripture], the *Prajñāpāramitā,* and will have deep faith and delight in it.' He further told Śāriputra, 'After I enter into nirvāṇa, in the latter five hundred years of the latter period of [of the Dharma], this most profound [scripture], the *Prajñāpāramitā,* will greatly further Buddhism in the northeast.' "[64]

According to the *Fu fazang jing* (Scripture of the Transmission of the Dharma Treasury),[65] after Śākya [muni] Tathāgata passed into nirvāṇa, the Dharma Eye was entrusted to Mahākaśyapa. Mahākaśyapa entrusted it to Ānanda, Ānanda entrusted it to Madhyāntika, Madhyāntika entrusted it to Śaṇavāsin, Śaṇavāsin entrusted it to Upagupta, Upagupta entrusted it to Dhṛtaka, Dhṛtaka entrusted it to Miccaka, Miccaka entrusted it to Buddhanandi, Buddhanandi entrusted it to Buddhamitra, Buddhamitra entrusted it to Pārśva Bhikṣu,[66] Pārśva Bhikṣu entrusted it to Puṇyayaśas, Puṇyayaśas entrusted it to Aśvaghoṣa, Aśvaghoṣa entrusted it to Kapimala, Kapimala entrusted it to Nāgārjuna, Nāgārjuna entrusted it to Kāṇadeva, Kāṇadeva entrusted it to Rāhula, Rāhula entrusted it to Saṇghānandi, Saṇghānandi entrusted it to Saṇghāyaśas, Saṇghāyaśas entrusted it to Kumārata, Kumārata entrusted it to Jayata, Jayata entrusted it to Vasubandhu, Vasubandhu entrusted it to Manora, Manora entrusted it to Haklena[yaśa], Haklena[yaśa] entrusted it to Siṁha Bhikṣu, Siṁha Bhikṣu entrusted it to Śaṇavāsa.

When Siṁha Bhikṣu had transmitted [the Dharma] to Śaṇavāsa, then he went from Central India to Kashmir. The king there was named Mihirakula.[67] This king did not believe in the Buddha-Dharma. He destroyed stūpas, demolished monasteries and slaughtered sentient beings, and honored the two heretics Momanni (Mani) and Mishihe (Messiah, i.e., Jesus).[68] At that time Siṁha Bhikṣu purposely came to convert this kingdom, and the pathless king with his own hands took up a sharp double-edged sword and swore an oath: "If you are a Holy One, the [other] masters must suffer punishment." Siṁha Bhikṣu then manifested a form whereby his body bled white milk. Momanni and Mishihe were executed, and as with ordinary men their blood spattered the ground. The king was inspired to take refuge in the Buddha, and he ordered the disciple of Siṁha Bhikṣu (the Dharma had already been transmitted to Śaṇavāsa) to enter South India to preach extensively and liberate beings.

The king then sought out and captured the disciples of the heretics Moman and Mishihe. When he had captured them, he set up stocks at court and suspended them by their necks, and the people of the entire country shot arrows at them. The king of Kashmir ordered that if there were [followers] of these creeds in any of the kingdoms, they should be driven from the kingdom. Owing to Siṁha Bhikṣu, the Buddha-Dharma flourished once again. Śaṇavāsa entrusted it to Upagupta, Upagupta entrusted it to Śubhamitra, Śubhamitra entrusted it to Saṅgharakṣa, Saṅgharakṣa entrusted it to Bodhidharmatrāta.[69] Thus, in the Western Kingdoms there were twenty-nine generations; excepting Dharmatrāta, there were twenty-eight generations.

There was a śramaṇa of the Eastern Capital (Luoyang), Master Jingjue, who was the disciple of Chan Master Shenxiu of Yuquan [monastery] and compiled the *Lengqie shizi xuemo ji* (Record of the Lineage of the Masters and Disciples of the *Laṅkāvatāra-sūtra]*) in one fascicle. He falsely alleged that the Trepiṭaka[70] Guṇabhadra was the first patriarch. I do not know his source, but he deluded and confused later students by saying [Guṇabhadra] was the Patriarchal Master Dharma's (i.e., Bodhidharma's) master. Guṇabhadra was from the first a scripture-translating Trepiṭaka, a student of the Lesser Vehicle, not a Chan Master. He translated the *Laṇkā-sūtra* in four fascicles, but he did not give an explanation of the *Laṇkā-sūtra* or transmit it to the Patriarchal Master Dharma. The Patriarchal Master Dharma, from the continuous line of direct transmission of the twenty-eight generations, inherited it from Saṅgharakṣa. Later at the Shaolin Monastery on Mt. Songgao, Great Master Huike personally asked Patriarchal Master Dharma about the succession of the direct transmission, and because there is this record [the matter] is clear. When this Master Jingjue falsely alleged that Guṇabhadra was the first patriarch he profoundly confused the study of the Dharma.

The *Lotus Sūtra* says: "Don't allow intimacy with Trepiṭakas, students of the Lesser Vehicle."[71] Trepiṭaka Guṇabhadra translated the *Laṇkā-sūtra* in four fascicles and called it the *Abatoubao Lenqie jing*.[72] In the Wei dynasty, Trepiṭaka Bodhiruci translated it in ten fascicles and called it the *Ru Lengqie jing*.[73] In the Tang dynasty, during the time of [Empress Wu] Zetian, Śikṣānanda translated the *Lengqie jing* in seven fascicles.[74] All of the above were translator-Trepiṭakas and not Chan masters. All of them transmitted the teachings of the written word. Patriarchal Master Dharma was in the lineage of the Chan Dharma (*zongtu Chanfa*). He did not bring a single word, [just] silently transmitted the mind-seal.

SECTION 4
The First Patriarch, Bodhidharmatrāta
(T. 51. 180C3–181A18)

梁朝弟一祖

菩提達摩多羅禅師者、即南天竺國王弟三子、幼而出家、早稟師氏、於言下悟。闡化南天、大作佛事。

是時觀見漢地衆生有大禅[75]性、乃遣弟子佛陀耶舎二人、往秦地説頓悟教法。秦中大德乍聞狐疑、都无信受、被擯出遂於盧山東林寺。時有法師遠公、問曰、「大德将何教来、乃被擯也？」於是二婆羅門申手告遠公曰、「手作拳、拳作手、是事疾否?」遠公答曰、「甚疾。」二婆羅門言、「此未為疾、煩悩即菩提即為疾。」遠公深達、方知菩提煩悩夲不異、即問曰、「此法彼國復従誰學?」二婆羅問[76]曰、「我師達摩多羅也。」遠公既深信已。還譯出禅門経一卷、具明大小乗禅法。西國所傳法者、亦具引禅経序上。二婆羅門譯経畢、同日滅度、葬于盧山、塔廟見在。

達摩多羅聞二弟子漢地弘化、無人信受、乃泛海而来至梁朝。武帝出城躬迎、昇殿問和上曰、「従彼國、将何教法来化衆生？」達摩大師答、「不将一字教来。」帝又問、「朕造寺度人、写経鑄像、有何功德？」大師答曰、「並无功德。」答曰、「此乃有為之善、非真實功徳。」武帝凡情不曉、乃辭出國。北望有大乗気。大師来至魏朝、居嵩高山、接引群品六年、學如雲奔如雨、衆如稻麻竹葦、唯可大師得其髓。

其時魏有菩提流支三藏光統律師於食中著毒餉。大師食訖、索盤吐[虫+也][77]一斗。又食著毒再餉、大師取食訖、於大槃石上座、毒出石裂。前後六度毒。大師告諸弟子、「我来本為傳法、今既得人、久住何益？」遂傳一領袈裟以為法信。語恵可、「我縁此毒、汝亦不免此難。至第六代、傳法者命如懸絲。」言畢遂因毒而終。毎常自言、「我年一百五十歳　。」實不知年幾也。大師云、「唐國有三人得我法、一人得我髄、一人得我骨、一人得我肉。得我髄者恵可、得我骨者道育、得我肉者尼惣持也。」　葬于洛州熊耳山。

時魏聘國使宋雲、於窓嶺逢大師、手提履一隻。雲問、「大師何處去？」答、「我歸夲國、汝國[78]王今日亡。」雲即書記之。雲又問大師、「大師去後、佛法付嘱誰人?」答、「我去後四十年、有一漢道人可是也。」

宋雲歸朝、舊帝果崩、新帝已立。雲告諸朝臣說、「大師手提一隻履、歸西國、言『汝舊國王亡。』實如所言。」諸朝臣不信、遂發大師墓、唯有履一隻。

蕭梁武帝造碑文：「西國弟子般若蜜多羅、唐國三人、道育、尼惣持等、唯恵可承衣得法。」[79]

LIANG DYNASTY, THE FIRST PATRIARCH

Chan Master Bodhidharmatrāta[80] was the third son of a South Indian king. He became a monk while still young, and as soon as he received instruction from his master he was immediately awakened. He preached in South India and greatly furthered Buddhism.

At a certain point, he ascertained that the beings of the land of the Han (China) were possessed of the Great Chan nature. So he dispatched two of his disciples, Buddha and Yaśas, to go to the land of the Qin[81] and explain the teaching of immediate awakening. When the worthies of the Qin first heard, they were doubtful and none would believe. [The disciples] were cast out and driven to Donglin Monastery on Mt. Lu. At that time, Dharma Master Lord Yuan (Huiyuan) was there, and he asked them, "Worthies, what Dharma have you brought, that you were thus cast out?" Thereupon, the two Brahmins put out their hands and said to Lord Yuan, "The hand changes to a fist and the fist changes to a hand. Does this happen quickly or not?" Lord Yuan responded, "Very quickly." The two Brahmins said, "This is not quick. Defilement is none other than bodhi. *This* is quick."[82] Lord Yuan was deeply impressed, and thereupon realized that bodhi and defilement are one and the same. Then he asked, "In this other country, from whom did you learn this Dharma?" The two Brahmins replied, "From our teacher Dharmatrāta." Lord Yuan [was moved to] a faith profound indeed.

[The two disciples] translated the *Chanmen jing* (Scripture of the Chan Teachings)[83] in one fascicle, which completely elucidates the Greater and Lesser Vehicles and the Chan Dharma. Those who transmitted the Dharma in the Western Kingdoms are also all included in the preface to the *Chan Scripture*.[84] When the two Brahmins had completed the translation, they both passed into extinction on the same day and were buried on Mt. Lu, where their stūpa even now remains.

When Dharmatrāta heard that his two disciples had gone to the land of Han to spread the Dharma but none would believe, he sailed across the sea and reached the Liang court. Emperor Wu came out of the city to welcome him personally. He had [Bodhidharma] ascend to the audience hall and asked the Venerable, "What teachings to convert beings have you brought from the other country?" Great Master Dharma replied, "I have not brought a single word." The emperor asked, "What merit have We gained in having monasteries built and people saved, scriptures copied and statues cast?" The Great Master responded, "No merit whatsoever." He replied [further], "This is contrived (*saṃskṛta*) goodness, not true merit."

Emperor Wu was a man of ordinary nature and did not understand. And so [Bodhidharma] left that country. Northward there was an atmosphere [more favorable] to the Great Vehicle. He came to the Wei, where he lived at Mt. Songgao[85] and received people of all degrees for instruction for six years; [86] students [gathered] like hastening clouds and like torrents of rain, the crowds [were thick as] rice, hemp, bamboo, or reeds. But only the Great Master Ke obtained the marrow [of Bodhidharma's teachings].

Now it happened that in the Wei the Trepiṭaka Bodhiruci and the Vinaya Master Guangtong put poison in some food which they offered [to Bodhidharma].[87] When the Great Master had finished eating he asked for a dish and vomited up a pint of snakes. Once again they offered him poisoned food. When the Great Master had taken the food and eaten it, he sat atop a massive boulder, and when the poison came out the boulder cracked.[88] Altogether they tried to poison him six times. The Great Master informed his disciples, "I originally came in order to pass on the Dharma. Now that I've gotten someone, what's the good of lingering?" Then he transmitted a *kāṣāya* robe as a verification of the Dharma transmission. He said to Huike, "My destiny is this poison; you also will not escape these tribulations. In the sixth generation, the life of the Dharma heir will be as a dangling thread."[89] He finished speaking and immediately died of the poison.[90] He himself used to say, "I am one hundred and fifty years old," but it was not known how old he actually was.

The Great Master said, "In the land of the Tang[91] there are three persons who have gotten my Dharma; one has gotten my marrow, one has gotten my bones, and one has gotten my flesh. The one who got my marrow is Huike, the one who got my bones is Daoyu, and the one who got my flesh is the nun Zongchi."[92] He was buried on Mt. Xionger in the Luo region.[93]

At that time, the Wei emissary Song Yun met the Great Master in the Pamirs. The Great Master was carrying one shoe in his hand.[94] Yun asked, "Great Master, where are you going?" [Bodhidharma] replied, "I am returning to my native country. Your king died today." Yun recorded this. Yun further asked the Great Master, "Great Master, once you are gone, to whom has the Buddha-Dharma been entrusted?" [Bodhidharma] replied, "Forty years after I've gone there will be a Chinese man of the Way, you can count on it."[95]

When Song Yun returned to court, the old emperor had [indeed] died and the new emperor was already established. Yun told the court officials, "The Great Master was carrying a single shoe, returning home to the Western Kingdoms. He said, 'The old king of your country has died,' and it is as he said." The court officials would not believe him, so they opened the Great Master's tomb—and there was only a single shoe.

Emperor Wu of the Xiao Liang wrote a memorial inscription, [which reads]: "His disciple in the Western Kingdoms was Prajñāmitara.[96] In the Tang Kingdom there are three persons: Daoyu, the nun Zongchi, and Huike, who alone received the robe and got the Dharma."[97]

SECTION 5

The Second Patriarch, Huike (T. 51. 181A19–181B18)

北齊朝弟二祖

惠可禅師、俗姓姬、武牢人也。時年四十、奉事大師六年。先名神光。初事大師夜、於大師前立、其夜大雪、至腰不移。大師曰、「夫求法者不貧軀命。」遂截一臂、乃流白乳。大師黙傳心契、付袈裟一領。

大師云、「我縁此毒、汝亦不免、善自保愛。」可大師問、「和上此法夲國承上所傳、囑付法者、請為再説。」「具如禅経序上説。」又問、「大師西國、誰人承後、亦傳信袈裟否?」大師答、「西國人信敬无有矯詐。承後者是般若波羅蜜多羅、承後不傳衣。唐國衆生有大乘性。詐言得道得果、遂傳袈裟以為法信。譬如轉輪王子灌其頂者、得七真寶、紹隆王位、得其衣者以表法正相承。」

可大師得付囑以後四十年、隠[山+皃][98]山洛相二州、後接引群品、道俗歸依不可稱數。経廿年開化時有難起、又被菩提流支三蔵光統律師徒[人+黨]欲損可大師。大師付囑僧璨、法已入司空山隠。可大師後佯狂於四衢城市説法、人衆甚多。菩提流支徒黨告可大師云妖異。奏勅令所司推問可大師、大師[99]答、「承實妖。」所司知衆疾、令可大師審。大師確答、「我實妖。」勅令城安縣令翟沖侃[100]、依法處刑。可大師告衆人曰、「我法至弟四祖、化為名相。」語已悲涙、遂示形身流白乳、肉色如常。所司奏帝、聞悔過、此真菩薩。挙朝發心、佛法再興。

大師時年一百七歳、其墓[101]葬在相州城安縣子陌河北五里東柳構、去墓一百步、西南十五里、吳兒曹口是。楞伽業都故事具載。弟子承後傳衣得法僧璨、釋後法琳[102]造碑文。[103]

NORTHERN QI DYNASTY, THE SECOND PATRIARCH[104]

Chan Master Huike had the lay surname Ji, and he was from Wulao.[105] When he was forty, he had served the Great Master [Bodhidharma] for six years. He had previously been called Shenguang.[106] When he first came [with the intention] to serve the Great Master, he stood before the Great Master in the night. That night there was a heavy snowfall and the snow rose up to [Huike's] waist, but he did not stir. The Great Master said, "He who would seek the Dharma must spare neither life nor limb." [Huike] then chopped off one of his arms, whereupon the blood flowed out as white milk.[107] The Great Master then silently transmitted the mind-pledge, and passed on to him a *kāṣāya* robe.

The Great Master said, "My destiny is this poison. You also will not escape [persecution], take good care of yourself. Great Master Ke asked, "Venerable, about this Dharma of yours that has been passed down through the generations in your native country, and those to whom the Dharma was entrusted—please explain it again." [Bodhidharma] replied, "All the particulars are as explained in the preface to the *Chan Scripture*." [Huike] further questioned the Great Master, "In the Western Kingdoms, to whom did you pass the succession, and did you also transmit the *kāṣāya* robe of verification to him, or not?" The Great Master replied, "The people of the Western Kingdoms are devout, they are not devious. My successor[108] there is Prajñāpāramitāra, and I have passed the succession to him without transmitting the robe. In the Tang Kingdom beings have the Great Vehicle nature, [yet there are some who] falsely claim to have obtained the Way and the fruit [of enlightenment], and so I have transmitted the robe for the sake of verification of the teachings.[109] It is like the consecration of the son of a Cakravartin (Wheel-Turning King), when he obtains the seven jewels and inherits his eminent position as King. Possession of the robe represents the true inheritance of the Dharma."[110]

After Great Master Ke obtained succession, for forty years he secluded himself at Mt. Huan and in the Luo and Xiang regions.[111] After that he received people of all degrees for instruction, and the lay and ordained who took refuge were innumerable. When he had been teaching for twenty years difficulties arose, again caused by the clique of the followers of the Trepiṭaka Bodhiruci[112] and Vinaya Master Guangtong, who wanted to harm Great Master Ke. When the Great Master had entrusted the Dharma to Sengcan, [Sengcan] went into seclusion at Mt. Sikong.[113] Great Master Ke then feigned madness, preaching the Dharma at the crossroads of the city marketplace.[114] People flocked to him in prodigious numbers. The clique of Bodhiruci's followers declared that Great Master Ke was uncanny and strange. They petitioned an imperial official, who interrogated [Huike]. Great Master Ke responded, "I confess that I truly am uncanny." The official knew that many were jealous, and he ordered that Great Master Ke be given an official hearing. The Great Master incontestably said, "I truly am uncanny." An imperial edict went to the District Magistrate of Cheng'an, Zhai Chongkan,[115] that [Huike] was to be executed in accordance with the law. Great Master Ke told the assembled crowd, "When my Dharma reaches the fourth patriarch it will become only nominal."[116] When he had spoken, he wept grievously and then manifested a form whereby his body bled white milk, though the color of his flesh was as usual. The official memorialized the emperor. When the emperor heard, he repented his error [and said], "This was a true bodhisattva." Everyone at court embarked upon the Way, and the Buddha-Dharma flourished once again.

At that time the Great Master was one hundred and seven.[117] His tomb was built in Cheng'an district in the Xiang region, five *li* north of the Zimou river at Dongliu canal. One hundred paces beyond the tomb and fifteen *li* southwest there is Wu'er Caokou. The *Lengqie Yedu gushi* records this.[118] His disciple, Sengcan, who received transmission of the robe and got the Dharma, succeeded him; later, Shi Falin wrote a memorial inscription.[119]

SECTION 6

The Third Patriarch, Sengcan (T. 51. 181B19–181C8)

随朝弟三祖

璨禅師、不知何處人。初遇可大師、璨示見大風疾、於衆中見。大師問、「從何處来、今有何事？」僧璨對曰、「故投和上。」可大師語曰、「汝大風患人、見我何益？」璨對曰、「身雖有患、患人心与和上心無有別處。」可大師知璨是非常人、便付法嘱[120]及信袈裟与僧璨。可大師曰、「汝善自保愛、吾有難、汝須避之。」璨大師亦佯狂市肆、後隠舒州司空山。

遭周武帝滅佛法、隠 [山+皃] 公山十餘年。此山比多足猛獸常損居人、自璨大師至、並移出境。

付法並袈裟与道信後、時有[山+皃]禅師月禅師定禅師巌禅師、来至璨大師所云、「達摩祖師付嘱後、此璨公真神璨也、定惠齊用、深不思議也。」

璨大師遂共諸禅師往隠羅浮山。三年後至大會齋、出告衆人曰、「吾今欲食。」諸弟子奉飲食。大師食畢、告衆人曰、「諸人歎言坐終為奇、唯吾生死自由。」語已[121] 一手攀會中樹枝掩[122] 然立化。亦不知年幾。塔廟在[山+皃] 山寺側。

弟子甚多、唯道信大師傳衣得法承後。薛道衡撰碑文。[123]

SUI DYNASTY, THE THIRD PATRIARCH[124]

Chan Master Can's place of origin is unknown. When he first encountered Great Master Ke, Can appeared to have palsy, and they met in the midst of a crowd. Great Master Ke asked, "Where are you from? Why are you here?" Sengcan replied, "Because I want to serve the Venerable." Great

Master Ke said, "For you, a person afflicted with palsy, what good is it to meet with me?" Can replied, "Although my body is afflicted, between the mind of the afflicted and the Venerable's mind, there is not any difference."[125] Great Master Ke realized that Can was no ordinary man and therefore entrusted the Dharma and the *kāṣāya* robe of verification to Sengcan. Great Master Ke said, "You must protect yourself well. I am involved in difficulties, but you must escape them." Great Master Can also feigned madness in the marketplace, and later he hid at Mt. Sikong in the Shu region.[126]

Evil times came when Emperor Wu of the Zhou was destroying the Buddha-Dharma, and [Sengcan] hid on Mt. Huangong[127] for over a decade. The mountain had been quite full of fierce wild animals who often preyed upon the people living there, but once Great Master Can arrived they all took themselves off to another area.

After [Sengcan] had entrusted the Dharma and the robe to Daoxin, the Chan Masters Huan, Yue, Ding, and Yan came to Great Master Can's place and said, "[Of all those] since Patriarchal Master [Bodhi]dharma passed on the Dharma, this Lord Can is a true spirit-gem. In him the simultaneous functioning of samādhi and prajñā are utterly inconceivable."[128]

Great Master Can subsequently went with the Chan masters to live in seclusion at Mt. Loufu.[129] After three years he went a Great Assembly vegetarian alms feast and came out and told the crowd, "I now wish to eat." His disciples served him food and drink. When the Great Master finished eating he told the crowd, "People exclaim that dying in a seated posture is a marvel, but I alone am free in birth and death." When he finished speaking, with one hand he grasped the branch of a tree that stood in the midst of the assembly and died instantly in a standing posture.[130] His age was also unknown. His stūpa is beside Mt. Huan temple.[131]

His disciples were very numerous but only Daoxin inherited the robe and got the Dharma, and was the successor. Xue Daoheng composed a memorial inscription.[132]

SECTION 7

The Fourth Patriarch, Daoxin (T. 51. 181C9–182A10)

唐朝弟四祖

信禅師、俗姓司馬、河内人也。少小出家、承事璨大師。璨大師知為特器、晝夜常坐不臥、六十餘年、脇不至席。神威奇特、目常不視、若欲視人、見者驚悚。

信大師於是大業年、遥見吉州、狂賊圍城百日已上、泉井枯涸。大師入城勧誘道俗、令行般若波羅蜜。狂賊自退、城中泉井再汎、學道者衆。

信大師遥見蘄州黄梅、破頭山有紫雲盖。信大師遂居此山、後改為雙峯山。

貞觀十七年、文武皇帝勅使於雙峯山、請信禅師入内。信禅師辞老不去。勅使廻見帝奏云、「信禅師辞老不来。」勅又遣再請。使至信禅師處、使云、「奉勅遣請禅師。」禅師苦辞老不去。語使云、「若欲得我頭任斬将、我終不去。」使廻見帝奏云、「須頭任斬将去、心終不去。」勅又遣使封刀来取信禅師頭。勅云、「莫損和上。使至和上處云、奉勅取和上頭、禅師去不去？」和上云、「我終不去。」使云、「奉勅云、若禅師不来、斬頭将来。」信大師引頭云[133]、「[石 + 斤] 取。」使返刀乙項。信大師唱言、「何為不[石 + 斤]、更待何時！」使云、「奉勅不許損和上。」信禅師大笑曰、「教汝知有人處。」

後時信大師大作佛事、黄開法門、接引群品。四方龍像造盡受歸依。経卅餘年、唯弘忍事之得意。付法及袈裟与弘忍訖、命弟子元一師、「与吾山側造龍龕一所、即須早成。」後問、「龍龕成否。」元一師答、「功畢。」

永徽二年閏九月廿四日、大師素無痾疾、奄然坐化。大師時年七十有二。葬後周年、石戸无故自開、大師容貌瑞厳、无改常日。弘忍等重奉神儀不勝感慕。乃就尊容加以漆布、自此已後更不敢閇。

弟子甚多、唯有弘忍傳衣得法後承[134]、中書令仕正倫撰碑文。[135]

TANG DYNASTY, THE FOURTH PATRIARCH[136]

Chan Master Xin's lay surname was Sima, and he was from east of the Yellow River.[137] He became a renunciant when very young and entered into the service of Great Master Can. Great Master Can knew that he was especially talented. He sat day and night without lying down; for over sixty years his sides never touched a mat. He had an exceptional spiritual presence. His eyes usually did not gaze out, [but] when he wanted to look at someone, that person would cower in fear.

In this manner, in the year Daye (605) Great Master Xin saw from afar [something that was taking place] in the Ji region. Bandits had been besieging a town for over a hundred days, and the spring-fed well had completely dried up. The Great Master entered the city and gave counsel and guidance to both lay and ordained. He had them carry out the practice of [chanting] the *Prajñāpārami[tā-sūtra].* The bandits withdrew of their own volition, and the town spring-fed well began to flow again. There were many who [were inspired to] study the Way.[138]

[Another time] Great Master Xin saw from afar that at Mt. Potou in Huangmei in the Qi region there was a canopy of purple clouds.[139] Great Master Xin thereupon went to live on this mountain, which was later renamed Mt. Shuangfeng.

In the seventeenth year of the Zhenguan era (643), Emperor Wenwu sent a messenger to Mt. Shuangfeng to invite Chan Master Xin to enter the imperial presence. Chan Master Xin pleaded old age and did not go. The messenger returned to the emperor and delivered the message, "Chan Master Xin pleads old age and will not come." The messenger was sent again, to repeat the invitation. He went to Chan Master Xin's place and said, "The emperor sends me to invite the Chan Master." The Chan Master earnestly pleaded old age and would not go, telling the messenger, "If you want my head you are welcome to behead me and take it, but I absolutely will not go." The messenger returned to the emperor and delivered the message, "He would allow his head to be cut off and taken, but his mind absolutely will not go." The emperor again sent off the messenger, [this time] wearing a sword with which to get Chan Master Xin's head. He ordered him, "Do not harm the Venerable." The messenger arrived at the Venerable's place and said, "The emperor orders me to get the Venerable's head. Will the Chan Master go or not?" The Venerable replied, "I absolutely will not go." The messenger said, "The emperor orders that if the Chan Master will not come, I am to cut off his head and bring it." Great Master Xin extended his head and said, "Chop it and take it." The messenger turned the blade and bent [Daoxin's] neck. Great Master Xin sang out, "Why don't you chop, how much longer must I wait?" The messenger replied, "The emperor ordered me not to harm the Venerable." Chan Master Xin gave a great laugh and said, "I've taught you to recognize someone who stays put."[140]

Great Master Xin thereafter greatly furthered Buddhism, extensively opened the Dharma-gates, and received people of all degrees for instruction. All the *hastināga*[141] of the four directions came to receive his teachings and take refuge. Over thirty years passed and only Hongren had served him and grasped his meaning, When [Daoxin] had transferred the Dharma and the *kāṣāya* robe to Hongren, he ordered his disciple Master Yuanyi, "Build a reliquary niche on the side of my mountain—and it must be done soon."[142] A while later he asked, "Is the reliquary niche completed or not?" Yuanyi replied, "It has been accomplished."

In the second year of the Yonghui era (651), on the twenty-fourth day of the intercalary ninth month, the Great Master, without ever having suffered from illness, died instantly in a seated posture. He was at that time seventy-two years old. After he had been entombed for a year, the stone door opened of itself for no reason. The Great Master's appearance was as composed and imposing as ever. Hongren and the others repeatedly paid obeisance to his remains[143] and they could not master their feelings of devotion. Subsequently, lacquered cloth was applied to the honored countenance. From that time forth, no one dared shut [the tomb door].

His disciples were very numerous, but only Hongren inherited the robe and got the Dharma, and was the successor. The Secretariat-Director Du Zhenglun composed a memorial inscription.[144]

SECTION 8

The Fifth Patriarch, Hongren (T. 51. 182A11–182B5)

唐朝第五祖

弘忍禅師、俗姓周、黄梅人也。七歳事信大師信[145]、年十三入道披衣。其性木訥沉厚、同學軽戲黙然无對。常勤作務、以禮下人。晝則混迹驅給、夜便坐攝至曉、未常懈倦。卅年不離信大師左右。身長八尺、容貌与常人絶殊。

得付法居馮茂山。在雙峯山東相去不遥。時人号為東山法門、即馮茂山也、非嵩山是也。時有狂賊可達寒奴戮等、圍繞州城数匝、无有路人、飛鳥不通。大師遥見来彼城、群賊退散、遞相言、「无量金剛、執杵趁我、怒目切齒。我遂奔散。」忍大師却歸馮茂山。

顕慶五年、大帝勅使黄梅馮茂山、請忍大師。大師不赴所請。又勅使再請不来。賜衣薬就馮茂山供養。後四十餘年、接引道俗、四方龍像、歸依奔湊。大師付囑恵能法及袈裟。

後至咸亨五年、命弟子玄賾師、「与吾起塔。」至二月十四日、問、「塔成否？」答「功畢。」大師云、「不可同佛、二月十五日入般涅槃。」又云、「吾一生教人无数、除恵能餘有十尒。神秀師、智詵師、智德師、玄賾師、老安師、法如師、恵蔵師、玄約師、劉主薄。雖不離吾左右、汝各一方師也。」後至上元二年二月十一日、奄然坐化、忍大師時年七十四也。

弟子[146]唯恵能傳衣得法承後。學士閭丘均撰碑文。[147]

TANG DYNASTY, THE FIFTH PATRIARCH[148]

Chan Master Hongren's lay surname was Zhou, and he was from Huangmei. At the age of seven he went to serve Master Xin, and at the age of thirteen he entered upon the Way and donned robes. He was by nature taciturn and imperturbable, and when his fellow students joked about, he remained silently unresponsive. He was always diligent in performing duties,[149] and toward others conducted himself with decorous humility. By day he secretly did things for others and by night he practiced sitting meditation until dawn; never was he negligent.[150] For thirty years he never left Master Xin. He was eight *chi*[151] tall, and his appearance was completely unlike that of ordinary people.

When he got the transmission of the Dharma he settled on Mt. Pingmao. It was not far east of Mt. Shuangfeng. What people of the time called "the East Mountain School" referred to Mt. Pingmao, not Mt. Song.[152] There was an occasion when the wild bandit Ke Dahan and his minions had heavily besieged a town in the region of Rao.[153] There was no way in—not even birds on the wing could get through. The Great Master saw this from afar and came to that town. The bandits fled in confusion, calling back and forth to one another, "Innumerable Vajrapāni carrying cudgels are stomping after us with fierce looks and gnashing teeth, so let us flee quickly." Great Master Ren then went back to Mt. Pingmao.[154]

In the fifth year of the Xianqing era (660), the Great Emperor [Gaozong] sent a messenger to Mt. Pingmao in Huangmei to invite Great Master Ren, but the Great Master did not attend [the audience] to which he had been invited. Again [the emperor] sent a messenger to invite him, but he did not come. [The emperor] then sent a gift of clothing and medicine as offerings to Mt. Pingmao [monastery].[155] Afterward, for over forty years,[156] [Hongren] received lay and ordained for instruction, and the *hastināga* of the four directions came to take refuge, hastening and gathering [like clouds]. The Great Master entrusted Huineng with the Dharma and the *kāṣāya* robe.

Later, in the fifth year of the Xianheng era, he ordered his disciple Master Xuanze, "Erect a stūpa for me." On the fourteenth day of the second month, he asked, "Is the stūpa done or not?" [Xuanze] replied, "It is completed." The Great Master said, "I can't very well enter *parinirvāṇa* on the fifteenth day of the second month, the same as the Buddha." He continued, "The people I have taught in the course of my life are countless, but besides Huineng there are just these ten: Master Shenxiu, Master Zhishen, Master Zhide, Master Xuanze, Master Laoan, Master Faru, Master Huizang, Master Xuanyue, and Liu Zhubu.[157] Although you never left me, each of you is but one aspect of a Master."[158] Later, on the eleventh day of the second month of the second year of the Shangyuan era (675), he died instantly in a seated posture. At the time, Great Master Ren was seventy-four years old.[159]

His disciples [were very numerous] but only Huineng inherited the robe and got the Dharma, and was the successor.[160] The scholar Lu Qiujun composed a memorial inscription.[161]

SECTION 9

The Sixth Patriarch, Huineng, Part 1 (T. 51. 182B6–182C16)

唐朝第六祖

韶州漕溪能禅師、俗姓慮、范陽人也。随父宦嶺外、居新州。年廿二、来至馮茂山、礼忍大師。初見大師、問、「汝従何来？」答、「従新州来、唯求作佛。」忍大師曰、「汝新州是 [犬+巢] 獠、若為作佛？」惠能答曰、「[犬+巢] 獠佛性与和上佛性豈異別否?」大師深知其能、再欲共語、為衆人在左右、令能隨衆。

踏碓八箇月碓聲相似不異。忍大師就碓上密說、直了見性。於夜間潛喚入房、三日三夜共語了、付嘱法及袈裟、「汝為此世界大師、即令急去。」大師自送、過九江驛看渡大江已、却迴歸。諸門徒並不知付法及袈裟与惠能。去三日、大師告諸門徒、「汝等散去、吾此間無有佛法、佛法流過嶺南。」衆人咸驚、遞相問[162]、「嶺南有誰？」潞州法如師對曰、「惠能在彼。」衆皆奔湊。

衆中有一四品官将軍、捨官入道、字惠明。久在大師左右、不能契悟。聞大師此言、即當曉夜倍逞奔趁、至大庚嶺上見能禅師。怕急、恐性命不存、乃将所傳衣[163]袈裟、過与惠明禅師。惠明禅師曰、「我本不為袈裟来。忍大師発遣之日、有何言教？願為我說。」能禅師具說心法直了見性。惠明師[164]聞法已、合掌頂礼。発遣能禅師、「急過嶺去、在後大有人来相趁。」其惠明禅師後居蒙山、所出弟子亦只看浄。

能禅師至韶州漕溪、四十餘年開化、道俗雲奔。後至景雲二年、命弟子玄楷、令新州龍山造塔。至先天元年、問、「塔[165]成否？」答、「已成。」其年九月、從漕溪却歸至新州。漕溪僧玄楷、智海等問、「和上已後、誰人得法承後、傳信袈裟？」和上答、「莫汝[166]問。已後難起極盛。我縁此袈裟、幾度合失身命。在信大師處三被度[167]偷、在忍忍[168]大師處三度被偸、乃至吾處六度被偸。竟无人偸得、我此袈裟、女子将去也。更莫問我。汝若欲知得我法者、我滅度後廿年外、竪我宗旨者即是得法人也。」

至先天二年、忽告門徒、「吾當大行矣。」八月三日夜、奄然坐化。大師春秋七十有六。漕溪溝澗斷流、泉池枯竭、日月無光、林木変白、異香氳氳、三日不絶。其年於新州國忌寺、迎和上神座、至十一月、葬於漕溪。

太常寺承韋據造碑文。至開元七年被人磨改別造碑。近代報脩侍郎宋鼎撰碑文。[169]

TANG DYNASTY, THE SIXTH PATRIARCH[170]

The lay surname of Chan Master Neng of Caoqi in Shaozhou was Lu, and he was from Fanyang.[171] After his father was posted to Lingwai, he lived in Xinzhou.[172] When he was twenty-two, he came to Mt. Pingmao to pay his respects to Great Master Ren. At their first meeting the Great Master asked, "Where did you come from?" [Huineng] replied, "I have come from Xinzhou. I want nothing else but to become a Buddha." Great Master Ren said, "You [people] from Xinzhou are Lao barbarians,[173] why would you become a Buddha?" Huineng replied, "Is there any difference between the Buddha-nature of a Lao barbarian and the Venerable's Buddha-nature?" The Great Master was deeply impressed by his ability. He wished to speak with him again, but because there were many people with him, he ordered Neng to follow after the crowd.

For eight months [Huineng] worked at treading the rice-hulling pestle, and the sounds of the pestle were consistent and unvarying. Great Master Ren went up to the pestle and instructed him secretly, and he directly saw his own nature.[174] In the night he was covertly summoned to [Hongren's] room, and when they had spoken together for three days and three nights, [Hongren] entrusted the Dharma and *kāṣāya* robe to him [and said], "You are the Great Master of this world, and thus I command you to depart quickly." The Great Master personally saw him off as far as Jiujiang station, and watched him cross the Great River (the Yangzi) before turning around and going home. None of the disciples knew that [Hongren] had passed the Dharma and robe to Huineng. After three days the Great Master announced to the disciples, "You can all disperse, there's no Buddha-Dharma in my vicinity, the Buddha-Dharma has flowed to Lingnan." The crowd was surprised, and asked each other, "Who is there in Lingnan?" Master Faru of Luzhou[175] replied, "Huineng is there." The crowd all hastened off [in pursuit].

Among the crowd there was one who had been a general of the fourth rank who had forsaken office to enter the Way, whose cognomen was Huiming.[176] He had long been with Great Master [Hongren], but had been unable to verify awakening. No sooner had he heard Great Master Ren's words, than by double-marches day and night he hastened in pursuit [of Huineng]. Atop Mt. Dayu[177] he met up with Chan Master Neng, who was terrified and feared for his life. So he took the *kāṣāya* robe [verifying] transmission of the Dharma and passed it over to Chan Master Huiming. Chan Master Huiming said, "It is not for the sake of the *kāṣāya* robe that I have come. On the day Great Master Ren sent you off, what words of teaching [did he give you]? I beg you to explain it for me." Chan Master Neng fully explained the mind-Dharma of directly realizing the nature. When Master Huiming had heard the Dharma, he put his palms together and made obeisance. He then urged Chan Master Neng, [saying] "Cross the mountains quickly, there are many people coming after you."[178] This Chan Master Huiming later settled on Mt. Meng,[179] but the disciples that came out of there also only "viewed purity."[180]

Chan Master Neng reached Caoqi in Shaozhou. He taught for over forty years, and the ordained and laity came hastening like clouds. Later, in the second year of the Jingyun era (711), he ordered his disciple Xuanjie to build a stūpa on Mt. Long in Xinzhou. In the first year of the Xiantian era (712), he asked "Is the stūpa was completed or not?" [Xuanjie] replied, "It is done." In the ninth month of that year, he left Caoqi and went back to Xinzhou.[181] The Caoqi monks Xuanjie, Zhihai,[182] and the others asked,

"After you, Venerable, who will get the Dharma succession and receive transmission of the *kāṣāya* robe of verification?" The Venerable replied, "Do not ask. After this, hardships will arise in great profusion. How often have we faced death on account of this *kāṣāya* robe? At Great Master Xin's place it was stolen three times, at Great Master Ren's place it was stolen three times, and now at my place it has been stolen six times. At last no one will steal this *kāṣāya* robe of mine, for a woman has taken it away. So don't ask me any more. If you want to know who gets my Dharma, twenty years after I have passed on the one who establishes my doctrine will indeed be the one who has gotten the Dharma."[183]

In the second year of the Xiantian era (713), he suddenly told his disciples, "I am at the point of the great undertaking." On the evening of the third day of the eighth month, he died instantaneously in a seated posture. The Great Master's springs and autumns numbered seventy-six. In Caoqi the canals and streams stopped flowing and the springs and ponds dried up. The sun and moon did not shine, and the forests turned white. There was an uncanny fragrant auspicious vapor that did not cease for three days and nights.[184] That year Guoen monastery of Xinzhou hosted the Venerable's corpse (*shenzuo* 神座), and in the eleventh month he was buried at Caoqi.

The administrative aide at Taichang monastery, Wei Ju,[185] composed a memorial inscription, but in the seventh year of the Kaiyuan era it was effaced by someone and another memorial was made.[186] It was restored recently, and the Gentleman-in-Attendance Song Ding composed a memorial inscription.[187]

SECTION 10
Dharma Master Daoan and Scripture Quotations
(T. 51. 182C17–183C1)

自教法東流三百年、前盡無事相法則。後因晉石勒時、佛圖澄弟子道安法師在襄陽。秦苻堅遥聞道安名、遂遣使伐襄陽、取道安法師。秦帝常重遇之、長安衣冠子弟為詩賦諷誦皆依附。「學不依道安法師、義不中難也、」此是。世智辯聡。後又造講説章門、作僧尼軌範、佛法憲章。受戒法則、條為三例。一曰行香定坐、二曰常六時礼懺、三曰每月布薩悔過。事相威儀、法事呪願讃歎等、出此道安法師。近代蜀僧嗣安法師、造「齋文」四卷、現今流行。

楞伽経云、「乃至有所立、一切皆錯乱、若見於自心、是則无違[188]諍。」

又云、「若依止少法、而有少法起。若依止於事、此法即便壞。」

又云、「随言而取義、建立於諸法、以彼建立故、死堕地獄中。」

又云、「理教中[189]求我、是妄垢悪離。[190]離聖教正理、欲滅或返增。是外道狂言、智者不應説。」

金剛経云、「離一切諸相即名諸佛。」

又云、「若以色見我、以音声求我、是人行邪道、不能見如来。」

思益経云、「『比丘、云何随佛教、云何随佛語？』『若称讃毀辱、其心不動、是随佛教。』又答云、『若不依文字語言、是名随佛語。』『比丘云何應受供養？』答言、『於法无所取者。』『云何消供養？』『不為世法之所牽者。』『誰人報佛恩？』答言、『依法脩行者。』」

諸小乗禅及諸三昧門不是達摩祖師宗旨。列名如後：白骨觀、数息觀、九相觀、五停心觀、日觀、月觀、樓臺觀、池觀、佛觀。又禅秘要経云、「人患熱病、想涼冷觀。患冷病、作[191]熱想觀。色想作毒蛇觀、不浄觀。愛好飲食、作蛇蛆觀。愛好衣、作熱鐵纏身觀。」諸餘三昧觀等。

禅門経云、「『坐禅觀中、見佛形像卅二相、種種光明、飛騰虚空、變見自在、為真實耶、為虚妄耶？』佛言、『坐禅見空无有物、若見於佛卅二相、種種光明、飛騰虚空、變見自在、皆是自心顛倒、繋着魔網、於空寂滅、見如是事即為虚妄。』」

楞迦経云、「如是種種相、墮於外道見。」

法句経云、「若學諸三昧、是動非坐禅、心随境界流、云何名為定？」

金剛三昧経云、「我不入三昧、不住坐禅、无生无行、不動不禅、是无生禅。」

思益経云、「不依止欲界、不住色无色、行如是禅定、是菩薩遍行。」

維摩経云維摩詰訶舍利弗林間晏坐、訶須菩提大迦葉不平等。

轉女身経云、「无垢光女訶天帝釋、『汝聲聞乗人、畏生死樂槃。』」

決定毗尼経云、「菩薩乗人持開通戒、聲聞乗人持盡遮戒盡護戒。」

藥師経云、「佛訶阿難、『汝聲聞人、如盲如聾、不識无上空義。』」

佛頂経云、「訶聲聞人得少為足此七。」

佛藏経云、「舍利弗、如来在世三寶一味、我滅度後分為五部。舍利弗、悪魔於今猶尚隠身、佐助調達破我法僧。如来大智見在世故、弊悪魔衆不能成其大悪。當来之世、悪[192]魔變身作沙門形。入於僧中種種耶説、令多衆生入於耶見為説邪法。尒時悪人為魔所迷各執所見、『我是彼非。』舍利弗、如来豫見未来世中、如是破法事故説是深経、悉斷悪魔諸所執着。」

『阿難、譬如悪賊於王大臣不敢自見、盜他物者不自言賊。如是阿難、破戒比丘成就非沙門法、尚不自言『我是悪人』況能向餘人説自言罪人。阿難、如是経者、破戒比丘随得聞時、自降伏則有慚愧、持戒比丘得自增長。』

大佛頂経云、「即時如来普告大衆及阿難言、『汝等有學縁覺聲聞、今日廻心趣大菩提無上妙覺。吾今已説真脩行法、汝猶未識脩奢摩他毗婆舍那。微細魔事魔境現前、汝不能識。洗心非正、落於邪見。或汝陰魔、或復天魔、或着鬼神、或遭魑魅。心中不明認賊為子。又復於中得少為足、如弟四禅無聞比丘、妄言證聖。天報巳畢、衰相見前。謗阿羅漢、身遭後有墮入阿鼻獄。』」

所以釋迦如来傳金襴袈裟。令摩訶迦葉在鶏足山、待弥勒世尊下生分付。今悪世時、學禅者衆。我達摩祖師遂傳袈裟表其法正、令後學者有其稟承也。

In the three hundred years after the Buddhist teachings came east, there was no formal standard at all. Later, around the time of Shi Le of the Jin, Fotudeng's disciple Dharma Master Daoan was at Xiangyang.[193] Fujian of the Qin heard of Daoan's fame from afar, and so he dispatched retainers to attack Xiangyang and capture Dharma Master Daoan. The Qin emperor often honored and met with him, and the sons of the nobility of Chang'an all went to him to recite their verses. [The saying] "If students don't rely on Dharma Master Daoan, they will not be able to make sense of difficulties"[194] refers to this; he had worldly wisdom and eloquence. Later he also established a method of organization for discourses, and made rules for monks and nuns and a set of statutes for the Buddha-Dharma. As for the rules for taking the precepts, he classified them into three sets: the first concerns circulating with incense and determining seating, the second concerns the regular six periods of repetition of the *vandana,* and the third concerns the monthly *uposatha* confession of transgressions.[195] Formal (*shixiang* 事相) deportment, the prayers and hymns used in services, etc., originated with this Dharma Master Daoan. In recent times there was the Shu (Sichuan) monk Dharma Master Sian, who made the *Zhaiwen* in four *juan* that is now very widely disseminated.[196]

The *Laṇkā-sūtra* says "Coming to something that stands [separately], everything is completely confounded. If you see it is [only] from your own mind, then there is no contention (*avivāda*)."[197]

Moreover, it says, "If you depend on inferior Dharma then inferior Dharma arises. If you depend on phenomena then the Dharma will be ruined."[198]

Moreover, it says, "If you follow after words and grasp meanings then you build on dharmas, and because of that construction, when you die you fall into Hell."[199]

Moreover, it says, "To seek the self in teachings is fantasy, it is 'wrong views.' If you part from the true principle of the holy teachings, then the delusions you want to extinguish will on the contrary increase, and this is heterodox crazy talk and should not be expounded by the wise."[200]

The *Vajracchedikā-sūtra* says, "Transcending all characteristics is called the Buddhas."[201]

Moreover, it says, "Someone who sees 'I' through form and seeks 'I' through sounds is taking a false path, and is unable to see the Tathāgata."[202]

The *Viśeṣacintibrahma-paripṛcchā-sūtra* says, "[Viśeṣacintibrahma asked the Buddha,] 'How do the bhikṣus follow the Buddha's teachings, how do they follow the Buddha's words?' [The Buddha replied,] 'One whose mind does not move whether praised or censured is following the Buddha's teachings.' He went on, 'Not relying on texts, characters, and words is called following the Buddha's words.'[203] [Viśeṣacintibrahma asked the Buddha,] 'How ought the bhikṣus receive offerings?' [The Buddha] replied, 'In the Dharma there is nothing that is taken.' [Viśeṣacintibrahma asked,] 'How does one use the offerings?' [The Buddha replied,] 'One is not involved in worldly dharmas.' [Viśeṣacintibrahma asked,] 'Who repays the Buddha's kindness?' [The Buddha replied,] 'One who practices according to the Dharma.'"[204]

The various Hīnayāna dhyānas and the various samādhi gates are not the tenets of the school of the Patriarchal Master [Bodhi]dharma; examples of their names are as follows: white bones contemplation (*vidagdhaka-samjñā*), counting breaths contemplation, nine visualizations contemplation,[205] five cessations of the mind contemplation,[206] sun contemplation, moon contemplation, tower contemplation, pond contemplation, Buddha contemplation.[207] The *Chan miyao jing* (Scripture of the Secret Essential Methods of Dhyāna) says, "A person who contracts a fever [does] the contemplation of visualizing cold. One who has chills does the contemplation visualizing heat. One with thoughts of carnal desire does the contemplation of poisonous snakes and the contemplations of impurity. One who loves food and drink does the contemplation of snakes and maggots. One who loves clothes does the contemplation of his body wrapped in hot iron."[208] There are various other samādhi contemplations.

The *Chanmen jing* says, "'In the midst of contemplation in seated meditation, [if] one sees an image of the Buddha's form with the thirty-two characteristics, of variegated radiance, soaring in the air and manifesting transformations at will—is this real or not?' The Buddha said, 'In seated meditation one sees emptiness, there are no things. If one sees the Buddha with thirty-two characteristics, of variegated radiance, soaring in the air and manifesting transformations at will, then this is all one's own mind tumbling over and over, bound up in a demon's net. In empty nirvāṇa, you see that such things are empty delusions.'"[209]

The *Laṇkā-sūtra* says, "These various characteristics [cause one] to fall into heterodox views."[210]

The *Dhammapada* says, "If one studies the various samādhis, this is activity and not the practice of seated meditation. If the mind follows the flow of the realm of sense-objects, how can this be called concentration?"[211]

The *Vajrasamādhi-sūtra* says, "[The Buddha said,] 'I do not enter samādhi and do not abide in seated meditation. No-birth and no-practice, neither activity nor meditation; this is birthless meditation.'"[212]

The *Viśeṣacintibrahma-paripṛcchā-sūtra* says, "Not dependent on the realm of desire (*kāma-dhātu*), not abiding in the realms of form or non-form (*rūpa-dhātu, ārūpya-dhātu*)—if one practices such samādhi, this is the universal practice of the bodhisattvas."[213]

The *Vimalakīrtinirdeśa-sūtra* says that Vimalakīrti rebuked Śāriputra for tranquil sitting (*niṣadya*) in the forest, and he rebuked Subhūti and Mahākāśyapa for non-equanimity.[214]

The *Strīvivarta-vyākaraṇa-sūtra* says, "The Unstained Radiant Woman rebuked Indra, 'You are one of the śrāvakas, fearing birth and death and delighting in nirvāṇa.'"[215]

The *Vinayaviniścaya-Upāliparipṛcchā-sūtra* says, "The bodhisattvas keep the all-inclusive precepts bestowed on them, whereas the śrāvakas keep each and every precept of convention (i.e. natural law) and each and every precept protecting [the Dharma]."[216]

The *Bhaiṣajyaguruvaiḍūryaprabharāja-sūtra* says, "The Buddha rebuked Ānanda, "You śrāvakas are as if blind and deaf, not recognizing the unsurpassed truth of emptiness."[217]

The *Śūraṃgama-sūtra* says, "[The Tathāgata] rebuked the śrāvakas for having gotten only a little, but taking it as fully sufficient."[218]

The *Buddhapiṭakaduḥśīlanirgraha-sūtra* says, "[The Buddha said,] 'Śāriputra, while the Tathāgata is still alive the Three Jewels are as one taste, but after I have crossed over to extinction it will split into five parts. Śāriputra, for the time being the demons conceal themselves and assist Devadatta's [efforts to] destroy myself, the Dharma, and the Saṅgha. Because the Tathāgata's great omniscience yet remains in the world, the loathsome demons are unable to accomplish great evils; in the coming age, [however,] demons will transform themselves and take the shapes of śramaṇas. Entering into the Saṅgha they will preach various heresies, and will cause many beings to enter into heterodox views due to having been taught false Dharma.[219] At that time evil people led astray by demons will each cling to their own views, [asserting] 'I am right and others are wrong.' Śāriputra, the Tathāgata presciently sees in the world to come such efforts to destroy the Dharma, and so teaches this profound scripture that will completely cut through that to which demons cling.'[220]

'Ānanda, take the example of an evil thief who dares not show himself before the King's ministers; though he steals the things of others he does not call himself a thief. Likewise, Ānanda, are those bhikṣus who break the precepts and establish a false śramaṇa Dharma yet do not say to themselves, 'I am an evil person,' much less are able to face others and admit to being sinners. Ānanda, such is the worth of this scripture that precept-breaking bhikṣus when they hear it will of their own accord give way and become ashamed, and precept-keeping bhikṣus will find themselves reaffirmed.'"[221]

The *Śūraṃgama-sūtra* says, "Then the Tathāgata advanced and addressed the assembly and Ānanda, saying, 'All you *śaikṣas*,[222] *pratyekabuddhas* and śrāvakas, today you must have a change of heart and hasten toward *mahābodhi,* the supreme mysterious awakening. I have already explained the Dharma of true practice, but you, as if unaware, practice *śamatha* and *vipaśyanā.* When the subtle works of demons and demon-realms appear before you, you are unable to recognize them. Cleansing the mind is not the point, you fall into wrong views. Sometimes it is the hidden demons of your own *skandhas,* sometimes you are turned back by the deva Māra, sometimes ghosts and spirits attach themselves to you, and sometimes you encounter evil demons of the wilds. Your mind is unclear, and you mistake these thieves for your own children. Moreover, if you return to the center and get a little but take it as sufficient, you are like a fourth dhyāna *assutavā-bhikkhu* (unlearned monk)[223] who is deluded and says that he has attained *arhatva.* When his heavenly reward is exhausted, the signs of decline appear before him. He has blasphemed against the arhats and meets with rebirth, falling into Avīci Hell.' "[224]

This is why Śākya-Tathāgatha transmitted the gold-embroidered robe. He ordered Mahākāśyapa to wait in Mt. Kukkuṭapāda until the World-honored Maitreya descends to be incarnated, and then hand it over to him. In this evil age, students of Chan are many. Our Patriarchal Master [Bodhi]dharma therefore transmitted a robe representing verification of his Dharma, and ordered that later students must have this [token of] inherited authorization.[225]

SECTION 11

Huineng, Part 2 (T. 51. 183C1–184A6)

忍大師當在黄梅馮茂山日、廣開法門、接引群品。當此之時、學道者千万餘人、其中親事不離忍大師左右者唯有十人。並是昇堂入室：智詵、神秀、玄賾、義方、智德、恵蔵、法如、老安、玄約、劉主薄等。並盡是當官領袖、盖國名僧。各各自言為大龍像、為言[226]得底、乃知非底也。

忽有新州人、俗姓盧、名恵能。年廿二、礼拜忍大師。**忍大師**[227]問、「汝従何来、有何事意？」恵能答言、「従嶺南来、亦無事意、唯求作佛。」大師知是非常人也。大師縁左右人多、「汝能随衆作務否？」恵能答、「身命不惜、何但作務？」遂随衆踏碓八箇月。大師知恵能根機純熟、遂默喚付法、及与所傳信袈裟、即令出境。

後恵能恐畏人識、常隠在山林、或在新州、或在韶州。十六七年在俗、亦不説法。後至南海制止寺、遇印宗法師講涅槃経。恵能亦在坐下、時印宗問衆聽人、「汝惣見風吹翻干、上頭翻動否？」衆答言、「見動。」或言、「見風動。」或言、「見翻動。」「不是風動、是見動。」如是問難不定。恵能於座下立、答法師言、「自是衆人妄想心動、動与不動、非是翻動。法夲无有動不動。」法師聞説驚愕、忙然不知是何言。問、「居士従何来？」恵能答、「本来不来、今亦不去。」

法師下高座、迎恵能就房、子細借問。恵能一一具説東山佛法、及有付嘱信袈裟。印宗法師見巳、頭面頂礼、歎言、「何期座下有大菩薩！」語已又頂礼、請恵能為和上。印宗法師自稱弟子。即与恵能禅師剃髪被衣已、自許弟子。及講下門従嘆言、「善哉善哉、黄梅忍大師法比聞流嶺南、誰知今在此間？衆人識否？」咸言、「不識。」印宗法師曰、「吾所説猶如瓦礫、今有能禅師、[228] 傳忍大師法門、喩若真金、深不思議。」

印宗法師領諸徒衆頂礼能禅師足。恐衆人疑、及請所傳信袈裟示衆人、并自身受菩薩戒。印宗師共大衆送能禅師歸漕溪。接引群品、廣開禅法。天下知聞、漕溪佛法最不思議。

One day at Mt. Pingmao in Huangmei, Great Master [Hong]ren was opening the Dharma gates wide, receiving people of all degrees for instruction. At this time his students were exceedingly numerous, but among them the close attendants who never left the side of Great Master Ren numbered only ten. All of them were [disciples who could] "ascend the hall and enter the chamber";[229] [they were] Zhishen, Shenxiu, Xuanze, Yifang, Zhide, Huizang, Faru, Laoan, Xuanyue, and Liu Zhubu.[230] They were one and all from the ranks of the elite, and were monks renowned throughout the entire country. Each said of himself that he was a great *hastināga* who had gotten the very depths, but we know that it was not very deep at all.

There was a certain man from Xinzhou whose lay surname was Lu and whose [Dharma] name was Huineng. When he was twenty-two he went to pay his respects to Great Master Ren. Great Master Ren asked, "Where have you come from, and with what intentions?" Huineng replied, "I have come from Lingnan, I have no intentions at all, I only seek to make a Buddha." The Great Master knew that this was no ordinary person, yet because there were so many people in attendance the Great Master said, "Are you able to join the crowd [of disciples] and do physical labor?" Huineng replied, "I would not begrudge even my life, what is mere physical labor to me?" And so he joined the crowd, and trod the rice-hulling pestle for eight months. When the Great Master knew that Huineng's potential was perfectly ripe, he secretly summoned him and passed on the Dharma, and gave him the *kāṣāya* robe of verification that had been transmitted. He then commanded him to leave the area.

After that, for fear of being recognized Huineng often hid in the mountain forests in Xinzhou or in Shaozhou.[231] For sixteen or seventeen years he remained a layman and never expounded on the Dharma. Then [one day] he arrived at Zhizhi monastery in Nanhai,[232] and it happened that Dharma Master Yinzong was expounding on the *Nirvāṇa-sūtra.*[233] As Huineng sat down, Yinzong asked the audience, "You all perceive the wind blowing the flag-staff—does the flag at the top of it move or not?" Everyone said, "We perceive movement." Some said, "We perceive the wind moving." Some said, "We perceive the flag moving." [Others said] "It is not the flag moving, it is perception that moves." They argued on in this manner and could not decide. [Then] Huineng stood up and replied to the Dharma Master, "It is these people's deluded minds that move and do not move, it is not the flag that moves. The Dharma is fundamentally without either movement or nonmovement."[234] When the Dharma Master heard this speech he was astounded, utterly at a loss to know what words were these. He asked, "Where does the layman come from?" Huineng replied, "Originally I have not come and also have never yet gone."

The Dharma Master descended from the high seat and invited Huineng to go to his room, [where] he carefully questioned him. Huineng went into full particulars about the East Mountain Buddha-Dharma and about having received the *kāṣāya* robe of verification. When Dharma Master Yinzong had seen [the robe], he made obeisance with his head to the ground and exclaimed "How could I have hoped that in my assembly there would be a great bodhisattva!" When he had said this he again made obeisance and begged Huineng to become a Venerable. Dharma Master Yinzong declared himself [Huineng's] disciple. Then he gave Chan Master Huineng [the ceremony of] tonsuring and robing, and when he was finished he pledged himself [to Huineng] as his disciple. Then he addressed his disciples, exclaiming, "How wonderful, how wonderful! I had recently heard that the Dharma of Master Ren of Huangmei had flowed to Lingnan, but who knew that [the Dharma heir] was now in our midst? Were any of you aware of it?" Someone said, "We were not aware of it." Dharma Master Yinzong said, "What I preach is like bits of rubble, but now here is Chan Master Neng, who has inherited the Dharma teachings of Great Master Ren; it is like pure gold, inconceivably profound."

Dharma Master Yingzong led the followers in making obeisance at the feet of Chan Master Neng. Fearing lest the crowd be in doubt he requested that the transmitted robe of verification be shown to the crowd, and together with them he himself received the bodhisattva precepts [from Huineng]. Dharma Master Yingzong, along with a great crowd, saw Chan Master Neng off when he returned to Caoqi. There he received people of all degrees for instruction and widely opened the Chan Dharma. All under Heaven have heard that the Caoqi Buddha-Dharma is the most inconceivable.

SECTION 12

Zhishen and Empress Wu (T. 51. 184A6–184B17)

後時大周立、則天即位、敬重佛法。至長壽元年、勅天下諸州各置大雲寺。二月廿日、勅使天冠郎中張昌期往韶州漕溪請能禅師、能禅師[235] 託病不去。則天後至万歳通天元年、使往再請能禅師、能禅師[236] 既不来、請上代達摩祖師傳信袈裟、朕於内道場供養。能禅師依請、即擎達摩祖師傳信袈裟与勅使。使廻得傳信袈裟、則天見得傳信袈裟来、甚喜悦、於内道場供養。

万歳通天二年七月、則天勅天冠郎中張昌期往資州徳純寺、請詵禅師。詵禅師[237] 授請赴京、内道場供養。久視年、使荊州玉泉寺請秀禅師、安州受山寺請玄賾禅師、随州大雲寺請玄約禅師、洛州嵩山會善寺請[238] 老安禅師。則天内道場供養。則天本請諸大徳、縁西國有三蔵婆羅門、則天常偏敬重之。

劍南智詵禅師、當有疾思念歸郷。　為関山阻遠、心有少憂。其邪通婆羅門云、「彼与此何殊？禅師何得思郷？」智詵答、「三蔵何以知之？」答云、「禅師但試舉意看、無有不知者。」詵又云、「去也看。」想身著俗人衣裳、於西市曹門看望。其三蔵云、「大徳僧人、何得著俗衣、市中而看？」詵又云、「好。看去也。」想身往禅定寺佛圖相輪上立。三蔵又云、「僧人何得登高而立。」詵云、「赭[239]廻好好、更看去也。」即當處依法想念不生。其三蔵於三界内尋看、竟不可得。三蔵婆羅門遂生敬仰、頂礼詵足、白和上言、「不知唐國有大乘佛法、今自責身心懺悔。」

則天見三蔵歸依詵禅師。則天諮[240]問諸大徳和上等、「有慾否？」神秀、玄約、老安、玄賾等皆言、「無慾。」則天問詵禅師、「和上有慾否？」詵禅師恐不放歸、順則天意答、「有慾。」則天答云、「何得有慾？」詵答云、「生則有慾、不生則無慾。」則天言下悟。又見三蔵歸依詵和上、則天倍加敬重。詵禅師因便奏請歸郷。勅賜新翻花厳経一部、弥勒繡像及幡花等、及将達摩祖師信袈裟。則天云、「能禅師不来、此上代袈裟亦奉上和上。将歸故郷、永為供養。」

則天至景龍元年十一月、又使内侍将軍薛間[241]至曹溪能禅師所宣口、勅云、「将上代信袈裟奉上詵禅師、将受持供養。今別将摩納袈裟一領、及絹五百疋、充乳薬供養。」

Later, the Great Zhou [dynasty] was established and [Empress Wu] Zetian ascended the throne, who greatly revered the Buddha-Dharma. In the first year of the Changshou era (692),[242] she decreed that every region in the empire should establish a Dayun monastery. On the twentieth day of the second month, she sent Zhang Changqi, director of the Ministry of Personnel, to Caoqi in Shaozhou in order to invite Chan Master Neng [to court].[243] Chan Master Neng pleaded illness and did not go.[244] Later, in the first year of the Wansui Tongtian era (696), Zetian sent a messenger to invite Chan Master Neng again. When Chan Master Neng did not come, she requested the *kāṣāya* robe of verification transmitted by the First Patriarch [Bodhi]dharma, so that she might make offerings to it in the palace chapel.[245] Chan Master Neng agreed to this request and gave the *kāṣāya* robe of verification transmitted by the Patriarchal Master [Bodhi]dharma to the imperial messenger. The messenger returned with the transmitted *kāṣāya* robe of verification, and when Zetian saw that the transmitted *kāṣāya* robe of verification had arrived she was extremely pleased, and made offerings to it in the palace chapel.

In the seventh month of the second year of the Wansui Tongtian era (697), Zetian sent Zhang Changqi, director of the Ministry of Personnel, to Dechun monastery in Zizhou to invite Chan Master Shen.[246] Chan Master Shen accepted the invitation and went to the capital, and [the empress] made offerings to him in the palace chapel. In the [first year of the] Jiushi era (700), [the empress] sent [a message] to Yuquan monastery in Jingzhou to invite Chan Master Xiu,[247] to Shoushan monastery in Anzhou to invite Chan Master Xuanze,[248] to Dayun monastery in Suizhou to invite Chan Master Xuanyue,[249] and to Huishan monastery on Mt. Song in Luozhou to invite Chan Master Laoan.[250] Zetian made offerings to them in the palace chapel. Zetian originally invited all these worthies because of a certain Trepiṭaka Brāhmana from the Western Regions, whom Zetian habitually relied upon and greatly revered.

At that time Chan Master Zhishen of Jiannan was ill and thought about returning to his native place. Because it was so far beyond the mountain passes, he felt a little melancholy. That heretic magician Brāhmana said to him, "What difference is there between 'here' and 'there'? How can the Chan Master pine for his native place?" Zhishen replied, "How does the Trepiṭaka know about it?" [Brāhmana] answered, "The Chan Master has only to try and bring something to mind, there is nothing I do not know." Shen replied, "Go ahead and try."

He imagined himself dressed in layman's garb, looking toward the section office of the western market. That Trepiṭaka said, "Bhadanta, how can you, a monk, wear layman's clothing and gaze into the midst of the city?" Shen said, "Good, go ahead and try [again]." He imagined himself going to the Buddha-relic stūpa at Chanding monastery and standing on the highest disk of the spire. The Trepiṭaka again said, "How can a monk climb so high and stand there?" Shen said, "This one will be really good, try again." Then, right where he was, by relying on the Dharma he produced no thoughts at all. That Trepiṭaka searched all through the triple-world, but in vain.[251] Thereupon, Brāhmana Trepiṭaka was filled with reverence, and he bowed down his head at Shen's feet and said to the Venerable, "I did not know that in the country of Tang there was Mahāyāna Buddha-Dharma. Now I rebuke myself body and mind and repent."

Zetian saw that the Trepiṭaka had taken refuge in Chan Master Shen. Zetian submitted a question to all the bhadanta: "Do the Venerables have desires, or not?"[252] Shenxiu, Xuanye, Laoan, and Xuanze all said, "We have no desires." Zetian asked Chan Master Shen, "Does the Venerable have desires, or not?" Chan Master Shen, fearing that he would not be allowed to return home, complied with the will of Zetian and replied, "I have desires." Zetian responded, "How can the Venerable have desires?" Shen replied,

"That which is born has desire. That which is not born has no desire." At these words, Zetian was awakened. Moreover, seeing that the Trepiṭaka took refuge in the Venerable Shen doubled her deep reverence.

Chan Master Shen therefore took the opportunity to petition that he be allowed to return to his native place. [The empress] ordered that he be given the new translation of the *Avataṃsaka-sūtra* in one part,[253] an embroidered image of Maitreya, and fine banners[254] and such, as well as having him take the *kāṣāya* robe of verification of the Patriarchal Master [Bodhi]dharma. Zetian said, "As Chan Master Neng did not come, I also offer up this robe of the first patriarch to the Venerable. Take it back to your native place and perpetually make offerings to it."

In the eleventh month of the first year of the Jinglong era (707),[255] Zetian again sent a messenger, the Palace Attendant General Xue Jian,[256] to make a proclamation at Chan Master Neng's place in Caoqi. The empress's message was: "We have offered up the first patriarch's *kāṣāya* robe of verification to Chan Master Shen, and he has undertaken to maintain the offerings. We now separately make offerings of one *kāṣāya* robe of fine *mona* cloth,[257] five hundred rolls of silk, and provision of 'milk medicine.'"[258]

SECTION 13

Chan Master Zhishen (T. 51. 184B18–184C2)

資州徳純寺智詵禅師、俗姓周、汝南人也。随祖宦至蜀。年十歳、常好釋教、不食薫[259]莘、志操高標、不為童戯。年十三、辞親入道。初事玄奘法師、學経論。後聞雙峰山忍大師、便辞玄奘法師、捨経論、遂於馮茂山投忍大師。大師[260]云、「汝兼有文性。」

後歸資州徳純寺、化道衆生。造虚融觀三巻、縁起一巻、般若心疏一巻。後至万歳通天二年七月、則天勅天冠郎中張昌期、於徳純寺請。遂赴西京、後因疾進表、却歸徳純寺。首尾卅餘年化道衆生。長安二年六月、命處寂、「扶侍吾。」遂付信衣云、「此衣是達摩祖師所傳袈裟、則天賜吾、吾今付汝。善自保愛。」至其年七月六日夜、奄然坐化、時年九十四。

Chan Master Zhishen of Dechun Monastery in Zizhou had the lay surname Zhou, and was from Runan.[261] He accompanied his grandfather when the latter was posted to Shu (Sichuan). When he was ten years old [Zhishen] was very partial to the Buddhist teachings, did not eat strong and pungent foods, resolutely adhered to a lofty standard, and did not engage in childish play. When he was thirteen he left his family and entered the Way. First he served Dharma Master Xuanzang, with whom he studied the scriptures and treatises.[262] Later, on hearing of Great Master

Ren of Mt. Shuangfeng, he left Dharma Master Xuanzang, abandoned the scriptures and treatises, and offered himself as disciple to Great Master Ren at Mt. Pingmao. The Great Master said, "You both have a literary nature."[263]

Later, [Zhishen] returned to Dechun monastery in Zizhou and taught the Way for the many beings.[264] He composed the *Xurong guan* (Contemplation on Union with Emptiness) in three fascicles, the *Yuanqi* (Dependent Arising) in one fascicle, and the *Banruoxin shu* (Commentary on the Heart Scripture) in one fascicle.[265] Later, in the seventh month of the second year of the Wansui Tongtian era (697), [Empress Wu] Zetian sent Zhang Changqi, director of the Ministry of Personnel, to Dechun monastery to invite [Zhishen]. So he went up to the Western Capital, but later, due to illness, he petitioned the empress and was allowed to return to Dechun monastery. He taught the Way for the many beings for over thirty years altogether. In the sixth month of the second year of the Chang'an era (702) he ordered Chuji, "Hold me up." He thereupon entrusted him with the robe of verification, saying, "This robe is the *kāṣāya* robe transmitted by the Patriarchal Master [Bodhi]dharma. Zetian bestowed it on me, and I now entrust it to you. You must protect yourself well."[266] On the evening of the sixth day of the seventh month of that year, he died instantly in a seated posture. He was ninety-four years old.

SECTION 14

Chan Master Chuji (T. 51. 184C3–184C16)

處寂禅師、綿州浮城縣人也。俗姓唐、家代好儒。常習詩礼、有分義孝行。年十歳父亡。歎曰、「天地既无、我聞佛法不可思議、抜生死苦。」乃投詵和上、詵和上問、「汝從何来？」答、「故投和上来。」和上知非常人。

當赴京日、遂擔大師至京、一肩不移。身長八尺、神情稟然。於衆獨見其首、見者欽貴。

後還居資州徳純寺、化道衆生廿年。後至開元廿四年[267]四月、密遣家人王鍠、喚海東无相禅師。付嘱法及信袈裟云、「此[268]衣是達摩祖師信衣。則天賜詵和上、詵和上与吾、吾轉付汝。善自保愛、看好山住去。」後至其年五月廿七日、告諸門徒、「吾不久住。」至夜半子時、奄然坐化。處寂大師[269]時年六十八。

Chan Master Chuji was from Foucheng District in Mianzhou.[270] His lay surname was Tang, and his family had for generations favored Confucianism. Chuji diligently studied the *Book of Odes* and the *Book of Rites*, and he had moral integrity and filial piety. When he was ten his father died.

He lamented, "There is nothing in Heaven and earth! I have heard that the Buddha-Dharma is inconceivable and roots out the suffering of life and death." And so he offered himself as disciple to the Venerable Shen.[271] The Venerable Shen asked, "Where do you come from?" Chuji replied, "I come in order to offer myself to the Venerable." The Venerable knew he was no ordinary person.

When they went to the capital, [Chuji] carried the Great Master all the way by himself, without switching with another person. He was almost seven feet tall, and his disposition was blessed. In a crowd only his head could be seen [above the rest], and whoever saw him looked up to him with respect.

Later he went back to live in Dechun monastery in Zizhou, where he taught the Way for the many beings for twenty years. In the fourth month of the twenty-fourth year of the Kaiyuan era (736) he secretly sent his servant Wang Huang to summon Chan Master Wuxiang from East-of-the-Sea (Korea). He entrusted him with the Dharma and the *kāṣāya* robe of verification, saying, "This robe is the robe of verification of the Patriarchal Master [Bodhi]dharma. Zetian bestowed it on the Venerable Shen, the Venerable Shen gave it to me, and I in turn entrust it to you.[272] You must protect yourself well. Go and find a good mountain and stay there."

Later, on the twenty-seventh day of the fifth month of that year, he told his disciples, "I will not long remain." In the middle of the night during hour of the rat, he died instantly in a seated posture. Great Master Chuji was sixty-eight years old.[273]

SECTION 15

Chan Master Wuxiang (T. 51. 184C17–185B14)

劍南城都府浄泉寺无相禅師、俗金姓[274]、新羅王之族、家代海東。昔在夲國、有季妹、初聞礼娉、授刀割面、誓志歸真。和上見而歎曰、「女子柔弱、猶聞雅操。丈夫剛強、我豈無心？」遂乃削髪辞親。浮海西渡乃至唐國。尋師訪道、周遊[水+步]歷、乃到資州德純寺、礼唐和上。唐和上有疾遂不出見、便燃一指為燈、供養唐和上。唐和上知其非常人、便留左右二年。

後居天谷山。却至德純寺、唐和上遣家人王鍠、密付信衣、「此衣是達摩祖師傳衣。則天賜与詵和上、詵和上与吾、吾付囑汝。」金和上得付法及信衣、遂居天谷山石巖下。草衣節食、食盡餐土、感猛獸衛護。後章仇大夫請開禅法。居淨眾寺、化道衆生廿餘年。

後至寶應元年五月十五日、忽憶白崖山無住禅師、「吾有疾計此合来看吾。」数数問左右人、「無住禅師何為不来？吾将年邁。」密使工人董璿、「将吾信衣及餘衣十七事、密送与无住禅師。善自保愛。未是出山時、更待三五年間、太平即出。」遥付囑訖。

至五月十九日命第子、「与吾取新浄衣、吾欲沐浴。」至夜半子時、儼然坐化。是日、日月无光、天地變白。法幢摧折、禅河枯涸。衆生失望、學道者無依。大師時年七十九。

金和上、每年十二月正月、与四衆百千万人受縁。厳設道場、處高座説法。先教引聲念佛、盡一氣絶聲停念訖。説云、「無憶、無念、莫妄。無憶是戒[275]、無念是定、莫妄是恵。此三句語即是惣持門。」

又云、「念不起猶如鏡面、能照万像。念起猶如鏡背、即不能照見。」

又云、「須分明知起、須知起滅、須知滅此知須不間斷、即是見佛。譬如二人同行、倶至他國。其父将書教誨。一人得書、尋讀已畢、順其父教[276] 不行非法。一人得書、尋讀已畢、不依教示、熾行諸悪。一切衆生、依无念者、是孝順之子、着文字者、是不孝之子。」

又云、「譬如有人酒醉而臥。其母来喚、欲令還家。其子為酔迷乱、悪罵其母。一切衆生无明酒酔、不信自身見性成佛道。」

又起信論云、「『心真如門、心生滅門。』无念即是真如門、有念即是生滅門。」

又云、「无明頭出、般若頭没。无明頭没、般若頭出。」

又引涅槃経云、「家犬野鹿。家犬喩妄念、野鹿喩佛性。」

又云、「綾本来是絲、无有文字。巧児織成、乃有文字。後折却還是本絲。絲喩佛性、文字喩妄念。」

又云、「水不離波、波不離水。波喩妄念、水喩佛性。」

又云、「擔麻人伴轉逢銀所。一人即捨擔取銀。餘人言、『我麻擔已定、我終不能棄。』又至金所、棄銀取金。諸人云、『我麻擔已定、終不能捨。』金喩涅槃、麻喩生死。」

又云、「我此三句語是達摩祖師本傳教法、不言是詵和上唐和上所説。」

又言、「許第子有勝師之義。縁詵唐二和上不説了教、曲承信衣。」

金和上所以不引詵唐二和上説處。每常座下教戒真言、「我達摩祖師所傳此三句語是惣持門、念不起是戒門、念不起是定門[277]、念不起恵門。无念即是戒定恵具足、是過去未来見[278]在、恒沙諸佛、皆從此門入。若更有別門、無有是處。

Chan Master Wuxiang of Jingzhong Monastery in Chengdu City Prefecture in Jiannan had the lay surname Kim and was from a clan of Silla princes, his family went back for generations East-of-the-Sea (i.e., Korea).[279] Formerly, when he was in his homeland, he had a younger sister. When she first heard of her betrothal ceremony, she picked up a knife,[280] slashed her face, and vowed her determination to "return to the true."[281] The Venerable [Wuxiang] saw this and cried, "Girls are pliant and weak, yet she knows the meaning of sticking to chastity. Fellows are hard and strong—how can I be so lacking in spirit?"[282] He thereupon took the tonsure and left his kin, crossed the sea westward and arrived in the Kingdom of Tang.[283] He sought out masters and inquired about the Way, he wandered around and passed through until he reached Dechun monastery in Zizhou and made obeisance to the Venerable Tang (Chuji). The Venerable Tang was ill and did not come out to greet him, and so Wuxiang burned one of his fingers as a candle and dedicated it as an offering to the Venerable Tang.[284] The Venerable realized that this was no ordinary man, and kept him at his side for two years.

Wuxiang later lived in the Tiangu Mountains.[285] Meanwhile, back at Dechun monastery, the Venerable Tang sent his servant Wang Huang [to Wuxiang] and secretly entrusted to him the robe of verification, saying, "This robe is the robe transmitted by the Patriarchal Master [Bodhi]-dharma. Zetian bestowed it upon the Venerable Shen, the Venerable Shen gave it to me, and I entrust it to you."[286] The Venerable Kim, having been entrusted with the Dharma and the robe of verification, lived beneath a cliff in the Tiangu Mountains. His clothing was of grass and his diet sparse, and when there was no food left he ate earth. The wild beasts were moved to protect him.[287] Later, the Grand Master Zhangqiu [Jianqiong 兼瓊][288] requested that he open the Chan Dharma. Living at Jingzhong Monastery, Wuxiang taught the Way for the many beings for more than twenty years.

On the fifteenth day of the fifth month of the first year of the Baoying era (762), [Wuxiang] suddenly thought of Chan Master Wuzhu of the Baiyai mountains[289] and [thought], "I am ill. Surely[290] [Wuzhu] will come to see me." Time and again he asked his attendants, "Why hasn't Chan Master Wuzhu come? I am growing old." He secretly sent the laborer Dong Xuan, [saying], "Take my robe of verification and seventeen other items of clothing, and secretly deliver them to Chan Master Wuzhu. He must protect himself well. It is not yet time for him to come out of the mountains, he should wait three to five more years, and when he hears that there is peace throughout the land then he can come out." [Thus] the transmission was settled from afar.[291]

On the nineteenth day of the fifth month, [Wuxiang] ordered his disciples, "Bring me a new, clean robe, I wish to bathe." In the middle of the night during the hour of the rat (11 P.M.–1 A.M.), he died solemnly in a seated posture. On that day, the sun and moon gave no light and heaven and earth turned white. The Dharma banners' [poles] snapped and the Nairanjanā River[292] dried up. All beings were bereft and students of the Way had no one on whom to rely. At that time, the Great Master was seventy-nine years old.[293]

The Venerable Kim, every twelfth and first month, administered the "receiving of conditions"[294] for countless numbers of people of the four assemblies. The *bodhimaṇḍa*[295] sanctuary was magnificently arranged, and [Wuxiang] occupied the high seat to expound the Dharma. He would first lead a vocal recollection of the Buddha. As the recitation ended at the end of an exhalation and the cessation of sound, he would expound, "No-recollection, no-thought, and 'do not be deluded': no-recollection is *śīla,* no-thought is samādhi, and 'do not be deluded' is prajñā.[296] These three phrases are the gates of perfectly maintaining [the precepts]."[297]

He also would say, "When thoughts do not arise it is like the mirror's face, able to reflect the myriad images. When thoughts arise it is like the mirror's back, unable to reflect."

He also would say, "In an instant one distinguishes cognition arising, in an instant cognition arises and is extinguished, and if in the instant cognition is extinguished this cognition-instant is not interrupted, this then is seeing the Buddha. To illustrate; two men were fellow travelers, and both arrived in another country. Their fathers sent them letters of instruction and admonition. One received his letter, and once he had read it he obeyed his father's instructions and did not do anything that was against the law. The other man also received his letter, and once he had read it he did not comply with the instructions given but heedlessly did all evil. Among the many beings, those that rely on no-thought are the filial, obedient sons; those that are attached to texts and characters are the unfilial sons."

He also said, "To illustrate; there was a man who was lying in a drunken stupor. His mother came calling for him, wishing to get him to return home. But the son, in his drunken confusion, viciously cursed his mother. Beings are drunk on the wine of ignorance[298] and do not believe that they themselves can see the nature and achieve the Way of the Buddha."

He would also [quote] the *Arousal of Faith,* saying, "'The mind is the gate of thusness. The mind is the gate of birth and extinction.'[299] No-thought is none other than the gate of thusness. The existence of thought is none other than the gate of birth and extinction."

He also would say, "When a bit of ignorance emerges, a bit of prajñā sinks. When a bit of ignorance sinks, a bit of prajñā emerges."

He would also quote the *Nirvāṇa-sūtra,* saying, "'The domestic dog and the wild deer'—the domestic dog illustrates delusive thinking, and the wild deer illustrates the Buddha-nature."[300]

He would also say, "Damask is originally silk thread without any 'texts and characters' (i.e., design).[301] Only after a skillful child has woven it does it have a design. Later, when it is torn up it returns to the original silk thread. The silk thread illustrates the Buddha-nature, the design illustrates delusive thinking."

He would also say, "Water is not separate from waves and waves are not separate from water. The waves illustrate delusive thinking, the water illustrates the Buddha-nature."[302]

He would also say, "A band of men were carrying hemp, and along the way they came across a place where there was silver. One man then threw away his load and picked up the silver. The others said, 'It has already been determined that we carry hemp, we will never discard it.' Further on they came to a place where there was gold, [and the one man] discarded the silver and picked up the gold. The others said, 'It has already been determined that we carry hemp, we will never throw it away.' The gold illustrates nirvāṇa, the hemp illustrates birth-and-death."[303]

He also would say, "These three phrases of mine are teachings that were originally transmitted by the Patriarchal Master [Bodhi]dharma. I do not say that this is what was taught by the Venerable Shen (i.e., Zhishen) or the Venerable Tang (i.e., Chuji)."

He also said, "It has been permitted that the disciple has understanding surpassing that of his masters. Because the Venerables Shen and Tang did not expound the ultimate teaching, I have by a winding course inherited the robe of verification."

The Venerable Kim thus did not draw from areas in which the Venerables Shen and Tang had expounded. Whenever he taught the precepts from the high seat he said directly, "These three phrases of mine that were transmitted by the Patriarchal Master [Bodhi]dharma are the gates of completely maintaining [the practice]. The non-arising of thought is the gate of *śīla,* the non-arising of thought is the gate of samādhi, the non-arising of thought [is] the gate of prajñā. No-thought is thus the complete fulfillment of *śīla,* samādhi, and prajñā; it is the gate through which all the Buddhas of the past, present, and future, [countless as] the Ganges sands, have entered. It is not possible that there could be any other gates."

SECTION 16

The Venerable Shenhui (T. 51. 185B14–185C26)

東京荷澤寺神會和上每月作壇場、為人說法、破清浄禅立如来禅。立知見[304]。立言説、為戒定恵不破言説。云、「正説之時即是戒、正説之時即是定、正説之時即是恵。」説无念法、立見性。

開元年中、滑臺為天下學道者定宗旨。會和上云、「若更有一人説、會終不敢説也。」為會和上不得信[305]衣。

天寶八年中、洛州荷澤寺亦定宗旨。被崇遠法師問、「禅師於三賢十聖脩行、證何地位？」會答曰、「涅槃経云、『南无純陁、南无純陁、身同凡夫、心同佛心。』」會和上却問遠法師、「講涅槃[306]経来、得幾遍？」遠法師答、「四十餘遍。」又問、「法師見佛性否？」法師答、「不見。」會和上云、「師子吼品云、『若人不見佛性、即不合講涅槃経、若見佛性、即合講涅槃経。』」遠法師却問、「會和上見佛性否？」會答、「見。」又問、「云何為見為復眼見、耶耳鼻等見耶？」會答、「見無尒許多[307]、見只没[308]見。」又問、「見等純陁否？」會答、「比量見、比即比於純陁、**[量即]**[309]量等純陁、不敢定斷。」又被遠法師問、「禅師上代袈裟傳否？」會答、「傳。若不傳時、法有斷絶。」又問、「禅師得否？」答、「不在會處。」遠法師又問、「誰得此袈裟？」會答、「有一人得、已後自應知。此人若説法時、正法流行邪法自滅。為佛法事大[310]、所以隠而未出。」

會和上在荊府時、有西國人迦葉賢者、安樹提等廿餘人。向會和上説法處問、「上代信袈裟、和上得否？」答、「不在會處。」却問賢者等、「從何處来？」迦葉答、「從劍南来。」問、「識金禅師否？」迦葉答、「盡是金和上第子。」會和上問説、「汝金禅師教人教道如何？」迦葉答、「无明頭出、涅槃頭没、般若頭出、无明頭[311] 没。有念猶如鏡面。」會和上叱之、「莫説此閑言語！汝姓迦葉、是婆羅門種姓、計合利根、乃是尿床婆羅門耳。」

會和上云、「汝劍南詵禅師是法師、不説了教。唐禅師是詵禅師第子、亦不説了教。唐禅師第子梓州趙法師是[312]、陵州王是律師、已[313] 西表是法師。益州金是禅師、説了教亦不得。雖然不説了教、佛法只在彼處。」

郎中馬雄使到漕溪礼能和上塔。問守塔老僧、「上代傳信袈裟何在？」玄楷答[314]老師答、「能和上在、玄楷師智海師[315]等問能和上、『承上袈裟傳否？佛法付嘱誰人？』能和上答、『我衣女子将也。我法我死後廿年外、竪立宗旨、是得我法人也。』」

The Venerable Shenhui of Heze monastery in the Eastern Capital [Luoyang] would set up an [ordination] platform every month and expound on the Dharma for people, knocking down "Purity Chan" and upholding "Tathāgata Chan."[316] He upheld direct experience and verbal explanation—regarding precepts, meditation, and wisdom, he did not knock down verbal explanation. He said, "Just as I am speaking now is none other than *śīla,* just as I am speaking now is none other than samādhi, just as I am speaking now is none other than prajñā." He expounded the Dharma of no-thought and upheld seeing the nature.

In the middle of the Kaiyuan era, at Huatai[317] he set forth the cardinal tenets of the school for students of the way from throughout the land. The Venerable Hui said, "There is yet someone who will explain it [fully], I really cannot presume to explain it."[318] This is because the Venerable Hui did not get the robe of verification.

In the middle of the eighth year of the Tianbao era (749), he also set forth the cardinal tents of the school at Heze monastery in Luozhou (Luoyang).[319] He was asked by Dharma Master Chongyuan, "Regarding the three virtues and ten holinesses,[320] what level of practice can you testify to?" Hui replied, "The *Nirvāṇa-sūtra* says, 'Homage to Cunda, homage to Cunda, his body was that of an ordinary mortal, his mind was the same as the Buddha's mind.'"[321]

The Venerable Hui then asked Dharma Master Yuan, "How many times now have you lectured on the *Nirvāṇa-sūtra?*" Dharma Master Yuan replied, "Over forty times." [Hui] asked, "Has the Dharma Master perceived Buddha-nature or not?" The Dharma Master replied, "I have not perceived it." The Venerable Hui said, "In the 'Lion's Roar' section [of the *Nirvāṇa-sūtra*] it says, 'If one has not perceived Buddha-nature, then one is not fit to lecture on the *Nirvāṇa-sūtra.* If one has perceived Buddha-nature, only then is one fit to lecture on the *Nirvāṇa-sūtra.*'"[322]

Dharma Master Yuan then asked, "Has the Venerable Hui perceived Buddha-nature or not?" Hui [i.e., Shenhui] replied, "I have perceived it." [Yuan] asked, "In what way do you perceive, is it by the eyes that you have perceived, or by the ears or the nose, etc., that you have perceived?" Hui replied, "Perceiving is not so quantifiable, perceiving is simply perceiving." [Yuan] asked, "Do you perceive the same as Cunda, or not?" Hui replied, "I perceive by inference (*biliang jian* 比量見). Comparison (*bi* 比) means 'comparable to Cunda,' estimation/knowing (*liang* 量) is 'equivalent to Cunda.' I dare not make a final conclusion."[323]

He was further questioned by Dharma Master Yuan, "Chan Master, has the First Patriarch's *kāṣāya* robe been transmitted or not?" Hui replied, "It has been transmitted. When it is not transmitted, the Dharma will be broken off." [Yuan] asked, "Has the Chan Master got it or not?" [Shenhui] replied, "It is not at my place." Dharma Master Yuan asked, "Who has got this *kāṣāya* robe?" Hui replied, "Someone has got it. In due course it should be apparent. When this person expounds on the Dharma, the true Dharma will flow forth and false Dharmas will perish of themselves. In order to further the great work of the Buddha-Dharma, he is hidden and has not yet come out."[324]

When the Venerable Hui was in Jing subprefecture,[325] there were men of the Western Kingdoms, the Bhadra (Elder) Kaśya, Anshuti, and about twenty others, who went up to the place where the Venerable was expounding on the Dharma and asked, "The First Patriarch's *kāṣāya* robe of verification—has the Venerable got it or not?" [Shenhui] replied, "It is not at my place." He then asked the Bhadra and the others, "Where have you come from?" Kaśya replied, "We have come from Jiannan." [Shenhui] asked, "Do you know Chan Master Kim?" Kaśya replied, "We are all the Venerable Kim's disciples." The Venerable Hui asked, "Explain how Chan Master Kim teaches people to study the Way." Kaśya replied, "'When a bit of ignorance emerges, a bit of nirvāṇa sinks, when a bit of prajñā emerges, a bit of ignorance sinks. When there is thought it is like the face of a mirror.'"[326] The Venerable Hui shouted at him, "Don't speak such empty prattle! Your name is Kaśya, a Brāhmanical sort of name, [so one would think that] surely you had some intelligence, but you are nothing but a bed-wetting Brāhman!"

The Venerable Hui said, "Your Chan Master Shen of Jiannan was a Dharma Master who did not expound the ultimate teaching. Chan Master

Tang was Chan Master Shen's disciple, and he also did not expound the ultimate teaching. Of Chan Master Tang's disciples, Zhao of Zizhou[327] is a Dharma Master, Wang of Lingzhou[328] is a Vinaya Master, and Biao of Baxi[329] is a Dharma Master. Kim of Yizhou[330] is a Chan Master, but he also did not manage to expound the ultimate teaching. Although he did not expound the ultimate teaching, the Buddha-Dharma is only at his place."[331]

Director Ma Xiong was sent to Caoqi to pay respects to the Venerable Neng's stūpa. He asked the old monk who was guarding the stūpa, "Where is the *kāṣāya* robe of verification transmitted by the First Patriarch?" The old monk replied, "When the Venerable Neng was alive, Master Xuanjie, Master Zhihai, and the others asked the Venerable Neng, 'Has the *kāṣāya* robe of succession been transmitted or not? To whom has the Buddha-Dharma been entrusted?' The Venerable Neng replied, 'A woman has taken my robe away. As for my Dharma, twenty years after my death [the one who] establishes the cardinal tenet of the school is the one who will have gotten my Dharma.'"[332]

SECTION 17

Discourses of the Venerable Wuzhu (T. 51. 185C26–186A14)

劍南成都府大暦保唐寺无住和上、每常為[333]學道四衆、「百千万人及一人、無有時節、有疑任問。處座說法、直指見性。以直心為道場、以発行為道場、以深心為道場、以無染為道場、以不取為道場、以不捨為道場。以无為為方便、以廣大為方便、以平等為方便。以離相為火、以解脱為香。以无罣碍是懺悔、以无念為戒、以无為无[334] 所得為定、以不二為恵。不以嚴設為道場。」

和上云、「一切衆生本来清淨、本来圓満、添亦不得、減亦不得。為順一念漏心、三界受種種身。假善知識直指本性。見性即成佛道、着相即沈輪[335]。為衆生有念、假說无念。有念若无、无念不自。滅三界心、不居寂地、『不住事相、不无功用。』但離虚妄、名為解脱。」

又云、「有心即是波浪、无心即是外道。順生死即是衆生垢、依寂即是涅槃動。不順生、不依寂地、『不入三昧、不住坐禅、无生无行、心无得失。』影體倶非、性相不立。」

Whenever the Venerable Wuzhu of the Dali[336] Bao Tang monastery in Chengdu sub-prefecture in Jiannan[337] addressed students of the Way of the four assemblies, [he would say], "Whether a multitude or a single person, regardless of the time, if you have doubts you may confide your questions to me. I am occupying the seat and explaining the Dharma [so that you] directly see your own natures. Regard direct mind as the *bodhimaṇḍa* (*daochang* 道場). Regard aspiration to practice as the *bodhimaṇḍa.* Regard the profound mind as the *bodhimaṇḍa.* Regard the unstained as the *bodhimaṇḍa.* Regard not-grasping as the *bodhimaṇḍa.* Regard not-rejecting as the *bodhimaṇḍa.* Regard nonaction as expedient means. Regard the vast as expedient means. Regard equanimity as expedient means. Regard transcendence of characteristics as the fire and regard liberation as the incense. Regard nonobstruction as repentance. Regard no-thought as the precepts, nonaction and nothing to attain as meditation, and nonduality as wisdom. Do not regard the constructed ritual arena as the *bodhimaṇḍa.*"[338]

The Venerable said, "All beings are fundamentally pure and fundamentally complete and can be neither augmented nor reduced. By allowing one thought to defile the mind, in the Three Worlds you will take on the various kinds of bodies. Provisionally, 'Good Friends' point directly to fundamental nature. Seeing the nature is thus the Way of becoming a Buddha, and attachment to characteristics is thus sinking into the cycle [of birth and death].[339] It is because beings have thought that one provisionally teaches no-thought, but if there is no presence of thought, then no-thought itself is not.[340] Extinguishing the mind of the Three Worlds but not dwelling in stillness, 'not abiding in characteristics but not without efficacy.'[341] Simply separating from empty delusion is called liberation."

He further said, "The presence of mind is 'ocean waves,' but no-mind is heterodoxy. Complying with birth-and-death is the stain of beings, but depending on stillness is the movement of nirvāṇa.[342] Not complying with birth, not depending on stillness, 'not entering samādhi, not abiding in seated meditation, there is no-birth and no-practice, and the mind is without loss or gain.'[343] Shadow and body are both negated, and neither nature nor characteristics are set up."

SECTION 18

Wuzhu and Wuxiang (T. 51. 186A15–187C7)

和上鳳翔郿縣人也。俗姓李、法号无住、年登五十。開元年代、父朔方展効。時年廿、膂力過人、武藝絶輪[344]。當此之時、信安王充河朔両道節度使。見和上有勇有列、信安王留充衙前遊弈先峯官。和上每自歎、「在世栄華、誰人不樂? 大丈夫兒、未逢善知識。一生不可虚弃。」遂乃捨官宦、尋師訪道。忽遇白衣居士陳楚璋、不知何處人也。時人号為維摩結化身。説頓教法。和上當遇之日、密契相知、默傳心法。和上得法已、一向絶思斷慮、事相並除。三五年間、白衣脩行。

天寶年間、忽聞范陽到次山有明[345]和上、東京有神會和上、太原府有自在和上、並盡是第六祖師第子、説頓教法。和上當日之時亦未出家。遂往太原、礼拜自在和上。自在和上説、「淨中无浄想[346]、即是真浄佛性。」

和上聞法已、心意快然、欲辞前途。老和上共諸律師大德、苦留不放、「此真法棟樑。」便与削髪披衣。

天寶八年、受具戒已、便辞老和上、向五臺山清涼寺、経一夏。聞説到次山明和上縦由、神會和上語音[347]、即知意况、亦不往礼。

天寶九載、夏満出山至西京、安國寺崇聖寺往来。

天寶十載、従西京却至北霊州、居賀蘭山二年。忽有商人曹[玉+襃]礼拝問、「和上曾到劍南、識金和上否？」答云、「不識。」[玉+襃]云、「和上相貌、一似金和上。鼻梁上有黶、顔状与此間和上相貌、更無別也。應是化身。」和上問曹[玉+襃]、「居士従劍南来、彼和上說何教法？」曹[玉+襃]答、「說无憶无念莫忘[348]。第子當日之時、受縁訖辞、金和上問瓌、『何處去？』[玉+襃]答云、『父母在堂、欲帰覲省。』金和上語瓌、『正不憶不念惣放却、朗朗蕩蕩[349]、看有汝父母否。』[玉+襃]當日之時、聞己未識、今呈和上。」和上聞説豁然、遥与金和上相見。遂乃出賀蘭山至北霊州出行文、往劍南礼金和上。遂被留、後姚嗣王不放。大德史和上、辯才律師、恵荘律師等諸大德並不放来。

至德二年十月、従北霊州黙出。向定遠城及豊寧、軍使楊含璋處出行文。軍使苦留、問和上、「佛法為當只在劍南、為復此間亦有？若彼此一種、緣何故去？」和上答、「若識心見性、佛法遍一切處。无住為在學地、善知識在劍南、所以遠投。」軍使又問和上、「善知識是誰？」和上答、「是无相和上、俗姓金、時人号金和上也。」軍使頂礼、便出行文。和上漸漸南行至鳳翔、又被諸大德苦留不放、亦不住。又取太白路山[350]、入住太白山経一夏。夏満、取細水谷路出至南梁州。諸僧徒衆苦留不住。

乾元二年正月、到成都府浄衆寺。初到之時逢安乾師、引見金和上。金和上見非常歓喜。金和上遣安乾師作主人。安置在鐘樓下院住。其時正是受縁之日、當夜随衆受縁。只経三日三夜。金和上每日於大衆中、高聲唱言、「縁何不入山去、久住何益？」左右親事第子恠、「金和上不曽有如此語、縁何忽出此言？」无住和上、黙然入山。金和上憶、「縁何不来。」空上座、秦上座、欲得相識、「恐後相逢、彼此不知是誰。」

和上向倪朝説、「吾雖此間、每常与金和上相見。若欲不相識、對面千里。吾重為汝說一縁起。佛昔在日、夏三月忉利天為摩耶夫人說法時、十六大國王及一切衆生悉皆憶佛。即令大目犍連往忉利天請佛。佛降下閻浮時、須菩提在石室中。聞佛降下即欲出室、自念云、『我聞世尊、『若在三昧、即是見吾。若来縦見吾色身、有何所益？』』便即却入三昧。是時連華色比丘尼、擬除悪名、即欲在前見佛。諸大國王、龍神八部、闔匝圍遶、无有路入。化身作大轉輪王千子圍遶、龍神國王悉皆開路。連華色比丘尼還作本身、圍遶世尊己、合掌説偈、『我初見佛、我初礼佛。』説偈己、作礼而立。尒時世尊告比丘尼、『於此會中、汝最在後。』比丘尼白世尊、『於此會中、无有阿羅漢、云何言我在後？』世尊告比丘尼、『須菩提在石室中常在三昧、所以先得見吾法身。汝縦来見色身、所以在後。』佛有明文、无住所以不去。」

同住道逸師、習誦礼念、和上一面[351]向絶思斷慮、入自證境界。道逸共諸同住小師、白和上云、「逸共諸同住、欲得六時礼懺、伏願和上聽許。」和上語道逸等、「此間粮食並是絶縁、人般運深山中。不能依法脩行、欲得學狂、此並非佛法。」和上引佛頂経云、「『狂心不歇、歇即菩提、勝浄明心、本周法界。』无念即是見佛、有念即是生死。若欲得礼念即出山。平下大有寛閑寺舍、任意出去。若欲得同住、一向无念。得即任住、不得即須下去。」

道逸師見不遂本意、辞和上出天蒼山。来至益州浄衆寺、先見空上座等説、「山中无住禅師不行礼念、只空閑坐。」何空等聞説、倍常驚恠、「豈是佛法！」領道逸師見金和上。道逸礼拝未了、何空等諮金和上云、「天蒼山无住禅師只空閑坐。不肯礼念、亦不教同住人礼念。豈[352]有此事、可是佛法！」金和上叱何空道逸等、「汝向後！吾在學地時、飯不及喫、只空閑坐。大小便亦无功夫。汝等不識、吾當天谷山日亦不礼念、諸同學嗔吾並出山去。无人送粮、惟錬土為食、亦无功夫出山、一向閑坐。孟寺主聞諸同學説吾閑坐、便向唐和上讒吾。唐和上聞説吾閑坐、倍加歎喜。吾在天谷山[353]亦不知讒。聞唐和上四大違和、吾從天谷山来至資州徳純寺。孟寺主見吾来、不放寺入[354]。唐和上聞吾来、使人喚吾至堂前。吾礼拝未訖、唐和上便問、『汝於天谷山作何事業？』吾答、『一物不作、只没忙。』唐和上報吾、『汝忙、吾亦忙矣！』唐和上知、衆人不識。」

和上云、「居士、達摩祖師一支佛法流在劍南、金和上即是。若不受縁、恰似宝山空手帰。」璿聞已、合掌起立、「第子即入成都府受縁去。」和上山中知金和上遥憶彼即知意。遂向璿説、「此有茶芽半斤、居士若去将此茶芽為信、奉上金和上、傳无住語頂礼金和上。金和上若問无住、云无住未擬出山。」

和上山中知金和上遥憶彼即知意。遂向璿説、「居士、達摩祖師一支佛法流在劍南、金和上即是。若不受縁、恰似宝山空手帰。」璿聞已、合掌起立、「第子即入成都府受縁去。」和上云、「此有茶芽半斤、居士若去将此茶芽為信、奉上金和上、傳无住語頂礼金和上。金和上若問无住、云无住未擬出山。」[355]

璿即便辞和上、将所奉茶芽。至建已月十三日、至成都府浄衆寺。為金和上四體違和、輒无人得見。董璿逢菩提師、引見金和上。具陳无住禅師所奉茶芽、傳頂礼金和上。金和上聞説及見茶芽、非常歎喜、語董璿、「无住禅師既有信来、何得不身自来？」董璿答、「无住禅師来日云未擬出山。」金和上問董璿、「汝是何人？」璿誑金和上答、「是无住禅師親事第子。」金和上向璿云、「帰白崖山日、吾有信去、汝須見吾来。」

至十五日、見金和上、璿云「欲帰白崖山、取和上進止。」其時發遣左右親事第子、「汝等惣出堂外去。」即喚董璿入。璿依命入堂[足+胡]跪合掌。[356] 金和上将袈裟一領、人間罕守勿有。呈示、「此是則天皇后与詵和上、詵和上与唐和上、唐和上与吾、吾傳将付与无住禅師。此衣久遠已来保愛、莫遣人知。」語已悲涙哽咽、「此衣嫡嫡相傳付授、努力努力！」即脱身上袈裟、覆膊裙衫坐具、共有十七事。「吾将年邁。汝将此物密送无住禅師、傳吾語、『善自保愛、努力努力！未是出山時。更待三五年間、自有貴人迎汝即出。』」便即発遣董璿、「急去莫教人。」見璿去、後金和上獨語云、「此物去遅、到頭還達。」金和上正語之時左右无人。堂外第子聞和上語聲一時入堂、問金和上、「云何獨語？」「吾只没語。」為金和上四大違和、諸人見已有擬便問、「和上承上所傳信衣何在？和上佛法付嘱誰人？」金和上云、「吾法无住處去。衣向木頭上掛着、无一人得。」金和上向諸人言、「此非汝境界、各着本處去。」

元年建巳月十五日、改為寶應元年五月十五日、遥付嘱法[357]訖。至十九日命第子、「与吾取新净衣裳、吾今沐浴。」至夜半子時、嚴然坐化。

The Venerable was from the Mei district of Fengxiang.[358] His family name was Li. His Dharma name was Wuzhu, and his years amounted to five decades.[359] During the Kaiyuan era (713–741), his father distinguished himself serving in the army at Shuofang. When [Wuzhu] was twenty, his physical strength surpassed that of other men and he excelled in the arts of war. At the time, Prince Xin'an[360] (d. 743) served as military commissioner of the He[bei] and Shuo[fang] circuits.[361] Seeing that the Venerable was brave and ardent, Prince Xin'an retained him as the Patrolling Grand Lance Officer at the Yamen.[362] The Venerable always lamented to himself, "Who among men is not delighted by worldly glory? I am a 'real hero,' but I have yet to meet a 'good friend.' One can't frivolously waste one's life." So he gave up his official position to search for a teacher from whom to inquire about the Way. He chanced to meet the white-robed layman Chen Chuzhang, whose origins are unknown.[363] People then called him an incarnation of Vimalakīrti.[364] He expounded the Dharma of the sudden teaching. From the moment that he met the Venerable [Wuzhu] he privately sealed their mutual understanding, and silently transmitted the mind-Dharma. Having obtained the Dharma, the Venerable completely cut through thinking and ceased all restless anxiety, abandoning phenomena and characteristics. For three to five years, [Wuzhu] practiced as a white-robed [layman].

During the Tianbao era (742–755) [Wuzhu] chanced to hear of the Venerable Ming of Mt. Daoci in Fanyang,[365] the Venerable Shenhui of the Eastern Capital (Luoyang), and the Venerable Zizai of Taiyuan subprefecture,[366] all of whom were disciples of the sixth Patriarchal Master [Huineng] and taught the Dharma of the sudden teaching. At the time, the Venerable was not yet a renunciant. Then he went to Taiyuan and made obeisances to the Venerable Zizai. The Venerable Zizai taught, "In the midst of purity to be without the marks of purity, this is the true purity of the Buddha-nature." As soon as the Venerable heard the Dharma he made up his mind, and he wanted to renounce his former path. The old Venerable [Zizai] and all the Vinaya masters and worthies earnestly detained him and would not let him go, [saying], "This is the ridge-pole of the true Dharma." And so he took the tonsure and donned a robe.[367]

In the eighth year of the Tianbao era (749), when he had received the complete precepts he left the old Venerable [Zizai] and went to Qingliang monastery on Mt. Wutai,[368] where he spent one summer. He heard expositions concerning the "traces of the way" of the Venerable Ming of Mt. Daoci and about the import of the sayings of the Venerable Shenhui. Because he understood their meaning, he did not go to pay his respects to them.

In the ninth year of the Tianbao era (750), at the end of the summer he left the mountains and reached the Western Capital (Chang'an), where he came and went between the Anguo and Chongsheng monasteries.

In the tenth year of the Tianbao era (751), he retraced his steps from the Western Capital to North Lingzhou and lived at Mt. Helan for two years.[369] It happened that there was a merchant [named] Cao Gui who came to pay his respects [to Wuzhu] and asked, "Has the Venerable ever been to Jiannan? Do you know the Venerable Kim?" [Wuzhu] answered, "I don't know him." Gui said, "Your features are exactly like those of the Venerable Kim. You [both] have a mole above the bridge of your nose, and the shape of your face so resembles that of the Venerable in our locale that one could even say there is no difference. It must be a transformation-body."

The Venerable asked Cao Gui, "So the layman has come from Jiannan. [Tell me], what doctrine does that Venerable teach? Cao Gui replied, "'No-recollection, no-thought, and do not forget.'[370] Once, after receiving the bodhisattva precepts [during a retreat] and the Venerable Kim asked me, 'Where are you going?' I answered, 'My honored father and mother are still living, so I wish to return home to see them.' The Venerable Kim told me, 'Just not recollecting, not thinking, relinquishing everything, clear and vast—see whether your father and mother are there or not.' That is certainly what I heard at the time, but I do not yet understand it. Now I submit it to you, Venerable." When the Venerable heard this teaching he understood clearly, and from afar he met the Venerable Kim face-to-face. Consequently, he left Mt. Helan and went to North Lingzhou [in order] to be issued traveling papers to go to Jiannan and pay his respects to the Venerable Kim. It turned out that he was detained, and after that Prince Yaosi would not let him go. The Worthy Venerable Shi, the Vinaya Master Biancai, the Vinaya Master Huizhuang and the other worthies all refused to let him go.[371]

In the tenth month of the second year of the Zhide era (757) [Wuzhu] quietly left North Lingzhou, and on his way to Dingyuan city he got to Fengning,[372] where the Military Commander Yang Hanzhang issued his traveling papers.[373] The military commander earnestly tried to keep him and asked the Venerable, "Is the Buddha-Dharma only in Jiannan, or is it also here? If 'there' and 'here' are one, then why do you go?" The Venerable replied, "If one knows the mind and sees the nature, then the Buddha-Dharma pervades all places. But I am still at the stage of learning, and my 'good friend' is in Jiannan, so I will go far away and submit myself to him."

The military commander further asked the Venerable, "Who is your 'good friend'?" The Venerable replied, "The Venerable Wuxiang; his lay surname is Kim, and these days people call him the Venerable Kim." The military commander prostrated himself and then issued the traveling papers.

The Venerable gradually made his way south to Fengxiang.[374] There also the worthies earnestly tried to keep him from going, but again he did not stay. Then he took the Mt. Taibai road, entered Mt. Taibai and stayed the summer there.[375] At the end of the summer he took the Xishui Valley road and came out in Nanliangzhou.[376] The monks and disciples earnestly tried to keep him, but he did not stay.

In the first month of the second year of the Qianyuan era (759), [Wuzhu] reached Jingzhong (Pure Assembly) monastery in Chengdu subprefecture. When he first arrived he met Master Anqian, who led him in to see the Venerable Kim. When the Venerable Kim saw him he was extremely pleased. The Venerable Kim delegated Master Anqian to act as host, and he arranged for Wuzhu to stay in a cloister below the bell-tower.[377] This was during a bodhisattva precepts [retreat], and that night [Wuzhu] followed the crowd and received the precepts. It lasted only three days and three nights.[378]

Every day in the midst of the great assembly the Venerable Kim would intone in a loud voice, "Why do you not go into the mountains, what good is it to linger?" His attendant disciples considered this strange, [and said,] "The Venerable Kim has never said anything like this before. Why would he suddenly come out with these words?" But the Venerable Wuzhu quietly entered the mountains. [Later] the Venerable Kim longed for him [and said,] "Why doesn't he come?" Preceptor Kong and Preceptor Qin wanted to be able to recognize [Wuzhu, and so they said,] "We fear that one day we might chance to meet but not know who he is."

[From the mountains] the Venerable [Wuzhu] faced toward them with a keen glance and exclaimed, "Although I am here, the Venerable Kim and I see each other constantly. Even if we wish not to know each other, we are face to face [though separated by] a thousand *li*. With my regards, I will preach a parable for you."

"Long ago when the Buddha was alive, when he spent the three months of the summer retreat in Trāyastriṃśa Heaven expounding the Dharma for [his mother] Mahāmāyā, the sixteen great kings and all beings longed for the Buddha. So they sent Mahāmaudgalyāyana to Trāyastriṃśa Heaven to ask the Buddha [to return]. When the Buddha was to descend to Jambudvīpa, Subhuti was [meditating] in a stone cell. When he heard that the Buddha was to descend he wanted to leave his cell, but then thought to himself, 'I have heard the World-Honored One [say], 'If you are in samādhi, then this is seeing me. If you come rushing to see my form body, where is the benefit?' [Subhuti] therefore reentered samādhi.

"At that time, the Bhikṣunī Utpalavarṇā (Lianhuase),[379] being determined to expunge the reputation [of her sex],[380] desired to be the first to greet the Buddha. All the kings of great kingdoms and the eight divisions of nāgas and divinities had completely encircled [the Buddha] in circumambulations, and there was no path through. [The nun] transformed herself into the thousand sons of a Great Cakravartin King and surrounded [the company], and the nāgas, divinities, and kings opened a path. Utpalavarṇā Bhikṣuṇī then returned to her original form, and when she had circumambulated the World-Honored One, she joined her palms and spoke a gāthā: 'I am the first to greet the Buddha, I am the first to make obeisance to the Buddha.' Having spoken the gāthā, she made obeisance and stood up. At that, the World-Honored One told the bhikṣuṇī, 'In this company, you are last.' The bhikṣuṇī said to the World-Honored One, 'In this company there are no arhats, why do you say I am last?' The World-Honored One told the bhikṣuṇī, 'Subhuti is in a stone cell continuously in samādhi, and so he was first, being able to see my Dharma-body. You came rushing to see my form-body, and so you are last.' "[381] [Wuzhu concluded,] "The Buddha has given a clear mandate, and that is why I do not go [to see the Venerable Kim]."

Master Daoyi, [Wuzhu's] fellow inmate [at the mountain hermitage], practiced chanting [scripture], worship, and recitation [of the Buddha's name], while the Venerable [Wuzhu] completely cut through thinking and ceased all anxiety, and entered into the field of self-validating [enlightenment]. Daoyi, accompanied by all the minor masters who were their fellow-inmates, said to the Venerable, "I, together with all our fellow inmates, want you to join us in the six daily periods of worship and repentance. We humbly beg the Venerable to listen and accede." The Venerable said to Daoyi and the others, "Because here we are altogether cut off from provisions, people carry them on foot deep into the mountains. You can't rely on legalistic practice—you want to get ravings by rote, but this is not the Buddha-Dharma at all." The Venerable quoted the *Śūraṅgama-sūtra,* " 'The raving mind is not at rest. At rest, it is bodhi. Peerless pure bright mind fundamentally pervades the Dharmadhātu.'[382] No-thought is none other than seeing the Buddha. The presence of thought is none other than birth-and-death. If you want to practice worship and recitation, then leave the mountains. On the plains there are gracious and easeful temple-quarters, and you are free to go. If you want to stay with me, you must utterly devote yourself to no-thought. If you can, then you are free to stay. If you cannot, then you must go down."

As Master Daoyi's views did not go along with [Wuzhu's] fundamental intent, he took leave of the Venerable and left Mt. Tiancang.[383] Arriving at Jingzhong monastery in Yizhou, he met with Preceptor Kong and the others and said, "Chan Master Wuzhu in the mountains doesn't practice worship or recitation, he just sits in vacuity. Hekong and the others heard this with manifold amazement, [exclaiming] "How could this be the Buddha-Dharma!" They took Master Daoyi to see the Venerable Kim. Before Daoyi had finished making obeisances, Hekong and the others informed the Venerable Kim, "Chan Master Wuzhu of Mt. Tiancang just sits in vacuity. He is not willing to worship and recite, and neither will he teach his fellow inmates to worship and recite. What is this? How could this be the Buddha-Dharma!"

The Venerable Kim exploded at Hekong, Daoyi, and the others, "You get out! When I was at the stage of learning, I wouldn't get around to eating, I just sat in vacuity. I didn't even make an effort to shit or piss. You don't realize that when I was at Mt. Tiangu, I didn't worship or recite, either. All my fellow-students got angry with me and left the mountain. No one sent provisions and I had only smelted earth as food. But even then I didn't make an effort to leave the mountain, and I devoted myself to sitting in idleness. When Abbot Meng heard from my fellow-students that I was sitting in idleness, he immediately went to the Venerable Tang to slander me. When the Venerable Tang heard I was sitting in idleness he was overjoyed. Meanwhile I was at Mt. Tiangu and knew nothing of the slander. Hearing that the Venerable Tang was gravely ill, I came from Mt. Tiangu to Dechun monastery in Zizhou. Abbot Meng saw me coming and would not let me enter the monastery. [But] the Venerable Tang heard that I had come and sent someone to summon me to appear before his hall. I had not yet completed my obeisance when the Venerable Tang asked me, 'At Mt. Tiangu, how do you occupy yourself?' I replied, 'I don't do a thing. I am just oblivious.' The Venerable Tang retorted, 'You are oblivious, I am also oblivious!' The Venerable Tang knew, the others had no inkling."

From amid the mountains, the Venerable [Wuzhu] knew the Venerable Kim thought of him from afar, and he immediately knew [Wuxiang's] intentions. So the Venerable said to Xuan, "Layman, the direct tributary of the Buddha-Dharma of the Patriarchal Master [Bodhi]dharma has flowed to Jiannan; the Venerable Kim is it. If you do not receive the bodhisattva precepts [from him], it is just like returning from a mountain of treasure empty-handed." When Xuan heard this, he joined his palms and stood up, [saying] "Then your disciple will to Chengdu subprefecture to receive the bodhisattva precepts." The Venerable said, "Here is half a catty of bud-tea.[384] If you are going, then take this bud-tea as a token of faith and present it to the Venerable Kim. Convey Wuzhu's words and prostrations to the Venerable Kim. If the Venerable Kim should inquire after me, say the Wuzhu does not yet intend to come out of the mountains."

Xuan then took leave of the Venerable, taking the bud-tea that was to be offered [to Wuxiang]. On the thirteenth day of the month designated *si*,[385] he reached Jingzhong monastery in Chengdu subprefecture, but because the Venerable Kim was ill no one was allowed to see him. [However,] Dong Xuan chanced on Master Bodhi, who took him to see the Venerable Kim. [Dong Xuan] prepared and set out the bud-tea offered by Chan Master Wuzhu and conveyed [Wuzhu's] prostration to the Venerable Kim. When the Venerable Kim heard the message and saw the bud-tea, he was very pleased and said to Dong Xuan, "Since Chan Master Wuzhu has sent a token of faith to me, why didn't he come to me himself?" Dong Xuan replied, "On the day I set out, Chan Master Wuzhu said that he does not yet intend to leave the mountains." The Venerable Kim asked Dong Xuan, "And who are you?" Xuan lied to the Venerable Kim and replied, "I am Chan master Wuzhu's personal disciple." The Venerable Kim told Xuan, "On the day you go back to the Baiyai mountains, I have a token of faith to send, so you must come to see me."

On the fifteenth day, [Dong Xuan] went to see the Venerable Kim. He said, "I wish to return to the Baiyai mountains, I am at your command." That time [Wuxiang] sent away his personal attendant disciples, [saying,] "You must all leave the hall." Then he summoned Dong Xuan to enter; Xuan obeyed and entered the hall kneeling, with his palms joined. The Venerable Kim brought out a *kāṣāya* robe, [the one that] the rarest few among men have had in their keeping. He revealed it [and said,] "This was given to the Venerable Shen by Empress [Wu] Zetian. The Venerable Shen gave it to the Venerable Tang, the Venerable Tang gave it to me, and I transmit it to Chan Master Wuzhu. This robe has long been cherished, don't let anyone know of it." When he finished speaking he became choked with sobbing [and said,] "This robe has been passed from legitimate heir to legitimate heir, one must make utmost effort, utmost effort!" Then he took from his own person his *kāṣāya,* under and outer robes, and sitting cloth. Altogether there were seventeen things.[386] [He said,] "I am getting on in years. You take these things and convey them secretly to Chan master Wuzhu, and transmit my words: 'Take good care of yourself, and make utmost effort, utmost effort! It is not yet time to leave the mountains. Wait three to five years longer, and only leave when a person of consequence welcomes you.'"[387] At that he dispatched Dong Xuan, [saying,] "Go quickly, and do not let anyone learn of this."

After he had seen Dong Xuan go, the Venerable Kim said to himself, "These things will get there late, but they will get through in the end." The Venerable Kim said this when there was no one about. When the disciples outside the hall heard the Venerable's voice they entered the hall at once and asked the Venerable Kim, "Why were you talking all by yourself?" The Venerable said, "I was just muttering." Because the Venerable Kim was gravely ill, there were those who when they saw [this] decided to ask, "Where has the Venerable passed on the transmitted robe of verification?

To whom will the Venerable entrust the Buddha-Dharma?"[388] The Venerable Kim said, "My Dharma has gone to the place of nonabiding (*wuzhu*). The robe is hanging from the top of a tree, no one has got it." The Venerable Kim said to them, "This is not your sphere, you should each get back to your original place."

On the fifteenth day of the month designated *si* of the first year, that was changed to the fifteenth day of the fifth month of the first year of the Baoying era (762),[389] the investiture of the Dharma was completed from afar. On the nineteenth day, [Wuxiang] ordered his disciples, "Get me new, fresh clothes. I will bathe now." In the middle of the night in the hour of the rat, he died solemnly in a seated posture.

SECTION 19

Du Hongjian's Arrival in Shu (T. 51. 187C7–188B21)

副元帥黄門侍郎杜相公初到成都府日、聞金和上不可思議。金和上既化、合有承後第子。遂就浄衆寺、衡山寧國寺觀望、見金和上在日蹤跡。相公借問小師等、「合有承後第子、僧人得衣鉢者？」小師答、「亦无人承後。和上在日有両領袈裟、一領衡山寧國寺、一領留後[390]在浄衆寺供養。」相公不信、又問諸律師、「鴻漸遠聞金和上是大善知識、承上已来師師相傳授付囑衣鉢。金和上既化、承後第子何在？」律師答相公云、「金禅師是外國蕃人、亦无佛法。在日亦不多説法、語不能得正。在日雖足供養布施、只空是有福徳僧。縱有第子亦不閑佛法。」

相公高鑑、即知盡是嫉言。即廻帰宅、問親事孔目官馬良康然等、「知劍南有高行名僧大徳否？」馬良答云、「院内常見節度軍将説、蠶崖関西白崖山中有无住禅師、得金和上衣鉢、是承後第子。此禅師得[391]業深厚、亦不曽出山。」相公聞説向馬良等、「鴻漸遠聞金和上是大善知識。昨自到衡山寧國寺淨衆寺、問金和上親事第子。皆云无承後第子及得衣鉢。又問律師、咸言毀謗。據此蹤由、白崖山无住禅師、必是道者。」

即於大衙日問諸軍将等、「知此管内、有何名僧大徳否？」節度副使牛望仙、李虚應、帰誠王、董嘉會、張温、陰浴、張餘光、張軫、韋鸞、秦逖等諮相公、「白崖山中有无住禅師。金和上衣鉢在彼禅師處、不可思議。」相公問牛望仙、「君何以得知？」答云、「望仙高大夫差充石碑營使、為去道場不遠、数就頂礼、知不可思議。」相公又問、「適來言衣鉢在彼、誰知[392]的實？」

秦逖張鍠諮儔曰、「逖等充左右巡虞候、金和上初滅度日、両寺親事第子啾唧。囑何常侍向大夫説、『金和上信衣、不知的實、及不肯焚燒。』高大夫判付左右巡虞候推問、得實領過。當日初只得両領袈裟、両寺各得一領、信衣不知尋處。當日不知有蠶崖関西白崖山中有无住禅師。後被差充十将領兵馬上西山、打當狗城未進軍、屯在石碑營寄住。行營迫[393]道場、逖等諸軍将齎[394]供養到彼。見此禅師与金和上容貌[395]一種。逖等初見、将是金和上化身。借問逗留、知金和上衣鉢先遣人送。被隠二年不送、賣与僧。僧得衣、夜有神人遣還本主、『若不還必損汝命。』買人遞[396]相告報。後賣不得、還到本禅師處。逖等初聞當時推尋不知袈裟去處今在此間、即請頂礼。亦不生難、便擎袈裟出、呈示諸軍将官健等、所以知在彼處。」

相公聞説、「奇奇哉哉！僧等隠没佛法、不如俗人。俗人却欲得佛法流行。」節度副使李靈應、張温、牛望先、帰誠王、董嘉會、韋鸞、秦逖等、即衆連署状、請和上。相公向諸軍将知无住禅師、自有心請。相公差光祿卿慕容鼎為専使、即令出文牒。所在路次州縣、嚴擬幡花、僧道耆壽及音声。差一了事縣官就山同請。

文牒未出、浄衆寺寧國両寺小金師張大師聞請无住和上、惶怖无計。与諸律師平章、擬作魔事。先嚴尚書表第子簫律師等、嘱太夫人、奪金和上禅院為律院、金和上禅堂為講律堂。小金師且苟[397]安身。与簫律師等相知計會、為律院立碑、都[398]昂撰文。律師張知足与王英耀、及小金師張大師、嘱都昂郎中。律師英耀、共王謇侍御同姓、相認為兄第。

嘱崔僕射任夫人設齋。食訖小金師即擎裴僕射所施納袈裟、呈示僕射及夫人。小金師悲涙云、「此是承上信衣。」僕射、「旰由来不知此事、請无住禅師。相公意重、不関旰事。」都昂王謇曲黨、恐奪律院、廻顧問諸律師、「此山僧无住禅師、有何道業？」英耀律師等答、「若據此无住禅師无有知解。若請此僧深不益緇流。」尚書問、「縁何不益緇流。」答云、「有一工人於汶川刻鏤功徳平、得袈裟一領計直廿千文。被彼禅師奪工人衣不還。云、『是金和上与我。』 不行事相礼念。據此蹤由、即是不益緇流。」僕射向諸律師云、「旰先在西山兵馬、具知意況。律師等何用相[399] 誣？」語已離席。魔黨失色无計。魔事便息。

As soon as the Lord Minister Du [Hongjian],[400] vice-marshal and vice-director of the chancellery, first arrived in Chengdu Superior Prefecture, he heard that the Venerable Kim was inconceivable. As the Venerable Kim had passed on, [Du Hongjian] expected that he had left a successor. So he went to Jingzhong Monastery and to Ningguo Monastery on Mt. Heng[401] to look around, and he saw the Venerable Kim's mortal remains. The Lord Minister took the opportunity to ask the lesser masters, "Surely there is a successor-disciple, a monk who received the robe and bowl?" The lesser masters replied, "There was no one at all to succeed him. When the Venerable was alive he had two *kāṣāya* robes; [now] one is at Ningguo monastery on Mt. Heng and one remains at the Jingzhong monastery receiving dedicatory offerings." The Lord Minister did not believe them, and further questioned the Vinaya masters, "I had heard from afar that the Venerable Kim was a great 'Good Friend' who was entrusted with the robe and bowl that have been passed down from master to master. Now that the Venerable Kim has passed on, where is his successor-disciple?" The Vinaya masters told the Lord Minister, "Chan master Kim was a foreign barbarian, entirely lacking the Buddha-Dharma. While alive he did not lecture on the

Dharma much, and his words were unable to attain the truth. Although while he was alive the offerings and donations were sufficient, [among his disciples] only Kong is a monk with merit.[402] The rest of his disciples are unfamiliar with the Buddha-Dharma."

The Lord Minister was highly perceptive, and he knew that these were no more than jealous words. Thereupon he returned home, and he asked his personal clerks Ma Liang and Kang Ran, "Do you know of any exemplary monks or worthies in Jiannan?" Ma Liang replied, "At the governmental court I have often heard the military commissioner and commanders say that west of the Canyai pass in the Baiyai mountains,[403] there is Chan master Wuzhu who has got the Venerable Kim's robe and bowl and is his successor-disciple. This Chan master is virtuous and genuine, and he never leaves the mountains." When the Lord Minister heard this he said to Ma Liang and the others, "I had heard from afar that the Venerable Kim was a great 'Good Friend.' Yesterday I went myself to Ningguo monastery of Mt. Heng and Jingzhong monastery, and I asked the Venerable Kim's personal disciples. They all said there was no successor-disciple who had the robe and bowl. Then I asked the Vinaya masters, and they all slandered [the Venerable Kim]. Based on this evidence, Chan master Wuzhu of the Baiyai mountains must indeed be a man of the Way."

So when he next went to the district headquarters he asked all the army officers, "In this jurisdiction, do you know of any famous monks or worthies?" The Military Vice-Commissioners Niu Wangxian, Li Xuying, Gui Chengwang, Dong Jiahui, Zhang Wen, Yin Yu, Zhang Yuguang, Zhang Zhen, Wei Luan, and Qin Ti reported to the Lord Minister, "In the Baiyai mountains there is the Chan master Wuzhu. The Venerable Kim's robe and bowl are at his place, and he is inconceivable." The Lord Minister asked Niu Wangxian, "How did you come to know this?" He replied, "The High Grand Master sends me to serve at the Shibei encampment. Because it is not far from [Wuzhu's] holy place, I often go to make obeisance, and thus I know he is inconceivable." The Lord Minister inquired further, "You just spoke of the robe and bowl being there, but who knows if this is really true?"

Qin Ti and Zhang Huang reported together,[404] "We are the acting Patrolling Inspectors of the Left and Right. On the day that the Venerable Kim passed into extinction, his personal attendant disciples of both monasteries were all abuzz. They delegated Attendant-in-Ordinary He to tell the Grand Master, 'Until we know the truth regarding the Venerable Kim's Robe of Verification, we are unwilling to cremate him.' The High Grand Master sent us Patrolling Inspectors of the Left and Right out to investigate, we were in charge of getting to the truth. At first we were only able to get two *kāṣāya;* the two monasteries each had one robe, and we did not know where to search for the Robe of Verification. At the time, we did not know that west of the Canyai pass in the Baiyai mountains there is Chan master Wuzhu. Later, we were appointed file leaders to lead cavalry up into the western mountains. We were about to attack Danggou city (i.e., the Tibetans) but had not yet advanced our troops, and we were quartered at the Shibei encampment. The encampment was close to his place of practice and, accompanied by the other generals, we went there bearing dedicatory offerings. We saw that this Chan master looked exactly like the Venerable Kim. When we first saw him it was as if he were a transformation body of the Venerable Kim. We ventured to question him and remained for some time, and we learned that the Venerable Kim's robe and bowl[405] had previously been dispatched to him via a messenger. [The messenger] hid them for two years and did not deliver them, and then sold them to a monk. When the monk obtained the robe, that night a spirit appeared who told him to send it back to its original owner, [saying] 'If you do not return it, you are most certainly throwing away your life.' The buyer exchanged it, giving an account of what had happened. After that [the messenger] couldn't sell it, and restored it to the original Chan master's place. As soon as we heard that the robe our previous searching had not discovered was now in the immediate vicinity, we asked to make obeisance. Without reservations, [Wuzhu] carried the robe out aloft and revealed it to all the army officers and soldiers, so we know it is at that place."

When the Lord Minister heard this he said, "Astounding, quite astounding! Monks would hide the Buddha-Dharma, unlike a layman. A layman, rather, wants the Buddha-Dharma to flow forth." The Military Vice-Commissioners Li Lingying, Zhang Wen, Niu Wangxian, Gui Chengwang, Dong Jiahui, Wei Luan, and Qin Ti collectively signed a petition inviting the Venerable [to come down from the mountains]. The Lord Minister was swayed by the army officers who knew Chan Master Wuzhu, and was himself moved to request him to come. The Lord Minister sent the Imperial Entertainments Chief Minister Murong Ding as a special messenger and ordered that an official document be issued. At each region and district along the way there were fine pennants splendidly arranged, and monks and Daoists, elders and the aged chanted together. [He also] sent a highly competent district official to go to the mountains and make the collective invitation.

Before the official document had been issued, Master Xiaojin and Great Master Zhang of the Jingzhong and Ningguo monasteries heard of the invitation to the Venerable Wuzhu, and they were deeply alarmed and utterly at a loss. They organized all the Vinaya masters and proposed an evil deed. First, Minister Yan's[406] cousin Vinaya Master Xiao and others got the Grand Mistress to take away the Venerable Kim's Chan cloister and make it a Vinaya cloister, and take the Venerable Kim's Chan hall and make it a Vinaya hall. Master Xiaojin was then temporarily safe. Vinaya Master Xiao and others were in on the plan; they had a stele erected for the Vinaya cloister, and Du Ang wrote the inscription. The Vinaya masters Zhang Zhizu and Wang Yingyao, as well as Master Xiaojin and Great Master Zhang, got Director Du Ang to do it. [This was probably due to the fact that] Vinaya master [Wang] Yingyao and the Attendant Censor Wang Jian had the same surname, and they recognized each other as brothers.

They got the official wife of Vice-Director Cui[407] to arrange a vegetarian feast. When they had finished eating, Master Xiaojin raised up a fine linen *kāṣāya* that Vice-Director Pei had donated and displayed it to the vice-director and his wife. Weeping, Master Xiaojin said, "This is the Robe of Verification that has been passed down." The Vice-Director said, "I was not aware of this before, when I invited Chan Master Wuzhu. But the Lord Minister's mind is made up, and he will not heed such as I."

The treacherous clique of Du Ang and Wang Jian, fearing that their Vinaya cloister would be taken away, turned around and asked all the Vinaya masters, "This mountain monk 'Chan master Wuzhu'—what sort of spiritual practice does he have?" Vinaya Master Yingyao replied, "To rely on this Chan Master Wuzhu would be unwise. Inviting this monk would be profoundly disadvantageous to the clergy as a whole." The minister [Yan] asked, "Why would it be disadvantageous for the clergy?" [Yingyao] replied, "There is a craftsman on the Min river[408] who is an inlay-artisan of average skill. He got a *kāṣāya* [as payment] that had an estimated value of twenty thousand cash. The craftsman's robe was taken away by that Chan master and was never returned. [Wuzhu] claimed, 'This was bestowed on me by the Venerable Kim.' [Moreover], he does not practice the forms of worship and recitation. Based on this evidence, it would be disadvantageous for the clergy [were he to be invited]." The Vice-Director said to the Vinaya masters, "Previously, when I was with the cavalry in the western mountains, I learned the whole situation. Why do you Vinaya masters resort to slander?" So saying, he left his seat. [The faces of] the malicious clique drained of color, they were utterly at a loss. Their evil deed was thus thwarted.

SECTION 20

Du Hongjian and Wuzhu Meet (T. 51. 188B21–189B22)[409]

永泰二年九月廿三日、光祿卿慕容鼎專使縣官僧道等、就白崖山請和上。傳相公、僕射、監軍請礼頂、願和上:「不捨慈悲、為三蜀蒼生、作大橋樑、」殷懃苦請。和上知相公深閑佛法愛慕大乘、知僕射仁慈寬厚、知監軍敬佛法僧。審知是同緣同會、不逆所請。即有幡花寶蓋。諸州大德、恐和上不出白崖山、亦就山門同来赴請。即賫輿迎和上令坐輿中、和上不受、步步徐行。欲出之日、茂州境内六廻震動、山河吼虫鳥鳴。百姓互相借問、「是何祥瑞?」見有使来迎和上、當土僧尼道俗、再請留和上。専使語僧俗等、「是相公僕射意重為三蜀蒼生。豈縁此境、約不許留?」

當和上未出山日、寇盗競起、諸州不熟、穀米勇貴、万姓惶惶。相公僕射迎和上出山、所至州縣、穀米倍賤、人民安楽、率境豊熟、寇盗盡除、晏然無事。和上[410]到州史迎、至縣縣令引路。家家懸幡、戸戸焚香、咸言、「蒼生有福。」道俗满路、唱言、「无相和上去、无住和上来。此即是佛佛授手、化化不絶、燈燈相傳、法眼再明。法幢建立、大行佛法矣!」

相公令都押衙欽華遠迎和上。欽押衙傳相公語云、「鴻漸忽有風疾不得遠迎、至日頂礼。」劍南西川節度使左僕射兼御使大夫成都尹崔公、令都虞候王休崴、少府監李君昭、衙前虞候杜瑋等傳僕射語。頂礼和上、「第子是地主、自合遠迎。縁相公風疾所以第子及監軍使不敢先来。伏願和上照察。」傳語已一時便引和上至空恵寺安置。

是九月廿九日到十月一日、杜相公、呉監軍、諸郎官侍御、東川留後杜[411]郎中杜濟、行軍杜蔵、経邛南使中丞鮮于叔明、郎中楊炎、杜亞、都昂、馬雄、岑参、觀察判官員外李布、員外柳子華、青苗使呉郁、祖**庸**[412]使韋夏有、侍御狄博濟、崔伉、崔倜、王謇、蘇敞、司馬廉両少尹成賁白子昉、両縣令班**遜**[413]、李融捕賊官、惣来空恵寺門。

即都虞候王休崴、相公都押衙欽華、衛擇交先来白和上云、「相公[414]来謁和上。」和上答、「来即従他来。」押牙等白和上、「國相貴重、應須出迎。」和上答、「不合迎。迎即是人情、不迎即是佛法。」押衙又欲語、相公入院見和上容儀不動、儼然安徉。[415]相公頓身下階、作礼合掌、問信起居。諸郎官侍御未曾見有此事。乍見和上不迎不起、両両相看問、「縁何不迎不起?」郎中楊炎、杜亞久事相公、深識意旨、亦閑佛法。語諸郎官侍御、「觀此禅師、必應有道、相公自鑒、何用恠耳。」是日門外節度副使、都虞侯、捕賊官、乍聞和上見相公不起不迎、戦懼失色、流汗霢霂。使人潜聴、更待進止。見相公坐定言笑[416]、和上説法、相公合掌叩額。諸郎官侍御等喜[417]、門外人聞已便即无憂。

相公初坐問和上、「因何至此問?」和上答云、「遠故投金和上。」相公又問、「先在何處?今来遠投金和上、説何教法?」答无住、[418]「曽臺山抱腹**寺**、[419]并汾等州、及賀蘭山坐。聞金和上説頓教法、所以遠投。」相公問和上、「金和上説无憶无念莫忘、是否?」和上答云、「是。」相公又問、「此三句語、為是一為是三?」和[420]上答、「是一不三。无憶是戒、[421]无念是定、莫妄是恵。」又云、「念不起戒門、念不起是定門、念不起恵門。无念即戒定恵具足。」相公又問、「既一妄字、為是亡下女、為是亡下心?」和上答、「亡下女。」「有證處否?」和上答。「有。」即引法句経云、「説諸精進法、為増上慢説。若无増上慢、无善无精進。若起精進心、是妄非進精[422]。若能心不妄、精進无有涯。」

相公又[423]聞説、白和上、「見庭前樹否?」和上答、「見。」相公又問和上、「向後墻外有樹、見否?」和上答、「見。非論前後、十方世界悉見悉聞。」庭前樹上[亞+鳥]鳴。相公又問和上、「聞[亞+鳥]鳴否?」

和上答、「此見聞覺知、是世間見聞覺知。維摩経云、「『若行見聞覺知、是即見聞覺知。法離見聞覺知。』無念即无見、无念即无知、為衆生有念、假説无念、正[424]无念之時、无念不自。」又引金剛[425]三昧経云、「『尊者大覺尊、説生无念法。无念无生心、心常生不滅。』又維摩経云、『不行是菩提、无憶念故。』『常求无念、實相智恵。』楞伽経云、『聖者内所證、常住於无念。』佛頂経云、『阿難、汝麈挙心、塵勞先起。』又云、『見猶離見、見不能及。』思益経云、『云何一切法正、云何一切法邪? 若以心分別、一切法邪。若不以心分別、一切法正。无心法中、起心分別、普皆是邪。』楞伽経云、『見佛聞法皆是自心分別。不起見者、是名見佛。』」

相公聞説、頂礼和上。白和上云、「鴻漸初聞。和上未下山日、鴻漸向浄衆寺寧國寺觀金和上蹤跡。是大善知識、即知劍南更合有善知識。鴻漸遍問諸師僧、金和上三句語及妄字、皆云亡下作心、三句語各別。不決第子所疑。鴻漸問諸軍将、『劍南豈无真僧?』无有一人祇對得者、節度副使牛望先[426]、秦逖諸軍将齊諮鴻漸、説和上徳業深厚。所以遠迎、伏願和上不捨慈悲、与三蜀蒼生作大良縁。」語已頂礼、「第子公事有限、為僕射諸節度副使、未得礼拜和上。鴻漸未離劍南、每日不離左右。」語已辞去。

On the twenty-third day of the ninth month of the second year of the Yongtai era (766),[427] the Imperial Entertainments Chief Minister Murong Ding acting as special messenger, the district officials, Buddhists, Daoists, and such, all went to Mt. Baiyai to invite the Venerable [Wuzhu]. Conveying the invitations and obeisances of the Lord Minister (Du Hongjian), the Vice-Director, and the Army Supervisor, they implored the Venerable: "Do not forsake mercy, for the sake of beings of the Three Shu,[428] make a 'Great Bridge,'"[429] they beseeched him fervently. The Venerable knew that the Lord Minister profoundly defended the Buddha-Dharma and cherished the Mahāyāna,[430] he knew that the Vice-Director was benevolent and generous, and he knew that the Army Supervisor honored the Buddha, Dharma, and Saṅgha. He judged that these were associates of the same karmic destiny and did not turn down the invitation. And so there were "fine pennants and a jeweled parasol" (i.e., a procession befitting a Buddha). All the worthies of the region, fearing that the Venerable would not come out from Mt. Baiyai, also went to the mountain gate to join in the invitation. They welcomed the Venerable with a jeweled sedan-chair and would have had him sit in it; but the Venerable declined and proceeded step by step in a slow and dignified manner. When he was about to leave, the earth quaked six times in the Mao Zhou area,[431] the mountains and rivers roared, and the insects and birds cried out. The ordinary people all asked one another, "What good omens are these?" When they saw that official representatives had come to welcome the Venerable, then the local monks, nuns, followers of the Way, and laypersons redoubled their pleas that the Venerable remain. The special messenger told the monks and laypersons and the others, "The Lord Minister and the Vice-Director consider this important for the benefit of all the beings of the Three Shu. Of what account is this area, when we have promised not to let him be detained?"

When the Venerable had not yet come out of the mountains, outlaws and thieves were running rampart, all the regions were uncivilized, the cost of grain and rice was rising ever higher, and the masses were very anxious. When the Lord Minister and Vice-Director invited the Venerable to come out of the mountains, wherever he went the cost of grain and rice fell by half, the people were content and happy, all the territory was refined and civilized. The outlaws and thieves were completely eradicated, and all progressed peacefully and without incident. When the Venerable arrived in a region, officials came to welcome him; when he came to a district, the district magistrate came to guide him along the road. Every household hung out banners, at each doorway they burned incense, and everyone said, "All beings are blessed with good fortune." Followers of the Way and laypersons filled the roads, chanting "The Venerable Wuxiang has gone, the Venerable Wuzhu has come. Thus it is that Buddha upon Buddha confers his hand, the teachings are taught without interruption, lamp lights lamp in succession, and the Dharma-eye is redoubled in brilliance. The Dharma-banner is established—indeed a great work of the Buddha-Dharma!"

The Lord Minister sent his Chief Warrant-Officer Qin Hua to welcome the Venerable from afar. Warrant-Officer Qin conveyed the Lord Minister's message, saying "Hongjian has suddenly caught a chill, and is unable to come to welcome you from afar. He will pay his obeisances when you arrive." The Governor of Chengdu, Lord Cui, Military Commissioner of the Jiannan West River Command, and concurrent Vice-Director of the Left and Censor-in-Chief, ordered Inspector-in-Chief Wang Xuiyan, Director of Imperial Manufactories[432] Li Junzhao, Local Inspector Du Zhang, and others to convey the Vice-Director's message. Making obeisances to the Venerable [they said on Lord Cui's behalf] "I, your disciple, am lord of the locality, and it would be proper if I myself were to welcome you from afar. However, owing to the Lord Minister's illness, your disciple and the Army Supervisor do not dare to go before him. We humbly beg the Venerable to favor us with his gracious understanding." So saying, [the delegates] immediately conducted the Venerable to Konghui monastery[433] and settled him there.

From the twenty-ninth day of the ninth month to the first day of the tenth month, the Lord Minister Du, Army Supervisor Wu, all the Directors and Attendant-Censors, the East River Capital Liaison Representative Director Du Ji, Adjutant Du Zang, the Commissioner South of the Qiong [River] and Vice-Censor Xianyu Shuming, Directors Yang Yan, Du Ya, Du Ang, Ma Xiong, and Chen Can, the Surveillance Commissioner's Supernumerary Administrative Assistant Li Bu, Supernumerary Liu Zihua, the "Green Sprouts" Official[434] Wu Yu, Special Supply Commissioner Wei Xiayou, Attendant Censors Di Boji, Cui Kang, Cui Ti, Wang Jian, and Su Chang, Cavalry Adjutant Inspector and Double Vice-Governor, the Honorable Bo Zifang, Double District Magistrate Ban Xun, and Li Rong, the Thief-Catching Officer, all came to the gates of Konghui monastery.[435]

The Inspector-in-Chief Wang Xuiyan and the Lord Minister's chief lackeys Qin Hua and Wei Zhejiao came first to tell the Venerable, "The Lord Minister is coming to present himself to the Venerable." [Wuzhu] replied, "If he's coming then it's up to him." The lackeys told the Venerable, "A minister of state is a very important person, you ought to go out and welcome him." The Venerable said, "It would not be appropriate to welcome him. 'Welcoming' is human feelings. 'Not welcoming' is the Buddha-Dharma."

The lackeys wanted to say more, but [at the moment] the Lord Minister entered the cloister and saw that the Venerable's demeanor was unmoving, majestically composed. The Lord Minister bowed at the lower level, made obeisance with palms joined, and politely inquired after [Wuzhu's] "rising and resting" (i.e., his health and comfort). None of the directors and attendant-censors had ever seen such a thing. When they first saw that the Venerable neither welcomed [the minister] nor rose, they looked at one another and asked, "Why does he neither welcome [the minister] nor rise?" The Directors Yang Yan and Du Ya had long served the Lord Minister, they were very familiar with his will, and moreover defended the Buddha-Dharma. They said to all the directors and attendant-censors, "Observe this Chan master—he must certainly possess the Way. The Lord Minister can look after himself, why take offense?" When the military vice-commissioner, inspector-in-chief, and thief-catching officer outside the door first heard that the Venerable met the Lord Minister without rising or welcoming him, they trembled with fear and lost color, and were soaked through with perspiration. The attendants listened secretly, waiting for [orders] to advance and punish [Wuzhu]. [However,] they saw the Lord Minister take a seat, talking and smiling; the Venerable spoke on the Dharma, and the Lord Minister joined his palms and touched his forehead to the ground. All the directors and attendant-censors were delighted, and once the people outside the door heard about it, they were no longer grieved.

When he was first seated the Lord Minister asked, "Why did the Venerable come here?" The Venerable said, "I came from afar in order to submit myself to the Venerable Kim." The Lord Minister further asked, "Where were you before? Since you came from afar to submit yourself to the Venerable Kim, what Dharma did he teach?" Wuzhu replied, "I have been at Baofu monastery at Tai shan, as well as Fenzhou and other areas, and I sat at Mt. Helan.[436] I heard that the Venerable Kim taught the Dharma of the Sudden Teaching, and so I came from afar to submit myself to him."

The Lord Minister asked the Venerable, "The Venerable Kim taught 'no-recollection, no-thought, and do not forget,' isn't that so?" The Venerable replied, "Yes."[437] The Lord Minister further asked, "These three phrases, are they one or are they three?" The Venerable replied, "They are one, not three.[438] No-recollection is *śīla,* no-thought is samādhi, and 'do not be deluded' is prajñā." He spoke further, "The non-arising of thought is the gate of *śīla,* the non-arising of thought is the gate of samādhi, the non-arising of thought is the gate of prajñā. No-thought is thus the complete fulfillment of *śīla,* samādhi, and prajñā."[439]

The Lord Minister asked further, "Regarding the character *wang,* is it [the one with] *nu* 女 below *wang* 亡, or with *xin* 心 below *wang?*" The Venerable replied, "*Nu* below *wang.*" [The Lord Minister asked,] "Do you have any evidence, or not?" The Venerable replied, "I have." Then he quoted the *Dhammapada,* "If you preach about the Dharma of 'good effort' (*vīrya*), you are preaching out of self-conceit (*adhimāna*). If you are without self-conceit there is no 'good' and no 'good effort.' If you arouse the mind of 'good effort,' this is delusion and not good effort. If you are able [to experience] mind without delusion, then good effort has no limit."[440]

The Lord Minister heard this teaching, then said to the Venerable, "Do you see the tree in front of the courtyard or not?"[441] The Venerable replied, "I see it." The Lord Minister further questioned the Venerable, "Outside the wall behind us there is a tree, can you see it or not?" The Venerable replied, "I see it. Do not discuss 'in front' and 'behind'; in the world of the ten directions, I see everywhere and hear everything." Atop the tree in front of the courtyard, a crow called. The Lord Minister again asked the Venerable, "Do you hear the crow call or not?"

The Venerable replied, "This seeing, hearing, perceiving, and knowing [that you are getting at] is worldly seeing, hearing, perceiving, and knowing. The *Vimalakīrti-sūtra* says, 'If you go about seeing, hearing, perceiving, and knowing, then this is seeing, hearing, perceiving, and knowing. The Dharma transcends seeing, hearing, perceiving, and knowing.'[442] No-thought is thus no-seeing, no-thought is thus no-knowing. It is because beings have thought that one provisionally teaches no-thought, but at the time of true no-thought, no-thought itself is not."[443] He went on to quote the *Vajrasamādhi-sūtra,* "'The Most Honored Greatly Enlightened One expounded the Dharma of producing no-thought. [Regarding] the mind of no-thought and non-production, the mind is constantly producing and never extinguished.'[444] Further, the *Vimalakīrti-sūtra* says, 'Not-practicing is bodhi, because it is without recollection.'[445] 'Always seek no-thought, the wisdom characterized by actuality.'[446] The *Lankā-sūtra* says, 'The Holy One's inner reference point is to constantly abide in no-thought.'[447] The *Śūraṃgama-sūtra* says, 'Ānanda, if you initiate the mind [even] for a short time, the suffering due to defilements will have [already] arisen first.'[448] Further, it says, 'So long as sight is separate from seeing, then seeing cannot be attained.'[449] The *Viśeṣacinta-sūtra* says, 'How is it that all dharmas are true, and how is it that all dharmas are wrong? If one makes distinctions with the mind, then all dharmas are wrong. If one does not make distinctions with the mind, all dharmas are true. In the midst of no-mind dharmas, once one gives rise to distinctions of mind everything is wrong.'[450] The *Lankā-sūtra* says, 'Seeing the Buddha and hearing the Dharma is your own mind making distinctions. One for whom 'seeing' does not arise—this is called seeing the Buddha.'"[451]

After the Lord Minister had listened to this teaching, he made obeisance to the Venerable. He said to the Venerable, "I have heard you speak for the first time. When you, Venerable, had not yet descended from the mountains, I went to Jingzhong monastery and Ningguo monastery and viewed the Venerable Kim's mortal remains. He was a great 'Good Friend,' so I knew that somewhere in Jiannan there had to be a 'Good Friend.' I asked every one of the masters and monks in turn about the Venerable Kim's three phrases and the *wang* character, and they all said that *wang* was written with *xin* underneath it, and that the three phrases were separate. They did not settle your disciple's doubts. I asked all the army officers, 'In Jiannan is there really no genuine monk?' There was not a single person who disagreed: the Military Vice-Commissioners and Directors Niu Wangxian and Qin Ti and all the army officers reported unanimously to me that the Venerable was virtuous and genuine. So I have welcomed you from afar, and I humbly beg the Venerable not to forsake mercy; create great 'good causes' for the beings of the Three Shu." He ceased speaking and made obeisance, [then continued], "Your disciple is constrained by public affairs, and the Vice-Director and all the military vice-commissioners have not yet been able to pay obeisance to the Venerable. So long as I am in Jiannan, I will not fail to attend you daily." So saying, he took his leave.

SECTION 21

Cui Gan Visits Wuzhu (T. 51. 189B22–190B16)

僕射知相公歓喜云、「和上不可思議。」即共任夫人及節度軍将頂礼和上。起居問訊訖、坐定處分都押衙、放諸軍将同聴和上説法。時有无盈法師清原法師、僧中俊哲、在衆而坐。

和上引佛頂経云、「『阿難、一切衆生従无始来、種種顛倒、業種自然、如悪叉聚。諸脩行人不能得成无上菩提。乃至別成[452]聲聞縁覺、及成外道諸天、魔王眷属。皆由不知二種根本、錯乱脩習、猶如煮沙欲成嘉饌。縦経塵劫、終不能得。云何二種？阿難、一者无始生死根本、則汝今者与諸衆生、用攀縁心為自性。二者无始菩提涅槃元[453]清浄體。則汝今者識精无明、能生諸縁。縁所遺者、由失本明。雖終日行、而不自覺、枉入諸趣。』」

和上又説、「一切衆生本来清浄、本来圓満。上至諸佛下至一切含識、共同清浄性。而[454]為衆生一念妄心、即染三界。為衆生有念、假説无念、有念若无、无念不自。无念即无生、无念即无滅、无念即无愛、无念即无憎[455]、无念即无取、无念即无捨、无念即无高、无念即无下、无念即无男、无念即无女、无念即无是、无念即无非。正无念之時、无念不自。心生即種種法生、心滅即種種法滅。如其心然、罪垢亦然、諸法亦然。正无念之時、一切法皆是佛法、无有一法離菩提者。」

又云、「因妄有生、因生[456] 妄有滅。生滅名妄、滅妄名真、是稱如来无上菩提及大涅槃。」

和上説法已、儼然不動。僕射聞説合掌、白和上云、「旰是地主。自合遠迎、為公事不獲。願和上勿責。旰先是西山兵馬使、和上在白崖山蘭若、元是當家。若有所須、專差衙前虞侯衹供和上。」

和上答云、「脩行般若波羅蜜、百无所須。」又云、「汝但辦心、諸天辦供[457]。何等心辦、不求心、不貪心、辦不受心、辦不染心。梵天不求、梵天自至、果報不求、果報自至。无量珍寶不求自至。」又云、「知足大富貴、少欲最安樂。」

僕射聞和上説、合掌頂礼。清原法師作礼、白和上、「小師一聞法已、疑網頓除。今投和上、願悲慈攝授和上。」然无盈法師據傲、[458]懔然色變。和上問无盈法師、「識主客否？」无盈法師答、引諸法相、廣引文義。和上云、「法師不識主客。強認前塵、以流注生滅心自為知解。猶如煮沙、欲成嘉饌、計劫只成熱沙。只是自誑誑他。楞伽経云、『随言而取義、建立於諸法、已彼建立故、死隨[459] 地獄中。』」

无盈法師聞説、側身偏坐。和上問法師、「无記有幾種？」法師答、「異熟无記、變易无記、工巧无記、威儀无記。」和上又問、「何者是有記？」法師答、「第六意識是有記。」

和上云、「第六意識[460]是顛倒識。[461]一切衆生、不出三界、都由意識。意不生時、即超三界。剃頭削髪、盡是佛第子、不可學有記、不可學无記。今時法師、盡學无記、不信大乘。云何是大乘？内自證不動、是无上大乘。我无上大乘、超過於名言、其義甚明了、愚夫不能覺。覺者覺諸情識空寂无生、名之為覺。」

无盈法師聞説杜口无詞。和上云、「无記有二種、一者有覆无記、二者无覆无記。第六意識、至眼等五識、盡属有覆无記。第六識已下至八識、盡属无覆无記。並是強名言之。又加第九識是清浄識、亦是妄立。」

和上引楞伽経云、「『八九種種識、如海衆波浪。習氣常増長、槃根堅固依。心随境界流、如鉄於磁[462]石。』『如水瀑流盡、波浪即不起、如是意識滅、種種識不生。』『種種意生身、我説為心量。』『得无思想法、佛子非聲聞。』」

无盈法師聞説、唯稱「不可思識。」和上又問、「楞伽経云、『已楔出楔』此義云何？」无盈法師答云、「譬如搬木、先以下大楔、即下小楔、令出大楔。」和上報法師、「既小楔出大楔、大楔[463]既出、小楔還在。云何以楔出楔[464]？」

法師更無詞敢對。和上即解、「楔喻衆生煩悩、楔假諸佛如来言教。煩悩既无、法即不自。譬如有病、然与處方。病得愈、方藥並除。然今法師執言教法、如病人執方、而不服藥。不捨文字、亦如楔在木中。楞伽経云、『譬如以指指物、小児觀指不觀於物。』随言説指而生執着、乃至盡命、終不能捨文字之指取弟一義。[465]」

和上又問法師三寶四諦義、又問三身義。法師更不敢對、唯稱和上不可思議。僕射聞説法已、倍加歡喜、「第子當日恐和上久在山門、畏祇對相公不得、深憂直縁。三川師僧、無一人稱相公意者。相公一見和上、向第子説、真實道者、天然特達、与諸僧玄殊、讃歎不可思議。第子聞相公説、喜躍不勝。是第子有福、登時无憂。」諸軍将並喜慰、不可説、頂礼去。

Vice-Director [Cui][466] learned that the Lord Minister had joyfully declared, "The Venerable is unfathomable." He immediately went with his wife Ren[467] and the military commissioners and army officers to make obeisances to the Venerable. When they had inquired after [Wuzhu's] "rising and resting," the officers were seated in sections, and [Cui] permitted all the army officers to listen with them to the Venerable expounding the Dharma. At that time Dharma Master Wuying and Dharma Master Qingyuan, eminently sagacious among monks, were seated among the assembly.[468]

The Venerable quoted the *Śūraṃgama-sūtra:*

> [The Buddha said], "Ānanda, all beings since beginningless time [experience] every kind of reversal; by the kind of deed [destinies] are self-determined, as numerous as *rudrākṣa* seeds.[469] Not all those who practice are able to attain unsurpassed bodhi. They may instead become śrāvakas, pratyekas, may become [denizens of] non-Buddhist heavens, or retainers of the Demon-King. This is all due to not knowing the two kinds of roots, and practicing in error and confusion. It is like boiling sand and wanting it to become fine viands. Although an eon as long as the number of atoms of a world ground to dust may elapse, it is in the end impossible. What are the two kinds [of roots]? Ānanda, the first is the root of beginningless birth and death. Thus, you, along with all beings, presently take the mind that grasps after conditions (*ārabhaṇa*) as yourself. The second is beginningless bodhi-nirvāṇa, originally pure substance. With you at present the consciousness essence is un-illuminated, and thus you are able to be born in various conditions. Those who forget conditions consequently lose their original luminosity. Even though you practice day in and day out, if you are not self-aware, you will vainly enter into every destiny."[470]

The Venerable continued, "All beings are fundamentally pure and fundamentally complete. From the Buddhas at the upper end down to sentient beings, all are of the same pure nature. However, with a single thought [produced by] the deluded mind of beings, the Three Worlds are dyed. It is because beings have thought that one provisionally teaches no-thought, but if there is no presence of thought, then no-thought itself is not.[471] No-thought is thus no-birth, no-thought is thus no-extinction. No-thought is thus no-love, no-thought is thus no-hate. No-thought is thus no-grasping, no-thought is thus no-abandoning. No-thought is thus no-high, no-thought is thus no-low. No-thought is thus no-male, no-thought is thus no-female. No-thought is thus no-true, no-thought is thus no-false. At the time of true no-thought, no-thought itself is not. 'When the mind is produced then the various dharmas are produced, when the mind is extinguished then the various dharmas are extinguished.'[472] 'As one's mind is, so also are the stains of wrongdoing, so also are all dharmas.'[473] At the time of true no-thought, 'all dharmas are the Buddha-Dharma,'[474] there is not a single dharma separate from bodhi."

[Wuzhu] went on, "Due to delusion there is birth, due to delusion there is extinction. Birth and extinction are called delusion, extinguishing delusion is called true reality. This is designated as the Tathāgatha, unsurpassed bodhi, and the great nirvāṇa."

When the Venerable had expounded the Dharma, he [sat] majestically unmoving. The Vice-Director had listened with joined palms, and [now] he addressed the Venerable, "I am lord of the locality, and it would have been proper if I myself were to have welcomed you from afar, but due to official matters I was prevented. I beg the Venerable not to blame me. When I was a cavalry officer in the western mountains, the Venerable was in a hermitage in the Baiyai mountains, and so from the outset you have been the head of the family. If there is anything you need, I have specially deputed the local inspector to respectfully make offerings to the Venerable."

The Venerable said, "One who cultivates the Prajñāparamitā needs nothing whatsoever." He went on, "If you only [offer with] discriminating mind, then the Heavens discriminate your offerings. Howsoever the mind discriminates, [one maintains] not-seeking mind and not-coveting mind; discriminating [one maintains] not-receiving mind, discriminating [one maintains] not-staining mind. If the Brahmaloka is not sought, the Brahmaloka is reached of itself; if karmic reward is not sought, karmic reward is reached of itself.[475] The incomparably precious jewel unsought is reached of itself." He went on, "Knowing satisfaction is great wealth and honor, having few desires is the greatest peace and happiness."[476]

When the Vice-Director heard the Venerable's words, he joined his palms and touched his forehead to the ground in obeisance. Dharma Master Qingyuan made obeisance and said to the Venerable, "Once I heard [your] Dharma, the net of doubt was suddenly removed.[477] I now submit myself to the Venerable, I beg to receive mercy and compassion from the Venerable." But Dharma Master Wuying succumbed to pride, and, shaking, he changed color. The Venerable asked Dharma Master Wuying, "Do you recognize host and guest or not?"[478] Dharma Master Wuying replied, drawing from various Dharma forms and widely quoting exegetical literature. The Venerable said, "The Dharma Master does not recognize host and guest. Concentrating on sense-objects, you take the flowing mind of birth and extinction itself as understanding.[479] 'It is like boiling sand wishing it to become fine viands'—however many kalpas [it boils], it will only become hot sand. It is only deceiving yourself and deceiving others. The *Laṇkāsūtra* says: 'If you follow after words and grasp meanings then you build on dharmas, and because of that construction, when you die you fall into Hell.' "[480]

When Dharma Master Wuying heard this talk, his body tilted to one side so that he sat off-kilter. The Venerable asked the Dharma Master, "How many kinds of *avyākṛta* (categories of morally neutral) are there?" The Dharma Master replied, "*Vipāka-avyākṛta* (morally neutral results from good or evil causes), *pariṇama-avyākṛta* (morally neutral death and rebirth), *śilpa-avyākṛta* (morally neutral arts and skills), and *īryāpatha-avyākṛta* (morally neutral postures and physical movements)." The Venerable asked, "What is *vyākṛta* (category of morally good or bad)?" The Dharma Master replied, "The sixth consciousness (*manovijñāna*) is *vyākṛta*."

The Venerable said, "The sixth consciousness is the *viparyāsa* (delusion) consciousness. [The reason that] the many beings do not exit the Three Worlds is all due to the consciousnesses. When thought is not produced, then the Three Worlds are released. Those who shave their heads and cut their hair are all disciples of the Buddha, they can't [waste time] studying *vyākṛta* and *avyākṛta*. Dharma masters these days all study *avyākṛta*, they don't have faith in the Mahāyāna. 'What is the Mahāyāna? Internally self-confirmed and unmoving, this is the unsurpassed Mahāyāna. My 'unsurpassed Mahāyāna' goes beyond names and words, its meaning is [for those of] profound understanding, fools are unable to realize it.'[481] 'Realization' is realization that all feelings and consciousnesses are void, tranquil, and unborn—this is what I call realization."

When Dharma Master Wuying heard this he shut his mouth wordlessly. The Venerable said, "There are two kinds of *avyākṛta*. One is *nivṛta-avyākṛta* (morally neutral with hindrances preventing realization). The other is *anivṛta-avyākṛta* (morally neutral without hindrances). [From] the sixth consciousness to the five consciousnesses of sight and the other [senses], all belong to the category of *nivṛta-avyākṛta*. From the sixth consciousness to the eighth consciousness, all belong to the category of *anivṛta-avyākṛta*. Both are phrases [arising from] the compulsion to name. Further adding a ninth consciousness that is a pure consciousness is also setting up delusion."[482]

The Venerable quoted from the *Laṇkā-sūtra:* "'The eighth and ninth and the various consciousnesses are like the ocean's many breaking waves. Habits continually increase, solid and dense as tangled roots. The mind follows the flow of one's conditioned state like iron to a lodestone.'[483] 'As when a cascade of water runs out the waves do not arise, likewise when the consciousnesses are extinguished, the various consciousnesses are not produced.'[484] 'The bodies produced by the various thoughts, I explain as the conditioned mind's apprehension.'[485] '[One who] attains the nonconceptual Dharma is a disciple of the Buddha and not a *śrāvaka.*'"[486]

When Dharma Master Wuying heard this teaching, he only said admiringly, "Inconceivable." The Venerable further inquired, "The *Laṇkā-sūtra* says, 'Using a wedge to push out a wedge.'[487] What does this mean?" Dharma Master Wuying replied, "It is like splitting wood—first one drives in a large wedge, then one drives in a small wedge, forcing out the large wedge." The Venerable responded to the Dharma Master, "When the small wedge pushes out the large wedge, while the large wedge is out, the small wedge is still in. Why does one use a wedge to push out a wedge?"

The Dharma Master again didn't dare utter a word. So the Venerable explained, "The [large] wedge illustrates the wedge of the defilements of the many beings, and the [small] wedge is a simile for the Buddhas' and Tathāgatas' verbal teachings. When there are no defilements, the Dharma does not of itself [remain]. It is like having an illness and receiving a prescription. If the illness is cured, the prescription and the medicine are both discarded. Thus, Dharma masters now who grasp at the Dharma of verbal teachings are like a sick person who grasps a prescription but is unable to swallow the medicine. Not abandoning texts and characters is like a wedge remaining in the wood. The *Laṇkā-sūtra* says, 'It is like using a finger to point at something. A small child looks at the finger and does not look at the object.' If one follows the pointing of verbal explanation and conceives an attachment to it, then at the end of one's life one is ultimately unable to relinquish the finger of texts and characters and grasp the cardinal meaning."[488]

The Venerable further questioned the Dharma Master, [asking him about] the meaning of the Triple Jewel and the Four [Noble] Truths, and he also asked about the meaning of the Three Bodies of the Buddha. The Dharma Master still didn't dare reply and only said admiringly that the Venerable was inconceivable. When the Vice-Director had heard the explanation of Dharma, his delight was redoubled. [He said,] "That day [when you met the Lord Minister] I was afraid lest the Venerable's long sojourn in the mountain monastery should make him overawed by the Lord Minister and unable [to speak]. I was deeply grieved due to these causes. Among the monks of the Three Rivers[489] there was not one who corresponded to the Lord Minister's intent. As soon as the Lord Minister had seen you, Venerable, he said to me that you were a genuine man of the Way, inherently perspicacious, and altogether different from the other monks, and he sighed in praise that you were inconceivable. When I heard the Lord Minister's words, my joy was unsurpassed. It was my good fortune, and from that moment my sorrows were no more." The army officers were also moved to joy; they could not speak, and they touched their foreheads to the ground in obeisance and departed.

SECTION 22

Dialogue with Chan Master Tiwu (T. 51. 190B16–190C18)

時有東京體无師、僧中俊哲。處處尋師。戒律威儀及諸法事、聰明多辨[490]。亦稱禅師、是聖善寺弘政禅師第子。共晉原竇承、什邡李去泰、青城蘇承、判官周洽等、尋問和上。直至禅堂、和上見来相然已各坐。

體无問和上、「是誰第子、是誰宗旨？」答、「是佛宗旨、是佛第子。」和上報、「闍梨削髪被衣、即是佛第子、何用問師宗旨？『依了義経、不依不了義経。』有疑任問。」體无知和上是金和上第子、乃有毀言、「希見劍南人[491] 不起心。禅師打人云不打、嗔人云不嗔。有施来受言不受。體无深不解此事。」

和上答、「脩行般若波羅密、不見報恩者、不見作恩者。已无所受、而受諸受。未具佛法、亦不滅受。无住従初發心迄至于今、未曾受人[492]毛髪施。」體元聞説、視諸官面云、「禅師言語大曷。」和上問體无、「闍梨既口認禅師。云何起心打人、起心嗔人、起心受施？」體无自知失宗旨、瞿然失色、量久不語。問和上、「解楞伽経否。」和上答云、「解是不解。」

諸官相黨語和上、「禅師但説、何用相詰？」和上報諸官人、「若説恐諸官不信。」官人答言、「信。」和上即説、「我若具説、或有人聞、心即狂乱、狐疑不信。」即引楞伽経云、「愚夫樂妄説、不聞真實恵。言説三界本、真實滅苦因。言説即變異、真實離文字。於妄想心境、愚生二種見。不識心及縁、即起二妄想。了心及境界、妄想即不生。」

體无救義引法華経有三乘。和上引楞伽経云、「『彼愚癡人説有三乘、不説唯心、无諸境界。』『心无覺智心[493] 生動念即魔網。』」又引思益経云、「云何一切法正、云何一切法邪？若以心分別、即一切法邪。若不以心分別、一切法正。无心法中起心分別、普皆是邪。」

At that time there was a Master Tiwu of the Eastern Capital (Luoyang), eminently sagacious among monks.[494] He had sought out masters everywhere. [He was notable in] adherence to the precepts, imposing comportment, and all matters of the Dharma, and he was astute and eloquent.

He was also designated a "Chan master," and he was a disciple of Chan Master Hongzheng of Shengshan monastery [in Luoyang].[495] Together with Dou Cheng of Jinyuan, Li Qutai of Shifang, Su Cheng of Qingcheng, the Administrative Assistant Zhou Xia and others,[496] he came seeking to question the Venerable. [They] proceeded directly to the Meditation Hall, and when they had each greeted the Venerable individually, they took their seats.

Tiwu asked the Venerable, "Whose disciple are you, and whose doctrines [do you adhere to]?" The Venerable replied, "I [adhere to] the Buddha's doctrines. I am the Buddha's disciple." The Venerable declared, "Ācārya, you cut your hair and wear robes and are thus the Buddha's disciple. What use is it to ask about teachers and doctrines? 'Rely on scriptures of the complete meaning, do not rely on scriptures of incomplete meaning.'[497] If you have some doubts, then question as you will."

Tiwu knew that the Venerable was the Venerable Kim's disciple, but his words were malicious: "I wish to observe that the people of Jiannan do not arouse the [true] mind. The Chan masters [hereabouts] strike people and call it not-striking, berate people and call it not-berating, and when they receive donations they say 'not-received.' I am deeply perplexed by these matters."

The Venerable replied, "Practicing Prajñāpāramitā one does not see the one who is awarded favor and does not see the one who extends favor. It is because already there is nothing to receive that one receives all one receives. The not-yet-complete Buddha-Dharma is also endlessly received. From the time when I first put forth the mind up until the present, I have never received a single hair in donations."

When Tiwu heard this he looked around at the officials and said, "The Chan master speaks with a big voice." The Venerable asked Tiwu, "So the Ācārya verbally recognizes a Chan master! Why would one arousing the mind strike people, arousing the mind berate people, and arousing the mind receive donations?" Tiwu knew himself that he had lost doctrinal [ground]. He was taken aback and lost color, and for a long while he did not speak. Then he asked the Venerable, "Do you comprehend the *Laṇkā-sūtra* or not?" The Venerable replied, "Comprehending is not-comprehending."

The officials exclaimed in concert to the Venerable, "The Chan master alone should expound [on the Dharma], what point is there in questioning each other?" The Venerable told the officials, "If I expound [on the Dharma], I am afraid you officials will not believe." The officials replied, "We believe!" The Venerable then explained, "If I were to expound completely, anyone who heard it would become disturbed in mind, and would fall prey to doubt and not believe."[498] Then he quoted from the *Laṇkā-sūtra,* saying, "A fool delights in delusive preaching and does not hear true wisdom. 'Verbal explanation is the origin of the Three Worlds, the real extinguishes the cause of suffering. Verbal explanation is flux, the real transcends texts and characters.'[499] In a deluded state of mind, the foolish give rise to the two kinds of views. If you do not recognize mind and causes, then you give rise to the two delusions. If you understand mind and the field of conditions, then delusion is not produced."[500]

Tiwu, attempting to redeem himself, quoted the *Saddharmapuṇḍarīka-sūtra* (*Lotus Sūtra*) regarding the "Three Vehicles." The Venerable quoted the *Laṇkā-sūtra,* saying: " 'Those idiots teach that there are three Vehicles, they do not explain that there is only mind, and no field of conditions whatsoever.'[501] 'The mind that is unaware produces active thinking, which is the demons' net.' "[502] He also quoted from the *Viśeṣacintā-sūtra,* "How is it that all dharmas are true, and how is it that all dharmas are wrong? If one makes distinctions with the mind, then all dharmas are wrong. If one does not make distinctions with the mind, all dharmas are true. In the midst of no-mind dharmas, once one gives rise to distinctions of mind everything is wrong."[503]

SECTION 23

Dialogue with Chan Master Huiyi (T. 51. 190C18–22)

有恵憶禅師、時人号李山僧。問和上云、「以北禅師、云何入作?」和上答、「禅師亦不南、亦不北、亦不入作、亦不出作。没得没失、不流不注、不沈不浮、活鱍鱍。」恵憶聞已、合掌叩頭而坐。

There was Chan master Huiyi, whom people in those days called "the monk of Plum Mountain."[504] He asked the Venerable, "As for the Northern Chan masters, how do they go about 'entering'?"

The Venerable replied, "A Chan master is neither 'Southern' nor 'Northern,' he neither enters nor exits.[505] One has neither gain nor loss; not flowing and not fixed, not sinking and not floating, lively like a fish jumping!"[506] When Huiyi heard this, he joined his palms and knocked his head [on the ground], then sat down.

SECTION 24

Dialogue with Masters Yijing, Zhumo, and Tangwen

(T. 51. 190C22–191A27)

有義浄師、處黙師、唐蘊師、並是恵明禅[507]師第子。来欲得共和上同住。和上問、「闍梨解何経論?」唐蘊師答、「解百法論、曽為僧講。」和上請説。唐蘊答、「内有五箇无為、外有五箇有為、惣攝一切法。」和上引楞伽経云、「无智恒分別有為及无為。若諸脩行者、不應起分別。経経説妄想、終不出於名。若離於言説、亦无有所説。」

唐蘊語義浄師、「請闍梨更問。」義浄即問和上、「禅師作沒[508]生坐禅？」和上答、「不生、只沒禅。」義浄自不會、問處黙、「此義云[510]何？」處黙亦不會。更令義浄師別問。和上知[509]不會、遂問義淨、「闍梨解何経論？」答、「解菩薩戒、曽為僧講。」和上問、「戒已何為體、以何為義？」其義浄无詞可對、便出穢言、「非我不解、直為試你。如似你禅、我嫌不行。」處黙連聲、「我嫌你鈍不作、我嫌悶不行、我嬾嫌[511]不作、我慵嫌[512]不入！」

和上語諸僧、「『如如之理、具一切智。』『我无上大乘、超過於名言。其義甚明了、愚夫不覺知。』无住与諸闍梨説一緣起。有聚落、於晨朝時有一孩[513]子啼叫聲。隣人聞就看、見母嗔打。隣人問、『何為打之?』母云答、[514]『為尿床。』隣人叱母、『此子幼稚、何為打之?』又聞一啼哭聲。隣人就問、見一丈夫年登卅、其母以杖鞭之。隣人問、『緣何鞭?』母答云、『尿床。』隣人聞説言、『老漢多應故尿、直須痛打。』如此僧等類、『譬如象馬攏悷不調。加諸楚毒、至乃[515]徹骨。』」

和上再為説、「欲[516]求寂滅樂、當學沙門法。『无心離意識、是即沙門法。』諸闍梨削髪披衣、自言我是佛第子、不肯學沙門法。只[517]言慵作嬾[518]作、嫌鈍不入。此非沙門釋子、是野干之類。佛有明文、『未来世當有身着於袈裟、妄説於有无、毀壊我正法。』『譬如以指指物、愚癡凡夫、觀指不觀於物。』随言説指而生執着、乃至盡命、終不能捨文字之指。『随言而取義、建立於諸法、以彼建立故、死墮地獄中。』」諸僧聞説、忙然失色辭去。

There were Master Yijing, Master Zhumo, and Master Tangwen, who were all disciples of Chan master Huiming.[519] They came wishing to stay with the Venerable. The Venerable asked, "Ācārya, what scriptures and treatises have you explicated?" Master Tangwen replied, "I have explicated the *Baifa lun* (Treatise on One Hundred Dharmas),[520] I have lectured on it for the monks." The Venerable invited him to expound on it. Tangwen replied, "Inside there are five [kinds of] *asaṃskṛta* (the unconditioned), outside there are five [kinds of] *saṃskṛta* (conditionality) altogether they encompass all dharmas." The Venerable quoted the *Laṅkā-sūtra*, saying: "'Those without wisdom constantly make a distinction between *saṃskṛta* and *asaṃskṛta*.'[521] 'Those who practice must not give rise to distinctions.'[522] 'Scripture after scripture expounds delusory concepts, in the end none depart from [mere] designations. If you transcend verbal explanation then there is nothing to explain.'"[523]

Tangwen said to Master Yijing, "Please, Ācārya, you ask next." So Yijing asked the Venerable, "Chan master, how do you produce seated meditation (*zuochan*)?" The Venerable replied, "Not producing, this is 'Chan.'"

Yijing didn't understand it himself, and he asked Zhumo, "What does this mean?" Zhumo didn't understand either. Instead he told Master Yijing to ask something else. The Venerable knew they didn't understand, and so he asked Yijing, "Ācārya, what scriptures and treatises have you explicated?" He replied, "I have explicated the *Pusa jie* (Bodhisattva Precepts),[524] I have lectured on it for the monks." The Venerable asked, "What is the substance of the precepts, and what is their meaning?" Yijing had no words with which to reply, and then he burst out with invective: "It is not that I don't understand, it was only in order to test you. Your sort of 'Chan'—I despise [such] 'not-practicing'!" Zhumo chimed in, "I despise your dull 'not-doing,' I despise [your] stupefying 'not-practicing,' I despise [your] lazy 'not-doing,' I despise [your] slovenly 'not-entering!' "

The Venerable addressed the monks, " 'The principle of suchness (tathatā) encompasses all wisdom.'[525] 'My unsurpassed Mahāyāna goes beyond names and words. Its meaning is [for those of] profound understanding, fools do not comprehend it.'[526] I will tell the Ācārya an instructive tale. At dawn in a small village there was the sound of a little girl crying. A neighbor heard and went to take a look, and saw the mother angrily hitting [the child]. The neighbor asked, 'Why are you hitting her?' The mother replied, 'Because she wet the bed.' The neighbor scolded the mother, 'This child is very young, why are you hitting her [for that]?' Once again the sound of crying was heard. The neighbor went to inquire, and saw a fine fellow well-nigh thirty years old whose mother was beating him with a cudgel. The neighbor asked, 'What are you beating him for?' The mother replied, 'He wet the bed.' The neighbor heard this and said, 'As he is a grown man he probably did it deliberately, so you certainly should beat him severely.' It is this way when the monks are 'like elephants and horses, contentious and uncooperative. It compounds the sharp poisons so that they penetrate to the bone.' "[527]

The Venerable once again expounded for them, "If you seek the bliss of tranquil extinction, you must learn the śramaṇa's Dharma. 'The no-mind of transcending consciousness, this is precisely the śramaṇa's Dharma.'[528] You Ācārya shave off your hair and put on robes and say to yourselves, 'I am the Buddha's disciple,' but you are unwilling to learn the śramaṇa's Dharma. You just say, 'slovenly doing, lazy doing, I despise dull not-entering.' This is not the śramaṇa lion, this is a kind of wild dog. The Buddha made a prediction: 'In generations to come there will be those whose bodies wear the *kāṣāya*, [but who] delusively preach 'being' and 'non-being' and harm my true Dharma.'[529] 'It is like using a finger to point at something. An ignorant common person looks at the finger and does not look at the object.' If one follows the pointing of verbal explanation and conceives an attachment to it, then at the end of one's life one is ultimately unable to relinquish the finger of texts and characters.[530] 'If you follow after words and grasp meanings then you build on dharmas, and because of that construction, when you die you fall into Hell.' "[531]

When the monks heard this they were confused, lost color, and fled.

SECTION 25
Dialogue with Master Jingzang (T. 51. 191A28–B17)

西京勝光寺浄蔵師、聞和上不可思議、遠投和上。和上[532]問、「**云何**[533]知不可思議？」浄蔵師**答**、[534]「知金和上衣鉢傳授和上。」和上[535]問、「云何以知之？」浄蔵答云、「僧俗咸言云、和上嫡嫡相傳授、得金和上法。小師多幸有福得遇和上。」語已作礼。

和上問、「先學何経論？」答云[536]、「小師曾看維摩章疏、亦學坐禅是太白宗旨。」和上即為説法、「无意是道、不觀是禅。不取亦不捨、境来亦不縁。若看章疏、即是想念喧動。若學太白宗旨、宗旨坐禅、即是意想攀縁。若欲得此間住、一生来所學者、盡不在心。」問浄蔵、「得否？」答「得。和上慈悲指授、一取和上規模。」

和上觀浄蔵堪為法器、即重再説法、「一物在心、不出三界。『有法是俗帝、[537]无性第一義。』『離一切諸相、即名諸佛。』无念即无相、有念即虚妄。无念出三界、有念在三界。无念即无是、无念即无非、无念即无自、无念即无他。自他倶離、成佛菩提。正无念之時、无念不自。」

浄蔵聞説、歓喜踊躍、即請和上改法号。名超蔵、不離左右扶持。

Master Jingzang of Shengguang monastery in the Western Capital (Chang'an)[538] heard that the Venerable was inconceivable and came from afar to submit himself to the Venerable. The Venerable asked, "How did you know that I am inconceivable?" Jingzang replied, "I knew that the Venerable Kim transmitted his robe and bowl to the Venerable." The Venerable asked, "How did you know this?" Jingzang replied, "Monk and layman alike say that Venerable was invested with the transmission from legitimate heir to legitimate heir, and has got the Venerable Kim's Dharma. I am blessed with great good fortune to be able to meet the Venerable." When he finished speaking, he made obeisance.

The Venerable asked, "What scriptures and treatises have you studied?" [Jingzang] replied, "I have read a commentary on the *Vimalakīrti-sūtra,* and I also studied seated meditation [according to] the doctrines of [Mt.] Taibai."[539] The Venerable then expounded the Dharma for him: "Non-intention is the Way, not contemplating is Chan. Neither grasped nor rejected, objects arrive and yet are not caused. If you read commentaries, thus is the clamor of conceptualization set in motion. If you 'study the doctrines of [Mt.] Taibai,' you doctrinalize seated meditation, and thus intentions and conceptions climb up like vines. If you want to stay here, let nothing whatsoever of what you have studied so far remain in your mind." He asked Jingzang, "Can you do that or not?" [Jingzang] replied, "I can. In compassion, Venerable, bestow your guidance on me, I will take you as my model."

The Venerable saw that Jingzang was a truly worthy vessel of the Dharma, and so he once more expounded the Dharma for him: "If there is but one thing in your mind, you will not depart from the Three Worlds. 'The existence of dharmas is conventional truth, and no-nature is the cardinal meaning.'[540] 'Transcending all characteristics is called the Buddhas.'[541] No-thought is thus no-characteristics, presence of thought is thus empty delusion. No-thought departs the Three Worlds, thought remains in the Three Worlds. No-thought is thus no-true, no-thought is thus no-false. No-thought is thus no-self, no-thought is thus no-other. If you transcend both self and other you achieve Buddha-awakening.[542] At the time of true no-thought, no-thought itself is not."

When he heard this teaching Jingzang leapt for joy, and then he asked the Venerable to change his Dharma-name. He was named Chaozang, and he constantly attended [the Venerable], never leaving his side.

SECTION 26
Dialogue with Master Zhiyi (T. 51. 191B18–C2)

隴州開元寺覺禅師弟子知一師、時人号質直僧。来投和上。和上[543]問、「汝従何来？」知一師答、「従隴州来。」和上問、「是誰弟子？」知一師答、「是覺和上弟子。」「覺和上是誰弟子？」「是老福和上弟子。」和上云、「説汝自脩行地看。」知一師即呈本師教云、「看浄。」

和上即為説法、「法无垢浄、云何看浄？此間淨由不立、因何有垢？看浄[544]即是垢、看垢即是淨。妄想是垢、无妄想是浄。取我是垢、不取我是浄。无念即无垢、无念即无浄。无念即无非。无念即无自、无念即无他。自他倶離、成佛菩提。正自之時、自亦不自。」

知一師聞説、言下悟。於説法[545]處、更不再移。和上見知一師志性淳厚、有忠孝心。便為改号名超然。不離左右、楽行作務。

Master Zhiyi, disciple of Chan Master Jue of Kaiyuan monastery in Longzhou, was designated by his contemporaries as a monk of upstanding character.[546] He came to submit himself to the Venerable. The Venerable asked, "Where did you come from?" Master Zhiyi replied, "I came from Longzhou." The Venerable asked, "Whose disciple are you?" Master Zhiyi replied, "I am the disciple of Master Jue." [The Venerable asked,] "Whose disciple is the Venerable Jue?" [Zhiyi replied,] "He is the disciple of the Venerable Old Fu."[547] The Venerable said, "Tell me about your own stage of practice." Master Zhiyi revealed the teachings of his original master and said, "Viewing purity."[548]

The Venerable then expounded the Dharma for him: "The Dharma has neither stain nor purity, how does one 'view purity'? Right here purity was never established, why would there be stains? Viewing purity is in fact stains, viewing stains is in fact purity. Delusive thinking is stains, no-delusive thinking is purity. Grasping 'I' is stain, not grasping 'I' is purity. No-thought is thus no-stain, no-thought is thus no-purity. [No-thought is thus no-true,] no-thought is thus no-false.[549] No-thought is thus no-self, no-thought is thus no-other. If you transcend both self and other you achieve Buddha-awakening.[550] At the time of true self, self itself is not."

When Master Zhiyi heard [the Venerable's] teaching he was enlightened at his words. He never moved from the place in which he heard the Dharma talk. The Venerable saw that Master Zhiyi had a determined nature and was utterly sincere, and had a loyal and filial heart. Thus he changed his name to Chaoran. [Chaoran] never left [the Venerable's] side, and he served him with delight.

SECTION 27

Dialogue with Master Zhongxin (T. 51. 191c2–15)

登州忠信師、博覧詩書、釋性儒雅。捨諸事業、来投和上、「忠信是海隅邊境、遠投和上。」語已作礼。和上答、「道无遠近、云何言遠？」忠信啓和上、「生死事大、聞和上有大慈悲、故投和上。不縁衣食、伏願照察。」和上問、「學士多足思慮、若能捨得、任住此間。」忠信答云、「朝聞道夕死可矣。身命不惜、何但文字？」

和上即為説法、「『尊者大覺尊、説生无念法。无念无生心、心常生不滅。』於一切時中自在、勿逐勿轉。不沈不浮、不流不注、不動不揺、不来不去、活鱍鱍。『行坐惣是禅。』」忠信師聞説、儼然不動。和上見已、即知悟解大乘。改名号超寂。山中常秘密、夜即作務。不使人知、明即却来舊處。

Master Zhongxin of Dengzhou[551] was widely read in the [*Classics of*] *Poetry* and *Documents*, and his Buddhist character was learned and refined. He abandoned all worldly affairs and came to submit himself to the Venerable, [saying]: "I am from a frontier region at the edge of the sea, I have come far to submit myself to the Venerable." So saying, he made obeisance. The Venerable replied, "The Way has neither far nor near, why do you speak of 'far'?" Zhongxin explained to the Venerable, "The matter of life and death is great, I heard that the Venerable has great compassion and therefore I came to submit myself to the Venerable. It is not for the sake of clothing and food, I humbly beg you to deign to consider me." The Venerable asked [him to consider, saying], "Scholars are too full of anxious thought. If you are able to abandon gain, I will allow you to stay here." Zhongxin replied, "'If one hears of the Way in the morning one can die in the evening.'[552] I don't care about my own life, how could I be concerned about texts and characters?"

The Venerable then expounded the Dharma for him, "'The Most Honored Greatly Enlightened One expounded the Dharma of producing no-thought. [Regarding] the mind of no-thought and non-production, the mind is constantly producing and never extinguished.'[553] At all times self-present, do not retreat and do not turn. Not sinking and not floating, not flowing and not fixed, not moving and not shaking, not coming and not going, lively like a fish jumping![554] 'Walking and sitting, everything is meditation.'"[555]

When Master Zhongxin heard [the Venerable's] talk, he sat stern and unmoving. When the Venerable saw this, he knew he had awakened to the Mahāyāna. He changed [Zhongxin's] name to Chaoji. At the mountain (i.e., monastery) [Chaoji] would often secretly perform acts of service at night. He didn't let anyone know and when it was light would come back to his old place.

SECTION 28

Dialogue with Dharma Master Falun

(T. 51. 191C15–192A7)

有法輪法師。解涅槃章疏、[556]博學聡明。傍顧无人、自言弟一。故就山門、共和上問難。遥見和上、神威奇特、与諸僧不同。法輪師向前作礼、問訊起居和上。和上遥見、知是法師、即遣坐已。和上問、「法師解何経論?」答云、「解涅槃経。」和上問、「云何解涅槃経?」法師即引諸章疏。

和上説云、「非是涅槃経、此並是言説。『言説三界本、真實滅苦因。言説即變異、真實離文字。』高貴得[557]王菩薩問、『世尊、云何名大般涅槃?』佛言、『盡諸動念、思想心息。如是法相、名大涅槃。』云何將言説妄想、已為涅槃? 若如此説、即是不解。云何言解涅槃?」法輪聞説、无詞敢對。

和上云、「『有法是法[558]是俗帝、[559]无性弟一義。』言解即是繫、聡明是魔施。无念即无繫、无念即无縛。无念是涅槃、有念是生死、无念是聡明、有念是暗鈍。无念即无彼、无念即无此。无念即无佛、无念无衆生。般若大悲智、无佛无衆生。『无有涅槃佛、亦无佛涅槃。』若明此解、是真解者。若不如此解、是着相凡夫。」法輪師聞説、啓顙帰依、「小師傳迷日久。今日得遇和上、暗眼再明。伏願和上慈悲攝授。」

There was a Dharma Master Falun who explicated *Nirvāṇa-sūtra* commentaries and was extensively learned and brilliant.[560] He took account of no one else and considered himself "number one." So he went to [Wuzhu's] temple to dispute with the Venerable. When he saw the Venerable from a distance, [he thought the Venerable] looked mysterious and unusual, unlike other monks. Master Falun approached and made obeisance, and inquired after the Venerable's health. When the Venerable saw [Falun] from a distance he knew he was a Dharma master, so he merely had him take a seat. The Venerable asked, "What scriptures and treatises does the Dharma Master explicate?" [Falun] replied, "I explicate the *Nirvāṇa-sūtra.*" The Venerable asked, "How do you explicate the *Nirvāṇa-sūtra?*" The Dharma Master then quoted from various commentaries.

The Venerable expounded, saying, "These are not the *Nirvāṇa-sūtra,* these are all just verbal explanations. 'Verbal explanation is the origin of the Three Worlds, the real extinguishes the cause of suffering. Verbal explanation is flux, the real transcends texts and characters.'[561] The Bodhisattva 'King of Lofty Noble Virtue' asked, 'World-honored One, what is the *mahāparinirvāṇa?*' The Buddha said, 'Exhausting all movement of thought, the mind of conceptualization ceases. Such a Dharma-characteristic is called the *mahāparinirvāṇa.*'[562] Why lecture on deluded conceptualization as nirvāṇa? If you expound thus, it is really not explicating. How can you say that you explicate nirvāṇa?" When Falun heard [the Venerable's] talk, and there was not a word he dared utter in reply.

The Venerable said, "'The existence of dharmas is conventional truth, and no-nature is the cardinal meaning.'[563] Verbal explication is thus attachment, and mental brilliance is a demonic device. No-thought is thus no-attachment, no-thought is thus no-bondage. No-thought is nirvāṇa, thinking is birth and death; no-thought is mental brilliance, thinking is dullness. No-thought is thus no 'that,' no-thought is thus no 'this.' No-thought is thus no Buddha, no-thought is no beings. In the great compassionate wisdom of prajñā, there are no Buddhas and no beings. 'There is neither nirvāṇa-Buddha nor Buddha-nirvāṇa.'[564] Those who understand this explication are the true explicators. If you do not explicate like this, then you are just a common fellow attached to characteristics." When Master Falun heard [the Venerable's] talk, he knocked his forehead on the ground and [requested] refuge, [saying], "I, a petty master, have transmitted deceptions for a long time, but now I have been able to meet the Venerable and my darkened eyes are again illuminated. I humbly beg the Venerable to compassionately accept me."

SECTION 29

Dialogue with the Brothers Yixing and Huiming

(T. 51. 192A7–24)

綏州禅林寺僧是[565]兄第二人、並持法華経、時人号史法華。兄法名一行師、[566]第名恵明師。来投和上。和上[567]問、「従何處来？先學何教法？」恵明師云、「従綏州来。持法華経、日誦三遍。」和上問云、「安樂行品、『一切諸法、空无所有、无有常住、亦无起滅、是名智者親近處。』」恵明等聞説、「小師迷没、只解依文誦習、未識義理。伏願和上接引盲迷。」

和上即為説法、「『諸法寂滅相、不可以言宣示。』『法不可示、言詞相寂滅。』『離相滅相、[568]常寂滅相、終歸於空。』『常善入於空寂行、』『恒沙佛蔵一念了。』若欲得住山中、更不得誦習。常閑[人+登][人+登]、[569]得否？」恵明等兄第知習誦是不究竟、故投和上。

和上[570]即為再説、「无念即无生、无念即无死。无念即无遠、无念即无近。无念即是史法華、有念即是法華史。无念即是転法華、有念即是法華転。正无念之時、无念不自。」恵明等聞已、心意快然。便住山中、楽作務。

At the Chanlin monastery in Suizhou[571] there were two monks who were brothers who both maintained the *Lotus Sūtra,* such that people at that time called them chroniclers of the *Lotus.*[572] The elder brother's Dharma name was Master Yixing, and the younger was named Master Huiming.[573] They came to submit to the Venerable. The Venerable asked them, "Where do you come from? What teachings have you studied previously?" Master Huiming said, "We came from Suizhou. We maintain the *Lotus Sūtra,* every day we recite it three times." The Venerable asked, "In the 'Peaceful Joyful Practice' section it says, 'All dharmas are empty and without any being, they have no permanent abode and no arising or extinction. This is called the intimate place of the wise.'[574] [What can you say about that?]" Huiming and his brother heard this and said, "We are sunk in delusion, all we understand is the practice of recitation by relying on the text, we have not yet realized the meaning. We humbly beg the Venerable to guide us in our blindness."

The Venerable then expounded the Dharma for them: "'Dharmas have the characteristic of tranquil extinction and cannot be presented verbally.'[575] 'The Dharma cannot be expressed, the characteristic of words is tranquil extinction.'[576] 'Transcending characteristics and extinguishing characteristics, forever the characteristic of tranquil extinction, finally returning home to emptiness.'[577] 'Always completely enter the practice of empty tranquility.'[578] 'The Buddha-Treasury [of scriptures numerous as] the Ganges sands are completely understood in a single thought.'[579] If you want to stay at the mountain (i.e., monastery), you can never practice recitation. Always at ease and indifferent; are you able to do this or not?" Huiming and his brother realized that practicing recitation was not the ultimate, therefore they submitted themselves to the Venerable.

The Venerable then expounded for them once more: "No-thought is thus no-birth, no-thought is thus no-death. No-thought is thus no-distance, no-thought is thus no-proximity. No-thought is none other than chronicling the Lotus, thought is none other than Lotus chronicles. No-thought is none other than revolving the Lotus, thought is none other than Lotus revolutions.[580] At the time of true no-thought, no-thought itself is not." When Huiming and his brother heard this, their minds were made up instantly. So they stayed at the monastery and delighted in doing service.

SECTION 30
Dialogue with Changjingjin and Liaojianxing (Female Disciples) (T. 51. 192A24–B18)

慶州慕容長史夫人并女、志求大乘。舉家大小並相随、来礼拜和上。和上問夫人、「従何處来？」答、「第子遠聞和上有大慈悲、故来礼拜。」和上即為說種種法要。其女聞說、合掌[足+胡][581] 跪啓和上、「第子女人、三障五難、不自在身。今故投和上、擬截生死源。伏願和上、指示法要。」和上語云、「若能如此、即是大丈夫兒、云何是女？」和上為說要法[582] 、「无念即无男、无念即无女。无念即无障、无念即无礙。无念即无生、无念即无死。正无念之時、无念不自、即是截生死源。」女人聞說、目不瞬動、立不移處。食頃間、和上知此女人有决定心。与法号常精進、母号政[583] 遍知。落髪脩行、尼僧中為道首。

後引表妹姓韋、是蘇宰相女孫。聡明黠恵、博學多知、問无不答。来礼拜和上、和上[584] 見有剛骨志操、即為說法、「是法非因非縁、无非不非、无是非是。『離一切相即一切法。』『法過眼耳鼻舌身心。法離一切觀行。』无念即无行、无念即无觀。无念即无身、无念即无心。无念即无貴、无念即无賤。无念即无高、无念即无下。正无念之時、无念不自。」

女人聞說、合掌白和上、「第子女人、罪障深重、今聞法已、垢障消除。」語已悲泣雨涙。便請法号、名了見性。得号已、自落髪披衣、尼師中為首。

The wife and daughter of Administrator Murong of Qingzhou were determined to seek the Mahāyāna.[585] Accompanied by the entire family, young and old, they came to pay obeisance to the Venerable. The Venerable asked the wife, "Where did you come from?" She replied, "Your disciple heard from afar that the Venerable had great compassion, so we came to pay obeisance."

The Venerable then expounded various essentials of the Dharma for them. When the daughter had heard his talk, she knelt on one knee with her palms joined and explained to the Venerable, "Your disciple is a woman with the three obstructions and five difficulties,[586] and a body that is not free. That is why I have come now to submit to the Venerable, I am determined to cut off the source of birth and death. I humbly beg the Venerable to point out the essentials of the Dharma."

The Venerable said, "If you are capable of such [resolution], then you are a great hero (*dazhangfu er* 大丈夫兒), why are you 'a woman'?" The Venerable expounded the essentials of the Dharma for her: "No-thought is thus no 'male,' no-thought is thus no 'female.' No-thought is thus no-obstruction, no-thought is thus no-hindrance. No-thought is thus no-birth, no-thought is thus no-death. At the time of true no-thought, no-thought itself is not. This is none other than cutting off the source of birth and death."

When the daughter heard his talk, her eyes did not blink and she stood absolutely still. In an instant, the Venerable knew that this woman had a resolute mind. He gave her the Dharma name Changjingjin (Ever-Pure Progress), and her mother was named Zhengbianzhi (Right Knowledge). They took the tonsure and practiced, and became leaders among nuns.

Later, they brought a younger female cousin with the surname Wei, who was the grand-daughter of Grand Councilor Su.[587] She was quick-witted and clever, extensively learned and knowledgeable, and when asked a question she was never without an answer. She came to pay obeisance to the Venerable, and the Venerable saw that she was obdurate and determined on chastity,[588] and so he expounded the Dharma for her: "This Dharma is not caused and conditioned, it has neither false nor not-false, and has neither truth nor not-truth. 'Transcending all characteristics is thus all Dharmas.'[589] 'The Dharma is beyond eye, ear, nose, tongue, body, and mind, the Dharma transcends all contemplation practices.'[590] No-thought is thus no-practice, no-thought is thus no-contemplation. No-thought is thus no-body, no-thought is thus no-mind. No-thought is thus no-nobility, no-thought is thus no-lowliness. No-thought is thus no-high, no-thought is thus no-low. At the time of true no-thought, no-thought itself is not."

When the woman heard his talk, she joined her palms together and told the Venerable, "Your disciple is a woman whose obstructions from transgressions are very weighty, but now that I have heard the Dharma, stain and obstruction are completely eliminated." So saying she wept grievously, a rain of tears. She then requested a Dharma name, and she was named Liaojianxing (Completely Seeing the Nature). When she had been named, she tonsured herself and donned robes, and became a leader among nuns.

SECTION 31

Excerpts and Quotations, Part 1 (T. 51. 192B18–193A15)

「誰人報佛恩？依法脩行者。誰人銷供養？世事不牽者。誰人堪供養？於法无所取者。」若能如此、自有天厨供養。

和上向諸第子説、「攝己従他、万事倶和。攝他従己、万事不己。」

又説偈、「一念毛輪觀自在。勿共同學諍道理。見鏡[591]即是丈夫児、不明即同畜生類。」「但脩自己行、莫見他邪正。口意不量他、三業自然浄。欲見心佛國、普敬真如性。」「善男子、於恪[592]惜心盡、即道眼心開、明如日。若有毛輪許惜心者、其道眼即被翳障。此是黒暗之大坑、无可了了實知難出。」

又説偈、「我今意况大好、行住坐臥倶了。看時无物可看、畢竟无言可道。但得此中意况、高抵木枕到暁。」

和上所引、諸経了義、无旨心地法門、並破言説。和上所説、説不可説。今願同學、但依義脩行、莫着言説。若着言説、即自失脩行分。

金剛経云、「若取法相、即着我人衆生。若取非法相、即着我人衆生。是故不應取法、不應取非法。以是義故、如来常説、『汝等比丘、知我説法、如筏喩者、法尚應捨、何况非法？』」

華嚴経云、「譬如貧窮人、日夜数他寳、自无一銭分。於法不脩行、多聞亦如是。如聾設音樂、彼聞自不聞。於法不脩行、多聞亦如是。如盲設衆象、彼見自不見。於法不脩行、多聞亦如是。如飢設飲食、彼飽自腹餓。於法不脩行、多聞亦如是。譬如海舩師、能渡於彼岸、彼去自不去。於法不脩行、多聞亦如是。」

法句経云、「説食之人、終不能飽。」

佛頂経云、「阿難縦強記、不免落邪思。覺觀出思惟、身心不能及。歴劫多聞、不如一日脩无漏法。」

方廣経云、「一念乱禅定、如煞三千界、満中一切人。一念在定、如活三千界、満中一切人。」

維摩経云、「『心不住内、亦不在外、是為宴坐。若能如此者、佛即印可。』『无以生滅心、説實相法。』『法過眼耳鼻舌身心、法離一切觀行。法相如是、豈可説乎？』」是故文殊師利菩薩讃維摩詰无有言説、「是真入不二法門。」

和上説、「无念法、法本不自。」

又云、「知見立知、即无明本。知見无見、思即涅槃、无漏真浄。」

又破知病、「知行亦寂滅、是即菩提道。」

又破智病、「智求於智不得智。『无智亦无得、已[593] 无所得故、即菩提薩埵。』」

又云、「圓滿菩提、歸无所得。『无有少法可得、是名阿耨多羅三藐三菩提。』」

又破本病、「云何為本？一切衆生本来清净、本来圓滿。有本即有利、為有利故、心有採集。識家得便、便即輪廻生死。本離離他、即无依止。己他俱利、成佛菩提。佛无根境相、不見名見佛『於畢竟空中、熾然建立。』」

又破净病、涅槃病、自然病、覺病、觀病、禅病、法病、「若住此者、即為有住是病。法不垢不淨、亦无涅槃佛、法離觀行。『超然露地坐、識蔭般涅槃。』『遠離覺所覺。』『不入三昧、不住坐禅、心无得失。』」

又破一病、「『一亦不為一、為一破諸数。』『一根既返源、六根成解脱。』『制之一處、无事不辦。』『参羅及万像、一法之所印。』『一本不起、三用無施。』『其心不計、是有力大觀。』汝等當離己衆他衆、己即是自性、他即是妄念。妄念不生、即是自他俱離、成佛菩提。」

"Who repays the Buddha's kindness? One who practices according to the Dharma. Who consumes offerings? One who is not involved in worldly affairs. Who is worthy of offerings? In the Dharma there is nothing that is taken."[594] If one is able to practice in this way, one naturally has offerings from Heaven's kitchen.

The Venerable explained to his disciples, "If one restrains oneself and indulges others, the ten thousand things will all be in harmony. If one restrains others and indulges oneself, the ten thousand things are not [as] oneself."

He also spoke in [these] gāthās: "'In a hair's-turn instant of thought, one contemplates self-presence. Do not debate principles of the Way with fellow-students. Seeing the mirror[-like nature of the field of cognition] one is none other than a great hero, but if one is unclear then one is just the same as the mass of beings.' 'Just cultivate your own practice and do not look at the errors or correctness of others. If you do not assess others by word or thought, then the three categories of action (thought, word and deed) are naturally pure. If you want to see the Buddha-land of the mind, everywhere revere suchness-nature.' 'Good sons, when the stingy mind is exhausted, then the mind of the eye of the Way opens, bright as the sun. If one has even a hair's-turn of stingy mind, then one's eye of the Way will be covered over. This is the great pit of darkness that cannot be completely plumbed, from which it is truly difficult to emerge.'"

He also spoke [this] gāthā: "Now the quality of my intention is very good; walking, staying still, sitting, and lying down are all complete. When seeing there is not a thing to be seen, in the end there is not a word that can be spoken. Only attain this quality of intention and [rest upon] the high wooden pillow until dawn."[595]

What the Venerable quoted was the complete meaning of the scriptures, the tenet-less 'Dharma-gate of the mind-ground.'[596] At the same time, he broke down verbal explanation. What the Venerable taught was teaching the unteachable. Now I beg my fellow-students to rely only on the essential meaning in practicing, do not become attached to verbal explanation. If one is attached to verbal explanation, then one loses for oneself the [fortunate] allotment of [being able to] practice.

The *Vajracchedikā-sūtra* says: "If you grasp at Dharma-characteristics, this is attachment to 'I,' 'others,' and 'beings.' If you grasp at what are not Dharma characteristics, this is attachment to 'I,' 'others,' and 'beings.' For this reason, one ought not grasp at the Dharma, and one ought not grasp at what is not the Dharma. It is because of this essential meaning that the Tathāgata often said, 'All you bhikṣus, know that my preaching the Dharma is like the simile of the raft—if even the Dharma ought to be abandoned, how much more so what is *not* the Dharma?' "[597]

The *Avataṃsaka-sūtra* says: "It is like a poor person day and night counting the treasure of others, himself lacking even a single piece of cash. Amid the Dharma but not practicing—the well-versed (*bahu-śruti*) are also like this. It is like a deaf person setting up musical [instruments]; others hear but he himself does not hear. Amid the Dharma but not practicing—the well-versed are also like this. It is like a blind person setting up a collection of images; others see but he himself does not see. Amid the Dharma but not practicing—the well-versed are also like this. It is like a starving person setting out drink and food; others fill up but his own belly is empty. Amid the Dharma but not practicing—the well-versed are also like this. It is like an ocean-going ship-master who is able to cross to the other shore; others go but he himself does not go. Amid the Dharma but not practicing—the well-versed are also like this."[598]

The *Dhammapada-sūtra* says, "A person who preaches about food will never be satiated by it."[599]

The *Śūraṃgama-sūtra* says: "Although Ānanda was strong in memorization, he did not avoid falling into wrong views. Awakened contemplation[600] departs from conceptualization, body and mind cannot reach it. To be well-versed through successive kalpas is not equal to one day's practice of non-outflow Dharma."[601]

The *Fangguang jing* says, "When a single thought disturbs samādhi, it is like destroying three thousand worlds filled with people. When a single thought is in samādhi, it is like reviving three thousand worlds filled with people."[602]

The *Vimalakīrti-sūtra* says, " 'The mind does not abide inside and also does not exist outside—this is quiet sitting. Those who are able to [sit] like this, the Buddhas will validate.'[603] 'One cannot teach the Dharma characterized by actuality with the mind of birth-and-death.'[604] 'The Dharma is beyond eye, ear, nose, tongue, body and mind, the Dharma transcends all contemplation practices. Dharma of this character—how could one teach it?'[605] This is why the bodhisattva Manjuśrī praised Vimalakīrti's nonverbal exposition, [saying] "This is directly entering the gate of the nondual Dharma."[606]

The Venerable explained, "The Dharma of no-thought [is that] the Dharma is fundamentally nonsubjective."

He also said, "Cognizance setting up cognition is thus the origin of ignorance. [But if there is] cognizance without seeing, thinking is then nirvāṇa, absolute purity without outflows."

He also broke down the "knowing" illness: "Knowing-practice is also tranquil extinction, this is precisely the Way of bodhi."

He also broke down the "wisdom" illness: "Wisdom seeking after wisdom does not attain wisdom. 'No wisdom and also no attainment; because there is nothing to attain this is in fact 'bodhisattva.'"[607]

He also said, "Perfect bodhi is returning to nothing-to-attain. 'When there is not the least Dharma that can be attained, this is called *anuttara-samyak-saṃbodhi.*'"[608]

He also broke down the "fundamental" illness: "What is 'fundamental?' All beings are fundamentally pure, fundamentally perfect and complete. Where there is origin there is benefit, and because there is benefit, the mind gathers and collects. [When] the home of consciousness gains conveniences, conveniences are thus the cycle of birth-and-death. Fundamental transcendence transcends 'other,' thus there is nothing on which to depend. Self and other both benefit, you achieve Buddha-awakening.[609] The Buddha does not have the characteristic of the roots of the field of sense-cognition; not-seeing is called seeing the Buddha 'in the midst of ultimate emptiness, gloriously established.'"[610]

He also broke down the "purity" illness, "nirvāṇa" illness, "spontaneity" illness, "realization" illness, "contemplation" illness, "dhyāna" illness, and "Dharma" illness: "One who abides in 'this' has the illness of abiding in this. The Dharma is neither stained nor pure, nor is there any nirvāṇa or Buddha, the Dharma transcends contemplation practice. 'Eminently "sitting on dewy ground," the factor of consciousness (*vijñāṇa-skandha*) [attains] final liberation (*parinirvāṇa*).'[611] 'One far transcends realization as something realized.'[612] 'Not entering samādhi, not abiding in seated meditation, the mind is without gain or loss.'"[613]

He also broke down the "one" illness, "'Even 'one' is not as one, as one it breaks down all numbers.'[614] 'Once 'one' root returns to the source, the six roots attain release.'[615] 'If you determine it in 'one' place, there is nothing that is not differentiated.'[616] 'Everything around you on up to the ten thousand appearances are imprinted by one Dharma.'[617] '"One" fundamentally does not arise, and the three functions have no actualization.'[618] 'When the mind does not calculate, this is energetic great contemplation.'[619] All of you ought to transcend [notions of] self and others; 'self' is one's own nature, 'other' is deluded thinking.[620] When deluded thinking does not arise, then this is 'transcending both self and other, achieving Buddha-awakening.'"[621]

SECTION 32

Excerpts and Quotations, Part 2 (T. 51. 193A15–B2)

和上每説言「有縁千里通、无縁人對面不相識。但識法之時、即是見佛、此諸経了義経。」

和上坐下、尋常教戒諸學道者。恐着言説、時時引稲田中螃蠏問、衆人不會。

又引王梵志詩、「恵眼近空心、非開髑髏孔。對面説不識、饒你母姓董。」

有数老人白和上、「第子盡有妻子男女眷属。罄捨投和上學道。」和上云、「道无形段可脩、法无形段可證。只没閑不憶不念、一切時中惣是道。」問老人、「得否？」老人黙然不對、為未會。和上又説偈、「婦是没耳枷、男女蘭單杻。你是没價奴、至老不得走。」

又有釼南諸師僧欲往台山礼拜、辞和上。和上[622]問言、「大徳何去？」僧答、「礼文殊師利。」和上云、「大徳、佛在身心、文殊不遠。妄念不生、即是見佛。何勞遠去？」諸師僧欲去。和上又与説偈、「迷子浪波波、巡山礼土坡。文殊只没在、背佛覔弥陀。」

The Venerable always said, "If there is a karmic cause it will penetrate a thousand *li;* if there is no cause, then even people facing each other will not recognize one another. When one is only conscious of the Dharma, this in none other than 'seeing the Buddha,' this is all the scriptures of complete meaning."[623]

When the Venerable took his seat, he usually taught the precepts to all those studying the Way. Fearing that they would get attached to verbal explanation, from time to time he would quote the crabs in the paddy-field and ask about it, but the assembly didn't understand.

He also quoted Brahmacarya Wang's poem: "The eye of wisdom is close to the mind of emptiness, not the holes that open into your skull. You don't recognize what [the person] facing you says, it doesn't matter that your mother's surname is respectable."[624]

There were some old men who told the Venerable, "We, your disciples, have wives and children, and young male and female household dependents. We wish to give them up entirely and submit to the Venerable and study the Way." The Venerable said, "The Way does not have any particular form that can be cultivated, the Dharma does not have any particular form that can be validated. Just unrestricted no-recollection and no-thought, at all times everything is the Way." He asked the old men, "Do you get it?" The old men were silent and did not answer, because they didn't understand. The Venerable expounded a gāthā: "Your wife is an earless shackle, your young are rattling manacles. You are a worthless slave, you have reached old age and cannot escape."

Another time, some masters and monks of Jiannan wanted to go to [Wu]tai shan to pay obeisance, and they took their leave of the Venerable. The Venerable asked, "Worthies, where are you going?" The monks replied, "To pay our respects to Mañjuśrī." The Venerable said, "Worthies, the Buddha is in body and mind, Mañjuśrī is not far. When deluded thoughts are not produced, this is none other than 'seeing the Buddha.' Why take the trouble to go so far?" The masters and monks wanted to leave. The Venerable expounded a gāthā for them: "Lost children restlessly dashing like waves, circling the mountain and paying obeisance to a pile of earth. Mañjuśrī is right here, you are climbing the Buddha's back to search for Amitābha."[625]

SECTION 33

Tea Gāthā (T. 51. 193B2–19)

和上呷茶次、是日幕府郎官侍御卅人礼拜訖、坐定問、「和上大愛茶？」和上云、「是。」便説茶偈、「幽谷生霊草、堪為入道媒。樵人採其葉、美味入流坯。静慮澄虚識、明心照會臺。不勞人氣力、真聳法門開。」

諸郎官因此問、「和上縁何不教人讀経念佛礼拜？第子不解。」和上云、「自證究竟涅槃、亦教他人如是。不将如来不了教。廻自己解、己悟初學。佛印是人得真三昧者。」

和上説訖、儼然不動。諸郎官侍御咸言歎、「未曾有也。」問、「和上縁何不教事相法？」和上答、「『大乘妙理至理控[626]曠。有為衆生而不能入。』経教旨衆生本性。見性即成佛道、着相即沉輪。」『心生即種種法生、心滅即種種法滅。』轉経礼拜皆是起心。起心即[627] 是生死、不起即是佛見。[628]」

又問、「和上若依此教、人得否？」和上云、「得。起心即是塵勞、動念即是魔網。『一切有為法、如夢幻泡影、如露亦如電。應作如是觀。』」諸官聞説、疑網頓除。咸言為第子。

Once when the Venerable was drinking tea, [a party of] thirty Directors and Censors of the Secretariat came to pay their respects, and when they had done this they took seats and asked, "Venerable, you really love tea, [don't you]?" The Venerable said, "Yes."[629] Then he recited a tea-gāthā for them:

The obscure valley produces the mysterious herb that serves as a medium for entering the Way.
Wood-cutters gather its leaves, the delicious flavor flows into an earthen vessel.
It tranquilizes worries and clarifies void consciousness, brightens the mind and illuminates the terrace of understanding.
Without wearing down one's vital energy, it directly moves the Dharma-gates to open.

Upon this, the Directors asked, "Venerable, why do you not teach people to read scriptures, recollect the Buddha, and perform devotions? We, your disciples, do not understand." The Venerable said, "One validates final nirvāṇa for oneself, I also teach others like this. Do not hold onto the Tathāgata's incomplete teaching. Returning to one's own understanding, self-awakening initiates training. The Buddhas validate this person as one who has attained true samādhi."

When the Venerable finished speaking, [he sat] imposing and motionless. The directors and censors sighed together, "This is unprecedented!" They asked, "Venerable, why do you not teach the phenomenal forms of the Dharma?" The Venerable replied, "'The subtle principle of the Mahāyāna reaches principle's empty extent. Beings involved in conditionality are unable to enter it.'[630] The teachings of the scriptures point to the fundamental nature of beings. Seeing the nature is thus the Way of becoming a Buddha, attachment to characteristics is thus sinking into the cycle [of birth and death].[631] 'When the mind is produced then the various dharmas are produced, when the mind is extinguished then the various dharmas are extinguished.'[632] Transmitting the scriptures and performing devotions are all arousals of the mind. Arousing the mind is precisely birth and death, not arousing the mind is precisely seeing the Buddha."

They asked further, "If the Venerable teaches by relying on this, do people get it?" The Venerable said, "They do. Arousing the mind is precisely defilements, movement of thought is precisely the demons' net.[633] 'All dharmas involved in conditionality are like the froth of dream-visions, like dew and like lightning. You ought to contemplate them thus.'"[634] When the officials heard his talk, the net of doubt was suddenly removed. All together they said they would become his disciples.

SECTION 34

Dialogue with Daoists (T. 51. 193B120–194A20)

又有道士数十人、山人亦有数十人、法師律師論師亦有廿人、皆是劍南領袖。和上問道士云、「『道可道非常道、名可名非常名。』豈不是老君所說？」道士云、「是。」和上云、「尊師解此義否？」道士黙然无對。

和上又問、「『為學日益、為道日損。損之又損之、已[635]至於无為。无為无不為。』」

又問、「莊子云、『生生者不生、煞生者不死。』」道士盡不敢對。和上云、「時今道士、无有一人學老君者、只學謗佛。」道士聞已、失色合掌。

和上又問諸山人、「夫子說易否？」山人答云、「說。」又問、「夫子說仁義礼智信否？」答言、「說。」又問、「易如何？」山人並不言。和上即為說云、「易言『无思也无為也、寂然不動、感而遂通。』此義如何？」山人不敢對。和上更說云、「易『不變不易』是衆生本性。『无思也无為也、寂然不動』是衆生本性。若不變不易、不思不想、即是行仁義礼智信。如今學士不見本性、不識主客。強識前塵、已為學問、大錯。夫子說无思无為、大分明。」

山人問、「和上、『感而遂通』義如何？」和上答云、「『梵天不求、梵天自至。』果報不求、果報自至。煩惱已盡、習氣亦除、梵釋龍神、咸皆供敬。是故如来入城乞食、一切草木皆悉頭低、一切山河皆傾向佛。何況衆生？此是『感而遂通』也。」山人一時礼和上、並願為第子。

和上又問道士云、「『上得[636]不失得、是以有得。下得不失得、是以无得。』此義如何？」道士云、「請和上為說。」和上說云、「上得之人无所得心。為无所得、即是菩提薩埵。无有少法可得、是名阿耨多羅三[637]藐三菩提。即是上得之義。『下得不失得、是以无得。』下得之人為有所求。若有所求、即有煩惱。煩惱[638]之心、即是失得。此是失得之義也。」

又云、「『為學日益、為道日損。』若有學心、惟憎塵勞生死、此是不益也。『為道日損、損之又損之。已[639]至於无為、无為[640]不為。』『道』即本性。至道絶言、妄念不生、即是『損之』。観見心王時、一切皆捨離、即是『又損之』。『以至於无為。』性空寂滅時、是法是時見。『无為无不為』、即是不住无為。脩行无起、不已[641]无起為證。脩行於空、不以空為證、即是『无不為』義也。又莊子云、『生生者不生。』妄念不起、即是『不生』。『煞生者不死。』『不死』義者、即是无生。」

又云、「『道可道非常道』、即是衆生本性。言說不及、即『非常道』。『名可名非常名』、亦是衆生本性。但有言說、都无實義、但名但字。法不可說、即『非常名』也。」[642]

道士聞說已、合掌問、「和上若如此說、即佛道无二。」和上言、「不然。莊子、老子、盡說无為无相、說一說浄、說自然。佛即不如此、說因縁自然俱為戲論。『一切賢聖皆以无為法、而有差別。』佛即不住无為、不住无相。以住於无相、不見於大乘。二乘人三昧酒醉、凡夫人无明酒醉。聲聞人住盡智、縁覺[643]浄智。如來之智恵、生起无窮盡。莊、老、夫子說、与共聲聞等。佛[644]呵聲聞人、『如盲如聾』。『預流、一来果、不還、阿羅漢果[645]、是等諸聖人、其心悉迷惑。』佛即不墮衆数、超過一切。法无垢浄、法无形相、法无動乱、法无處所、法无取捨。是以超過孔丘、荘子、老子[646]。『佛常在世間、而不染世法。不分別世故、[647]敬礼无所観。』孔老所説、多有所着。盡是聲聞二乗境界。」道士作礼、盡為第子。黙然信受聴法。

Another time [Wuzhu was visited by] scores of Daoist priests and scores of recluses,[648] and also twenty Dharma masters, Vinaya masters, and Treatise masters. They were all "collars and sleeves" (leading figures) in Jiannan. The Venerable asked the Daoists, "'The Way that can be spoken/trodden is not the constant Way, the names that can be named are not the constant names.'[649] Is this not what Laojun (Laozi) taught?" The Daoist answered, "It is." The Venerable said, "Do you, Honored Masters, understand the meaning or not?" The Daoists were silent and did not reply.

The Venerable further asked [about the meaning of]: "'To undertake learning one increases day by day, to undertake the Way one decreases day by day. Decreasing it and further decreasing it, one finally arrives at nondoing. In nondoing, there is nothing that is not done.'"[650]

He also asked, "The *Zhuangzi* says, 'That which produces life is not born, that which destroys life does not die.' [What does this mean?]"[651] None of the Daoists dared reply. The Venerable said, "Among Daoists nowadays, not one studies Laojun, they only study vilification of the Buddha." When the Daoists heard this, they lost color and joined their palms together.

The Venerable then asked the recluses, "Did not Fuzi (Confucius) explain the *Yijing?*" The recluses answered, "Yes, he did." The Venerable further asked, "Did not Fuzi teach benevolence, righteousness, propriety, wisdom and faith?"[652] They answered, "He did." The Venerable asked, "What about the [cardinal meaning of] the *Yijing?*" The recluses were all speechless. The Venerable then expounded for them: "The *Yijing* says, 'Nonconceiving and nondoing, tranquil and unmoving; stimulated, the [response] that follows pervades all.'[653] What is the meaning of this?" The recluses dared not reply. The Venerable explained further, "In the *Yijing,* 'Not transforming, not changing' is the fundamental nature of beings. 'Nonconceiving, nondoing, tranquil and unmoving' is the fundamental nature of beings. If one does not transform and does not change, does not conceptualize and does not imagine, this is the practice of benevolence, righteousness, propriety, wisdom, and faith. These days scholars do not see fundamental nature, they do not recognize host and guest. They concentrate on sense-objects and take this as scholarly inquiry, a great mistake.[654] Fuzi explained nonconceiving and nondoing, [he had] great discernment."

The recluses asked the Venerable, "'Stimulated, the [response] that follows pervades all'—what does this mean?" The Venerable replied, "If the Brahmaloka is not sought, the Brahmaloka is reached of itself; if karmic reward is not sought, karmic reward is reached of itself.[655] The defilements are completely exhausted, the seeds [in the *ālayavijñāna,* storehouse consciousness] are also removed, and Brāhma, Indra, the nāgas and devas are all moved to do reverence. For this reason, when the Tathāgata entered a town to eat, all the grasses and trees bowed their heads, and all the mountains and rivers leaned towards the Buddha. How much more so the many beings? This is 'stimulated, the [response] that follows pervades all.'" The recluses all made obeisance to the Venerable at once, and all desired to become his disciples.

The Venerable further questioned the Daoists, saying, "'When those of high virtue do not lose virtue, it is because of having virtue. When those of low virtue do not lose virtue, it is because of being without virtue.'[656] What does this mean?" The Daoists said, "Please, Venerable, explain it for us." The Venerable explained, "A person of high virtue has a mind of 'nothing to attain.' 'Because there is nothing to attain, this is in fact "bodhisattva."'[657] 'When there is not the least Dharma that can be attained, this is called "*anuttara-samyak-saṃbodhi.*"'[658] This is the meaning of high virtue. [As for] 'When those of low virtue do not lose virtue, it is because of being without virtue'; a person is of low virtue is one who seeks after something. If one is seeks after something then one has defilements. The mind of defilements is precisely 'losing virtue.' This is the meaning of 'losing virtue.'"

He went on, "[Regarding] 'To undertake learning one increases day by day.'[659] If one has the mind of learning this only adds to the defilements of birth-and-death, and this is not 'increase.' [Regarding] 'To undertake the Way one decreases day by day. Decreasing it and further decreasing it, one finally arrives at nondoing. In nondoing, there is nothing that is not done.' The Way is fundamental nature. Reaching the Way cuts off words, deluded thoughts are not produced, and this is precisely 'decreasing it.' When one contemplates the Mind King,[660] one parts with everything altogether, and this is 'further decreasing it.' [Regarding] 'One finally arrives at nondoing'—when one experiences the emptiness of the nature in nirvāṇa, this Dharma is at this time seen. 'In nondoing, there is nothing that is not done'—this means not abiding in nondoing. Practicing non-arising, one does not make non-arising into evidence. Practicing in emptiness, one does not make emptiness into evidence, and this is the meaning of 'nothing that is not done.' [The Venerable continued,] "Furthermore, [as for] Zhuangzi saying 'that which produces life is not born.'[661] When deluded thoughts do not arise, this is precisely 'not born.' [Regarding] 'That which destroys life does not die.' The meaning of 'does not die' is precisely 'unborn.'"

[The Venerable] went on, "[Regarding] 'The Way that can be spoken is not the constant Way.' This is precisely the fundamental nature of beings. Verbal explanation does not reach it, thus this is 'not the constant Way.' 'The names that can be named are not the constant names' is also the fundamental nature of beings. 'With only verbal explanation there is no true meaning at all,'[662] 'only names, only characters.'[663] The Dharma cannot be explained, this [is the meaning of] 'not the constant names.'"

When the Daoists had heard his talk, they joined their palms and asked the Venerable, "If one explains it like this, then this means 'Buddhism and Daoism are not two.'" The Venerable said, "Not so. Zhuangzi and Laozi covered nondoing and no-characteristics, the one, purity, and spontaneity. The Buddha is not like this, he taught that both causation and spontaneity are idle theories. 'All worthies and saints accord with the Dharma of nondoing, yet there are differences.'[664] The Buddha thus does not abide in nondoing and does not abide in no-characteristics. Abiding in no-characteristics, one does not see the Mahāyāna. Persons of the two vehicles (i.e., pratyekabuddhas and śrāvakas) are drunk on the wine of samādhi, and common persons are drunk on the wine of ignorance.[665] Śrāvakas abide in the wisdom of complete [removal of defilements]. Pratyekabuddhas abide in the wisdom of tranquil purity. The Tathāgata's wisdom keeps arising without depletion. Zhuang[zi]'s, Lao[zi]'s, and Fuzi's teachings are to be lumped together with those of the Śrāvakas. The Buddha rebuked the Śrāvakas, [saying they were] 'as if blind, as if deaf.'[666] 'Stream-entrants, once-returners, nonreturners, and arhats are all saints, yet their minds are completely deluded.'[667] The Buddha thus does not sink into the crowd, but transcends all. The Dharma is without stain or purity, the Dharma is without form or feature, the Dharma is without restless disturbance, the Dharma is without a location, the Dharma is without grasping or discarding. Therefore it transcends Kong Qiu (Confucius), Zhuangzi, and Laozi. 'The Buddha is always in the world, yet is not stained by worldly dharmas. Due to not separating "the world" [from the ultimate], we do reverence without having anything to contemplate.'[668] What Kong [Fuzi] and Lao[zi] taught all had something attached. All of it is the sphere of Śrāvakas, the two vehicles." The Daoists did obeisance, and all of them became his disciples. With silent faith they received [the opportunity to] listen to the Dharma.

SECTION 35

Dialogue with Dharma Masters (T. 51. 194A20–194B1)

又問諸法師、「云何是佛寶、云何是法寶、云何是僧寶？」法師黙然不語。和上説云、「知法即是佛寶、離相即是法寶、无為即是僧寶。」

又問法師、「法无言説、云何説法？『夫説法者、无説无示。其聽法者、无聞无得。』『无法可説、是名説法。』『常知如来不説法者、是具足多聞。』法師云何説法？」法師答曰、「般若有三種。一文字般若、二實相般若、三觀照般若。」和上答云、「『一切諸文字、无實无所依。俱同一寂滅、本来无所動。』『我法无實无虚。』『法離一切觀行。』」諸法師互相視面、无詞可言。

He also asked the Dharma masters, "What is the Buddha-Jewel, what is the Dharma-Jewel, what is the Saṅgha-Jewel?" The Dharma masters were silent and did not speak. The Venerable explained, "Knowing the Dharma is precisely the Buddha-Jewel, transcending characteristics is precisely the Dharma-Jewel, and nondoing is precisely the Saṅgha-Jewel."[669]

He also asked the Dharma masters, "The Dharma is without verbal explanation, how does one explain the Dharma? 'One who explains the Dharma does so without explaining and without manifestation. Those who listen to the Dharma do so without hearing and without obtaining.'[670] 'That there is no Dharma that can be explained is called explaining the Dharma.'[671] 'Those who always know that the Tathāgata does not explain the Dharma are called complete hearers [of the Dharma].'[672] How do the Dharma masters explain the Dharma?" A Dharma master replied, "There are three kinds of prajñā. One is the prajñā of texts and characters, the second is the prajñā characterized by actuality, and the third is the prajñā of contemplating radiance."[673] The Venerable replied, "'Texts and characters have nothing actual and nothing on which to depend. Altogether unified in tranquil extinction, fundamentally there is nothing that moves.'[674] 'My Dharma is without actuality and without void.'[675] 'The Dharma transcends all contemplation practice.'"[676] The Dharma masters all looked at each other, unable to say a word.

SECTION 36

Dialogue with Vinaya Masters (T. 51. 194B1–194C15)

和上問律師、「云何是戒律？云何是決定毗尼、云何是究竟毗尼？戒以何為體、律以何為義？」律師盡不敢答。和上問律師、「識主客否？」律師云、「請和上為説主客義。」

和上答、「来去是客、不来去是主。想念不生、即没主客、即是見性。『千思万慮』不益道理、徒為動乱、失本心王。若无思慮、即无生滅。律是調伏之義、戒非青黄赤白。非色非心、是戒體。戒是衆生本性、本来圓満、本来清淨。妄念生時、即『背覺合塵』、即是犯戒律。妄念不生、即背塵合覺、即是戒律満足。念不生時、即是究竟毗尼。念不生時、即是决定毗尼。念不生時、即是破壊一切心識。『若見持戒、即破戒。戒非戒二見一相。能知此者、即是大道師。』『見犯重罪比丘、不入地獄、見清浄行者、不入涅槃。若住如是是見[677] 平等見。』」

「今時律師説觸説浄、説持説犯。作相授戒、作相威儀、及以飯食皆作相。『假使作相、即与外道五通等。若无作相、即是无為。不應有見。』妄想是垢、无妄想是浄。取我是垢、不取我是浄。顛倒是垢、不顛倒是浄。持犯但束身、非身无所束。非无[678]遍一切、云何獲圓通?『若説諸持戒、无善无威儀。戒性如虚空、持者為迷倒。』『心生即種種法生、心滅即種種法滅。』『如其心然、罪垢亦然、諸法亦然。』今時律師只為名聞利養。如猫伺鼠、細歩徐行、見是見非、自称戒行。此並是滅佛法、非沙門行。楞伽経云、『未来世當有身着於袈裟、妄説於有无、毀壊我正法。』未来世、於法我[679]中、而為出家、妄説毗尼、壊乱正法。寧毀尸羅、不毀正見。尸羅生天、增諸結縛、正見得涅槃。」律師聞説、惶悚失色、戰悚不安。

和上重説、「『離相滅相、常寂滅相、終歸於空。』『常善入於空寂行。』『恒沙佛蔵、一念了。』佛只許五歳學戒律。五歳已、捨小乗師、訪大乗師、學无人我法。若不如此、佛甚呵責。」律師聞已、疑網頓除、白和上、「小師傳迷日久、戒律盡捨、伏願慈悲攝受。」一時作礼、雨淚而泣。

和上云、「不憶不念、一切法並不憶、佛法亦不憶、世間法亦不憶、只没閑。」問、「得否?」律師咸言、「得。」和上云、「實若得時、即是真律師、即是見性。正見之時、見猶離見。見不能及、即是見佛。正見之時、見亦不自。」和上更為再説、「起心即是塵勞、動念即是魔網。只没閑、不沉不浮、不流不轉、活鱍鱍。一切時中、惣是禅。」律師聞已、踴躍歎喜、黙然坐聽。

The Venerable asked the Vinaya masters, "What are the Vinaya precepts? What is *Vinayaviniścaya* and what is *Vinayottara?*[680] What is the substance of the precepts, and what is the meaning of the Vinaya?" None of the Vinaya masters dared answer. The Venerable asked the Vinaya masters, "Do you recognize host and guest or not?"[681] The Vinaya masters said, "We request the Venerable to explain the meaning of 'host and guest' for us."

The Venerable replied, "Coming and going is 'guest,' not coming and going is 'host.' If conceptualizations are not produced, then there is neither host nor guest, and this is precisely 'seeing the nature.' The 'thousand thoughts and ten thousand anxieties'[682] do not benefit the principle of the Way, and merely due to agitation one loses the fundamental Mind-King. If there are no thoughts and anxieties then there is no birth-and-death.

The significance of the Vinaya is to regulate and subdue, and the precepts are not blue, yellow, red or white. Not color/desire and not mind, this is the substance of precepts, this is the fundamental nature of beings, fundamentally complete, fundamentally pure. When deluded thoughts are produced, then one 'turns away from awakening and adheres to dust,'[683] and this is precisely 'violating the Vinaya precepts.' When deluded thoughts are not produced, then one turns away from dust and adheres to awakening, and this is precisely 'fulfilling the Vinaya precepts.' When thoughts are not produced, this is precisely *Vinayottara;* when thoughts are not produced, this is precisely *Vinayaviniścaya.* When thoughts are not produced, this is precisely destroying all mind-consciousnesses.[684] 'If one has views of upholding the precepts then one violates the precepts. Whether 'precepts' or 'not precepts,' the two views are a single characteristic. One who is able to know this is a great Master of the Way.'[685] 'One sees that the bhikṣus who commit grave offenses do not fall into Hell, and sees that those who practice purity do not enter nirvāṇa. If you abide in views like these, this is impartial seeing.' "[686]

"These days Vinaya masters preach about [sense] 'contact' and preach about 'purity,' preach about 'upholding' and preach about 'violating.' They make forms for receiving the precepts, they make forms for decorum, and even for eating food—everything is made into forms. 'If one makes forms, then one is the same as non-Buddhist [practitioners of] the five supramundane powers. If one does not make forms, this is precisely the unconditioned (*asaṃskṛta*). One ought not have views.'[687] False concepts are defilement, having no false concepts is purity. Grasping 'I' is defilement, not grasping 'I' is purity. Turning things upside down is defilement, not turning things upside down is purity. 'Upholding' and 'violating' are merely restraining the body, and it is not the body that has nothing to restrain. Unless there is nothing whatsoever, how does one capture absolutely everything? 'If what one preaches is all about upholding the precepts, one has neither goodness nor decorum. The nature of the precepts is like emptiness, and those who uphold them are confounded by them.'[688] 'When mind is produced then various dharmas are produced, when the mind is extinguished then various dharmas are extinguished.'[689] 'As one's mind is, so also are the stains of wrongdoing, so also are all dharmas.'[690] Nowadays Vinaya masters are only motivated by fame and benefits. Like cats stalking mice, they take mincing steps and creep along, seeing 'true' and seeing 'false' with their self-styled precepts practice. This is really the extinction of the Buddha-Dharma, it is not the practice of the śramaṇa. The *Laṇkā-sūtra* says, 'In generations to come there will be those whose bodies wear the *kāṣāya,* [but who] delusively preach 'being' and 'nonbeing' and harm my true Dharma.'[691] In generations to come, in my Dharma [there will be those who] having left home delusively preach the Vinaya and ruin the true Dharma. Better that one should destroy *śīla,* and not destroy true-seeing. *Śīla* [causes] rebirth in Heaven, adding more [karmic] bonds, while true-seeing attains nirvāṇa." Hearing his talk, the Vinaya masters looked frightened and lost color and were trembling and uneasy.

The Venerable expounded again, "'Transcending characteristics and extinguishing characteristics, forever the characteristic of tranquil extinction, finally returning home to emptiness.'[692] 'Always completely enter the practice of empty tranquillity.'[693] 'The Buddha Treasury [of scriptures numerous as] the Ganges sands are completely understood in a single thought.'[694] The Buddha only permitted five years of study of the Vinaya precepts. After five years [the disciple was to] abandon Hīnayāna masters and seek Mahāyāna masters, and study the Dharma of no 'others' or 'self.' If [disciples] did not [practice] like this, the Buddha would severely rebuke them."[695] When the Vinaya masters heard this, the web of doubt was suddenly removed, and they told the Venerable, "We petty masters have transmitted deceptions for a long time, [now] we utterly forsake the precepts and Vinaya, and we humbly beg that you compassionately accept us." They made obeisances in unison, while weeping a rain of tears.

The Venerable said, "[As for] not-recollecting and not-thinking, [this means] not-recollecting any Dharma at all, not-recollecting either the Buddha-Dharma or worldly dharmas, so much at ease."[696] He asked, "Do you get it?" The Vinaya masters said in unison, "We get it." The Venerable said, "When you truly get it, then you will indeed be genuine Vinaya masters, and this is precisely 'seeing the nature.' At the time of true seeing, seeing is like transcendence of seeing. When seeing is inadequate, this is precisely 'seeing the Buddha.' At the time of true seeing, even seeing itself is not." The Venerable expounded for them yet again, "Arousing the mind is precisely defilement, movement of thought is precisely the demons' net.[697] So much at ease, not sinking and not floating, not flowing and not revolving, lively like a fish jumping! At all times, everything is meditation."[698] When the Vinaya masters had heard they leapt with joy, [then] sat silently listening.

SECTION 37

Dialogue with Treatise Masters (T. 51. 194C16–195A2)

和上問諸法師論師、「作何學問？」論師答、「解百法。」和上説、「解一百法是一百箇計、惣不解是无計。无計即无念。无念即无受、无念即无自、无念即无他。為衆生有念、假説无念。正无念時、无念不自。」

又問論師、「更解何経論？」答、「解起信論。」和上説云、「起即不信、信即不起。」又問論師、[699]「以何為宗。」論師不語。

和上云、「論以摧邪顯正為宗。論云、『離言説相、離名字相、離心縁相。』『離念相者等虚空、遍法界无所不遍。』如今論師只解口談藥方。不識主客、以流注生滅心解経論、大錯。論云、『離言説』即着言説、『離名字』即着名字。只解渾㗻[食+追]子、不知棗素。楞伽経云、『乃至有心轉、是即為戲論。不起分別者、是人見自心。』『以无心无[700] 意无受行、而悉摧伏諸外道。』『達諸法相无罣礙、[701]稽首如空无所依。』」論師聞説、合掌作礼。

The Venerable asked the Dharma masters and Treatise masters, "What branch of study do you pursue?" The Treatise masters replied, "We explicate the *Baifa* [*lun*]."[702] The Venerable expounded, "Explicating the one hundred Dharmas is one hundred separate calculations,[703] and not explicating at all is no-calculation. No-calculation is thus no-thought. No-thought is thus no-receiving, no-thought is thus no-self, no-thought is thus no-other. It is because beings have thought that one provisionally teaches no-thought, but at the time of true no-thought, no-thought itself is not."[704]

He further questioned the Treatise masters, "What other scriptures and treatises do you explicate?" They replied, "We explicate the *Treatise on the Arousal of Faith*." The Venerable said, "Arousing is precisely not faith, faith is precisely not-arousing." He further questioned the Treatise masters, "What do you take to be 'doctrine'?" The Treatise masters did not speak.

The Venerable said, "The treatise takes destroying the false and displaying the true as 'doctrine.'[705] The treatise says, 'Transcending the characteristic of verbal explanation, transcending the characteristic of names and characters, transcending the characteristic of mind and causes.'[706] 'Transcending the characteristic of thought is equal to void emptiness; in the entire Dharmadhatu, there is nowhere that is not encompassed.'[707] Nowadays Treatise masters merely explicate verbal prescriptions. They do not recognize host and guest, and they explicate scriptures and treatises with the mind of the flux of birth and death, a great error. The treatise saying 'transcend verbal explanation' is in fact attachment to verbal explanation, [and saying] 'transcend names and characters' is in fact attachment to names and characters. [It is like] only explicating an impure [diet] of dumplings, and not knowing the simple [diet] of jujube. The *Laṇkā-sūtra* says: 'As for the revolving of the mind, this really makes for frivolous treatises. If one does not give rise to distinctions, this person sees his own mind.'[708] 'With no *xinyi* 心意 (consciousness and discrimination), and no *shouxing* 受行 (perception and volition),[709] then one fully brings down all heterodoxies.'[710] 'Thoroughly penetrating all Dharma characteristics without hindrance, one bows one's head to the ground like emptiness, without anything on which to depend.'"[711] When the Treatise masters heard his talk, they joined their palms and made obeisance.

SECTION 38
Trading Quotations with Masters Daoyou, Mingfa, and Guanlu
(T. 51. 195A2–12)

又有道幽師、旻法師、冠[712]律師。法名嗣遠[713]。問和上、「禅師経云、[714]『貪着禅味、是菩薩縛。』」

和上答、「諸法師取相着相、是衆生繋。」

「又経云、『鈍根浅智人、着相憍慢者、如斯之等類、云何而可度？』」

和上言、「経云、『離相滅相、常寂滅相。』律師法師、惣違佛教。着相取相、妄認前塵、以為學問。如犬逐塊、塊即増多。无住即不如此。如師子放塊尋人、塊即自息。想念喧動、壊其善根。悟性安禅、即无漏智。『若於外相求、縦経塵劫、終不能得。』於内覺觀、刹那頃便成阿耨多羅三藐三菩提。」

There were also Master Daoyou, Master Mingfa, and Master Guanlu. (Their Dharma names were long passed down.)[715] They asked the Venerable [to explain], "The *Chanshi jing* says, 'Attachment to the taste of meditation is the bondage of the bodhisattva.'"[716]

The Venerable replied, "That Dharma Masters grasp after characteristics and are attached to characteristics is the bondage of the many beings."

[The masters went on,] "Another scripture says, 'People of dull roots and shallow wisdom, those arrogant ones attached to characteristics; regarding this type, how can one say that they can be saved?'"[717]

The Venerable said, "A scripture says, 'Transcending characteristics and extinguishing characteristics, forever the characteristic of tranquil extinction.'[718] Vinaya masters and Dharma masters all disregard the Buddha's teachings. They are attached to characteristics and grasp after characteristics, misrecognize sense objects, and take this as scholarly inquiry.[719] It is like a dog chasing clods of earth—the clods just increase. I, Wuzhu, am not like that. I am like a lion who leaves the clods and goes after the person [throwing them], and the clods then cease on their own.[720] Conceptualizations are noisily active and destroy one's good roots. Awakening to one's nature in peaceful meditation is thus non-outflow wisdom. 'If one seeks after external characteristics, endless kalpas go by and in the end one is unable to attain [wisdom].'[721] In inner awakened contemplation,[722] in an instant one attains *anuttara-samyak-saṃbodhi.*"

SECTION 39

Taking on Chan Disciples While Drinking Tea

(T. 51. 195A12–29)

又時有廣慶師、悟幽師、道宴師、大智師。已上並是堅成禅師第子。来至和上[723]坐下。是時和上呷茶次。悟幽師向和上説、「呷茶三五椀合眼坐。恰似壮士把一痩人腰、着急 [日+空][日+空] 地大好。」和上語悟幽師、「莫説閑言語、永淳年不喫泥 [食+專] 飩。」悟幽聞語失色。和上云、「阿師今将世間生滅心測度禅、大癡愚。此是『龍象蹴蹋、非驢所堪。』」

和上語悟幽師、「无住為説一箇話。有一人高 [土+追] 阜上立。有数人同伴路行、遥見高處有人立 。[724] 遞[725] 相語言、『此人必失畜生。』有一人云、『失伴。』有一人云、『採風涼。』三人共爭不定、来至高處問 [土+追] 上人、『失畜生否？』答云、『不失。』又問、『失伴否？』亦不失伴。又問、『採風涼否？』亦不採風涼。『既惣无、縁何高立 [土+追] 上？』答、『我只没立。』」和上語悟幽師、[726] 「无住禅、不沉不浮、不流不注、而實有用。用无生寂、用无垢淨、用无是非。活鱍鱍、一切時中、惣是禅。」

Another time there were Master Guangjing, Master Wuyou, Master Daoyan, and Master Dazhi. All of the above were disciples of Chan master Jiancheng.[727] They came to the Venerable and sat down. The Venerable was drinking tea at the time. Master Wuyou said to the Venerable, "Drinking three or five cups of tea and sitting with eyes closed. . . . Just like a strong fellow grabbing an emaciated man by the waist, it seems rather affected and pretentious." The Venerable told Master Wuyou, "Don't indulge in idle talk. You didn't eat mud dumplings in the [famine of the] Yongchun era (682–683).' "[728] (I.e., "You young whippersnapper.") Wuyou heard this and lost color. The Venerable said, "You, Master So-and-So, bring a worldly, birth-and-death mind to try to fathom Chan—really stupid. This [is like] 'a kick from a *hastināga* is not something an ass can bear.' "[729]

The Venerable told Master Wuyou, "Wuzhu will tell you a story. There was a man standing on a high earthen mound. There were a number of people traveling along the road together, and from afar they saw there was man standing on the high place. They talked about it among themselves, [one man said] 'This man surely has lost an animal.' There was a man who said, 'He lost his group.' There was a man who said, 'He's enjoying the coolness of the wind.' The three argued together without deciding. They reached the high place and asked the man on the mound, 'Did you lose an animal?' He replied, "No, I didn't.' Again they asked, 'Did you lose your group?' But neither had he lost his group. Again they asked, 'Were you enjoying the coolness of the wind?' But neither was he enjoying the coolness of the wind. [They asked,] 'Then if it is none of these, why are standing up high on the mound?' He replied, 'I'm just standing.'"[730] The Venerable told Master Wuyou, "Wuzhu's Chan is not sinking and not floating, not flowing and not fixed, but it truly has function. It functions without birth or tranquil [extinction],[731] functions without stain or purity, and functions without 'is' or 'is not.' Lively like a fish jumping; at all times, everything is meditation."[732]

SECTION 40
Dialogue with Master Xiongjun (T. 51. 195A29–B3)

有雄俊法師、問「和上、禅師入定否？」和上云、「定无出入。」問、「禅師入三昧否？」答云、「『不入三昧、不住坐禅、心无得失。』一切時中惣是禅。」

There was Dharma Master Xiongjun,[733] who asked, "Venerable, does a Chan master enter meditation?" The Venerable said, "In meditation there is neither exiting nor entering" [Master Xiongjun] asked, "Does a Chan master enter samādhi?" [The Venerable] replied, "'Not entering samādhi, not abiding in seated meditation, the mind is without gain or loss.'[734] At all times, everything is meditation."[735]

SECTION 41
Dialogue with Master Fayuan, Accompanied by His Mother (T. 51. 195B3–22)

又有隴右法縁師、俗姓魯。[736] 遠聞和上[737]、将母相随、至白崖山、礼拜和上。和上[738] 問、「講説何経論？」答云、「講金剛般若波羅蜜経。」和上問、「用誰疏論？」答云、「用天親、无着論、暉、壇、達等師疏。」和上問、「経云、『一切諸佛、及諸佛阿耨多羅三藐三菩提法、皆従[739] 此経出。』云何是此経？黄蘗是此経、紙是此経、墨是此経？」法縁師答云、「實相般若、觀照般若、文字般若。」

和上語法縁師、「一切諸文字无實无所依。俱同一寂滅、本来无所動。法離一切觀行。経云、『我法无實无虚。』『若言如来有所説法[740]、即為謗佛。』」法師答云、「法縁依章疏説。」和上語法縁師、「天親、无著、暉、壇等疏、何如佛説？」法縁師答、「不如。」和上云、「既不如、縁何不依佛教？経云、『離一切諸相、即名諸佛。』『若以色見我、以音聲求我、是人行邪道、不能見如来。』此経者即是此心。見性成佛道。无念即見性、无念无煩悩。无念即无自、无念即无他。无念即无佛、无念无衆生。正无念之時、无念不自。」

法師聞已、合掌白和上、「法緣多幸得遇和上。法緣老親伏願慈悲攝授。」便住山中、不離左右。

There was also Master Fayuan of Longyou,[741] whose secular surname was Lü. From afar he heard of the Venerable and, bringing his mother along with him, he arrived at the Baiyai mountains and made obeisance to the Venerable.[742] The Venerable asked, "On which scriptures and treatises do you lecture?" He replied, "I lecture on the *Jingangbanruopoluomi jing* (*Vajracchedikā-sūtra*)." The Venerable asked, "Whose commentaries and treatises do you use?' He replied, "I use the treatises by Vasubandhu and Asaṅga, and the commentaries of Masters Hui, Tan, and Da."[743] The Venerable asked, "The [*Vajracchedikā*] sūtra says, 'The Dharma of all the Buddhas and all the Buddhas' *anuttara-samyak-saṃbodhi* (unsurpassed enlightenment) come from this scripture.'[744] What is this scripture? Is it *tāla* tree leaves,[745] is it ink, is it paper?" Master Fayuan replied, "The prajñā characterized by actuality, the prajñā of contemplating radiance, and the prajñā of texts and characters."[746]

The Venerable told Master Fayuan, "'Texts and characters have nothing actual and nothing on which to depend. Altogether unified in tranquil extinction, fundamentally there is nothing that moves.'[747] 'The Dharma transcends all contemplation practice.'[748] The [*Vajracchedikā*] sūtra says, 'My Dharma is without actuality and without void.'[749] 'If anyone says the Tathāgata preached any Dharma, then they slander the Buddha.'"[750] The Dharma master replied, "I rely on the explanations of essays and commentaries." The Venerable said to Master Fayuan, "The [treatises of] Vasubandhu and Asaṅga, and the commentaries of Hui and Tan et al.—are they as good as the Buddha's explanations?" Master Fayuan replied, "They are not." The Venerable said, "Since they are not as good, why don't you rely on the Buddha's teachings? The [*Vajracchedikā*] sūtra says, 'Transcendence of all characteristics is precisely called the Buddha.'[751] 'Someone who sees 'I' through form and seeks 'I' through sounds is taking a false path, and is unable to see the Tathāgata.'[752] The words of this scripture are none other than this mind. Seeing the nature is the Way of becoming a Buddha. No-thought is thus seeing the nature, no-thought is no-defilements. No-thought is thus no-self, no-thought is thus no-other. No-thought is thus no-Buddha, no-thought is no-beings. At the time of true no-thought, no-thought itself is not."

When Master Fayuan heard this, he joined his palms and said to the Venerable, "I am exceedingly glad that I have been able to meet the Venerable. Fayuan and his aged relative (i.e., my mother and I) humbly beg you to compassionately accept us."[753] And so they stayed in the mountains and never left [the Venerable's] side.

SECTION 42
Discourse to Lay Donors (T. 51. 195B23–C13)

「般若波羅蜜、不見報恩者、不見作恩者。无住行无縁慈、行无願慈、行不熱慈、行无恩[754]慈。亦不彼亦不此、不行上中下法、不行有為无為、實不實法。不為益不為損、无大福无小福。以无所授、而授諸授。未具佛法、亦不滅授。『若欲懺悔者、端坐觀實相。』无念即實相、有念即虚妄。懺悔呪願、皆是虚妄。」

和上又說、「『誰人報佛恩？依法脩行者。誰人堪授供養[755]？世事不牽者。誰人消供養？於法无取者。』无念即无取、无念即无捨[756]。无念即无垢、无念即无浄。无念即无繋、无念即无縛。无念即无自、无念即无他。正无念之時、无念不自。无念即是般若波羅蜜。『般若波羅蜜者、是大神呪、是大明呪、是无上呪、是无等等呪。能除一切苦、真實不虚。』何其壇越、拔妄見之源、悟无生之體？卷重雲而朗恵日、業障頓祛。廓妄想以空心、寂然不動。真如之義、非理非事、无生无滅、不動不寂。二諦雙照、即真見佛。壇越但依此法、无慢斯須、雖開塞阻遥、即常相見无異也。儻違此義、流注根塵、思慮競生、貪染過度。縦常對面、楚越難以喩焉。

[The Venerable said,] "In the Prajñāpāramitā, one does not see the one who repays the kindness nor does one see the one who does the kindness. I, Wuzhu, practice unconditioned compassion, practice desireless compassion, practice not-grasping compassion, and practice causeless compassion. It is neither that nor this, I do not practice upper, middle, and lower Dharma, do not practice 'conditioned and unconditioned' or 'real and unreal' Dharma. It is not for the sake of increase and not for the sake of decrease, there is no great good fortune and no small good fortune. With nothing that is received, one yet receives all that is received. In the uncompleted Buddha-Dharma, there is also no end to receiving. 'If you want to confess and repent, sit properly and contemplate the characteristic of actuality.'[757] No-thought is thus the characteristic of actuality, thought is thus empty delusion. Confessing and repenting and intoning prayers, all this is empty delusion."

The Venerable expounded, "'Who repays the Buddha's kindness? One who practices according to the Dharma. Who is worthy to receive offerings? One who is not involved in worldly affairs. Who consumes offerings? In the Dharma there is nothing that is taken.'"[758] No-thought is thus no-taking, no-thought is thus no-discarding. No-thought is thus no-stain, no-thought is thus no-purity. No-thought is thus no-bonds, no-thought is thus no-ties. No-thought is thus no-self, no-thought is thus no-other. At the time of true no-thought, no-thought itself is not. No-thought is thus

Prajñāpāramitā. 'Prajñāpāramitā is the mantra of great spirit, is the mantra of great illumination, is the unsurpassed mantra, is the unequalled mantra. It is able to do away with all suffering, it is true reality and not void.'[759] How about if you *dānapati* (lay donors) root out the source of delusory views and awaken to your unborn substance? Like the roiling of thick clouds and the sun of bright wisdom, the veil of karma will suddenly roll back.[760] Cut back delusory conceptualization by emptying the mind, tranquilly not moving. The meaning of tathāta is neither principle nor phenomena, it is unborn and undying, it is not moving and not still. If one experiences the twin illumination of the Two Truths, then one truly sees the Buddha. If you *dānapati* would only rely on this Dharma this instant without delay, then even if the border is closed[761] and we are kept far apart, we will always see each other without any alienation. If you dare disregard this meaning, you will be swept along by sense-defilements, anxieties and strife will be produced, and the stain of arrogance will be unlimited. Then, though we might often be face to face, it is as difficult to meet as the states of Chu and Yue.[762]

SECTION 43

Portrait-Eulogy and Final Scene (T. 51. 195C15–196B6)

大曆保唐寺和上傳

頓悟大乘禅門門人写真讃文并序。[763]

山人孫寰述曰、「『道也无名』、悟道者方知得本。法也无相、識法者乃達其源。得本即道、知道體妙有无生。識法即源、見法性圓明自他[764]在。在无所在、在非彼此之方。生无所生、生非有无之際。

故釋迦文佛說十二部之分法、惣了於心、即說无所說。我和上指八万門之塵積、直教見性、乃至[765]无所指。矧知法離言說法、非言說不明。法離見聞、法非見聞不顯。『因言顯義、得義亡言。』是知[766] 順言說者、言顯而法亡、返見聞者、言亡而法顯。无言无我、无我无為。无為之體如如、如如之理不一、不一不自、寔曰菩提。『勝浄明心、周於法界。』

即我和上處其門傳其法。示无念之義、不動不寂。說頓悟之門、无憶无念。每謂門人曰、『法即如是、非言說所及。吾祖師達摩多羅傳此法要、嫡嫡相授。是諸佛之秘門、是般若波羅蜜。亦名第一義、亦名不二門、亦名見性、亦名真如、亦名涅槃、亦名禅門。如是之名是過去諸如来之假說、真實之義无有名字。』

時門人得教如說脩行而味之。共相歎曰、『蕩蕩乎、如覩太虛之寥廓、无[767] 无纖无埃。洋洋乎、若視滄溟之浩 [水+羔]、[768] 无際无涯。深知道言不及、微妙无名。感荷大師愍我迷愚、示我正法、不由階漸、真至菩提。若遇諸學、我須轉示、不有師相、曷以顯諸？』

遂嘿召良工、繪事真跡。容光煥然、相好成就。覩貌者可以摧邪、依法者可以至妙。更深處而未測。稽首瞻仰、強為讃云、

『最上乘法、无理非事。善説多門、皆歸不二。迦葉得之、西弘於佛域。達摩授之、東流於漢地。事即千有餘載、聖乃卅有四、嫡嫡相承、代代相次。得法契於道源、傳衣表於真偽。吾師密授、堂堂顯示、豁諸佛之密秘門、啓大乘之了義。不順有為、不依无記、離性離相、不愚不智、義非有无、有无非義。逆凡夫心、越賢聖意、行過三乘、頓超十地。非因非果、无他无自。『用无生寂、』影體俱離。見无明暗、无念即是。

遂召良工、潛為繪事。挫毫生相、覩巍巍之應身、離相窮言、見汪汪之法器。得猶天錫、骨与世異。嘿妙良哉！宛得真氣、貌惶惶而欲言、目瞬瞬而将視。「仰之弥高、瞻之弥貴。」不有吾師、此法将墮。』」

大曆九年六月三日、告諸門徒、「与吾取新浄衣、吾欲沐浴。」沐浴訖着衣、問第子、「齋時到未？」答、「到。」約束諸門徒第子、「若是孝順之子、不得違吾言教。吾當大行。吾去後不得頻眉、不得同世間不脩行人。哭泣着服及頻眉者、即不是吾第子。哭泣即是世間法、佛法即不然。離一切諸相、即是見佛。」

語已奄然坐化。大師春秋六十有一。

曆代法寶記一卷

ACCOUNT OF THE VENERABLE OF THE DALI BAO TANG MONASTERY

Portrait-eulogy, with preface, composed for a disciple of the Chan teachings of sudden awakening in the Mahāyāna

The mountain man Sun Huan states: "'The Dao is nameless,'[769] those who awaken to the Dao only then know they have attained the origin. 'The Dharma is without characteristics,'[770] those who recognize the Dharma then penetrate its source. Attaining the origin is thus the Dao, and one knows that the substance of the Dao is wondrous being[771] and birthlessness. Recognizing the Dharma is thus the source, and one sees that the nature of the Dharma is perfect luminosity and spontaneity. Existence is without anything that exists, existence is not orientation to 'that' or 'this.' Birth is without anything that is born, birth is not the limit of being or nonbeing.

Because the twelve divisions of Dharma[772] that Śākyamuni Buddha preached are complete in the mind, his exposition is without anything that is expounded. Our Venerable, as he pointed out the eighty thousand gates of the mound of dust,[773] was directly teaching 'seeing the nature,' and so he pointed without anything at which to point. How well he knew that the Dharma transcends the Dharma of verbal explanation, yet it is not that verbal explanation does not illuminate. The Dharma transcends seeing and hearing, but it is not that the Dharma is not manifest in seeing and hearing. 'Rely on words to make the meaning manifest, and having gotten the meaning forget the words.'[774] Thus, those who follow verbal explanations manifest words and forget the Dharma, while, on the contrary, those who see and hear forget the words and manifest the Dharma. Without words there is no 'I,' without 'I' there is nondoing. The substance of nondoing is suchness, the 'principle of suchness'[775] is not one; not one and not self, this is truly bodhi. 'Peerless pure bright mind pervades the Dharmadhātu.'[776]

Just so did our Venerable ground his teachings and transmit his Dharma. He displayed the meaning of no-thought, not moving and not still. He expounded the teaching of sudden awakening, no-recollection, and no-thought. He often told his disciples, 'The Dharma is just this, it is not something verbal explanation can reach. Our Ancestral Master Dharmatrāta (Bodhidharma) transmitted these essentials of the Dharma, passed from legitimate heir to legitimate heir. It is the secret teaching of the Buddhas, it is the Prajñāpāramitā. It is also called "the number one meaning," "the nondual gate,"[777] "seeing the nature," "suchness," "nirvāṇa," and "the Chan teachings." Names such as these are the provisional teachings of the Tathāgatas of the past, but the meaning of true reality has no name.'

Sometimes we disciples, obtaining the teaching and practicing according to his explanation, would get a taste of it. Then we would sigh to each other, 'How magnificent! It is like gazing at the empty expanse of the Great Void, without particle or speck of dust. How oceanic! It is as if looking out over the utter limitlessness of the Vast Deep, without boundary or shore. Words cannot touch deeply knowing the Dao, subtle mystery,[778] nameless. We are full of gratitude toward our Great Master for having pity on our delusion and dullness, for showing us the true Dharma not through gradual steps but directly arriving at bodhi. If we meet other students we should turn about and show [the true Dharma], but without the characteristics of our master, how are we to manifest it?'

Accordingly, we secretly summoned a fine artist to paint [the Venerable's] portrait. His appearance is lustrous, his characteristics are fine and successfully rendered. Those who gaze at the portrait are able to destroy evil, those who rely on the Dharma are able to attain the mystery. The deeper places [of his Dharma] I have not yet fathomed. Bowing my head to the ground and raising my gaze with reverence, I exert my strength to speak this eulogy:

The highest vehicle of the Dharma is neither principle nor phenomena. The many gates of the good teaching all return to nonduality. [Mahā]kāśyapa attained it, and it spread westward to Buddha-regions; [Bodhi]dharma received it, and it flowed eastward to the land of the Han. These are matters spanning over one thousand years, the holy ones for thirty-four generations have passed it from legitimate heir to legitimate heir, from one generation to the next. The Dharma they obtained tallies with the Dao's source, the robe they transmitted clearly shows true and false. Our teacher secretly received it and graciously displayed it, opening the secret mysterious gates of the Buddhas and revealing the complete meaning of the Mahāyāna. Not following conditionality (*saṃskṛta*), not relying on *avyākṛta,*[779] transcending qualities and characteristics, not 'dull' and not 'wise,' the true meaning is not being or nonbeing, being and nonbeing are not the true meaning. Contrary to the mind of the ordinary man, going beyond the intent of the virtuous holy ones, [our] practice exceeds the three vehicles and suddenly leaps over the ten *bhūmis* (stages). It is neither cause nor result, it has neither other nor self. 'It functions without birth or tranquil [extinction],'[780] reflection and substance are altogether transcended. Seeing is without bright or dark, no-thought is precisely this.

Accordingly we summoned the fine artist, secretly he made the painting. [The artist] brandished his brush and produced the characteristics, and gazing at the majestic response-body transcending characteristics and emptied of words, we see the expansive vessel of the Dharma. His attainments are like Heaven's gifts, his bones (i.e., intrinsic qualities) are not like those of this world. How silently mysterious and fine! [The portrait] seems to be truly breathing, the face quivers and wants to speak, the eyes dance and are about to see. 'I look up and it is ever loftier, I venerate and it is ever more dear.'[781] Without our master, this Dharma will sink."

On the third day of the sixth month of the ninth year of the Dali era (774), [the Venerable] told his disciples, "Bring me a fresh clean robe, I wish to bathe." When he had bathed and put on the robe, he asked his disciples, "Is it the time of abstinence (i.e., noon) yet?" They answered, "Yes." He bound all his disciples to a promise: "If you are filial obedient children you will not disobey my teachings. I am at the point of the great practice. After I am gone you are not to knit your brows [in distress], you are not to act like worldly and untrained persons. Those who weep, wear mourning garments, and knit their brows shall not be called my disciples. Weeping is precisely the way of the world, the Buddha-Dharma is not thus. 'Transcending all characteristics; this is precisely seeing the Buddha.'"[782]

When he finished speaking, he passed away while remaining in a seated position. The Great Master's springs and autumns amounted to sixty-one.

Lidai fabao ji, in one fascicle.

Notes

NOTES TO CHAPTER 1 (PP. 3–16)

1. Kong Yingda 孔穎達 (574–648), preface to his *Chunqiu zhengyi* 春秋正義 (Spring and Autumn Annals Commentary), in Yang 1961: 52.
2. *Beishan lu,* T. 52 (2113) 611a–613a; Shenqing's criticisms are discussed in chapter 7.
3. McRae 1986: 11.
4. Wuzhu and his disciples were later designated as the "Bao Tang" lineage, derived from the name of the temple they occupied, the Dali Bao Tang si 大曆保唐寺. In connection with this name, Chan scholar Yanagida Seizan surmises that Wuzhu's patron, the imperial minister Du Hongjian 杜鴻漸 (709–769) may have been responsible for installing Wuzhu in a temple with an imperial designation, and possibly imperial support. See Yanagida 1967: 286–287. The Bao Tang monastery was in Yizhou 益州, the Chengdu area of Sichuan. Regarding use of the character *li* 曆, see Part 2, n2.
5. The accepted belief was that the robe was enshrined at Huineng's temple in Shaozhou 韶州. The earliest extant text claiming that Huineng received the robe is the *Putidamou nanzong ding shifei lun* 菩提達摩南宗定是非論 (Treatise Determining the True and False about the Southern School of Bodhidharma), a record of Shenhui's 神會 (684–758) 732 debate. Shenhui states that it was not necessary to transmit the robe after Huineng and that the robe was in Shaozhou; see Hu [1958] 1970: 280–282.
6. Seo 1969: 49.
7. Nāgasena was a Buddhist teacher who was said to have instructed the Indo-Greek King Milinda (r. c. 163–150 B.C.E.). Nāgasena illustrated the doctrine of no-self by drawing the king's attention to his own carriage, demonstrating that the carriage could not be identified by any one of its constituent parts and was merely a designation for the composite. See *Milindapañha* (The Questions of King Milinda) 2.1: 1–2, trans. in Rhys Davids [1890] 1992: 40–46.
8. See *Lidai fabao ji,* T. 51 (2075) 195c14–15, 180c2–3, and 180c6. Regarding *da Chan xing* (180c6), the *Taishō* edition "corrects" this term to the phrase *dasheng xing* 大乘性 (Mahāyāna nature), but the *Lidai fabao ji* manuscripts have 大禪性.

9. The complete or nearly complete texts of the *Lidai fabao ji* are: P. 2125; S. 516; P. 3717; and Jinyi 津藝 304 (*Tianjinshi yishu bowuguan cang Dunhuang Tulufan wenxian* 4: 324–349). On the discovery and publication of the *Lidai fabao ji* texts and fragments known before 1997, including fragments newly identified by Rong Xinjiang, see Rong 1997: 235–242. The fragments are: S. 5916; S. 1611; S. 1776; S. 11014 (title only; see Rong 1997: 241–242); part of P. 3727; Jinyi 103 (*Tianjinshi yishu bowuguan cang Dunhuang Tulufan wenxian* 2: 199); Ch. 3934r (a fragment from Turfan material collected during the German expeditions of 1902–1914, now in the Staatsbibliothek in Berlin; see Nishiwaki 1997: 138–139); F. 261 (a fragment at the Institute of Oriental Studies of the Russian Academy of Sciences, St. Petersburg, in *E cang Dunhuang wenxian* 5: 42–43; see Rong 1997: 237–241); and the manuscript from the "Ishii" collection. The Ishii manuscript was listed as item no. 20 in Kawase Kazuma's 川瀬一馬 1942 catalogue of the collection of Ishii Mitsuo 石井光雄, the *Ishii Sekisuiken bunko zenbon shomoku* 石井積翠軒文庫善本書目. An article in the *Mainichi Shimbun* in 1976 revealed that the manuscript was in the possession of Hamada Noriaki 濱田德昭. His collection was subsequently divided between the Tōyō Bunkō and the National Diet Library, but part of it ended up in a bookstore; see Tanaka Ryōshō 1983: 395; Rong 1997: 237. The current location of the original manuscript is unknown, but when I was studying with Yanagida Seizan at Hanazono College in 1992, he allowed me to photocopy a reproduction of what he identified as the Ishii manuscript. This manuscript has portions taken from *Lidai fabao ji* sections 10 through 29; the copyist appears to have wanted extracts of Wuzhu's lectures and quotations from scripture. The beginning of the manuscript is damaged, and the end appears to have been torn off. While in Beijing in 2000, I gave a copy to Rong Xinjiang, and he subsequently published an article explaining the history of the Ishii manuscript and reproducing the entire text; see Rong 2002.
10. Texts showing the influence of the *Lidai fabao ji* include P. 2776; P. 2680; P. 3727; P. Tib. 116; P. Tib. 121; P. Tib. 813; P. Tib. 699; see Rong 2001: 349–357 and Ueyama 1981.
11. The *Lidai fabao ji* is listed in the Dunhuang manuscript of a catalogue of the library of the Sanjie 三界 monastery at Dunhuang, the *Jian yiqie ruzangjing mulu* 見一切入藏經目錄, written by Daozhen 道真 in 934. One copy of the catalogue is now in the Beijing library collection; see Oda 1989: 555–576 (the entry of the title *Lidai fabao ji* occurs on p. 560). Rong Xinjiang and other scholars have raised the question of whether the Dunhuang Chan manuscript listed therein can be considered a part of the lost "Chan Canon" (*Chan zang* 禪藏) compiled by Zongmi; see Rong 1997: 242. On the *Chan zang*, see Gregory 1991: 322–323.
12. See Rong 1999–2000 on the nature of the materials in the library cave. Rong also advances the theory that the cave was sealed because of fear of invasion by the Islamic Karakhanids, who destroyed Khotan in 1006, resulting in a wave of refugees to Dunhuang; ibid.: 272–275.
13. The following Chan transmission accounts are roughly contemporaneous with the *Lidai fabao ji*: the *Baolin zhuan* 寶林傳 (Transmission of the Baolin [Temple]); see Tanaka Ryōshō 2003; the *Caoqi dashi zhuan* 曹溪大師傳 (Biography of the Great Master of Caoqi), in ZZ. II, 19, 5: 483–488; and early versions of the *Liuzu tan jing* 六祖壇經 (Platform Sūtra of the Sixth Patriarch); see Komazawa daigaku Zenshūshi kenkyūkai 1978 and Yang 1993. Earlier "proto-Chan" genealogical texts are discussed in chapter 5.
14. *Jingde chuangdeng lu*, T. 51 (2076).

15. See Foulk 1987, 1992, and 1993.
16. For a bibliography of Yanagida's extensive work on Chan and related topics I refer the reader to Faure 1994. See also Faure 1988, 1989, 1991, and 1997; McRae 1986; and Broughton 1999.
17. For examples of studies that interrogate historiography and ideology with regard to Buddhism, see Faure 1993; Lopez 1995b.
18. For an overview of institutional Buddhism in the Tang, see Weinstein 1987a.
19. See Twitchett 1973 and 1979; Peterson 1973 and 1979; Dalby 1979; Hartman 1986.
20. See Hu 1932; Gernet [1949] 1977; McRae 1987. The dates for Shenhui are based on the recently discovered Longmen stele of 765. See Takeuchi 1985.
21. Sharf 2002: 42. Sharf focuses on the affinities between the Niutou *Jueguan lun* 絕觀論 (Treatise on Transcendence of Cognition) and the mid-seventh century *Baozang lun* 寶藏論 (Treasure Store Treatise), the subject of his study. Other Niutou-related expressions of this literary culture include the *Wuxin lun* 無心論 (Treatise on No-mind), *Xinxin ming* 信心銘 (Inscription on Faith in Mind), *Xinming* 心銘 (Inscription on Mind), and *Xinwang ming* 心王銘 (Inscription on the Mind King); see ibid.: 47–51. Sharf does not include the *Lidai fabao ji* in this family of texts, but the affinities between their signature style of discourse and Wuzhu's sermons are discussed in the section on Daoists in chapter 7.
22. For a fuller discussion of the problem of reification of Chan, see Faure 1991: 317–318.
23. See "Religious Rejections of the World and Their Directions," in Gerth and Mills 1946: 328–350. Weber emphasizes the constricting effect of a cumulative process of rationalization and resolution of contradictions, but the history of Chan also provides good examples of the regenerative effect of repeated enactments of a foundational polemic.
24. I was told that Jeffrey Broughton had completed an English translation of the *Lidai fabao ji*, but when I attempted to communicate with him about my project I did not receive a reply. The only other translation of *Lidai fabao ji* is Yanagida Seizan's (1976a) annotated translation into Japanese. As I explain in the preface to the translation, I consulted Yanagida's translation throughout the process of translating the text into English and I make extensive use of his annotations. My translation of the *Lidai fabao ji* is based on S. 516. Throughout, I cite page and line numbers in the *Taishō* canon edition, T. 51 (2075) 179a–196b, because it is the standard source for the Chinese canon and the most readily available, but its *Lidai fabao ji* is not the best redaction. The *Taishō* editors claim that P. 2125 is the base text, with notes on the variations in S. 516, but there are many misprints and unannotated alterations of the text; see Kondō 1974.
25. The term was first used by Martin Luther to condemn Johann Agricola's more extreme position regarding reliance on salvation by faith and grace alone. The original form of the belief that grace superseded law was attributed to St. Paul, who taught that faith in Christ freed the early Christians from observing the laws of the Old Testament.
26. *Lidai fabao ji*, T. 51 (2075) 186a4 (section 17) and 194b22 (section 36).

NOTES TO CHAPTER 2 (PP. 17–54)

1. Works consulted include Tang [1938] 1991; Zürcher 1959; Tsukamoto 1985; Kenneth Chen 1973; and Wright 1990. *The Chinese Transformation of Buddhism* and *The Buddhist Conquest of China* are the titles of Chen's and Zürcher's works, respectively, and

represent sides in the debate over which was more transformed by their encounter—"Buddhism" or "China."

2. The topic of nuns is taken up in chapter 6 and in my forthcoming book on nuns in the early Tang.
3. Brown 1988.
4. Borrowed from systems analysis, "tangled hierarchy" refers to circular causality between hierarchical levels. For a now-classic discussion of the conundrum of the relationship between absolute and cultural in claims of mystical experience, see Katz 1978.
5. For a discussion of Indian, Chinese, Japanese, and Western ideological constructs integral to the definition of Mahāyāna, see Silk 1994: 1–52 and Nattier 2003.
6. Lamotte [1958] 1988: 64; from *Dīgha Nikāya* II: 100.
7. Taking up the literary aspect of this dynamic, Sharf points out the coinherence of orthodoxy and heterogeneity in Buddhist works with reference to Mikhail Bakhtin's discussion of centripetal and centrifugal forces in the text. Centripetal forces favoring centralization and conservatism reflect "the urge towards verbal-ideological unity," while centrifugal decentralizing forces are expressed in the individual and radical. Bakhtin stresses the necessary mutual activation of these forces: "every concrete utterance of a speaking subject serves as a point where centrifugal as well as centripetal forces are brought to bear." See Sharf 2002: 139–140. Thus, as in Faure's notion of the "will to orthodoxy," differential, polemical, and sectarian representations are as much implicated in the ongoing creation of orthodoxy as unitary and conservative ones.
8. T. 51 (2075) 179a–196b.
9. *Lengqie shizi ji,* T. 85 (2837).
10. The *Lidai fabao ji* gives these specific dates for Daoxin, Hongren, and Huineng, but does not give dates for Bodhidharma, Huike, or Sengcan. Dates for Bodhidharma's death vary from text to text; see Reference section, Chen [1939] 1991: 38. Huike's dates are based on *Jingde chuandeng lu* 淨德傳燈錄 (Record of the Transmission of the Lamp [compiled in] the Jingde era), T. 51 (2076); see Chen [1939] 1991: 42. Sengcan's date of death is given as 592 in the recently discovered memorial inscription reported in Chen 1985. However, Chen Jinhua suggests that the stele is likely to be a later fabrication (personal communication, December 2003).
11. *Sishier zhang jing* 四十二章經, T. 17 (784).
12. *Lidai fabao ji,* T. 51 (2075) 179a14–24 (section 1). For all quotations from *Lidai fabao ji,* the reader should consult the translation in part 2 for full annotations.
13. Ibid.: 179c9–17 (section 2).
14. Ibid.: 179b12–19. Of course, proper ordination would have been impossible within the terms of the legend, for the rules of Buddhist ordination require the presence of a minimum of ten monks, and the aspirant must also demonstrate knowledge of the full monastic code; see Chen 1964: 45. There is no historical basis for Emperor Ming's dream and the conversion of his court, but his brother appears to have led a Huang-Lao devotional group that included Buddhist images in its worship; see Tsukamoto 1985: 49–50, 60–64.
15. *Lidai fabao ji,* T. 51 (2075) 179b20–c9.
16. *Gaoseng zhuan* biography of Daoan, T. 50 (2059) 353c. The visitor was later affirmed to be the wandering arhat Piṇḍola, as discussed below.
17. Biography of Buddhabhadra, in *Gaoseng zhuan,* T. 50 (2059) 335a–b.
18. *Gaoseng zhuan,* T. 50 (2059) 359b7–15 and 360b7–16.
19. For a summary of the Chinese Vinaya and monastic codes, see Yifa 2003: 3–8.

20. *Chu sanzang ji ji,* T. 55 (2145) 20a–21b. Sengyou describes the four Vinaya translations produced in the early fifth century and notes that the fifth was as yet unavailable. The four are: (1) *Sarvāstivāda Vinaya* (*Shisong lu* 十誦律) T. 23 (1435), trans. c. 404–406 by Kumārajīva鳩摩羅什, Puṇyatara 弗若多羅, Dharmaruci 曇摩流支; (2) *Dharmaguptaka Vinaya* (*Sifen lu* 四分律) T. 22 (1428), trans. c. 410–412 by Buddhayaśas 佛陀耶舍; (3) *Mahāsaṅghika Vinaya* (*Mohosengqi lu* 摩訶僧祇律) T. 22 (1425), trans. c. 416–418 by Faxian 法顯 and Buddhabhadra 佛馱跋陀羅; (4) *Mahīśāsaka* Vinaya (*Mishasebuhexi wufen lu* 彌沙塞部和醯五分律) T. 22 (1421), trans. c. 424 by Buddhajīva 佛陀什. The final Vinaya, the *Mūlasarvāstivāda Vinaya* (*Genben shuoyiqieyou bu lu* 根本說一切有部律), was translated by the pilgrim monk Yijing (635–713) in c. 700–703. Yifa gives an account of the process by which the *Dharmaguptaka Vinaya* had become the main Vinaya text in use in China by the seventh century (2003: 5–8). For an account of Vinaya translations within the larger context of transmission of the Nikāyas in China, see Wang 1994.
21. *Chu sanzang ji ji,* T. 55 (2145), preface by Dharmaraksa at 80c20–81a25; preface by Daoan at 80a16-c19. Dharmaraksa was active at the Eastern Jin capital at the end of the fourth century.
22. Hirakawa 1960: 524.
23. *Shisong biqiu jieben,* S. 797; corresponds to *juan* 27 and 28 of the *Sarvāstivāda Vinaya,* T. 23 (1435). See Kuo 1994: 45–46; Tsukamoto 1959.
24. *Gaoseng zhuan,* T. 50 (2059) 403b.
25. Ibid.: 324c15–325a12. On the possibility of oral transmission of the *prātimokṣa,* see Zürcher 1959: 32.
26. *Gaoseng zhuan,* T. 50 (2059) 325a6–9. The *Gaoseng zhuan* passage also mentions the third-century monk Saṅghavarman 康僧鎧, to whom Zhisheng 智昇 (658–740) attributes a translation of a *karmavācana* text; see *Kaiyuan shijiao lu,* T. 55 (2154) 487a3. However, Hirakawa argues that the extant text, T. 22 (1432), was compiled after the introduction of the Dharmaguptaka Vinaya in 410; see Hirakawa 1970: 203.
27. Biography of Fotudeng, in *Gaoseng zhuan,* T. 50 (2059) 383b–387a, trans. in Wright [1948] 1990. Walter Liebenthal argues that Fotudeng was probably a rendering of the name "Buddha Mātanga" (1947).
28. *Chu sanzang ji ji,* T. 55 (2145) 80a29–b1.
29. Sources for the following discussion are: *Gaoseng zhuan* biography of Daoan, T. 50 (2059) 351c3–354a17, trans. in Link 1958; Tang [1938] 1991: 187–228, 242–277; Zürcher 1959: 185–204; Tsukamoto 1985: 655–756.
30. *Gaoseng Faxian zhuan* 高僧法顯傳 (Biography of the Eminent Monk Faxian), a.k.a. *Foguo ji* 佛國記 (Record of Buddhist Kingdoms), T. 51 (2085).
31. *Gaoseng zhuan,* T. 50 (2059) 352c, trans. in Link 1958: 25.
32. *Lidai fabao ji,* T. 51 (2075) 182c17–25 (section 10). The *Lidai fabao ji* account is clearly derived from the passage on Daoan's regulations in his *Gaoseng zhuan* biography (T. 50 [2059] 353b23–27) or some other source based on it, but the section on monastic regulations is rather garbled. For a discussion of Daoan's regulations, see Yifa 2003: 10–13.
33. In this and other *Lidai fabao ji* sections criticizing attachment to form, three related terms are used: (1) *shixiang* 事相, phenomenal or ritual aspects as opposed to the noumenal or doctrinal; (2) *shi* 事 by itself, used more for the ritual aspect, and (3) *xiang* 相 by itself, usually meaning characteristics ("marks") or features, externals, the contingent as opposed to the absolute.
34. *Lidai fabao ji,* T. 51 (2075) 182c28–183a1 (translation section 10).

35. "He Fangguang-Guangzan luejie xu 合放光光讚略解序" (Preface to a summary of the collated *Pañcaviṁśatisāhasrikā-sūtra*), in *Chu sanzang ji ji,* T. 55 (2145) 48a29–b1, trans. in Zürcher 1959: 193, with minor modifications.
36. *Chu sanzang ji ji,* T. 55 (2145) 62c18–20. The letter is not attributed, but Zürcher argues that it must be from Daoan (1959: 392n81).
37. See Daoan's "Anpan zhuxu 安般注序," in the *Chu sanzang ji ji,* T. 55 (2145) 43c4–24; "Ren benyusheng jing xu 人本欲生經序," in ibid.: 45a14–b2; "Shiermen jing xu 十二門經序," in ibid.: 45b26–46a13; "Da shiermen jing xu 大十二門經序," in ibid.: 46a14–46b18; "Daoxing jing xu 道行經序," in ibid.: 47a12–c3; "Daodi jing xu 道地經序," in ibid.: 69a27–c18.
38. *Lidai fabao ji,* T. 51 (2075) 183a11–13 (translation section 10).
39. First published in 1938, Tang's work on the introduction of Buddhism to China, *Han Wei Liang Jin Nanbei chao Fojiaoshi* 漢魏兩晉南北朝佛教史, remains an invaluable resource. It has influenced, among others, Erik Zürcher, Arthur Wright, Kenneth Chen, and Stanley Weinstein, whose books on Six Dynasties and Tang Buddhist history are the standard English language sources. Tang argues that during the period of North-South division (317–589) the "wisdom" aspect flourished in the south and practice atrophied, while in the north the reverse was true. More recently, scholars have argued that while cultural differences between the northern and southern regimes produced distinctive developments in both Buddhism and Daoism, the interactions are too complex to be well-served by Tang's heuristic characterization. See, for example, Shinohara 1994: 482.
40. *Ānāpānasmṛti-sūtra* (Scripture of the Mindfulness of Breathing) T. 15 (602).
41. Full title: *Pratyutpannabuddhasaṃmukhāvasthitasamādhi-sūtra,* a.k.a. *Sūtra of Bhadrapāla,* T. 13 (416), (417), (418), (419).
42. *Śūraṅgamasamādhi-sūtra,* T. 15 (642).
43. Tang [1938] 1991: 766–771.
44. We may place the apocryphal *Śūraṅgama-sūtra,* T. 19 (945), within this eighth-century context; it was often cited in Chan works, including *Lidai fabao ji,* as scriptural support for the notion of an all-inclusive formless practice. Like other apocrypha, the *Śūraṅgama-sūtra* derived its pedigree as an authentic translation through being identified with works of the same or similar titles, and clearly drew on the prestige of the above *Śūraṅgamasamādhi-sūtra.*
45. For discussion of the concept of "one-practice samādhi" in this connection, see Faure 1986c.
46. *Chu sanzang ji ji,* T. 55 (2145) 44a19–23. Such uses of Chinese concepts to explicate the relationship between non-duality and practice would continue to develop in ever more sophisticated ways; Southern School Chan simplification of practice to nondual realization, "seeing the nature" (*jianxing* 見性), is sometimes portrayed as a sinification of Buddhism in Daoist terms, and in chapter 6 we return to this issue when exploring the treatment of Daoism in the *Lidai fabao ji.*
47. *Jin shu* (114), trans in Rogers 1968: 160–161.
48. *Chu sanzang ji ji,* T. 55 (2145) 52c3–9.
49. Biography of Sengguang, in *Gaoseng zhuan,* T. 50 (2059) 355a.
50. Biography of Daoan, in *Gaoseng zhuan,* T. 50 (2059) 353a.
51. Regarding Daoan's bibliographic methods, see Zürcher 1959: 195.
52. Biography of Daoan, in *Gaoseng zhuan,* T. 50 (2059) 353b, trans. in Link 1958: 34–35, with minor modifications.

53. For sources on Piṇḍola, see T. 32 (1689) 784b–c; T. 49 (2030) 13a; Lévi and Chavannes 1916; and Strong 1979. Bernard Faure attests to the continuity of his role in medieval and modern Japanese monastic practice: "Another well-known testimony to ritual correctness is the Arhat Piṇḍola, whose acceptance of the ritual offerings in the monastery's kitchen and bathroom serves to overcome the doubts of the monks as to their spiritual progress" (1991: 279).
54. Biography of Daoan, in *Gaoseng zhuan,* T. 50 (2059) 353c. The association between bathing and *memento mori* can still be seen in the inscriptions of East Asian monastery bath-houses.
55. Ibid.: T. 50 (2059) 352a27–29, trans. in Link 1958: 18, with minor modifications.
56. There are divergent traditions regarding the succession of authority after the Buddha's death. See Lamotte 1988: 202–212. The Aśoka texts include an account of the transmission of five Dharma masters, from Mahākāśyapa to Upagupta. There are two variant Chinese translations of the legend of Aśoka, the Mauryan king who reigned in the mid-third century B.C.E. The first is the *Ayu wang zhuan* 阿育王傳 (*Aśokavadāna,* Biography of King Aśoka), T. 50 (2042), translated by An Faqin 安法欽 in the early fourth century. The second is *Ayu wang jing* 阿育王經 (*Aśokarājasūtra,* Scripture of King Aśoka), T. 50 (2043), translated by Saṅghapāla 僧伽婆羅 in 512. See Strong 1983 and Li 1993. For a genealogy of Vinaya masters stemming from the Buddha's disciple Upali, see the *Mahāsaṅghika Vinaya* (*Mohosengqi lu* 摩訶僧祇律) T. 22 (1425) 492c–493a, translated c. 416–418 by Faxian and Buddhabhadra; and Buddhaghosa's *Samantapāsādikā* (*Shanjian lu piposha* 善見律毘婆沙) T. 24 (1462) 684b–685a, translated c. 488 by Saṅghabhadra.
57. T. 15 (618). Demiéville argues that *Damoduoluo chan jing* was misnamed in the *Lidai sanbao ji* 歷代三寶記 (T. 49 [2034] 71a), for in the text itself it is identified as a manual of practice, or *Yogācārabhūmi* (see T. 15 [618] 301b22), rather than a *Dhyāna sūtra,* and is the work of Dharmatrāta's disciple Buddhasena, Buddhabhadra's master (Demiéville 1978: 46). Buddhabadra's own preface makes no mention of Buddhasena, but the *Gaoseng zhuan* does say that Buddhabhadra studied with him when he was young (T. 50 [2059] 334c18).
58. See McRae 1986: 79–82. In the *Chu sanzang ji ji,* two lists are found in Sengyou's record of Sarvāstivāda masters (T. 55 [2145] 88c–90a), and two are found in Huiyuan's and Huiguan's respective prefaces (ibid.: 65c–66a and 66c–67a). Buddhabhadra's list in the translation of the *Damoduoluo chan jing* is at T. 15 (618) 301c; Huiyuan's preface is also included, with the list at ibid.: 301a–b. I discuss these lists further in chapter 4 in connection with the *Lidai fabao ji*'s list of Indian patriarchs.
59. Biography of Buddhabhadra, in *Gaoseng zhuan,* T. 50 (2059) 334b–335c.
60. See McRae 1986: 299nn.199, 201. On the basis of the greater sophistication of the transmission scheme found in the later of the two Aśoka translations, and in the Kashmiri lineages discussed below, McRae speculates that a theory of transmission may have evolved in Kashmir during the fourth and fifth centuries.
61. *Chu sanzang ji ji,* T. 55 (2145) 65c5–12.
62. Ibid.: T. 55 (2145) 65c12–28.
63. That is, the Later Qin 後秦 (385–417).
64. *Lidai fabao ji,* T. 51 (2075) 180c5–17 (translation section 4).
65. Buddhayaṣas's *Gaoseng zhuan* biography immediately precedes that of his contemporary, Buddhabhadra, T. 50 (2059) 333c15–334b25. Buddhayaṣas's biography provides an interesting counterpoint to that of Buddhabhadra; like Buddhabhadra, he

was known at court in Chang'an for his strict observance of the precepts, but unlike Buddhabhadra he remained there as an honored guest. He had been Kumārajīva's teacher in Kashgar and was invited to Chang'an at Kumārajīva's urging, but he initially refused, saying that he would not come unless the emperor promised not to make him live with women, the fate that Kumārajīva suffered.

66. Given the indeterminacy of number in literary Chinese, one must ask, is it one stūpa or two? However, this is the implication of the "twins" motif that is established throughout the passage.
67. For example, in their role as the messengers of Bodhidharma, they could be compared to the "Boys of Good and Evil" who attend King Yama.
68. There is a precedent for use of *Damoduoluo chan jing* in an account of the Chan patriarchs, as it is also mentioned in the *Chuan fabao ji,* T. 85 (2838) 1291a.
69. However, Zongmi cites this scripture "translated" by Buddha and Yaśas as a source for the transmission of introductory methods of seated meditation such as taught by Shenxiu; see *Chanyuan zhuquanji duxu* 禪源諸詮集都序 (Prolegomenon to the Collection of Expressions of the Chan Source), T. 48 (2015) 404a1–3. He appears to have gotten his misapprehensions about the origins and nature of the scripture from *Lidai fabao ji;* see Yanagida 1967: 311–312.
70. *Lidai fabao ji,* T. 51 (2075) 183a19–22 (translation section 10); from the *Chanmen jing,* S. 5532, in Suzuki 1968–71: 3: 334. One might note that, according to this view of visionary experience, the dream of Emperor Ming would certainly fall into the category of delusion.
71. The *Chanmen jing* is related to several other Northern School Chan apocrypha that display Esoteric elements and a pre-Shenhui style of subitism; see Faure 1997: 125–128.
72. *Lidai fabao ji,* T. 51 (2075) 183a24–25; from the *Vajrasamādhi-sūtra,* T. 9 (273) 368a12–13 and 370b3.
73. *Lidai fabao ji,* T. 51 (2075) 183b15.
74. The pretext was the above-mentioned affair of Buddhabhadra's vision of "five ships setting out from his native country" (*Gaoseng zhuan,* T. 50 [2059] 335a21; b1; b14).
75. Two famous *Gaoseng zhuan* stories about Kumārajīva's chastity underscore this point. It is said that Kumārajīva was sought and taken captive in the war that destroyed his homeland, Kucha. The victorious Qin general Lu Guang 呂光 then decided to assault the monk's integrity by plying him with a princess and strong drink. When the latter had caused Kumārajīva to succumb to the former, he was then forced to ride unruly animals. Kumārajīva's chief virtue in the face of all indignities was that he "did not change color." The general desisted, but what eventually won him over was Kumārajīva's skill in accurate prediction. Much later in life, enjoying prestige as an honored translator in the court of the Later Qin 後秦 emperor Yao Xing 姚興 (r. 393–416), Kumārajīva was made to live in luxurious quarters with ten beautiful women in order that his talent might be transmitted to the next generation physically as well as spiritually (*Gaoseng zhuan* biography of Kumārajīva, T. 50 [2059]: 330a–333a). As will be seen later in stories about Shenxiu and Zhishen, the continence of monks could become an arena in which the conflict between secular and monastic authority was played out.
76. On the translation enterprise, see *Gaoseng zhuan,* T. 50 (2059) 332a25–c3.
77. Ibid.: 332c24–333a6.
78. *Lidai fabao ji,* T. 51 (2075) 179c23–28 (translation section 2). This passage does not appear in the *Jin shu,* but contains elements from Huiyuan's biography in the *Gao-*

seng zhuan and the account of the 402–404 bowing controversy in the *Hongming ji* 弘明集, discussed below.

79. Regent for Emperor Cheng 成 (r. 325–342).
80. This summary of the bowing controversy of 340 is based on Zürcher 1959: 106–110, 160–163; Tsukamoto 1985: 339–346.
81. The "five relationships" are the foundational reciprocal relationships, as defined by Mencius: parent and child, ruler and minister, husband and wife, older and younger siblings, and older and younger friends.
82. From the first edict promulgated by Yu Bing on behalf of the emperor Cheng. The full debate is found in the *Hongming ji* 弘明集, T. 52 (2102) 79b-80b. The documents are also found in the *Ji shamen buying bai su dengshi* 集沙門不應拜俗等事, T. 52 (2108) 443c–444c. This passage is from the *Hongming ji,* T. 52 (2102) 79b12–15; trans. in Zürcher 1959: 160–163, with minor modifications.
83. From the second edict by Yu Bing on behalf of the emperor, in the *Hongming ji,* T. (2012) 80a19–20; trans. in Zürcher 1959: 160–163, with minor modifications.
84. From the second memorial of He Chong 何充 (292–346) et al., in the *Hongming ji,* T. (2012) 80a8–6; trans. in Zürcher 1959: 160–163, with minor modifications.
85. The letters and treatise are discussed further below.
86. Huan Xuan enlisted the aid of the abbess Miaoyin 妙音, who had a reputation for erudition and literary talent. Through her intercession he was able to have a pawn rather than a rival general appointed governor of a key territory which he later overran, slaughtering the weaker incumbent. See *Biqiuni zhuan* 比丘尼傳 biography of Miaoyin, T. 50 (2063) 936; trans. in Tsai 1994: 33–34. The story may be didactic in the "praise and blame" manner of biographies of moral failures in the *Shiji* 史記, but it indicates that nuns as well as monks were involved in politics.
87. *Gaoseng zhuan* biography of Huiyuan, T. 50 (2059) 360b16; see also the biography of Huichi 慧持, in ibid.: 361c14; and the biography of Daozu 道祖, ibid.: 363a13. See Zürcher 1959: 214, 397nn175–176.
88. See Zürcher 1959: 397n177.
89. Biography of Huiyuan, in the *Gaoseng zhuan,* T. 50 (2059) 360b18–28; trans. in Zürcher 1959: 250, with minor modifications.
90. *Tang shu* 唐書 (1) 17.
91. The *Dao seng ge* is no longer extant; see Weinstein 1987: 11–27.
92. *Tang shu* (127) 3579.
93. *Tang huiyao* (47); see Yanagida 1967: 287–288.
94. Weinstein 1987: 90–97.
95. All the letters are found in the *Hongming ji,* T. 52 (2102) 80b–85c, and in the *Ji shamen buying bai su dengshi* 集沙門不應拜俗等事, T. 52 (2108) 444c–448c. A version of the exchange is found in the *Gaoseng zhuan* biography of Huiyuan, T. 50 (2059) 360c. The following account is based on the *Hongming ji,* and adaptation of two previous translations: Zürcher 1959: 231–239, 256–264 and Tsukamoto 1985: 836–844.
96. *Hongming ji,* T. 52 (2102) 80b21–23.
97. Ibid.: 81a2–4.
98. Ibid.: 81a18–21.
99. Ibid.: 81b25–28.
100. The treatise is found in the *Hongming ji,* T. 52 (2102) 29c–32b and in the *Ji shamen buying bai su dengshi,* T. 52 (2108) 449a–451b. An abbreviated version is found in the *Gaoseng zhuan* biography of Huiyuan, T. 50 (2059) 360c–361a; trans. in Hurvitz 1957.

101. *Hongming ji,* T. 52 (2102) 84a23–27.
102. Ibid.: 32a16–27.
103. Ibid.: 32a27–b6; trans. in Hurvitz 1957: 112–113, with minor modifications.
104. The biography of Daoyi 道壹 (d. c. 398) quotes his letter to the official charged with summoning him to return to the capital from his mountain monastery, in which he says that because monks are free from ordinary desires, ties, and delusions, they should not be subjected to ordinary duties and registration. He in effect claims extraterritoriality: "Thus, the people of a strange land are not ten thousand *li* away—wearing coarse clothing and shaking pewter [ringed staves] they spread out over Heaven's own country" (*Gaoseng zhuan,* T. 50 [2059] 357a16–28).
105. Huiyuan's biography claims two occasions on which he harbored known rebels, enemies of Huan Xuan and Liu Yu, respectively, and yet was praised for his nonpartisanship by these potentially dangerous military leaders whose authority he had flouted. See the *Gaoseng zhuan,* T. 50 (2059) 359b7–15 and 360b7–16, for the incidents involving Liu Yu and Huan Xuan, respectively.
106. Ibid.: 359b15–18.
107. Besides Huiyuan's letters to Huan Xuan concerning regulation of the clergy, four nonextant prefaces on monastic regulations are attributed to him in Lu Cheng's 陸澄 *Falun mulu* 法論目錄; *Chu sanzang ji ji,* T. 55 (2145) 84a3–5.
108. *Gaoseng zhuan,* T. 50 (2059) 360a8–14; *Chu sanzang ji ji,* T. 55 (2145) 20a28–b18.
109. *Gaoseng zhuan,* T. 50 (2059) 361a29–b5.
110. Regarding the spatial features of the Han cosmological system, Faure writes, "In actual practice, Chinese cosmology was probably a spatially and temporally discontinuous whole, whose cohesion has been somewhat exaggerated by traditional Sinology. At any rate, it was later reinterpreted, adapted, and subverted by the popular tradition and by religious Taoism. However, its fundamental intuition was never questioned—namely, that space is complex and unstable, that it is not always or everywhere the same; now diluted, now concentrated, it constitutes a 'hierarchized federation of heterogeneous expanses.' Even after the cosmological structure itself had collapsed, the perception of a 'qualitative,' heterogeneous space remained prevalent" (1987: 345).
111. See ibid.
112. *Gaoseng zhuan,* T. 50 (2059) 358a22–28.
113. Biography of Daoan, in ibid.: 352a13–15.
114. Biography of Huiyuan, in ibid.: 358b12–c3.
115. Faure 1987: 346.
116. Zürcher 1959: 127.
117. Raoul Birnbaum's experience of the monasteries of modern Wutai shan attests to a very similar mix of the criminal and the cultivated, and he points out that the extremes of both groups would tend to gravitate to the same monasteries, sharing a taste for the most difficult of access (lecture at Stanford University, March 16, 1995).
118. *Hongming ji,* T. 52 (2102) 85c14–17.
119. An example is this story purported to date from the Eastern Jin: "The tiger's ravages ceased from then on. The local inhabitants transformed the temple of the soil god into a Buddhist monastery where they invited Fa-an to reside, making over the surrounding fields and gardens as permanent assets for his community" (*Shenseng zhuan* 神僧傳, T. 50 [2064] 958b; trans. in Gernet 1995: 114).

120. Gernet 1995: 94–152.
121. Loosely based on the *Viśeṣacintibrahma-paripṛcchā-sūtra*, T. 15 (586) 37b3–8.
122. *Lidai fabao ji*, T. 51 (2075) 192a24–b20 (translation section 31).
123. For the following discussion I rely on Rogers 1968.
124. Ibid.: 52.
125. Ibid.: 69–73.
126. *Jin shu* (114); trans. in ibid.: 160–161.
127. In chapter 5 I discuss Anna Seidel's work regarding the important role that Daoist talismans and myths played in supporting dynastic legitimacy.
128. Rogers 1968: 54–58.
129. See Puett 2001: 73–76.
130. Rogers 1968: 58.

NOTES TO CHAPTER 3 (PP. 55–90)

1. *Lidai fabao ji*, T. 51 (2075) 193b6–b10 (translation section 33).
2. See Gernet 1995.
3. *Majjhima Nikāya* III: 253–257, trans. in Nāṇamoli and Bodhi 1995: 1102–1106.
4. Hao Chunwen's (1998) analysis of Dunhuang documents demonstrates that clerics continued to have close social and economic ties with their lay families.
5. See Gombrich 1988 and Brown 1982 and 1988 for discussions of the complexity of the lay-monastic relationship in the contexts of Theravāda Buddhism and Late Antique Christianity, respectively.
6. From the *Vimalakīrti-sūtra*, T. 14 (475) 540a18–19.
7. From the *Vajracchedikā-sūtra*, T. 8 (235) 751c15.
8. Based on the *Nirvāṇa-sūtra*, T. 12 (374) 520b8–9.
9. Based on the *Dashengyi zhang*, T. 44 (1851) 699a20–21 ff.
10. From the apocryphal *Dhammapada*, T. 85 (2901) 1435a13–14.
11. From the *Vajracchedikā-sūtra*, T. 8 (235) 750b29.
12. From the *Vimalakīrti-sūtra*, T. 14 (475) 540a17.
13. *Lidai fabao ji*, T. 51 (2075) 194a23–b1 (translation section 35).
14. See Davidson 1990; Lopez 1995.
15. Davidson 1990: 292; Lopez 1995: 37. For versions of this story in the Vinaya, see Lamotte 1988: 552–558.
16. Davidson 1990: 292–293. Legend does designate a single exception, the Buddha's cousin Ānanda, his constant attendant. However, even Ānanda's versions had to be approved by the assembly.
17. Davidson 1990: 294.
18. Ibid., from the Pali Vinaya, trans. in Oldenberg 1879: 4:15.
19. Lopez 1995: 36.
20. Davidson 1990: 294.
21. Ibid.: 299.
22. Ibid.: 300; Lopez 1995: 26.
23. Davidson 1990: 300.
24. Ibid.: 301–302.
25. Lopez 1995: 27.

26. Steven Katz (1978) pointed out the ways in which traditions are reflected in the visions of mystics, in spite of the standard claim that such experiences are unmediated and ineffable.
27. Davidson 1990: 302; from the *Majjhima Nikāya* 3: 9–11; trans. in Ñāṇamoli and Bodhi 1995: 881–882.
28. Davidson 1990: 302.
29. *Majjhima Nikāya* III: 11–13; trans. in Ñāṇamoli and Bodhi 1995: 883–884. A related discussion of the criteria for good and bad teachers is found in the *Lohicca-sutta, Dīgha Nikāya* I: 224–234; there the attainment of supernormal powers is not included in the criteria.
30. Although the subject is far too complex to be explored in this context, the Esoteric (*Zhenyan* 真言) orientation to the use of powers is of course quite different. Charles Orzech argues that early soteriologically based categorizations of supramundane powers as "noble" or "ignoble" evolved into the complex Esoteric system of two interdependent yet divergently oriented cosmologies, characterized by the interaction between powers of transmutation/world-mastery and powers of vision/world-transcendence. See Orzech 1998: 50–55.
31. Hubbard 2001: 43. The quotation is from *The Book of the Gradual Sayings* (*Aṅguttara Nikāya*), trans. E.M. Hare (London: Pali Text Society, 1973), 3: 133. A reader protested the use of "runes" to translate what is probably the Sanskrit term *vedala,* for which there appears to be no good translation.
32. Hubbard 2001: 44; see *Aṅguttara Nikāya* III: 134.
33. Lopez 1995: 28.
34. Davidson 1990: 308.
35. Ibid.: 312.
36. Ibid.
37. Ibid.: 316.
38. Lopez 1995: 44n17.
39. Ibid.: 38.
40. Ibid.: 39, 47n67; from *Sutta Nikāya* XII: 65.
41. An example of this is the *Sigālaka-sutta, Dīgha Nikāya* III: 180–193.
42. Lopez 1995: 39.
43. *Wuyi shi jie* 無憶是戒; *Lidai fabao ji,* T. 51 (2075) 189a15–18.
44. *Da fangguang fo huayan jing* 大方廣佛華嚴經; (*[Buddha]avataṃsaka-sūtra*), T. 9 (278) and 10 (279). The five basic precepts of Buddhism are not killing, not stealing, not indulging in sexual misconduct, not lying, and not taking intoxicants. The *Avataṃsaka* virtues included the first four, to which are added: not slandering, not speaking harshly, not speaking frivolously, not being covetous, not being moved to anger, and not entertaining false views. See Cleary 1993: 714–721; Mochizuki: 1570–1573.
45. Early Chinese translations of the *Daśabhūmika-sūtra,* excerpted from the *Avataṃsaka,* helped to spur interest in the notion of bodhisattva precepts. See Demiéville 1929–30: 142–143.
46. Hirakawa 1960: 534. Hirakawa also discusses the apparent ambivalence of the *Mahāprajñāpāramitā-śāstra,* which lauds the superior efficacy of Mahāyāna precepts but does not detail special bodhisattva precepts. Although separate precepts for lay and ordained are prescribed in one section, in another context the all-inclusive ten precepts are advocated for both; ibid.: 543n28; *Dazhi du lun* 大智度論, T. 25 (1509) 161a–c; 395b.

47. On the other side of the coin, scholars are also reexamining the Pāli scriptures for evidence of inclusiveness in the earliest Buddhist communities. Freiberger (2000) argues that the Pāli scriptures show coexisting institutional and non-institutional tendencies in the early Saṅgha. Passages that he cites in support of a non-institutional, individualistic tendency include: *Aṅguttara Nikāya* (AN) I: 189, 6–15 (lay practice and spiritual development); AN III: 207, 1–3 (lay practice retreats); *Sutta Nikāya* (SN) IV: 281, 11–283, 19; SN IV: 302, 20–304, 20; AN V: 185, 2–189, 8 (laymen instructing others, including ascetics). See ibid. and Samuels 1999.
48. Nattier 2003: 3–9.
49. Ibid.: 171–192.
50. Ibid.: 107–110.
51. Groner 1990b: 223.
52. *Wenshushili wen jing* 文殊師利問經, T. 14 (468). See Groner 1990b: 234.
53. The history of Chinese translations of these texts is complex. The *Yogācārabhūmi-śāstra* is one of a group of texts of the Vijñaptimātra school of Asaṅga and Vasubandhu. It was not translated into Chinese in its entirety until the seventh century, as the *Yuqie shidi lun* 瑜伽師地論, T. 30 (1579), by Xuanzang 玄奘, who also translated the related precepts texts T. 24 (1499) and T. 24 (1501). However, there are two fifth-century translations of the *Bodhisattvabhūmi* section of the *Yogācārabhūmi-śāstra,* (1) the *Pusadichi jing* 菩薩地持經, T. 30 (1581), trans. c. 414–421 by Dharmakṣema 曇無讖, and (2) the *Pusa shanjie jing* 菩薩善戒經, T. 30 (1582), trans. c. 431 by Guṇavarman 求那跋摩. Excerpted from (2) by the same translator, the *Youpoli wen pusa shoujiefa* 優波離問菩薩受戒法, T. 30 (1583), is a separate one-fascicle ordination-method text. In addition, there is another translation by Dharmakṣema, the *Pusa jieben* 菩薩戒本, T. 24 (1500), a precepts text that appears to be compiled from parts of both the *Bodhisattvabhūmi* and the *Yogācārabhūmi-śāstra.* See Demiéville 1929–30: 144–145; Tang [1938] 1991: 827; Hirakawa 1960: 536–539; Kuo 1994: 39–40.
54. *Pusadichi jing,* T. 30 (1581) 913b. See Demiéville 1929–30: 144–145; Hirakawa 1960: 526–530.
55. For a discussion of the different schema for reconciling Hīnayāna and Mahāyāna precepts under the rubric of the Three Groups of Pure Precepts, see Groner 1990b: 225–227.
56. Hirakawa 1960: 531–532.
57. Groner 1990b: 229, 230n20; see *Yuqie shidi lun,* T. 30 (1579) 589c.
58. From the *Vajrasamādhi-sūtra,* T. 9 (273) 371a10.
59. *Lidai fabao ji,* T. 51 (2075) 190c22–191a11 (translation section 24). The final quotation in the passage is from the *Laṅkā-sūtra,* T. 16 (672) 633a24–25.
60. *Lidai fabao ji,* T. 51 (2075) 191a20–22.
61. T. 40 (1811). See Yanagida 1976a: 238.
62. Liangzhou 涼州, in present-day Gansu.
63. *Gaoseng zhuan,* T. 50 (2059) 336b10–19.
64. Present-day Datong 大同 in Shanxi.
65. On *Pusadichi jing,* T. 30 (1581) and the *Pusa jieben,* T. 24 (1500), see note 53 on bodhisattva precepts texts, above. Regarding *Youposaijie jing* 優波塞戒經 (*Upāsakaśīla-sūtra*), T. 24 (1488), Ono Hōdo 大野法道 characterizes it as a "Mahāyānization" of the advice for laypersons in the *Sigālaka-sutta* (*Dīgha Nikāya* III: 180–193). See Ono [1954] 1963: 206 and Tokuno 1994: 127nn40, 41.
66. See Groner 1990b: 227.

67. *Gaoseng zhuan,* T. 50 (2059) 336a11–19.
68. Funayama Toru has shown that Daojin is the same as the Fajin 法進 (d. 444) included in the self-immolators section in the *Gaoseng zhuan,* T. 50 (2059) 404a–b; see Funayama 1995: 16–21.
69. The seven-day repentance retreat would become a standard part of Chinese practice ritual, and Chen Jinhua argues that the forms practiced in Dharmakṣema's community were probably derived from the repentance chapter in Dharmakṣema's translation of the *Jin guangming jing* 金光明經 (*Suvarṇaprabhāsa-sūtra*), T. 16 (663) 336b–339a; see Chen Jinhua 2002: 68–75.
70. *Gaoseng zhuan,* T. 50 (2059) 336c19–27.
71. See, for example, the story of Dharmakṣema subduing demons in ibid.: 336b8–14.
72. Huiyuan's group is often referred to as the White Lotus Society (*Bailian she* 白蓮社), but this was a much later designation; see Tanaka 1990: xvi. Although this group was the basis for Huiyuan's designation as first patriarch of the Pure Land school, in his time the practice of visualization of Buddha-lands did not have the territorial implications it would assume in later centuries. This can be seen in the caves of Kizil, Dunhuang and Yungang, where the paradises of Amitābha, Maitreya, and Bhaiṣajyaguru adorn the walls of the same cave and individual paradise scenes are sometimes impossible to identify as one or the other.
73. Tsukamoto 1985: 844–847.
74. *Pratyutpannabuddhasaṃmukhāvasthitasamādhi-sūtra* (a.k.a. *Bhadrapāla-sūtra*) T. 13 (416), (417), (418) & (419). T. 13 (418) is considered a late second-century translation by Lokakṣema 支婁迦讖; see Harrison (1990: 209–272) for a detailed discussion of the different versions of the text, and Sharf (2002: 313–314n111) for a summary.
75. T. 13 (418) 905c27–906a3. Sharf quotes the corresponding (but not identical) passage from the later Jñānagupta translation of 594–595, T. 13 (416); see Sharf 2002: 118.
76. T. 13 (418) 905a27–b5; modified from Hurvitz's translation in Tsukamoto 1985: 851.
77. *Dasheng dayi zhang* 大乘大義章, T. 45 (1856) 134b5–21. Kumārajīva's reply is from 134b22–135a11. Kumārajīva's response is rather technical, but he admits that these are difficult questions.
78. Zürcher 1959: 220.
79. Tsukamoto 1985: 855.
80. See Fuller-Sasaki et al. 1971.
81. I am deeply indebted to the work of Kyoko Tokuno. However, I am as yet unable to abandon entirely the term "apocryphal scripture" for her recommended term, "indigenous scripture." See Tokuno 1994: 1–7. I find it necessary to maintain a distinction between Buddhist works that were avowedly indigenous (like the *Lidai fabao ji*) and those that claimed to be translations or compilations of Indian sūtras and that attempted to retain some of the formal qualities of foreign scriptures. The choice to use "apocryphal" does not mean that we now privilege Indian scriptures, but acknowledges that Chinese Buddhists through the Tang did in fact privilege texts with a certified Indian pedigree, however freely they may have used texts suspected or known to be indigenous. I sympathize with Charles Orzech's (1998: xiv) objection that "apocryphal" carries with it the unwelcome baggage of Christian notions of textual authority. Should we therefore also abandon the use of the terms "canonical" or even "scriptural" with reference to Buddhist texts? (Orzech himself does not.) However, I agree that it is essential that we continue to question our usages.
82. Tokuno 1994: 195.

83. T. 24 (1484). For an annotated French translation and commentary, see De Groot 1893. The *Fanwang jing* was alleged to have been translated by Kumārajīva. A postface included in the *Chu sanzang ji ji* claims that, on completion of the translation, Kumārajīva administered the bodhisattva precepts to three hundred people (T. 55 [2145] 79b27–c5). However, internal evidence suggests that the *Fanwang jing* could not have been compiled before 431, and a Dunhuang manuscript establishes a terminus ad quem of no later than 480.
84. T. 24 (1485). See Appendix, no. 13.
85. Groner 1990a: 255.
86. Although the *Fanwang jing*'s canonical authenticity was called into doubt in the sixth century, it was made into the basis of ordination in the Tendai sect in Japan and continues to be used in Taiwan to this day. The ten major precepts of the *Fanwang jing* are prohibitions against: killing, stealing, indulging in sexual misconduct, lying, drinking alcohol, speaking about the transgressions of the fourfold assembly, praising oneself and denigrating others, injuring another through one's avarice, harboring aversion and refusing repentance, and speaking ill of the Three Jewels. The forty-eight minor precepts are too lengthy to summarize, but several of them are discussed individually.
87. *Fanwang jing*, T. 24 (1484) 1004a23–24. Filial obedience is also repeated as the first of the vows in the thirty-fifth precept (ibid.: 1007b27).
88. Ibid.: 1008c4–6.
89. Ibid.: 1007a3–22.
90. Ibid.: 1007c3–1008a12.
91. Ibid.: 1009b16–17.
92. Groner 1990a: 255.
93. *Fanwang jing*, T. 24 (1484) 1008b1–3; trans. in Groner 1990a: 256.
94. Groner 1990a: 256.
95. *Fanwang jing*, T. 24 (1484) 1008c9–11. The roles of ordination officiants are discussed briefly at the end of this section.
96. *Fanwang jing*, T. 24 (1484) 1008b21–28.
97. Groner 1990a: 256.
98. Ibid.: 257. Japanese Tendai use of the *Fanwang jing*, rather than the Vinaya, as the basis of ordination created complications due to its inclusivity; see Groner 2002: 247.
99. *Yingluo jing*, T. 24 (1485) 1021b13. See Groner 1990b: 230.
100. T. 10 (281).
101. Bokenkamp 1990: 123–125, 135. For a summary of the *Yingluo jing*'s textual history, see ibid.: 141–142n30.
102. Ibid.: 137; *Yingluo jing*, T. 24 (1485) 1018c8–21.
103. Groner 1990b: 232.
104. It is difficult to tell if the practice was already highly developed at the time of Dharmakṣema or if the shape of later practice was retroactively reflected on the prime disseminator of the bodhisattva precepts.
105. *Pusadichi jing*, T. 30 (1581) 912b–913a. See also *Pusa shanjie jing*, T. (1583) 1014a–c and *Yuqie shidi lun*, T. 30 (1579) 521b; discussed in Kuo 1994: 40–45 and Groner 1990b: 227–229.
106. *Zhancha shanwuyebao jing* 占察善惡業報經 (Book of Divining the Requital of Good and Evil Actions), T. 17 (839) 904c. Whalen Lai (1990) argues that this is a late sixth-century text of Northern origins.

107. *Fanwang jing,* T. 24 (1484) 1006c5–15. For the passage of similar import in the *Yingluo jing,* see T. 24 (1485) 1020c4–10.
108. T. 9 (277). The translation is attributed to Dharmamitra 曇摩蜜多, a Kashmiri monk active in Jiangkang from 424 to 442. For further discussion of bodhisattva precepts practice in the south, see Funayama 1995.
109. Texts vary as to whether *ācārya* is translated (*shi* 師), or transliterated (*asheli* 阿闍梨).
110. Kuo 1994: 43–45. See *Guan Puxianpusa xingfa jing,* T. 9 (277) 393c11–25.
111. Groner 1990b: 238.
112. *Lidai fabao ji,* T. 51 (2075) 193a15–19.
113. The extant manuscripts of the *Tiwei jing* are from Dunhuang, S. 2051 and P. 3732. Kyoko Tokuno's analysis of the Dunhuang manuscripts and the extensive citations in other works from the sixth through the eighth centuries demonstrates two major lines of textual affiliation and shows that the text continued to be revised through the seventh century (1994: 82–100). The work cited here includes her annotated translation based on S. 2051 and P. 3732.

    The earliest reference to the *Tiwei jing* is in the *Chusanzang ji ji,* where it is already listed as suspect. The reference even gives the name of the compiler, the monk Tanjing 曇靖 and the period of compilation, 452–464; see T. 55 (2145) 39a 24–25. Discussed in the biography of Tanyao 曇曜 (d. c. 485), Tanjing's motivation was said to be his realization that with all the older scriptures lost in the fires of the persecution, something was needed for the instruction of the people (*Xu Gaoseng zhuan* 續高僧傳 [Continued Biographies of Eminent Monks], T. 50 [2060] 428a5–12).
114. *Youposaijie jing,* T. 24 (1488), previously mentioned in the section on Dharmakṣema.
115. Trapuṣa is the only interlocutor in the *Tiwei jing,* and Ballika, who appears in some versions of the title, is seldom mentioned in the text. See Tokuno 1994: 100, 111–117, 128n44. The legend of Trapuṣa and Ballika as the first recipients of the Buddha's teaching was known from translations of *Jātaka* stories, and the motif appears in the Yungang caves.
116. Tokuno 1994: 222.
117. Ibid.: 114, 119, 125n29, 155–156, 208–209.
118. Ibid.: 169–174, 250–256.
119. Ibid.: 305.
120. Ibid.: 105, 168, 283–286.
121. Ibid.: 286.
122. Ibid.: 275–280.
123. *Xu Gaoseng zhuan,* T. 50 (2060) 428a7–21. Whalen Lai links *Tiwei jing*–based lay associations with Northern Wei governmental Saṅgha-households, but it is not clear to me what evidence he has for this (1987b: 13–14).
124. See Yampolsky 1967: 144–145. I have often relied on Yampolsky's translation and excellent research, but find that some changes were necessary in this case. The text is problematic, and Yampolsky's interpretation made it appear to contradict the nondual message of contiguous sections.
125. This exchange is first found in the *Lidai fabao ji.*
126. *Lidai fabao ji,* T. 51 (2075) 181b19–24.
127. The encounter between Hongren and Huineng is probably based on the account in Shenhui's "Miscellaneous Dialogues"; see Suzuki and Kōda 1934: 60.
128. *Jingde chuandeng lu,* T. 51 (2076) 220c22–23.

NOTES TO CHAPTER 4 (PP. 91–135)

1. On this terminology, see Hubbard 2001: 17, 50.
2. In speaking of Buddhism during the period of north-south division, the question of the biases of one's sources becomes especially acute. For background on Northern Wei monks, translations, and texts, we are greatly indebted to Sengyou's *Chusanzang ji ji* and Huijiao's *Gaoseng zhuan,* both written in the south during the first half of the sixth century. The relationship between Sengyou's and Huijiao's circumstances and their work has been studied elsewhere; suffice it to say that the north-south divide did play a role in their presentation of material, and they bequeathed to later scholars a sense of dichotomy between the doctrinal sophistication of southern monks versus the rigorous ascesis of northern monks, along with a certain distaste for the extremes of the latter. For example, see Tang [1938] 1991; Wright [1954] 1990 ; Link 1960; Makita 1973 and 1975. For a counterargument, see Shinohara 1994.
3. From the *Guan Puxianpusa xingfa jing,* T. 9 (277) 393b11.
4. *Lidai fabao ji,* T. 51 (2075) 195b22–29 (translation section 42).
5. *Wei shu* 魏書 (114) 3025–3062. For an English translation of the Buddhist section and Tsukamoto Zenryū's annotations, see Hurvitz 1956.
6. T. 51 (2092); trans. in Wang 1984.
7. Tuoba Gui reigned from 336 to 409 and was enthroned as emperor of the Wei in 398; see Hurvitz 1956: 50–51. The Tuoba 拓跋 (Tabghatch) people were from the northeast of present-day Shanxi. For a linguistic analysis of their origins, see Boodberg [1936] 1979.
8. Hurvitz 1956: 53.
9. Mather 1979.
10. Hurvitz 1956: 70.
11. Ibid.: 73. Tsukamoto has a note to the effect that Gaozong, the posthumous title of Emperor Wencheng (r. 452–465) should be changed to Gaozu, the posthumous title of Emperor Xiaowen (r. 471–498). However, Wei Shou has been discussing Gaozong, and in the next passage notes the accession of Xianzu (r. 465–471), so it is not clear why Tsukamoto believes Wei Shou to be in error here.
12. There is some disagreement regarding the dates and sequence of construction of the caves; see Caswell 1988: 6–20.
13. See Soper 1959, Sato 1978, Caswell 1988, Fraser 2003, and Abe 2002.
14. Conferral of the bodhisattva precepts probably played a part in practices carried out in the caves and in the city temples of Pingcheng and Luoyang. From a variety of textual and artistic traces, it is apparent that Buddhist art was intimately linked with practices of visualization, repentance and bodhisattva precepts ordination like those discussed in chapter 3. The spate of apocryphal scriptures of the latter half of the fifth century suggests that these already-flourishing practices were given added impetus by the postpersecution mood of reverence for the power of karmic retribution.
15. Caswell 1988: 16–20, 27–28, 65–66, 91–97.
16. Chen 1964: 154–158. On the latter half of the Northern Wei, see also Tsukamoto [1942] 1974 and Jorgensen 1979: 17–44.
17. Hurvitz 1956: 80–81.
18. *Luoyang qielan ji;* trans. in Wang 1984: 202, 215–246.
19. Hurvitz 1956: 87.

20. Brown [1976] 1982: 181.
21. Ibid.
22. Ibid.: 181–182.
23. Employing the "return from death" device often used in Chinese didactic tales, the *Luoyang qielan ji* story is purported to be the testimony of the monk Huining 惠凝 (a.k.a. Huiyi 慧嶷), who came back to life after being dead for seven days. Reporting on the underworld king Yama's dealings with newly arrived monks, Huining tells how an ascetic meditator and a reciter of the *Nirvāṇa-sūtra* were instantly allowed to ascend to paradise, but an important lecturer and a fund-raising enthusiast for scriptures and images were led away to a dark and unpleasant place. Finally, a high-ranking official-turned-monk came up for judgment and was told: "As Grand Warden, you impaired justice, twisted the law, and robbed people's properties. Even if you claim to have built the temple, it was not due to your efforts [because the expenses are from others]. So it is senseless for you to talk about it!" Then he too was led away. Yang Xuanzhi claims that Huining's story resulted in an official change of policy whereby greater imperial favor was awarded to meditators, and this message is reinforced in other stories demonstrating that true merit is gained through simple, dedicated practice, not expensive projects (*Luoyang qielan ji;* trans. in Wang 1984: 75–76).
24. From a complaint about clerical excesses in a memorial included in the *Shilao zhi;* see Hurvitz 1956: 96.
25. Jorgensen 1979: 25–26. Faqing asserted that murder of enemies caused his followers to progress through the stages of the bodhisattva path.
26. Hurvitz 1956: 90.
27. Orzech speculates that the *Renwang jing* description of the decline of the Dharma as a time when "soldiers and slaves will be made *bhikṣu*" is a criticism of these effects of Tanyao's state Buddhism (1998: 120 and 287–288).
28. Hurvitz 1956: 40–42.
29. For an excellent discussion of Han debates on the nature of rulership, see Puett 2001.
30. See Nattier 1991: 33–37, 91–94; Hubbard 2001: 36–54.
31. See Nattier 1991: 147–169.
32. An excursus on fifth-century Chinese eschatology is beyond the scope of the present discussion, but interested readers may find useful introductions in Stein 1979; Seidel 1984a and 1984b; Mollier 1990; Bokenkamp 1994; and Strickmann 2002: 50–62.
33. T. 50 (2058) 297a–322b. For the following section on the *Fu fazang zhuan,* I am greatly indebted to discussions with Elizabeth Morrison and John Kieshnick when we read the text in our reading group at Stanford in 1994–1995. I am also indebted to Elizabeth Morrison for her 1996 paper on the topic "Contested Visions of the Buddhist Past and the Curious Fate of an Early Medieval Buddhist Text."
34. The line of transmission is serial with the exception of one collateral transmission in the third generation, to Madhyāntika in addition to Śaṇavāsa. The two were often mistakenly treated as sequential third and fourth patriarchs in works (like the *Mohe zhiguan* and the *Lidai fabao ji*) that relied on the *Fu fazang zhuan,* resulting in a scheme of twenty-four patriarchs. See Tanaka 1983: 61–66.
35. The text was utilized in a variety of devotional contexts besides Chan; for a discussion of the many incarnations of the *Fu fazang zhuan,* see ibid.: 61–105.

36. *Chu sanzang ji ji,* T. 55 (2145) 13b6–12.
37. T. 49 (2034) 85a25. Maspéro claims that a terminus ad quem of 481 has been established for this nonextant catalogue (1911: 129).
38. *Lidai sanbao ji,* T. 49 (2034) 85b4–6.
39. *Baolin zhuan* fascicle 8, in the *Zhongguo fojiao congshu: Chanzong bian,* 1: 18: 659.
40. *Chuanfa zhengzong lun,* T. 51 (2080) 774a28–b9.
41. Ibid.: 774a10–17.
42. Maspéro 1911: 139–146.
43. Ibid.: 130–138.
44. The *Aśokarāja-sūtra* was first translated by Saṅghapāla 僧伽婆羅 in 512 as the *Ayu wang jing* 阿育王經 (Scripture of King Aśoka), T. 50 (2043). There are also accounts of the Buddha's disciples in An Faqin's 安法欽 early fourth-century translation of the *Aśokavadāna, Ayu wang zhuan* 阿育王傳 (Biography of King Aśoka), T. 50 (2042), but the *Fu fazang zhuan* is more similar to the *Aśokarāja-sūtra.* However, while both the *Aśokavadāna* and the *Fu fazang zhuan* present a transmission from Mahākāśapa 摩訶迦葉 to Ānanda 阿難 to Saṇavāsa 商那和修 to Upagupta 優波鞠多(T. 50 [2042] 121a24–26), the *Aśokarāja-sūtra* makes Śaṇavāsa's 舍那婆私 co-disciple Madhyāntika 末田地 into the senior Dharma-heir and includes him in the lineal transmission (T. 50 [2043] 152c15–20). The latter version is the one followed by the *Lidai fabao ji.*
45. T. 12 (383) 1013b16–1014a3; see Morrison 1996: 13. The *Fu fazang zhuan* shares four names with the *Mahāmāyā-sūtra:* Mahākśapa, Upagupta, Aśvaghoṣa and Nāgārjuna.
46. I have visited this site twice and had rubbings made of the carvings of the patriarchs and the dedicatory inscription. For a published description, see Ding 1988.
47. Huiguang and Bodiruci are considered founders of the southern branch of the Dilun tradition. Their *Xu Gaoseng zhuan* biographies show master-disciple affiliations based on exegesis and practice of the tenets of Vasubandhu's *Daśabhūmi-vyākhyāna* (*Shidi jing lun* 十地經論), T. 26 (1522), a commentary on the chapter on the ten stages of the bodhisattva path in the *Avataṃsaka-sūtra.* Chen Jinhua's analysis of the evidence leads him to conclude that Huiguang's dates should be considered later than the standard dates of 468–537, and he suggests "after 491–after 560" as an approximation (2002: 25–26).
48. That is, the thirty-five Buddhas of confession, such as those expounded in the *Jueding pini jing* 決定毘尼經 (*Upālipariprcchā*), T. 12 (325); see discussion below in the section on the Sanjie movement.
49. Henansheng gudai jianzhu baohu yanjiusuo 河南省古代建築保護研究所 (Henan Research Institute for the Preservation of Ancient Architecture) 1991: 15–18, 293; see also Ding 1988. Kenneth Chen claims that Siṁha Bhikṣu's murder is portrayed in caves 9 and 10 at Yungang, but he gives no reference for this identification (1964: 167). I have not been able to locate this image in published works on the caves. In April 2005 I visited the caves and attempted to find the image; caves 9 and 10 are not completely accessible, but I checked every cave and every surface I could access. Many thanks to the Friends of the Art Museum of the Chinese University of Hong Kong for inviting me on the tour that enabled me to carry out this search.
50. Regarding the twenty-five patriarchs cave, see Tanaka 1983: 66–72; regarding the twenty-nine patriarchs cave, see ibid.: 73–75; Ding 1988: 19.
51. See Yanagida 1967: 136–138.

52. In his study on the *Platform Sūtra,* Philip Yampolsky provides a useful chart of the patriarchal lists found in eighth-century Chan works in comparison with these two main source texts (1967: 8–9).
53. Buddhabhadra's "lineage" in his preface to the *Damoduoluo chan jing* is found at T. 15 (618) 301c6–9. In the *Chu sanzang ji ji,* the names in Huiyuan's preface are at T. 55 (2145) 65c9–12 and 66a11 and Huiguan's are at ibid.: 66c5–7, 21–25, and 67a2–3.
54. Sengyou's record is included in the *Chu sanzang ji ji,* T. 55 (2145) 88c–90a. For a detailed comparison of Sengyou's record and the *Fu fazang zhuan,* see Funayama 2000.
55. *Āryavasumitrabodhisattvasaṃghīti-śāstra* (Treatise compiled by the Venerable Bodhisattva Vasumitra), T. 28 (1549); *Chu sanzang ji ji,* T. 55 (2145) 71c8–72a8. See Demiéville 1954: 366–368.
56. The *Fuzhu fazang zhuan lue chao* is preserved in S. 5981, P. 2791, and P. 3212, and a later, modified version appears in P. 3913. See Tanaka 1981: 168.
57. P. 3913. See Tanaka 1983: 102–103; 1981: 164–169. On the identification of Bodhidharma as Guanyin in the *Baolin zhuan,* see Jorgensen 2005: 218.
58. One might also note the significance these groups of numbers in the "proto-Tantric" *Guanding jing* 灌頂經 (Book of Consecration). This apocryphon includes a passage in which the Buddha teaches his audience the names of supernatural protectors, whose *dhāraṇi*-like names are composed of the Chinese characters used for transcription of Sanskrit. He gives the names of the seven Buddhas up to and including himself, the eight great bodhisattvas, the ten great disciples, thirty-five dragon kings, twenty-eight spirit generals (plus two of their mothers and three of their daughters), and twenty-four demon commanders (*guishi* 鬼師) (T. 21 [1331] 517c7–519a16). The notion of thirty-five as a full set (as seen in the thirty-five Buddhas of confession or the thirty-five dragon kings) may have had some bearing on the way that patriarchal genealogies were constructed in the eighth century, for twenty-eight Indian patriarchs plus seven Chinese patriarchs (or twenty-nine and six), or alternatively seven Buddhas of the past plus twenty-eight patriarchs, add up to a pantheon of thirty-five.
59. See Yampolsky 1967: 30. "Śubhamitra" also appears in the Dunhuang manuscript of the *Platform Sūtra;* see ibid.: 179.
60. *Putidamo nanzong ding shifei lun,* in Hu [1958] 1970: 294–295.
61. Yanagida (1983b: 28) attributes further confusion over the first patriarch's name to the influence of the *Lidai fabao ji,* noting that use of the name Dharmatrāta for Bodhidharma appears in the *Caoqi dashi zhuan* (ZZ. II, 19, 5: 484a), the *Yuanjue jing dashu chao* (ZZ. I, 14, 3: 276d), and the *Zongjing lu* 宗鏡錄 (T. 48 [2016] 939b). Finally, the *Jingde chuandeng lu* claims that the first patriarch's original Dharma name was Dharmatrāta, but when he received transmission from Prajñātāra it was changed to Bodhidharma (T. 51 [2076] 217a).
62. *Lidai fabao ji,* T. 51 (2075) 180a16–b15.
63. The *Baolin zhuan* accounts of the Indian patriarchs are elaborations of the *Fu fazang zhuan* versions. The Indian patriarchs take up most of the first six of the text's original ten fascicles (the extant text is missing fascicles 7, 9, and 10); see *Zhongguo fojiao congshu: Chanzong bian,* 1:18: 514–636.
64. *Ayu wang jing* (*Aśokarāja-sūtra*), T. 50 (2043) 154c–155a; trans. in Li 1993: 115–117.
65. *Fu fazang zhuan,* T. 50 (2058) 302c2–303a7.
66. Ibid.: 321c20–322b28.

67. Mihirakula was the second ruler of the conquering Hūṇa people (related to the Hepthalites) who ruled northwest India and Kashmir from the end of the fifth century and well into the sixth. The exceptional cruelty of this ruler and his known persecution of Buddhists led to speculation that his reign, and the consequent exodus of monks, may have been responsible for the late sixth-century development of the "decline of the Dharma" theme in China. Nattier argues that while this may have been a factor, the literature of decline is also strongly associated with the very prosperity of the Saṅgha during the peaceful Kushan rule of the second and third centuries (1991: 110–117; 224–227). Linda Penkower cites Yamada Meiji's argument that the scale and duration of Mihirakula's violent reign was limited (2000: 250). However, even if the actual impact was slight, the rumor of terror may have traveled far and grown in the telling. If the "Miduoluojue 彌多羅掘" of the *Fu fazang zhuan* is indeed Mihirakula, this is an indication of sixth-century origins.
68. The *Lidai fabao ji* is the only account of Siṁha Bhikṣu's murder in which Mani and Jesus are named. In a forthcoming article, Rong Xinjiang gives the historical background for appearances of these figures in Chinese texts and notes that the *Lidai fabao ji* seems to be the earliest extant text to mention both together. He outlines the contexts in which Mani and Jesus are mentioned, focusing on the *Laozi huahu jing* 老子化胡經, and he chronicles shifts in attitude that can be discerned in each context. Generally speaking, the *Huahu jing* presents Manichaeism more sympathetically, while the *Lidai fabao ji* condemns both (Rong, forthcoming). In an earlier article, Rong also discusses the possible negative influence of this *Lidai fabao ji* passage on the Tibetan king Trhi Songdetsen's (r. 754–797) attitude toward Manichaeism, and suggests that this is but one effect of Chinese xenophobia following the An Lushan rebellion (755–762). Since the Tang restoration depended on Uighur armies, the central government was forced to adopt tolerant policies (in contrast to Xuanzong's edict of 732 criticizing Manichaeism and barring Chinese from practicing it). However, Rong argues that the similar Northern military backgrounds of Wuzhu and his patron Du Hongjian would probably have created a Bao Tang prejudice against foreign religions, and the Shuofang area from which they originated was riddled with tensions between Buddhists versus Manichaeans and Christians. See Rong 2001; see also Uray 1983; Lieu 1992; Scott 1995; Pelliot 1996; Forte 2000.
69. *Lidai fabao ji*, T. 51 (2075) 180a29–b12 (translation section 3).
70. *Fu fazang zhuan*, T. 50 (2058) 321c14–18.
71. Yuanjue 緣覺, self-enlightened Buddha, one of the two "inferior" vehicles according to Mahāyāna soteriology.
72. *Fu fazang zhuan*, T. 50 (2058) 320a3–16.
73. Ibid.: 320a16–22.
74. *Lidai fabao ji*, T. 51 (2075) 181c4–6.
75. On Zhiyi's biography, see Satō 1961 and 1981, and Hurvitz [1962] 1980.
76. Chen Jinhua 1999: 58.
77. Ibid.: 61.
78. Ibid.: 153–157.
79. Selected secondary works on Zhiyi's system include: Satō 1961 and 1981; Hurvitz [1962] 1980; Sekiguchi 1969; Chappell and Ichishima 1983; Stevenson 1986 and 1987; Swanson 1989; Donner and Stevenson 1993.
80. Penkower 2000: 268–274.

81. On lineage in the preface of the *Mohe zhiguan,* see T. 46 (1911) 1a13-c1; trans. in Donner and Stevenson 1993: 100–107; see also their discussion of Tiantai lineage, pp. 22–24, 33–39. The prediction of the future circumstances of Dharma transmission is a scriptural topos indicating a profound link between the bestower and the subject of the prediction; see, for example, the Buddha's predictions about Upagupta in the *Ayu wang jing* (*Aśokarāja-sūtra*), T. 50 (2043) 149b–1150a.
82. *Mahāprajñāpāramitā-śāstra,* T. 25 (1509), attributed to Nāgārjuna but probably compiled in China by Kumārajīva. See Lamotte 1944–80.
83. Penkower 2000: 248–256.
84. Ibid.: 261–262.
85. T. 9 (262) 32b–34c.
86. Penkower 2000: 263.
87. Ibid.: 262.
88. Penkower 2000: 263.
89. Donner and Stevenson 1993: 35.
90. Penkower 2000: 264.
91. T. 46 (1916) 485–486; see Kuo 1994: 62–64.
92. Chen Jinhua argues that when Zhiyi administered confessional rituals, he probably relied on the *Jin guangming jing*-based traditions of Dharmakṣema's group, as transmitted through the disciples of Dharmakṣema's contemporary Xuangao 玄高 (d. 444) (2002: 73). Xuangao was one of the monks said to have been executed at the outset of the Northern Wei persecution, and his disciples fled south to escape. See the biography of Xuangao in the *Gaoseng zhuan,* T. 50 (2059) 397a3–398b11.
93. Faure 1986c. For discussion of the Tiantai influence on Chan, see Sekiguchi 1969; Yanagida 1969b; Donner 1987; McRae 1992a; Faure 1997: 49–58. On the emergence of Pure Land, see Tanaka 1990 and Gómez 1996, and on Pure Land and Chan, see Shih 1992.
94. T. 8 (245) and (246). See Orzech 1998 for a study and annotated translation of the *Renwang jing.*
95. Zhiyi's nuanced use of the *Renwang jing* in his correspondence with the Sui emperors is instructive in this regard; see Chen Jinhua 1999: 130–132.
96. Charles Orzech surmises that this imperial recognition is the reason that three translations of the *Renwang jing* appear in late sixth-century catalogues linked to the names of three famous translators (only the one attributed to Kumārajīva is extant), though earlier it had been listed as an anonymous translation (1998: 125–128). See also De Visser 1935:2: 116–189.
97. Donner and Stevenson 1993: 10.
98. In characterizing this syntax as reflexive, I highlight the dynamic identity between levels (i.e., kings and bodhisattvas). Charles Orzech, using the term "recursivity," focuses on the dynamic distinction between levels, a form of tangled hierarchy whereby kingship is a marker for the ritually reenacted gesture of deference to the Saṇgha (1998: 99–107). Like ambiguous images, these contrasting views from the perspectives of identity versus distinction are interdependent and instigate continuous alternation. However, the "identity" aspect was key to the Southern School patriarchal mystique, which implied the union of bodhisattva monk and bodhisattva king and the hidden continuity of a lineage of world-turning wheel-turners.
99. On the relationship between Indian and Chinese notions of the periods of the Dharma, see Nattier 1991.

100. Ibid.: 128. On regulation of the Saṅgha by the state, see especially the last section of the "Kumārajīva translation" of the *Renwang jing,* T. 8 (245) 833b12–834a7.
101. Orzech 1998: 55. Regarding the provenance of the text, see ibid.: 119–121. There are two "translations" extant, one attributed to Kumārajīva and the other attributed to Bukong 不空 (Amoghavajra, 705–774). For a description of the creation of the *Renwang jing*'s pedigree, see ibid.: 125–128.
102. Ibid.: 55.
103. *Renwang jing,* T. 8 (245) 829c29–830a7, translation attributed to Kumārajīva.
104. Orzech 1998: 87.
105. Ibid.: 99–107; Orzech 1989: 21–22.
106. *Renwang jing,* T. 8 (246) 844b14–15, translation attributed to Bukong; in Orzech 1998: 272.
107. Orzech 1996: 376.
108. *Renwang jing,* T. 8 (246) 844c6–9; trans. in Orzech 1998: 273.
109. T. 55 (2147), completed in 594 by Fajing 法經.
110. Prophetic passages were regarded as an indication that a scripture was spurious; see Tokuno 1994: 21–22. There are other instances of Emperor Wen's selective tolerance of prophetic texts, as with his sanction of the prophetic passages in a translation by Naredrayaśas that were clearly meant to reveal the Sui emperor as an avatar of the popular messiah-bodhisattva Candraprabha kumāra (Yueguang tongzi 月光童子); see *Dehu zhangzhe jing* 德護長者經 (*Śrīgupta-sūtra*), T. 14 (545) 849b; Zürcher 1982: 25–26; Wang-Toutain 1994.
111. Zürcher 1981: 41.
112. Zürcher 1982: 18n33; Hubbard 2001: 68–72. The argument that *mofa* had begun in 434 is found in the *Nanyue Si dachanshi lishi yuanwen* 南嶽思大禪師立誓願文, T. 46 (1933) 786b ff., compiled in 558. However, the attribution of this text to Huisi is the subject of dispute; see Hubbard 2001: 69n42.
113. Orzech 1998: 133.
114. Orzech 1996: 373; 1989: 23. There is also a striking later example of amalgamation of Chan patriarchs with protector deities. In the twelfth-century "Dali Scroll" from Yunnan (*Daliguo Fanxiang juan* 大理國梵像卷, Picture of Buddhist Images from the Country of Dali), the sixteen kings of the *Renwang jing,* the Chan patriarchs, the sixteen arhats, and Tantric deities are portrayed. Thus the Chan patriarchs were assimilated into a pantheon of national security icons; see Berger 1994: 97 and McRae 1992b. A ninth-century Dali ruler is also included in the Chan lineage; see Li Lincan 1982: 96, panel 55; Chapin 1971.
115. Girard 1977.
116. See Beckwith 1987: 143–172, for an account of this struggle from the expansion of the Tibetan empire after the An Lushan rebellion until 851.
117. An assessment of the extent of the influence of Zhenyan trends in late eighth-century Buddhism, though germane, is beyond the scope of the present study. I recommend Orzech's detailed treatment of Bukong's milieu, teachings, ritual works, and legacy (1998: 135–206); see also Chou 1945. For a critique of reifications of Zhenyan, see Sharf 2002: 263–278.
118. Yanagida 1976a: 209.
119. *Lidai fabao ji,* T. 51 (2075) 193a26–193b2. See Weinstein 1987a: 80–83.
120. *Lidai fabao ji,* T. 51 (2075) 185c5–8 (translation section 16). The debate is most prominently featured in Dugu Pei's *Putidamo nanzong ding shifei lun;* for a likely model for

this dialogue, in which Shenhui hints that he himself is the Dharma heir, see Hu [1958] 1970: 286.

121. For a summary of texts and practices common in Xinxing's milieu, see Hubbard 2001: 233.

122. Biography of Xinxing, in *Xu gaoseng zhuan* T. 50 (2060) 560a. Hubbard speculates that possible reasons for his renunciation of vows could have included the conflict between the Vinaya and Xinxing's physical labor and social welfare work, or it may have been involuntary, due to the Northern Zhou persecution. If due to the latter, however, one must ask why he did not seek re-ordination after the persecution (2001: 10).

123. Ibid.: 19–24.

124. Ibid.: 20–21.

125. Ibid.: 22. This surmise is based on the attribution to Xinxing of two "Seven Roster Buddhanāma" texts in the *Kaiyuan shijiao lu,* T. 55 (2154) 678c. One of the source texts for the "Seven Roster Buddhanāma" is the *Jueding pini jing* (*Vinayaviniścaya-Upālipariprcchā-sūtra*), which is one of the source texts claimed in the *Lidai fabao ji* (see Appendix, no. 8). However, not surprisingly, the *Lidai fabao ji* authors make no reference to the rite or to the eschatological ideology and repentance practice explicated in the text.

126. Hubbard 2001: 76–92.

127. Orzech 1998: 90–91. There is no Sanskrit equivalent for *Dao zhongxing,* but this is found in the *Yingluo jing* as part of a system of five seed-natures (T. 24 [1485] 101b25–26).

128. Orzech 1998: 91.

129. Hubbard 2001: 18.

130. T. 51 (2082) 788b; trans. in Hubbard 2001: 18.

131. Hubbard 2001: 39–41.

132. See ibid.: 101–102.

133. Ibid.: 102.

134. *Lidai fabao ji,* T. 51 (2075) 190a3–5 (translation section 21).

135. S. 2446. Attributed to Xinxing, this text is one of the most important of the extant Sanjie sources. For a textual history and summary, see Hubbard 1986: 207–213.

136. See Hubbard 2001: 104–120, and also his translation of another Sanjie text summarizing the four Buddhas, the *Pufa sifo* 普法四佛 (The Refuge of the Four Buddhas of the Universal Dharma), in ibid.: 247–256.

137. From the *Dui gen qixing fa;* see Hubbard 2001: 134.

138. Ibid.: 135–136.

139. Ibid.: 140–147.

140. The Sanjie cloisters are known from an edict of 725 banning them (ibid.: 214–215).

141. Ibid.: 34–35.

142. On the "sixteen inexhaustible practices, see ibid.: 176 and 258–259. Historical development of the *wujinzang* is bound up with the history of the fundamental Buddhist practice of pious donation. Examining Indian antecedents legitimating the commercial activities of the clergy, Jacques Gernet surveyed the various Vinayas and found that the *Mahāsaṅghika Vinaya* was especially supportive of using surplus donations as capital (called *wujinwu* 無盡物 or *wujincai* 無盡財) for profitable ventures to benefit the monasteries or for social welfare (1995: 158–166). Two key Mahāyāna scriptures promulgated the notion of the inexhaustible storehouse of the bodhisattva's merit,

and were frequently quoted to support the institution of the *wujingzang;* these are the *Avataṃsaka-sūtra,* especially the "Ten Inexhaustible Storehouses' section, T. 10 (279) 111a27–115a6, and the *Vimalakīrtinirdeśa-sūtra,* especially the gāthās in the eighth fascicle, T. 14 (474) 550b.

However, the notion that an accumulation of small donations could be stockpiled to relieve the wants of the poorest also harks back to Chinese social welfare societies, such as those formed in the Daoist millenarian movements of the Han. The above-mentioned "Saṇgha households" instituted by the Northern Wei incorporated elements of the Buddhist model of the for-profit charitable institution, along with elements of the Chinese social welfare collective. Prior to the Sanjie movement, one of the most successful Chinese deployments of the virtuous cycle of temple donations was through the monasteries supported by Emperor Wu of the Liang (r. 502–549); see Chen 1964: 124–128. Kenneth Chen states that Liang Wudi established thirteen *wujinzang,* but does not cite a source for this claim (ibid.: 126), while Gernet claims that the earliest use of the term is found in the *Xu gaoseng zhuan* biography of the monk Jizang 吉藏 (549–623), T. 50 (2060) 514a (1995: 216).

143. Hubbard 2001: 28.
144. The two texts are: (1) *Wujingzang fa lueshuo* 無盡藏法略說 (Abridged Explanation of the Dharma of the Inexhaustible Storehouse), S. 190, attributed to Xinxing, trans. in Hubbard 2001: 257–263, and (2), a commentary on the foregoing, the *Dasheng fajie wujingzang fa shi* 大乘法界無盡藏法釋 (Commentary on the Dharma of the Inexhaustible Storehouse of the Mahāyāna Universe), S. 721, trans. in Hubbard 2001: 264–288.
145. T. 85 (2870); Hubbard 2001: 166.
146. Hubbard 2001: 172–173.
147. Ibid.: 174; complete translation on pp. 264–288.
148. Ibid.: 177n81.
149. Ibid.: 174–175.
150. Ibid.: 72–74, 190–195.
151. Ibid.: 195–221.
152. Lai 1992: 7; quoted in Hubbard 2001: 215.
153. Development of various types of economic activities associated with Buddhist monasteries is extensively documented in Gernet's magisterial (if biased and occasionally unreliable) *Buddhism in Chinese Society.* One of Gernet's arguments is that Buddhist engagement in commerce and lending was part of the development of a currency-based alternative to the traditional land-based economy, and that Buddhism's rapid growth exacerbated the tension between the two economies. Hubbard also notes that the controversy over the Sanjie Inexhaustible Storehouses reflects underlying anxieties and tensions in the newly urban, currency-based economy of north China in the fifth and sixth centuries (2001: 151–152).
154. Ibid.: 211–219.
155. This characterization of the Sanjie and Bao Tang is an adaptation of Faure's structuralist reading of Bodhidharma and Sengchou as "symmetrical figures that imply each other (1993: 130).
156. T. 53 (2122).
157. Shinohara 2000: 302. The following works also give an account of Daoxuan's vision describing the heavenly Jetavana: the *Zhong Tianzhu Sheweiguo Zhihuansi tujing* 中天竺舍衛國祇桓寺圖經 (Diagram Scripture of the Jetavana in the Kingdom of Śrā-

vastī in Central India), T. 45 (1899) 883–896; the *Luxiang gantong zhuan* 律相感通傳 (Traditions of Vinaya-related Miracles), T. 45 (1898) 874–882; and the *Daoxuan lushi gantong lu* 道宣律師感通錄 (Record of Miraculous Instruction Given to Vinaya Master Daoxuan), T. 52 (2107) 435–442. There is another work by Daoxuan that is related to T. 45 (1899) but makes no mention of visionary instruction and may have been written prior to the experience. This is the *Guanzhong chuangli jietan tujing* 關中創立戒壇圖經 (Diagram Scripture on Establishing the Ordination Platform in Central China), T. 45 (1892). See Shinohara 2000: 301–302. For a discussion of the transmission of a version of the text in Japan, see Forte 1988a: 51–52.

158. Shinohara 2000: 304.
159. Jetavana was a royal garden in Kośala that was purchased by a rich merchant and given to the Buddha as a rainy season retreat. In the scriptures, it is the setting for many of the Buddha's sermons.
160. *Fayuan zhulin,* T. 53 (2122) 353c26–354b11. In summarizing these passages, I consulted both the text and Koichi Shinohara's translations in his unpublished article, "Imagining the Jetavana in Medieval China."
161. The structure is clearly influenced by another of Daoxuan's interests, the legend of Aśoka's stūpas; see Shinohara 2000: 328–338. In the *Aśokāvadāna,* Aśoka visits the sites of the life of the Buddha, and at each site there is an object that Aśoka then enshrines in veneration. On this motif of enshrinement, Daoxuan builds a more complex narrative of entrusting and preserving the true Dharma in times of threat by reproducing stūpas that contain objects used by the Buddhas, and important scriptures. Shinohara points out that there is an unresolved tension between the claim that the objects used by the Buddha preserve the teaching, and the claim that efficacy lies with the copies of stūpas and scriptures, especially the Vinaya (ibid.: 304–306).
162. *Fayuan zhulin,* T. 53 (2122) 560a29–b9.
163. For a discussion of the womb symbology of the robe, see Faure 1995: 361–364.
164. *Fayuan zhulin,* T. 53 (2122) 560b28–c23.
165. Ibid.: 560c29–561a5.
166. Shinohara, "Imagining the Jetavana," p. 48.
167. Shinohara 2000: 314–327.
168. *Fayuan zhulin,* T. 53 (2122) 562c26–28.
169. See Seidel 1983.
170. McRae (1998) discusses ordination platform activities as a "movement" in which Shenhui participated. With regard to "cultic objects," McRae also notes that the ritual censor and water pitcher discovered in Shenhui's grave "bear silent witness to the importance of initiations in his life" (ibid.: 51n13).
171. Shinohara 2000: 338–339.
172. The motif of the gold-embroidered robe comes from a separate legend, as discussed in chapter 5.
173. Yanagida 1985: 406–408. Shinohara's discussion of Yanagida's argument is in an earlier version of "The Kasaya Robe of the Past Buddha Kasyapa in the Miraculous Instruction Given to the Vinaya Master Daoxuan (596~667)," but was not included in the published version (2000).
174. *Jingde chuandeng lu,* T. 51 (2076) 437c29–438a4.
175. For the texts of the Platform *Sūtra,* see Komazawa daigaku Zenshūshi kenkyūkai 1978; for a textual history, see Yanagida 1974a: 459, and for an English translation and analysis, see Yampolsky 1967.

176. See Yanagida 1985: 407–408. The full title of the text of Shenhui's address is: "Nanyang heshang dunjiao jietuo chanmen zhiliao xing tanyu 南陽和上頓教解脫禪門直了性壇語" (The Platform Address of the Venerable of Nanyang on Directly Comprehending the Nature According to the Chan Approach of Emancipation in the Sudden Teaching), hereafter referred to as the *Tanyu*. The text was compiled c. 720, and the extant Dunhuang manuscripts are: (a) Beijing *han* 81, in Suzuki (1968–71) 3: 290–317; (b) P. 2045 (part 2) in Hu [1958] 1970: 225–252; (c) Dunhuang museum ms. no. 77. For a more recent annotated edition of Shenhui's works, see Yang 1996.

177. Biographies of Huizhong appear in the *Song gaoseng zhuan*, T. 50 (2061) 762b–763b, and the *Jingde chuandeng lu*, T. 51 (2076) 244a–245a. However, John McRae questions the veracity of the claim that Huizhong was Huineng's disciple (in a comment on this manuscript, 2004).

178. *Biyan lu*, T. 48 (2003) cases 18 and 99; trans. in Cleary and Cleary 1977: 1: 115–122; 2: 628–635.

179. *Song gaoseng zhuan*, T. 50 (2061) 762c4–5; unpublished translation by John Kieschnick.

180. "Master function" is a coinage based on Michel Foucault's discussion of the "author function." See "What Is an Author?" in Rabinow 1984: 101–120. Figures such as Zhiyi or Daoxuan serve functions similar to those that Foucault assigns to "founders of discursivity," who are established as representatives of the possibility of a certain realm of discourse and also its limitations and standards. Foucault writes: "The author allows a limitation of the cancerous and dangerous proliferation of significations within a world where one is thrifty not only with one's resources and riches, but also with one's discourses and their significations. The author is the principle of thrift in the proliferation of meaning" (ibid.: 118). For discussion of a related issue, the proliferation and limitation of relics and representations of masters, see Faure 1991: 148–178.

NOTES TO CHAPTER 5 (PP. 136–193)

1. *Lidai fabao ji* T. 51 (2075) 180b29–c2 (translation section 3).
2. Faure 1986b: 188.
3. Japanese studies of Bodhidharma include Sekiguchi 1957; Yanagida 1967 and 1969a. Studies in Western languages include Broughton 1999; Jorgensen 1979; Faure 1986a; and McRae 1986: 15–29. Jorgensen's massive 2005 study of Huineng's hagiographies is a valuable new addition to the body of work on the Chan patriarchs, but unfortunately my book was already in press by the time I began reading Jorgensen's work so I was unable to add detailed references.
4. T. 50 (2060).
5. Falin wrote the *Poxie lun* 破邪論 and *Bianzheng lun* 辯正論 (T. 52 [2109] and [2120]), and his treatises are also included in Daoxuan's *Guang hongming ji* 廣弘明集, T. 52 (2103) 160–168. The *Guang hongming ji* and Sengyou's *Hongming ji* 弘明集 are large compendia of Six Dynasties, Sui, and early Tang Buddhist polemical works and apologia.
6. Weinstein 1987a: 32–34. John McRae recommends an M.A. thesis by Andrew Junker on this stage of the bowing controversy, but unfortunately I was not able to obtain it; see Junker 2000.
7. See Chen 2002: 120–122.

8. In this regard, one should recall that Daoxuan was also influential in setting out guidelines for monastic ritual and regulations based on the traditions of the *Dharmaguptaka Vinaya.* His example clearly inspired Daoshi's monumental *Fayuan zhulin.* In Yifa's *The Origins of the Monastic Code in China,* she traces the history of certain sets of monastic regulations that may have been precursors to the *Chanyuan qinggui* 禪苑清規 (Rules of Purity for Chan Monasteries), the disputed Chan monastic code that is the focus of her study. She discusses Daoan's regulations and the regulations Huiyuan was reputed to have written, as well as Zhiyi's rules for novices (2002: 8–23). However, she considers the most important influence on the *Chanyuan qinggui* to have been Daoxuan's guidelines and monastic regulations in his commentaries on the *Dharmaguptaka Vinaya* (ibid.: 23–28).
9. Regarding the Sui-Tang transition and Buddhism, see Chen 1999; Twitchett, ed., 1979; Wright 1973; Weinstein 1973 and 1987a: 3–37; Boodberg [1938–39] 1979: 265–349.
10. See Broughton 1999: 53–75.
11. For example, in the *Xu gaoseng zhuan* Ratnamati 勒那摩提 appears as a translator at Yongning monastery in Bodhiruci's 菩提流支 biography, but there is a separate biography for his doppelgänger Ratnamati 勒那漫提 the thaumaturge who wields a variety of miraculous powers at the same monastery in the same period; compare *Xu gaoseng zhuan* T. 50 (2060) 429a5–9 and 644a13–b24. Wright (1957) has shown that Huijiao did the same, but in Huijiao's case the bisection was due to political and geographic factors when a northern monk took a different Dharma-name after fleeing to the southern court. McRae also suggests that a lost part of Shenxiu's early career may be rediscovered in accounts of the monk "Weixiu" 威秀, who is recorded as having represented the clergy in the bowing controversy of 662 (1986: 48–50).
12. *Ji Shenzhou sanbao gantong lu* 集神州三寶感通錄, T. 52 (2106) 423a18–19.
13. *Guang hongming ji,* T. 52 (2103) 284c–286b. See Weinstein 1987a: 32–33.
14. Shinohara 1991: 83.
15. See Yanagida 1967: 7–11.
16. *Xu gaoseng zhuan,* T. 50 (2060) 551b27–c26.
17. For an explanation of the extant texts of the *Erru Sixing,* see Broughton 1999: 121n12; see also his annotated translation, ibid.: 8–12. For an annotated Japanese translation and collated edition of six of the texts, see Yanagida 1969a.
18. See Broughton 1999: 8–12, 53–57.
19. Ibid.: 70–74.
20. Ibid.: 38–52, 83–95, 118.
21. This observation was made in one section of an unpublished manuscript that Prof. Yanagida gave me in 1993, a section that appears to be a revision and expansion of Yanagida 1970. Yanagida and others have also raised questions about the identity of the dhyāna master "Dharma 達摩" who appears as an early teacher of the Liang monk Sengfu 僧副 (464–524) and was said to be skilled in contemplation practice (*guanxing* 觀行); see the *Xu gaoseng zhuan,* T. 50 (2060) 550b3–4. Even though the two references occur close together at the beginning of the fascicle devoted to fifth- and sixth-century practitioners, Daoxuan makes no connection between Bodhidharma and the dhyāna master Dharma, but this may be another thread in the Bodhidharma legend. Sengfu was later included in Chan lore as a minor disciple of Bodhidharma's; see Broughton 1999: 138–39n6.
22. Regarding Bhadra's establishment on Song shan, see the *Shilao zhi;* trans. in Hurvitz 1956: 82, and the *Xu gaoseng zhuan,* T. 50 (2060) 551a21–b26.

23. See Faure 1986b: 195–196. Transmission of the *Laṅkāvatāra-sūtra* was one of Bodhidharma's distinguishing characteristics, but the *Lidai fabao ji* authors took great pains to distinguish Bodhidharma's transmission from mere translations of the text; see *Lidai fabao ji*, T. 51 (2075) 180b16–c2. Nevertheless, the translation by Śikṣānanda is used extensively in the *Lidai fabao ji;* regarding the different *Laṅkā* translations, see Appendix, no. 18. In a subsequent section of this chapter there is further discussion of the *Laṅkāvatāra-sūtra* transmission and early Chan.
24. Daoxuan's overview is found in a treatise known as "Xichan lun 習禪論," attached to the meditator's section in the *Xu gaoseng zhuan*, T. 50 (2060) 595c26–597b23.
25. Chen 2002: 151–152.
26. *Xu gaoseng zhuan*, T. 50 (2060) 596c; trans. in Chen 2002: 156.
27. *Xu gaoseng zhuan*, T. 50 (2060) 596c; trans. in Chen 2002: 172.
28. Chen 2002: 172–175.
29. Ibid.: 178–179.
30. This is the only point on which I feel compelled to question Chen's analysis, for I find his work to be extremely valuable. His delicate analysis of homologies between the relic campaigns of Sui Wendi and Wu Zetian, his attention to the important dimension of kinship relations, and his exposition on the background of the monk Tanqian and the Chandingsi enterprise should make this work a cornerstone of Sui-Tang Buddhist studies.
31. See, for example, the reference to Layman Xiang 向 in the biography of Huike: *Xu gaoseng zhuan*, T. 50 (2060) 552a27–b7.
32. Ibid.: 552a6–7.
33. Yanagida 1970: 145–165.
34. *Xu gaoseng zhuan*, T. 50 (2060) 552a11–23. See Broughton 1999: 57–60.
35. *Xu gaoseng zhuan*, T. 50 (2060) 596c11.
36. Ibid.: 596c5–7.
37. Ibid.
38. Ibid.: 598a27–b1. Tanlun was also called Wolun 臥倫 (Sleeping Lun), a jibe from fellow monks that is reminiscent of the criticism Wuzhu received for his own ceaseless sitting practice. Tanlun was said to have bested his master in debate, and Chen Jinhua cites Chen Yinque's argument to the effect that this debate was the model for the Chan story of the contest between Huineng and Shenxiu (see Chen 2002: 197–198).
39. *Xu gaoseng zhuan*, T. 50 (2060) 598b15–16; cited in Chen 2002: 198.
40. *Xu gaoseng zhuan*, T. 50 (2060) 597a25–26.
41. In the *Putidamo nanzong ding shifei lun*, in Hu [1958] 1970: 261–262. See Yanagida 1985: 379–381.
42. John McRae argues that Shenhui's disavowal of merit and pious donation was an effective fundraising strategy in a milieu in which other Buddhist monks were engaged in soliciting donations. He further suggests that this disinterested stance was integral to Chan's success in the Song (2002: 137–138).
43. *Lidai fabao ji*, T. 51 (2075) 180c19–23 (translation section 4). In contrast, an earlier trace of Bodhidharma appeared in the *Luoyang qielan ji* with quite a different kind of attitude, reverent in awe before Empress Ling's Yongning monastery: "The monk Bodhidharma of the Western Regions was a native of Persia. He came from the desolate frontier to visit China. Having seen the golden plates making dazzling reflections of the sunlight and shining into the clouds, and having heard the ringing of bejeweled bells lofted into the sky by the wind, he sang praises of this extraordinary artistic

achievement. . . . He chanted *namah*—an expression of complete submission to the Buddha—and held his palms together for several days after having seen it" (trans. in Wang 1984: 20–21).

44. The difference between drama and *dhūta* was not lost on later Confucian critics, one of whom commented acerbically, "Had he truly given himself, then the Buddha should have taken him, of which there is no indication" (quoted in Gernet 1995: 243).
45. In Chen Jinhua's recent monograph on the Renshou era relic-distribution campaign of Emperor Wen of the Sui, he notes the role that the Aśokan model played in the ideology of the campaign (2002: 75–77).
46. Strong 1983: 200–201.
47. For an explanation of the history of the smile-flower transmission motif in Chan literature, see Foulk 1999: 253–258.
48. Strong 1983: 287–292.
49. For a discussion of the ambivalence toward self-immolation in Chinese Buddhism, see Jan 1965; see also Benn 2001.
50. For an example of a similar act of self-sacrifice, see the biography of Puyuan 普圓, in the *Xu gaoseng zhuan,* T. 50 (2060) 680b–c.
51. *Lidai fabao ji,* T. 51 (2075) 181a19–23 (translation section 5).
52. *Xu gaoseng zhuan,* T. 50 (2060) 552b22–29. Broughton helpfully clarifies differences between the two different layers of Daoxuan's account of Huike (1999: 56–65).
53. Faure 1986b: 192–194.
54. *Chuan fabao ji,* in Yanagida 1971: 365.
55. *Lengqie shizi ji,* T. 85 (2837) 1286a14–16.
56. *Putidamo nanzong ding shifei lun,* in Hu [1958] 1970: 263.
57. *Baolin zhuan* fascicle 8, in *Zhongguo fojiao congshu: Chanzong bian,* 1.18: 638–639 and 648–649.
58. *Jingde chuandeng lu,* T. 51 (2076) 219b8–23.
59. *Baolin zhuan* fascicle 8, in *Zhongguo fojiao congshu: Chanzong bian,* 1: 18: 649–650 and 653.
60. *Jingde chuandeng lu,* T. 51 (2076) 220c14–23.
61. In Vinaya regulations for ordination, the aspirant is asked a series of questions to determine whether there are obstacles (*antarāyika dharmas*) to his or her ordination, and this includes probing questions regarding physical abnormalities or diseases. The questions asked of female aspirants were especially restrictive; see Hirakawa 1999: 61–62. In the *Da Song sengshi lue* 大宋僧史略 (The Song Dynasty Compendium of Monastic History), Zanning stresses that Mahāyāna "unrestricted" (*fangdeng* 方等) precepts ceremonies were open even to those with the physical or karmic hindrances that would debar them from Vinaya ordination. Instead, a participant is accepted because he or she is able to generate bodhicitta (T. 54 [2176] 250c5). McRae points out that Shenhui also emphasizes generation of bodhicitta as the aim of the precepts ceremony (1998: 57).
62. The issue of Huineng's identity as a "southern barbarian" or ethnic minority is a fascinating topic beyond the scope of the present study. However, related political circumstances shed some light on underlying issues involved in the dispute over the patriarchy. After Empress Wu's reign, there was a power struggle between the great clans of northwestern China who were restored to power by Xuanzong, and the civil servants, a large number of them from the south, who had been recruited through the empress's exam system. Gernet outlines a pivotal historical incident in which

the protagonists epitomize this conflict. The civil servant Zhang Jiuling (673–740), whom Gernet characterizes as a "creole born in the tropics," was opposed in 736 by the northern aristocrat Li Linfu (patron of An Lushan), who gained the post of prime minister and virtually ruled the empire from that time until his death in 752. See Gernet 1982: 259. The opposition between Huineng and Shenxiu bears some resemblance to this political and ethnic struggle. Huineng was also a "creole from the south" and a self-made or self-realized man, albeit an illiterate. Shenxiu's milieu and source of support was among the northern aristocracy, although he was also favored by the empress. The most telling difference, of course, is that in the Chan version, the southern barbarian won.

63. *Lidai fabao ji,* T. 51 (2075) 181b22 (translation section 6).
64. Broughton adds the negative from P. 3018, not present in Yanagida's edition (see note 65) (1999: 128n97).
65. *Record II* is a synoptic text of Beijing *su* 99 and S. 2715 (in Yanagida 1969a: 217–224); this translation is based on Broughton 1999: 42, with minor modifications. For an account of the extant manuscripts, see ibid.: 121n12. In the *Record II* dialogue one can see a rendering of the immediacy-in-dialogue that would become characteristic of the Chan literary style, but traces remain of the expository style of the standard question-and-answer format.
66. Strickmann 2002: 48.
67. Ibid.: 46.
68. *Lidai fabao ji,* T. 51 (2075) 181c19–29 (translation section 7).
69. Zongmi's criticism is further discussed in chapter 6.
70. *Lidai fabao ji,* T. 51 (2075) 181a23 (translation section 5). Lore about the Buddha's robe transmission usually involves either the *kāṣāya* or the *saṃghāṭī. Kāṣāya* was originally a generic term for monk's robes, designating their reddish-brown color. The prescribed monk's robes are the inner (*antarvāsa*) and outer (*uttarāsaṅga*) everyday robes, and the "great" (*saṃghāṭī*) robe used only for formal occasions and teaching. For a discussion of the complex symbolism of the *kāṣāya* in China and Japan, see Faure 1995.
71. The story of Bodhidharma's poisoning appears in the *Chuan fabao ji* (Yanagida 1971: 360) and then in Shenhui's "Miscellaneous Dialogues" (Suzuki and Kōda 1934: 54). Shenqing's extended criticism of this story is discussed in chapter 7.
72. On Bodhiruci and Guangtong, see the notes to translation section 4. On Yanagida's surmise, see his 1967: 315.
73. *Lidai fabao ji,* T. 51 (2075) 180c26–181a4 (translation section 4).
74. Ibid.: 181a7–8. The *Lidai fabao ji* appears to be the earliest source for Bodhidharma's characterization of his students, which was repeated in the *Baolin zhuan,* Zongmi's *Zhonghua chuanxindi chanmen shizi chengxi tu* 中華傳心地禪門師資承襲圖, the *Zutang ji* 祖堂集, and the *Jingde chuandeng lu.* For a discussion of the evolution of this theme from the *Baolin zhuan* onward, see Foulk 1999: 232–236.
75. Thompson 1988: 95–108.
76. *Lidai fabao ji,* T. 51 (2075) 181a5–17.
77. Ibid.: 181a26–b2 (translation section 5).
78. See Lamotte 1988: 625–629 and Michel Strickmann's discussion (2002: 113–119) of Buddhist *abhiṣeka* in the context of the *Guanding jing* 灌頂經 (Book of Consecration), T. 21 (1331). Strickmann claims that this work was written or adapted in c. 457 by the monk Huijian (1990: 90–93).

79. Seidel 2003.
80. *Fayuan zhulin,* T. 53 (2122) 560c29–561a5.
81. Faure 1995: 343. Seventh-century Vinaya traditions regarding the robe are represented in the *Fayuan zhulin,* T. 53 (2122) and Yijing's *Nanhai jiguinei fazhuan* 南海寄歸內法傳 (Transmission of the Dharma in the Southern Archipelago), T. 54 (2125); trans. in Takakusa, [1896] 1966.
82. In an apocryphal prophecy interpolated into the *Dehu zhangzhe jing,* T. 14 (545), it is said that the messianic figure Candraprabha kumāra would be reborn as King Daxing 大行 in China, a ruler clearly meant to be recognized in Emperor Wen of the Sui. It is said that the power of King Daxing's great faith and great virtue in revering the Buddha's almsbowl would cause the object itself to be transmitted to the "Great Sui," where it would receive constant pious offerings and further the spread of Buddhism. This is linked to the Buddha's confirmation of King Daxing's status as a Cakravartin king and his future Buddhahood. See Chen 2002: 115–116; Wang-Toutain 1994.
83. Seidel 1983: 368.
84. Ibid.: 369.
85. Seidel 2003.
86. Ibid.
87. *Putidamo nanzong ding shifei lun,* in Hu [1958] 1970: 284–285. For Shenhui's claim that the robe was not transmitted in India, see ibid.: 296.
88. In the *Baolin zhuan,* robes do appear at several key junctures. Zhiju includes Shenhui's story that Kāśyapa wears the Buddha's gold-embroidered robe to await Maitreya, but does not claim that this is a representation of the authority of the patriarchal robe (*Baolin zhuan,* fascicle 1, in the *Zhongguo fojiao congshu: Chanzong bian,* 1.18: 515 and 520). Notably, the twenty-fourth patriarch Siṁha Bhikṣu gives his disciple Basiasita 婆舍斯多 a robe in addition to the gāthā that seals each transmission in the *Baolin zhuan* (fascicle 5, p. 609, and fascicle 6, p. 691). When Basiasita transmits the Dharma to the twenty-sixth patriarch, Puṇyamitra 不如密多, Puṇyamitra asks why the robe has been enshrined in a stūpa in the king's palace and not transmitted to him. Basiasita replies that he received the robe because of difficulties, alluding to the persecutions by Mihirakula. He tells Puṇyamitra, "You have no difficulties, of what use is the robe?" (fascicle 6, p. 630). Finally, Bodhidharma transmits his robe to Huike as verification, and this robe is passed to Sengcan and Daoxin (fascicle 8, pp. 639, 640, 649, 650, 654). However, the gāthās remain the primary seal of transmission.
89. *Lidai fabao ji,* T. 51 (2075) 183b26–c1 (translation section 10).
90. *Xu gaoseng zhuan,* T. 50 (2060) 666a3–c24. For fuller discussion of *Xu gaoseng zhuan* biographies and *Laṅkā* transmission, see Hu 1935; Yanagida 1967: 19–30; McRae 1986: 24–29; and Faure 1989: 42–53.
91. *Xu gaoseng zhuan,* T. 50 (2060) 666b15. This a variant of the second character in the name of Huike's disciple in the eventual Chan lineage, Sengcan 僧璨; see McRae 1986: 280–281n40.
92. *Xu gaoseng zhuan,* T. 50 (2060) 666b24.
93. The use of the lamp as a symbol of transmission may have been derived from the *Vimalakīrti-sūtra* passage on the inexhaustible lamp (*wujindeng* 無盡燈), in which Vimalakīrti tells the women of Mara's palace that the Dharma can be found anywhere it is practiced, and that they too are manifesting the inexhaustible lamp (T. 14 [475] 543b17–24).

94. *Xu gaoseng zhuan,* T. 50 (2060) 666c17–19.
95. Faure 1989: 47–48.
96. Hu 1935: 211–212.
97. *Xu gaoseng zhuan,* T. 50 (2060) 552a27 sq.
98. Ibid.: 552b20–22.
99. Ibid.: 552b29–c1. In the *Lidai fabao ji* Huike laments that by the fourth patriarch, his Dharma will become merely nominal (T. 51 [2075] 181b12).
100. See McRae 1986: 280–282n40. Chen Jinhua argues that Daocan 道璨 (*Xu gaoseng zhuan,* T. 50 [2060] 669c) is most likely to have been the Can chanshi 璨禪師 cited as Huike's main disciple in Huike's *Xu gaoseng zhuan* biography (T. 50 [2060] 666b15); see Chen 2002: 45n97.
101. Biography of Daoxin, in *Xu gaoseng zhuan,* T. 50 (2060) 606b2–28; trans. in McRae 1986: 31–32.
102. *Xu gaoseng zhuan,* T. 50 (2060) 606b22. In the mid-eighth century, a series of inscriptions would claim Daoxin and his "Bodhidharma" lineage for the Niutou branch of Chan, claiming that the putative Niutou founder Farong 法融 (594–657) was Daoxin's disciple. As Albert Dalia points out, Farong's own *Xu gaoseng zhuan* biography (ibid.: 603c–605b) and those of his codisciples point to affiliations with Sanlun exegesis rather than a meditation specialization trend. See Dalia 2003.
103. The epitaph for Faru can be found in the *Jinshi xubian* 金石續编 6: 2a–b; annotated edition in Yanagida 1967: 487–496. See also McRae 1986: 85–86; Faure 1989: 54.
104. On Huiyuan's preface, see the section on Buddhabhadra in chapter 2.
105. Yanagida 1967: 487–488.
106. Ibid.: 487.
107. Ibid.: 489.
108. *Da Tang Zhongyue dong Xianjusi gu dade Gui heshang ji dechuang* 大唐中嶽東閑居寺故大德珪和尚紀德幢 (Banner Recording the Virtue of the Tang Late Worthy Reverend Gui of East Xianju Monastery on Zhongyue). *SKSL* Series I, vol. 7: 4849a–4850b.
109. *Chuan fabao ji,* T. 85 (2838), P. 2634, P. 3858, P. 3559 (the only complete manuscript). See the annotated Japanese translation in Yanagida 1971: 327–435, and the annotated English translation in McRae 1986: 255–269. See also Yanagida 1969a: 47–57; 1971: 3–45; McRae 1986: 86–88; Faure 1989: 65–67. On dating of the text, see Yanagida 1967: 48. On recently discovered fragments, see Rong 1997: 231–232.
110. *Chuan fabao ji,* in Yanagida 1971: 396, trans. in McRae 1986: 265.
111. Yanagida 1971: 420; trans. in McRae 1986: 268.
112. Yanagida 1971: 355–356; trans. in McRae 1986: 259.
113. Yanagida 1971: 365 and 420; trans. in McRae 1986: 261 and 269.
114. Yanagida 1971: 360; trans. in McRae 1986: 259.
115. Faure 1997: 162–163. McRae questions Faure's statement that this is "specifically Chinese" (from a comment on this manuscript, spring 2004). I think his point is well taken, given more recent studies on Indian Mahāyāna elitism (Nattier 2003) and Indian approaches to stūpa veneration (Schopen 2004: 329–359), as well as the ideology found in the *Fu fazang zhuan* (the "Indian-ness" of which is difficult to determine).
116. Yanagida 1971: 346; trans. in McRae 1986: 257.
117. "Twelve Former Worthies" is found in P. 3559, where it immediately follows the *Chuan fabao ji.* See Yanagida 1963: 55. For discussion of the identities of the twelve worthies, see Yanagida 1963; McRae 1986: 84–85; Faure 1989: 54–55n97.

118. Early use of the term *Dongshan famen* 東山法門 is primarily associated with the *Lengqie shizi ji*, the subject of the following discussion. See also Song Zhiwen's 宋之問 memorial about Shenxiu (in Yanagida 1967: 507) and Zhang Yue's 張說 epitaph for Shenxiu (in ibid.: 497–516). The latter work also includes the same list of patriarchs as the *Chuan fabao ji*, except that Faru's name is omitted and Shenxiu becomes the sixth patriarch.
119. Hongren's monastery was located on the eastern of the Twin Peaks (Shuangfeng 雙峰) in Qizhou 蘄州, in modern Huangmei 黃梅, Hubei.
120. *Lengqie shizi ji*, T. 85 (2837), P. 4564, P. 3294, P. 3537, P. 3436, P. 3703, S. 2054, S. 4272. See the annotated edition and Japanese translation in Yanagida 1971: 47–326 and the annotated French translation in Faure 1989: 85–182. See also Yanagida 1967: 58–100; 1971: 3–45; McRae 1986: 88–91; Faure 1989.
121. *Lengqie shizi ji*, in Yanagida 1971: 268.
122. Yanagida 1971: 295. At the very end of the *Lengqie shizi ji* there is a passage on four disciples of Shenxiu in the eighth generation, and among the four is the master Puji 普寂, who would become the focus of Shenhui's most virulent criticism; see ibid.: 320–321. Faure discerns several layers in the composition of the *Lengqie shizi ji* and surmises that this final passage may well be a later addition by a disciple of one of the eighth generation masters (1989: 179n1).
123. The list of disciples is: Shenxiu, Zhishen, Liu Zhubu 劉主簿, Huizang 慧藏, Xuanyue 玄約, Laoan, Faru, Huineng, Zhide 智德, and Yifang 義方 (Yanagida 1971: 273). For Confucius' discussion of his disciples, see the *Analects*, trans. in Waley 1938: 153. I am indebted for this observation about disciples to Jeffrey Broughton's unpublished manuscript "Proto-Chan Texts," pp. 410–411n42. Broughton also compares Hongren's evaluation to the trope of the ten great disciples of the Buddha.
124. *Lengqie shizi ji*, in Yanagida 1971: 273. Jingjue quotes this version of Hongren's final words from Xuanze's work, the lost *Lengqie renfa zhi* 楞伽人法志.
125. Yanagida 1971: 273. *Dan yifang renwu* 但一方人物 could also be translated as "a person of only one direction."
126. Yanagida 1971: 273.
127. *Lidai fabao ji*, T. 51 (2075) 180b16–25 (translation section 3).
128. Ibid.: 182a29–182b3. In the context of the *Lengqie shizi ji*, *yifang* is more likely to mean "local" masters, as translated in Faure 1989: 166.
129. *Lidai fabao ji*, T. 51 (2075) 184a25–b9. See further discussion of this passage in the "Robes Purple and Gold" section of this chapter.
130. See Faure 1988: 51–55.
131. Wuzhu's relationship with Laoan's disciple Chen Chuzhang 陳楚璋 is discussed in chapter 6.
132. *Zhu banruopoluomiduo xin jing* 注般若波羅蜜多心經 (Commentary on the *Prajñāpāramitā-hṛdaya-sūtra*). Two Dunhuang manuscripts are extant: S. 4556 and a recently discovered copy from a private collection, which is now in the Peking University Library collection. For an annotated edition, see Yanagida 1967: 594–624.
133. Yanagida 1967: 597. A *kāṣāya* made of *mona* 摩 (磨) 納 (fine linen or cotton) was a valuable gift item, and such a robe is mentioned in a series of dubious references to imperial gifts made to Hongren's heirs; see note on the *mona* robe in translation section 12. The motif of a *mona* robe either given to or given by Hongren's disciples with a link to Wu Zetian's court may be considered one of the many threads from which the Chan patriarchal robe was woven.
134. Faure 1997: 137.

135. T. 8 (232) and (233). Zhiyi referred to this scripture as the source of the one-practice samādhi, which he equates with the first of four types of samādhi, the "constantly sitting" (*Mohe zhiguan,* T. 46 [1911] 11a25). For a fuller discussion of the connections between one-practice samādhi, Zhiyi, Daoxin, and the *Lengqie shizi ji,* see Faure 1986.
136. *Lengqie shizi ji,* in Yanagida 1971: 298.
137. *Lengqie shizi ji,* in Yanagida 1971: 186.
138. *Lengqie shizi ji,* in Yanagida 1971: 287. The quotation is from the *Rulai zhuangyan zhihui guangming ru yiqie fojingjue jing* 如來莊嚴智惠光明入一切佛境界經 (*Sarva-buddha-viṣayāvatāra-jñānālokālaṃkāra-sūtra*), T. 12 (357) 248a. See note in Yanagida 1971: 294.
139. *Lengqie shizi ji,* in Yanagida 1971: 287–288. See the *Laṅkā-sūtra,* T. 16 (670) 484a. (Hongren's reference is closest to a phrase in Guṇabhadra's four-*juan* version; see Yanagida 1971: 295.) McRae discusses Hongren's style of teaching through "questions about things" and its anticipation of the later kōan style; see McRae 2000.
140. See the *Nirvāṇa-sūtra,* T. 12 (374) 581a, the passage on Mazu and Huairang in the *Jingde chuandeng lu,* T. 51 (2076) 240c18–23 (and also 247a13–16), and Dōgen's 道元 (1200–1253) *Bendōwa* 辦道話 and *Sansui-kyō* 山水經 in the *Shōbōgenzō* 正法眼藏 (Treasury of the True Dharma Eye), T. 82 (2582).
141. Faure 1997: 174.
142. See for example epitaphs for Yifu 義福 (661–736), in QTW (280) 6.3596–3598, and Jingxian 景賢 (660–723), in QTW (362) 8. 4650. For a discussion of Shenxiu's descendents, see Faure 1988: 87–137; 1989: 179–182, and McRae 1986: 61–71.
143. QTW (231) 5.2953–2954. (There are also other versions extant, see Yanagida 1967: 497; Faure 1988: 41–42n3.) For an annotated edition, see Yanagida 1967: 497–516.
144. Ibid.: 498. The phrase is a quotation from the *Yijing* (ibid.: 505n). This passage has been the source of some scholarly speculation as to the cause and duration of Shenxiu's seclusion, see Faure 1988: 29. It is possible that Shenxiu's personal mystery was transfigured into an element of the patriarchal mystique when the motif of the heir-in-hiding was elaborated in the *Platform Sūtra.*
145. Yanagida 1967: 498.
146. Ibid.: 499. The last phrase is also quoted from the *Yijing* (ibid.: 507n).
147. *Dazhao chanshi taming* 大照禪師塔銘 (Stūpa Inscription for Chan Master Dazhao), in QTW (262) 6.3360–3363.
148. S. 2512. Edition in Tanaka 1983: 555. For a discussion of materials on Puji, see ibid.: 549–555.
149. See Faure 1997: 87.
150. See, for example, the passage in the *Putidamo nanzong ding shifei lun,* wherein Shenhui says that Puji falsely claims to represent the Southern School and accuses him of having tried to destroy the real Southern School by sending one of his followers disguised as a monk to steal the head of Huineng's mummy. It is said that the numinous substance of the mummy broke three swords without sustaining any damage. This incident was alleged to have taken place in 714. Shenhui then charges Puji with sending another follower to deface Huineng's stele and carve a new inscription stating that Shenxiu was the sixth patriarch and inherited the robe (Hu [1958] 1970: 288–289). The *Jingde chuandeng lu* also includes a story (set in 722) of a failed attempt to steal Huineng's head, but this time the perpetrator is a Korean monk who pays a boy to steal it so that he can take it back to Korea and worship it (T. 51 [2076] 236c15–21).
151. Faure 1997: 182.

152. McRae 1986: 235–253; 1987: 227–278; Faure 1988: 167–178; 1991: 11–78. Moreover, McRae shows that before 730 Shenhui was affiliated with and participated in the discourse of the religious community that he would later excoriate as the "Northern School" (1987: 237–246).
153. Faure 1988: 57–83, 139–149, 154–155.
154. Faure 1997: 48.
155. Ibid.: 87.
156. The *Putidamo nanzong ding shifei lun* has been dated to c. 745. The Dunhuang manuscripts P. 2045 (part 1), P. 3047 (part 2), and P. 3488 (part 1) were collated and edited in Hu [1958] 1970: 260–314. Cf. later related works: (1) *Dunwu wushang banruo song* 頓悟無生般若頌, c. 750, S. 468, in Hu [1930] 1970; also known as the *Xianzong ji* 顯宗記 (Record of the Manifestation of the Doctrine) in the *Jingde Chuandeng lu*, T. 51 (2076) 458c25–459b6; abbreviated variant *Xianzong lun* 顯宗論 in the *Zongjing lu*, T. 48 (2016) 949a26–b7; (2) *Luojing Heze Shenhui dashi yu* 洛京荷澤神會大師語 (The Words of the Great Master Heze Shenhui of Luoyang), in the *Jingde chuandeng lu*, T. 51 (2076) 439b20–440a2.
157. McRae 1987: 236.
158. On Suzong and Shenhui, see Weinstein 1987a: 65. On the Longmen stele, see Takeuchi 1985.
159. See Hu 1932; 1953; Suzuki 1949; 1953; Yanagida 1967; 1985; Gernet [1949] 1977; Yampolsky 1967; McRae 1987; and Faure 1988.
160. See McRae 1986; 1987; Faure 1988.
161. That is, in the *Nanyang heshang dunjiao jietuo chanmen zhiliao xing tanyu* 南陽和上頓教解脫禪門直了性壇語. McRae takes note of Yanagida's stress on Shenhui's doctrine as one of sudden teaching rather than sudden enlightenment: Shenhui's emphasis was not on the instantaneous nature of the moment of enlightenment, nor its place in the path. Rather, Shenhui implicitly claimed that the "sudden teaching" was like the ultimate level of teaching in a hierarchy of teachings, bringing complete and ultimate understanding all at once to those with the capacity to receive it (Yanagida 1985: 390–391, discussed in McRae 1998: 60–61).
162. *Lidai fabao ji*, T. 51 (2075) 185c8–17 (translation section 16).
163. McRae 1987: 256.
164. Faure 1991: 77; see pp. 53–78.
165. *Lidai fabao ji*, T. 51 (2075) 195b27–195c13 (translation section 42).
166. *Lidai fabao ji*, T. 51 (2075) 185b14–18 (translation section 16).
167. See *Nanyang heshang dunjiao jietuo chanmen zhiliao xing tanyu* 南陽和上頓教解脫禪門直了性壇語; Hu [1958] 1970: 229–230.
168. *Lidai fabao ji*, T. 51 (2075) 185b19–20.
169. Ibid.: 185b23–24. Based on the *Nirvāṇa-sūtra*, T. 12 (374) 372b26–27. For the same passage in the *Putidamo nanzong ding shifei lun*, see Hu [1958] 1970: 276.
170. Ibid.: 277; trans. in McRae, forthcoming, Part 2, "Definition of the Truth" (pp. 285–286).
171. *Lidai fabao ji*, T. 51 (2075) 185b28–c8 (translation section 16). In adjacent passages, Shenhui is made to repeat twice more that he does not have Huineng's robe.
172. I do not know quite what to make of the figure of the "Great Master Cunda" (純陁大師) who appears in the chronological pictorial representation of the transmission of the robe in the Dali scroll. In the scroll, he appears as the third patriarch after Shenhui; Li Lincan 1982: 95, panels 52 and 53.

173. McRae 2002: 141–142; and forthcoming, chapters 2 and 3.
174. Madhyamaka (Middle Path) is the Buddhist school founded on Nāgārjuna's treatises. (Mādhyamika is the agent form.) The classic example of Mādhyamika-style dialectic is Nāgārjuna's tetralemma: successive propositions (such as existence, nonexistence, both existence and nonexistence, and neither existence nor nonexistence) are deconstructed to show that the intrinsic contradictions of language and conceptualization are the source of experience of illusory duality.
175. Suzuki 1968: 3: 248; trans. in McRae, forthcoming, Part 2, "Dialogues on Miscellaneous Inquiries of the Reverend [Shenhui] of Nanyang" (p. 292). See *Heze heshang wenda za zhengyi* 荷澤和上問答雜徵義 (Miscellaneous Dialogues of the Venerable of Heze) in the bibliography for a description of the manuscripts under this title.
176. Dunhuang Mogao Cave 445, north wall, and Yulin Cave 25. See *Dunhuang Mogao ku* 敦煌莫高窟 (The Mogao Caves at Dunhuang) 1987 (reprint), vol. 3, plate 175; Dunhuang yanjiu yuan 敦煌研究院 1993: 32 sq.
177. *Jingang sanmei jing* 金剛三昧經, T. 9 (273). On the origins of the *Vajrasamādhi* and its relation to early Chan, see Buswell 1989; Liebenthal 1956. Buswell has convincingly argued that the *Vajrasamādhi* was composed in Silla in the latter decades of the seventh century, when there were close cultural ties between the Korean peninsula and mainland China. The text weaves together *tathāgatagarbha* thought and teachings associated with the East Mountain school, and the blend is rendered so convincingly in authentic sūtra style that it was considered a translation of a lost Sanskrit original until this century. Although the *Vajrasamādhi* was probably composed before or during the reign of Wu Zetian it was still listed as "nonextant" in the Buddhist canon produced under her auspices in 695, and yet it was apparently widely known and officially accepted in China by the time of its inclusion in the Kaiyuan canon of 730 (1989: 171–181).
178. Ibid.: 220.
179. McRae 1998: 66.
180. It is clear that Shenhui used passages from the *Vajrasamādhi-sūtra,* and it is quite possible that he took the pattern for Bodhidharma's robe from the inconceivable "robe of the Tathāgatas." Yanagida has drawn attention to textual and conceptual links between the *Vajrasamādhi* and Shenhui's works. There are several places in Shenhui's writings where passages and lines are taken from the *Vajrasamādhi* but not identified as quotations. For example, a section of his "Miscellaneous Dialogues" is composed of a pastiche of passages from the second and third fascicles of the *Vajrasamādhi,* but the section is identified instead as a quotation from a *Prajñāpāramitā* text, the *Sheng Tian Wang banruo [poluomi] jing* 勝天王般若[波羅蜜]經. (Compare the *Vajrasamādhi,* T. 9 (273) 366c21–23; 367a4–6; 367c20–24; 368a18–21 to the "Miscellaneous Dialogues," in Suzuki and Kōda 1934: 52.) The passages from the *Vajrasamādhi* are grafted onto an abbreviated section from the second fascicle of the *Sheng Tian Wang banruo jing.* (Compare the *Sheng Tian Wang banruo [poluomi] jing,* T. 8 (231) 693c24–694a14 to Suzuki and Kōda 1934: 51–52.) Furthermore, the *Vajrasamādhi* text has been changed slightly in places, apparently to render it more compatible with Shenhui's doctrine of sudden practice. For example, consider the following *Vajrasamādhi* line: *De wufa jing, shi wei dasheng* 得五法淨，是謂大乘. (Attaining purification of the five dharmas, this is called the Mahāyāna) (T. 9 [273] 366c23). In the "Miscellaneous Dialogues," "five dharmas" is changed to "the Dharma-Eye" *fayan* 法眼 (Suzuki and Kōda 1934: 52 l. 9). The difference is not great, but purification of the five dharmas (another term for the

five aggregates, the physical and mental elements comprising the phenomenal world) connotes gradual practice, while purification of the Dharma-Eye (inherent wisdom) connotes the integral, undifferentiated qualities associated with sudden practice (from lectures at the International Institute for Zen Buddhism in Kyoto, 1993).

181. Yampolsky 1967: 159.
182. Yanagida 1967: 181–212; see McRae 1994: 68–71.
183. Yanagida 1985: 404–17; see McRae 1994: 94–96.
184. From lectures at the International Institute for Zen Buddhism in Kyoto, 1993.
185. *Liuzu tanjing* 六祖壇經 (Platform Sūtra of the Sixth Patriarch); see Komazawa Daigaku Zenshūshi kenkyūkai 1978, and Yampolsky 1967.
186. S. 5475; trans. in Yampolsky 1967: 133.
187. *Lidai fabao ji*, T. 51 (2075) 182b13–16 (translation section 9).
188. S. 5475; trans. in Yampolsky 1967: 176.
189. *Lidai fabao ji*, T. 51 (2075) 182c4–8 (translation section 9).
190. The term used for "woman" is *nuzi* 女子. McRae (forthcoming, ch. 2) claims that this meant "girl" and was a derogatory reference to Empress Wu, but in a personal communication in Kyoto in 1992 Antonino Forte argued that this term simply meant "woman." In either case, it does not seem a respectful way to refer to an empress, but the *Lidai fabao ji* presentation of Wu Zetian is otherwise favorable.
191. For a discussion of Bao Tang antinomianism as a natural extension of Shenhui's doctrines, see Faure 1991: 64.
192. See *Chuang Tzu;* trans. in Watson 1964: 92–94.
193. *Lidai fabao ji*, T. 51 (2075) 184a25–b9 (translation section 12).
194. In later Chan lore, Laoan, under his other names Huian 慧安 or Daan 大安, appears in roles that mirror Zhishen's in stories of a type one might call "the adventures of Hongren's disciples at Wu Zetian's court." In the *Fozu tongji* 佛祖統記 (Sequential Record of the Buddhas and Patriarchs) there is a story of a contest between Huian and a mind-reading prophetess in which the latter is finally baffled by encountering no-thought. See T. 49 (2035) 370a26-b5. In the *Zutang ji* 祖堂集 (Anthology from the Patriarchal Hall) there is an episode in which Huian and Shenxiu are offered a bath by Wu Zetian, who intends to gauge their naked reaction to the female bathing attendants. She is duly impressed by Huian's manifest (or nonmanifest) attitude of "no-desire." See *Zutang ji* 18, in Yanagida 1974: 348a.
195. The *Song gaoseng zhuan* account is as follows:

> At that time, there was a certain Chuji who was an extraordinary man. Wu Zetian once summoned him to the palace and conferred on him a nine-piece *mona* robe. Chuji could predict events and was never wrong. Before Wuxiang had arrived, Chuji said, "There is a guest coming from abroad. He will appear tomorrow. You should sweep up and prepare to attend to him." The next day, sure enough, Wuxiang arrived. It was at that time that Chuji gave him the name Wuxiang. In the middle of the night, Chuji gave Wuxiang the *mona* robe. With this robe, Wuxiang entered deep into a ravine and sat in meditation beneath a cliff. There were two black bulls that locked horns relentlessly right in front of where he was sitting. One came very close to where Wuxiang was and put its hairy hoof up his sleeve. The hoof was cold as ice. The bull pushed his hoof in so that it rubbed against the monk's stomach, but Wuxiang did not move in the slightest. (T. 50 [2061] 832b15–21; translation by John Kieschnick, with minor modifications)

196. *Caoqi dashi zhuan*, ZZ. II, 19, 5: 487b. In a version of this story in the *Jingde chuangdeng lu*, it is said that Suzong has Huineng's robe and bowl brought to court in 760; however, in 765 his successor Daizong has a dream of Huineng, who requests that the robe and bowl be returned (T. 51 [2076] 236c26–27).
197. *Tang shu* (183) 4742; trans. in Forte 1976: 4–5.
198. For a discussion of the significance of Wu Zetian's bestowal of the purple robe, see Forte 2003. Forte mentions evidence of Daoist precedents.
199. Chen Jinhua argues that Wu Zetian's ideological campaign was in fact modeled after that of her ancestral relative Sui Wendi (2002: 109–148).
200. See Forte 1976: 156. The commentary is the *Dayun jing Shenhuang shouji yishu* 大雲經神皇授記義疏 (Commentary on the Meaning of the Prophecy About [Her Majesty] Shenhuang in the Great Cloud Scripture), S. 6502; trans. in Forte 1976: 183–238.
201. Jan Nattier points out that notions of Maitreya as a world-ruler stem from the Chinese apocrypha, whereas in canonical sources there is no blending of spiritual and political rule, the latter remaining strictly subordinate. This is symbolized by the disappearance of the seven-jewel talismans of the Cakravartin's rule when Maitreya is enlightened (1988: 34).
202. Forte 1976: 153–159, 199–200.
203. Trans. in ibid.: 199–200. For a discussion of this prophetic stone inscription conveniently "discovered" in 688, see ibid.: 191n50.
204. Ibid.: 19–20.
205. For discussion of the Indian sources, see Seidel 2003; Jaini 1988: 74–76; Miyaji 1989: 45–48; and Silk 1994: 54–68.
206. *Fu fazang zhuan*, T. 50 (2058) 300c11–13. Though this version conforms to the notion that the Buddha and the arhats in nirvāṇa are utterly "beyond," later in the narrative Ānanda tells King Aśoka that when Maitreya comes, Mahākāśyapa's body will rise in the air and perform eighteen transformations (ibid.: 301a9–13).
207. Xuanzang's version has been shown to be quite different from both Indian and Chinese canonical sources; see Silk 1994: 61.
208. *Da Tang xiyu ji*, T. 51 (2087) 919b24–c24.
209. For discussion of the founding of the nuns' order and the Buddha's prediction, see Nattier 1991: 28–37.
210. Silk 1994: 62. For another discussion of the versions of Mahāprajāpatī's gift, see Jaini 1988: 62.
211. *Putidamo nanzong ding shifei lun*, Hu [1958] 1970: 285; *Lidai fabao ji*, T. 51 (2075) 183b26–c1.
212. For a discussion of Maitreya and Ajita, see Lamotte 1988: 699–710.
213. Silk 1994: 61.
214. Forte 1976: 253.
215. S. 6502, reproduced in Forte 1976, plate 1. Translation adapted from Forte's in ibid.: 185. The inability to obtain rebirth as Mahābrahman, Indra, Māra, a Cakravartin, or a Buddha constituted the "five obstacles" of female form, here circumvented by the proviso that the territory ruled will be only a quarter of that of a Cakravartin. However, by taking the title "Divine Sovereign of the Golden Wheel" (金輪聖神皇帝) in 693, Wu Zetian was clearly identifying herself with a Golden-Wheel Cakravartin.
216. *Puxian pusa shuo ci zhengming jing* 普賢菩薩說此證明經 (Scripture of Attestation Spoken by the Bodhisattva Samantabhadra), T. 85 (2879). For textual analysis and partial translation, see Forte 1976: 271–280.

217. Forte 1976: 276.
218. Forte 1988a: 205.
219. Ibid.: 209–219.
220. Ibid.: 232. In spite of the suspicious timing, Forte concurs with the empress's stated conviction that the fire was accidental (ibid.: 64–66).
221. Ibid.: 230.
222. Ibid.: 68.
223. Faure 1988: 38–41.
224. See Tonami 1988. I am also indebted to a talk given by Stephen Teiser, "On the Idea of a Chinese Buddhist Canon," Stanford University, March 1995.
225. *Tang huiyao* 唐會要, 47 and 49; *Fozu tongji* 佛祖統記, T. 49 (2035) 374–375. See Tonami 1988: 31–32 and Faure 1997: 76–80.
226. Tonami 1988: 39–45. However, after the An Lushan rebellion, Suzong and successive emperors issued edicts that once again exempted the clergy from paying obeisance to their parents and the emperor (Weinstein 1987a: 34–35).
227. Ibid.: 110–111; 188–189n20–22.
228. Jorgensen 1987: 103–114.
229. Ibid.: 108.
230. *Dunwu wushang banruo song* 頓悟無生般若頌, S. 468; Hu [1930] 1970: 195.
231. It is therefore somewhat ironic that, in order to quell the disputes that Shenhui's claims precipitated among the Saṅgha, his heir Zongmi appealed to a 796 edict by Emperor Dezong 德宗 confirming Shenhui's status as seventh patriarch. See *Yuanjue jing dashu chao,* ZZ. I, 14: 277b–c. The earliest source to refer to Shenhui as the seventh patriarch is the Longmen stele of 765. See McRae 1987: 237. Two other recently discovered inscriptions shed light on Shenhui's life and his status as the seventh patriarch, see Jan 1994 and Tanaka 1998.
232. *Zhengming jing,* T. 85 (2879) 1366b9–17. Adapted from partial translation in Forte 1976: 280.
233. The *Lidai fabao ji* also highlights Wuzhu's relationship with the prominent imperial minister in Sichuan, Du Hongjian 杜鴻漸 (709–769). Although he is considered to have been Wuzhu's follower, his role is that of primary patron rather than close personal disciple.
234. *Lidai fabao ji,* T. 51 (2075) 192a24–b20.

NOTES TO CHAPTER 6 (PP. 194–252)

1. *Lidai fabao ji,* T. 51 (2075) 193a16 (translation section 32).
2. *Lidai fabao ji,* T. 51 (2075) 195b1 (translation section 40).
3. I am indebted for the kingship/kinship image to a paper by Mihwa Choi (1996).
4. It is perhaps not irrelevant that in the flowering of fiction during the Ming and the Qing, authors of novels and dramas often employed a symbolic object, such as a stone or a hairpin, to tie together the different generations, groups, and levels of the story.
5. McRae argues that incorporation of the genealogical mode was one reason for Chan's popularity (1992a: 359).
6. However, one cannot go too far with the "Protestant" analogy—the other faces of formlessness have been revealed by Bernard Faure's (1991: 132–178) and Robert Sharf's (1992) work on Chan mummies and relics.

7. See Hartman 1986: 161. Scholars have also discerned Chan influences at work in the construction of Neo-Confucian lineages. See McRae 1992a: 359–360; Wilson 1995.
8. For a discussion of four Song Chan genres (*chuandeng lu, yulu, qinggui,* and *gongan*), see Poceski 2000: chap. 1. For a discussion of the emergence of the Chan *yulu* genre and its relation to earlier Buddhist genres, see Berling 1987. For a related discussion of the "encounter" versus "mārga" paradigms of cultivation, see McRae 1992, and on Neo-Confucian *yulu,* see Gardiner 1991.
9. See Mather 1976.
10. For a fascinating study of connections among early medieval genres, see Campany 1996. On the relationship between *qingtan* and Buddhist treatises, see Zürcher 1959: 93–94.
11. *Lidai fabao ji,* T. 51 (2075) 193a18–19 (translation section 32).
12. Weinstein 1987a: 59–65.
13. Groner 1990b: 235. For a discussion of sixth- to seventh-century bodhisattva ordination manuals as they relate to Zhanran's 湛然 (711–782) *Fanwang jing*-based ordination manual, see ibid.: 235–245.
14. *Chusanzang ji ji,* T. 55 (2145) 92c-93a. See Kuo 1994: 47.
15. *Guang hongming ji,* T. 52 (2103) 305c; trans. in Kuo 1994: 48 (French), 230 (English). A commentary gives the date of the ceremony as 591, before the future Emperor Yang murdered his father, Emperor Wen, in 604 (T. 46 [1934] 803b–804b).
16. See Stevenson 1986.
17. Groner 1990b: 239.
18. Ibid.: 244.
19. Ibid.: 245.
20. Groner 1990a: 268–272.
21. *Dasheng wusheng fangbian men,* S. 2503 (T. 85 [2834]), P. 2058, P. 2270. On Japanese editions of the text, see McRae 1986: 327–330n161. For a composite translation, see ibid.: 171–196.
22. Groner 1990b: 246.
23. T. 85 (2834) 1273b16–29. Trans. in McRae 1986: 171–172.
24. That is, the *Nanyang heshang dunjiao jietuo chanmen zhiliao xing tanyu* 南陽和上頓教解脫禪門直了性壇語 (The Platform Address of the Venerable of Nanyang on Directly Comprehending the Nature According to the Chan Approach of Emancipation in the Sudden Teaching).
25. Hu [1958] 1970: 226–228.
26. Chinese text in ibid.: 229, trans. in McRae forthcoming, *Platform Sermon* (pp. 272–273).
27. Chinese text in Hu [1958] 1970: 228; trans. in McRae 2002: 143. McRae argues that Shenhui was not a "Zen Master" according to the current cultural stereotype of a teacher who trains students in spiritual self-cultivation but was, rather, an inspirational figure who excelled at exhortation, histrionic debate, and doctrinal strategy.
28. Yampolsky 1967: 125. Yanagida argues that the formulation of the formless precepts in the *Platform Sūtra* shows the influence of the Madhyamaka/*Prajñāpāramitā* approach of the Oxhead school (1967: 154).
29. Yampolsky 1967: 141–146.
30. Ibid.: 141.
31. Ibid.: 147.
32. Groner 1990b: 249.

33. *Fangdeng* (Skt. *vaipulya*) broad or extensive, was often used to mean Mahāyāna, but in his *Da Song sengshi lue* 大宋僧史略 (The Song Dynasty Compendium of Monastic History) Zanning explains that it refers to loosely structured Mahāyāna precepts ceremonies open to all, in contrast to Vinaya ceremonies, which were exacting in form and restricted to those who were physically and mentally qualified for ordination (T. 54 [2176] 250c5). See McRae 1998: 57; Gregory 1991: 42n57.
34. ZZ. I, 14: 278c5–12; trans. by Foulk in Gregory 1991: 41–43.
35. *Lidai fabao ji*, T. 51 (2075) 186c6–7 (translation section 18).
36. Gregory notes, "First, both the Ching-chung tradition and its Sheng-shou subtradition were powerful institutions within the world of Szechwanese Buddhism during the second half of the eighth century and the beginning of the ninth. . . . Second, there was nothing distinctively 'Ch'an' about either the practice or the institutional life of the Ching-chung ssu or the Sheng-shou ssu, and in this regard both temples seem to have been conventional establishments" (1991: 51).
37. *Lidai fabao ji*, T. 51 (2075) 185c26–186a5 (translation section 17).
38. *Weimojie suo shuo jing* 維摩詰所說經 (*Vimalakīrtinirdeśa-sūtra*, Scripture on the Expositions of Vimalakīrti), T. 14 (475); trans. in Watson 1997: 54; for translation of the entire passage on the *bodhimaṇḍa* see pp. 54–56.
39. The *Platform Sūtra* uses the ordination platform to good effect as the stage upon which Huineng tells his own story, but I know of no evidence that transmission stories were generally told to audiences at precepts ceremonies.
40. Zongmi's account is as follows: "[Laoan] had four disciples, all of whom were high in the path and famous. Among them there was the lay disciple Chen Chuzhang (the other three were Teng Teng, Zizai, and Pozao Duo), at that time styled Chen Qige. There was a monk named Wuzhu. He met Chen, who instructed him and guided him to awakening. [Wuzhu] was also singular in his determination. Later, he traveled within Shu and encountered Preceptor Kim's instruction in Chan, even attending his assembly. [Wuzhu] merely asked questions and seeing that it was not a matter of changing his previous awakening, wanted to transmit it to those who had not yet heard it. Fearing that it was improper to have received the succession from a layman, he subsequently recognized Preceptor Kim as his master" (*Yuanjue jing dashu chao*, ZZ. I, 14: 278d; Kamata 1971: 305; trans. in Broughton 2004: 21–22, with minor modifications). See also *Zhonghua chuanxindi chanmen shizi chengxi tu* 中華傳心地禪門師資承襲圖 (Chart of the Master-Disciple Succession of the Chan Gate that Transmits the Mind Ground in China), ZZ. II, 15: 435a; Kamata 1971: 289; Gregory 1991: 15, 248, and 318.
41. *Lidai fabao ji*, T. 51 (2075) 186a21–24 (translation section 18).
42. Ibid.: 186a24–c4. There are few traces of Wuzhu outside the *Lidai fabao ji* itself; the notice on Wuzhu in the *Jingde chuandeng lu* (T. 51 [2076] 234b10–235a7) is based on the *Lidai fabao ji*. The sources for Zongmi's references to Wuzhu and the Bao Tang probably included the *Lidai fabao ji*, but in any case he does not give further biographical information about Wuzhu. Wuzhu's notice in the *Jingde chuandeng lu* is discussed in chapter 7.
43. As discussed below, there is a controversy over the phrase *mowang* (莫忘 or 莫妄), and here the use of 莫忘 (do not forget) does not accord with assertions made later in the *Lidai fabao ji*.
44. *Lidai fabao ji*, T. 51 (2075) 186b8–17 (translation section 18).

45. In Zongmi's account, there is a consistent transmission of teachings emphasizing *śīla*, samādhi, and prajñā in the Jingzhong lineage that runs from Zhishen, through Chuji, to Wuxiang and his four disciples. Wuzhu is not included in the list: "Tang [i.e., Chuji] produced four sons, the preeminent of which was Preceptor Kim of Jingzhong monastery in the superior prefecture of Chengdu, Dharma name Wuxiang. He greatly spread this teaching. (As to Kim's disciples, Zhao 召 of that monastery [i.e., Jingzhong], Ma 馬 of Mount Changsong 長松, Ji 季 of Suizhou 遂州, and Ji 季 of Tongquan 通泉 county all succeeded him)" (*Yuanjue jing dashu chao,* ZZ. I, 14: 278b–c; trans. in Broughton 2004: 19, with minor modifications). Yanagida claims that "Zhao" is a mistaken designation for Jingzhong Shenhui, whose patronym was Shi 石 (1967: 338).
46. *Lidai fabao ji,* T. 51 (2075) 185b6–13 (translation section 15).
47. Ibid.: 189a17–18 (translation section 20).
48. *Yuanjue jing dashu chao,* ZZ. I, 14: 278c; trans. in Broughton 2004: 19 (with minor modifications).
49. *Yuanjue jing dashu chao,* ZZ. I, 14: 278d.
50. *Nanyang heshang dunjiao jietuo chanmen zhiliao xing tanyu,* in Hu [1958] 1970: 228–229.
51. *Lidai fabao ji,* T. 51 (2075) 185c20–21 (translation section 16).
52. Ibid.: 186c2–9 (translation section 18).
53. McRae also notes what he calls "the pattern of inspiration followed by departure" that is discernible in accounts of those who received teachings from Shenhui. He suggests that "short training tenures" appear to be associated with masters of sudden enlightenment, citing the example of the monk Xuanjue 玄覺 who stayed with Huineng for only one night (2002: 133). However, the *Lidai fabao ji* deployment of the "inspiration and departure" pattern is in some ways even more radical, as Wuzhu and Wuxiang only have one brief initial meeting and then never see each other again.
54. *Lidai fabao ji,* T. 51 (2075) 186c9–13 (translation section 18).
55. Ibid.; 186c13–28 (translation section 18).
56. Ibid.; 193a15–20 (translation section 32).
57. Ibid.; 185a2–7 (translation section 15).
58. Ibid.; 187a27–b14 (translation section 18).
59. Ibid.; 187b14–26 (translation section 18).
60. Ibid.; 187c2–3 (translation section 18).
61. Ibid.; 188a15–23 (translation section 19).
62. Ibid.; 188b13–21 (translation section 19).
63. See Gregory 1991: 35–52.
64. Biography of Jingzhong Shenhui, in the *Song gaoseng zhuan,* T. 50 (2061) 764a27–28. In Wuxiang's *Song gaoseng zhuan* biography, it is said that when asked about the succession on his deathbed, Wuxiang took up a brush and wrote out an inscrutable passage in verse (ibid.: 832c22–23). Huibao 慧寶 (c. early Northern Song), the monk who wrote the interlinear commentary to the *Beishan lu,* claims that Shenhui received Wuxiang's Dharma but that his disciples also included "Nanyin Huiguang 南印慧廣 and the monks An 安 and Liang 梁" (T. 52 [2113] 611b11). These names are not cited in notices for Wuxiang in the *Song gaoseng zhuan* or the *Jingde chuandeng lu.* However, in the *Song gaoseng zhuan* biography of Jingzhong Shenhui, Wuxiang apparently refers to one of his disciples when he laments that Dechong Huiguang 德充慧廣 has gone off the deep end of the Dharma (T. 50 [2061] 764a29–b1). As noted above, Zongmi

has a different list of Wuxiang's disciples: Jingzhong Zhao 召 (possibly should be Shi 石), Ma 馬 of Mount Changsong 長松 (i.e., Mazu), Ji 季 of Suizhou 遂州, and Ji 季 of Tongquan 通泉 (*Yuanjue jing dashu chao*, ZZ. I, 14: 278b–c).

65. Regarding the Zongmi–Heze Shenhui issue, dispute over the significance of claims in various sources is quite complex, see Yanagida 1967: 340–347.
66. Gregory 1991: 35–52; see also Yanagida 1988.
67. Gregory 1991: 48.
68. Ibid.: 50.
69. See Foulk 1987, 1992, 1993, and 1999.
70. Gregory 1991: 51.
71. Biography of Wuxiang, in the *Song gaoseng zhuan*, T. 50 (2061) 832b–833a.
72. *Lidai fabao ji*, T. 51 (2075) 186a15–b9 (translation section 18).
73. Ibid.: 187a8–27 (translation section 18).
74. Faure 1991: 31.
75. This term refers to Bourdieu's (1984) analysis of social strategy.
76. Derrida 1978: 279.
77. *Zheng wunian zhi shi, wunian bu zi* 正無念之時無念不自. For one of many examples, see *Lidai fabao ji*, T. 51 (2075) 192a22.
78. Derrida 1978: 280.
79. From the *Śūraṃgama-sūtra*, T. 19 (945) 121a2.
80. Based on a gāthā in the *Zhufa benwu jing*, T. 15 (651) 763a7–8.
81. *Lidai fabao ji*, T. 51 (2075) 194b8–16 (translation section 36). Final quotation based on the *Wenshu shuo banruo jing*, T. 8 (232) 728b23–25.
82. Intriguing as these texts are, the fact that they include so many of the features of late eighth-century Chan literature—colloquialism, subitism, Daoist influence, and criticism of reified notions of meditation and transgression—may well mean that they are later than Broughton claims. Broughton appears to believe that the *Records* predate early eighth-century "proto-Chan" literature and claims "internal evidence" for early eighth-century provenance. However, stylistic features and doctrinal issues point to a late eighth-century milieu, and according to the stratigraphy of Dunhuang Chan documents that Broughton himself lays out, the earliest materials were copied c. 750–78 (1999: 96–118). At the same time, one cannot rule out the possibility that some of the material in these texts is from an earlier strata of lore that is then reflected in Shenhui's and the *Lidai fabao ji* accounts.
83. Ibid.: 44, following Beijing *su* 99.
84. *Zhujing yaochao*, T. 85 (2819) 1195a20–22.
85. *Lidai fabao ji*, T. 51 (2075) 187b23–24 (translation section 18).
86. See the biographies of Du Hongjian in the *Tang shu* (108) 3282–3283 and *Xin Tang shu* (126) 4422–4423. See also Yanagida 1976a: 197; Weinstein 1987a: 79; Backus 1981: 82–83.
87. *Lidai fabao ji*, T. 51 (2075) 188c26–189a3 (translation section 20).
88. Emperor Zhongzong was said to have praised a monk for not rising to greet him; see Weinstein 1987a: 49.
89. *Śūraṃgama-sūtra*, T. 19 (945) 121b25–26.
90. *Lidai fabao ji*, T. 51 (2075) 186c28–187a8 (translation section 18).
91. Ibid.: 187a16–19 (translation section 18).
92. Ibid.: 190b24–190c4 (translation section 22).
93. Ibid.: 194b13–17 (translation section 36).

94. Based on the *Viśeṣacintibrahma paripṛcchā-sūtra,* T. 15 (586) 37b3–8.
95. *Lidai fabao ji,* T. 51 (2075) 195b27–195c13 (translation section 42).
96. Ibid.: 195b28 (translation section 42).
97. *Yuanjue jing dashu chao,* ZZ. I, 14: 278d; Kamata 1971: 306–307; trans. in Broughton 2004: 21–23 (with minor modifications). For an excellent study of Zongmi's life and thought, see Gregory 1991; his discussion of the Bao Tang appears on pp. 248–252. For a description of Zongmi's commentaries on the *Yuanjue jing,* see ibid.: 320–321. Zongmi's implicit *panjiao* (classification of the teachings) is made clearer in his later work, the *Chanyuan zhu quanji duxu* 禪源諸詮集都序 (Prolegomenon to the Collection of Expressions of the Chan Source), T. 48 (2015). In this work, the Bao Tang is one of four schools on the lowest level of three types of teachings; see Broughton 2004: 14–33.
98. *Mieshi* is further discussed in chapter 7, in the context of Shenqing's related criticism of the Bao Tang.
99. Gregory 1991: 247.
100. Ibid.: 251–252.
101. *Lidai fabao ji,* T. 51 (2075) 186c18–28 (translation section 18).
102. *Gaoseng Faxian zhuan* 高僧法顯傳 (Biography of the Eminent Monk Faxian), a.k.a. *Foguo ji* 佛國記 (Record of Buddhist Kingdoms), T. 51 (2085) 859c12–15; trans. in Beal [1884] 1981: xl; and in Giles [1923] 1959: 24–25. Both the Beal and Giles translations state that the Buddha used his powers to change her into a Cakravartin and then placed her so that she could see him first. However, the Chinese text says that she used her own spiritual powers to transform and place herself.
103. Falk 1980: 219.
104. Other cases of parallels between the *Lidai fabao ji* and the *Records of the Bodhidharma Anthology* are noted in chapter 5 and in previous and subsequent sections of this chapter.
105. Broughton 1999: 47. Regarding the *Record III* texts, see ibid.: 121n12. Broughton identifies the first scriptural quotation as a line from the *Fangguang banruo jing* 防光般若經, T. 8 (221) 105c, the second is from that sūtra or the twenty-five thousand or eight-thousand line versions of the *Prajñāpāramitā-sūtra,* T. 8:363b–c or T. 8:578b, and the third is unidentified.
106. *Jingde chuandeng lu,* T. 51 (2076) 219c; trans. in Broughton 1999: 132n136.
107. *Lidai fabao ji,* T. 51 (2075) 181a7–8 (translation section 4).
108. *Miaofa lianhua jing* 妙法蓮華經 (*Saddharmapuṇḍarīka-sūtra*), T. 9 (262) 35c (Kumārajīva's translation); trans. in Watson 1993: 187–189. For an insightful discussion of the use of this passage in Chan literature, see Levering 1982: 22–27.
109. *Vimalakīrti-sūtra,* T. 14 (475); trans. in Watson 1997: 90–92.
110. I refer interested readers to selected works on the topic; see Horner [1930] 1975; Paul [1974] 1980, and 1979; Falk & Gross 1980; Levering 1982 and 1992; Murcott 1991; Cabezón 1992; Gross 1993; Tsai 1994.
111. *Biqiuni zhuan* 比丘尼傳 (Biographies of Nuns), T. 50 (2063); trans. in Tsai 1994: 19. The two main characters are Tanmojieduo 曇摩羯多 (Dharmagupta, identification unclear, perhaps the same as Tanmojueduo 曇摩崛多 known to have been active in the Later Qin 後秦 [384–417]), and the nun Zhu Jingjian 竺淨檢, c. 292–c. 361.
112. *Baolin zhuan,* fascicle 1, *Zhongguo fojiao congshu: Chanzong bian,* 1.18: 514.
113. See Horner [1930] 1975: 345–361.
114. Falk 1980: 220–223.

115. See Li Yuzhen 1989 and Georgieva 2000. My current project centers on Tang inscriptions for nuns.
116. *Platform Sūtra;* trans. in Yampolsky 1967: 159.
117. *Lidai fabao ji,* T. 51 (2075) 193a20–26 (translation section 32).
118. This is the only mention of a disciple who joined Wuzhu while he was still in the mountains, from 759 to 766.
119. *Vajracchedikā-sūtra,* T. 8 (235) 752a17–18.
120. *Lidai fabao ji,* T. 51 (2075) 195b3–22 (translation section 41). For discussion of mothers in Chinese Buddhism, see Cole 1998; Faure 1991: 245–246.
121. *Lidai fabao ji,* T. 51 (2075) 184c17–21 (translation section 15).
122. Ibid.: 192a24–b7 (translation section 30).
123. From the *Vimalakīrti-sūtra,* T. 14 (475) 540a16–17.
124. Loosely based on the *Viśeṣacintibrahma-paripṛcchā-sūtra,* T. 15 (586) 37b3–8.
125. *Lidai fabao ji,* T. 51 (2075)) 192b7–b20 (translation section 30–31).
126. Levering 1992: 137–156.
127. Levering 1992: 151. Levering focuses on Dahui's use of the term *dazhangfu* 大丈夫. In the *Lidai fabao ji,* Changjingjin is called a 大丈夫兒, the *er* 兒 making the masculinity of the term even more explicit. This is also the term used when Wuzhu refers to his military accomplishments before he decides to become a monk (T. 51 [2075] 186a20). In that context, it refers to Wuzhu's physical strength as well as his brave martial character.
128. See Fuller-Sasaki et al. 1971.
129. Faure 1998b: 27–30.
130. Ibid.: 37.
131. Tsai 1994: 67–68.
132. Faure himself notes the sectarian agendas at work in this inscription, which was written some forty years after the deaths of the nuns, and well after Shenhui's criticism of Puji had become widely disseminated; see ibid.: 30–36.
133. Self-tonsuring later became a form of devotional practice among Japanese noblewomen during the Heian period; see Groner 2002: 246–282. There is also an interesting passage featuring self-tonsuring in the second fascicle of the *Baolin zhuan,* wherein a group of Daoist immortals convert to Buddhism and are taught that they can recollect the Buddha (*nianfo*) on their own and tonsure themselves, without relying on Daoist rites (*Zhongguo fojiao congshu: Chanzong bian,* 1.18: 534–535).

In his recent study of the hagiographies of Huineng, Jorgensen (2005: 562) makes the following responses to my surmise about the possibility of authorship by the female disciples: (1) Cui Gan was said to have raped the wives and daughters of the officials in the region, and therefore would not have received such a favorable portrayal at the hands of a woman; (2) the colloquial language of the *Lidai fabao ji* would be "unseemly" for a pious laywoman. (Regarding a third point, I agree with Jorgensen that the anonymity of the *Lidai fabao ji* is not unusual enough to carry much weight, and had already altered my hypothesis accordingly.)

Let me state at the outset that I am not immovably wedded to my hypothesis. However, certain counterarguments do seem plausible. The charges against Cui Gan are in the *Tang shu* ([117] pp. 3397–3402), where it is also made clear that Cui Gan was an upstart who seriously challenged imperial power in Sichaun, was given a post in Chang'an in order to weaken his hold on Chengdu, and was assassinated for treason. It is not unknown for the official histories to exaggerate or fabricate charges of perversion against those who challenged established authority. Moreover, are we to accept the implication that a male disciple of Wuzhu's would have been more likely to draw a favorable portrait of a notorious rapist?

I find Jorgensen's point about the incongruity of the language of the *Lidai fabao ji* to be as interesting as it is irresolvable. Since the writings of pious laywomen have not been preserved, we do not really know what kind of language they might have used. One could also argue that a person not trained for an official position may have been less constrained by stylistic norms and may have felt more free to record Wuzhu's language and earthy stories as they were told, without literary polish.

134. Recent works that engage such issues in the context of Chinese Buddhist and Daoist studies include Bell 1992; Faure 1993; Teiser 1994; Clarke 2000; Sharf 2002; Hymes 2002.
135. Sørensen 2004: 323.
136. For more detail see Barrett 1996; Bokenkamp 1997: 1–148; Little 2000: 13–93; Kirkland 1997–1998 and 2002.
137. Yanagida 1967: 301–302. For examples of such Buddhist-Daoist contests, see the biography of Sengnu 僧衄 of Xinzhou 新州 in the *Xu gaoseng zhuan,* T. 50 (2060) 630b25–631a3; the biography of Wei Yuansong 衛元嵩 of Yizhou 益州, in ibid.: 657c6–658a24; and the biography of Baoqiong 寶瓊 of Yizhou, in ibid.: 688a10-b6.
138. See Hu 1989 and 1994; Schipper 1985; Verellen 1992; Cahill 1993; Little 2000; Howard 2001. Of particular interest for Tang-era Daoism in Sichuan, Hu Wenhe's work gives an excellent overview of surviving Buddhist and Daoist caves and inscriptions.
139. *Xu ji gujin fodao lun heng* 續集古今佛道論衡, T. 52 (2105) 397b25–401c25. See Appendix, no. 30.
140. *Lidai fabao ji,* T. 51 (2075) 179a22–b12 (translation section 1).
141. Franciscus Verellen argues that Du Guangting's *Daojiao lingyan ji* 道教靈驗記 (Record of Evidential Miracles in Support of Daoism) borrowed the format of Buddhist tales of karmic retribution and efficacious devotion in order to collect a body of Daoist counter-evidence (1992: 227–233). Du's *Lidai chongdao ji* 歷代崇道記 (The Veneration of the Way by [Sovereigns of] Succeeding Ages) was presented to the Emperor Xizong 僖宗 at his court-in-exile in Chengdu in 885. The work chronicles miraculous Daoist manifestations confirming the legitimacy of the Tang dynasty, in honor of its imminent restoration after the four-year Huang Chao 黃巢 rebellion; see Verellen 1994.

These two works include the following accounts of miraculous events in eighth-century Sichuan. In 731, Changdao guan 常道觀 on Mt. Qingcheng 青城山 (Guanxian, Sichuan) was restored to Daoist hands, after encroaching Buddhists were expelled from the site by supernatural disturbances; *Daojiao lingyan ji,* in Verellen 1992: 246–247. In 729, Buddhists holding a vegetarian feast at a convent in Shuzhou 蜀州 (southwest of Chengdu) were rude to an uninvited Daoist guest, who disappeared into the Buddha Hall. The Buddhists then discovered that his image and images three of the Daoist directional animals had been miraculously engraved in one of the wooden pillars of the hall (ibid.: 252–253). This tale is also in the *Lidai chongdao ji,* where the manifestation and image are identified as the Most High Lord Lao (Verellen 1994: 129). In 756, while on inspection in Shu, the Emperor Xuanzong himself saw a manifestation of the divinity Hunyuan (the Emperor of Undifferentiated Beginning, Hunyuan huangdi 混元皇帝). The divinity also made another appearance in Lizhou 利州; these were seen as signs that An Lushan would be defeated, and the Daoist "Blessing the Tang" temple (Fu Tang guan 福唐觀) was established in Chengdu. In 757, the massive and radiant "true form" of Hunyuan appeared to an assembly praying for the blessing of the Tang in Maozhou 茂州, Sichuan (*Lidai chongdao ji,* in Verellen 1994: 134–135). In 794, a female Daoist adept named Xie Ziran 謝自然 ascended to heaven in broad daylight, after receiving instructions from the Queen Mother of the West on Mt. Jinquan 金泉 in Sichuan. After three months, she returned to make a report to the prefect Li Jian 李堅 before ascending to heaven again (ibid.: 136–137). Du also gives an involved account of the restoration of the above-mentioned Qingyang gong in Chengdu (ibid.: 140–151).

142. *Lidai fabao ji,* T. 51 (2075) 179c4–9 (translation section2). See also Appendix, no. 6. Guangming tongzi is a version of Yueguang tongzi 月淨童子, the Chinese translation of Candraprabha kumāra. Sumedha was a previous incarnation of the Buddha, but the use of this name is probably due to the correspondence between Rujia 儒家 (Confucianism) and *rutong,* a translation of Māṇava, "young man."
143. The *Huahu jing* is no longer extant in its original form. For a discussion of this and related works, see Zürcher 1959: 288–320; Seidel 1984b; Kohn 1991; Schipper 1994.
144. In the *Hongming ji* 弘明集, T. 52 (2102) 1a28–7a22. See Appendix, no. 32.
145. *Lidai fabao ji,* T. 51 (2075) 179c9–180a2 (translation section 2).
146. Tanaka 1983: 526–530; see also his subsequent discussion of approaches to Daoism in related Chan histories. The *Lidai fabao ji* is notable for including a large number of works linked to Six Dynasties Buddhist-Daoist polemics in its prefatory bibliography; see Appendix, nos. 6, 25, 26, 29, 30, 31, 32, 33, 34, and 35.
147. See Xiong 1996; Sharf 2002: 71–76.
148. Xiong 1996.
149. Barrett 1996: 72.
150. See Xiong 1996; Barrett 1996; Kirkland 1997–98.
151. The famous first line of the *Daode jing.*
152. *Lidai fabao ji,* T. 51 (2075) 193b20–25 (translation section 34). The *Daode jing* (chapter 48) line is: 損之又損、以至於无為。无為而无不為。
153. Sharf's study is focused on the *Baozang lun* 寶藏論 (Treasure Store Treatise), T. 45 (1857). The *Baozang lun* is attributed to Kumarājīva's student Sengzhao 僧肇 (374–414), but is likely to have been composed in the eighth century(Sharf 2002: 31–39). The text combines *chongxuan* thought with a rhetorical style associated with Niutou-school Chan, and these background discourses shared a proclivity for Mādhyamika dialectics.
154. Ibid.: 60; regarding the notion of a *chongxuan* school as a construct of modern scholarship, see pp. 56–59.
155. Ibid.: 59–62.
156. For descriptions of the eleven persons whom Du Guangting associated with the *chongxuan* category, see ibid.: 53–56.
157. The phrase in the *Daode jing* (chapter 48) is: *sun zhi you sun* 損之又損. The *Lidai fabao ji,* S. 516 has: *sun zhi you sun zhi* 損之又損之. The *Taishō* version has 損之有損之, following P. 2125 (T. 51 [2075] 193b24–25).
158. See Sharf 2002: 65–66. As noted in chapter 2, the classic example of Mādhyamika dialectic is Nāgārjuna's four-stage deconstruction of the notion of being.
159. See Robinet 1997: 194. See also Kohn 1987; Kirkland 1997–98: 101–114.
160. *Lidai fabao ji,* T. 51 (2075) 193c24–28 (translation section 34).
161. *Jingde chuandeng lu,* T. 51 (2076) 457a11–13. "Mind-King Bodhisattva" is also the name of the interlocutor in the *Vajrasamādhi-sūtra,* T. 9 (273), which Wuzhu frequently quotes.

162. In the *Zhuangzi*, chapter 6, "The Great Ancestral Teacher": "Letting limbs and body sink, dismissing cleverness and intelligence, parting from form and leaving knowledge, one is in accord with the great pervasiveness. This is what I call sitting and forgetting."
163. *Daozang* 1036; see Kohn 1987.
164. We also find the juxtaposition of *chongxuan*/Madhyamaka discourse on emptiness and an apophatic understanding of meditation in the Dunhuang text that Broughton styles *Record III*. Its opening passages include the following statements: "Therefore: 'Dharmas and knowing are both void; this is called the voidness of voidness.' . . . Dharma Master Zang says: 'The one for whom in all dharmas there is nothing to be apprehended is called the person who is cultivating the path. Why? As one whose eyes see every form, his eyes do not apprehend any form. As one whose ears hear every sound, his ears do not apprehend any sound. . . . The sutra says: 'No dharma can be apprehended, and even nonapprehension cannot be apprehended'" (Broughton 1999: 45). Regarding the *Record III* texts, see ibid.: 121n12. The first quotation is based on a comment by Kumārajīva in the *Zhu weimojie jing* 注維摩詰經, T. 38 (1775) 372c, and the second is unidentified.
165. *Daozang* 641.
166. Robinet 1997: 203–204.
167. *Daozang* 400.
168. Robinet 1997: 205–207.
169. This is adapted from a line in the first part of the *Xici zhuan* 繫辭傳 (Commentary on the Appended Phrases), traditionally but not reliably attributed to Confucius. The original passage refers to the nonaction of the *Yijing* itself; see Lynn 1994: 63.
170. *Lidai fabao ji*, T. 51 (2075) 193c2–8 (translation section 34).
171. P. 2392. For an annotated French translation of the *Benji jing*, see Wu 1960; for a complete list of the 81 Dunhuang manuscripts of the text, see pp. 2–3. See also Kaltenmark 1979.
172. This may be based on a passage in the apocryphal *Shanhaihui pusa jing* 山海慧菩薩經, T. 85 (2891) 1407a6–7.
173. *Lidai fabao ji*, T. 51 (2075) 193c8–13 (translation section 34).
174. As noted in chapter 4, Puett (2001) provides an invaluable window into the complex use of classics and commentaries in the Han political-philosophical debates on the nature of the ruler.
175. Sharf 2002: 77–88; see also the discussion of *xiang* 象, "schemata," on pp. 147–149.
176. Lynn 1994: 137; quoted in Sharf 2002: 83.
177. Sharf 2002: 88–93.
178. Ibid.: 111–114.
179. On "heteroglossia" and Chinese Buddhist polemics, see ibid.: 140.
180. *Lidai fabao ji*, T. 51 (2075) 194a5–8 (translation section 34).
181. *Daode jing*, chapter 42.
182. Hu [1929] 1970: 99; McRae forthcoming, part 2, 3 (pp. 274–275), "Dialogues on Miscellaneous Inquiries of the Reverend [Shenhui] of Nanyang."
183. Hu [1929] 1970: 143–144; McRae forthcoming, part 2, 3 (p. 331).
184. From the *Laṅkā-sūtra*, T. 16 (672) 597c1–2.
185. From a gāthā in the *Rulai zhuangyan zhihui guangming ru yiqie fojingjie jing*, T. 12 (357) 248a3–4.
186. *Lidai fabao ji*, T. 51 (2075) 194a13–19 (translation section 34).

NOTES TO CHAPTER 7 (PP. 253–296)

1. Faure 1993: 26–27.
2. Jiang 1996: 77–92.
3. In the *Putidamo nanzong ding shifei lun,* Shenhui fulminates against Puji for setting up a Hall of Seven Patriarchs on Mt. Song and following the *Chuan fabao ji* in placing both Faru and Shenxiu in the sixth generation with no mention of Huineng (Hu [1958] 1970: 288–289).
4. Foulk and Sharf 1994: 172–177. For a discussion of the placement of portraits of monks and prominent secular figures in monastery portrait halls, see Jiang 1996: 82–86.
5. See Cole 1996: 310–312.
6. The oldest extant example is the statue of the abbot Hongbian 洪辯 (restored to Mogao Cave 17), whose reliquary portrait-statue was made around the time of his death in 861. On this statue and portrait-statues in general, see Ma 1978; Whitfield 1995: 329–331; and Brinker and Kanazawa 1996: 83–93. On the related practice of venerating mummies of Buddhist masters, see Sharf 1992; Faure 1991: 148–178; 1992.
7. *Song gaoseng zhuan,* T. 50 (2061) 832c24–833a3. A reference to a clay portrait of Huineng completed while he was still alive is in the *Jingde chuandeng lu,* T. 51 (2076) 755b.
8. Namely, Vajrabodhi 金剛智 (669–741), Śubhakarasiṃha 善无畏 (637–735), Bukong 不空 (705–774), Yixing 一行 (673–727), and Huiguo 惠果 (746–805). See Shi 1976.
9. All the portraits are 212.7 x 150.9 cm, in color on silk. See ibid.: 32; Siren 1956: 113; *Tōyō bijutsu* (Asiatic Art in Japanese Collections), vol. 1, p. 6.
10. Stein painting 163, in Waley 1931: 161; see Whitfield 1982: 2: 330–331 and plate 51.
11. Brinker and Kanazawa 1996: 157.
12. See Shi 1976: 33.
13. *Dayunsi Yi gong xie zhenzan* 大雲寺逸公寫真讚 (Portrait-Eulogy for Lord Yi at Dayun Monastery), in QTW (917.13) 9557. See Jiang 1996: 78.
14. *Zhuangzi,* chap. 21, 7:36b; trans. in Chan 1963: 210. As it is taken from one of the "outer chapters," this passage could be from as late as the fourth century and does indeed seem akin to a *qingtan* 清談 (pure conversation) anecdote.
15. For a fuller discussion of the aesthetics and economics of the artist's function, see Fraser 2004.
16. See Cahill 1987; Sullivan 1979: 140–143; and Brinker and Kanazawa 1996: 37–45.
17. Sullivan 1979: 156–158.
18. Brinker and Kanazawa 1996: 122–124, 143–148, and 218–219.
19. Held in the National Palace Museum collection in Taiwan, the scroll is known as the *Dali guo Fanxiang juan* 大理國梵像卷 (Picture of Buddhist Images from the Country of Dali). See Li Lincan 1982; Chapin 1971.
20. John McRae (1992b) has analyzed the political implications of the Chan lineage in the scroll.
21. Nanyin may have used the name Weizhong in order to be taken for Heze Shenhui's disciple of that name (705–782) and thus may be the source of the confusion over Zongmi's claim to be Heze Shenhui's successor through Nanyin/Weizhong. See Yanagida 1988: 215–242; Gregory 1991: 33–52.
22. The Worthy Mai ? cha 買■ 差, the Great Master Chuntuo 純陁 (Cunda), the monk Faguang 法光, Mahārāja (a king of Nanzhao), the monk Candragupta (a ninth-century Buddhist missionary to Nanzhao), and an unidentified śramaṇa (Chapin 1971: 259–263; Li Lincan 1982: 27–28).

23. A somewhat similar row of eight monks is featured in an early tenth-century Dunhuang painting and may also reflect the arrangement of a local lineage, though these are probably symbolic donor figures rather than portraits. The monks appear at the bottom of a scroll painting of Amitābha's Pure Land (Pelliot collection of the Musée Guimet no. 17673, 141 cm x 84.2 cm), their identifying cartouches are not filled in, and they occupy the register normally used to portray those who commissioned the painting and the deceased to whom the painting was dedicated. See Giès 1995: 1: 320–321, pl. 19.
24. Chapin 1971: 172.
25. See Berger 1994; McRae 1992b.
26. Brinker and Kanazawa 1996: 26–27.
27. *Zengaku daijiten*, p. 1074d.
28. See Brinker and Kanazawa 1996: 157–166.
29. Anon., color on silk, collection of the Yale University Art Gallery.
30. An example of this is the famous Case 19 in the *Biyan lu* 碧巖錄 (Blue Cliff Record), T. 48 (2003). The "Case" states: "Whenever anything was asked, Master Zhu Di would just raise one finger." The lengthy commentary then informs us,

    This kind of Chan is easy to approach but hard to understand. People these days who just hold up a finger or a fist as soon as they're questioned are just indulging their spirits. It is still necessary to pierce the bone, penetrate to the marrow, and see all the way through in order to get it. At Zhu Di's hermitage there was a servant boy. While he was away from the hermitage, he was asked, "What method does your master usually use to teach people?" The servant boy held up a finger. When he returned, he happened to mention this to the Master. Zhu Di took a knife and cut off the boy's finger; as he ran out screaming, Zhu Di called to him. The boy looked back, whereupon Zhu Di raised his finger; the boy opened up and attained understanding. Tell me, what truth did he see? (trans. in Cleary and Cleary 1977: 1: 123–128)

31. *Lidai fabao ji*, T. 51 (2075) 195c15–16 (translation section 43).
32. Ibid.: 196a13–18 (translation section 43).
33. *Gaoseng zhuan*, T. 50 (2059) 326b4–5.
34. P. 3726. See Rao 1994: 133–134. The piece begins with identification of the compiler: "Composed by the Buddhist Military Commission Officer of the Great Fan 蕃 (i.e., the period of Tibetan rule, 786–848), Gua 瓜 [*zhou* 州] and Sha 沙 [*zhou*] Frontier Prefect of Two States, Assistant Secret Envoy Zhizhao 智照." Zhizhao's name appears on a number of Dunhuang manuscripts, but he is otherwise unknown. Regarding the official titles, both Zhizhao's military title and the Venerable Du's clerical title were established during the Tibetan period; the Venerable Du's title (Du falu 都法律) was a high clerical office. See Zheng 1992: 221–223n2, 4, and 5. Rong Xinjiang surmises that P. 3726 ought to have been the first page of P. 4660, which is a collection of *zhenzan* for prominent clerics and laymen of Dunhuang. Ikeda On has dated P. 4660 to the early ninth century; Rong suggests instead that it was not all compiled at the same time, but was a collection of individual sheets arranged in chronological order. The Venerable Du 杜 may be the same as a monk listed with the same surname in P. 2729, which is dated 788. See Rong 1994: 354.
35. That is, the great translator Kumarājīva (344–413) and Kāśyapamātaṅga, the legendary first Buddhist monk in China.
36. *Longhua yihui* 龍華一會 refers to the version of the legend of Maitreya found in the *Pusa chu tai jing* 菩薩處胎經 (abbreviated title), T. 12 (384). When Maitreya descends

from Tuṣita and is born in the next age, he will attain enlightenment under the Long-hua tree (Nāgapuṣpa, *Mesuma ferrea L.*) and preach to three successive assemblies; the first assembly will contain those of the highest level.

37. There are three alternate versions of this poem used in other *Dunhuang zhenzan;* see Rao 1994: 134n13.
38. QTW (389.14) 3956.
39. That is, Hongzhou 洪州, present-day Nanchang 南昌, capital of Jiangxi 江西. About a decade after this piece was written, Mazu Daoyi 馬祖道一 (709–788) would take up residence there.
40. "Former" (*qian* 前) here probably designates his former office rather than indicating that he was no longer alive at the time the piece was written. In any event, the portrait was painted and displayed while he was still alive.
41. Possibly referring to poems written on the painting by others.
42. There are other inscriptions referring to this practice; see Jiang 1996: 82. Early occasional portraits of this type do not survive, but there is a contemporary tomb mural portrait of the court official Gao Yuangui 高元珪 (d. 756); he is shown seated in a chair, flanked by a female attendant. See Zhang 1995: 148–153.
43. "Lun hua liu fa 論畫六法" (On the Six Methods of Painting), *Lidai minghua ji* (1.22), compiled in 847; SKQS 812: 289.
44. Foulk and Sharf 1994: 196.
45. For a discussion of the genres of image-inscriptions included in *yulu,* see Brinker and Kanazawa 1996: 131–132.
46. Foulk and Sharf 1994: 200.
47. Brinker and Kanazawa 1996: 38.
48. Ibid.: 162.
49. Ibid.: 159.
50. Foulk and Sharf 1994: 196.
51. See Fraser 2004: 206–212.
52. *Lidai fabao ji,* T. 51 (2075) 196a22–26 (translation section 43). The quotation is an adaptation of Yan Hui's praise of virtue in the *Lunyu* 論語, 9.10; see Waley 1938: 140.
53. For a discussion of the use of portraits in "Patriarchs' Halls" (*zutang* 祖堂) and the controversy over the function of individually owned portraits, see Brinker and Kanazawa 1996: 116–118.
54. Ibid.: 155.
55. *Lidai fabao ji,* T. 51 (2075) 196a11–12 (translation section 43).
56. Foulk and Sharf 1994: 184.
57. See Jiang 1996: 80–81.
58. Foulk and Sharf 1994: 186.
59. Cole 1996: 311.
60. A lay association also mentioned in other Dunhuang documents; see Ji 1998: 428.
61. Mao 邈, cognate for 貌 in Dunhuang texts.
62. *Shengyi* 生儀. I have not yet been able to locate this term, but it might be another type of image of the deceased, as *zhenyi* 真儀 was another designation for "portrait" in Dunhuang texts. Shengyi could possibly refer to an earlier portrait done while the monk was still alive, as in a phrase from P. 4600: *Hui shengqian zhi yingxiang* 繪生前之影像. See Jiang 1996: 84–85, for a discussion of the different types of portrait designations.
63. P. 2856 verso; in Tang and Lu 1986–90: 4: 123–124.
64. Cole 1996: 310–312.

65. Jay 2001.
66. See, for example, Teiser 1988; Faure 1991: 179–208; and Cole 1998.
67. From a conversation with Rong Xinjiang at Peking University, spring 2001.
68. Cole 1996: 313–314.
69. *Lidai fabao ji*, T. 51 (2075) 196a26 (translation section 43).
70. Faure 1991: 136–137; on relics and mummies in Chan, see pp. 132–178.
71. Ray 1994: 52. See also Eck 1981.
72. Schopen 2004: 329–359. Faure has made similar points with regard to the competition over the "flesh-bodies" or mummified remains of Chan and Zen masters.
73. Sharf 2002: 120–121.
74. *Song gaoseng zhuan*, T. 50 (2061) 832c24–833a3.
75. Faure 1991: 159.
76. Foulk and Sharf 1994: 195.
77. See Yampolsky 1967: 141–143.
78. Sharf 2002: 10–12, 97–111.
79. *Dasheng silun xuanyi* 大乘四論玄義 (ZZ. 74. 34b7–8 and 34d11–18); trans. in Sharf 2002: 123. (Jizang is identified as the author of the quote, but the text title and citation refer to Junzheng's work.)
80. *Lidai fabao ji*, T. 51 (2075) 186b8–17 (translation section 18).
81. Ibid.: 193a26–193b2 (translation section 32).
82. *Linji lu* 臨濟錄 (Record of Linji); trans. in Watson 1993b: 38–39.
83. *Lidai fabao ji*, T. 51 (2075) 185c29–186a5 (translation section 17).
84. The practice of Buddha-visualization is criticized on the same grounds in the Niutou school-related *Jueguan lun* 絕觀論 and in the *Baozang lun* 寶藏論; see Sharf 2002: 44–45.
85. Faure 1991: 177–178.
86. *Yangqi fanghui heshang houlu* 楊崎方會和尚後錄, T. 47 (1994) 642b5–13; trans. in Foulk and Sharf 1994: 203. However, I have substituted "portrait" for Foulk and Sharf's translation, "true image," because I think by the Song *zhenxiang* simply meant portrait.
87. *Beishan lu*, T. 52 (2113) 611a25–b1.
88. Ibid.: 611b8–9.
89. Ibid.: 611b21–23.
90. Ibid.: 611b23–25.
91. Ibid.: 611b26–c4.
92. *Aśokavadāna*, T. 50 (2042) 121a9-19; *Aśokarāja-sūtra*, T. 50 (2043) 162b2–19.
93. *Baolin zhuan* fascicle 2, in *Zhongguo fojiao congshu: Chanzong bian*, 1.18: 530. On the basis of a phrase-search, this passage did not turn up in the *Fu fazang zhuan* or the *Jingde chuandeng lu*.
94. *Beishan lu*, T. 52 (2113) 611c13–16.
95. Ibid.: 611c16–19. Given that the *Lidai fabao ji* was unknown to him, the commentator Huibao is understandably confused, and notes: "What is narrated here deviates from both the *Baolin zhuan* and the *Gaoseng zhuan*."
96. It is not clear how Shenqing arrives at his chronology for Siṁha Bhikṣu, but the reign of terror of Mihirakula is indeed thought to have been c. late fifth to early sixth centuries. Qisong (1007–1072), previously mentioned in the section on the *Fu fazang zhuan*, takes issue with Shenqing on this and other points. He defends the *Lidai fabao ji* version without appearing to know the text itself, and he cites the *Baolin zhuan*

dating of Siṁha Bhikṣu's death in order to argue that Shenqing must have confused King Qi 齊 of the Former Wei (r. 239–254) with the Southern Qi 齊 dynasty. (The *Baolin zhuan* includes meticulous spurious Chinese dates for the deaths of all the Indian patriarchs.) See Qisong's *Chuanfa zhengzong lun*, T. 51 (2080) 775b14–21.

97. Shenqing is clearly referring to the *Lidai fabao ji* version, though the story is also alluded to in the *Baolin zhuan* (fascicle 8, *Zhongguo fojiao congshu: Chanzong bian*, 1.18: 639, 641, and 649). Huibao protests the defamation of Bodhiruci and calls for a thorough interrogation of the perverse errors of the *Baolin zhuan* (*Beishan lu*, T. 52 [2113] 612a6–9).
98. *Beishan lu*, T. 52 (2113) 612a18–21. In the same vein, Shenqing subsequently denounces a story that the second patriarch, Huike, was poisoned by a monk whom he had slandered (ibid.: 612b8–11), but this story is found in neither the *Lidai fabao ji* nor the extant *Baolin zhuan*.
99. *Beishan lu*, T. 52 (2113) 612a27–b2.
100. Ibid.: 612b7–c4.
101. Ibid.: 612c7–8.
102. Ibid.: 612c11–16.
103. Ibid.: 612c22–27.
104. *Pohuai yiqie xin* 破壞一切心 [識], from *Lidai fabao ji*, T. 51 (2075) 179a4, repeated in section 36 (194b13).
105. *Lidai fabao ji*, T. 51 (2075) 189c15 (section 21), 193b15 (section 33), and 194b24 (section 36). The quotation is from the *Qixin lun*, T. 32 (1666) 577b22–23.
106. This of course brings to mind the famous "tree in the courtyard" line by Zhaozhou 趙州 in Case no. 37 of the *Wumen guan* 無門關, in *Zen no goroku* 18: 133.
107. *Nanyang heshang dunjiao jietuo chanmen zhiliao xing tanyu*, in Hu [1958] 1970: 241.
108. Loosely based on the *Vimalakīrti-sūtra*, T. 14 (475) 546a23–24.
109. *Lidai fabao ji*, T. 51 (2075) 189a27–b3 (translation section 20); quotation from the *Vajrasamādhi-sūtra*, T. 9 (273) 369a23–24.
110. *Jingde chuandeng lu*, T. 51 (2076) 234b10–235a7. The *Fozu lidai tongzai* version of 1341 closely follows the *Jingde chuandeng lu*; see T. 49 (2036) 600b9–601a3.
111. *Jingde chuandeng lu*, T. 51 (2076) 234c2–9.
112. QTW (780) 8: 8141–8142.
113. See *Tang shu* (165) and *Xin Tang shu* (163).
114. 靜 is a mistake for Jingzhong 淨眾.
115. Zhizang's (735–814) biography is appended to Mazu's in the *Song gaoseng zhuan*; see T. 50 (2061) 766c.
116. Yanagida 1967: 339–340; see also Jorgensen 2005: 490–491.
117. QTW (780) 8. 8141a. Hereafter, in-text citations will be used for this piece. I also consulted the annotations in the *Sibu beiyao, Fannan wenji bubian* 10: 1–24.
118. See note in translation section 15.
119. The twelfth year of the Xingyuan era is nonexistent; 784 was the only Xingyuan year. However, Zanning also mentions Huanxi's ordination in his *Da Song sengshi lue* 大宋僧史略, and there he gives the date as the "twelfth year of the Zhenyuan 貞元 era," i.e., 796 (T. 54 [2126] 252a24–25).
120. *Song gaoseng zhuan*, T. 50 (2061) 891c5–12.
121. Ibid.: 785b8.
122. See Weinstein 1987a: 138.
123. *Song gaoseng zhuan*, T. 50 (2061) 785b11.

124. Ibid.: 832b–833a.
125. Minn 1991.
126. *Lidai fabao ji*, T. 51 (2075) 185a11–15 (translation section 15).
127. Fazhao wrote a treatise on *nianfo* practice, the *Jingtu wuhui nianfo songjing guanxing yi* 淨土五會念佛誦經觀行儀 (The Pure Land Five-Rhythm Buddha-Recollection Liturgy and Visualization Practice Ceremony), T. 85 (2827). Zongmi, in his section on the "South Mountain Buddha-Recollection Gate Chan Lineage" (Nanshan nianfomen chanzong 南山念佛門禪宗), notes a tradition of chanting *nianfo* that stems from Chuji's teacher Zhishen (i.e., the lineage claimed by the *Lidai fabao ji*), and he notes similarities with the practices of Wuxiang's community; see *Yuanjue jing dashu chao*, ZZ. I, 14: 279c; Broughton 2004: 23–24. See also Satō 1963; Tsukamoto 1976: 325–332 and 520–565; Broughton 1983; Weinstein 1987a: 73–74; Stevenson 1996.
128. See Yanagida 1967: 340–341.
129. Gregory 1991: 45–46; from the *Song gaoseng zhuan*, T. 50 (2061) 830c13–14; Wei Gao's epitaph for the parrot is in the QTW (453.11–13).
130. Backus 1981: 69–100.
131. Beckwith 1987: 108–172.
132. P. Tib. 116, P. Tib. 121, P. Tib. 813, and P. Tib. 699; see Ueyama 1981.
133. Ba Sangshi was Chinese; he was the son of a Chinese envoy to the Tibetan court who remained in Tibet in the entourage of the future Tibetan emperor Trhi Songdetsen (Broughton 1983: 5).
134. The history and dating of this chronicle of the bSam yas monastery is complex, but there is reason to believe that its account of Wuxiang may stem from eighth-century documents; see Kapstein 2000: 72 and 212–214.
135. Eg-chu appears to be a transcription of Yizhou 益州, i.e., the Chengdu area; see ibid.: 72.
136. Yamaguchi Zuihō (1984) traces the process by which Wuxiang and his tiger became one of the eighteen arhats in Tibet.
137. This is an interesting claim, implying that Wuxiang was being trained by a still more powerful master. There is a distorted reflection of this theme in the *Song gaoseng zhuan* biography of Wuxiang (cited in chapter 5), where it is said that Wuxiang's master Chuji was never wrong in his predictions. Moreover, the biography also has a version of the animal-taming motif: Wuxiang, meditating in the night, remains impervious even when an aggressive bull puts its hoof up his sleeve (*Song gaoseng zhuan*, T. 50 [2061] 832b15–21).
138. Kapstein 2000: 71.
139. Ibid.: 71–72.
140. Broughton 1983: 7.
141. Ibid.: 7–8.
142. The following is a representative selection of works on Chan in Tibetan texts: Demiéville 1978 and 1979; Yamaguchi 1973 and 1984; Obata 1974, 1976a, and 1976b; Okimoto 1975 and 1976; Ueyama 1974; Kimura 1981; Broughton 1983; Mala and Kimura 1988; Tanaka and Robertson 1992. For an excellent bibliography of Japanese scholars' works on Tibetan Chan texts, see Ueyama 1981.
143. For materials on the arguments used in the debate, see Demiéville 1952; Tucci [1958] 1986; Ruegg 1989; Gómez 1991, 1983a, and 1983b.
144. The Chinese texts are P. 4646 and S. 2672 (fragment); it is probable that these represent a text that was augmented and rearranged over time. For a translation and photo-

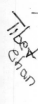

copy of P. 4646 see Demiéville 1952, and for analyses of the two Chinese manuscripts see Demiéville 1973a: 320–346 and Imaeda 1975. Fragments of Moheyan's arguments are also found in the following Tibetan Dunhuang manuscripts: P. Tib. 116 (verso), P. Tib. 117 (verso), P. Tib. 812, P. Tib. 813; S. 468, S. 709; see Gómez 1983b.

145. Obata 1976a: 332–334. Moheyan's phrase is found in P. 4646, folio 135a; see Demiéville 1952: plate X. As noted above, Wuzhu's phrase is: "*Zheng wunian zhi shi, wunian bu zi* 正無念之時無念不自." Obata and other scholars also stress the significance of Moheyan's and the *Lidai fabao ji* authors' use of the same quotations from the *Śūraṅgama*, *Vajracchedikā*, and *Vimalakīrti* scriptures. Many of Moheyan's quotations are also found in a Dunhuang compendium of scriptural excerpts that support subitism, the text known as the *Zhujing yaochao* 諸經要抄 (Digest of Scriptures), T. 85 (2819); see Obata 1976a: 332–334. The *Zhujing yaochao* was clearly an important source for the *Lidai fabao ji* authors; see translation section 10. This confluence supports the notion that late eighth-century Chan subitism was gaining substance as a distinct school of thought and practice. Kimura Ryūtoku (1981) argues that Moheyan brought the *Zhujing yaochao* to Tibet, and that some later Tibetan works also show evidence of having drawn from this compendium.

146. *Dunwu dasheng zhenglijue*, P. 4646, folios 136b–138b; Demiéville 1952: plates XII–XIV.

147. *Lidai fabao ji*, T. 51 (2075) 189a17–19 (translation section 20).

148. For example, see *Dunwu dasheng zhenglijue*, P. 4646, folio 137a; Demiéville 1952: plate XII.

149. *Dunwu dasheng zhenglijue*, P. 4646, folios 157b–158a; Demiéville 1952: plate XXXII.

150. Gómez 1983b: 94–103.

151. See Tanaka and Robertson 1992: 58–59.

152. Kapstein 2000: 72–73.

153. Yanagida 1976a: 166. The *bodhimaṇḍa* passage is discussed in chapter 6; *Lidai fabao ji*, T. 51 (2075) 185c26–186a5 (translation section 17).

154. Tibetan title: *Cig-char yang-dag-pa'i phyi-mo'i tshor-ba*. *The Sudden Awakening* is a Chinese work translated into Tibetan some time in the first half of the ninth century, but the Tibetan manuscript is much longer than the extant Chinese manuscripts (P. 2799, P. 3922, S. 5533, and Ryūkoku University collection 50); see Tanaka and Robertson 1992: 58–59.

155. Neatly capturing the dilemma of the not-yet enlightened yet nondual mind, the Chinese manuscript P. 2799 asserts that these two are actually the same person (Tanaka and Robertson 1992: 60).

156. P. Tib. 116, folio 231.2; trans. in Tanaka and Robertson 1992: 71.

157. Kapstein 2000: 75–78.

158. Tanaka and Robertson 1992: 65.

159. *Yuanjue jing dashu chao*, ZZ. I, 14: 279a–b. In addition to Zongmi's writings, other sources on Mazu include a recently discovered inscription composed in 791; a stele inscription for Mazu by Quan Deyu 權德輿 (759–818), in QTW (501); the abovementioned stele inscription by Li Shangyin 李商隱, in QTW (780); and biographies in the *Zutang ji* 祖堂集 (Anthology from the Patriarchal Hall), in Yanagida 1974: 4: 33–44, and the *Song gaoseng zhuan*, T. 50 (2061) 766a–c. See Poceski 2000: chap. 3 for a discussion of these sources and Mazu's biographical information.

160. Minn 1991. The biographies of the Korean monks are in *juan* 17 of the *Zutang ji* (Yanagida 1974: 1625–1631).

161. See Minn 1991; he discusses the writings of Hu Shi and of Japanese scholars on the subject. See also Yanagida 1967: 335–340; 1978.
162. *Yuanjue jing dashu chao*, ZZ. I, 14: 279a–b; trans. in Broughton 2004: 27.
163. Broughton 2004: 27.
164. Poceski 2000: chap. 2.
165. *Song gaoseng zhuan*, T. 50 (2061) 770c.
166. Kondō Ryōichi (1968) and Griffith Foulk (1993) have argued that there is no evidence that Baizhang wrote a monastic code. Yifa, however, argues that it was possible that Baizhang wrote a monastic code, but that it could not have been called the *Baizhang qinggui*. Moreover, she argues that both the practices of Baizhang's community and the later *Chanyuan qinggui* were grounded in the Vinaya and were not as revolutionary as they were claimed to be (2003: 28–37).
167. Though the *Baolin zhuan* fascicles that are most relevant to the Hongzhou school are missing (fascicles 9 and 10), Shiina Kōyū (1980a and 1980b) has identified quotations from the missing sections that are found in later texts.
168. *Baolin zhuan* fascicle 8 includes a spurious eulogy that gives an account of the lineages of Huike's secondary disciples; *Zhongguo fojiao congshu: Chanzong bian*, 1.18: 653. Two later texts that are considered to be further steps toward the *chuandeng lu* genealogical format are the *Zutang ji* of 952 and the *Zongjing lu* 宗鏡錄 (Record of the Mirror of Truth) of 961.
169. A variation on an oft-quoted line from the *Vajracchedikā-sūtra*, T. 8 (235) 750b9.
170. *Lidai fabao ji*, T. 51 (2075) 196a27–196b5 (translation section 43).
171. Sutton 1996: 242.
172. Ibid.: 243.

NOTES TO PART 2

1. Only P. 2125, S. 516, and P. 3717 preserve the first section. P. 2125 is intact, but the first parts of both S. 516 and P. 3717 are damaged, a common occurrence because the first part of a scroll is the outermost and most vulnerable layer. As far as it is possible to judge, the three texts follow the same sequence.
2. Regarding the title of the text, the Dunhuang manuscripts of the *Lidai fabao ji* all use 暦 rather than the standard 歷. Yanagida said he had once speculated that this was a clue that the text was written during the Dali 大暦 era (766–779), but then he changed his mind and thought it must be a Dunhuang variant usage (from a conversation at the International Research Institute for Zen Buddhism, Kyoto, 1990).
3. In section 36 the phrase *pohuai yiqie xinshi* 破壞一切心識 is used (T. 51 [2075] 194b13).
4. The subtitles reflect the *Lidai fabao ji* authors' identification with themes important to Shenhui and the Southern School. For example, *cuixie xianzheng* 摧邪顯正 echoes a phrase found in Jizang's吉藏 (549–623) *Sanlun xuanyi* 三論玄義 (Essentials of the Three Treatises) (T. 45 [1852] 1a14), stating that when all false views are eradicated, the true appears of itself. Shenhui's criticism of Northern School style is in part an appropriation of this Sanlun emphasis on radical negation, a criticism of the developmental approach to awakening. The use of *ding shifei* 定是非 echoes Dugu Pei's 獨孤沛 record of Shenhui's debate, the *Putidamou nanzong dingshifei lun*. In his preface, Dugu Pei uses the term "*Shizi xuemai zhuan* 師資血脈傳" to designate the latter

part of the *Putidamo nanzong ding shifei lun* (Hu [1958] 1970: 260). Other elements in the *Lidai fabao ji* subtitles reflect the characteristic Southern school themes of lineage and sudden awakening.

5. P. 2125 has 雑, and it is the *Saṃyuktāgama-sūtra* that includes a passage on transmission of the robe. See Appendix, no. 2.
6. The first two characters in this title should be reversed: 瑞應経.
7. The apparent repetition is due to the reversed order of two titles in the two texts: in P. 2125 the *Bhaiṣajyarāja-sūtra* comes before the *Vajracchedikā-sūtra*, and in S. 516 it comes after the *Vajracchedikā-sūtra*.
8. See Appendix for a descriptive bibliography of these works.
9. P. 2125 (here supplementing a missing portion of S. 516) has 申壬, but P. 3717 has the correct order, *renshen* 壬申.
10. In S. 516, 形 is consistently written 刑.
11. P. 2125 has the correct character, 尊.
12. 者 added interlinearly in P. 2125.
13. In S. 516 知 is often written 如, and the first 如 has been changed to 知 in P. 2125.
14. Interlinear character unclear in S. 516; P. 2125 has 置於壇上.
15. Character unclear in S. 516, could be 示; P. 2125 has 為.
16. P. 2125 has 歎.
17. An interlinear mark indicates that 漢於 should be reversed, to read 於漢地.
18. 五 added interlinearly.
19. The extant version, titled *Hanfa bennei zhuan* 漢法本内傳, is included in the *Xu ji gujin fodao lun heng* 續集古今佛道論衡 (Continued Anthology of Past and Present Buddhist-Daoist Debates), T. 52 (2105) 397b25–401c25. It is also preserved in the Dunhuang manuscripts P. 3376, P. 2626, and P. 2862. See Appendix, no. 30. The *Lidai fabao ji* account of the introduction of Buddhism to China follows, with some abbreviation, the versions found in the *Hanfa neizhuan* and the *Mouzi lihuo lun* 牟子理惑論 (Mouzi's Treatise Settling Doubts), T. 52 (2102) 4c26–5a8. The *Hanfa neizhuan* is analogous to the *Gaoseng zhuan* 高僧傳 (Biographies of Eminent Monks) story of the two monks, the dream, and the embassy (T. 50 [2059] 322c15–323a23), but it adds the contest with the Daoists. The *Gaoseng zhuan* version derives from the *Mouzi lihuo lun*, which in turn derives from the earliest extant source, the *Yu sishierzhang jing* 序四十二章経 (Preface to the Scripture in Forty-Two Sections), T. 55 (2145) 42c19–28, c. mid-third century. This was later incorporated into the *Chu sanzang ji ji* 出三藏記集 (Collection of Notes Concerning the Translation of the Tripiṭaka) of 515.
20. Hou Han Mingdi 後漢明帝 = Xianzong 顯宗 (r. 57–75). Emperor Ming's embassy is briefly related in the *Xiyu zhuan* 西域傳 (Account of the Western Regions) section of the *Hou Han shu* 後漢書 (c. 445) (88) 2922. Fu Yi is referred to by name in the earliest version of the story in the *Yu sishierzhang jing*, and also in the *Mouzi lihuo lun*, *Gaoseng zhuan*, and *Hanfa neizhuan* versions. The *Hou Han shu* version of the embassy merely has an unnamed "someone" (*huo* 或) as the source of information. According to his biography, Fu Yi was beginning to be known under Emperor Ming but seems not to have held office under him. He wrote Emperor Ming's funeral elegy, *Xianzong song* 顯宗頌, but that was in his capacity as archivist under Emperor Zhang 章 (r. 76–88). His rise to fame was in the service of the latter emperor (*Hou Han shu* [80] 2610–2613).
21. These dates are quoted from a passage in the *Hanfa neizhuan*, T. 52 (2105) 397c14–398a9, quoting from the nonextant *Zhou shu yiji* 周書異記 (Supplement to the Zhou

History). The *jiayin* 甲寅, twenty-fourth year of the reign of King Zhao 昭 of the Zhou, has been correlated to 958 B.C.E., and the *renshen* 壬申, fifty-second year of King Mu 穆 of the Zhou, has been correlated to 878 B.C.E. These dates are based on reconstructions of the chronology of the *Zhushu jinian* 竹書紀年 (Annals Written on Bamboo), a chronicle dating from the fourth century B.C.E. that included a history of the Zhou. There is some debate as to how much of the original is preserved in the present work of that title; see Lowe 1993: 39–47. Zürcher surmises that the *Zhou shu yiji* author changed the date of the occurrence recorded in the original *Zhushu jinian* for the last (fifty-first) year of the reign of King Zhao to the twenty-fourth year, in order to link it to the Buddha's birth date and therefore achieve the requisite eighty year span between this date and the date of a miraculous occurrence in the reign of King Mu which was linked to the Buddha's death date (1959: 286–287). As is shown by a story in the *Xu gaoseng zhuan* 續高僧傳 (T. 50 [2060] 624c26) regarding a court debate in which the *Zhou shu yiji* is quoted, these dating schemes were important in debates with the Daoists in order to prove that the Buddha's teaching had precedence. When the *Lidai fabao ji* authors next quote the *Zhou shu yiji,* they (or unknown intermediate sources) make an error, and thus there is a contradiction between the death date here and the one given at the end of the section.

22. In the various sources, there are slight variations in the names and the titles given for the men sent to India. For a discussion of the confusion over names, see Chavannes 1905: 546–548.
23. The *Sishier zhang jing* 四十二章經, T. 17 (784), is traditionally held to be China's earliest translated sūtra, but it was probably compiled as an introduction to Buddhism sometime during the Eastern Jin (317–420), with the names of the two translators spuriously added. See translation by Robert Sharf in Lopez 1996: 360–371.
24. Regarding Jiashemateng 迦葉摩騰 and Zhu Falan 竺法蘭, see *Gaoseng zhuan* 高僧傳 (Biographies of Eminent Monks), T. 50 (2059) 322c15–323a23.
25. *Shengdian gongyang* 昇殿供養. Only officials of the fifth rank and above, and sixth-rank archivists, were permitted to "ascend to the hall," and in the Han this specifically refers to the audience hall in the emperor's living quarters, the *qingliang dian* 清涼殿. Note the contrast with the *Lidai fabao ji* passage in which Emperor Wu of the Liang honors Bodhidharma and similarly invites him to *sheng dian,* and the famous "no merit" dialogue ensues (T. 51 [2075] 180c18–23). The Bodhidharma episode is reminiscent of Song Chan encounter dialogues in which the Master's *shang tang* 上堂 "ascending the hall" signals his readiness to engage in challenging dialogue.
26. Baima si 白馬寺 is traditionally held to be China's first Buddhist monastery, but there is no clear-cut evidence supporting this claim.
27. Here one might assume that Huo shan refers to the mountain in Hunan that during the Han was renamed Heng shan 衡山, the southern peak of the standard five marchmounts, for the *Hanfa neizhuan* refers to "the Daoist of the Southern Peak, Chu Shanxin" (T. 52 [2105] 398b29). However, Bailu shan and especially Huo shan are frequently mentioned in the Daoist canon, and a Daoist work listing sacred places, the *Dongtian fudi yuedu mingshan ji* 洞天福地嶽瀆名山記, says: "Huo shan is the central peak . . . and it is in Jinzhou 晉州 (Shanxi)" (*Daozang* 599.5a). Of Bailu shan it says: "Contemplating-Celestial-treasures (Tianbao guan 天寶觀) Bailu shan is in Hangzhou 坑州 (Zhejiang)" (ibid.: 10b). In any case, the *Hanfa neizhuan* author clearly intended to implicate as many famous Daoists, sites, and scriptures as possible in the conclusive defeat.

28. The bulk of the extant version of the *Han fa ben neizhuan* is devoted to a series of debates between Chu Shanxin and the proponents of Buddhism, including Kāśyapamātaṅga and the emperor. Chu Shanxin and Fei Shucai are otherwise unknown.
29. Taishang 太上, "Most High," can be a designation for the Dao itself, or it can refer to manifestation of the Dao as the deity Taishang Daojun 太上道君 (Lord of the Dao Most High), also called Taishang Laojun 太上老君 (Lord Lao Most High). This deity is in some texts identified with the body of the universe, and Laozi is one of its many manifestations in human form. The epithets *xuwu* 虛無 (void) and *ziran* 自然 (spontaneous) are commonly applied to this deity.
30. In the corresponding passage from the *Han fa ben neizhuan,* T. 52 (2105) 397b25–401c25, there is a more detailed description of the Daoists' ritual: "They set up three altars on the east side of the avenue on an east-west axis, and on each altar they opened twenty-four pickets. On the west altar they placed the *Taishang lingbao tianzun jing* 太上霊寶天尊経, 369 *juan* in all; on the middle altar they placed treatises of Huang-Lao from twenty-seven schools, 235 *juan* in all; and on the east altar they set out food offerings and libations for the ancestral spirits."

    In the *Taishang dongyuan shenzhou jing* 太上洞淵神咒經, *Daozang* 335: 18: 1a–13a, there is a description of a specific ritual involving three altars and twenty-four pickets, with deity names and geomantic prescriptions. The ritual was for the purpose of obtaining relief from calamities. For a discussion of the general background and significance of such rituals, see Schipper and Wang 1986. The most germane passage is as follows:

    > The outer limit of the ritual area is a square called the Outer Altar. The real dimensions of the square may differ, but the symbolic numbers attached to it are always the same: twenty-four pickets, placed at the corners and at equal intervals along the sides, create a demarcation line with twenty-four interspaces. These represent the Twenty-four Energy Nodes; constructed around the equinoxes and solstices, these divided the tropical year of 360 days into twenty-four periods of fifteen days. This cycle is of paramount importance in the Taoist liturgical tradition, as it not only structures the religious year but also provides the fundamental grid for the organization of the community and the geographical network of dioceses. (Ibid.: 189)

    It is important to note that burning of the texts was the prescribed denouement of the ritual, rather than a sign of inefficacy: "It ends with the dispersion of the altar and the combustion of the Real Writs and all other writings (including the name tablets of the divine agents and the holy books recited during the service) in a great holocaust" (ibid.: 195).
31. Pavilion, 行殿 *xingdian,* denotes a temporary palace or dais for the emperor, used when traveling. Examples of adornment with various combinations of the "seven precious gems, " *qibao* 七寶, are found throughout Buddhist literature. Commonly the treasures are: *jin* 金 gold; *yin* 銀 silver; *liuli* 琉璃 beryl; *boli* 玻璃 crystal; *chequ* 硨磲 nacre; *manao* 瑪瑙 carnelian; *zhenzhu* 真珠 pearl; and *meigui* 玫瑰 ruby. See Schaefer 1963: 222–249.
32. Taishang tianzun 太上天尊. The *Taishang lingbao tianzun jing* 太上靈寶天尊經 is mentioned by name in the *Hanfa neizhuan* (T. 52 [2105] 400c7) description of the Daoists' altar preparations. According to this work, Taishang tianzun is equivalent to Lingbao tianzun, "The Sacred Jewel Celestial Venerables." This is a collective name for

all the divinities of the Lingbao, a movement that transformed Daoism in the sixth century. The title Tianzun is an ancient one, often appended to the names of Daoist divinities.

33. *Fanyin* 梵音. *Brahmasvara,* one of the thirty-two characteristics of the Buddha. This can be synonymous with both *fanyu* 梵語 (Sanskrit) and *fanbai* 梵唄, a special musical style of chanting scripture; see the detailed explanation in *Hōbōgirin* II: 133–135.
34. *Chujia gongde jing* 出家功德経, T. 16 (707). The translation of this text is attributed to Dharmaratna. In the parallel passage in the *Hanfa neizhuan* (T. 52 [2105] 401b22–24), the doctrines that the two Dharma Masters expound are arranged in a *panjiao* 判教, or classification of the teachings, in five levels: (1) the teachings of men, Heaven, Hell, causes and conditions (*ren tian diyu yinyuan* 人天地獄因縁); (2) Hīnayāna; (3) Mahāyāna; (4) extinguishing sins by repentance (*zhanghui miecui* 懺悔滅罪); and (5) the merit of renunciation (*chujia gongde* 出家功德) advocated in the *Chujia gongde jing.*
35. See Appendix, no. 1. In the biography of Dharmaratna in the *Gaoseng zhuan,* T. 50 (2059) 323a 12–13, this title is the fourth listed in the names of the five scriptures he was said to have translated: *Shididuanjie* 十地斷結, *Fobensheng* 佛本生, *Fahaizang* 法海藏, *Fobenxing* 佛本行, and *Sishierzhang* 四十二章.
36. Kaṇṭhaka is the name of the horse that carried the Buddha when he left home, and Chandaka is the name of the Buddha's charioteer.
37. *Guiwei zhi sui er yue shi wu ri* 癸未之歲二月十五日. The dates here agree with neither the *Hanfa neizhuan* as quoted in the earlier part of the *Lidai fabao ji* nor the *Zhou shu yiji* as quoted in the *Hanfa neizhuan.* It is in part a simple problem of transposed years, for if we switch the year of leaving home to *guiwei* and the year of death to *renshen,* counting from his birth in a *jiayin* 甲寅 year, this would make the Buddha thirty years old when he left home in a *guiwei* year, and eighty when he died in a *renshen* 壬申 year. A death date of *renshen* year, second month, fifteenth day agrees with the *Hanfa neizhuan,* T. 52 (2105) 398a7–9. However, the *Hanfa neizhuan* does not have *guiwei* year, second month, eighth day as the date of leaving home. Instead, it claims that the Buddha left home at nineteeen (to add to the confusion, this is also a *renshen* year), and in the guiwei year, at age thirty, "achieved the way" 成道 (ibid.: 397c26–398a1). A marginal note in P. 2125 changing *guiwei* (癸未) to *yiwei* (乙未) shows that someone was concerned about this date, but the change does not really seem to help. In any case, according to the *Hanfa neizhuan* the Buddha died in 878 B.C.E.
38. This last line foreshadows the quotation from the *Qingjing faxing jing* 清浄法行経 that immediately follows.
39. S. 516 error: redundant 我.
40. An interlinear mark indicates that these characters should be reversed, to 然後.
41. An interlinear mark indicates that these characters should be reversed, to 形像.
42. 佛 added interlinearly.
43. The text has 晉法, but an interlinear mark indicates that this should be reversed to 法晉, corrected here for the sake of correct punctuation.
44. See Appendix, no. 6.
45. *Guangjing tongzi* 光淨童子 is probably meant to be identified with *Yueguang tongzi* 月淨童子, the Chinese translation of Candraprabha kumāra. In a passage interpolated in the Dharmarakṣa translation of the *Candraprabhakumāra-sūtra,* T. 14 (534), it is said that Candraprabha kumāra will be reborn in China to spread Buddhism; see Zürcher 1981 and 1982.

46. Mingyue Rutong 明月儒童. Sumedha was a previous incarnation of the Buddha, but the use of this name is probably due to the correspondence between Confucianism, Rujia 儒家, and *rutong*, a translation of Māṇava, "young man" (Yanagida 1976a: 57). For a discussion of the identification of bodhisattvas with Confucius and Yanhui, see Zürcher 1959: 313–317.
47. *Shi, Shu, Li, Yue* 詩書礼楽. The *Classic of Changes* and the *Spring and Autumn Annals* are omitted, and the lost *Classic of Music* is added.
48. This passage is taken, with some variation, from the *Mouzi lihuo lun* 牟子理惑論 (Mouzi's Treatise Settling Doubts) in the *Hongming ji* 弘明集, T. 52 (2102) 1a28–7a22. See Appendix, no. 32.
49. This is no doubt the Qin Jing 秦景 mentioned in other versions; see note 22 in section 1.
50. Zhang Qian was known as one of the emissaries sent on an exploratory mission to the Yuezhi 月氏 under Emperor Wu of the Han in the second century B.C.E.; see *Shiji* 史記 (123). The Han accounts of his mission make no mention of Buddhism, but a number of Six Dynasties works claim him as an early source of Chinese knowledge about Indian Buddhism. Qin Jing, a.k.a. Jing Lu 景盧, was a Chinese envoy to the Yuezhi court in 2 B.C.E., and was said to have received instruction on a Buddhist scripture; see Zürcher 1959: 24.
51. Da Yuezhi 大月支 = 月氏, a nomadic people of West Transoxania who were instrumental in introducing Buddhism to the Chinese in the Later Han.
52. 蘭臺 Lan Tai, the archives of the Han palace.
53. This passage does not appear in the *Jinshu* 晉書; as discussed in chapter 2, it reflects passages in the *Gaoseng zhuan* biography of Huiyuan, T. 50 (2059) 360b18–28, and the *Hongming ji*, T. 52 (2102) 29c–32b and 80b–85c. As noted, Huan Xuan was the virtual ruler of the Eastern Jin territories from 397 to 404.
54. Quoted in the *Falin biezhuan* 法琳別傳, T. 50 (2051) 211b26–27; see Appendix, no. 26.
55. It looks as if someone may have tried to change 道 to 導; P. 2125 has 道.
56. 経 added interlinearly.
57. 多 added interlinearly.
58. Interlinear marks indicate that 苾芻 should be repeated.
59. In P. 2125 this name is rendered as Pārśva Bhikṣuni 脇比丘尼 in both places.
60. 口云 is used in the sense of 咒云.
61. Repetition of 達摩祖師 indicated by interlinear marks.
62. Repetition of 法 indicated in P. 2125.
63. *Da fangguang fo huayan jing* 大方廣佛華嚴經 (*Avataṃsaka-sūtra*); see Appendix, no. 14. This is not a direct quotation, but it appears to be a summary or paraphrase of a long passage in the "Entering the Dharmadhātu" (Ru fajie 入法界) section. The passage elaborately evokes the various transformations through which the Dharma is disseminated, see T. 10 (279) 435b9–435c27. The list of demons presented in the *Lidai fabao ji* recalls the detailed lists found in works of demonology such as the *Moni luotan jing* 摩尼羅壇經 (*Maṇiratna*), T. 21 (1393); see Strickmann 2002: 109–113.
64. *Dabanruopoluomiduoxin jing* 大般若波羅蜜多心経 (*Mahāprajñāpāramitā-sūtra*); see Appendix, no. 15. This is also a summary of a much longer passage, in which the Buddha tells Śāriputra how after his nirvāṇa the Dharma will spread to each direction in turn. The entire passage is found in T. 7 (220), fascicle 508, 593c20–594c17, and the line pertaining to Buddhism in the northeast is 594b26.

65. The following is loosely based on the *Fufazang yinyuan zhuan* 付法藏因縁伝 (Account of the *Avadāna* [Causes and Conditions] of the Transmission of the Dharma Treasury), T. 50 (2058). See Appendix, no. 24, and the section on this text in chapter 3.
66. Xie 脇 is a translation of the name Pārśva. The use of the nickname "Sides" Bhikṣu derives from the entry on Pārśva in the *Fu fazang zhuan,* where it is said that his sides never once touched the ground (T. 50 [2058] 314c). This austerity is also attributed to the fourth Chan patriarch, Daoxin.
67. Miduoluojue 彌多羅掘, probably Mihirakula, the second ruler of the Hūṇa people (related to the Hepthalites) who ruled northwest India and Kashmir in the fifth and sixth centuries; see note 67 in the *Fu fazang zhuan* section of chapter 4.
68. The *Lidai fabao ji* is the only account of Siṁha's murder in which these identifications are made. The significance of the appearance of Mani and Jesus in the *Lidai fabao ji* are discussed in note 68 in the *Fu fazang zhuan* section of chapter 4.
69. See the discussion in chapter 4 regarding the background of this unique form of Bodhidharma's name.
70. Trepiṭaka is the title of a master of the Tripiṭaka. In the *Lengqie shizi ji* it has precisely the opposite meaning; it is used for a person who transmits Chan in the correct line of transmission from India (Yanagida 1976a: 66).
71. *Miaofa lianhua jing* 妙法蓮華經 (*Saddharmapuṇḍaarīka-sūtra, Lotus Sūtra*), T. 9 (262) 37b23–24: 亦不親近, 增上慢人, 貪著小乘, 三藏學者.
72. That is, the *Lengqie abaduoluo baojing* 楞伽阿跋多羅寶経, T. 16 (670); see Appendix, no. 18, on the *Laṅkā* translations.
73. T. 16 (671).
74. That is, the *Dasheng ru Lengqie jing* 大乘入楞伽経, T. 16 (672).
75. The standard phrase would be 大乘 (Mahāyāna), but both S. 516 and P. 2125 have 大禅.
76. Correction to 門 indicated interlinearly.
77. [虫+也] is the vulgate form of 蛇; see Morohashi 10.2.
78. 汝國 added interlinearly.
79. The last line is written in half-space small characters.
80. 菩提達摩多羅, i.e., Bodhidharma. Use of the name Bodhidharmatrāta, unique to the *Lidai fabao ji,* was criticized in Shenqing's *Beishan lu,* T. 52 (2113) 611b21–24. However, the portmanteau patriarch was later to become quite popular as an arhat in Tibet; see Demiéville 1978: 45–49.
81. That is, the Later Qin 後秦 (385–417).
82. The locus classicus for this dialogue is the passage in the *Lotus Sūtra* in which the seven-year-old daughter of the Nāga king demonstrates her enlightenment; see Watson 1993a: 188. It is also possible that the *Lidai fabao ji* authors were inspired by a passage in the apocryphal *Śūraṃgama-sūtra,* T. 19 (945) 109c14–22; see Appendix, no. 9.
83. The *Chanmen jing* 禪門經, a.k.a. *Chanyao jing* 禪要經 (P. 4646, S. 5532), is a Dunhuang apocryphal scripture of the early eighth century associated with the "Northern School." See Appendix, no. 16; Yanagida 1961; Faure 1988: 154–155. However, as discussed in chapter 2, the *Lidai fabao ji* authors apparently confused the *Chanmen jing* with the so-called *Damoduoluo chan jing,* T. 15 (618). The *Damoduoluo chan jing* is a long list of Hīnayāna dhyānas divided into categories, with a discursive final section that is more "Mahāyānist," including visualization of Buddha-lands. Moreover, the

key "preface" referred to in the next sentence is the preface to the *Damoduoluo chan jing*.

84. The line "西國所傳法具引禪經序上 All the Dharmas transmitted from the Western Kingdom are quoted in the preface of the Chan Scripture," echoes Shenhui in the *Putidamo nanzong ding shifei lun:* "據禪經序中具明西國代數 [This is] according to the *Chan Scripture* preface, which elucidates the complete patriarchal succession of the Western Regions" (Hu [1958] 1970: 295). Although much of the *Lidai fabao ji* account of Bodhidharma (with the exception of the Buddha/Yaśas story) is taken from Shenhui, here the authors must have felt compelled to alter Shenhui's statement for the sake of consistency, because Shenhui's list of seven patriarchs preceding Bodhidharma derived from Buddhabhadra's preface to the *Damoduoluo chan jing* (T. 15 [618] 301c) was expanded considerably in the *Lidai fabao ji.*
85. The reference to Bodhidharma residing on Mt. Song is from the *Chuan fabao ji* and is taken up by all the later biographies of Bodhidharma; see Yanagida 1971: 354.
86. The reference to receiving students for six years is from the "Miscellaneous Dialogues," in Suzuki and Kōda 1934: 54.
87. In the *Xu gaoseng zhuan* Bodhidharma is an insubstantial figure when contrasted with his famous near-contemporary Bodhiruci (d. 527 or 535); see the *Xu gaoseng zhuan,* T. 50 (2060) 428a22–429c5. Bodhiruci and his disciples formed the nucleus of a group sponsored by the Northern Wei court for the translation and study of new Yogācāra and Pure Land-related scriptures, and he was later designated the founder of the Northern branch of the Dilun 地論 (Daśabhūmika) School. Guangtong (a.k.a. Huiguang 慧光) was considered a patriarch of the Southern branch; see his biography in the *Xu gaoseng zhuan,* T. 50 (2060) 607b18—608b29.
88. Interestingly, in a seventh-century "Book of Spellbinding" by Sun Simo, we find the following phrases in an incantation for treatment of poisoning: "In my hands I grasp hills and mountains, in my mouth I hold a hundred toxins, in my heart I bear centipedes. When I spit on heaven, heaven must turn. When I spit on earth, earth sinks and opens. When I spit on stone, it shatters and crumbles" (trans. in Strickmann 2002: 29).
89. The reference to "dangling thread" is found in the "Miscellaneous Dialogues" (Suzuki and Kōda 1934: 54) and is meant as a prediction of the persecutions suffered by Huineng.
90. This version is more elaborate than the versions in the *Chuan fabao ji* (Yanagida 1971: 360) and in the "Miscellaneous Dialogues" (Suzuki and Kōda 1934: 54), neither of which attempt to name the poisoners. The poisoning story is ridiculed in Shenqing's *Beishan lu,* T. 52 (2113) 612a1–6.
91. Anachronistic reference to China.
92. In the Song *Shimen zhengtong* 釋門正統, it was said that the nun Zongchi was the former incarnation of the monk Baoyu 抱玉 (c. mid-eighth century); ZZ. 2, 3: 448d, see Yanagida 1967: 317–318. Her name means "Grasping All" and is also a translation of dhāraṇī.
93. Xuanyang 宣陽 prefecture in present-day Henan province,.
94. Leaving a tomb empty save for some personal effect is a topos associated with Daoist masters. This was borrowed much earlier for Fotudeng's biography, in which only his staff and bowl remain in his tomb and he is sighted in the desert (*Gaoseng zhuan,* T. 50 [2059] 387a14–17). There is no meeting with Bodhidharma in the account of Song Yun's mission in the *Luoyang qielan ji,* but the emissaries do encounter a pra-

tyekabuddha's shoe enshrined in a stūpa; see *Luoyang qielan ji;* trans. in Wang 1984: 222.

95. This is a pun incorporating Huike's name: 可是也. See examples of this usage in Zhang 1985: 42–43 and 51–52.
96. This name is taken from the *Putidamo nanzong ding shifei lun,* in Hu [1958] 1970: 295. However, in the next section the *Lidai fabao ji* manuscript has it as Prajñāpāramitara 般若波羅蜜多羅.
97. Shenhui's version in the "Miscellaneous Dialogues" makes the claim that Emperor Wu of the Liang wrote an inscription, but does not give a text (Suzuki and Kōda 1934: 55). Yanagida discusses the *Lidai fabao ji* stele-inscription attributions at length; see Yanagida 1967: 321–322 regarding attributions of inscriptions for Bodhidharma.
98. *Xian* 峴 (a cognate of *huan* 山 + 完) is the character used here in Shenhui's "Miscellaneous Dialogues"; see Suzuki and Kōda 1934: 56. *Huan* [山+完] is used in the *Chuan fabao ji* in this context; see Yanagida 1971: 169. It is now commonly written 皖. The name and location of this mountain is under dispute; see notes below.
99. Marks for repetition of 大師 added interlinearly.
100. 侃 = [人+ 品].
101. 墓 added interlinearly.
102. Should be 後釋法琳.
103. The last line is in half-space small characters.
104. As discussed in chapter 5, there are basically two lines of derivation for biographical accounts of Huike. One is the *Putidamo nanzong ding shifei lun* and "Miscellaneous Dialogues" accounts via the *Chuan fabao ji,* and the other is the *Lengqie shizi ji* via the *Xu gaoseng zhuan.*
105. West Fanshui 汜水 district, Yingyang 榮陽 prefecture, Henan province. It was originally written Humo 虎牢, but in the Tang *hu* was a taboo character due to its presence in the name of a Tang ancestor (Yanagida 1976a: 81).
106. This originates with the *Putidamo nanzong ding shifei lun,* where it is said that Huike gained his new Dharma name after Huike's severed arm offering was met with Bodhidharma's laconic response, "*Ru ke* 汝可" (You can, you'll do) (Hu [1958] 1970: 263).
107. See chapter 5 for a discussion of the various versions of this scene.
108. The *Lidai fabao ji* uses 承後者, a term coined by Shenhui (Yanagida 1976a: 81).
109. This is an elaboration of Shenhui's account in the *Putidamo nanzong ding shifei lun;* see Hu [1958] 1970: 296.
110. In the *Putidamo nanzong ding shifei lun,* Shenhui uses the simile of the Cakravartin's universal rule to argue that there cannot be two patriarchs per generation (Hu [1958] 1970: 282).
111. Shenhui's version in the "Miscellaneous Dialogues" claims that Huike secluded himself at Mt. Huan or Xian (峴) in Shuzhou 舒州 (Anhui) in order to escape the Northern Zhou persecution (Suzuki and Kōda 1934: 56). Yanagida asserts that this is the same as Mt. Huan (山 + 完), where Daoxin is said to have gone (Yanagida 1976a: 81). The Luo region corresponds to present-day Luoyang district in Henan, and the Xiang region corresponds to the Anyang district in Henan.
112. In all the Chan historical texts after the *Baolin zhuan,* Bodhiruci is replaced by Dharma Master Bianhe 辨和, a scholar-monk who lectured on the *Nirvāṇa-sūtra* (Yanagida 1976a: 82).
113. See section 6.

114. This episode is based on Shenhui's "Miscellaneous Dialogues," which cites the nonextant *Yang Lengqie Yedu gushi* 楊楞伽鄴都故事 (Yang Lengqie's Stories from Ye) (Appendix, no. 37) as a source; see Suzuki and Kōda 1934: 56.
115. There is no record of this person, but the Cheng'an district was in Xiang region, where the Sanjie (Three Stages) movement flourished in the Sui and early Tang. By the late eighth century, the area was probably associated with Wu Zetian's suppression of the Sanjie sect, and the *Lidai fabao ji* authors may have been trying to draw a link between this persecution and Huike's martyrdom (Yanagida 1976a: 82).
116. In the *Xu gaoseng zhuan*, T. 50 (2060) 552b29-c1, Huike's lament refers to the cheapening of the transmission of the *Laṅkā* scripture. As discussed in chapter 5, rival claims to a "*Laṅkā*" lineage were disputed in "proto-Chan" biographies and texts.
117. This claim originated with the *Lidai fabao ji* and became the standard version (Yanagida 1976a: 82).
118. A nonextant geographical work on Ye; see Appendix, no. 37.
119. A full text of this interesting inscription, undoubtedly fabricated, is included in fascicle 8 of the *Baolin zhuan;* in *Zhongguo fojiao congshu: Chanzong bian*, 1.18: 651–653. See Yanagida 1967: 323–234, regarding the *Lidai fabao ji*'s inscription attribution for Huike.
120. 付法囑 should be reversed: 付囑法.
121. Manuscript has 自語由已, here corrected to 自由語已.
122. Written 掩, but should be 奄, as in section 7, on Daoxin's death.
123. The last two lines are in half-space small characters.
124. Accounts of Sengcan as the patriarch in between Huike and Daoxin began with the *Chuan fabao ji* (T. 85 [2838] 1291b4 and c1) and were further developed in the *Lengqie shizi ji* (T. 85 [2837] 1286b8–11) and Shenhui's "Miscellaneous Dialogues" (Suzuki and Kōda 1934: 57). Traditionally attributed to Sengcan, references to the *Xinxin ming* 信心銘 (Inscription on Faith in the Mind) did not appear until the early ninth century. Sharf cites the citation in Chengguan's 澄觀 *Huayan* commentary (T. 36 [1736] 282c4–5) as the most reliable basis for establishing a terminus ad quem; see Sharf 2002: 298n58. See also Kajitani et al. 1974: 2–29 and 184–191.
125. This exchange is first found in the *Lidai fabao ji,* no doubt modeled after the famous initial exchange between Huineng and Hongren in Shenhui's "Miscellaneous Dialogues"; see Suzuki and Kōda 1934: 60.
126. Mt. Sikong is in northeast Taihu 太湖 district, Anhui province. The *Chuan fabao ji* says that Sengcan went into seclusion at Mt. Huangong 皖公, but then adds a note that Mt. Huangong was also called Mt. Sikong 思空, thus confusing two different but nearby mountains (Yanagida 1971: 169). Mt. Huangong is also in Anhui, in the northwest of the Huaining 懷寧 district in the area formerly known as Shuzhou 舒州. This is the location of Sengcan's death as named in a recently discovered but perhaps unreliable stele inscription for Sengcan; see note 131.
127. Huike also went into hiding on this mountain; see previous section.
128. The first half is a pun on Sengcan's name, which means Saṅgha-gem, and the praise also means he is an heir in the true spirit of Bodhidharma. The second half might be based on a phrase about Sengcan in the *Chuan fabao ji*: "*Can dinghui qimin, shenxue rizhi* 璨定恵齊泯、深學日至. In Can there was a blending of samādhi and prajñā, and every day he realized this profound practice." See Yanagida 1971: 372.
129. Mt. Loufu is on the border between Dianbai 電白 district and Bolou 博羅 district, in Guangdong province; it was considered a Daoist sacred site (Yanagida 1976a: 85).

130. This episode is from the *Lengqie shizi ji*, T. 85 (2837) 1286b15–16.
131. This accords with the two inscriptions discovered in 1982 at what is believed to be the site of Sengcan's reliquary stūpa, published in *Wenwu*, no. 4 (1985): 8. The first inscription reads: "Made in the twelfth year of Kaixing in the Great Sui (592)." The second reads: "In the seventh month, in the twelfth year of Kaixing in the Great Sui, Master Sengcan passed away in a cave on Mt. Huangong in Shu [zhou]. Having built a stūpa and made offerings, Daoxin recorded [this]" (trans. in Sørensen 1991: 91). Sørensen points out that the traditional date for Daoxin's birth (580) would make him twelve at the time of Sengcan's death, necessitating a reconsideration of Daoxin's dates (ibid.: 92). However, Chen Jinhua considers the inscription to be inauthentic (in a conversation in December 2003).
132. 薛道衡 Xue Daoheng, cognomen Yuanqing 元卿, was an official who served the Northern Qi, Northern Zhou, and Sui emperors, and he was ordered to commit suicide by Sui Yangdi (r. 605–617); see *Bei shi* 北史 (36), *Sui shu* 隋書 (57). He is mentioned in other monks' biographies, but the claim that he wrote an inscription for Sengcan is a fabrication. Dugu Ji 獨孤及 (725–777) wrote two of the earliest inscriptions about Sencan: (1) the *Shuzhou Shanyusi shangfang chanmen disanzu Can dashi taming* 舒州山谷寺上方禪門弟三祖璨大師塔銘 (Memorial Inscription at Shanyu Temple in Shuzhou for the Third Patriarch of the Highest Chan School, Great Master Can), in QTW (392) 3991; and (2) the *Shuzhou Shanyusi juejita Sui gu Jingzhi chanshi beiming bing xu* 舒州山谷寺覺寂塔隋故鏡智禪師碑銘并序 (Memorial Inscription, with Preface, of the Funerary Stūpa at Shanyu Temple in Shuzhou for the Former Chan Master Jingzhi of the Sui), written in 773, in QTW (390) 3972–3974. See Yanagida 1967: 324–327 for a discussion of inscriptions for Sengcan.
133. 云 is in P. 2125 and seems to be written interlinearly in S. 516.
134. Should be 承後.
135. The last line is in half-space small characters.
136. The biographies of Daoxin in early Chan literature are largely based on the entry in the *Xu gaoseng zhuan*, T. 50 (2060) 606b2–28. The *Lidai fabao ji* version is also influenced by the versions in the *Chuan fabao ji* (Yanagida 1971: 376–385), and the "Miscellaneous Dialogues" (Suzuki and Kōda 1934: 58–59). See Chappell 1983b.
137. Henei 河内 = Qinyang 沁陽 prefecture in Henan.
138. The story of Daoxin delivering a town from bandits originates with the version in the *Xu gaoseng zhuan*, T. 50 (2060) 606b9–13, and the *Lidai fabao ji* version is closest to that of the "Miscellaneous Dialogues" (Suzuki and Kōda 1934: 58). An echo of this story also made its way into Tibetan accounts of the sixteen Chinese arhats (Yanagida 1976a: 90).
139. Mt. Potou is probably the former name of one of the peaks that became known as Shuangfeng 雙峰, the seat of the East Mountain School, in Hubei.
140. This story of Daoxin's refusal of the invitation of Emperor Taizong (r. 627–650; the *Lidai fabao ji* uses his posthumous title, Wenwu 文武) originated with the *Lidai fabao ji* and was taken up in later Chan accounts. The use of humor and dialogue contrasts with the doctrinal explication in the *Lengqie shizi ji* entry on Daoxin, and it anticipates the "encounter dialogue" style of Song Chan (Yanagida 1976a: 90–91).
141. "Elephant-Dragons," an epithet for peerless monks.
142. The "Miscellaneous Dialogues" account is the first to mention a Master Yuanyi, but he plays a minor role; see Suzuki and Kōda 1934: 58. Daoxuan's *Xu gaoseng zhuan* account says that Daoxin ordered Hongren to build him a reliquary; this reflects the practices

of Daoxuan's time, when it was common for the group of prominent disciples to record their names in inscriptions on reliquary niches dedicated to their masters. Beginning with the *Chuan fabao ji* and even more in the "Miscellaneous Dialogues," the singular Dharma-heir takes precedence over those who have a reliquary niche built and inscribed (Yanagida 1976a: 91).

143. *Shenyi* 神儀, lit. divine appearance.

144. Jingjue quotes a memorial inscription by Du Zhenglun in his *Zhu banruopoluomiduo xin jing* 注般若波羅蜜多心經 (Commentary on the *Prajñāpāramitāhṛdaya-sūtra*), and Enchin 円珍, who was in China from 853 to 858, lists a "Du Zhenglun song Shuangfengshan Xin chanshi beiwen yiben" 杜正倫送雙峰山信禪師碑文一本 (Memorial Inscription of Du Zhenglun's Farewell to Chan Master Xin of Mt. Twin Peaks, one book) in his *Nyū Tō guhō mokuroku* 入唐求法目録 (Catalogue of Texts from Travels into Tang China to Seek the Dharma), T. 55 (2172) 1101a19; see Yanagida 1971: 385; 1967: 327–333.

145. An unnecessary 信 was added by the copyist.

146. In previous sections this is part of a formula that begins 第子甚多, so here the lack of 甚多 may be a copyist error.

147. The last line is in half-space small characters.

148. The *Chuan fabao ji* (Yanagida 1971: 386–389) and *Lengqie shizi ji* (T. 85 [2837] 1289b11–1290a18) give the earliest accounts of Hongren, and the *Lidai fabao ji* is particularly dependent on the latter, despite criticism of Jingjue expressed in the section on Bodhidharma. The list of Hongren's disciples given in the *Lengqie shizi ji* was clearly important for the Bao Tang lineage, for it is the only supporting evidence that Zhishen, Wuxiang's great-grandfather in the Dharma, was a student of Hongren's (Yanagida 1976a: 95).

149. *Zuowu* 作務; this term has been used in support of the argument that physical labor was a special feature of Chan monasteries from the time of Daoxin, supposedly as a form of spiritual training and in the spirit of self-sufficiency that is mandated in the *Chanyuan qinggui* 禪苑清規 (Rules of Purity for Chan Monasteries) of 1103. However, scholars have begun to question this Japanese sectarian reading of early Chan texts. Here *zuowu* probably simply means the duties that novices and monks were expected to perform, a common feature in most Buddhist monasteries.

150. This description of Hongren's character is taken almost verbatim from the *Chuan fabao ji;* see Yanagida 1971: 386. The style is noticeably more refined and literary than the basic diction of the *Lidai fabao ji.*

151. A *chi* is approximately 14 cm. To say someone is eight *chi* tall is a trope to describe a distinguished man (Yanagida 1976a: 95).

152. This is based on the "Miscellaneous Dialogues" (Suzuki and Kōda 1934: 59).

153. Rao = Poyang 鄱陽 prefecture, Jiangxi.

154. This story of bandits is a *Lidai fabao ji* innovation, clearly modeled on the older story of Daoxin's rout of bandits in the previous section. The *Lidai fabao ji* authors were fond of taking a classic story and fashioning another episode to prefigure or echo it. This method of repeating motifs to create a sense of destiny or cosmic design is found in popular Buddhist works like the *Jātakas,* was also used in the *Fu fazang jing,* and may be said to be a common device in popular literature in general. Regarding the bandit they chose to feature, he apparently enjoyed a long life in popular and official memory. According the *Zizhi tongjian* 資治通鑑 (182), Ke Dahan began his career of banditry in 615 (eleventh year of the Daye 大業 era) and plundered the districts of Jingmian 荊沔 and Shannan 山南.

155. This story is also a *Lidai fabao ji* innovation. In 660 Gaozong suffered a stroke and thereafter his attention turned more toward the Daoists, but he continued to support Buddhism. In 659 he made contributions to the monks at Famen temple, in 660 he sponsored a devotional processional in Luoyang for the famous Famen temple finger-bone relic and in 661 ordered the repair of temples at Wutai shan (Weinstein 1987a: 37).
156. Since Hongren died fifteen years later, this should be read as a trope echoing the traditions regarding the length of the Buddha's teaching career or an approximation of Hongren's span as a teacher. If Hongren left Daoxin sometime after age thirty-seven and died at seventy-four, then he taught for about thirty-seven years.
157. This is based on the *Lengqie shizi ji*, but the names are rearranged and one is left out (no. 10, Yifang 義方); this is probably due to copyist error, as this leaves the count short. In the *Lidai fabao ji* Huineng is set aside from the herd, and in the *Lengqie shizi ji* this special treatment is reserved for Xuanze, who was Jingjue's teacher and compiled the work on which the *Lengqie shizi ji* was based. The *Lengqie shizi ji* list is as follows: Shenxiu, Zhishen, Liu Zhubu, Huizang, Xuanyue, Laoan, Faru, Huineng, Zhide, Yifang (T. 85 [2837] 1289c11–15). Regarding these masters, see Yanagida 1971: 282. A second version of the list occurs later in the *Lidai fabao ji* (section 11), where Zhishen is promoted to the head of the list: Zhishen, Shenxiu, Xuanze, Yifang, Zhide, Huizang, Faru, Laoan, Xuanyue, Liu Zhubu.
158. The *Lengqie shizi ji* has Hongren make a couple of disparaging remarks about masters in the list of ten: "The best are all dead, there are only ten remaining who carry on my way," and (regarding Faru, Huineng, and Zhide) "Although these [masters] taken together would be a fit teacher, they [each] are no more than one aspect of a figure" (Yanagida 1971: 273). The *Lidai fabao ji* authors exempt Huineng from this depreciation, but, interestingly, they allow Zhishen to remain. This may reflect the *Lidai fabao ji* authors' ambivalence about their ancestor, who provided an important link to Hongren but is otherwise treated as a lesser trustee of the robe on its journey to Wuzhu; see Yanagida 1976a: 97–98.
159. This passage, beginning with "the fifth year of the Xianheng era," is based closely on the *Lengqie shizi ji* (Yanagida 1971: 273). Regarding the dates of Hongren's death, see ibid.: 389.
160. In the *Lengqie shizi ji* it is Shenxiu who is Hongren's heir, and in the *Chuan fabao ji* it is Faru; see chapter 5 for a review of the versions of succession found in these "proto-Chan" texts.
161. The reference to this inscription is first found in the "Miscellaneous Dialogues," which claims that it was in Huangmei (Suzuki and Kōda 1934: 59–60). There is a short notice on the poet Lu Qiujun appended to the biography of Chen Zimao 陳子昴 in the *Tang shu* (190) 5025. Enchin's *Nyū Tō guhō mokuroku* lists a *Tang Qizhou Ren chanshi beiwen* 唐蘄州忍禪師碑文 (Memorial Inscription for the Tang Dynasty Chan Master Ren of Qizhou), but it is not known if this is the inscription referred to by Shenhui. See Yanagida 1967: 327–333.
162. 問 added interlinearly.
163. P. 2125 has 法 instead of 衣; the former makes more sense in this context.
164. 師 added interlinearly.
165. 塔 added interlinearly.
166. An interlinear mark indicates that 莫汝 should be reversed to 汝莫
167. An interlinear mark indicates that 被度 should be reversed to 度被.
168. The repetition of 忍 is apparently a copyist error.

169. The last three lines are in half-space small characters.
170. On Huineng's biographical materials in the *Platform Sūtra* and Shenhui's writings, see Yampolsky 1967; Yang 1993 and 1996.
171. Wang Wei's 王維 epitaph for Huineng disputes the claim that Huineng hailed from the Lu family, a prominent clan in Fanyang (*Liuzu Neng chanshi beiming* 六祖能禪師碑銘, *Tang wen cui* 唐文粹 [63]; see Jorgensen 2005: 145).
172. Caoqi is in Guangdong, Qujiang 曲江 prefecture. Fanyang is in northern Hebei. Xinzhou is in Guangdong, Xinxing 新興 prefecture (Yanagida 1976a: 101). Lingwai 嶺外 is the same as Lingnan 嶺南, in southwestern Guangdong, and this posting far from the capital would be a demotion.
173. "Lao" designated an aboriginal tribe in the southwest, now the largest ethnic minority in China (Yanagida 1976a: 104).
174. Commentators have noted the pregnancy and childbirth metaphors here; see ibid.: 104.
175. This is the Faru whose claim to the patriarchy was advanced in the *Chuan fabao ji* and rejected by Shenhui in the *Putidamo nanzong ding shifei lun.*
176. In the "Miscellaneous Dialogues," his surname is given as Chen 陳 (Suzuki and Kōda 1934: 61).
177. South Dayu prefecture in Jiangxi (Yanagida 1976a: 102).
178. This episode, including the dialogue between Huineng and Huiming, originates with the "Miscellaneous Dialogues" (Suzuki and Kōda 1934: 61–62). The scene atop Mt. Dayu became more elaborate in later versions of the *Platform Sūtra,* but the early Dunhuang manuscript of the *Platform Sūtra* does not yet include any dialogue (Yanagida 1976a: 105).
179. Northeast Yichun 宜春 prefecture in Jiangxi (ibid.: 102).
180. This disparagement of Huiming's teaching is an innovation of the *Lidai fabao ji.*
181. In the "Miscellaneous Dialogues" it says, "He withdrew to his former dwelling on Mt. Long in Xinzhou and built a stūpa" (Suzuki and Kōda 1934: 62).
182. The "Miscellaneous Dialogues" have Xuanjie 玄楷 and Zhiben 智本 rather than Zhihai 智海 (ibid.: 62). (Yanagida claims that the *Lidai fabao ji* manuscripts have Lijie 立楷 instead of Xuanjie [1976a: 105]. However, if one compares the manuscripts what appears to be the character *li* is an abbreviated form of *xuan*.)
183. In the "Miscellaneous Dialogues" the speech about succession is given after the date, the third day of the eighth month of the second year of Xiantian (Suzuki and Kōda 1934: 62). The main *Lidai fabao ji* innovation is the phrase "a woman has taken it away," which foreshadows the *Lidai fabao ji* authors' elaborate fabrication about Zhishen in Wu Zetian's court (see section 12). The "Miscellaneous Dialogues" has Huineng making a prediction about someone forty years later, and in the *Lidai fabao ji* the span is changed to twenty years. The former span appears to be keyed to Shenhui's proselytizing in c. 756, while the latter appears to be keyed to Shenhui's challenge at the great assembly at Dayun monastery in 732. This is because the *Lidai fabao ji* authors use the Dayun assembly scene to have Shenhui predict Wuzhu as the true heir; see section 16.
184. This account of strange phenomena is modeled after the account of the death of the Buddha in the *Mahāparinirvāṇa-sūtra;* this device is also used in the description of Wuxiang's death in section 15.
185. By imperial decree, Taichang temple was in charge of ancestral memorial rites. Wei Ju is unknown outside of a textual filiation derived from Shenhui—he is first mentioned in the "Miscellaneous Dialogues," where he is identified as a palace administrative

aide, *dianzhong cheng* 殿中承. The "Miscellaneous Dialogues" claims that Wei Ju's original inscription was rubbed out, and the restored inscription was at Caoqi and summarized the six generations of Dharma and robe transmission (Suzuki and Kōda 1934: 63; Yanagida 1976a: 106).

186. The *Putidamo nanzong ding shifei lun* claims that Shenxiu's disciple Puji sent his disciple Wu Pingyi 武平一 to efface the inscription on Huineng's stele and substitute another that said Shenxiu was the sixth patriarch; see Hu [1958] 1970: 289. Not surprisingly, Wu Pingyi's biography in the *Xin Tang shu* (119) makes no mention of such an episode, but the biography of Huineng in the *Song gaoseng zhuan* credits Wu Pingyi with a poem praising Huineng (T. 50 [2061] 755b25–26).

187. The claim that Song Ding wrote an inscription first appears in the *Lidai fabao ji* and is also in the *Song gaoseng zhuan* (T. 50 [2061] 755b). He was the person responsible for inviting Shenhui to Luoyang in 745 (Weinstein 1987a: 65). He is mentioned in the *Tang shu* in connection with Dong Xieman 東謝蠻 but is not given a full biography; see *Tang shu* (197)5275 and (222) 6320. According to the *Jinshi lu* 金石錄 of Zhao Mingcheng 趙明誠 in the Song, there was such a stele erected in 762 (Yanagida 1976a: 107).

188. P. 2125 has 為, but in S. 516 this variant wei 違 is used.

189. 中 added interlinearly.

190. 悪離 should be 悪見. P. 2125 and P. 3717 have the same mistake.

191. 作 added interlinearly.

192. 悪 added interlinearly.

193. Shi Le 石勒 was first ruler of the Later Zhao and died some thirty years before Daoan came to Xiangyang.

194. The version in the *Lidai fabao ji* (不依道安法師義不中難) loses the rhyme and rhythm of the *Gaoseng zhuan* original: *Xue bu shi An yi bu zhong nan* 學不師安義不中難 (T. 50 [2059] 353a15–16). Link credits Lyman Van Slyke for this translation: "If students be not pupils of An, difficult meanings will vex them anon." See Link 1958: 31.

195. The account of Daoan's teachings is condensed from his biography in the *Gaoseng zhuan*, T. 50 (2059) 351c3–354a17; see especially 353b23–27. Interestingly, this division into categories lends itself to phenomenological abstraction, as the first category concerns ordering ritual space, the second concerns ritual time, and the third concerns definition of the community.

196. The implicit point of this passage is that the forms in common use are all constructed in particular places and times and are not the eternal Buddha-Dharma.

197. From the translation by Śikṣānanda, the version most often quoted by the *Lidai fabao ji* authors: *Dasheng ru lengqie jing* 大乘入楞伽經, T. 16 (672) 619b23–24; see Appendix, no. 18. Hereafter referred to as the *Laṅkā-sūtra*.

198. As with many of the passages below, the *Lidai fabao ji* authors appear to have taken this from a favorite source, the Dunhuang compendium known as the *Zhujing yaochao* 諸經要抄 (Digest of Scriptures); see T. 85 (2819) 1196b28–29. The line is actually a pastiche of two different lines from fascicle seven of the *Laṅkā-sūtra*, T. 16 (672) 634c13 and 634c21.

199. *Laṅkā-sūtra*, T. 16 (672) 610a27–28; also found in the *Zhujing yaochao*, T. 85 (2819) 1195b1–2. The *Lidai fabao ji* authors use this quote twice more (T. 51 [2075] 190a6–7 [section 21] and 191a26–27 [section 24]). It is also included in the *Dunwu dasheng zhenglijue* 頓悟大乘正理決 (Verification of Sudden Awakening in the Mahāyāna), the account of the Lhasa debate from the Chinese perspective (P. 4646 and S. 2672; Yanagida 1976a: 118).

200. This passage is assembled from different couplets in a long gāthā in fascicle 7 of the *Laṅkā-sūtra,* T. 16 (672) 639b21 and 639c12–13. Two pairs of couplets from the gāthā were spliced together in the *Zhujing yaochao,* T. 85 (2819) 1197a9–11, but the *Lidai fabao ji* authors leave out the second couplet of the first pair.
201. *Jingangbanruopoluomi jing* 金剛般若波羅蜜經 (*Vajracchedikā-sūtra*), T. 8 (235) 750b9; see Appendix, no. 23. Also in the *Zhujing yaochao,* T. 85 (2819) 1194b2. This phrase is used three more times in the *Lidai fabao ji,* T. 51 (2075) 191b12 (section 25), 195b16 (section 41), and 196b4 (section 43). In the last instance the quotation is altered, and these are said to be Wuzhu's last words: 離一切諸相即是見佛. The phrase was a favorite with subitists in both China and Tibet; it appears in Shenhui's "Miscellaneous Dialogues" (Suzuki and Kōda 1934: 26) and his *Tanyu* (Hu [1958] 1970: 235), it was used six times in the above-mentioned *Dunwu dasheng zhenglijue,* and it also appears in P. Tib. 116 (Yanagida 1976a: 118).
202. *Vajracchedikā-sūtra,* T. 8 (235) 752a17–18; also in the *Zhujing yaochao,* T. 85 (2819) 1194a14–15. This is quoted again, along with the preceding phrase, in section 41, T. 51 (2075) 195b16–17. It is also used in Shenhui's *Guanxin lun* 觀心論 and in the *Xiuxin yaolun* 修心要論 attributed to Hongren (Yanagida 1976a: 118).
203. Loosely based on the *Sheng siyifantian suowen jing* 勝思益梵天所問經 (*Viśeṣacintibrahma-paripṛcchā-sūtra*), T. 15 (586) 47c11–13. Of the three translations, the *Lidai fabao ji* version is closest to the Kumārajīva translation, see Appendix, no. 19. Also in the *Zhujing yaochao,* T. 85 (2819) 1196a15–17.
204. Loosely based on the *Viśeṣacintibrahma-paripṛcchā-sūtra,* T. 15 (586) 37b3–8; this part does not appear in the *Zhujing yaochao.* Different arrangements of these phrases are used three times: T. 51 (2075) 183a9–10 (this section), 192b18–20 (section 31), and 195b29–c2 (section 42).
205. One of the "contemplations of impurity," the "Nine Visualizations" (usually rendered 九想) refers to the well-known contemplation of the nine stages of corpse decay in order to overcome attachment to the physical; contemplation of white bones is the eighth stage.
206. The "Five Cessations" is one of the larger categories of contemplation practices, and includes the contemplations of impurity and breath counting; these practices are designed to counteract greed, anger, ignorance, delusion of self, and disordered mind (*Zengaku daijiten*: 346d).
207. The last five contemplations are included in the sixteen contemplations in the popular *Guan wuliangshou jing* 觀無量壽經 (*Amitāyurbuddhānusmṛti-sūtra*), T. 12 (365); see Nakamura 1980: 662c–d. These contemplations are depicted frequently in Dunhuang murals and scrolls.
208. = *Chan miyaofa jing* 禪秘要法經, T. 15 (613). This is not a direct quotation, but these improvised examples reflect the general tenor of the scripture; see ibid.: 246a15–b17 and 251a 13–14.
209. From the *Chanmen jing,* S. 5532; in Suzuki 1968–71: 3: 334. See Appendix, no. 16.
210. *Laṅkā-sūtra,* T. 16 (672) 602a28.
211. *Faju jing* 法句經, T. 85 (2901) 1435a21–22; see Appendix, no. 11.
212. *Jingang sanmei jing* 金剛三昧經 (*Vajrasamādhi-sūtra*), T. 9 (273) 368a12–13 and 370b3; see Appendix, no. 10. Different versions of this pastiche are used four times in the *Lidai fabao ji*: T. 51 (2075) 183a25 (this section); 186a13–14 (section 17); 193a9–10 (section 31); and 195b2 (section 40). Here an introductory "I" is added to signal that it is the Buddha speaking; the original is couched as the Buddha's instructions to the bodhisattva Xinwang.

213. *Viśeṣacintibrahma-paripṛcchā-sūtra*, T. 15 (586) 37c17–18.

214. This is a summary of a passage in the *Weimojie suo shuo jing* 維摩詰所說經 (*Vimalakīrtinirdeśa-sūtra*), T. 14 (475) 521c3ff; see Appendix, no. 21. The first part is also commented on by Shenhui in his "Miscellaneous Dialogues" (Suzuki and Kōda 1934: 14–15).

215. There is nothing precisely corresponding to this line, but a similar passage can be found in the Dharmamitra translation, *Foshuo zhuan nushen jing* 佛說轉女身經, T. 14 (564) 916b22–24; see Appendix, no. 7.

216. *Juedingpini jing* 決定毘尼經 (*Vinayaviniścaya-Upālipariprcchā-sūtra*), T. 12 (325) 40b7–8 is a near match; see Appendix, no. 8. Notably, the thrust of the section is that the bodhisattvas receive all-at-once the essence of the precepts (*kaitongjie* 開通戒), while *śrāvaka*s are obsessed with transgressions and distinctions.

217. See Appendix, no. 22; the extant texts do not include this phrase. It is used again in section 34, T. 51 (2075) 194a13.

218. In the *Lidai fabao ji*, *Foding jing* 佛頂経 and *Dafoding jing* 大佛頂経 both refer to the Tang apocryphal *Śūraṃgama-sūtra*, T. 19 (945); see Appendix, no. 9. This phrase appears frequently in the scripture, as for example in the final quotation in this section; see T. 19 (945) 147a28. It is not clear why the *Lidai fabao ji* manuscripts include *ciqi* 此七 at the end of the phrase, but it appears to be an error and I leave it untranslated.

219. The passage in the *Lidai fabao ji* is actually a pastiche of the three sections from the original, with minor variations; see the *Fozang jing* 佛藏經 (*Buddhapiṭakaduḥśīlanirgraha-sūtra*), T. 15 (653) 790a26–b2. See Appendix, no. 12.

220. Ibid.: 790b5–8.

221. Ibid.: 803b21–26; also in the *Zhujing yaochao*, T. 85 (2819) 1195c2–7.

222. Arhats-in-training who have not yet reached the fourth and final level, *arhatva*.

223. This means a monk who practices samādhi but does not study, and who therefore mistakes the fourth level of dhyāna meditation for nirvāṇa. The *icchantika* Sunakṣatra is a classic example from the *Nirvāṇa-sūtra;* he falls into Avīci Hell because he mistakes the fourth level of dhyāna for nirvāṇa and then holds that there is no nirvāṇa, and that the arhats will also be reborn.

224. From the *Śūraṃgama-sūtra*, T. 19 (945) 147a21–b1.

225. This claim about the gold-embroidered robe is based on Shenhui's *Dingshifei lun*, in Hu [1958] 1970: 285. See discussion in chapter 5.

226. Should be reversed: 言為.

227. P. 2125 has interlinear marks indicating that 忍大師 should be repeated.

228. 師 added interlinearly.

229. That is, disciples privileged to engage in public dialogue with the master and seek private instruction.

230. As noted, there is a similar list of Hongren's disciples in section 8 at the scene of Hongren's passing, but here Zhishen is promoted to the head of the list, as he is the protagonist of the next two sections.

231. Wang Wei's 王維 epitaph for Huineng claims that he lived among commoners as a laborer during this time (*Liuzu Neng chanshi beiming* 六祖能禪師碑銘; see Yanagida 1967: 540; Jorgensen 2005: 145).

232. A.k.a. *Guangxiao si* 光孝寺, this is one of the oldest and most eminent temples in Nanhai, located in present-day Qingzhou city. It was established in 362, its famous ordination platform was established in c. 439, and Paramārtha was said to have planted a slip of the Bodhi tree there in 502. It was renowned for scripture translation, and it was purported to be where the apocryphal *Śuramgama-sūtra* was translated.

The *Guangxiao si yifa taji* 光孝寺瘞髮塔記 (Reliquary Inscription for the Interment of [Huineng's] Hair at Guangxiao Monastery) features Huineng's meeting with Yinzong, and it includes a verse in which Paramārtha predicts that 160 years after his death an incarnated bodhisattva (i.e., Huineng) will come to the Bodhi tree that he planted (Yanagida 1967: 535–536; Jorgensen 2005: 720). However, Jorgensen argues that the latter work is a post-Tang forgery (ibid.: 726–728).

233. Yinzong 印宗 (627–713) was preeminent in study of the *Nirvāṇa-sutra* in the south; see his biography in the *Song gaoseng zhuan* (T. 50 [2061] 731b8–26). The *Lidai fabao ji* story of his encounter with Huineng may have been inspired by the mention in Wang Wei's *Liuzu Neng chanshi beiming* (Yanagida 1967: 540; Jorgensen 2005: 147).
234. The flag-and-wind dialogue may have originated with the *Lidai fabao ji* and is further elaborated in the *Caoqi dashi zhuan* (*ZZ*. II, 19, 5: 484c) and in the Yuan dynasty *Liuzu tanjing* (*T*. 48 [2008] 349c10–350a2). It probably made its way to Tibet through the medium of the *Lidai fabao ji;* see Yanagida 1983a: 16–17.
235. Interlinear marks indicate repetition of 能禅師.
236. Interlinear marks indicate repetition of 能禅師.
237. Interlinear marks indicate repetition of 詵禅師.
238. 請 missing only in S. 516.
239. 赭 is a vulgate variant of zhe 這 (Yanagida 1976a: 135).
240. 諮 added interlinearly.
241. P. 2125 has 簡, which would be more likely to be used in a name.
242. As is well-known, Gaozong's widow Wu Zetian (623–705) established her own Zhou dynasty in 690, supplanting the Tang heirs. In official historical sources, she also established the Dayun monasteries in 690; see Forte 1976:3–54. Yanagida claims that 692 is a deliberate falsification on the part of the *Lidai fabao ji* authors (Yanagida 1976a:134), but one must keep in mind that we do not know what sources the *Lidai fabao ji* authors used for their fabrications (and the story of her inviting Zhishen to court is almost certainly a fabrication). The Tang archives were destroyed by An Lushan in 756, and the earliest extant official account of the Dayun proclamation is in the *Tang shu* (completed in 945) and is based on the sketchy coverage of Empress Wu's reign in the *Guo shi* 國史 compiled by Liu Fang in 760.
243. Zhang Changqi was the brother of the two lovers of Empress Wu, Zhang Changzong 張昌期 and Zhang Yizhi 張易之. See *Tang shu* (78) 2706; *Xin Tang shu* (72) 2718 and (104) 4014. Including his name is the *Lidai fabao ji* authors' innovation; see Jorgensen 2005: 158.
244. The circumstances surrounding the invitation vary according to the sources, but all agree that Huineng declined to go. See Wang Wei's *Liuzu Neng chanshi beiming,* in Jorgensen 2005: 148; the *Caoqi dashi zhuan* 曹溪大師傳, ZZ. II, 19, 5: 486; and *Tang shu* (191) 5109.
245. *Nei daochang* 内道場. On the practice of having a private chapel where monks expounded on scripture for the Imperial household, see Chen 2004. It was in the imperial chapel in Luoyang that the Empress Wu's clerical supporters presented the *Dayun jing* commentary to her; see Forte 1976: 3.
246. There is no seventh month of the second year of Wansui Tongtian, the reign name was changed after fourteen months. There is no other record claiming that Zhishen was invited to court (Yanagida 1976a: 134).
247. Jingzhou = northwest Dangyang 當陽 prefecture, in Hubei. In Shenxiu's (d. 706) epitaph it is recorded that he was invited to court by Empress Wu in this year (700); *Jingzhou Yuquansi Datong chanshi beiming bing xu* 荊州玉泉寺大通禪師碑銘并序 (Stele

Inscription for Chan Master Datong [Shenxiu] of Yuquan Monastery in Jingzhou, with preface), in QTW (231) 5.2953–2954; Yanagida 1976a: 134.

248. Anzhou = southwest Yingshan 應山 prefecture, in Hubei. In Jingjue's preface to the *Lengqie shizi ji,* he says that in the second year of Jinglong 景龍 (708) Xuanze (d.u.) was invited to court at Chang'an by Zhongzong and subsequently went on to Luoyang, where Jingjue became his disciple (T. 85 [2837] 1283a6–8).

249. Suizhou = Suiyang 隨陽 prefecture, in Hubei. There is no other record claiming that Xuanyue (d.u.) was invited to court (Yanagida 1976a: 135).

250. Mt. Song is near Luoyang, in Henan. In the *Fozu lidai tongzai* 佛祖歷代通載 it is claimed that Huian (a.k.a. Laoan, 582–709) was invited to court in the first year of the Tiance wansui 天冊萬歲 era (695) (T. 49 [2036] 584b9 and b15).

251. As noted in chapter 5, this encounter is reminiscent of a mind-reading contest in the *Zhuangzi;* see trans. in Watson 1964: 92–94. In the *Fozu tongji* 佛祖統記 (Sequential Record of the Buddhas and Patriarchs) there is a similar story of a mind-reading contest between Huian and a prophetess who calls herself a bodhisattva (T. 49 [2035] 370a26–b5). (I am indebted to John Kieschnick for this reference.) The *Lidai fabao ji* story may have been the model for a story of a contest of powers between Huineng's disciple Huizhong 慧忠 (d. 775) and a Trepiṭaka in Suzong's court; this is found in Huizhong's biography in the *Jingde chuandeng lu,* where the episode is also made the subject of *wenda* 問答 "encounter" dialogue (T. 51 [2076] 244a13–24).

252. As noted in chapter 5, in the *Zutang ji* 祖堂集 (Anthology from the Patriarchal Hall) there is an episode in which Empress Wu makes Huian and Shenxiu take a bath with female bathing attendants, and Huian is successful in manifesting "no-desire" (*Zutang ji* [18], in Yanagida 1974: 348a).

253. This would refer to the translation in 80 *juan,* c. 695–699, by Śikṣānanda, T. 10 (279); see Appendix, no. 14. In Śikṣānanda's biography in the *Song gaoseng zhuan,* it is claimed that Empress Wu composed a preface for the translation and wrote the title in her own hand (T. 50 [2061] 718c25–26).

254. *Fanhua* 幡花 is mentioned as a kind of offering in several sources and probably means banners of fine cotton, which was a relatively rare material in the Tang.

255. This is impossible, as Empress Wu died in the eleventh month of the first year of Shenlong 神龍, 705. This episode probably originated with the *Lidai fabao ji,* and it was taken up in later sources with further permutations of the anachronism. The *Caoqi dashi zhuan* states that in the third year of the Shenlong 神龍 era (707, the same as the first year of the Jinglong era cited in the *Lidai fabao ji*), Emperor Gaozong (d. 683) sent a *mona* (linen) *kāṣāya* and five hundred rolls of silk to Huineng as an offering (*Caoqi dashi zhuan,* ZZ. II, 19, 5: 486b). In the *Song gaoseng zhuan* it is said that in the third year of the Shenlong era Huian (Laoan, 582–709) received a *mona* robe at court (*Song gaoseng zhuan,* T. 50 [2061] 823c13). In the *Song gaoseng zhuan* version it is not clear whether the empress or her son Zhongzong 中宗 (r. 705–710) was supposed to have made the bestowal, since 707 was during Zhongzong's reign and the passage merely states that Huian received the robe when he came to court to be honored. In the *Jingde chuandeng lu,* it is said that in the first year of the Shenlong era Zhongzong invited Laoan and Shenxiu to court to honor them. They tell him that Huineng has got the robe and the Dharma, and the imperial messenger Xue Jian is dispatched to invite Huineng to court, and he declines. A dialogue between Huineng and the messenger ensues, and Xue Jian is enlightened. He returns to court and reports Huineng's words, and the emperor sends Huineng a *mona kāṣāya,* five hundred rolls of silk, and a jeweled bowl (T. 51 [2076] 235c25–236a24). A version with the same

date as the *Lidai fabao ji*, and the claim that the invitation was extended by both Wu Zetian and Zhongzong, appears in the Yuan edition of the *Liuzu tanjing*, T. 48 (2008) 359c12–360a22.

256. *Neishi* 內侍 is a common designation for eunuchs (Hucker 4237). Xue Jian 薛間 is previously unknown, but in the above-mentioned versions of the story in the *Jingde chuandeng lu* and the Yuan *Liuzu tanjing*, he receives teachings from Huineng and is enlightened.

257. *Mona* 摩納 was a prized cloth, probably fine linen from Korea (see Nakamura: 1280d). Wang Wei's epitaph for Huineng mentions the sending of a *baina* 百納 robe (*Liuzu Neng chanshi beiming*, in Yanagida 1967: 540). As noted above, a *mona* robe is one of the imperial offerings given to Huineng in the stories in the *Caoqi dashi zhuan*, the *Jingde chuandeng lu*, and the Yuan dynasty *Liuzu tanjing*. The *Fozu tongji* (T. 49 [2035] 370b12–14) mentions that an alms-bowl, *mona* robe, and fine tea were conferred on Huineng in the first year of Wansui tongtian (696), the year that the *Lidai fabao ji* authors claim Empress Wu obtained Bodhidharma's robe from Huineng. Zanning, compiler of the *Song gaoseng zhuan*, may have been modifying the *Lidai fabao ji* story when he claimed that Empress Wu gave Chuji a *mona* robe that he then gave to Wuxiang (T. 50 [2061] 832b15–19). See Jorgensen 2005: 288–89 for a related set of speculations on the mona robe.

258. *Ruyao* 乳藥. The term originally referred to a poison used for suicide, but later referred to an herb (or fungus) with magically efficacious properties that was given as an auspicious gift. Morohashi 1. 396.

259. The manuscript has *xun* 薰 (fragrance), but it is likely that *hun* 葷 (garlic, meat, strong foods) is meant.

260. Repetition of 大師 indicated by interlinear marks.

261. A prefecture in Henan.

262. Zhishen was thirteen in 621, and Xuanzang (602–664) received the precepts at Konghui 空惠 monastery in Chengdu at around that time, at age twenty. So it is unlikely that Zhishen could have become his disciple. Xuanzang left Shu the following year, in 622, and there is no mention of Zhishen leaving Shu until he went to Mt. Shuangfeng (Yanagida 1976a: 138). In any case, the name Xuanzang represents scholasticism and often serves as a trope in Chan treatises.

263. This is taken from the biography of Hongren in the *Lengqie shizi ji*, in which Hongren says that, among his disciples, both Zhishen and Liu Zhubu 劉主簿 have a literary nature (Yanagida 1971: 273).

264. In the biography of Weikuan 惟寬 in the *Song gaoseng zhuan*, there is an appended notice for Baoxiu 寶修 of Zizhou that says that he studied with a master at Dechun monastery who had studied with Hongren, possibly referring to Zhishen (T. 50 [2061] 768b4–6).

265. The first two works are nonextant, but the last one has survived; see Yanagida 1972a. The commentary shows the influence of Xuanzang's Yogācāra.

266. The only contemporaneous mention of this master-disciple relationship was probably based on the *Lidai fabao ji* itself; this is Lu Wen's 呂溫 inscription for Chuji's disciple Chengyuan 承遠, the *Nanyue Mituosi Chengyuan heshang bei* 南嶽彌陀寺承遠和尚碑, in QTW (630) (Yanagida 1976a: 138).

267. 四年 added interlinearly.

268. Text has 此云, corrected for the sake of punctuation.

269. 師 added interlinearly.

270. Mianzhou = Mianyang 綿陽 prefecture, Sichuan.
271. The biography of Chuji in the *Song gaoseng zhuan* claims that he was the disciple of Baoxiu 寶修 (T. 50 [2061] 836b8).
272. The biography of Chuji in the *Song gaoseng zhuan* does not make any claims about transmission, but includes an episode in which Chuji correctly predicts a visit from Wuxiang (T. 50 [2061] 836b14–16). It is also claimed that Zetian summoned Chuji to the capital and gave him a *saṃghāṭi* robe made of *mona* cloth (ibid.: 836b10). The *Lidai fabao ji* authors claim that a robe of this material was given by Zetian to Huineng; see section 12.
273. The *Lidai fabao ji* dates for Chuji are thus 669–736. In the *Song gaoseng zhuan* biography it is claimed that Chuji died in Kaiyuan 22 (734) at the age of eighty-seven, thus making his dates 648–734 (T. 50 [2061] 836b28). The *Taishō* edition of the *Lidai fabao ji* also has the year as Kaiyuan 22 (184c10), which is an error; the Stein and Pelliot manuscripts of the *Lidai fabao ji* have Kaiyuan 24.
274. An interlinear mark indicates that 金姓 should be reversed to 姓金.
275. 戒 added interlinearly.
276. 教 added interlinearly.
277. 念不起是定門 added interlinearly.
278. In S. 516, 現 is regularly written as 見.
279. The most extensive biography of Wuxiang is found in the *Song gaoseng zhuan*, T. 50 (2061) 832b—833a. The *Song gaoseng zhuan* biography also says that Wuxiang was the third son of a king, but this rank, also attributed to Bodhidharma, may well be a trope. In the *Song gaoseng zhuan* there is a similarly named monk Wulou 無漏 (d. 762) who was also said to be a Korean with the surname Kim, to be the third son of a king, and to be noted for asceticism (T. 50 [2061] 846a24-c12). Jan Yün-hua argues that both could have been third sons, but of different kings, as there were four reign changes during the period in question (1990: 44–45).
280. Yanagida surmises that *shou dao* 授刀 in the manuscript should be changed to *jiang dao* 將刀, as translated here (1976a: 150).
281. *Guizhen* 歸貞: to attain awakening, or to die.
282. This story of Wuxiang's sister is a *Lidai fabao ji* innovation that was not taken up by any other source.
283. According to the *Song gaoseng zhuan* he arrived in China in Kaiyuan 16 (728) and immediately obtained a meeting with Emperor Xuanzong (T. 50 [2061] 832b13–14). The *Song gaoseng zhuan* also claims that Wuxiang was honored by Xuanzong in Chengdu after the emperor fled to Sichuan (ibid.: 832b29). Jan Yün-hua points out a possible corroborating notice in a Korean chronicle, the *Dongguo tongjian* 東國通鑑, which says that the son of a Korean king had an audience with Xuanzong in 728 (1990: 46). However, the *Dongguo tongjian* was compiled in 1485, and Jan does not discuss the sources on which it is based.
284. Taking the "Bhaiṣajya-rāja" chapter of the *Lotus Sūtra* as inspiration, this form of self-immolation is frequently mentioned in hagiographies and is still practiced to this day.
285. Tiangu shan 天谷山, southwest Guan 灌 district in Sichuan.
286. The *Song gaoseng zhuan* version of the story is that Wuxiang had an audience with Zhishen when he entered Shu; however, as Jan Yün-hua points out, this would have been impossible, as Zhishen died in 702 and Wuxiang arrived in China in 728 (1990: 46). In the *Song gaoseng zhuan* the narrative shifts to Chuji without any indication that

Chuji was Zhishen's disciple, and Chuji is said to have received a nine-piece *mona* robe from Wu Zetian, to have predicted Wuxiang's arrival at his monastery (this echoes a passage in Chuji's *Song gaoseng zhuan* biography; see note 272), to have given Wuxiang his Dharma name, and to have given the *mona* robe to Wuxiang in the middle of the night (T. 50 [2061] 832b15–19).

287. There are two passages involving beasts in the *Song gaoseng zhuan* biography of Wuxiang; it is said that he remained in meditation even when two bullocks fought nearby and one put its hoof on his stomach, and it is said that he washed himself and offered his naked body as a meal for two tigers, who thereafter became his companions (T. 50 [2061] 832b19–25). In Tibet, Wuxiang morphed into an arhat with a tiger companion; see Yamaguchi 1984.

288. The *Song gaoseng zhuan* notes that it was through the good offices of Zhangqiu Jianqiong 章仇兼瓊 that Wuxiang was invited to Emperor Xuanzong's court in exile in Shu (T. 50 [2061] 832b28–29). He is also mentioned as Wuxiang's patron in Li Shangyin's memorial inscription (QTW [780] 8.8141c). Although the *Lidai fabao ji* does not elaborate, this distinction greatly enhanced Wuxiang's prestige in Shu and is mentioned in Tibetan sources. Zhangqiu was a military commissioner in Yizhou (Sichuan) and was lauded for his participation in the war against the Tibetans. There are numerous references to him in the Tang histories; see especially *Tang shu* (196) 5234–5235, and *Xin Tang shu* (216) 6086. Yanagida notes that he was among those known as "slick Buddhists" (*ning fojia* 佞佛家), politicians who used their Buddhist affiliations for political advantage (1983a: 21).

289. According to the *Lidai fabao ji* Wuzhu was there for eight years, from 759 to 766. Baiyai 白崖 (White Cliff) was not an uncommon place name. Yanagida (1976a: 152) identifies these Baiyai mountains as the same ones noted in the biography of Fajin 法進 in the *Xu gaoseng zhuan*, located in the Changlong 昌隆 (a.k.a. Changming 昌明) district of Minzhou 綿州, in modern Sichuan's Zhangming 彰明 prefecture, northeast of Chengdu. The *Jingde chuandeng lu* notice for Wuzhu mistakenly locates them in Nanyang 南陽 (T. 51 [2076] 234b11). The problem with Yanagida's identification is that in section 19 Wuzhu's Baiyai mountains are said to be west of the Canyai 蠶崖 pass, which is in Guan 灌 prefecture, northwest of Chengdu. Both sites are in the mountains bordering the western plateau and would have been part of the contested frontier in Wuzhu's day, but the Zhangming location is twice as far from Chengdu and is not near the Canyai pass.

290. Yanagida suggests that the word order of the manuscript be changed from the incomprehensible *ji ci he lai* 計此合來 to the colloquially comprehensible 計合此來; *jihe* means "surely" (1976a: 152).

291. This scene is repeated at greater length in Wuzhu's biography in section 18, where it is clarified that Dong Xuan was originally dispatched by Wuzhu. Note that the *Lidai fabao ji* authors establish a precedent for indirect transmission via servants by claiming that the transmission between Chuji and Wuxiang was also accomplished in this manner.

292. A river that flows past Gayā; this trope is drawn from the account of the Buddha's *pairinirvāṇa* in the *Nirvāṇa-sūtra.*

293. The *Lidai fabao ji* has Wuxiang's dates as 684–762, but the *Song gaoseng zhuan* says he died in 756 at the age of seventy-seven, rendering the dates 680–756 (T. 50 [2061] 832c20–21).

294. *Shouyuan* 受緣 appears to refer to a kind of precepts ceremony.

295. *Daochang* 道場 was a term for the ritual space set up for bodhisattva precepts retreats. As discussed in chapter 6, Zongmi describes Wuxiang's precepts ceremony in great detail.
296. *Wuyi wunian mowang* 無憶無念莫妄. The last character, *wang* (false or delusion), is disputed, as is further developed in section 20.
297. *Zongzhi men* 總持門: *zongzhi* is a translation of *dhāraṇī*, and *zongzhi men* usually refers to esoteric teachings. Here it seems to correspond to the sense of *dhāraṇī* as "perfectly maintained, unbroken practice," such as it appears in the *Vimalakīrti-sūtra* (*Zengaku daijiten*: 731).
298. In section 34, it is said that common persons are "drunk on the wine of ignorance" (T. 51 [2075] 194a11).
299. *Dasheng qi xin lun* 大乘起信論 (Treatise on Arousal of Faith in the Mahāyāna), T. 32 (1666 and 1667), an apocryphon attributed to Aśvaghoṣa. See Hakeda 1967: 31.
300. In the *Nirvāṇa-sūtra*, the metaphors of deer and dog are used to illustrate the intractability of the mind—the fearless domestic dog represents the passion of anger, difficult to get rid of, while the shy forest deer represents compassion, easy to lose (T. 12 [374] 453c26–28).
301. *Wenzi* 文字 is a pun, meaning both "texts and characters" and design.
302. Waves and ocean are well-known Yogācāra similes for the nonduality of the turbulent sense-consciousnesses and the unfathomable storehouse consciousness; see, for example, the use of this metaphor in a gāthā in the *Laṅkāvatāra-sūtra*, T. 16 (670): 484b9–485a9.
303. This is based on a story in the *Dīrghāgama*, T. 1 (1) 45b3–c1.
304. 立知見 added interlinearly.
305. 信 added interlinearly.
306. 槃 added interlinearly.
307. 尒許多 is colloquial, meaning an indeterminate number (Yanagida 1976a: 161).
308. 只沒 is a colloquial compound with the same meaning as 只, "only" (ibid.).
309. The authors were summarizing from the *Putidamo nanzong ding shifei lun*, in Hu [1958] 1970: 277. It is necessary to add these two characters in order to replicate the meaning of the *Putidamo nanzong ding shifei lun* passage.
310. 事大 should be reversed to 大事.
311. 頭 added interlinearly.
312. 法師是 should be 是法師.
313. 已 should be 巴 (Yanagida 1976a: 163).
314. 玄楷答 is clearly a copyist's mix-up with the next sentence. There are some interlinear marks that probably mean an editor or reader noticed the interpolation.
315. 師 added interlinearly.
316. "Purity Chan" is a reference to *kanjing* 看淨, "viewing purity," a practice associated with the Northern School. McRae points out that for Shenxiu this meant the ultimate pure mind or reality (thus no different from *jian foxing* 見佛性, seeing Buddha-nature) and was not used dualistically as Shenhui and his heirs claimed (1986: 229–230). The *Laṅkā-sūtra* classifies four types of dhyāna, of which *tathāgata-dhyāna* (如來禪) is the highest, and in the gāthā this is referred to as *rulai qingjing chan* 如來清淨禪 (T. 16 [672] 602a10–25). Zongmi, in his *Chanyuan zhu quanji duxu*, uses the term *qingjing rulai chan* to designate the highest type of dhyāna (*Zengaku daijiten*: 994–995).
317. Hua 滑 prefecture, in Henan. The assembly referred to is the *wuzhe dahui* 無遮大會 (unrestricted great assembly) of 732 at Dayun 大雲 monastery in Huatai.

318. In the *Putidamo nanzong ding shifei lun* there is an assertion with similar wording and exactly the opposite import; denouncing Puji's claim to the "Southern lineage," Shenhui says that he himself is the only one who can explain its tenets and establish the true Dharma (Hu [1958] 1970: 293).
319. Shenhui settled at Heze monastery in 745, but this exchange is taken from the record of Shenhui's debate in 732.
320. *Sanxian shisheng* 三賢十聖 refers to the divisions of the bodhisattva path according to the *Avataṃsaka-sūtra;* the fifty-two stages are divided into three levels, and the "ten holinesses" means the ten *bhūmis* (Yanagida 1976a: 161).
321. *Dabanniepan jing* 大般涅槃經 (*Nirvāṇa-sūtra*), T. 12 (374) 372b26–27; Appendix, no. 17. The same quote is used in the *Putidamo nanzong ding shifei lun;* in Hu [1958] 1970: 276.
322. The *Nirvāṇa-sūtra* passage says that if a person can explain the *Nirvāṇa-sūtra,* it means that he has seen Buddha-nature (T. 12 [374] 526a29–b1). The *Lidai fabao ji* authors have conflated different parts of the *Putidamo nanzong ding shifei lun* to make the exchange more confrontational; compare Hu [1958] 1970: 277 and 311.
323. This passage is adapted from the *Putidamo nanzong ding shifei lun,* in Hu [1958] 1970: 277; see discussion in chapter 5. Shenhui uses the technical terminology of Buddhist logic and analysis of cognition; the means of knowledge are divided into categories such as direct perception, knowledge based on the scriptures, inference, and deduction of error.
324. The comparable passage in the *Putidamo nanzong ding shifei lun* indirectly alludes to Shenhui's own inheritance of the transmission; see Hu [1958] 1970: 286.
325. Jiangling 江陵 prefecture, in Hubei. During Shenhui's period of exile from 753 to 756, he moved to Jingzhou in 754 (Yanagida 1976a: 162).
326. This is a deliberately garbled version of Wuxiang's teachings as given in the previous section.
327. Santai 三臺 prefecture, in Sichuan.
328. Renshou 仁壽 prefecture, in Sichuan.
329. Mianyang 綿陽 prefecture, in Sichuan.
330. The Chengdu area.
331. The *Lidai fabao ji* authors make Shenhui the mouthpiece for this negative assessment of Wuxiang's or Wuzhu's rivals in Sichuan, who are otherwise unknown. According to the Chan ranking of masters, a Dharma master was lowest, a Vinaya master was in the middle, and a Chan master was the highest; this is expressed in the *Shisike song* 十四科頌 attributed to the Liang monk Baozhi 寶誌 (*Jingde chuandeng lu,* T. 51 [2076] 451b19–c1229).
332. This episode at Huineng's stūpa is a fiction created by the *Lidai fabao ji* authors. However, the *Putidamo nanzong ding shifei lun* has a dramatic scene in which one of Puji's disciples tries to steal the robe, and Huineng laments, "At Great Master Ren's place this *kāṣāya* was stolen three times, and Great Master Ren said that at Great Master Xin's place it was stolen once. This would-be thief stole nothing at all. Because of this *kāṣāya,* south and north, ordained and lay, and zenith and nadir are confused, and sword and cudgel often confront one another" (Hu [1958] 1970: 293). The *Caoqi dashi zhuan* has the most extensive account of the installation of the robe in a stūpa in Caoqi (Jorgensen 2005: 703–704).
333. 為 probably should be 謂.
334. 无 added interlinearly.

335. 輪 probably should be 淪.
336. Identification of Wuzhu with the Dali 大曆 era (766–779) Bao Tang monastery indicates the recent founding or rededication of the monastery.
337. According to Li Shangyin's 李商隱 (813–858) *Tang Zizhou huiyijingshe nanchanyuan sizhengtang beiming* 唐梓州慧義精舍南禪院四證堂碑銘 (QTW 780) and the *Jingde chuandeng lu* (T. 51 [2076] 226c16), the Bao Tang monastery was in Yizhou, but the exact location is unclear. Weinstein (1987a: 138) notes that after the Huichang era persecution (841–846) many monasteries were restored with "patriotic, if bland, names" like Bao Tang or Tang'an (Tranquility of the Tang). For example, in the *Tang huiyao* 唐會要 (49) there is the record of a petition submitted at the end of the persecution, when Emperor Wuzong 武宗 was dying; one entry in the petition reads: "first month of the sixth year of the Huichang era: Bodhi monastery changed to Bao Tang monastery." Therefore, by the latter half of the ninth century the identity of Wuzhu's Dali-era Bao Tang monastery could have been confused with other more recently designated sites.
338. Wuzhu's reinterpretation of the bodhisattva precepts ritual is based on the well-known *bodhimaṇḍa* passage in the *Vimalakīrti-sutra,* T. 14 (475) 542c13–543a8. A few lines from the beginning of this sermon were translated into Tibetan, in Pelliot Tib. 116; Yanagida 1976a: 166.
339. These two sentences are used again in section 33 (T. 51 [2075] 193b13–14), but there it is the scriptures that point, rather than "Good Friends."
340. A different version of the passage from "All beings are fundamentally pure" to "no-thought itself is not" is given in T. 51 (2075) 189c8–10 (section 21). There two repetitions of the line "it is because beings have thought that one provisionally teaches no-thought, but if there is no presence of thought, then no-thought itself is not"; see T. 51 (2075) 186a9 (this section) and 189c9–10 (section 21). There are two repetitions of a close variation, "it is because beings have thought that one provisionally teaches no-thought, but at the time of true no-thought, no-thought itself is not"; see T. 51 (2075) 189b1–2 (section 20) and 194c19–20 (section 37).
341. *Vajrasamādhi-sūtra,* T. 9 (273) 371a3.
342. This appears to be a misconstrual of a gāthā in the *Vajrasamādhi-sūtra,* 覺本無生, 離眾生垢, 覺本無寂, 離涅槃動 (awareness is fundamentally unborn, transcending the stains of beings; awareness is fundamentally non-still, transcending the movement of nirvāṇa) (T. 9 [273] 368c27–28).
343. *Vajrasamādhi-sūtra,* T. 9 (273) 368a12–13 and 370b3. Versions of this pastiche are used four times in the *Lidai fabao ji:* T. 51 (2075) 183a25 (section 10); 186a13–14 (this occurrence); 193a9–10 (section 31); and 195b2 (section 40).
344. 輪 should be 倫.
345. 明 added interlinearly.
346. 想 should be 相.
347. P. 2125 has 意 instead of 音.
348. P. 2125 has 妄.
349. The repetition of 朗 and 蕩 is indicated interlinearly.
350. 路山 should be 山路, interlinear marks indicate reversal.
351. Interlinear marks indicate that this 而 is a mistake.
352. Text has 豈念, interlinear marks indicate reversal.
353. 山 added interlinearly.
354. 寺入 should be 入寺, interlinear marks indicate reversal.

355. The dialogue is clearly out of sequence. The text in boldface is the reconstruction in Kim Kugyŏng's collated edition (see Kim 1935) and my translation follows the reconstruction.

356. This line (蹐 . . . 掌) only occurs in S. 516 and P. 3717. The character here represented by [足+胡] is possibly a cognate of 踞.

357. 法 added interlinearly.

358. Still named Mei 郿 prefecture, in Shaanxi. Not surprisingly, Wuzhu's biography is the most detailed account in the *Lidai fabao ji*. The *Lidai fabao ji* was no doubt a source for Zongmi's more critical discussion of Wuzhu (Kamata 1971: 306) and for the *Jingde chuandeng lu* notice on Wuzhu (T. 51 [2076] 234b10–235a7), which is discussed in section 20. Wuzhu was not included in the *Song gaoseng zhuan*.

359. I think this may be an indication that someone started to write the *Lidai fabao ji* while Wuzhu (714–774) was still alive, based on Wuzhu's own account. Yanagida translates this to mean that he was fifty years old when he took the tonsure (1976a: 177), but the text claims he took the tonsure before 749 (and he would have been thirty-four in 749). Nor can we conclude that he spent fifty years as a monk, because then he would have been ten when he was ordained.

360. Prince Xin'an was the grandson of Emperor Taizong's son Wu Wangke 吳王恪; he became Prince Xin'an in 724; his biography is in the *Tang shu* (76) and *Xin Tang shu* (80) (Yanagida 1976a: 184).

361. The Shuofang circuit is in present-day Ningxia, and the Hebei circuit is in the area of present-day Beijing.

362. *Yaqian* 衙前 positions were relatively low ranking (Hucker 7846), but *youyi* 遊弈 officers were cavalry scouts for garrisoned government troops, chosen from among the common soldiers for their skill and bravery (Yanagida 1976a: 184).

363. See the discussion of Zongmi's version of Wuzhu's lineage in chapter 6.

364. At this time the trope of the enlightened lay master was becoming popular; Huineng and Layman Pang are the best-known examples.

365. In Fanyang 范陽 prefecture, Hebei. No other reference to Ming of Mt. Daoci can be found (Yanagida 1976a: 185).

366. = Taiyuan 太原 prefecture, Shanxi. The list of Huineng's heirs in the *Jingde chuandeng lu* includes a Chan master Zizai of Bingzhou 並州, which was in Taiyuan subprefecture (T. 51 [2076] 235b2).

367. Yanagida says that the *Lidai fabao ji* claims that Wuzhu was heir to three lineages; Wuxiang's, Chen Chuzhang's, and Zizai's (1983b: 24). However, the *Lidai fabao ji* only claims that Wuzhu was tonsured under Zizai, not that he received transmission from him.

368. In Wutai 五臺 prefecture, near Taiyuan, in Shanxi. Perhaps the most famous Buddhist pilgrimage site in China, Mt. Wutai was considered the home of Manjuśri.

369. In western Ningxia 寧夏 district, in Ningxia. Mt. Helan had a long-standing reputation as a sacred area (Yanagida 1976a: 186).

370. *Wuyi wunian mowang* 無憶無念莫忘; these phrases are discussed in chapter 6. As noted above, P. 2125 has 妄 here, meaning false or deluded. In the next section, Wuzhu's claim that Wuxiang meant 妄 and not 忘 forms part of his discussion with Du Hongjian (189a14–21), so use of 忘 here points either to an editing error or is meant to show that Cao Gui misunderstood.

371. The identities of Prince Yaosi, the Venerable Shi, and Vinaya Master Huizhang are unclear. Vinaya Master Biancai, however, may be Biancai of Longxing 龍興 monastery in

Shuofang who is given a biography in the *Song gaoseng zhuan,* T. 50 (2061) 806a7–b8. The possibility of connection between Biancai and Wuzhu is suggested by the *Song gaoseng zhuan* assertion that Biancai was established in Longxing monastery by Du Hongjian, Wuzhu's patron (ibid.: 806a21).

372. In Xixiang 西鄉 prefecture, Shaanxi.
373. Yang Hanzhang is otherwise unknown.
374. That is, back to his home district.
375. Southern Mei 郿 prefecture, Shanxi. Mt. Taibai 太白 was a Daoist sacred site and also a place known for Buddhist meditation training. It is often mentioned in *Xu gaoseng zhuan* biographies as a place where monks lived in hermitages or did their initial training; see, for example, the biographies of Daopan 道判, in T. 50 (2060) 516c19–517b15; Daolin 道林, in ibid.: 579c4–580a3; Daoan 道安, in ibid.: 628a9–630b24; Faan 法安, in ibid.: 651c26–652b10; and Tongda 通達, in ibid.: 655b7–19.
376. Nanliangzhou 南梁州 = Langzhong 閬中 prefecture, in western Sichuan.
377. "Below" here refers to the axis of the temple buildings, so the cloister was outside the main temple complex.
378. The reference to three days and three nights may be meant as a parallel to the story of the transmission between Hongren and Huineng, in which Huineng was in Hongren's room for three days and three nights.
379. There were numerous *avadāna* (morality tales) concerning this nun, for example, the Dunhuang manuscript *Lianhuase ni chujia yinyuan* 蓮花色尼出家因緣, Beijing *han* no. 29.
380. The phrase *eming* 惡名 could also refer to her name, which in Chinese would have ambiguous connotations for a nun. In the name Lianhuase 蓮華色, literally "the color of the Lotus," the character for "color," *se* 色, is also used for the "form body" (*se shen* 色身) of the Buddha that she rushes to see, and it also means "sexual passion."
381. A version of this episode is found in the *Ekottarāgama,* T. 2 (125) 707c5–708a20, as well as in several later sources more likely to have been known by the *Lidai fabao ji* authors. The *Dazhi du lun* version is very close to the *Lidai fabao ji* version (T. 25 [1509] 137a, trans. in Lamotte 1944–80: 2: 634–636. There is also a brief account in the *Da Tang xiyu ji,* T. 51 (2087) 893b.
382. *Śūraṅgama-sūtra,* T. 19 (945): 121b25–26; the scripture has 狂性 instead of 狂心. This is also quoted in another Dunhuang text, the *Faxing lun* 法性論 (Suzuki 1968–71: 2: 444; Yanagida 1976a: 187).
383. Location unclear; perhaps a peak in the Baiyai mountains.
384. According to a personal communication from John Kieschnick, the *Lidai fabao ji* contains the earliest references to Chinese monks drinking tea. Tea was a special product of Sichuan, and the general popularity of tea-drinking was said to have spread after the An Lushan rebellion, perhaps as a result of Emperor Xuanzong's sojourn in Chengdu. There are two other passages concerning tea in the *Lidai fabao ji.* In one of them Wuzhu composes a gāthā in praise of tea (section 33, 193b4–6), and in another, Wuzhu is roused to ire in defense of tea (section 39, 195a14–17).
385. That is, the fourth month of the first year of the Baoying 寶應 era, 762. In 761 Emperor Suzong (r. 756–762) had issued a proclamation that reign names were to be abolished and months were to be designated by the stems and branches system. However, he died on the eighteenth day of the *si* month of that "nameless year" (i.e., five days after Dong Xuan arrived at Jingzhong monastery) and it was subsequently changed to the fourth month of the first year of the Baoying era (Yanagida 1976a: 188).

386. A monk's kit has eighteen items, of which the three robes are #3, and the sitting cloth is #6. It is not clear why seventeen is specified here.
387. This is obviously intended to predict Wuzhu's meeting with Du Hongjian.
388. That is, they interpreted his talking to himself as a sign of decrepitude and imminent death.
389. So this should read *jian wu yue* 建午月; the month designated *wu* = the fifth month.
390. 後 has interlinear marks indicating that it should be elided.
391. 得 is probably an error; the phrase is written with 德 in section 20.
392. 知 added interlinearly.
393. P. 2125 has 近, which makes more sense here.
394. Both S. 516 and P. 2125 have a cognate character that is not in the available character sets.
395. Both S. 516 and P. 2125 have a cognate character that is not in the available character sets.
396. Both S. 516 and P. 2125 have a cognate character that is not in the available character sets.
397. An interlinear mark indicates that 且苟 should be reversed to 苟且.
398. Alternatively, the character read here as *du* 都 could be a cognate of *xi* 郤.
399. 相 added interlinearly.
400. Due to the support that the eunuch general Du Hongjian 杜鴻漸 (709–769) gave to Suzong (r. 756–762) at his base at Lingwu 靈武 in Ningxia province during the An Lushan rebellion, Du was promoted to the rank of vice-marshal. He later served as chancellor to both Suzong and Dezong (r. 762–779), and he was sent to Shu in 766 to put down an uprising by the cavalry officer Cui Gan 崔旰. In order to quell the uprising, Du criticized Cui's cowardice in his capacity as military commissioner; see the biographies of Du Hongjian in the *Tang shu* (108) 3282–3284, and *Xin Tang shu* (126) 4422–4424. There is an epitaph for Du written by his famous fellow-minister Yuan Zai 元哉, who was also a devout Buddhist and was largely responsible for the stability of the Tang during the Dali era (766–779); see *Gu Xiangguo Du Hongjian shendao bei* 故相國杜鴻漸神道碑, in QTW (369) (Yanagida 1976a: 197).
401. These monasteries, along with the Daci 大慈 and Bodhi 菩提 monasteries, are mentioned in the *Song gaoseng zhuan* biography of Wuxiang as having been built with the patronage of Chengdu District Director Yang Yi 楊翌. As other hermitages are mentioned as having been constructed "outside the district," these four main monasteries were assumed to have been in the Chengdu district (T. 50 [2061] 832c5–6). For a discussion of the site of the Jingzhong monastery in present-day Chengdu, see Minn 1991.
402. This Kong could be the same as the Preceptor Hekong 何空上座 mentioned in section 18 (T. 51 [2075] 187a10–11).
403. In Guan 灌 prefecture, northwest of Chengdu; see note in section 15.
404. There is no Zhang Huang 張鍠 in either of the lists of officers that appear in this passage, but Zhang Wen 張温 is listed twice. It is possible that 鍠 is a mistake for 温, but it is also possible that it is being used as a cognate for 惶, which would render the translation Yanagida chose: "Qin Ti spoke fearfully" (1976a: 195). However, his translation depends on treating the subsequent character, *chou* 儔, as an error; see ibid.: 198.
405. The bowl is not specifically mentioned among the items Wuxiang sent to Wuzhu, and Shenhui's account of transmission emphasizes only the robe. This may be the earliest

mention of the "robe and bowl" in a Chan transmission episode, but they are also mentioned together in the nearly contemporaneous *Caoqi dashi zhuan* (ibid.: 197).

406. This probably refers to Yan Wu 嚴武, a military commissioner of Jiannan who broke down the Tibetan resistance at Danggou city; *Xin Tang shu* (192); see Yanagida 1976a: 198.

407. *Lidai fabao ji*, section 21, is devoted to Wuzhu's audience with Cui Gan and his wife; see notes to that section.

408. A famous river in Sichuan that flows near Chengdu.

409. The meeting between Du Hongjian and Wuzhu is included as an episode in both the *Jingde chuandeng lu*, T. 51 (2076) 234b10–235a7, and the *Fozu lidai tongzai*, T. 49 (2036) 600b9–601a3. The *Fozu lidai tongzai* follows the *Jingde chuandeng lu* version rather than the *Lidai fabao ji* itself. In these versions, the content and tenor of the dialogue are considerably altered to reflect later Chan sensibilities; one of the more interesting alterations is discussed in chapter 7.

410. 上 added interlinearly.

411. This additional 杜 appears to be an error.

412. P. 2125 has this character *yong;* S. 516 has a cognate character that is not in the available character sets.

413. Both P. 2125 and S. 516 have a cognate character [孫 + 心] that is not in the available character sets.

414. 相公 added interlinearly.

415. It appears that *yang* 佯 is an error or is being used as a cognate for *xiang* 祥.

416. The character here appears to be a variant of 笑; it is written in the same unconventional form in S. 516, P. 2125, and P. 3717.

417. 喜 is written in an unconventional form, with the heart radical underneath.

418. P. 2125 has the correct word order, 无住答.

419. P. 2125 includes the necessary 寺.

420. 和 added interlinearly.

421. 戒 added interlinearly.

422. An interlinear mark indicates that 進精 should be reversed to 精進.

423. 又 added interlinearly, but it seems unnecessary.

424. 正 added interlinearly.

425. *Gang* written with 罡 instead of 岡 on the left.

426. In section 19, this name was consistently rendered with the character 仙 rather than 先.

427. In the *Fozu lidai tongzai* and in the *Jingde chuandeng lu* notice on Wuzhu, T. 51 (2076) 234b14, the year is listed as the first year of the Dali era. However, the reign name was changed to Dali only in the eleventh month of the Yongtai era.

428. This refers to greater Sichuan province; the name derives from the traditional division of the province into Shujun 蜀郡, Guang Han 廣漢, and Jianwei 犍為 (Yanagida 1976a: 209).

429. "Great Bridge" is an epithet indicating the power of the Buddhas to save beings; see, for example, the phrase in the *Xumati zhangzhe jing* 須摩提長者經, T. 14 (530) 807a4: "All the Buddhas of the past became 'great bridges' for the sake of all beings, their great compassion causing all to be joined."

430. Du Hongjian's devotion to Buddhism is professed in numerous sources, including the *Tang shu* and *Zizhi tongjian*. The *Song gaoseng zhuan* notes his devotion to Vajrabodhi 金剛智 (669–741), Bukong 不空 (705–774), Biancai 辯才 (723–778), and Dayi

大義 (691–779); see Yanagida 1967: 285; 1976a: 209. However, no source, aside from the *Lidai fabao ji* and the above-mentioned derivative sources, mentions a connection with Wuzhu. Du's biography cites a poem that he is said to have spontaneously composed at a dinner with friends in his later years: "I often wish to pursue Chan principles, tranquilly able to ladle from transformation's source" (*Tang shu* [108] 3284).

431. Mao Zhou 茂州 is immediately north of the area where Wuzhu's Baiyai mountains were probably located and may have been the administrative region in which they were included.
432. Hucker 5098.
433. A famous monastery in Chengdu, said to have been established in the Han. Before the Tang it was called Longyuan 龍淵 monastery (Yanagida 1976a: 210).
434. The term "green sprouts" refers to an extra tax that was levied at about the same time as this episode, due to government insolvency. It was called "green sprouts" because it was collected just as the plants were sprouting, not after the harvest; a "green sprouts official" was therefore a tax collector and no doubt an especially unpopular one (Morohashi 12.116).
435. There are no records for most of these people. However, Yang Yan 楊炎, Du Ya 杜亞, and Du Ji 杜濟 are mentioned in various places in the *Tang shu* and *Xin Tang shu*, and their participation in Jiannan politics and military campaigns can be seen in the biographies of Du Hongjian and Cui Gan; see *Tang shu* (108) 3282–3283; (117) 3398–3401. Chen Can 岑参 is also mentioned in *Xin Tang shu* (72) 2671. Ma Xiong was mentioned in section 16 as the person who went to Cao Qi and asked about Huineng's robe.
436. Baofu monastery is on Mt. Jie 介 in Jinyang 晉陽, and Fenzhou is in the Fenyang 汾陽 district of Shanxi. Mt. Helan is in Ningxia and was mentioned as part of Wuzhu's itinerary in section 18.
437. Since the *Lidai fabao ji* manuscripts use the characters 莫忘 rather than 莫妄 for Du Hongjian's question, Wuzhu's affirmative reply here does not square with his subsequent explanation.
438. All the *Lidai fabao ji* manuscripts have 是一不三. However, in the *Jingde chuandeng lu* (234b25) and the *Fozu lidai tongzai* (600b14) this is changed to 非一非三, "not one, not three," which reflects the Song Chan paradigm shift favoring paradox over the "one practice" motif of the eighth century.
439. A line describing the Dharmadhātu as no-recollection (*wuyi* 無憶) and no-thought in the *Wenshushili xing jing* 文殊師利行經 (*Mañjuśrīvikāra-sūtra*) may have served as a source for this rubric (T. 14 [471] 513c14–16). Furthermore, there is a passage equating *wusi* 無思 with *śīla*, *wunian* with samādhi, and *wuwang* 無妄 with prajñā in the *Sanbao sidi wenda* 三寶四諦問答 (Dialogue on the Three Jewels and Four Truths), in the Ryūkoku University collection of Dunhuang manuscripts (Yanagida 1976a: 211). These may or may not have been direct influences, but interpreting the three aspects of practice in terms of no-thought was clearly an important matter for the Chan schools of Wuzhu's day; see the discussion of the "three phrases" in chapter 6.
440. From the apocryphal *Dhammapada*, T. 85 (2901) 1435a19–21. The *Lidai fabao ji* version is slightly different from the original, but the only change in meaning occurs in the first line: the scripture has 說諸精進業 (preach about the karma of good effort), whereas the *Lidai fabao ji* has 說諸精進法. This quotation was used in both the "Northern School" *Dasheng wu fangbian* (Suzuki 1968–71: 3: 216) and the subitist *Dunwu yaomen* (*Zen no goroku*, no. 6: 112); it was meant to point out that the concept of meritorious practice mired the practitioner in attachment to purity. Thus, Wuzhu's

use of this phrase in connection with *mowang* squares with his interpretation of "delusion" not as defilements but as objectification of merit (Yanagida 1976a: 211–212).

441. This "tree in the courtyard" dialogue is discussed in chapter 7, in the context of Shenqing's criticism of the *Lidai fabao ji.*
442. The import of the *Vimalakīrti-sūtra* passage is that seeking the Dharma means practice without attachment to any object; the Kumārajīva translation has 法不可見聞覺知、若行見聞覺知是則見聞覺知非求法也 (T. 14 [475] 546a23–24). None of the translations have the rather dualistic phrase 法離見聞覺知.
443. This is the first appearance of Wuzhu's signature phrase "at the time of true no-thought, no-thought itself is not"; altogether it is used nine times: T. 51 (2075) 189b2 (this occurrence), 189c14, 191b16, 192a22, 192b4, 192b14–15, 195c19–20, 195b20, and 195c4–5. As noted, there are two repetitions of the line "it is because beings have thought that one provisionally teaches no-thought, but at the time of true no-thought, no-thought itself is not," in T. 51 (2075) 189b1–2 (this section) and 194c19–20 (section 37). There are two repetitions of the variant line "it is because beings have thought that one provisionally teaches no-thought, but if there is no presence of thought, then no-thought itself is not"; see T. 51 (2075) 186a9 (section 17) and 189c9–10 (section 21).
444. *Vajrasamādhi-sūtra,* T. 9 (273) 369a23–24. Also used in section 27, T. 51 (2075): 191c9–10.
445. *Vimalakīrti-sūtra,* T. 14 (475) 542b25.
446. Ibid.: 554b24. The original (in the Kumārajīva translation) is slightly different: 常求无念實相智恵行. This was a popular phrase; it was also quoted in the *Dasheng kaixin xianxing dunwu zhenzong lun* 大乘開心顯性頓悟真宗論 (Suzuki 1968–71: 3: 322) and the *Faxing lun* 法性論 (ibid.: 2: 445). See Yanagida 1976a: 212.
447. *Laṅkā-sūtra,* T. 16 (672) 628c19.
448. *Śūraṃgama-sūtra,* T. 19 (945) 121b2.
449. Ibid.: 113a18.
450. This appears to be a gloss of a *Viśeṣacinta-sūtra* passage, T. 15 (586) 36b24–28; it is used again in section 22, T. 51 (2075) 190c15–18.
451. This appears to be a gloss of the *Laṅkā-sūtra* passages T. 16 (672) 588c8–9 and T. 16 (671) 516b25–28.
452. 成 added interlinearly.
453. The S. 516 copyist does not clearly distinguish 无 and 元, but here the meaning requires 元; see Yanagida 1976a: 213.
454. 而 added interlinearly.
455. 无念即无憎 added interlinearly.
456. 生 added interlinearly, probably intended to replace 妄.
457. 供 added interlinearly.
458. The manuscript has 心 + 敖, which is not in the available character set.
459. Here S. 516 has *sui* 隨, but the correct character *duo* 墮 appears in the previous use of this quotation, T. 51 (2075) 183a1 (section 10).
460. 識 added interlinearly.
461. 識 added interlinearly.
462. P. 2125 has 礠; S. 516 has a character not in the available character set, 次 + 凡. The *Laṇkā-sūtra* also has 礠 (T. 16 [672] 625a29).
463. Repetition of 大楔 is indicated interlinearly.
464. 出楔 added interlinearly.
465. 取弟一義 added interlinearly.

466. Cui Gan 崔旰, a.k.a. Cui Ning 崔寧, was originally from Henan, and he used his military position to become a virtual ruler in the Shu region. As noted, Du Hongjian was sent in to control him, but his military power in the area remained uncontested. There is no other record indicating the kind of Buddhist devotion and humble behavior we find him exhibiting in the *Lidai fabao ji.* His biography is in *Tang shu* (117) 3397–3404.

467. Cui Gan's wife, Ren, is mentioned in his biography as having bravely fought rebels during an attack on Chengdu while Cui Gan was away at court; see *Tang shu* (117) 3402.

468. Dharma Master Wuying and Dharma Master Qingyuan are otherwise unknown (Yanagida 1976a: 222).

469. Rosaries are made of these seeds, which form in triplets and illustrate the simultaneity of illusion, action, and suffering. They also fall in clusters and thus illustrate numerousness, as here (Nakamura: 19c).

470. *Śūraṃgama-sūtra,* T. 19 (945) 108b28-c8; the quotation is close but not exact.

471. The passage "All beings are fundamentally pure and fundamentally complete . . . then no-thought itself is not" was also used in Wuzhu's sermon in section 17, T. 51 (2075) 186a6–9. The middle section, "From the Buddhas," etc., is similar to a passage in the *Erru sixing* 二入四行; see Yanagida 1969a: 31 ff. As noted, there two repetitions of the line "it is because beings have thought that one provisionally teaches no-thought, but if there is no presence of thought, then no-thought itself is not"; T. 51 (2075) 186a9 (section 17) and 189c9–10 (this section). There are two repetitions of a close variation, "it is because beings have thought that one provisionally teaches no-thought, but at the time of true no-thought, no-thought itself is not"; T. 51 (2075) 189b1–2 (section 20) and 194c19–20 (section 37).

472. From the *Dasheng qixin lun,* T. 32 (1667) 586a10–11. This phrase was popular in early Chan works, and it was used by Chan masters who are included in the *Lidai fabao ji;* Zhishen used it in his *Banruoxinjing shu* 般若心經疏 and Shenhui quotes it in his first response in the *Putidamo nanzong ding shifei lun* (Hu [1958] 1970: 261). It is used three times in the *Lidai fabao ji,* T. 51 (2075) 189c15 (this section), 193b14–15 (section 33), and 194b23–24 (section 36).

473. From the *Vimalakīrti-sūtra,* T. 14 (475) 541b20. This phrase is used again as a set piece with the previous quotation in section 36, T. 51 (2075) 194b24.

474. From the *Vajracchedikā-sūtra,* T. 8 (235) 751b2.

475. This sentence echoes a passage in the apocryphal *Shanhaihui pusa jing* 山海慧菩薩經, T. 85 (2891) 1407a6–7. The phrase is used again, T. 51 (2075) 193c9 (section 34).

476. This is a paraphrase of several lines in the *Fo yijiao jing* 佛遺教經, T. 12 (389) 1111c4–6, in a section devoted to this theme, entitled "Zhizu gongde 知足供德."

477. This is a trope, as, for example, found in a gāthā in the *Lotus Sūtra:* "When the bodhisattva hears this Dharma, the net of doubt is completely removed" (T. 9 [264] 143a11).

478. "Host and guest" is used to represent the teaching that the fundamental nature, "host," is covered by adventitious defilements, "guest." However, in Chan texts it is used in a polemical sense to criticize gradualist dualism that reifies original purity or "host." Wuzhu uses this as a testing question again in T. 51 (2075) 194b4–6 (section 36).

479. In section 34 (ibid.: 190a4), Wuzhu criticizes Confucian scholars for "not recognizing host and guest," and "concentrating on sense-objects."

480. This gāthā from the *Laṅkā-sūtra,* T. 16 (672) 610a27–28, is first quoted in T. 51 (2075) 183a1 (section 10) and again in 191a26–27 (section 24).

481. Pastiche from the *Laṅkā-sūtra,* T. 16 (672) 630b7 and 633a24–25. The last part ("my unsurpassed Mahāyāna," ff.) is repeated again in T. 51 (2075) 191a10–11 (section 24). In the *Zhujing yaochao,* T. 85 (2819) 1196a12–14, the order of the phrases is reversed.
482. For an introduction to the Yogācāra system of consciousnesses, see Nagao 1991.
483. From the *Laṅkā-sūtra,* T. 16 (672) 625a27–29.
484. In the *Zhujing yaochao,* T. 85 (2819) 1196c20–21. This deviates slightly from the first line in the *Laṅkā-sūtra* versions used in the *Lidai fabao ji:* the seven-fascicle *Laṅkā-sūtra* has 如大瀑流盡, T. 16 (672) 606a14–15, and the four-fascicle *Laṅkā* has 如水大流盡, T. 16 (670) 496b5–6, whereas the *Lidai fabao ji* and *Zhujing yaochao* both have 如水瀑流盡.
485. From the *Laṅkā-sūtra,* T. 16 (672): 610a2. Also found in the Dunhuang manuscript of the *Jueguan lun* 絕觀論; see Suzuki 1968–71: 2: 190. The *Lidai fabao ji* and the *Jueguan lun* share the same slight deviation from the original: 種種意生身、我説為心量, while the *Laṅkā-sūtra* has 種種意成身、我説是心量 (Yanagida 1976a: 225).
486. From the *Laṅkā-sūtra,* T. 16 (672) 610b28. The *Laṅkā* has 得无分別法 rather than 得无思想法.
487. This is not found in any of the three *Laṅkā-sūtra* translations, although there is a similar phrase in T. 16 (672) 601c18: 如因 (打 + 丁 + 屑) 出 (打 + 丁 + 屑). *Xie* 楔 and *xie* 屑 are homonyms with some of the same meanings.
488. Quotation from the *Laṅkā-sūtra,* T. 16 (672) 616a22–23, followed by Wuzhu's comments; a slightly different version of the quotation and Wuzhu's commentary are used again in section 24, T. 51 (2075) 191a24–25.
489. That is, the Jiannan area.
490. All the manuscripts have 辨, but it is likely that this represents the cognate 辯.
491. P. 2125 has 人.
492. P. 2125 has 一 instead of 人, which makes more sense here.
493. Interlinear marks indicate that this 心 should be deleted.
494. Chan master Tiwu is otherwise unknown.
495. Chan master Hongzheng 弘政 (or 宏正) of Shengshan 聖善 monastery in Luoyang is mentioned in two stele inscriptions. The first is the *Gu Zuoxi dashi bei* 故左溪大師碑 (Stele of the Late Great Master Zuoxi) by Li Hua 李華 (d. c. 766), in QTW (320) 2241–2242. The relevant line reads: "There were eight generations [from Bodhidharma] to Chan master Hongzheng of Shengshan monastery of the Eastern Capital, and this is what is known as the Northern School." The second is Dugu Ji's inscription for Sengcan written in 773, the *Shuzhou Shanyusi juejita Sui gu Jingzhi chanshi beiming.* It says that among Puji's disciples, Hongzheng was one who had spontaneous wisdom (QTW [390] 3973). (Dugu Ji's inscriptions for Sengcan are noted in section 6.)
496. These persons are otherwise unknown, but they appear to have been local officials. Jinyuan 晉原 was in the Chongqing 崇慶 district of Sichuan, Shifang 什邡 was in the north of the Chengdu district, and Qingcheng 青城 was in the southern part of the Guan 灌 district of Sichuan, near Mt. Tiangu where Wuxiang practiced (Yanagida 1976a: 230).
497. From the *Vimalakīrti-sūtra,* T. 14 (475) 556c10. This is part of what was known as the "four supports" (*siyi* 四依): "Rely on the essential meaning, do not rely on words. Rely on wisdom, do not rely on [sense] consciousnesses. Rely on scriptures of the complete meaning, do not rely on scriptures of incomplete meaning. Rely on the Dharma, do not rely on persons" (ibid.: 556c9–10).
498. From the *Vajracchedikā-sūtra,* T. 8 (235) 751a5–6, with minor discrepancies.

499. In the *Zhujing yaochao,* T. 85 (2819) 1196a10. These phrases are used again in section 28, T. 51 (2075) 191c22–23.
500. In the *Zhujing yaochao,* T. 85 (2819) 1196a9–12. This passage appears to be a gloss of the last gāthā in fascicle 4 of the seven-fascicle *Laṅkā-sūtra;* see T. 16 (672) 614b10–29.
501. In the *Zhujing yaochao,* T. 85 (2819) 1195a26.
502. This phrase appears in Jingjue's commentary to the *Heart Sūtra,* the *Zhu banruopoluomiduo xin jing,* and it appears to be a gloss of a couplet in the *Dazhidu lun,* T. 25 (1509) 118a6–7 (Yanagida 1976a: 231). A variation on this phrase is used in sections 33 and 36.
503. As noted at the first appearance of this passage in section 20, this seems to be a gloss of the passage found in the *Viśeṣacintā-sūtra,* T. 15 (586) 36b24–28.
504. There is no other record of this monk (Yanagida 1976a: 232).
505. Here and elsewhere, Wuzhu's teachings on meditation practice echo the *Wusheng xing* 無生行 (Birthless Practice) section of the *Vajrasamādhi-sūtra,* T. 9 (273) 367b20–368b1. The line "neither entering nor exiting" can be found at ibid.: 367c13.
506. The *Lidai fabao ji* appears to be the earliest Chan text to use the term *huopopo* 活鱍鱍 "lively like a fish jumping." It was used in the *Linji lu* 臨濟錄 and thereafter became a popular epithet (T. 47 [1985] 498c10). Yanagida discusses the phrase's importance in the context of the Sichuan-style dynamic Chan popularized by Mazu and his heirs (Yanagida 1976a: 30; 1983a: 39–41). Variations on Wuzhu's phrases "not flowing and not fixed . . . lively like a fish jumping" are used four times; T. 51 (2075) 190c21 (this section), 191c11–12 (section 27), 194c14 (section 36), and 195a27–28 (section 39).
507. 禅 added interlinearly.
508. 没 is used colloquially in Dunhuang texts in the way that 麼 would later be used. 只没 in the next line is thus equivalent to *zheme* 這麼. See Jiang [1959] 1988: 515.
509. 知 added interlinearly.
510. 闍梨 added interlinearly.
511. 嫌 added interlinearly. 嬾嫌 should be reversed to 嫌嬾, as in the previous verb-object examples.
512. 慵嫌 should be reversed to 嫌慵, as above.
513. In the manuscript, 孩 is written with the 女 radical rather than the 子 radical.
514. 云答 should be reversed, as is indicated by an interlinear mark.
515. 至乃 should be reversed, as is indicated by an interlinear mark.
516. 欲 added interlinearly.
517. S. 516 could be 口 or 只, but P. 2125 has 只.
518. 身 added interlinearly.
519. These disciples are otherwise unknown. Their master is possibly Fochuan Huiming 佛川慧明 (697–780), for whom there remains an inscription, *Tang Huzhou Fochuan si gu Dashi taming* 唐湖州佛川寺故大師塔銘 (Stūpa Inscription for the Former Great Master of Fochuan Monastery in Huzhou, Tang dynasty), in QTW (917), and a biography in the *Song gaoseng zhuan,* T. 50 (2061) 876a23-c5. In the former it is said that he was a codisciple of Yongjia Xuanjue 永嘉玄覺 and Shenhui, and in the latter it is said that he had three disciples, Huijie 慧解, Huimin 慧敏, and Ruzhi 如知. Fochuan monastery is in the northern part of Huzhou (Zhejiang province, Wuxing 吳興 district) (Yanagida 1976a: 237).
520. The *Treatise on One Hundred Dharmas* refers to Xuanzang's translation of the *Dasheng baifa mingmen lun* 大乘百法明門論 (*Mahāyānaśatadharmaprakāśamukha-sūtra*), T. 31 (1614). This is an abbreviation based on Vasubandhu's division of all dharmas into five classes of one hundred dharmas in the *Yogācārabhūmi-sūtra,* T. 30

(1579). Many people were lecturing on the *Baifa lun* at that time, one frequently sees it mentioned in monks' biographies (Yanagida 1976a: 237). Wuzhu deprecates it again in T. 51 (2075) 194c16–17 (section 37).

521. From the *Laṅkā-sūtra,* T. 16 (672) 631c23; also in the *Zhujing yaochao,* T. 85 (2819): 1197a6–7.
522. From the *Laṅkā-sūtra,* T. 16 (672) 631a7.
523. From the four-fascicle *Laṅkā-sūtra,* T. 16 (670) 505b8–9.
524. As noted in chapter 3, it is possible that the *Pusa jie* meant here is Zhiyi's commentary on the *Fanwang jing,* the *Pusa jie jing shu* 菩薩戒經疏, T. 40 (1811) (Yanagida 1976a: 238).
525. From the *Vajrasamādhi-sūtra,* T. 9 (273) 371a10. However, the scripture reads "encompasses all Dharmas" (*fa* 法) instead of "all wisdom" (*zhi* 智). This is quoted three times in the *Dunwu dasheng zhenglijue* and constitutes an important motif in that work (Yanagida 1976a: 238).
526. From the *Laṅkā-sūtra,* T. 16 (672) 633a24–25; also in the *Zhujing yaochao,* T. 85 (2819) 1196a12–13. A slightly different version appears in section 21, T. 51 (2075) 190a15–16.
527. From the *Vimalakīrti-sūtra,* T. 14 (475) 553a14.
528. In the *Zhujing yaochao,* T. 85 (2819) 1196b11–12; from the *Le yingluo zhuangyan fangbianpin jing* 樂瓔珞莊嚴方便品經, T. 14 (566) 931b26. See Appendix, no. 7.
529. From the *Laṅkā-sūtra,* T. 16 (672) 633c26–27, in the *Zhujing yaochao,* T. 85 (2819): 1195a24–25; quoted again in section 36, T. 51 (2075) 194b27–28.
530. Quotation from the *Laṅkā-sūtra,* T. 16 (672): 616a22–23, followed by Wuzhu's comments; a slightly different version of the quotation and Wuzhu's commentary was used in section 21, T. 51 (2075) 190b6–8.
531. From the *Laṅkā-sūtra,* T. 16 (672) 610a27–28; first quoted in T. 51 (2075) 183a1 (section 10) and used again in 190a6–7 (section 21).
532. Repetition of 和上 indicated by interlinear marks.
533. 云何 is not in S. 516 but is in P. 2125 and the other manuscripts.
534. 答 is not in S. 516 but is in P. 2125 and the other manuscripts.
535. Repetition of 和上 indicated by interlinear marks.
536. 答云 added interlinearly.
537. 帝 ought to be 諦, as in P. 2125.
538. Jingzang is otherwise unknown (Yanagida 1976a: 241).
539. In section 20 it is said that Wuzhu spent a summer at Mt. Taibai during his wanderings (T. 542 [2075] 186b29).
540. From the *Laṅkā-sūtra,* T. 16 (672) 632a29. This phrase is used again in T. 51 (2075) 191c27–28 (section 28).
541. From the *Vajracchedikā-sūtra,* T. 8 (235) 750b9; also in the *Zhujing yaochao,* T. 85 (2819) 1194b2. This phrase and a variation are used four times: T. 51 (2075) 183a4 (section 10), 191b12 (this section), 195b16 (section 41), and 196b4 (section 43).
542. Variations on the sentence "if you transcend both self and other you achieve Buddha-awakening" are used four times: T. 51 (2075) 191b15 (this section); 191b28 (section 26); 193a4 (section 31); and 193a15 (section 31).
543. Repetition of 和上 indicated interlinearly.
544. Interlinear marks indicate repetition of 看净, but this would be redundant.
545. 法 added interlinearly.
546. Master Zhiyi and Chan Master Jue are not otherwise known (Yanagida 1976a: 244).
547. "Old Fu" probably refers to the well-known Northern School master Yifu 義福 (661–736), who was commemorated in several inscriptions (see especially QTW [280]

6.3596–3598), was mentioned in the *Tang shu* (191) 511, and has a biography in the *Song gaoseng zhuan,* T. 50 (2061) 760b7–29. See Yanagida 1971: 323–324. He is not elsewhere known as "Old Fu," but he is referred to as "Big Fu" (distinguishing him from Huifu 慧福, "Little Fu") in the *Dunwu dasheng zhenglijue* (Yanagida 1976a: 244).

548. *Kanjing* 看淨, "viewing purity," is part of Shenhui's oft-repeated negative characterization of Northern School practice: "freeze the mind to enter concentration, fix the mind to view purity, activate the mind for external illumination, and concentrate the mind for internal realization." For a critical discussion of Shenhui's summary, see McRae, forthcoming, pp. 153–163.
549. Though the text does not include the first part of this set phrase, we see the couplet used in very similar contexts in T. 51 (2075) 189c13–14 (section 21) and ibid.: 191b14–15 (section 25). The end of Wuzhu's discourse in this section repeats his discourse in section 25, except for the variation on his signature phrase "at the time of true no-thought, no-thought itself is not."
550. Variations on the sentence "if you transcend both self and other you achieve Buddha-awakening" are used four times in the *Lidai fabao ji:* T. 51 (2075) 191b15 (section 25); 191b28 (this section); 193a4 (section 31); and 193a15 (section 31).
551. Zhongxin is not otherwise known. Dengzhou corresponds to Mouping 牟平 district at the northernmost edge of the Shandong peninsula, and it was indeed quite remote from the Chinese central regions (Yanagida 1976a: 247).
552. A well-known quotation from the "Liren 里仁" section of the *Lunyu,* 4.8.
553. From the *Vajrasamādhi-sūtra,* T. 9 (273) 369a23–24; also used in section 20, T. 51 (2075) 189b2–3.
554. Variations on Wuzhu's phrases "not flowing and not fixed . . . lively like a fish jumping" are used four times: T. 51 (2075) 190c21 (section 23), 191c11–12 (this section), 194c14 (section 36), and 195a27–28 (section 39).
555. The *Chanmen jing* says that if one realizes that one's true substance is the same as emptiness, then when walking, staying still, sitting, or lying down (*xing zhu zuo wo* 行住坐臥) there is nothing that is not meditation (Yanagida 1976a: 247). In the two subsequent *Lidai fabao ji* sections in which *huopopo* (lively like a fish jumping) is used, a variation on this phrase is appended: "一切時中惣是禪 At all times, everything is meditation." See T. 51 (2075) 194c14–15 (section 36), and 195a28–29 (section 39).
556. In S. 516, 疏 is written with the 足 radical.
557. 得 should be 德, as in the *Nirvāṇa-sūtra* section named for this bodhisattva, fascicles 21–26 (T. 12 [374] and [375]). See Appendix, no. 17.
558. Interlinear marks indicate that 是法 should be omitted.
559. S. 516 and P. 3717 have 帝, but this should be 諦 as in P. 2125.
560. There is no other record of Falun (Yanagida 1976a: 250).
561. In the *Zhujing yaochao,* T. 85 (2819) 1196a10. These phrases were used in section 22, T. 51 (2075): 190c10–11.
562. This dialogue is not found in the *Nirvāṇa-sūtra,* though one would expect to find it in the Bodhisattva "King of Lofty Noble Virtue" sections, T. 12 (374) fascicles 21–26. However, the key phrase "exhausting all movement of thought . . . is called the *mahāparinirvāṇa*" is found in the "Yingjin huanyuan 應盡還源" section of the *Dabanniepan jing houfen* 大般涅槃經後分 (Latter Part of the *Mahāparinirvāṇa-sūtra*), translated in the Tang by Jñānabhadra, T. 12 (377) 904c11–12.
563. From the *Laṅkā-sūtra,* T. 16 (672) 632a29. This phrase was used in T. 51 (2075) 191b12 (section 25).

564. From the four-fascicle *Laṅkā-sūtra,* T. 16 (670) 480b6–7. This was also quoted in the *Lengqie shizi ji* account of Guṇabhadra, T. 85 (2837) 1284b10.
565. Interlinear marks indicate that 是 should be omitted.
566. P. 2125 has 師.
567. Interlinear marks indicate repetition of 和上.
568. 滅相 added interlinearly.
569. See Morohashi 1: 925.
570. Interlinear marks indicate repetition of 和上.
571. In Suide 綏德 district, Shaanxi province.
572. Mahāyāna scriptures promulgated the belief that recitation gained merit, and the popularity of this practice was further augmented by such works as the *Fahuachuan ji* 法華傳記 (Record of Accounts of the Lotus), T. 51 (2068), compiled in the Tang by Sengxiang 僧詳. This work contained stories of miracles that resulted from recitation of the *Lotus*.
573. The two brothers are otherwise unknown (Yanagida 1976a: 253).
574. This is indeed from the "Anlexing 安樂行" section of the *Lotus,* T. 9 (262) 37c13–15.
575. From the *Lotus,* T. 9 (262) 10a4. Also quoted in Jingjue's preface to the *Lengqie shizi ji;* see Yanagida 1971: 77.
576. From the *Lotus,* T. 9 (262) 5c25.
577. From ibid.: 19c4–5. (The middle phrase in the scripture is longer: 究竟涅槃常寂滅相 "In final nirvāṇa, forever the characteristic of tranquil extinction.") This quotation is used three times: T. 51 (2075) 192a16 (this section), T. 51 (2075) 194c2–3 (section 36), and partially in T. 51 (2075) 195a6–7 (section 38).
578. From the *Vimalakīrti-sūtra,* T. 14 (475) 538a13. This phrase is used again in T. 51 (2075) 194c3 (section 36).
579. From the *Renwang jing* 仁王經 (Scripture of Humane Kings), T. 8 (245) 827c21. This phrase is used again in T. 51 (2075) 194c4 (section 36). Thus, the identical sequence of three quotations is repeated in section 36. The *Vimalakīrti* phrase that the *Lidai fabao ji* authors use is also similar to the *Renwang jing* phrase that precedes this one.
580. In the *Platform Sūtra* dialogue between Huineng and the *Lotus* practitioner Fada 法達, there is a discussion of "revolving the Lotus/Lotus revolutions" that is similar in import to Wuzhu's sermon. See Yampolsky 1967: 167–168.
581. See Morohashi 10: 939.
582. Interlinear mark indicates that 要法 should be reversed, to 法要.
583. 政 should be 正, as in P. 2125.
584. Repetition of 和上 indicated by interlinear marks.
585. Administrator Murong may be the same as the Imperial Entertainments Chief Minister Murong Ding 慕容鼎 who was the official representative sent to welcome Wuzhu when he came out of the mountains; see T. 51 (2075) 188a27 (section 19) and 188b22 (section 20). Qingzhou was in the present-day Qingyang 慶陽 district of Gansu province.
586. *Sanzhang wunan* 三障五難 refers to the three obstructions of greed, anger, and ignorance and the traditional difficulties endured by women: namely, the necessity of leaving her own family to be married into another's, menstruation, pregnancy, childbirth, and the obligation to wait on a man; see *Śīgālovāda-sutta, Dīgha Nikāya (DN)* III. 180–193. Alternatively, there are five obstacles specific to women, who cannot be reborn as a Mahābrahman, Indra, Māra, Cakravartin, or Buddha.

587. Grand Councilor Su may or may not be the official with the surname Su mentioned in section 20, Attendant Censor Su Chang 蘇敞, T. 51 (2075) 188c26. (Su Cheng of Qingcheng is mentioned in T. 51 (2075) 190b19 (section 22), but he is not given any ranking.)

588. A similar term is applied to Wuxiang's sister, *yacao* 雅操; see T. 51 (2075) 184c20. *Zhicao* 志操 is not applied to the male disciples of Wuzhu, but it does occur in praise of Chuji, where it follows his other virtues of not eating meat or pungent foods (T. 51 [2075] 184b20).

589. This could be an inversion of a line in the *Śūraṃgama-sūtra*, T. 19 (945) 142c2: 即一切法離一切相.

590. From the *Vimalakīrti-sūtra*, T. 14 (475) 540a16–17. In the scripture, there are two more characterizations of the Dharma in between the two quoted here: "*Fa wu gaoxia, fa changzhu bu dong* 法無高下, 法常住不動. The Dharma is without high or low, the Dharma abides eternally unmoving." This quotation is used again in T. 51 (2075) 192c22 (section 31), and "the Dharma transcends all contemplation practices" is used twice more: 194a29 (section 35) and 195b12 (section 41).

591. The three main manuscripts all have *jing* 鏡 (mirror), but *jing* 境 (objects/realm of cognition) is added interlinearly in P. 2125. The former is sometimes used as a metaphor for the latter; see Demiéville 1987.

592. The manuscript has a cognate character not in the available character set.

593. In the *Zhujing yaochao*, T. 85 (2819) 1196c4–5, and the *Heart Sūtra*, T. 8 (251) 848c14–15, this is written yi 以. See note 607.

594. Based on the *Viśeṣacintibrahma-paripṛcchā-sūtra*, T. 15 (586) 37b3–8; variations occur in sections 10 and 42. The phrase about Heaven's kitchen is reminiscent of the notion of being "fed by Heaven" in the "Signs of the Fullness of Power" chapter of the *Zhuangzi*; see Graham 1981: 82.

595. This gāthā is in the early-eighth century *Dunwu yaomen* 頓悟要門, in *Zen no goroku*, no. 6: 103 (Yanagida 1976a: 266).

596. In the *Fanwang jing*, the bodhisattva precepts are called the "mind-ground" precepts, and "the Dharma-gate of the mind-ground section" is used to refer to the *Fanwang jing* precepts; see T. 24 (1484) 1003b17–18, 1003b24, 1003c19, and 1009c10. In his *Chanyuan zhu quanji duxu* 禪源諸詮集都序, Zongmi instead identifies the "mind-ground" with Chan practice and Buddha-nature. He cites the *Fanwang jing* evocation of the "Dharma-gate of the mind-ground" as the foundation of the practice of the Buddhas and bodhisattvas, but he is referring to Chan rather than to the bodhisattva precepts of the original context (T. 48 [2015] 399b4–5). In each of these contexts the term is used as Wuzhu uses it, to refer to the essence or the foundation of the Dharma, but the identity of the foundation shifts.

597. From the *Vajracchedikā-sūtra*, T. 8 (235) 749b8–11. This is also quoted in Shenhui's *Tanyu* and "Miscellaneous Dialogues," and the *Dunwu yaomen*, in *Zen no goroku*, no. 6: 83 and 109 (Yanagida 1976a: 267).

598. An adaptation apparently based on two different translations of verses from the *Avataṃsaka-sūtra*, T. 9 (278) 429a3–14 and T. 10 (279) 68a25–b5. The "poor person" simile is also quoted in the Huike section of the *Lengqie shizi ji*, T. 85 (2837): 1286a4–5.

599. An adaptation of a simile in the apocryphal *Dhammapada*, T. 85 (2901) 1432b28–c1. This simile is alluded to in the Huike section of the *Lengqie shizi ji*, T. 85 (2837) 1286a3, immediately preceding the *Avataṃsaka* quotation noted above. The juxtaposition of

these similes in both works suggests that Wuzhu or the *Lidai fabao ji* authors were following the lead of the *Lengqie shizi ji* in this exhortation to practice.

600. *Jueguan* 覺觀 was the old translation for *vitarka* (coarse contemplation) and *vicāra* (subtle contemplation). However, in this quotation from the apocryphal *Śūraṃgama-sūtra,* the term appears to be used in a broader sense.

601. The first two sentences are composed of lines from verses in the *Śūraṃgama-sūtra,* T. 19 (945) 131a11 and 131a8.

602. I cannot confirm Yanagida's identification of this quotation as "a gāthā in the last fascicle" of the *Fangguang jing* (Yanagida 1976a: 267), as my searches through the texts referred to by this title proved fruitless: T. 3 (187), T. 12 (353), T. 24 (1489), T. 9 (278), and 10 (279).

603. From the *Vimalakīrti-sūtra,* T. 14 (475) 539c23–26. In the scripture, two more characterizations of "quiet sitting" are given before the line "*Ruo neng ruci zuozhe Fo suo yinke* 若能如此坐者佛所印可 Those who are able to sit like this are the ones the Buddha will validate." This is also quoted in Shenhui's *Putidamou nanzong dingshifei lun* (see McRae, forthcoming, section 20, p. 295), and the term *yinke* is used in the "Miscellaneous Dialogues" (ibid.: 278). The term *yinke* is used in the *Lengqie shizi ji* in a similar manner, to approve the kind of understanding that would be considered valid; T. 85 (2837) 1287c27–28 (Daoxin section) and 1290a14 (Hongren section). The notion of *yinke* 印可 (Jap. *inka*) bestowed on the disciple by the master would become very important in later Chan institutions.

604. From the *Vimalakīrti-sūtra,* T. 14 (475) 541a17.

605. From ibid.: 540a16–18, with several phrases left out. The first part was used in section 30, T. 51 (2075) 192b11–12. "The Dharma transcends all contemplation practices" is used twice more: 194a29 (section 35) and 195b12 (section 41).

606. From the *Vimalakīrti-sūtra,* T. 14 (475) 551c24. In this famous passage, Manjuśrī praises Vimalakīrti's silence.

607. From the *Zhujing yaochao,* T. 85 (2819) 1196c4–5, identified as a quotation from the *Heart Sūtra.* Both the *Lidai fabao ji* and the later Northern School *Dunwu zhenzong lun* 頓悟真宗論 (T. 85 [2835] 1279c29–1280a1) use the *Zhujing yaochao* version of this quotation, which differs in meaning from the scripture. In T. 8 (251) 848c14–15 (Xuanzang's translation, also the same in the translation of Prajñā et al., T. 8 [253] 849c12–13), the portion used in the *Zhujing yaochao* and the *Lidai fabao ji* is the end of one sentence and the beginning of another: "no wisdom and also no attainment. Because there is nothing to attain, the bodhisattva / relies on the *prajñāpāramitā.*" This is partially used again in T. 51 (2075) 193c17 (section 34).

608. From the *Vajracchedikā-sūtra,* T. 8 (235) 751c23. This is used twice in the *Lidai fabao ji:* T. 51 (2075) 192c29–193a1 (this section) and 193c17–18 (section 34). It is also quoted in full or in part in Moheyan's *Dunwu dasheng zhenglijue,* the Niutou school *Wuxin lun* 無心論, T. 85 (2831) 1269c7, and the *Dunwu yaomen,* in *Zen no goroku,* no. 6: 114 (Yanagida 1976a: 268).

609. Variations on the sentence "if you transcend both self and other you achieve Buddha-awakening" are used four times in the *Lidai fabao ji:* T. 51 (2075) 191b15 (section 25); 191b28 (section 26); 193a4 (section 31, this occurrence); and 193a15 (section 31).

610. From the apocryphal *Dhammapada,* T. 85 (2901) 1433c9. This phrase was used in a number of texts, including the *Platform Sūtra* and the *Dunwu yaomen,* in *Zen no goroku* no. 6, p. 16 (Yanagida 1976a: 268).

611. From the *Vajrasamādhi-sūtra*, T. 9 (273) 368c20. *Ludi zuo* 露地坐 (sitting on dewy ground) refers to the condition of escaping from defilements, as it was used in the *Lotus Sūtra* to describe the place where the children sat down after escaping from the Burning House (T. 9 [262] 12c15). (It also refers to living in the open, one of the twelve *dhūta*, extreme ascetic practices.)
612. From the *Laṅkāvatāra-sūtra*, T. 16 (672) 635a25; also quoted in the *Lengqie shizi ji*, T. 85 (2837) 1284b10, and the *Dunwu zhenzong lun*, T. 85 (2835) 1281b19.
613. Based on the *Vajrasamādhi-sūtra*, T. 9 (273) 368a12–13 and 370b3. Different versions of this pastiche are used four times in the *Lidai fabao ji*: T. 51 (2075) 183a25 (section 10); 186a13–14 (section 17); 193a9–10 (this section); and 195b2 (section 40).
614. From the apocryphal *Dhammapada*, T. 85 (2901) 1435a24, but there the second line is *wei yu po zhu shu* 為欲破諸数. In the *Lengqie shizi ji*, T. 85 (2837) 1289b3, it is quoted correctly.
615. From the *Śūraṃgama-sūtra*, T. 19 (945) 131a20–21; also in the *Zhujing yaochao*, T. 85 (2819) 1196c23–24, and quoted in the *Dunwu dasheng zhenglijue* (Yanagida 1976a: 268).
616. From the *Fo yijiao jing*, T. 12 (389) 1111a20. Wuzhu's discourse on "one" could be considered critical of notions such as the East Mountain teaching of *shouyi* 守一 (guarding the one), as, for example, expounded in the *Lengqie shizi ji*, T. 85 (2837) 1288a20–23. The *Vajrasamādhi-sūtra* has the phrase *zhi zhi yi chu* 制之一處 (T. 9 [273] 370c22) and is also the source for two subsequent phrases (see below). The "Zhenxingkong 真性空" section was clearly a source for Wuzhu's discourse on the one, but the discussion of "one" at the beginning of the *Vajrasamādhi* section develops the paradox of one and differentiation as creations of thought that are at the same time the actualization of function, especially realization of their unreality.
617. From the apocryphal *Dhammapada*, T. 85 (2901) 1435a23. This quotation appears in a number of related texts, including the preface of the *Lengqie shizi ji*, T. 85 (2837) 1283a29, the *Dunwu yaomen*, in *Zen no goroku*, no. 6: 92, and the *Baozang lun* 寶藏論 (Treasure Store Treatise), T. 45 (1857) 148c2. (Only the latter has *senluo* 森羅, rather than *canluo* 參羅.)
618. From the *Vajrasamādhi-sūtra*, T. 9 (273) 370c23.
619. Ibid.: 371a4. The scripture has *bu xi* 不繫, rather than *bu ji* 不計.
620. Possibly loosely based on the *Fo yijiao jing*, T. 12 (389) 1111c11–13.
621. Variations on the sentence "if you transcend both self and other you achieve Buddha-awakening" are used four times in the *Lidai fabao ji*: T. 51 (2075) 191b15 (section 25); 191b28 (section 26); 193a4 (section 31); and 193a15 (section 31, this occurrence).
622. Repetition of 和上 indicated interlinearly.
623. These comments on the relativity of distance and recognition echo the passage in section 18, in which Wuzhu addresses Wuxiang's attendants from his mountain retreat; see discussion in chapter 6.
624. This poem does not appear in the extant collection of Wang Fanzhi's 王梵志 (d. 670?) poems, some of which survived among the Dunhuang manuscripts (T. 85 [2863]). See also Xiang 1991 and Zhang 1983. Wang's poems were perhaps well-known in Sichuan Chan circles, as Zongmi also quotes a verse by Wang Fanzhi in his *Chanyuan zhu quanji duxu*, T. 48 (2015) 412d20–21.
625. In chapter 7, I draw attention to the similarity between this passage and a passage in the *Linji lu*. One could also note that although Wuzhu is critical of the practice of

pilgrimage to Wutai shan, in section 18 it is said that Wuzhu also spent a summer on the famous mountain.

626. 空 is probably the correct character, but both S. 516 and P. 3717 have 控, and this was apparently the original character in P. 2125 as well. However, in P. 2125 someone has blotted out the radical, leaving 空.

627. Repetition of 起心 is indicated by interlinear marks, and the character 即 is added interlinearly.

628. An interlinear mark indicates that 佛見 should be reversed, to 見佛.

629. Tea-drinking is one of the distinctive motifs of the *Lidai fabao ji;* in section 18 Wuzhu's gift of tea to Wuxiang is a key part of the narrative plot, and in section 39, Wuzhu upbraids a rude guest who mocks his tea-drinking habits. Yanagida notes that although dialogues arising in tea-drinking settings were frequent in later Chan/Zen records, this is the first such dialogue in a Chan context. He also notes that this scene marks a turn toward showing interactions between teacher and students in everyday settings, which was to become a hallmark of later Chan/Zen (1976a: 275).

630. From the *Chanmen jing* as quoted in the *Zhujing yaochao,* T. 85 (2819) 1196c1–2, except that the *Zhujing yaochao* has *miaoyi* 妙義 (subtle meaning) rather than *miaoli* 妙理.

631. These two sentences were used in section 17 (T. 51 [2075] 186a8–9; the *Taishō* version is missing some characters), but there it is "Good Friends" who point, rather than the scriptures.

632. From the *Dasheng qixin lun,* T. 32 (1667) 586a10–11. This phrase is used three times in the *Lidai fabao ji,* T. 51 (2075) 189c15 (section 21), 193b14–15 (this section), and 194b23–24 (section 36).

633. The phrase "arousing the mind . . . demons' net" is used again in section 36, T. 51 (2075) 194c13. The second phrase was used in section 22 and is from Jingjue's commentary to the *Heart Sūtra,* the *Zhu banruopoluomiduo xin jing* (Yanagida 1976a: 276).

634. This is a gāthā at the end of the *Vajracchedikā-sūtra,* T. 8 (235) 752b28–29.

635. This should be 以, as in *Dao de jing* section 48. In the discussion of this phrase below, there is further confusion of 已 and 以.

636. Throughout this passage, 得 is used for 德.

637. 三 added interlinearly.

638. Repetition of 煩惱 is indicated by interlinear marks.

639. As noted above, this should be 以, as in *Dao de jing* section 48.

640. 无 is missing; this line should be 无為无不為, as in the previous and subsequent references to the same line.

641. Although the S. 516 and P. 2125 both have 已, this should be amended to 以, matching the pattern of the subsequent line.

642. 也 added interlinearly.

643. 人住 should be added here (as in P. 2125), in order to follow the pattern of the previous line.

644. Interlinear marks indicate that one 佛 should be omitted.

645. Interlinear marks indicate that 果 should be omitted.

646. Interlinear marks indicate that 莊子 and 老子 should be reversed, so 老子 is first.

647. 不分別世故 has been added interlinearly.

648. Shanren 山人 referred to a kind of Confucian or literatus recluse.

649. The famous first line of the *Daode jing.*

650. The *Daode jing* (chapter 48) line is: 損之又損、以至於无為。无為而无不為。

651. Derived from the "Dazong shi 大宗師" section, where the order of the phrases is reversed: 殺生者不死、生生者不生。See Graham 1981: 87.
652. These are the key virtues as developed in the *Mengzi* 孟子; see 2A:6 and 6A: 16.
653. This is adapted from a line in the first part of the *Xici zhuan* 繫辭傳 (Commentary on the Appended Phrases), traditionally but not reliably attributed to Confucius. The original passage refers to the non-action of the *Yijing* itself; see Lynn 1994: 63.
654. In section 21 (T. 51 [2075] 193c7), Wuzhu criticized Dharma Master Wuying for "not recognizing host and guest," and "concentrating on sense-objects." In section 38 (ibid.: 195a8) he criticizes Vinaya and Dharma masters for deluded focus on sense-objects.
655. This echoes a passage in the apocryphal *Shanhaihui pusa jing* 山海慧菩薩經, T. 85 (2891) 1407a6–7: "This is like a person who practices direct mind with the perfection of energy (*vīrya*) and attains true liberation, and is moreover born in a heaven. This person did not seek liberation, liberation was reached of itself. He/she did not seek birth in a heaven, but birth in a heaven was reached of itself."
656. In the *Daode jing*, chapter 38, the line is as follows: 上德不德是以有德。下德不失德是以无德. The *Lidai fabao ji* version makes the two lines parallel (substituting 失 for 德 in the first half), but in the end Wuzhu's commentary could also be applied to the original.
657. From the *Zhujing yaochao*, T. 85 (2819) 1196c4–5; an extract from the *Heart Sūtra*, T. 8 (251) 848c14–15. This was used in section 31, T. 51 (2075) 192c28 where it was also used in conjunction with the next line. See note 607.
658. From the *Vajracchedikā-sūtra*, T. 8 (235) 751c23. This is used twice in the *Lidai fabao ji*: T. 51 (2075) 192c29–193a1 (section 31) and 193c17–18 (this section).
659. From the *Daode jing*, chapter 48.
660. This reference to the Mind King is briefly discussed in the "Discourse with Daoists" section of chapter 6.
661. See note 651.
662. This line is repeated seven times in the third fascicle of the *Śūraṃgama-sūtra:* T. 19 (945) 117c11, 118a2, 118a20, 118b10, 118c6, 119a5, and 119b2. It is also quoted in the *Linji lu*, T. 47 (1985) 506b22–23.
663. From the *Vajrasamādhi-sūtra*, T. 9 (273) 367c6.
664. From the *Vajracchedikā-sūtra*, T. 8 (235) 749b18.
665. This may be based on a passage in the *Vajrasamādhi-sūtra*, T. 9 (273) 370b15–17, in which it is said that those of the two vehicles taste samādhi and then reify it, like an alcoholic who is stupefied by drink and doesn't sober up. In Wuxiang's Dharma talk in section 15, he says that all beings are "drunk on the wine of ignorance" (T. 51 [2075] 185a23).
666. In section 10 (ibid.: 183b2–3) this is said to be a quotation from the *Bhaiṣajyaguru-vaiḍūryaprabharāja-sūtra*, but the extant texts do not include it.
667. From the *Laṅkā-sūtra*, T. 16 (672) 597c1–2.
668. As quoted in the *Zhujing yaochao*, T. 85 (2819) 1194b5–6. From a gāthā in the *Rulai zhuangyan zhihui guangming ru yiqie fojingjue jing* 如來莊嚴智惠光明入一切佛境界經 (*Sarvabuddhaviṣayāvatārañānālokālaṃkāra-sūtra*) (T. 12 [357] 248a3–4). In the scripture, the line "do reverence without anything to contemplate' is a regularly repeated refrain.
669. This may be based on a gāthā in the *Viśeṣacintabrahmaparipṛcchā-sūtra*, T. 15 (586) 37c13–14: 知法名為佛，知離名為法，知無名為僧。
670. From the *Vimalakīrti-sūtra*, T. 14 (475) 540a18–19.

671. From the *Vajracchedikā-sūtra*, T. 8 (235) 751c15. In context, this line refers to refutation of the possibility that the Dharma of the Tathāgatha would reify forms and characteristics. Also quoted in the *Dunwu dasheng zhenglijue* (Yanagida 1976a: 288).

672. Based on the *Nirvāṇa-sūtra*, T. 12 (374) 520b8–9. The line in the scripture is: "復除是事若知如来常不説法、是名菩薩具足多聞。 Again, discarding [even] this matter (i.e., knowing that the Tathāgatha is eternal and changeless), if one knows the Tathāgatha never explained the Dharma, this is called the bodhisattva's complete hearing [of the Dharma]." This passage in the scripture progresses from defining "complete hearing" as complete dissemination and explanation of the *Nirvāṇa-sūtra*, down to the final step of deconstruction quoted here. A version of this is quoted in the *Lengqie shizi ji*, T. 85 (2837) 1287b5–6 and in a work said to consist of Hongren's dialogues, the *Zuishangsheng lun* 最上乘論 (a.k.a. *Xiuxinyao lun* 修心要論), T. 48 (2011) 378a11–12. It is also used in the *Dunwu dasheng zhenglijue*, but is attributed to the *Laṅkā-sūtra* (Yanagida 1976a: 289).

673. This is based on the *Dashengyi zhang* 大乘義章, T. 44 (1851) 699a20–21 ff.; the passage is said to be an explanation of the three kinds of prajñā from the *Dazhidu lun*. In section 41, these three kinds of prajñā are put forth by Dharma master Fayuan, and Wuzhu's critique is constructed of the same phrases in a different order (T. 51 [2075] 195b9–12).

674. From the apocryphal *Dhammapada*, T. 85 (2901) 1435a13–14. This is Wuzhu's rebuttal of the "prajñā of texts and characters" and is quoted again in the similar exchange in T. 51 (2075) 195b10–11 (section 41). This is also quoted in Zhishen's *Banruoxinjing shu* (Yanagida 1976a: 289).

675. From the *Vajracchedikā-sūtra*, T. 8 (235) 750b29. The scripture has 此法 instead of 我法. This is Wuzhu's rebuttal of the "prajñā of actuality" and is quoted again in section 41, T. 51 (2075): 195b12.

676. From the *Vimalakīrti-sūtra*, T. 14 (475) 540a17. This is Wuzhu's rebuttal of the "prajñā of contemplating radiance." The phrase is used four times: T. 51 (2075) 192b12 (section 30), 192c22 (section 31), 194a29 (this section), and 195b12 (section 41).

677. An interlinear mark indicates that 是見 should be reversed, so the sentence should read: 若住如是見、是平等見。

678. An interlinear mark indicates that 非无 should be reversed to 无非.

679. An interlinear mark indicates that 法我 should be reversed to 我法.

680. As discussed in the *Juedingpini jing*, T. 12 (325) (see Appendix, no. 8), *Vinayaviniścaya* is Vinaya to remove the gravest transgressions, and *Vinayottara* means the highest Vinaya, referring to the view that the fundamental nature of all dharmas is pure.

681. Wuzhu used this as a testing question in section 21, T. 51 (2075) 190a2.

682. From the *Vajrasamādhi-sūtra*, T. 9 (273) 366c20.

683. From the *Śūraṃgama-sūtra*, T. 19 (945) 121a2.

684. This echoes part of one of the subtitles of the *Lidai fabao ji*: *Pohuai yiqie xin* 破壞一切心傳 (The Transmission . . . Destroying All Mind [Activities]).

685. Based on a gāthā in the *Zhufa benwu jing* 諸法本無經 (*Sarvadharmāpravṛttinirdeśa-sūtra*), T. 15 (651) 763a7–8. A different version is quoted in the *Zhujing yaochao*, T. 85 (2819) 1195a4–6. As discussed in chapter 6, the overall tenor of the foregoing discussion is very similar to a comment on *zhenjie* 真戒 (real precepts) in the same section of the *Zhujing yaochao*, T. 85 (2819) 1195a20–22.

686. Based on the *Wenshu shuo banruo jing* (*Saptaśatikāprajñāpāramitā-sūtra*), T. 8 (232) 728b23–25. The *Zhujing yaochao* misidentifies this passage as a quotation from the *Juedingpini jing;* see T. 85 (2819) 1197b1–4.
687. From the *Vimalakīrti-sūtra,* T. 14 (475) 541b2–3.
688. From the apocryphal *Dhammapada,* T. 85 (2901) 1435a16–17; also quoted in the *Zhujing yaochao,* T. 85 (2819) 1194c28–29. There is also a similar passage in the *Vajrasamādhi-sūtra,* T. 9 (273) 370b22–24.
689. From the *Dasheng qixin lun,* T. 32 (1667) 586a10–11. This phrase is used three times in the *Lidai fabao ji,* T. 51 (2075) 189c15 (section 21), 193b14–15 (section 33), and 194b23–24 (this section).
690. From the *Vimalakīrti-sūtra,* T. 14 (475) 541b20. This phrase is used again as a set piece with the previous quotation in T. 51 (2075) 189c15–16 (section 21).
691. From the *Laṅkā-sūtra,* T. 16 (672) 633c26–27; also in the *Zhujing yaochao,* T. 85 (2819) 1195a24–25. This was quoted in T. 51 (2075) 191a23 (section 24).
692. From the *Lotus Sūtra,* T. 9 (262) 19c4–5. This quotation is used three times: T. 51 (2075): 192a16 (section 29), T. 51 (2075) 194c2–3 (this section), and partially in section 38, T. 51 (2075) 195a6–7.
693. From the *Vimalakīrti-sūtra,* T. 14 (475) 538a13. This phrase was used in section 29, T. 51 (2075) 192a17, as a set piece with the above quotation.
694. From the *Renwang jing* 仁王經 (Scripture of Humane Kings), T. 8 (245) 827c21. This phrase was also used in section 29, T. 51 (2075) 192a17. Thus, the identical sequence of three quotations appeared previously, in section 29.
695. This passage on "five years of study" may be based on a note in the *Zhujing yaochao,* T. 85 (2819) 1194c17.
696. Read at face value, 只没閑 could also mean "only without barriers." However, since the *Lidai fabao ji* authors tend to use 只没 like 這麼, and tend to use 閑 like 間, I have chosen to translate it in this manner.
697. The phrase "arousing the mind . . . demons' net" was used in T. 51 (2075) 193b17 (section 33).
698. Variations on Wuzhu's phrases "not flowing and not fixed . . . lively like a fish jumping" are used four times; T. 51 (2075) 190c21 (section 23), 191c11–12 (section 27), 194c14 (this section), and 195a27–28 (section 39). The passage in section 27 also includes a variation on the phrase "everything is meditation," and sections 39 and 40 (195b3) repeat "everything is meditation" as it appears in this section.
699. S. 516 is missing this 師, but the other manuscripts have it.
700. An interlinear mark indicates that this 无 should be omitted.
701. S. 516 has a cognate not in the available character set.
702. The *Treatise on One Hundred Dharmas* refers to Xuanzang's translation of the *Dasheng baifa mingmen lun,* T. 31 (1614). It was mentioned in section 24, T. 51 (2075): 190c25.
703. This is a critique of the numerical approach that is used throughout the *Dasheng baifa mingmen lun.*
704. As noted, there are two repetitions of the line "it is because beings have thought that one provisionally teaches no-thought, but at the time of true no-thought, no-thought itself is not," in T. 51 (2075) 189b1–2 (section 20) and 194c19–20 (this section). There are two repetitions of the variant line "it is because beings have thought that one provisionally teaches no-thought, but if there is no presence of thought, then no-thought itself is not," in T. 51 (2075) 186a9 (section 17) and 189c9–10 (section 21).

705. This appears to be based on the introduction of three kinds of interpretation in the Liang translation of the *Qixin lun,* T. 32 (1666) 576a3–5. Note that *cuixie xianzheng* 摧邪顯正 is also included in one of the subtitles of the *Lidai fabao ji*.
706. From the *Qixin lun,* T. 32 (1666) 576a12.
707. Based on ibid.: 576b13. The line in the scripture is: 離念相者等虛空界無所不遍。There is a dialogue on this line, and the concept of *linian* 離念, in the *Dasheng wufangbian,* T. 85 (2834) 1273c23–1274b18. *Linian* was considered a characteristic Northern School practice, and it became the focus of Southern School criticism.
708. From the *Laṅkā-sūtra,* T. 16 (672) 613c18–19, with minor variations.
709. Yanagida glosses these terms in this manner (1976a: 299).
710. From the *Vimalakīrti-sūtra,* T. 14 (475) 537c18.
711. From ibid.: 538a14.
712. Both S. 516 and P. 2125 have a cognate that is not in the available character sets.
713. 法名嗣遠 is written in small characters.
714. One would think that this should be 禅門経, and P. 2125 has an interlinear 門. However, the quotation is from the *Vimalakīrti.*
715. These masters are otherwise unknown, but in P. 2125 Daoyou's name appears among the group of visiting Chan disciples.
716. The title *Chanshi jing* is unknown, but the quotation is from the *Vimalakīrti-sūtra,* T. 14 (475) 545b6. "Attachment to the taste of meditation" is also criticized in the *Dasheng wufangbian,* but there it is associated with followers of the two vehicles in contrast to the bodhisattvas (T. 85 [2834] 1274b23 and c15–20, 1275c9–11).
717. This is loosely based on a gāthā in the *Lotus Sūtra,* T. 9 (262) 9c7–8.
718. From ibid.: 19c4–5, somewhat abbreviated. This quotation is used three times: T. 51 (2075) 192a16 (section 29), T. 51 (2075) 194c2–3 (section 36), and partially in this section, 195a6–7.
719. In a similar line in section 34, Wuzhu criticizes scholars for focusing on sense-objects (ibid.: 193c7).
720. The reference to a person throwing clods at a lion is based on an example given in the *Mahāprajñāpāramitā-sūtra,* T. 7 (220) 939a28-b2.
721. Based on the *Chanmen jing;* a different version of this phrase is also found in the *Dunwu yaomen,* in *Zen no goroku,* no. 6: 8 (Yanagida 1976a: 303).
722. As noted in section 31, *jueguan* 覺觀 was the old translation for *vitarka* (coarse contemplation) and *vicāra* (subtle contemplation). However, it was used for a range of meanings in early Chan texts. In the discussion borrowed from the *Erru sixing* in the *Vajrasamādhi-sūtra,* the "entrance of principle" is equated with *jueguan* and contemplating Buddha-nature (T. 9 [273] 369c7–10).
723. 上 added interlinearly.
724. 有 and 立 were both added interlinearly.
725. S. 516 has a cognate not in the available character sets.
726. 師 added interlinearly.
727. These masters are otherwise unknown.
728. The famine of the Yongchun era was apparently a leading date for some time; see *Zizhi tongjian* (203) 6406–6407.
729. The phrase "a kick from a *hastināga* is not something an ass can bear" is from the *Vimalakīrti-sūtra,* T. 14 (475) 547a26. It is also used in the *Linji lu,* T. 47 (1985) 503a1, and in the *Zhengdao ge* (Jap. *Shōdōka*) 証道歌, in Kajitani et al. 1974: 65.
730. See Yanagida 1976a: 30 for a discussion of this story and Wuzhu's "as is" Chan.

731. "It functions without birth or tranquil [extinction]" is used again in the eulogy at the end; T. 51 (2075) 196a21 (section 43).
732. As noted, variations on these phrases appear four times; T. 51 (2075) 190c21 (section 23), 191c11–12 (section 27), 194c14–15 (section 36), and 195a27–28 (this section). "Everything is meditation" is repeated only a few lines further on, in section 40 (195b3).
733. The name Dharma Master Xiongjun is otherwise unknown, but in the "Miscellaneous Dialogues" the teachings of a Dharma master Jun 俊 of Xiangyang 襄陽 are presented to Shenhui for commentary, and it appears that this Dharma master was well-known; see McRae, forthcoming, pp. 303–305. The content of the passages in the "Miscellaneous Dialogues" bears no relation to the questions asked in the *Lidai fabao ji*.
734. From the *Vajrasamādhi-sūtra*, T. 9 (273) 368a12–13 and 370b3. Variations on this pastiche appear four times: T. 51 (2075) 183a25 (section 10), 186a13–14 (section 17), 193a9–10 (section 31), and 195b2 (this section).
735. As noted, variations on the phrase "everything is meditation" are used four times: T. 51 (2075) 191c12 (section 27), 194c14–15 (section 36), 195a28–29 (section 39), and 195b3 (this section).
736. The character in S. 516 could also be meant to represent Cao 曹.
737. 上 added interlinearly.
738. Repetition of 和上 indicated by interlinear marks.
739. 従 added interlinearly.
740. 法 added interlinearly.
741. P. 2125 has 隴州 instead of 隴右, and Longzhou is in the Long district of Shaanxi province.
742. Master Fayuan is otherwise unknown. This is the only mention of a disciple who joined Wuzhu while he was still in the Baiyai mountains, from 759 to 766. Thus, Fayuan could be one of Wuzhu's earliest disciples, which might account for the relatively gentle handling he receives and the unusually realistic tone of the dialogue.
743. Tianqin 天親 is the old translation for Vasubandhu's name (Shiqin 世親 is the new translation), and Wuzhu 无着 is the translation of Asaṅga. Their *Vajracchedikā* treatises were widely used, and there are five Chinese translations: T. 25 (1510–1514). Hui 暉 could refer to Yuanhui 圓暉 of Dayun 大雲 monastery; in the *Song gaoseng zhuan* it is said that he wrote commentaries on the *Vajracchedikā* and the *Avataṃsaka* (though none are extant); see T. 50 (2061) 734a11–22. Tan 壇 is unknown. Da 達 could refer to Baoda 寶達, the compiler of the *Jingang ying* 金剛暎 (T. 85 [2734]).
744. From the *Vajracchedikā-sūtra*, T. 8 (235) 749b24; also in the *Zhujing yaochao*, T. 85 (2819) 1197a16, and the *Dunwu yaomen*, in *Zen no goroku*, no. 6: 91. As is well known, Shenhui highly extolled the *Vajracchedikā-sūtra*, and it remained foundational for the Chan school.
745. *Huangnian* 黃蘗: Phallodendron amurence. The leaves of this tree were used to copy early scriptures (Nakamura: 129).
746. This is based on the *Dashengyi zhang*, T. 44 (1851) 699a20–21 ff. In section 35 there is a slightly different version of the same exchange: T. 51 (2075) 194a26–29. As in section 35, the following three quotations refute each categorization of prajñā, but not in the order in which Fayuan listed them.
747. From the apocryphal *Dhammapada*, T. 85 (2901) 1435a13–14. This was also quoted in the similar exchange in section 35, T. 51 (2075) 194a28–29.

748. From the *Vimalakīrti-sūtra,* T. 14 (475) 540a17. This phrase is used four times: T. 51 (2075) 192b12 (section 30), 192c22 (section 31), 194a29 (section 35), and 195b12 (this section).
749. From the *Vajracchedikā-sūtra,* T. 8 (235) 750b29. The scripture has 此法 instead of 我法. This was also quoted in the similar exchange in section 35, T. 51 (2075) 194a–29.
750. From the *Vajracchedikā-sūtra,* T. 8 (235) 751c13. The scripture has 若人言 instead of 若言.
751. From the *Vajracchedikā-sūtra,* T. 8 (235) 750b9; also in the *Zhujing yaochao,* T. 85 (2819) 1194b2. This phrase and a variation are used four times: T. 51 (2075) 183a4 (section 10), 191b12 (section 25), 195b16 (this section), and 196b4 (section 43).
752. *Vajracchedikā-sūtra,* T. 8 (235) 752a17–18; also in the *Zhujing yaochao,* T. 85 (2819) 1194a14–15. This was quoted along with the preceding phrase in section 10: T. 51 (2075) 183a5.
753. For a discussion of monks and their mothers, see Faure 1991: 245–246.
754. P. 2125 has 因, which makes more sense here.
755. P. 2125 has 養.
756. 无念即无捨 is added interlinearly.
757. From the *Guan Puxianpusa xingfa jing* 觀普賢菩薩行法經 (Scripture of the Methods of Contemplation of the Bodhisattva Samantabhadra), T. 9 (277) 393b11; also quoted in the Daoxin section of the *Lengqie shizi ji,* T. 85 (2837) 1287a8. Discussed in chapter 3, the *Guan Puxian jing* is a contemplation sūtra translated in the south in the fifth century. It promoted practices for self-administration of the bodhisattva precepts as well as contemplation of the emptiness of precepts and confession, and would have supported Wuzhu's teachings on formless practice. However, since this appears to be the only time it is quoted, the *Lidai fabao ji* authors may have taken the line from the *Lengqie shizi ji.*
758. Based on the *Viśeṣacintibrahma-paripṛcchā-sūtra,* T. 15 (586) 37b3–8. Variations on these phrases are used three times: T. 51 (2075) 183a9–10 (section 10), 192b18–20 (section 31), and 195b29–c2 (this section).
759. Well-known lines from the end of the *Heart Sūtra,* T. 8 (251) 848c18–20; also quoted in the *Putidamo nanzong ding shifei lun,* in Hu [1958] 1970: 301. However, there it is attributed to the *Sheng Tian Wang banruo jing* 勝天王般若經, T. 8 (231), where it does not appear. As noted in the previous section, there may be some mirroring of the *Ding shifei lun* in *Lidai fabao ji* sections 41 and 42.
760. It is possible that the *Lidai fabao ji* authors drew this metaphor from a passage in the Huike section of the *Lengqie shizi ji,* T. 85 (2837) 1285c3–12. The *Lengqie shizi ji* passage develops the *tathāgatagarbha* theme of the adamantine Buddha in the bodies of all beings that is obscured by the skandhas; the wind of wisdom disperses the clouds so that Buddha nature can shine forth. The *Lengqie shizi ji* cites the *Shidi jing* 十地經 (*Daśabhūmika-sūtra*) and the *Avataṃsaka,* though there is nothing quite like this passage in these works. (However, the *Avataṃsaka* does have frequent references to the clouds and rain of the Dharma purifying beings, as for example in fascicle 34, T. 9 [278] 615b4 ff.) The *Lengqie shizi ji* passage may, instead, be based on a passage in the *Zuishangsheng lun* (said to be the dialogues of Hongren) (T. 48 [2011] 377a24–b3).
761. The manuscripts all appear to have *kai* 開 (open) but Yanagida (1976a: 312) has chosen to amend this to *guan* 關 (closed), which does make more sense.
762. Two of the most powerful contenders during the Warring States period, Chu and Yue were one-time allies turned enemies, and Chu vanquished Yue in 333 B.C.E. This

line echoes Wuzhu's long-distance challenge in section 18 (186c12), one of his sayings in section 32 (193a16), and a line in the poem by Wang Fanzhi in the same section (193a20).

763. 并序 written in small characters.
764. An interlinear mark indicates that 他 should be omitted.
765. P. 2125 has 指, which makes more sense here.
766. P. 2125 has 是故, which makes more sense here.
767. This 无 is redundant and appears to be partially blotted out.
768. See Morohashi 7.150.
769. This wording does not appear as such in the *Daode jing,* though the Dao is frequently referred to as "nameless," as, for example, in chapter 41: "道隱無名 the Dao is hidden and nameless."
770. This phrase may be based on a section in the *Vimalakīrti-sūtra* (T. 14 [475] 540a9), in which the Dharma is described in a series of apophatic couplets, including the phrase 法無形相.
771. *Miaoyou* 妙有 was a key phrase in *chongxuan*-style exegesis; see the discussion in chapter 6.
772. This refers to the twelve categories of scriptural literature: *Sūtra* (discourses of the Buddha), *Geya* (recapitulating verses), *Gāthā* (verses), *Nidāya* (historical narratives), *Itivṛttaka* (past lives of the disciples), *Jātaka* (past lives of the Buddha), *Adbhuta-dharma* (tales of the Buddha's miracles), *Avadāna* (allegories), *Upadeśa* (dialogues on doctrine), *Udāna* (statements of the Buddha), *Vaipulya* (broad topics), and *Vyākaraṇa* (prophecies of the Buddha about the disciples' enlightenment).
773. In other words, the expedient means that eradicate the eighty-four thousand *kleśa,* defilements.
774. Based on a phrase in the "Outer Chapters" of the *Zhuangzi;* see Watson 1964: 140.
775. A line from the *Vajrasamādhi* (T. 9 [273] 371a10) in which the "principle of suchness" appears was quoted in section 24, T. 51 (2075) 191a9.
776. This is based on a line in the *Śūraṅgama-sūtra* (T. 19 [945] 121b26), from a passage quoted in section 18, T. 51 (2075) 187a5.
777. A phrase likely to have been based on the section in the *Vimalakīrti-sūtra,* 入不二法門 "Entering the Nondual Dharma Gate."
778. *Miaowei* 妙微; see Sharf 2002: 195–203, for a discussion of the Daoist background of the Chan use of this term.
779. *Avyākṛta* is a technical term from Abhidharma exegesis on the moral qualities of dharmas; it means morally neutral, not subject to karmic retribution. Wuzhu engages in a dialogue on this topic in section 21, T. 51 (2075) 190a7–21.
780. "It functions without birth or tranquil [extinction]" was used in section 39, T. 51 (2075) 195a27.
781. Adaptation of Yan Hui's praise of virtue in the *Lunyu* 論語, 9.10; see Waley 1938: 140.
782. This is a variation on a line from the *Vajracchedikā-sūtra* (T. 8 [235] 750b9) that is used three other times: T. 51 (2075) 183a4 (section 10), 191b12 (section 25), and 195b16 (section 41).

Appendix

TEXTS LISTED AT THE BEGINNING OF THE *LIDAI FABAO JI*

Note: Other texts are also used in the *Lidai fabao ji,* and these are identified in the translation annotations.

Categorical Overview

Scriptures: Nos. 1–5, 7, 8, 12, 14, 15, and 17–23 (16 texts)
Texts Related to Buddhist-Daoist Polemics: Nos. 6, 25, 26, and 29–35 (10 texts)
Unclear, but probably taken from a source related to Buddhist Daoist polemics: No. 36
Apocrypha: Nos. 9–11, 13, and 16 (5 texts)
Transmission History (purported translation, compiled in China): No. 24
Catalogue: No. 28
Geography (nonextant): No. 37
Biography (unknown): No. 27

1. *Benxing jing* 本行經 *Abhiniṣkramaṇa-sūtra* (Scripture of the Initial Steps on the Path)

   = *Fo benxing ji jing* 佛本行集經

   60 *juan,* Sui, trans. Jñānagupta 闍那崛多 (523–600). T. 3 (190).

   One of the best-known versions of the Buddha's biography is the *Buddhacaritakāvya-sūtra* by Aśvaghoṣa 馬鳴, the *Fo suoxing zan* 佛所行讃, T. 4 (192). However, the version translated by Jñānagupta was commonly used in the Tang and is most likely the one indicated here; Yanagida 1976a: 45.

2. *Za ahan jing* 雑阿含經 *Saṃyuktāgama-sūtra* (Miscellaneous Discourses)

   50 *juan,* Liu Song, trans. Guṇabhadra 求那跋陀羅 (394–468). T. 2 (99).

The dialogue in fascicle 44 is an important source for the notion of a link between receiving the Buddha's teachings and receiving the robe, see T. 2 (99) 317b29-c1. The same motif is used in the *Ayuwang zhuan*, T. 50 (2042) and in the *Fufazang yinyuan zhuan* (see no. 24); Yanagida 1976a: 45.

3. *Puyao jing* 普曜經 *Lalitavistara-sūtra* (Scripture of the Unfolding of the Divine Play [of the Buddha])

   8 *juan*, Western Jin, trans. in 308, Dharmarakṣa 竺法護 (b. 230?). T. 3 (186).

This is a Mahāyāna biography of the Buddha, which tells of the Buddha's descent from Tuṣita heaven and his birth as Śākyamuni. The Chan records commonly used the Dharmarakṣa translation; Yanagida 1976a: 45.

4. *Shuiying jing* 瑞應經 *Kumārakuśalaphalanidāna-sūtra* (Scripture of Auspicious Signs)

   = *Taizi shuiying benqi jing* 太子瑞應本起經

   2 *juan*, Wu, trans. c. 222–229, Zhiqian 支謙. T. 3 (185).

   For a comparison of nos. 3 and 4, see Matsuda 1988: 24–33.

5. *Wenshushili niepan jing* 文殊師利涅槃經 *Manjuśrī-parinirvāda-sūtra* (Scripture of the Final Nirvāṇa of Manjuśrī)

   = *Foshuo Wenshushili banniepan jing* 佛說文殊師利般涅槃經

   1 *juan*, Western Jin, trans. Nie Daozhen 聶道真 (in China c. 280–312). T. 14 (463).

6. *Qingjing faxing jing* 清浄法行經 (Scripture of the Practice of the Pure Dharma)

   1 *juan*, Six Dynasties apocryphon.

This work was long considered lost, but was recently rediscovered at Nanatsudera; see Ochiai 1991: 26. The earliest extant listing in a bibliography is under the "anonymous translations" section of the *Chusanzangji ji*, T. 55 (2145) 29a21. The first time it appears as a "suspected scripture" is in the *Zhongjing mu lu* 衆経目録, T. 55 (2147) 126b17. It was written as a Buddhist rebuttal to the Daoists' *Laozi hua Hu jing* 老子化胡経 (see no. 25), and is quoted mainly in works which advance the claim that Chinese sages of antiquity were manifestations of Buddhas and bodhisattvas; see Zürcher 1959: 316 and 438n133. Shenqing's *Beishan lu* (T. 52 [2113] 578c1–2) uses the same quotation as the one in the *Lidai fabao ji*.

7. *Wugouguang zhuan nushen jing* 無垢光轉女身經 *Strīvivarta-vyākaraṇa-sūtra* (Scripture of the Unstained Radiant Transformation of the Female Body)

   = *Foshuo wugou xiannu jing* 佛說無垢賢女經

   1 *juan*, Western Jin, trans. Dharmarakṣa. T. 14 (562).

   = *Foshuo fuzhongnu ting jing* 佛說腹中女聽經

   1 *juan*, Northern Liang, trans. Dharmakṣema 曇無讖 (385–433). T. 14 (563).

   = *Foshuo zhuan nushen jing* 佛說轉女身經

   1 *juan*, Liu Song, trans. Dharmamitra 曇摩蜜多 (356–442). T. 14 (564).

   = *Shunquan fangbian jing* 順權方便經

   2 *juan*, Western Jin, trans. Dharmarakṣa. T. 14 (565).

   = *Le yingluo zhuangyan fangbianpin jing* 樂瓔珞莊嚴方便品經

   1 *juan*, Later Qin, trans. Dharmayaśas 曇摩耶舍 (in China early fifth century). T. 14 (566).

8. *Juedingpini jing* 決定毘尼經 *Vinayaviniścaya-Upālipariprcchā-sūtra* (Scripture of the Inquiry of Upāli Regarding Determination of the Vinaya)

   1 *juan*, Western Jin, trans. Dharmarakṣa. T. 12 (325).

This is a separate translation of the *Youpo lihui* 優波離會 (*Vinayaviniścaya-Upālipariprcchā*), item 24 of the *Dabaoji jing* 大寶積経 (*Mahāratnakūṭa*), T. 11 (310). It explains that in the period of the decline of the Dharma, Maitreya protects the true Dharma and saves beings. This work was a source for the practice of taking the Mahāyāna precepts and extinguishing sins through repentance; Yanagida 1976a: 46.

9. *Dafoding jing* 大佛頂經 *Śūraṃgama-sūtra* (Scripture of the Crown of the Buddha's Head)

   = *Dafoding rulai miyin xiuzheng liaoyi zhupusai wanxing shoulengyen jing* 大佛頂如来密因修証了義諸菩薩万行首楞厳経

   10 *juan*, Tang apocryphon, claimed to be a translation by Pāramiti 般刺蜜帝 in 705. T. 19 (945).

This sūtra was frequently quoted in Chan works and the Tibetan documents that relate to Chan.

10. *Jingangsanmei jing* 金剛三昧經 *Vajrasamādhi-sūtra* (Scripture of Adamantine Concentration)

    1 *juan*, apocryphon compiled c. 650–665. T. 9 (273).

Robert Buswell has made a convincing argument that this work was produced by a Korean monk. One also finds it quoted in a few Tibetan works on sudden awakening, as Moheyan, the Chinese representative in the so-called debate of Lhasa, summarized his position by using quotations from this work. See Buswell 1989; Kapstein 2000: 75–78.

11. *Faju jing* 法句經 "*Dhammapada-sūtra*" (Verses on Dharma)

    = *Foshuo faju jing* 佛說法句經

    1 *juan*, T. 85 (2901). Early Tang apocryphon, with a separate commentary in one *juan*, T. 85 (2902).

Not to be confused with the *Faju jing* translated in the Wu dynasty, T. 4 (210), or the other versions of the *Dhammapada-Udānavarga*, T. 4 (211)–(213). See Tanaka 1983: 401–412; Mizuno 1961 and 1981; Willemen 1978.

12. *Fozang jing* 佛藏經 *Buddhapiṭakaduḥśīlanirgraha-sūtra* (Scripture in Which the Admonitions of the Buddha-Treasury Are Understood)

    3 *juan*, Later Qin, trans. Kumārajīva 鳩摩羅什 (344–413). T. 15 (653).

This work provided a scriptural antecedent for reinterpretation of key Buddhist rubrics, such as the Pure Precepts and recollection of the Three Jewels, in terms of no-thought, nonconceptualization, and nondiscrimination; Yanagida 1976a: 46.

13. *Yingluo jing* 瓔珞經 (Gem-Necklace Scripture)

    = *Pusa yingluo benye jing* 菩薩瓔珞本業經

    2 *juan*, apocryphon, translation attributed to Zhu Fonian 竺佛念 (Later Qin). T. 24 (1485).

    = *Pusa yinglou jing* 菩薩瓔珞經

    14 *juan*, also attributed to Zhu Fonian, T. 16 (656).

This text was probably composed in China in the fifth century, see Ono Hōdo [1954] 1963: 164–165. It explains the forty-two stage bodhisattva path and the threefold Pure Precepts, and it was used as a basis for the Tiantai school's teachings on the fifty-two stages and the threefold contemplation (emptiness, impermanence, and the Middle Way); Yanagida 1976a: 46–47.

14. *Huayan jing* 華厳経 *Avataṃsaka-sūtra* (Flower-Garland Scripture)

= *Da fangguang fo huayan jing* 大方廣佛華厳経 (*Buddha-avataṃsaka-sūtra*)

In three translations:

60 *juan,* Eastern Jin, trans. c. 418–421, Buddhabhadra 佛馱跋陀羅 (359–429). T. 9 (278).

80 *juan,* Tang, trans. c. 695–699, Śikṣānanda 實叉難陀 (652–710). T. 10 (279).

40 *juan,* Tang, trans. c. 798, Prajñā 般若. T. 10 (293).

As discussed in chapter 3, this scripture was a key source for bodhisattva precepts practice. Besides serving as the foundation of the Huayan school, it was also important in early Chan; for example, it was taken as the basis of the fifth gate of the Northern School's *Dasheng wufangbian* 大乘五方便 (The Five Expedient Means of the Mahāyāna), see McRae 1986: 193–194.

15. *Dabanruo jing* 大般若經 *Mahāprajñāpāramitā-sūtra* (Scripture of the Great Perfection of Wisdom)

600 *juan,* Tang, trans. 659, Xuanzang 玄奘 (602–664). T. 5–7 (220).

16. *Chanmen jing* 禅門經 (Scripture of the Chan Teachings)

= *Chanyao jing* 禅要經

1 *juan,* apocryphon, compiled c. end of seventh century, S. 5532, P. 4646.

Perhaps compiled during the reign of Empress Wu, this title appears in the section on spurious works in the *Kaiyuan shijiao lu* 開元釈教録 (see no. 28). The extant work is a summary of early Chan school teachings in the form of a sūtra, and it was often quoted in later Chan texts. See Yanagida 1961.

17. *Niepan jing* 涅槃經 *Mahāparinirvāṇa-sūtra* (Scripture of the Great Final Nirvāṇa)

= *Dabanniepan jing* 大般涅槃經

In two translations:

40 *juan,* Northern Liang, trans. Dharmakṣema. T. 12 (374).

36 *juan,* Liu Song, trans. Huiyan 慧嚴 (363–443) et al. T. 12 (375).

Along with the *Vajracchedikā-sūtra* (Diamond Sūtra), this scripture is fundamental to an understanding of Shenhui's thought. His phrase "see the nature and become Buddha" (*jianxing chengfo* 見性成佛) is from the Liang commentary to this sūtra by Baoliang 寶亮 et al., the *Dabanniepan jing jijie* 大般涅槃経集解, T. 37 (1763); Yanagida 1976a: 47.

18. *Lengqie jing* 楞伽經 *Laṅkāvatāra-sūtra* (Scripture of the Appearance of the Dharma in Laṅkā)

= *Lengqie aboduolou baojing* 楞伽阿跋多羅寶經

4 *juan,* Liu Song, trans. 443, Guṇabhadra (394–468). T. 16 (670).

= *Ru lengqie jing* 入楞伽經

10 *juan,* Northern Wei, trans. 513, Bodhiruci 菩提流支 (d. 527?). T. 16 (671).

= *Dasheng ru lengqie jing* 大乘入楞伽經

7 *juan,* Tang, trans. c. 704, Śiksānanda. T. 16 (672).

Although the early Chan schools used Guṇabhadra's translation, most of the *Laṅkā* quotations in the *Lidai fabao ji* are from the translation by Śikṣānanda.

19. *Siyi jing* 思益經 *Viśeṣacintabrahmaparipṛcchā-sūtra* (Scripture of the Inquiry of the Deity of Thinking)

= *Chixinfantian suowen jing* 持心梵天所問經

4 *juan,* Northern Jin, trans. Dharmarakṣa. T. 15 (585).

= *Siyifantian suowen jing* 思益梵天所問經

4 *juan,* Later Qin, trans. Kumārajīva. T. 15 (586).

= *Sheng siyifantian suowen jing* 勝思益梵天所問經

6 *juan,* Northern Wei, trans. Bodhiruci. T. 15 (587).

Kumārajīva's translation was the one most commonly used. This scripture was important to the early Chan school, and it is the basis of the fourth gate of the Northern school's *Five Expedient Means of the Mahāyāna;* see McRae 1986: 192–193. It was also much quoted in the Chinese account of the debate at Lhasa, the *Dunwu dasheng zhenglijue* 頓悟大乘正理決 (Verification of Sudden Awakening in the Mahāyāna). Yanagida 1976a: 47.

20. *Fahua jing* 法華經 *Saddharmapuṇḍarīka-sūtra* (Scripture of the Lotus of the True Dharma)

= *Miaofa lianhua jing* 妙法蓮華經

7 *juan,* Later Qin, trans. 406, Kumārajīva. T. 9 (262).

= *Zhengfahua jing* 正法華經

10 *juan,* Western Jin, trans. Dharmarakṣa. T. 9 (263).

= *Tianpin miaofa lianhua jing* 添品妙法蓮華經

7 *juan,* Sui, trans. Jñānagupta and Dharmagupta 達磨笈多. T. 9 (264).

21. *Weimo jing* 維摩經 *Vimalakīrtinirdeśa-sūtra* (Scripture on the Expositions of Vimalakīrti)

= *Foshuo Weimojie jing* 佛說維摩詰經

2 *juan,* Wu, trans. Zhiqian 支謙. T. 14 (474).

= *Weimojie suoshuo jing* 維摩詰所說經

3 *juan,* Former Qin, trans. Kumārajīva. T. 14 (475).

= *Shuowugoucheng jing* 說無垢稱經

6 *juan,* Tang, trans. Xuanzang. T. 14 (476).

This is one of the most frequently cited scriptures in all of Chan literature.

22. *Yaoshi jing* 藥師經 (Scripture of the Master of Medicine) *Bhaiṣajyaguruvaiḍūryaprabhāsapūrvapraṇidhānaviśeṣavistara-sūtra* (Elaboration on the Merit of the Previous Vows of the Medicine Master Who Shines Like an Emerald)

= *Foshuo Yaoshi rulai benyuan jing* 佛說藥師如来本願經

1 *juan,* Sui, trans. Dharmagupta. T. 14 (449).

= *Yaoshi liuliguang rulai benyuan gongde jing* 薬師瑠璃光如来本願功德經

1 *juan,* Tang, trans. Xuanzang. T. 14 (450).

= *Yaoshi liuliguang rulai benyuan gongde jing* 薬師瑠璃光七佛本願功德經

2 *juan,* Tang, trans. Yijing 義浄 (635–713). T. 14 (451).

23. *Jingangbanruo jing* 金剛般若經 *Vajracchedikā-sūtra* (Diamond Scripture)

= *Jingangbanruopoluomi jing* 金剛般若波羅蜜經

1 *juan,* Later Qin, trans. Kumārajīva. T. 8 (235)

1 *juan,* Northern Wei, trans. Bodhiruci. T. 8 (236).

1 *juan,* Chen, trans. Paramārtha 眞諦 (500–569). T. 8 (237)

= *Jingangnengduanbanruopoluomi jing* 金剛能斷般若波羅蜜經

1 *juan,* Sui, trans. Dharmagupta. T. 8 (238)

= *Foshuo nengduanjingangbanruopoluomi jing* 佛說能斷金剛般若波羅蜜經

1 *juan,* Tang, trans. Yijing. T. 8 (239)

Kumārajīva's translation was the most commonly used, and corresponds to the extant Sanskrit text. After Shenhui, the scripture became a mainstay of Southern School discourse and was widely quoted in Chan texts; Yanagida 1976a: 47.

24. *Fu fazang jing* 付法蔵經

= *Fu fazang yinyuan zhuan* 付法蔵因縁伝 (Account of the *Avadāna* [Causes and Conditions] of the Transmission of the Dharma Treasury)

6 *juan,* translation attributed to Kiṅkara 吉迦夜 and Tanyao 曇曜 (Northern Wei). T. 50 (2058).

This is a Buddhist transmission history compiled in China from a number of different sources. It narrates the sequential transmission of the Dharma from Mahākāśyapa to Siṁha Bhikṣu, and is the basis of the *Lidai fabao ji* authors' account of the transmission of the Indian patriarchs; see chapter 4 for a discussion of the *Lidai fabao ji* and the *Fufazang zhuan.*

25. *Daojiao xisheng jing* 道教西昇經 (Scripture of the Ascension to the West of the Daoist Teachings)

= *Laozi hua hu jing* 老子化胡经 (Scripture of Laozi's Conversion of the Barbarians)

2 *juan,* T. 44 (2139).

Claiming that Laozi went to India and became the Buddha, this apocryphon was said to have been written by the Daoist Wang Fu 王浮, who was defeated in the Buddhist/Daoist debate held during the reign of Emperor Hui (r. 291–307) of the Western Jin. This text was repeatedly banned, so there are different versions listed in the various catalogues. Erik Zürcher notes that it is difficult to separate fragments from the initial polemic in the third and fourth centuries from later interpolations, and the extant *Hua hu jing* seems to include passages stemming from both the Daoist and the Buddhist versions. One passage showing Buddhism as the superior teaching includes a lineage of transmission of Daoist teachings from Mahākāśyapa to the Daoist masters of the Han, and an account of Emperor Ming's dream; Zürcher 1959: 319–320. See also Kohn 1991.

As discussed in chapter 7, Wuzhu and the Bao Tang were clearly sensitive to Buddhist-Daoist polemics in Sichuan, where archaeological and textual records show a great deal of militant syncretism and mutual borrowing in the ninth and tenth centuries.

26. *Shi Falin zhuan* 釋法琳傳 (Biography of Shi Falin)

= *Tang hufa shamen Falin biezhuan* 唐護法沙門法琳別傳

3 *juan*, compiled by Yanzong 彥棕 in the second half of the seventh century. T. 50 (2051).

This work includes Falin's (572–640) memorial to the emperor Taizong (r. 626–649) regarding the injustice of the inferior status of Buddhism compared to Daoism (203a). Falin's *Poxie lun* 破邪論 T. 52 (2109) and *Bianzheng lun* 辨正論 T. 52 (2110) are also polemical treatises defending Buddhism. In connection with the issue of the precedence of Buddhism, the *Shi Falin zhuan* also includes an extensive discussion of the correlation between dates in the Buddha's life and dates in the Zhou dynasty (207a–208a), and thus may have been a source for the first section of the *Lidai fabao ji.*

27. *Shi Xushi ji* 釋虛實記 (Record of the Monk Shi Xushi)

This text has so far proved untraceable.

28. *Kaiyuan shijiao mu* 開元釋教目 (Buddhist Catalogue of the Kaiyuan Era [713–742])

= *Kaiyuan shijiao lu* 開元釋教録

20 *juan*, compiled by Zhisheng 智昇 in 730. T. 55 (2154).

The Buddhist literature included in the first Chinese canon (1,124 works, 5,048 *juan*) was established on the basis of this catalogue. Included in the section on Bodhiruci is a biography of Bodhidarma (541c), which is based on the version in the *Luoyang qielan ji.* Yanagida 1976a: 48.

29. *Zhou shu yiji* 周書異記 (Supplement to the Zhou History)

This Buddhist apocryphon correlated the Buddha's birth and death with dates in the reigns of two Zhou princes. It is nonextant, but is quoted in many works from the sixth century onward. Sources of quotations include the *Falin biezhuan* 釋法琳別傳 (no. 26, above), Daoxuan's *Ji gujin fodao lun heng* 集古今佛道論衡, T. 52 (2104), and Daoshi's *Fayuan zhu lin* 法苑珠林, T. 50 (2104). According to the *Xu gaoseng zhuan* biography of the Northern Wei monk Tanwuzui 曇無最, T. 50 (2060) 624c, when Tanwuzui and the Daoist Jiang Bin 姜斌 debated in court over which was earlier, Buddhism or Daoism, it was on the basis of the *Zhou shu yiji* and the *Hanfa neizhuan* that Buddhism was judged earlier. Yanagida 1976a: 48.

Erik Zürcher surmises that the *Zhou shu yiji* author based his chronology on events related in the *Zhushu jinian* 竹書紀年, a chronicle of Wei dating from the end of the fourth century B.C.E. that included a history of the earliest period. Only fragments of the original *Zhushu jinian* remain, and these have been incorporated into a later, spurious work. Based on a fragment preserved in the *Taiping yulan* (674.4b), which relates a miraculous celestial phenomenon and agrees almost exactly with a quotation from the *Zhou shu yiji,* Zürcher concludes that the author of the *Zhou shu yiji* changed the date of the celestial phenomenon in order to make it match the presumed date of the Buddha's death; see Zürcher 1959: 286–87.

30. *Hanfa neizhuan* 漢法內傳 (Inner Commentary on the Dharma in the Han)

= *Hanfa ben neizhuan* 漢法本內傳

Purporting to chronicle the introduction of Buddhism to China during the Later Han, this Buddhist apologetic work was compiled in the context of Buddhist-Daoist polemics of the third century. Due to its anti-Daoist thrust it was prohibited by Emperor Xuanzong 玄宗 (r. 712–756), but the scriptural cataloguer Zhisheng 智昇 (658–740) re-edited it and succeeded in getting it into the canon as part of his *Xu ji gujin fodao lun heng* 續集古今佛道論衡 (Continued Anthology of Past and Present Buddhist-Daoist Debates), T. 52 (2105) 397b25–401c25. The earliest extant work in which it is mentioned is the *Xu gaoseng zhuan* 續高僧傳 biography of Tanwuzui, noted above. The *Guang hongming ji* (*T.* 52 [2103] 174b19) claims that the *Hanfa neizhuan* was cited in the *Hou Han shu*, but it is not in the extant version. Moreover, the *Hou Han shu* is a fifth-century composition.

31. *Yin Xi neizhuan* 尹喜内傳 (Yin Xi's Inner Commentary)

= *Wushang miaodao Wen Shi zhenjing* 無上妙道文始眞経 (The Unsurpassed Subtle Dao of Wen Shi's True Scripture)

1 *juan*. *Daozang* 347.667.

Yin Xi (or Wen Shi) was the guard posted at the Hangu Pass 函谷関 who was said to have received the *Daode jing* 道德経 from Laozi. Purporting to be Yin Xi's own account, the *Yin Xi neizhuan* is a spurious work dating from the Tang, similar in type to the *Laozi hua hu jing* 老子化胡経 (no. 25); Yanagida 1976a: 49. See also Kohn 1991.

32. *Mouzi* 牟子 (The Book of Master Mou)

= *Mouzi lihuo lun* 牟子理惑論 (Mouzi's Treatise Settling Doubts)

The original two-*juan* version is not traceable after the Tang, but a one-*juan* version is included in the *Hongming ji* 弘明集, T. 52 (2102) 1a28–7a22. This was later included in the *Baizi quanshu* 百子全書 (2.1189b) under the title *Taiwei Mou Yong xuan* 太尉牟融撰 (Selected Writings of the Defender-in-chief Mou Yong).

According to the preface, it was written by the prefect Mou Yong at the end of the second century. However, there is no mention of it until the title appears in Lu Cheng's 陸澄 collection of Buddhist literature, the *Fa lun* 法論, which was compiled after 465. Thereafter, the work is frequently cited. For a more detailed discussion of the problems of its provenance, see Zürcher 1959: 13–15.

33. *Liezi* 列子 (The Book of Master Lie)

= *Chongxu zhidezhi jing* 沖虛至德眞経

3 *juan*. *Daozang* 348.668.

The name Lie Yukou 列禦冦 appears in the *Zhuangzi* 荘子, but the present-day *Liezi* is a stratified composite of ideas spanning eight centuries, from the end of the Warring States to the Eastern Jin. In addition to concepts pertaining to study of the Dao and immortals, the *Liezi* has elements in common with Buddhist thought. Yanagida 1976: 49.

34. *Fuzi* 苻子 (The Book of Master Fu)

Listed variously as 20 or 30 *juan*, this is a nonextant Daoist work written by Fu Lang 苻朗 in the latter part of the fourth century. Fu Lang was a nephew of Fu Jian 苻堅 (357–384), ruler of the Former Qin dynasty, and after the fall of the Former Qin he was made an official in the Jin court. (Zürcher 1959: 436n124 gives a summary of Fu Lang's biographical information.) Yan Kejun 嚴可均 later collected some fifty fragments of the *Fuzi*, mostly quotations from early encyclopedias, and published them in chapter 52 of his *Quan Jin wen* 全晋文. Apart from the statement that Śākyamuni was the master of Laozi, which is quoted in the *Fayuan zhulin* 法苑珠林, T. 53 (2122) 705c26, there are no other Buddhist ideas found among the fragments.

35. *Wu shu* 呉書 (The Wu History)

The *Wu shu* comprises fascicles 46–65 of the *Sanguo zhi* 三國志, but the official dynastic history has been lost. The extant spurious work probably dates from the second half of the sixth century, and it includes an account of the instructions in Buddhism given to the Prince of Wu and Kang Senghui's 康僧會 activities at the Wu court. It is quoted in many Buddhist apologia; see Maspéro 1910: 96–110. The *Lidai fabao ji* authors may have wanted to include the work due to its account of Emperor Ming of the Han and the contest between the Buddhists and the Daoists, which is quoted in the *Chuanfa ji* 傳法記, T. 52 (2105) 402a9–b17. The *Chuanfa ji* is the companion text to the *Hanfa neizhuan* in the *Xu ji gujin fodao lun heng* (no. 30, above).

36. *Bing gu lu* 并古録

It is probable that this is a miscopied citation, "bing Gujiu er lu 并古旧二録," from a list of titles in the *Falin biezhuan* 法琳別傳 that are cited as sources for the dates of the Buddha; T. 50 (2051) 207a17. This appears likely because the *Falin biezhuan* is one of the sources claimed by the *Lidai fabao ji* authors (no. 26), and the *Falin biezhuan* list includes two other *Lidai fabao ji* claimed sources, the *Zhou shu yiji* (no. 29) and the *Hou Hanfa bennei zhuan* 後漢法本内傳 (an alternative title for no. 30). *Gujiu er lu* probably refers to two *Lidai sanbao ji* entries, T. 49 (2034) 127b24 and 127c1, for two old catalogues of scriptures that are attributed to compilers in the Qin and the Former Han; see Yanagida 1967: 297.

A more remote possibility is that this refers to the two records, "Bing lu 并録," cited by Sengyou in his preface to the two lists of Sarvāstivāda masters; see *Chu sanzang ji ji*, T. 55 (2145) 89a15.

37. *Yang Lengqie Yedu gushi* 楊楞伽鄴都故事 (Yang Lengqie's Stories of Ye)

This is a nonextant geographical work by Yang Lengqie centered on Ye, the capital of the Northern Qi 北齊 (550–577). It appears to have included an account of Huike's activities in Ye, and it is quoted in the biography of Huike in Shenhui's "Miscellaneous Dialogues" (Suzuki and Kōda 1934: 56). In the *Taiping yulan* 太平御覧 there are references to what is probably the same work by three other titles: *Yecheng gushi* 鄴城故事, *Yang Lengqie Bei Qi Yedu gushi* 楊楞伽北齊鄴都故事, and *Bei Qi Yedu gushi* 北齊鄴都故事; see Yanagida 1967: 305n13. Paul Pelliot mentions that according to the *Shiwu jiyuan* 事物記原 there is a *Yecheng jiushi* 鄴城旧事 that tells the story of Emperor Ming's dream; Pelliot 1906: 394.

Abbreviations

Materials from Chinese historical sources and compendia are referenced by *juan* number in parentheses; page citations are from the Zhonghua shuju editions unless otherwise noted.

Romanization and diacritics: Because of variation in the romanization and diacritics systems used in the sources of quotations, there are some discrepancies in the rendering of Chinese, Sanskrit, and Pali terms. For direct quotations I retain the usage of the source, but where I have summarized or modified source material (indicated in the notes) I use Pinyin and standard Indic diacritics. In citing modern Chinese scholars, I use Pinyin unless the scholar is generally known by the Wade-Giles romanization of his name (i.e., Jan Yün-hua). For transliteration of Tibetan, I follow the usage of the source. Sanskrit and Pali words that have been identified by Roger Jackson as included in *Webster's Third New International Dictionary* are not italicized. See Jackson 1982.

Beijing = Dunhuang manuscripts in the National Library of China. Each manuscript in the original collection was identified according to its number within a batch of 100 manuscripts, and the batches were designated according to the sequence of characters in the *Qianziwen* 千字文 (Thousand-Character Classic).

Bussho = *Bussho kaisetsu daijiten* 佛書解說大辭典

Daozang = The Daoist canon, cited according to Schipper's numbering system

Hōbōgirin = Lévi, Sylvain, J. Takakusa, and Paul Demiéville, eds., *Hōbōgirin, Dictionnaire Encyclopédique du Bouddhisme d'après les sources chinoises et japonaises*

Hucker # = Entry number from *A Dictionary of Official Titles in Imperial China*

Jinyi 津藝 = Dunhuang and Turfan manuscripts in the Tianjin Art Museum collection. Texts in this collection are cited according to the document number, volume, and pages in the Shanghai guji publication, *Tianjinshi yishu bowuguan cang Dunhuang Tulufan wenxian* 天津市藝術博物館藏敦煌吐魯番文獻 (Dunhuang and Turfan documents held at the Tianjin Art Museum).

"Miscellaneous Dialogues" = Shenhui's *Heze heshang wenda za zhengyi* 荷澤和上問答雜徵義 (Miscellaneous Dialogues of the Venerable of Heze)

Mochizuki = *Mochizuki Bukkyō daijiten* 望月仏教大辭典

Morohashi = *Dai kanwa jiten* 大漢話辞典
Nakamura = *Bukkyōgō daijiten* 仏教語大辞典
P. = Dunhuang manuscripts in the Pelliot collection, Bibliothèque Nationale
P. Tib. = Tibetan Dunhuang manuscripts in the Pelliot collection, Bibliothèque Nationale
QTW = *Quan Tang wen* 全唐文
S. = Dunhuang manuscripts in the Stein collection, British Library
SKQS = *Siku quanshu* 四庫全書
SKSL = Yan Gengwang 嚴耕望, ed., *Shike shiliao xinbian* 石刻史料新編
T. = Takakusu Junjiro 高楠順次郎, ed., *Taishō shinshū daizōkyō* 太正新修大蔵経
Zengaku daijiten = Zengaku daijiten hensanshō 禅学大辞典編纂所, eds., *Zengaku daijiten* 禅学大辞典
ZZ. = Nakano Tatsue 中野達慧, ed., *Dai Nippon zokuzōkyō* 大日本続蔵経

Bibliography

REFERENCE AND COLLECTIONS

Chen Yuan 陳垣 ([1939] 1991). *Shishi yinian lu* 釋氏疑年錄 (Record of Dubious Dates of Buddhist Monks). Jiangsu: Jiangsu guangling guji.

E cang Dunhuang wenxian 俄藏敦煌文獻 (Dunhuang Documents Held in Russia [at the Institute of Oriental Studies of the Russian Academy of Sciences, St. Petersburg Branch]) (1995–99). 9 vols. Shanghai: Shanghai guji.

Huang Yongwu 黄永武, ed. (1981–86). *Dunhuang baozang* 敦煌寶藏 (Treasures from Dunhuang). 140 vols. Taibei: Xinwenfeng.

Hucker, Charles (1985). *A Dictionary of Official Titles in Imperial China.* Stanford: Stanford University Press.

Ji Xianlin 季羡林, ed. in chief (1998). *Dunhuangxue dacidian* 敦煌學大辭典 (Dictionary of Dunhuang Studies). Shanghai: Shanghai cishu.

Jiang Lihong 蔣禮鴻 ([1959] 1988). *Dunhuang bianwen ziyi tongshi* 敦煌變文字義通釋 (Comprehensive Explanations of the Meanings of Characters in Dunhuang *bianwen*). Shanghai: Shanghai guji.

Lévi, Sylvain, J. Takakusa, Paul Demiéville, and Hubert Durt, et al., eds. (1929–2003). *Hōbōgirin, Dictionnaire encyclopédique du Bouddhisme d'après les sources chinoises et japonaises.* 8 fascicles. Tokyo: Maison franco-japonaise.

Mochizuki Shinkyō 望月信亨 (1933–36). *Mochizuki Bukkyō daijiten* 望月仏教大辞典 (Mochizuki's Buddhist Dictionary). 10 vols. Tokyo: Sekai seitan kankū kyūkai.

Morohashi Tetsuji 諸橋轍 (1955–60). *Dai Kanwa jiten* 大漢和辞典 (Dictionary of Chinese). 12 vols. Tokyo: Daishukan shoten.

Nakamura Hajime 中村元 (1982). *Bukkyōgo daijiten* 仏教語大辞典 (Dictionary of Buddhist Terms). Reprint. Tokyo: Tōkyō shoseki.

Nakano Tatsue 中野達慧, ed. (1905–12). *Dai Nippon zokuzōkyō* 大日本続蔵経 (The Continued Buddhist Canon [Produced in] Japan). 150 vols. Kyoto: Zōkyō shoin.

Ono Genmyō 小野玄妙 (1932–36). *Bussho kaisetsu daijiten* 仏書解説大辞典 (Annotated Dictionary of Buddhist Works). Tokyo: Daitō shuppansha.

Takakusu Junjiro 高楠順次郎, ed. (1922–33). *Taishō shinshū daizōkyō* 太正新修大蔵経 (The New Edition of the Buddhist Canon [Produced in] the Taishō Era). 85 vols. Tokyo: Daizō shuppan kai.

Tang Geng'ou 唐耕耦 and Lu Xiongxi 陸雄斯, eds. (1986–90). *Dunhuang shehui jingji wenxian zhenji shilu* 敦煌社會經濟文獻真蹟釋錄 (Annotated Catalogue of Photos of the Social and Economic Documents of Dunhuang). 5 vols. Beijing: Center for Microfilm Copying of Documents, National Library.

Tianjinshi yishu bowuguan cang Dunhuang Tulufan wenxian 天津市藝術博物館藏敦煌吐魯番文獻 (Dunhuang and Turfan Documents Held at the Tianjin Art Museum) (1997–99). 7 vols. Shanghai: Shanghai guji.

Tōyō bijutsu 東洋美術 (Asiatic Art in Japanese Collections) (1967). Tokyo: Asahi shinbunsha.

Yan Gengwang 嚴耕望, ed. (1966–86). *Shike shiliao xinbian* 石刻史料新編 (A New Edition of Historical Materials Carved on Stone). Taibei: Xinwenfeng.

Zengaku daijiten hensanshō 禅学大辞典編纂所 (1985). *Zengaku daijiten* 禅学大辞典 (Dictionary of Zen Studies). Tokyo: Daishukan shoten.

Zhang Xiang 張相 (1985). *Shici quyu cihuishi* 詩詞曲語辭匯釋 (A Lexicon of Poetry and Song Lyrics). 3rd ed. Beijing: Zhonghua shuju.

PRIMARY SOURCES

Anban shouyi jing 安般守意經 (*Ānāpānasmṛti-sūtra*). T. 15 (602), trans. An Shigao 安世高.

Ayu wang jing 阿育王經 (*Aśokarāja-sūtra;* Sūtra of King Aśoka). T. 50 (2043), trans. in 512 by Saṅghapāla 僧伽婆羅.

Ayu wang zhuan 阿育王傳 (*Aśokāvadāna;* Biography of King Aśoka). T. 50 (2042), trans. early fourth century by An Faqin 安法欽.

Banruopoluomiduo xin jing 般若波羅蜜多心経 (*Prajñāpāramitā-hṛdaya-sūtra, Heart Sūtra*). T. 8 (251).

Banruo xin jing shu 般若心經疏 (Commentary on the *Heart Sūtra*). P. 2178, 4949; S. 839. By Zhishen 智詵 (609–702).

Banzhou sanmei jing 般舟三昧經 (*Pratyutpannabuddhasaṃmukhāvasthitasamādhi-sūtra,* a.k.a. *Bhadrapāla-sūtra*). T. 13 (418), trans. late second century by Lokakṣema 支婁迦識. Cf. T. 13 (416), (417), and (419); see Harrison 1990: 209–272.

Baolin zhuan 寶林傳 (Transmission of the Baolin [Temple]). 801, by Zhiju 智炬. In *Zhongguo fojiao congshu: Chanzong bian* 中國佛教叢書：禪宗編 (Compendium of Chinese Buddhism: Chan School), 1.18: 507–659. Reprint. Beijing: Jiangsu guji, 1993. See Tanaka 2003.

Baozang lun 寶藏論 (Treasure Store Treatise). C. late eighth century. T. 45 (1857).

Beishan lu 北山錄 (Record of North Mountain). 806, by Shenqing 神清. T. 52 (2113).

Benji jing 本際經 (Scripture of the Genesis Point). P. 2392, P. 3799.

Bianzheng lun 辯正論 (Treatise Discrimating the Truth). By Falin 法琳 (572–640). T. 52 (2120).

Biqiuni zhuan 比丘尼傳 (Biographies of Nuns). C. 516, by Baochang 寶唱. T. 50 (2063).

Biyan lu 碧巖錄 (Blue Cliff Record). T. 48 (2003).

Caoqi dashi zhuan 曹溪大師傳 (Biography of the Master of Caoqi). 781. ZZ. II, 19, 5: 483–488. In Komazawa daigaku Zenshūshi kenkyūkai 1978: 7–82.

Chan miyaofa jing 禪秘要法經 (Scripture of the Secret Essential Methods of Dhyāna). T. 15 (613), trans. Kumārajīva 鳩摩羅什.

Chanmen jing 禪門經 (Scripture of the Chan Teachings). P. 4646, S. 5532. Appendix, no. 16.

Chanyuan qinggui 禪苑清規 (Rules of Purity for Chan Monasteries). 1103, by Changlu Zongze 長蘆宗賾 (d. 1107?). ZZ. II, 19, 5.

Chanyuan zhu quanji duxu 禪源諸詮集都序 (Prolegomenon to the Collection of Expressions of the Chan Source). C. 833, by Guifeng Zongmi 圭峰宗密 (780–841). T. 48 (2015).

Chuan fabao ji 傳法寶紀 (Annals of the Transmission of the Dharma-Jewel). C. 713, by Du Fei 杜朏. T. 85 (2838); P. 2634, P. 3858, P. 3559.

Chuanfa zhengzong lun 傳法正宗論 (Treatise of the True Doctrine of Transmission of the Dharma). By Qisong 契嵩 (1007–1072). T. 51 (2080).

Chu sanzang ji ji 出三藏記集 (Collection of Notes on the Translation of the Tripiṭaka). 515, by Sengyou 僧祐. T. 55 (2145).

Da aluohan Nantimiduoluo suo shuo fachu ji 大阿羅漢難提密多羅所說法住記 (The Great Arhat Nandimitara Explains the *Bhūtatathatā*). T. 49 (2030).

Dabanniepan jing 大般涅槃經 (*Mahāparinirvāṇa-sūtra*). T. 12 (374) and (375). Appendix, no. 17.

Dabanniepan jing houfen 大般涅槃經後分 (Latter Part of the *Mahāparinirvāṇa-sūtra*). T. 12 (377), trans. in the Tang by Jñānabhadra.

Dabanruopoluomiduo jing 大般若波羅蜜多経 (*Mahāprajñāpāramitā-sūtra*). T. 5–7 (220). Appendix, no. 15.

Dafangdeng wuxiang jing 大方等無想經, a.k.a. *Dayun jing* 大雲經 (*Mahāmegha-sūtra*). T. 12 (387).

Dafangguang fo huayan jing 大方廣佛華嚴經 (*[Buddha]avataṃsaka-sūtra*). T. 9 (278), T. 10 (279), T. 10 (293). Appendix, no. 14.

Dafoding jing 大佛頂經 (*Śūraṃgama-sūtra;* Scripture of the Crown of the Buddha's Head). Tang apocryphon. T. 19 (945). Appendix, no. 9.

Dakkhiṇāvibhanga Sutta (The Exposition of Offerings). *Majjhima Nikaya* 3.255. Ñāṇamoli and Bodhi 1995: 1102–1106.

Damoduoluo chan jing 達摩多羅禪經 (The Dhyāna-Scripture of Dharmatrāta). T. 15 (618), trans. Buddhabhadra 佛馱跋陀羅 (359–429).

Daoxuan lushi gantong lu 道宣律師感通錄 (Record of Miraculous Instruction Given to Vinaya Master Daoxuan). By Daoxuan 道宣 (596–667). T. 52 (2107).

Dasheng baifa mingmen lun 大乘百法明門論 (*Mahāyānaśatadharmaprakāśamukha-śastra*). T. 31 (1614), trans. Xuanzang.

Dasheng dayi zhang 大乘大義章, a.k.a. *Jiumaluoshe fashi dayi* 鳩摩羅什法師大義 (Significant Points [Explained by] Dharma Master Kumārajīva), T. 45 (1856) (Letters of Huiyuan 慧遠 [334–416] and Kumārajīva).

Dasheng yi zhang 大乘義章 (Chapters on the Meaning of the Mahāyāna). By Huiyuan (523–592). T. 44 (1851).

Dasheng qixin lun 大乘起信論 (Treatise on Arousal of Faith in the Mahāyāna). Apocryphon attrib. to Aśvaghośa. T. 32 (1666) (trans. attrib. to Paramārtha) and (1667) (trans. attrib. to Śikṣānanda).

Dasheng wufangbian 大乘五方便 (The Five Expedient Means of the Mahāyāna), a.k.a. *Dasheng wusheng fangbian men* 大乘無生方便門 (Teachings on the Expedient Means of [Attaining] Birthlessness in the Mahāyāna). S. 2503 (T. 85 [2834]), S. 735 (in Suzuki 1968–71, vol. 3), P. 2058 (in Ui 1966), P. 2270, P. 2836.

Dasheng xinxing lun 大乘心行論 (Treatise on the Mind-Practice of the Mahāyāna). By Sengchou 僧稠 (480–560). P. 3559.

Da Song sengshi lüe 大宋僧史略 (The Song Dynasty Compendium of Monastic History). [978–999], by Zanning 贊寧. T. 54 (2126).

Da Tang xiyu ji 大唐西域記 (The Tang Dynasty Account of the Western Regions). By Xuanzang 玄奘 (602–664). T. 51 (2087).

Da Tang Zhongyue dong Xianjusi gu dade Gui heshang ji dechuang 大唐中嶽東閑居寺故大德珪和尚紀德幢 (Banner Recording the Virtue of the Tang Late Worthy Reverend Gui of East Xianju Monastery on Zhongyue). *Baqiongshi jinshi buzheng* 八瓊室金石補正, vol. 3 (53) 903a–904b. In SKSL, series I, vol. 7: 4849a–4850b.

Dayun jing Shenhuang shouji yishu 大雲經神皇授記義疏 (Commentary on the Meaning of the Prophecy About [Her Majesty] Shenhuang in the Great Cloud Scripture). S. 6502.

Dazhao chanshi daming 大照禪師塔銘 (Stūpa Inscription for Chan Master Dazhao [Puji]). QTW (262) 6.3360–3363.

Dazhidu lun 大智度論 (*Mahāprajñāpāramitā-śastra*). T. 25 (1509), attributed to Nāgārjuna, trans. Kumārajīva.

Dehu zhangzhe jing 德護長者經 (*Śrīgupta-sūtra*). T. 14 (545).

Dingguan jing 定觀經 (Scripture of Concentration and Meditation). *Daozang* 400.

Diqizu Dazhao heshang jimie ri zhai zan wen 第七祖大照和尚寂滅日齋讚文 (Funeral Eulogy for the Seventh Patriarch, the Venerable Dazhao [Puji]). S. 2512.

Duigenqi xingfa 對根起行法 (Practice Methods That Arise in Accord with Capacity). S. 2446, *Dunhuang baozang* 19.509a–538b.

Dunwu dasheng zhenglijue 頓悟大乘正理決 (Verification of Sudden Awakening in the Mahāyāna). Arguments of Moheyan 摩訶衍, comp. Wang Xi 王錫. P. 4646, S. 2672.

Dunwu wushang banruo song 頓悟無生般若頌 (Hymn to the Birthless Wisdom of Sudden Awakening). C. 750, by Shenhui 神會 (684–758). S. 468, in Hu [1930] 1970: 191–208; also known as the *Xianzong ji* 顯宗記 (Record of the Manifestation of the Doctrine), in *Jingde chuandeng lu,* T. 51 (2076) 458c25–459b6; abbreviated variant *Xianzong lun* 顯宗論 in the *Zongjing lu,* T. 48 (2016) 949a26–b7.

Dunwu yaomen 頓悟要門 (The Essentials of Sudden Awakening). Early eighth century, by Dazhu Huihai 大珠慧海. In *Zen no goroku* 禅の語録, no. 6. Tokyo: Chikuma shobō.

Dunwu zhenzong lun 頓悟真宗論 (Treatise on the True Lineage of Sudden Awakening). Compiled in the Tang, by Huiguang 慧光. T. 85 (2835).

Erru sixing lun 二入四行論 (Treatise on the Two Entrances and Four Practices). Attributed to Bodhidharma. S. 2715, S. 3375, S. 7159, P. 2923, P. 3018, P. 4634. In Yanagida 1969a.

Fahuachuan ji 法華傳記 (Record of Accounts of the Lotus). Compiled in the Tang by Sengxiang 僧詳. T. 51 (2068).

Fanwang jing 梵網經 (*Brahmajāla-sūtra;* Scripture of Brahma's Net). T. 24 (1484).

Fayuan zhulin 法苑珠林 (Jade Grove of the Dharma Garden). By Daoshi 道世. T. 53 (2122).

Fo yijiao jing 佛遺教經 (Teachings Left by the Buddha), a.k.a. *Fochui banniepan lueshuo jiaojie jing* 佛垂般涅槃略說教誡經, T. 12 (389), trans. attrib. to Kumārajīva.

Fozu lidai tongzai 佛祖歷代通載 (Comprehensive Register of the Buddhas and Patriarchs Through the Ages). 1341, by Nianchang 念常. T. 49 (2036).

Fozu tongji 佛祖統記 (Sequential Record of the Buddhas and Patriarchs). T. 49 (2035).

Fu fazang [yinyuan] zhuan 付法藏[因緣]傳 (Account of the [*Avādana*] of the Transmission of the Dharma Treasury). T. 50 (2058). Appendix, no. 24.

Gaoseng Faxian zhuan 高僧法顯傳 (Biography of the Eminent Monk Faxian), a.k.a. *Foguo ji* 佛國記 (Record of Buddhist Kingdoms). T. 51 (2085).

Gaoseng zhuan 高僧傳 (Biographies of Eminent Monks). C. 530, by Huijiao 慧皎. T. 50 (2059).

Guanding jing 灌頂經 (Book of Consecration). T. 21 (1331).

Guanfo sanmei hai jing 觀佛三昧海經 (Sūtra on the Sea of the Samādhi of Buddha Visualization). T. 15 (643).

Guang hongming ji 廣弘明集 (Expanded Anthology of Extended Brilliance). By Daoxuan. T. 52 (2103).

Guangxiao si yifa taji 光孝寺瘞髮塔記 (Reliquary Inscription for the Interment of [Huineng's] Hair at Guangxiao Monastery). By Facai 法才. QTW (912); in Yanagida 1967: 535–536.

Guan Mile pusa shangsheng Doushuaitian jing 觀彌勒菩薩上生兜率天經 (Scripture of the Visualization of Maitreya's Ascension to Tuṣita). T. 14 (452).

Guan Puxianpusa xingfa jing 觀普賢菩薩行法經 (Scripture of the Methods of Contemplation of the Bodhisattva Samantabhadra). T. 9 (277), trans. mid-fifth century, by Dharmamitra 曇摩蜜多.

Guanzhong chuangli jietan tujing 關中創立戒壇圖經 (Diagram Scripture on Establishing the Ordination Platform in Central China). By Daoxuan. T. 45 (1892).

Hanfa neizhuan 漢法內傳 (Inner Commentary on the Dharma in the Han), T. 52 (2105) 397b25–401c25. Appendix, no. 30.

Heze heshang wenda za zhengyi 荷澤和上問答雜徵義 (Miscellaneous Dialogues of the Venerable of Heze) in three manuscripts: (a) P. 3047 (part 1), in Hu [1930] 1970: 91–152; (b) the "Ishii" manuscript, in Suzuki and Kōda 1934 (synoptic edition of these two manuscripts found in Suzuki 1968–71: 3: 236–288); and (c) *Nanyang heshang wenda za zhengyi* 南陽和尚問答雜徵義 (Miscellaneous Dialogues of the Venerable of Nanyang), S. 6557, in Hu [1958] 1970: 426–452. By Shenhui.

Hongming ji 弘明集 (Anthology of Extended Brilliance). By Sengyou. T. 52 (2102).

Ji shamen buying bai su dengshi 集沙門不應拜俗等事 (*Anthology of [Reasons Why] Monks Should not Bow to the Laity and Related Matters*). Compiled in the Tang by Yan Cong 彥悰 T. 52 (2108).

Ji Shenzhou sanbao gantong lu 集神州三寶感通錄 (Collected Records of Triple-Jewel Miracles in China). By Daoxuan. T. 52 (2106).

Jian yiqie ruzangjing mulu 見一切入藏經目錄 (A Catalogue of All Scriptures Checked [in the Library of the Sanjie Temple in Dunhuang]). 934, by Daozhen 道真. In Oda 1989.

Jianbei yiqie zhide jing 漸備一切智德經 (*Daśabhūmika-sūtra*). T. 10 (285), trans. Dharmarakṣa.

Jie mo 羯磨 (*Karmavācanā*). T. 22 (1433).

Jin guangming jing 金光明經 (*Suvarṇaprabhāsa-sūtra*). T. 16 (663), trans. Dharmakṣema 曇無讖.

Jin shu 晉書 (Jin History). C. 646–648. Beijing: Zhonghua shuju, 1975.

Jingangbanruopoluomi jing 金剛般若波羅蜜經 (*Vajracchedikā-sūtra; Diamond Sūtra*). T. 8 (235)–(239). Appendix, no. 23.

Jingang sanmei jing 金剛三昧經 (*Vajrasamādhi-sūtra*). T. 9 (273). Appendix, no. 10.

Jingde chuandeng lu 淨德傳燈錄 (Record of the Transmission of the Lamp [Compiled in] the Jingde era). 1004, by Daoyuan 道原. T. 51 (2076).

Jingtu wuhui nianfo songjing guanxing yi 淨土五會念佛誦經觀行儀 (The Pure Land Five-Rhythm Buddha-Recollection Liturgy and Visualization Practice Ceremony). 774, by Fazhao 法照 (d. 820?). P. 2066; T. 85 (2827).

Jingzhou Yuquansi Datong chanshi beiming bing xu 荊州玉泉寺大通禪師碑銘并序 (Stele Inscription for Chan Master Datong [Shenxiu] of Yuquan Monastery in Jingzhou, with preface). QTW (231) 5.2953–2954.

Juedingpini jing 決定毘尼經 (*Vinayaviniścaya-Upālipariprcchā-sūtra;* Scripture of the Inquiry of Upāli Regarding Determination of the Vinaya). T. 12 (325), trans. Dharmarakṣa. Appendix, no. 8.

Jueguan lun 絕觀論 (Treatise on Transcendence of Cognition). C. late eighth century. P. 2732, P. 2074, P. 2885, P. 2045, Beijing *jun* 84, and the Ishii manuscript. See Tokiwa and Yanagida 1976.

Kaiyuan shijiao lu 開元釋教錄 (Buddhist Catalogue of the Kaiyuan Era [713–742]). T. 55 (2154). Appendix, no. 28.

Lengqie jing 楞伽経 (*Laṅkā[vatāra]-sūtra;* Scripture of the Appearance of the Dharma in Laṅkā). T. 16 (670), (671), and (672). Appendix, no. 18.

Lengqie shizi ji 楞伽師資記 (Record of the Masters and Disciples of the *Laṅkā[vatāra]-sūtra*). C. 720, by Jingjue 淨覺. T. 85 (2837); P. 4564, P. 3294, P. 3537, P. 3436, P. 3703, S. 2054, S. 4272.

Lidai fabao ji 曆代法寶記 (Record of the Dharma-Jewel Through the Generations). C. 780. T. 51 (2075).

Lidai minghua ji 歷代名畫記 (Record of Famous Painters Through the Generations). 847. SKQS vol. 812.

Lidai sanbao ji 歷代三寶記 (Record of the Three Jewels Through the Generations). T. 49 (2034).

Linji lu 臨濟錄 (Record of Linji) = *Zhenzhou Linji Huizhao chanshi yulu* 鎮州臨濟慧照禪師語錄, T. 47 (1985).

Liuzu Neng chanshi beiming 六祖能禪師碑銘 (Epitaph for the Sixth Patriarch, Chan Master Neng). C. 740, by Wang Wei 王維 (699–759). *Tang wen cui* 唐文粹 (63), in Yanagida 1967: 540.

Liuzu tanjing 六祖壇經 (Platform Sūtra of the Sixth Patriarch). C. late eighth c. Numerous texts, see Komazawa daigaku Zenshūshi kenkyūkai 1978, and Yang 1993.

Luoyang qielan ji 洛陽伽藍記 (A Record of Buddhist Monasteries in Luoyang). 547, by Yang Xuanzhi 楊衒之. T. 51 (2092).

Lüxiang gantong zhuan 律相感通傳 (Traditions of Vinaya-related Miracles). By Daoxuan. T. 45 (1898).

Miaofa lianhua jing 妙法蓮華經 (*Saddharmapuṇḍarīka-sūtra; Lotus Sūtra*). T. 9 (262)–(264). Appendix, no. 20.

Mingbao ji 冥報記 (Tales of Miraculous Retribution). C. 655, by Tanglin 唐林 (600–659). T. 51 (2082).

Mishasaibuhexi wufen lü 彌沙塞部和醯五分律 (*Mahīśāsaka Vinaya*). T. 22 (1421), trans. c. 438 by Buddhajīva 佛陀什.

Mohemoye jing 摩訶摩耶經 (*Mahāmāyā-sūtra;* Scripture of [the Buddha's Mother] Mahāmāyā). T. 12 (383), trans. c. 479–502.

Mohe zhiguan 摩訶止觀 (The Great Calming and Insight). By Tiantai Zhiyi. T. 46 (1911).

Mohosengqi lü 摩訶僧祇律 (*Mahāsaṅghika Vinaya*). T. 22 (1425), trans. c. 416–418 by Faxian 法顯 and Buddhabhadra.

Mouzi lihuo lun 牟子理惑論 (Mouzi's Treatise Settling Doubts). T. 52 (2102) 1a28–7a22. Appendix, no. 32.

Nanhai jiguinei fazhuan 南海寄歸內法傳 (Transmission of the Dharma in the Southern Archipelago). By Yijing 義淨. T. 54 (2125).

Nanyang heshang dunjiao jietuo chanmen zhiliao xing tanyu 南陽和上頓教解脫禪門直了性壇語 (The Platform Address of the Venerable of Nanyang on Directly Comprehending the Nature According to the Chan Approach of Emancipation in the Sudden Teaching). C. 720. Dunhuang manuscripts: (a) Beijing *han* 81, in Suzuki 1968–71, vol. 3: 290–317; (b) P. 2045 (part 2) in Hu [1958] 1970: 225–252; and (c) Dunhuang museum manuscript no. 77.

Neiguan jing 內觀經 (Scripture of Interior Meditation). *Daozang* 641.

Poxie lun 破邪論 (Treatise on Destroying the Heterodox). By Falin. T. 52 (2109).

Pusadichi jing 菩薩地持經 (*Bodhisattvabhūmi*). T. 30 (1581), trans. c. 414–421 by Dharmakṣema.

Pusa jieben 菩薩戒本 (*Bodhisattvaprātimokṣa*). T. 24 (1500), trans. Dharmakṣema.

Pusa shanjie jing 菩薩善戒經 (*Bodhisattvabhūmi*). T. 30 (1582), trans. c. 431 by Guṇavarman 求那跋摩.

Pusa shanjie jing 菩薩善戒經 (*Bodhisattvacāryanirdeśa*). T. 30 (1583), trans. Guṇavarman.

[Pusa] yingluo [benye] jing [菩薩]瓔珞[本業]經 (Scripture of the [Original Acts That Serve as] Necklaces [for the Bodhisattvas]). T. 24 (1485). Appendix, no. 13.

Putidamou nanzong ding shifei lun 菩提達摩南宗定是非論 (Treatise Determining the True and False about the Southern School of Bodhidharma). Record of Shenhui's 732 debate, by Dugu Pei 獨孤沛. P. 3047 (part 2), P. 2045 (part 1), and P. 3488 (part 1); in Hu [1958] 1970: 260–314.

Puxian pusa shuo ci zhengming jing 普賢菩薩說此證明經 (Scripture of Attestation Spoken by the Bodhisattva Samantabhadra). T. 85 (2879).

Qing Bintoulu fa 請賓頭盧法 (The Method for Propitiating Piṇḍola). T. 32 (1689).

Quan Tang wen 全唐文 (Complete Prose of the Tang Dynasty). 1814, Dong Gao 董誥 et al., eds. Beijing: Zhonghua shuju, 1983.

Renwang [banruopoluomi] jing 仁王[般若波羅蜜]經 (*[Prajñāpāramitā]* Scripture of Humane Kings). T. 8 (245), trans. Kumārajīva; T. 8 (246), trans. Bukong 不空 (a.k.a. Amoghavajra, 705–774).

Rulai zhuangyan zhihui guangming ru yiqie fojingjie jing 如來莊嚴智惠光明入一切佛境界經 (*Sarvabuddhaviṣayāvatārajñānālokālaṃkāra-sūtra*). T. 12 (357).

Shanjian lu piposha 善見律毘婆沙 (*Samantapāsādikā*). By Buddhaghosa. T. 24 (1462), trans. c. 488 by Saṅghabhadra.

Sheng Tian Wang banruo [poluomi] jing 勝天王般若[波羅蜜]經 (The *Prajñāpāramitā* Scripture of the King of the Surpassing Heaven). T. 8 (231).

Shi chan poluomi cidi famen 釋禪波羅蜜次第法門 (Explaining the Sequence of Dharma Gates to the *Pāramitā* [Perfection] of Meditation). By Tiantai Zhiyi. T. 46 (1916).

Shidi jing 十地經 (*Daśabhūmika-sūtra*). T. 10 (287).

Shiji 史記 (Records of the Historian). By Sima Qian 司馬遷 (145–86 B.C.E.). Beijing: Zhonghua shuju, 1959.

Shilao zhi 釋老志 (Treatise on Buddhism and Daoism). C. 550, by Wei Shou 魏收. Fascicle 114 of the *Wei shu* 魏書 (Wei History). Beijing: Zhonghua shuju, 1974: 3025–3062.

Shisong lü 十誦律 (*Sarvāstivāda Vinaya*). T. 23 (1435), trans. early fifth century by Kumārajīva 鳩摩羅什, Puṇyatara 弗若多羅, and Dharmaruci 曇摩流支.

Shizhu jing 十住經 (*Daśabhūmika-sūtra*). T. 10 (286), trans. Kumārajīva.

Shōbōgenzō 正法眼藏 (Treasury of the True Dharma Eye). By Dōgen 道元 (1200–1253). T. 82 (2582).

Shoulengyan sanmei jing 首楞嚴三昧 (*Śūraṃgamasamādhi-sūtra*). T. 15 (642), trans. c. 384–417 by Kumārajīva.

Sifen lü 四分律 (Dharmaguptaka Vinaya). T. 22 (1428), trans. c. 412 by Buddhayaśas 佛陀耶舍.

Sishier zhang jing 四十二章經 (Scripture in Forty-two Sections). T. 17 (784).

Siyifantian suowen jing 思益梵天所問經 (*Viśeṣacintibrahmaparipṛcchā-sūtra*). T. 15 (586), trans. Kumārajīva.

Song gaoseng zhuan 宋高僧傳 (Song Dynasty Biographies of Eminent Monks). 988, by Zanning. T. 50 (2061).

Taiping guangji 太平廣記 (The Comprehensive Record of the Taiping Era). 978, comp. Li Fang 李昉 et al. Reprint. Beijing: Zhonghua shuju, 1961.

Tang huiyao 唐會要(Record of the Social Institutions of the Tang). 961, by Wang Pu 王溥 (932–982). Ed. Yang Jialuo 楊家駱, 3 vols. Reprint. Taibei: Shijie shuju, 1974.

Tang shu 唐書 (Tang History). 945, by Liu Xu 劉昫. Reprint. Beijing: Zhonghua shuju, 1975.

Tang wen cui 唐文粹 (The Complete Literature of the Tang). By Yao Xuan 姚鉉 (968–1020). In *Sibu congkan* 四部叢刊 (1st series).

Tang zhongyue shamen Shi Faru chanshi xingzhuang 唐中岳沙門釋法如禪師行狀 (Epitaph for the Tang [Dynasty] Śramaṇa of the Central Peak, Dhyāna Master Shi Faru). C. 689. *Jinshi xubian* 金石續編, vol. 6, p. 2a–b; in Yanagida 1967: 487–88.

Tang Zizhou Huiyi jingshe nanchanyuan sizhengtang beiming 唐梓州慧義精舍南禪院四證堂碑銘 (Stele Inscription for the Four Exemplars Hall of the Southern Chan Cloister of Huiyi Monastery in Zizhou, Tang Dynasty), by Li Shangyin 李商隱 (813–858). QTW (780) 8.8141–8144. (Annotated edition in *Sibu beiyao: Fannan wenji bubian* 樊南文集補編 10: 1–24.)

Tiwei [Boli]jing 提謂[波利]經 (Scripture of Trapuṣa [and Ballika]). S. 2051, P. 3732.

Wang Fanzhi shiji 王梵志詩集 (The Collected Poems of Brahmacarya Wang), by Wang Fanzhi 王梵志 (d. 670?). T. 85 (2863).

Weimojie suoshuo jing 維摩詰所說經 (*Vimalakīrtinirdeśa-sūtra;* Scripture on the Expositions of Vimalakīrti). T. 14 (475)–(476). Appendix, no. 21.

Wei shu 魏書 (Wei History). Reprint. Beijing: Zhonghua shuju, 1974.

Wenshushili wen jing 文殊師利問經 (*Mañjuśrīparipṛcchā*). T. 14 (468).

Wenshushili xing jing 文殊師利行經 (*Mañjuśrīvikāra-sūtra*). T. 14 (471).

Wenshu shuo banruo jing 文殊說般若經 (*Saptaśatikāprajñāpāramitā-sūtra*). T. 8 (232) and (233).

Wumen guan 無門關 (Gateless Barrier). In *Zen no goroku,* no. 18. Tokyo: Chikuma shobō.

Wuxin lun 無心論 (Treatise on No-Mind). C. late eighth century S. 5619; T. 85 (2831).

Xiande ji yu Shuangfeng shan ta ge tan xuanli shier 先德集於雙峰山塔各談玄理十二 (Twelve Former Worthies Gather at the Stūpa on Mt. Shuangfeng and Each Discusses the Mysterious Principle). P. 3559.

Xinming 心銘 (Inscription on Mind). C. late eighth century. In *Jingde chuandeng lu,* T. 51 (2076) 457b–458a.

Xin Tang shu 新唐書 (New Tang History). 1060, by Ouyang Xiu 歐陽修 and Song Qi 宋祁. Reprint. Beijing: Zhonghua shuju, 1975.

Xinwang ming 心王銘 (Inscription on the Mind King). C. late eighth century. In *Jingde chuandeng lu,* T. 51 (2076) 456c25–457a17.

Xinxin ming 信心銘 (Inscription on Faith in Mind). C. late eighth century. In *Jingde chuandeng lu,* T. 51 (2076) 457a18–b24. Also S. 4037, S. 5692, P. 2104, P. 4638.

Xu gaoseng zhuan 續高僧傳 (Continued Biographies of Eminent Monks). C. 664, by Daoxuan. T. 50 (2060).

Youpoli wen pusa shoujiefa 優波離問菩薩受戒法 (Upāli Asks a Bodhisattva to Explain the Precepts). T. 30 (1583), trans. Guṇavarman.

Youposejie jing 優波塞戒經 (*Upāsakaśīla-sūtra*). T. 24 (1488), trans. Dharmakṣema.

Yuanjue jing dashu chao 圓覺經大疏鈔 (Subcommentary to the Scripture of Perfect Enlightenment). 823–824, by Zongmi. ZZ. I, 14, 3.

Yuqie shidi lun 瑜伽師地論 (*Yogācārabhūmi-śāstra*). T. 30 (1579), trans. Xuanzang.

Zhancha shanwuyebao jing 占察善惡業報經 (Book of Divining the Requital of Good and Evil Actions). T. 17 (839).

Zhonghua chuanxindi chanmen shizi chengxi tu 中華傳心地禪門師資承襲圖 (Chart of the Master-Disciple Succession of the Chan Gate That Transmits the Mind Ground in China). By Zongmi. ZZ. II, 15.

Zhongjing mulu 眾經目錄 (Catalogue of Scriptures). 594, by Fajing 法經. T. 55 (2147).

Zhong Tianzhu Sheweiguo Zhihuansi tujing 中天竺舍衛國衹桓寺圖經 (Diagram Scripture of the Jetavana in the Kingdom of Śrāvastī in Central India). By Daoxuan. T. 45 (1899).

Zhu banruopoluomiduo xin jing 注般若波羅蜜多心經 (Commentary on the *Prajñāpāramitāhṛdaya-sūtra*). By Jingjue. S. 4556. In Yanagida 1967: 594–624.

Zhufa benwu jing 諸法本無經 (*Sarvadharmāpravṛttinirdeśa-sūtra;* Scripture of the Fundamental Non-Being of Dharmas). T. 15 (651).

Zhujing yaochao 諸經要抄 (Digest of Scriptures). T. 85 (2819). (Original title unknown, current title given by *Taishō* editors.) Photocopy of Dunhuang manuscript in Nogami, ed., 1972.

Zizhi tongjian 資治通鑑 (Comprehensive Mirror for Aid in Government). By Sima Guang 司馬光 (1019–86). 10 vols. Reprint. Beijing: Zhonghua shuju, 1976.

Zongjing lu 宗鏡錄 (Record of the Mirror of Truth). 961, by Yanshou 延壽. T. 48 (2016).

Zuishangsheng lun 最上乘論 (Treatise on the Highest Vehicle). Dialogues of Hongren 弘忍 (602–675). T. 48 (2011). A.k.a. *Xiuxinyao lun* 修心要論 (Treatise on Essentials of Cultivating the Mind), S. 2669, S. 3558, S. 4064, P. 3434, P. 3559, P. 3777.

Zun Poxumi pusa suoji lun 尊婆須蜜菩薩所集論 (*Āryavasumitrabodhisattvasaṃghītiśāstra;* Treatise compiled by the Venerable Bodhisattva Vasumitra). T. 28 (1549).

Zuowang lun 坐忘論 (Essay on Sitting and Forgetting). By Sima Chengzhen 司馬承禎 (646–735). *Daozang* 1036.

Zutang ji 祖堂集 (Anthology from the Patriarchal Hall). 952, by Jing 靜 and Yun 筠. In Yanagida, ed., 1974.

SELECTED SECONDARY SOURCES

Abe, Stanley K. (2002). *Ordinary Images.* Chicago: University of Chicago Press.

——— (1990). "Art and Practice in a Fifth-Century Chinese Buddhist Cave Temple." *Ars Orientalis* 20: 1–32.

App, Urs (1995). "On No-Mind, in One Fascicle, by Bodhidharma." *Eastern Buddhist* 28(1): 82–106.

——— (1994a). *Master Yunmen: From the Record of the Chan Teacher "Gate of Clouds."* Tokyo: Kodansha International.

——— (1994b). "Reference Works for Ch'an Research." *Cahiers d'Extrême-Asie* 7: 357–409.

——— (1993). "Recent English Publications about Chan, Sŏn, and Zen (1977–1992)." *Zenbunka kenkyūjo kiyō* 禅文化研究所紀要 19: 1–58.

Backus, Charles (1981). *The Nan-chao Kingdom and T'ang China's Southwestern Frontier.* Cambridge: Cambridge University Press.

Bagchi, Prabodh Chandra (1927). *Le canon bouddhique en Chine: Les traducteurs et les traductions.* 2 vols. Paris: Sino-Indica, Publications de l'Université de Calcutta, Librarie orientaliste Paul Geuthner.

Barrett, Timothy H. (1996). *Taoism Under the T'ang.* London: Wellsweep Press.

——— (1994). "The Emergence of the Taoist Papacy in the T'ang Dynasty." *Asia Major* (3rd series) 7: 89–106.

Beal, Samuel, trans. ([1884] 1981). *Si-yu-ki: Buddhist Records of the Western World. Translated from the Chinese of Hiuen Tsiang (A.D. 629).* Delhi: Motilal Banarsidass.

Beckwith, Christopher I. (1987). *The Tibetan Empire in Central Asia.* Princeton: Princeton University Press.

——— (1983). "The Revolt of 755 in Tibet." *Weiner Studien zur Tibetologie und Buddhismuskunde* 10: 1–16.

Bell, Catherine (1992). *Ritual Theory, Ritual Practice.* Oxford: Oxford University Press.

Benn, James A. (2001). "Burning for the Buddha: Self-Immolation in Chinese Buddhism." Ph.D. diss., University of California, Los Angeles.

Berger, Patricia (1994). "Preserving the Nation: The Political Uses of Tantric Art in China." In Marsha Weidner, ed., *Latter Days of the Law: Images of Chinese Buddhism 850–1850,* pp. 89–123. Lawrence: Spencer Museum of Art, University of Kansas.

Berling, Judith A. (1987). "Bringing the Buddha Down to Earth: Notes on the Emergence of Yu-lu as a Buddhist Genre." *History of Religions* 21(1): 56–88.

Birnbaum, Raoul (1990). "Secret Halls of the Mountain Lords: The Caves of Wu-t'ai Shan." *Cahiers d'Extrême-Asie* 5: 115–140.

——— (1986). "The Manifestation of a Monastery: Shen-ying's Experiences on Mount Wu-tai in T'ang Context." *Journal of the American Oriental Society* 106(1): 119–137.

——— (1984). "Thoughts on T'ang Buddhist Mountain Traditions and their Context." *T'ang Studies* 2: 5–23.

Bokenkamp, Stephen (1997). *Early Daoist Scriptures.* Berkeley: University of California Press.

——— (1994). "Time After Time: Taoist Apocalyptic History and the Founding of the T'ang Dynasty." *Asia Major* (3rd series) 7: 59–88.

——— (1990). "Stages of Transcendence: The Bhūmi Concept in Taoist Scripture." In Buswell, ed., *Chinese Buddhist Apocrypha*, pp. 119–147.

Boodberg, Peter ([1938–39] 1979). "Marginalia to the Histories of the Northern Dynasties." In Alvin P. Cohen, ed., *Selected Works of Peter Boodberg,* pp. 265–349. Berkeley: University of California Press.

——— ([1936] 1979). "The Language of the T'o-Pa Wei." In Cohen, ed., *Selected Works of Peter Boodberg,* pp. 221–239.

Bourdieu, Pierre (1984). *Distinction: A Social Critique of the Judgement of Taste.* London: Routledge and Kegan Paul.

Brinker, Helmut, and Hiroshi Kanazawa (1996). *Zen Masters of Meditation in Images and Writings.* Zürich: Artibus Asiae.

Broughton, Jeffrey L. (2004). "Tsung-mi's Zen Prolegomenon: Introduction to an Exemplary Zen Canon." In Steven Heine and Dale S. Wright, eds., *The Zen Canon: Understanding the Classic Texts,* pp. 11–51. Oxford: Oxford University Press.

——— (1999). *The Bodhidharma Anthology: The Earliest Records of Zen.* Berkeley: University of California Press.

——— (1983). "Early Ch'an Schools in Tibet." In Gimello and Gregory, eds., *Studies in Ch'an and Hua-yen,* pp. 1–68.

——— (n.d.). "Proto-Ch'an Texts."

——— (1975). "Kuei-feng Tsung-mi: The Convergence of Ch'an and the Teachings." Ph.D. diss., Columbia University.

Brown, Peter (1988). *The Body and Society: Men, Women, and Sexual Renunciation in Early Christianity.* New York: Columbia University Press.

——— (1983). "The Saint as Exemplar in Late Antiquity." *Réprentations* 1(2): 1–25.

——— (1982). *Society and the Holy in Late Antiquity.* Berkeley: University of California Press.

——— ([1976] 1982). "Eastern and Western Christendom in Late Antiquity: A Parting of the Ways." In Brown, *Society and the Holy in Late Antiquity,* pp. 166–195. Berkeley: University of California Press.

Buswell, Robert E., Jr. (1990). *Chinese Buddhist Apocrypha.* Honolulu: University of Hawai'i Press.

——— (1989). *The Formation of Ch'an Ideology in China and Korea: The Vajrasamādhi-Sūtra, A Buddhist Apocryphon.* Princeton: Princeton University Press.

Buswell, Robert E., Jr. and Robert M. Gimello, eds. (1992). *Paths to Liberation: The Mārga and Its Transformations in Buddhist Thought.* Honolulu: University of Hawai'i Press.

Cabezón, José Ignacio, ed. (1992). *Buddhism, Sexuality, and Gender.* Albany: State University of New York Press.

Cahill, James (1987). "Tung Ch'i-ch'ang's 'Southern and Northern Schools' in the History and Theory of Painting: A Reconsideration." In Gregory, ed., *Sudden and Gradual,* pp. 429–446.

Cahill, Susan (1993). *Transcendence and Divine Passion: The Queen Mother of the West in Medieval China.* Stanford: Stanford University Press.

Campany, Robert Ford (1996). *Strange Writing: Anomaly Accounts in Early Medieval China.* Albany: State University of New York Press.

Caswell, James O. (1988). *Written and Unwritten: A New History of the Buddhist Caves at Yungang.* Vancouver: University of British Columbia Press.

Chan, Wing-tsit (1963). *A Sourcebook in Chinese Philosophy.* Princeton: Princeton University Press.

Chang, Garma C.C., ed. (1983). *A Treasury of Mahāyāna Sūtras: Selections from the Mahāratnakūṭa Sūtra.* University Park and London: Pennsylvania State University Press.

Chapin, Helen B. (1971). *A Long Roll of Buddhist Images.* Ascona, Switzerland: Artibus Asiae. [Articles published in 1936–38, revised and annotated by Alexander Soper.]

Chappell, David W., ed. (1987). *Buddhist and Taoist Practice in Medieval Chinese Society: Buddhist and Taoist Studies II.* Honolulu: University of Hawai'i Press.

——— (1983). "The Teachings of the Fourth Chan Patriarch Tao-hsin (580–651)." In Lai and Lancaster, eds., *Early Chan in China and Tibet,* pp. 89–129.

——— (1977). "Chinese Buddhist Interpretations of the Pure Lands." In Michael Saso and David W. Chappell, eds., *Buddhist and Taoist Studies I,* pp. 23–53. Honolulu: University Press of Hawai'i.

Chappell, David W., and Masao Ichishima, eds. (1983). *T'ien-t'ai Buddhism: An Outline of the Fourfold Teachings.* Tokyo: Daiichi Shobō.

Chavannes, Edouard (1905). "Les pays d'Occident d'après le Wei lio." *T'oung pao* 6: 519–571.

Chen Hao 陳浩 (1985). "Sui Chanzong sanzu Sengcan taming zhuan 隋禪宗三祖僧璨塔銘磚 (The Inscribed Tile for the Stūpa of the Third Chan Patriarch Sengcan of the Sui Dynasty)." *Wenwu* 文物 1985(4): 8.

Chen, Jinhua (2004). "The Tang Buddhist Palace Chapels." *Journal of Chinese Religions* 32: 101–173.

——— (2002). *Monks and Monarchs, Kinship and Kingship: Tanqian in Sui Buddhism and Politics.* Kyoto: Italian School of East Asian Studies.

——— (1999). *Making and Remaking History: A Study of Tiantai Sectarian Historiography.* Tokyo: International Institute for Buddhist Studies.

Chen, Kenneth (1973). *The Chinese Transformation of Buddhism.* Princeton: Princeton University Press.

——— (1964). *Buddhism in China: A Historical Survey.* Princeton: Princeton University Press.

Choi, Mihwa (1996). "Scholarship on the Platform Sūtra in the Twentieth Century." Seminar paper, Columbia University.

Chou, I-liang (1945). "Tantrism in China." *Harvard Journal of Asiatic Studies* 8: 241–332.

Clarke, J.J. (2000). *The Tao of the West: Western Transformations of Taoist Thought.* London: Routledge.

Cleary, Thomas, trans. (1993). *The Flower Ornament Scripture.* Boston: Shambhala.

Cleary, Thomas, and J.C. Cleary, trans. (1977). *The Blue Cliff Record.* 3 vols. Boulder: Shambhala.

Cole, Alan (1998). *Mothers and Sons in Chinese Buddhism.* Stanford: Stanford University Press.

——— (1996). "Upside Down/Right Side Up: A Revisionist History of Buddhist Funerals in China." *History of Religions* 35(4): 307–338.

Collcutt, Martin (1983). "The Early Ch'an Monastic Rule: Ch'ing-kuei and the Shaping of Ch'an Community Life." In Lai and Lancaster, eds., *Early Chan in China and Tibet,* pp. 165–184.

Cowell, E.B. ([1895–1907] 1990). *The Jātaka: Stories of the Buddha's Former Births.* Delhi: Motilal Banarsidass.

Dalby, Michael T. (1979). "Court Politics in Late T'ang Times." In Twitchett, ed., *The Cambridge History of China, Vol. 3: Sui and T'ang China, 589–906, Part 1,* pp. 561–681.

Dalia, Albert A. (2003). "Mt. Ox-head, Fa-rong (牛頭法融): A Forgotten Exegesis Master in the Rise of Tang Buddhism." *Hualin* 華林 3: 313–330.

Davidson, Ronald M. (1990). "An Introduction to the Standards of Scriptural Authenticity in Indian Buddhism." In Buswell, *Chinese Buddhist Apocrypha,* pp. 291–325.

De Groot, J. J. M. (1893). *Le code du Mahāyāna en Chine: son influence sur la vie monacale et sur le monde laïque.* Amsterdam: Johannes Müller.

De Visser, M. W. (1935). *Ancient Buddhism in Japan: Sūtras and Ceremonies in Use in the Seventh and Eighth Centuries A.D. and Their History in Later Times.* 2 vols. Leiden: E. J. Brill.

Delahaye, Hubert (1983). "Les antécedents magiques des statues chinoises." *Revue d'esthétique* (n.s.) 5: 45–53.

Demiéville, Paul (1987). "The Mirror of the Mind." In Gregory, ed., *Sudden and Gradual,* pp. 13–40.

——— (1979). "L'introduction au Tibet du bouddhisme sinise d'après les manuscrits de Touen-houang (analyse de recents travaux japonais)." In Michel Soymié, ed., *Contributions aux études sur Touen-houang. Hautes études orientales* 10: 1–16. Geneva and Paris: Librairie Droz.

——— (1978). "Appendice sur 'Damoduolo' (Dharmatrā[ta])." In Jao Tsong-yi et al., ed., *Peintures monochromes de Tun-huang (Dunhuang baihua),* pp. 43–49. Paris: École Française d'Extrême-Orient.

——— (1973a). *Choix d'études bouddhiques* (1929–1970). Leiden: E. J. Brill.

——— (1973b). *Choix d'études sinologiques* (1921–1970). Leiden: E. J. Brill.

——— (1954). "La Yogāgcārabhūmi de Saṅgharakṣa." *Bulletin de l'École Française d'Extrême-Orient* 44(2): 339–436.

——— (1952). *Le Council de Lhasa: Une controverse sur le quiétisme entre les bouddhistes de l'Inde et de la Chine au VIIIe siècle de l'ère chrétienne.* Paris: Presses Universitaires de France.

——— (1929–30). "Bosatsukai." In *Hōbōgirin,* pp. 142–147. Tokyo: Maison Franco-Japonaise.

Derrida, Jacques (1978). *Writing and Difference.* Trans. Alan Bass. Chicago: University of Chicago Press.

Dien, Albert E., ed. (1990). *State and Society in Early Medieval China.* Stanford: Stanford University Press.

Ding Mingyi 丁明夷 (1988). "Beichao fojiaoshi de zhongyao buzheng 北朝佛教史的重要補正 (Important Additions and Corrections to the Buddhist History of the Northern Dynasties)." *Wenwu* 文物 4: 15–20.

Doniger, Wendy (1997). "The Implied Spider: Politics and Theology in Myth." *Religious Studies News* (February): 9.

Donner, Neal (1987). "Sudden and Gradual Intimately Conjoined: Chih-i's T'ien-t'ai View." In Gregory, ed., *Sudden and Gradual*, pp. 201–226.

——— (1976). "The Great Calming and Contemplation of Zhiyi: Chapter One, the Synopsis." Ph.D. diss., University of British Columbia.

Donner, Neal, and Daniel B. Stevenson (1993). *The Great Calming and Contemplation: A Study and Annotated Translation of the First Chapter of Chih-i's Mo-ho Chih-kuan.* Honolulu: University of Hawai'i Press.

Drège, Jean-Pierre (1991). *Les bibliothèques en Chine au temps des manuscrits.* Paris: École Française d'Extrême-Orient.

Dumoulin, Heinrich (1993). "Early Chinese Zen Reexamined: A Supplement to Zen Buddhism: A History." *Japanese Journal of Religious Studies* 20(1): 31–53.

——— (1988). *Zen Buddhism: A History.* Trans. James W. Heisig and Paul Knitter. New York: Macmillan.

Dunhuang wenwu yanjiusuo 敦煌文物研究所 (Dunhuang Cultural Research Institute) ([1980–82] 1987). *Dunhuang Mogaoku* 敦煌莫高窟 (The Dunhuang Mogao Caves). Zhongguo shiku Series, vols. 1–5. Beijing: Wenwu chubanshe.

Dunhuang yanjiu yuan 敦煌研究院 (1993). *Dunhuang shiku yishu: Yulinku dierwu ku fu diyiwu ku (Zhong Tang)* 敦煌石窟藝術：榆林窟第二五窟附第一五窟 (中唐) (Dunhuang Cave Art: Yulin Caves 25 and 15 [Mid-Tang]). Jiangsu: Jiangsu meishu.

Ebrey, Patricia Buckley, and Peter N. Gregory, eds. (1993). *Religion and Society in T'ang and Sung China.* Honolulu: University of Hawai'i Press.

Eck, Diana (1981). *Darśan: Seeing the Divine Image in India.* Chambersburg, PA: Anima Books.

Falk, Nancy A. (1980). "The Case of the Vanishing Nuns: The Fruits of Ambivalence in Ancient Indian Buddhism." In Falk and Gross, eds., *Unspoken Worlds*, pp. 207–224.

Falk, Nancy A., and Rita M. Gross, eds. (1980). *Unspoken Worlds: Women's Religious Lives in Non-Western Cultures.* San Francisco: Harper and Row.

Faure, Bernard (1998a). *The Red Thread: Buddhist Approaches to Sexuality.* Princeton: Princeton University Press.

——— (1998b). "Voices of Dissent: Women in Early Chan and Tiantai." *Zenbunka kenkyūjo kiyō* 禅文化研究所紀要 24: 25–66.

——— (1997). *The Will to Orthodoxy: A Critical Genealogy of Northern Chan Buddhism.* Phyllis Brooks, trans. Stanford: Stanford University Press.

——— (1995). "Quand l'habit fait le moine: The Symbolism of *Kāṣāya* in Sōtō Zen." *Cahiers d'Extrême-Asie* 8: 335–369.

——— (1994). "Bibliographie succincte de Yanagida Seizan." *Cahiers d'Extrême-Asie* 7: 45–50.

——— (1993). *Chan Insights and Oversights: An Epistemological Critique of the Chan Tradition.* Princeton: Princeton University Press.

——— (1992). "Relics and Flesh Bodies: The Creation of Ch'an Pilgrimage Sites." In Naquin and Yü, eds., *Pilgrims and Sacred Sites in China*, pp. 150–189.

——— (1991). *The Rhetoric of Immediacy: A Cultural Critique of Chan/Zen Buddhism.* Princeton: Princeton University Press.

——— (1989). *Le bouddhisme Ch'an en mal d'histoire: Genèse d'une tradition religieuse dans le Chine des T'ang.* Paris: École Française d'Extrême-Orient.

——— (1988). *La volunté d'orthodoxie dans le bouddhisme chinois.* Paris: Editions du CNRS.

——— (1987). "Space and Place in Chinese Religious Traditions." *History of Religions* 26(4): 337–356.

——— (1986a). *Le Traité de Bodhidharma.* Paris: Editions Le Mail.

——— (1986b). "Bodhidharma as Textual and Religious Paradigm." *History of Religions* 25(2): 187–198.

——— (1986c). "The Concept of One-Practice Samādhi in Early Ch'an." In Gregory, ed., *Traditions of Meditation in Chinese Buddhism,* pp. 99–128.

——— (1984). "La volunte d'orthodoxie: Généalogie et doctrine du bouddhisme Ch'an et l'école du Nord—d'après l'une de ses chroniques, le Leng-chia shih-tzu chi (début du 8e s.)." Ph.D diss., University of Paris.

Fitzgerald, Charles P. (1968). *The Empress Wu.* London: Cresset Press.

Forte, Antonino (2003). "On the Origin of the Purple *Kāṣāya* in China." In Giovanni Verardi and Silvio Vita, eds., *Buddhist Asia 1: Papers from the First Conference of Buddhist Studies Held in Naples in May 2001,* pp. 145–162. Kyoto: Italian School of East Asian Studies.

——— (2000). "The Chinese Title of the Manichaean Treatise from Dunhuang." Paper presented at the International Conference on Dunhuang Studies, Dunhuang, July 25–26.

——— (1992). "Chinese State Monasteries in the Seventh and Eighth Centuries." In Kuwayama Seishin, ed., *E Chō Gotenchikukyō den kenkyū,* pp. 213–258. Kyoto: Jinbun kagaku kenkyūjo.

——— (1988a). *Mingtang and Buddhist Utopias in the History of the Astronomical Clock: The Tower, Statue, and Armillary Sphere Constructed by Empress Wu.* Rome: Istituto Italiano per il Medio ed Estremo Oriente; Paris: École Française d'Extrême-Orient.

———, ed. (1988b). *Tang China and Beyond: Studies on East Asia from the Seventh to the Tenth Century.* Kyoto: Italian School of East Asian Studies.

——— (1976). *Political Propaganda and Ideology in China at the End of the 7th Century: Inquiry into the Nature, Authors, and Function of the Tunhuang Document S. 6502 Followed by an Annotated Translation.* Naples: Instituto Universitario Orientale.

Foulk, Theodore Griffith (1999). "Sung Controversies Concerning the 'Separate Transmission' of Ch'an." In Peter N. Gregory and Daniel A. Getz, Jr., eds., *Buddhism in the Sung,* pp. 220–294. Honolulu: University of Hawai'i Press.

——— (1993). "Myth, Ritual, and Monastic Practice in Sung Ch'an Buddhism." In Ebrey and Gregory, eds., *Religion and Society in T'ang and Sung China,* pp. 147–208. Honolulu: University of Hawai'i Press.

——— (1992). "The Ch'an Tsung in Medieval China: School, Lineage, or What?" *Pacific World,* n.s. 8: 18–31.

——— (1987). "The Ch'an School and Its Place in the Buddhist Monastic Tradition." Ph.D. diss., University of Michigan.

Foulk, Theodore Griffith, and Robert Sharf (1994). "On the Ritual Use of Ch'an Portraiture in Medieval China." *Cahiers d'Extrême-Asie* 7: 149–219.

Fraser, Sarah Elizabeth (2004). *Performing the Visual: The Practice of Buddhist Wall Painting in China and Central Asia, 618–960.* Stanford: Stanford University Press.

Freiberger, Oliver (2000). "Profiling the Sangha: Institutional and Non-Institutional Tendencies in Early Buddhist Teachings." *Marburg Journal of Religion* 5(1): 1–6.

Fujieda, Akira (1966; 1969). "The Tun-huang Manuscripts: A General Description." *Zinbun: Memoirs of the Research Institute for Humanistic Studies* 9(1966): 1–32; 10(1969): 17–39.

Fuller-Sasaki, Ruth, trans. (1975). *The Record of Lin-chi.* Kyoto: Institute for Zen Studies.

Fuller-Sasaki, Ruth, Yoshitaka Iriya, and Diana R. Fraser, trans. (1971). *The Recorded Sayings of Layman P'ang: A Ninth Century Zen Classic.* Tokyo: Weatherhill.

Funayama Toru 船山徹 (2000). "Ryō no Sōyū sen 'Satsubata shizi den' to Tōdai bukkyō 梁の僧祐撰「薩婆多師資伝」と唐代佛教 (Tang Dynasty Buddhism and the 'Account of the Sarvāstivāda Masters and Disciples' Compiled by Senyou of the Liang Dynasty)." In *Tōdai no shūkyō* 唐代の宗教 (Studies in Tang Religion), pp. 325–354. Kyoto: Jinbun kagaku kenkyūjo.

——— (1995). "Rikuchō jidai ni okeru bosatsukai no juyō katei—Ryū Sō • Nan Sei ki o chūshin ni 六朝時代における菩薩戒の受容過程—劉宋•南斉期を中心に (On the Acceptance of the Bodhisattva Precepts During the Six Dynasties Period: With Special Reference to the Liu Song and Nan Qi Periods)." *Tōhō gakuhō* 東方学報 67: 1–135.

Gardiner, Daniel K. (1991). "Modes of Thinking and Modes of Discourse in the Sung: Some Thoughts on the Yü-lu ('Recorded Conversations') Texts." *Journal of Asian Studies* 50(3): 574–603.

Ge Zhaoguang 葛兆光 (1995). *Zhongguo Chan suxiangshi—cong liu shiji dao jiu shiji* 中國禪思想史 —— 從六世紀到九世紀 (A History of Chinese Chan Thought—from the Sixth to Ninth Centuries). Beijing: Beijing daxue.

Georgieva, Valentina (2000). "Buddhist Nuns in China: From the Six Dynasties to the Tang." Ph.D. diss., University of Leiden.

Gernet, Jacques (1982). *A History of Chinese Civilization.* Trans. J. R. Foster. Cambridge: Cambridge University Press, from the French original published in 1972.

——— (1995). *Buddhism in Chinese Society: An Economic History from the Fifth to the Tenth Centuries.* Trans. Franciscus Verellen. New York: Columbia University Press, from the French original published in 1956.

——— (1951). "Biographie du Maître Chen-houei du Ho-tsö." *Journal Asiatique* 239: 59.

——— ([1949] 1977). *Entretiens du maître dhyāna Chen-houei du Ho-tsö (668–760).* Paris: École Française d'Extrême-Orient.

Gerth, H. H., and C.W. Mills, eds. (1946). *From Max Weber.* Oxford: Oxford University Press.

Giès, Jacques, ed. (1995). *Les arts de l'Asie centrale: la collection Paul Pelliot du musée national des arts asiatiques-Guimet.* 2 vols. Paris: Réunion des musées nationaux.

Giles, Lionel, ed. (1937). *Descriptive Catalogue of the Chinese Manuscripts from Tunhuang in the British Museum.* London: British Museum.

Giles, Lionel, trans. ([1923] 1959). *The Travels of Fa-hsien (399–414 A.D.), or Record of the Buddhistic Kingdoms.* London: Routledge and Kegan Paul.

Gimello, Robert M. (1992). "Chang Shang-ying on Wu-t'ai Shan." In Naquin and Yü, eds., *Pilgrims and Sacred Sites in China,* pp. 89–102.

Gimello, Robert M., and Peter N. Gregory, eds. (1983). *Studies in Chan and Hua-yen.* Honolulu: University of Hawai'i Press.

Girard, René (1977). *Violence and the Sacred.* Trans. Patrick Gregory. Baltimore: Johns Hopkins University Press, from the French original published in 1972.

Gombrich, Richard F. (1988). *Theravāda Buddhism: A Social History from Ancient Benares to Modern Columbo.* London: Routledge and Kegan Paul.

Gómez, Luis O. (1996). *The Land of Bliss: The Paradise of the Buddha of Measureless Light: Sanskrit and Chinese Versions of the Sukhāvatīvyūha Sutras.* Honolulu: University of Hawai'i Press; Kyoto: Higashi Honganji Shinshū Otani-ha.

——— (1991). "Purifying Gold: The Metaphor of Effort and Intuition in Buddhist Thought and Practice." In Gregory, ed., *Sudden and Gradual,* pp. 67–165.

——— (1983a). "Indian Materials on the Doctrine of Sudden Enlightenment." In Lai and Lancaster, eds., *Early Ch'an in China and Tibet,* pp. 393–434.

——— (1983b). "The Direct and Gradual Approaches of Zen Master Mahāyāna: Fragments of the Teachings of Mo-ho-yan." In Gimello and Gregory, eds., *Studies in Ch'an and Hua-yen*, pp. 69–167.

Graham, A. C., trans. (1981). *Chuang-tzŭ: The Inner Chapters*. London: George Allen & Unwin.

Granoff, Phyllis E., and Koichi Shinohara, eds. (1993). *Speaking of Monks: Religious Biography in India and China*. Oakville, ONT: Mosaic Press.

———. (1988). *Monks and Magicians: Religious Biographies in Asia*. Oakville: Mosaic Press.

Gregory, Peter (1994). "Tsung-mi's Perfect Enlightenment Retreat: Ch'an Ritual During the T'ang Dynasty." *Cahiers d'Extrême-Asie* 7: 115–147.

——— (1991). *Tsung-mi and the Sinification of Buddhism*. Princeton: Princeton University Press.

——— (1989). "Ch'an Practice in Szechwan in the Late T'ang." Paper presented at the Conference on Religion and Society in China, 750–1300, Hsi-lai Temple, Hacienda Heights, California.

——— (1983). "Chinese Buddhist Hermeneutics: The Case of Hua-yen." *Journal of the American Academy of Religion* 51(2): 231–249.

——— (1981). "Tsung-mi's Inquiry into the Origin of Man: A Study of Chinese Buddhist Hermeneutics." Ph.D. diss., Harvard University.

Gregory, Peter, ed. (1987). *Sudden and Gradual: Approaches to Enlightenment in Chinese Thought*. Honolulu: University of Hawai'i Press.

———. (1986). *Traditions of Meditation in Chinese Buddhism*. Honolulu: University of Hawai'i Press.

Groner, Paul (2002). *Ryōgen and Mount Hiei: Japanese Tendai in the Tenth Century*. Honolulu: University of Hawai'i Press.

——— (1990a). "The Fan-wang ching and Monastic Discipline in Japanese Tendai: A Study of Annen's *Futsū jubosatsukai kōshaku*." In Buswell, *Chinese Buddhist Apocrypha*, pp. 251–290.

——— (1990b). "The Ordination Ritual in the *Platform Sūtra* Within the Context of the East Asian Buddhist Vinaya Tradition." In *Fo Kuang Shan Report of International Conference on Ch'an Buddhism*, pp. 220–250. Gaoxiong, Taiwan: Foguang.

Gross, Rita (1993). *Buddhism After Patriarchy: A Feminist History, Analysis, and Reconstruction of Buddhism*. Albany: State University of New York Press.

Guisso, Richard W. L. (1978). *Wu Tse-T'ien and the Politics of Legitimation in T'ang China*. Bellingham: Western Washington University.

Haberman, David L., and Jan Nattier (1996). "Whatever Became of Translation?" *Religious Studies News* (November): 13.

Hakeda Yoshito S., trans. (1967). *The Awakening of Faith, Attributed to Asvaghosha*. New York: Columbia University Press.

Hao Chunwen 郝春文 (1998). *Tang houqi Wudai Songchu Dunhuang sengni de shehui shenghuo* 唐後期五代宋初敦煌僧尼的社會生活 (The Social Life of Buddhist Monks and Nuns in Dunhuang During the Late Tang, Five Dynasties and Early Song). Beijing: Zhongguo shehui kexue.

Harrison, Paul (1990). *The Samādhi of Direct Encounter with the Buddhas of the Present: An Annotated English Translation of the Tibetan Version of the Pratyutpanna-Buddha-saṃmukhāvasthita-Samādhi-Sūtra with Several Appendices Relating to the History of the Text*. Studia Philologica Buddhica Monograph Series, no. 5. Tokyo: International Institute for Buddhist Studies.

Hartman, Charles (1986). *Han Yü and the T'ang Search for Unity.* Princeton: Princeton University Press.

Henansheng gudai jianzhu baohu yanjiusuo 河南省古代建築保護研究所 (Henan Research Institute for the Preservation of Ancient Architecture) (1991). *Baoshan Lingquan si* 寶山靈泉寺. Zhengzhou: Henan renmin.

——— (1988). "Henan Anyang Lingquansi shiku ji Xiaonanhai shiku 河南安陽靈泉寺石窟及小南海石窟 (The Lingquan Temple Caves and Xiaonanhai Caves at Anyang in Henan Province)." *Wenwu* 文物 4: 1–14.

Hirai Shun'ei 平井俊栄 (1980). "Gozushū to Hotōshū 午頭宗と保唐宗 (The Niutou School and the Baotang school)." In Shinohara Toshio 篠原寿雄 and Tanaka Ryōshō 田中良昭, eds., *Tonkō Butten to Zen* 敦煌仏典と禅 (The Buddhist Scriptures from Dunhuang and Chan), pp. 199–220. Tokyo: Daitō.

Hirakawa Akira 平川彰 (1999). *Monastic Discipline for the Buddhist Nuns: An English Translation of the Chinese Text of the Mahāsāṃghika Bhikṣuṇī-Vinaya.* Patna: Kashi Prasad Jayaswal Research Institute.

——— (1970). *Ritsuzō no kenkyū* (Research on the *Vinaya-piṭaka*). Tokyo: Sankibō Busshorin.

——— (1960). "Daijōkai to bosatsukaikyō 大乗戒と菩薩戒経 (Mahāyāna Precepts and the Bodhisattva Precepts Scriptures). In *Tōyō shisōron shū* 東洋思想論集 (Collection of Essays on East Asian Thought), pp. 522–544. Tokyo: Fukui hakashi shōjukinen ronbunshū kankōkai.

——— (1955). "Kanyaku ritsuten seikaku 漢訳律典性格 (The Characteristics of Chinese Translations of the Vinaya)." *Indogaku bukkyōgaku kenkyū* 印度学仏教学研究 3(2): 16–23.

Horner, I.B. ([1930] 1975). *Women Under Primitive Buddhism: Laywomen and Almswomen.* Delhi: Motilal Banarsidass.

Hou, Ching-lang (1975). *Monnaies d'offrande et la notion de trésorerie dans la religion chinoise.* Paris: College de France, Institut des Hautes Études Chinoises.

Houston, Gary (1976). "Sources for a History of the bSamyas Debate." Ph.D. diss., Indiana University.

Howard, Angela Falco (2001). *Summit of Treasures: Buddhist Cave Art of Dazu, China.* Trumbull, CT: Weatherhill.

Hrdlickova, V. (1958). "The First Translations of Buddhist Sutras in Chinese Literature and Their Place in the Development of Storytelling." *Archiv Orientálni* 26: 114–144.

Hu Shi 胡適 ([1958] and [1930] 1970). *Shenhui heshang yizhi* 神會和尚遺集 (The Surviving Works of the Venerable Shenhui). Taibei: Hu Shi jinian guan.

——— (1962). "Ba Peixiu de Tang gu Guifeng Dinghui chanshi chuanfa bei 跋裴休的唐故圭峰定慧禪師傳法碑 (Stele on the Transmission of the Dharma of the Late Dhyāna Master Guifeng Dinghui of the Tang, by Ba Peixiu)." *Bulletin of the Institute of History and Philology* 34: 5–26.

——— (1953). "Ch'an (Zen) Buddhism in China: Its History and Method: Is Ch'an (Zen) Beyond Understanding?" *Philosophy East and West* 3(1): 3–24.

——— (1935). "Lengqiezong kao 楞伽宗考 (A Consideration of the Laṅkā School)." Reprinted in Yanagida, ed., *Ko Teki zengaku an,* pp. 153–195.

——— (1932). "The Development of Zen Buddhism in China." *Chinese and Political Science Review* 15(4): 475–505.

Hu Wenhe 胡文和 (1994). *Sichuan Daojiao Fojiao shiku yishu* 四川道教佛教石窟藝術 (Daoist and Buddhist Cave Art in Sichuan). Chengdu: Sichuan renmin.

——— (1989). "Sichuan Sui Tang shiqi de Daojiao moyai zaoxiang 四川隋唐時期的道教摩崖造像 (Daoist Cliff Images of the Sui-Tang Period in Sichuan)." *Chengdu Wenwu* 成都文物 23.

Huang Minzhi 黄敏枝 (1989). *Songdai fojiao shehui jingji shi lunji* 宋代佛教社會經濟史論集 (A Collection of Essays Concerning Song Dynasty Buddhist Socio-Economics). Shixue congshu 史學叢書. Taibei: Xuesheng shuju.

Huang Yansheng 黄燕生 (1989). "Tangdai Jingzhong-Bao Tang chanpa gaiqiu 唐代淨眾保唐禪派概述 (A Survey of the Jingzhong-Baotang Chan Sects of the Tang Dynasty)." *Shijie zongjiao yanjiu* 世界宗教研究 4: 66–80.

Hubbard, Jamie (2001). *Absolute Delusion, Perfect Buddhahood: The Rise and Fall of a Chinese Heresy.* Honolulu: University of Hawai'i Press.

——— (1986). "Salvation in the Final Period of the Dharma: The Inexhaustible Storehouse of the San-chieh-chiao." Ph.D. diss., University of Wisconsin.

Hurvitz, Leon [1962] (1980). *Chih-I (538–597).* Brussels: Institut Belge des Hautes Études Chinoises.

——— (1957). "'Render Unto Caesar' in Early Chinese Buddhism." *Sino-Indian Studies* 5(3–4): 80–114.

Hurvitz, Leon, trans. (1956). *Wei Shou: Treatise on Buddhism and Taoism: An English Translation of the Original Chinese Text of Wei-shu CXIV and the Japanese Annotation of Tsukamoto Zenryū.* Kyoto: Jinbun kagaku kenkyūjo.

Hymes, Robert (2002). *Way and Byway: Taoism, Local Religion, and Models of Divinity in Sung and Modern China.* Berkeley: University of California Press.

Imaeda, Yoshiro (1975). "Documents tibétains de Touen-houang concernant le Concile de Tibet." *Journal Asiatique* 263(1/2): 125–146.

Iriya Yoshitaka 入矢義高 (1955–56). "O bonshi ni tsuite 王梵志について (Regarding [the Poet] Wang Fanzhi)." *Chūgoku bungakuhō* 中国文学報 3(1955); 4(1956).

Jackson, Roger (1982). "Terms of Sanskrit and Pāli Origin Acceptable as English Words." *Journal of the International Association of Buddhist Studies* 5: 141–142.

Jaini, Padmanabh S. (1988). "Stages in the Bodhisattva Career of the Tathāgata Maitreya." In Alan Sponberg and Helen Hardacre, eds., *Maitreya, the Future Buddha,* pp. 54–90. Cambridge: Cambridge University Press.

Jan Yün-hua (Ran Yunhua) 冉雲華 (1994). "'Tang gu Zhaosheng si dade Huijian chanshi bei' kao 《唐故招聖寺大德慧堅禪師碑》考 (A Study and Transcription of the Stūpa Inscription of Chan Master Huijian of the Tang Dynasty)." *Chung-hwa Buddhist Journal* 7: 97–120.

——— (1990). "Donghai dashi Wuxiang zhuan yanjiu 東海大師無相傳研究 (A Study of the Biography of the Korean Master Wuxiang)." In his *Zhongguo fojiao wenhua yanjiu lunji* (An Anthology of Studies of Chinese Buddhist Culture), pp. 42–64. Taibei: Dongchu. (Originally published in *Dunhuang xue* 敦煌學 4[1979]: 47–60.)

——— (1989). "A Comparative Study of 'No-Thought' (*wu-nien*) in Some Indian and Chinese Buddhist Texts." *Journal of Chinese Philosophy* (16): 37–58.

——— (1988). "Portrait and Self-Portrait: A Case Study of Biographical and Autobiographical Records of Tsung-mi." In Granoff and Shinohara, eds., *Monks and Magicians: Religious Biographies in Asia,* pp. 229–246.

——— (1987). "Zongmi chuanfa shixi de zai jiantao 宗密傳法世系的再檢討 (A Reexamination of the Lineage of Chan Buddhism Given by Zongmi)." *Chung-hwa Buddhist Journal* 1: 43–57.

——— (1983). "Seng-ch'ou's Method of Dhyāna." In Gimello and Gregory, eds., *Studies in Ch'an and Hua-yen,* pp. 51–63.

——— (1980). "Tsung-mi's Questions Regarding the Confucian Absolute." *Philosophy East and West* 30(4): 495–504.

——— (1979). "Donghai dashi Wuxiang zhuan yanjiu 東海大師無相傳研究 (A Study of the Biography of the Korean Master Wuxiang)." *Dunhuang xue* 敦煌學 4: 47–60.

——— (1978). "Mu-sang and His Philosophy of No-thought." In *Proceedings of the 5th International Symposium,* pp. 55–86. Seoul: National Academy of Sciences of Korea.

——— (1977a). "Conflict and Harmony in Ch'an and Buddhism." *Journal of Chinese Philosophy* 4: 287–302.

——— (1977b). "The Power of Recitation: An Unstudied Aspect of Chinese Buddhism." *Studi Storico* 1(2): 289–299.

——— (1974). "Two Problems Concerning Tsung-mi's Compilation of Ch'an-tsang." *Transactions of the International Conference of Orientalists in Japan* 19: 37–47.

——— (1972). "Tsung-mi: His Analysis of Ch'an Buddhism." *T'oung Pao* 58: 1–54.

——— (1965). "Buddhist Self-Immolation in Medieval China." *History of Religions* 4: 243–268.

——— (1964). "Buddhist Historiography in Sung China." *Zeitschrift der Deutschen Morgenländischen Gesellschaft* 114(2): 360–381.

Jay, Nancy (2001). "Sacrifice as Remedy for Having Been Born of Women." In Elizabeth A. Castelli, ed., *Women, Gender, Religion: A Reader,* pp. 174–194. New York: Palgrave.

Jiang Boqin 姜伯勤 (1996). *Dunhuang yishu zongjiao yu liyue wenming* 敦煌藝術宗教與禮樂文明 (Dunhuang Arts, Religion, and 'Rites and Music' Civilization). Beijing: Zhongguo shehui kexue.

Jorgensen, John (2005). *Inventing Hui-neng, the Sixth Patriarch: Hagiography and Biography in Early Ch'an.* Leiden: Brill.

——— (1987). "The 'Imperial' Lineage of Ch'an Buddhism: The Role of Confucian Ritual and Ancestor Worship in Ch'an's Search for Legitimation in the Mid-T'ang Dynasty." *Papers on Far Eastern History* 35: 89–133.

——— (1979). "The Earliest Text of Ch'an Buddhism: The Long Scroll." M.A. thesis, Australian National University.

Jullien, François (1995). *The Propensity of Things: Toward a History of Efficacy in China.* New York: Zone Books.

Junker, Andrew (2000). "Clergy, Clan, and Country: Tang Dynasty Monastic Obeisance and Sacrificial Religion." M.A. thesis, Indiana University.

Kajitani Sōnin 梶谷宗忍 et al., eds. (1974). *Shinjinmei, Shōdōka, Jūgyūzu, Zazengi* 信心銘, 証道歌, 十牛図, 座禅儀 (The Inscription on Faith in the Mind, Song of the Authentic Way, Ten Oxherding Pictures, and Significance of Seated Meditation). *Zen no goroku,* no. 16. Tokyo: Chikuma shobō.

Kaltenmark, Max (1979). "Notes sur le Pen-tsi king." In Michel Soymié, ed., *Contributions aux études sur Touen-houang. Hautes études orientales* 10: 91–98. Geneva and Paris: Librairie Droz.

Kapstein, Matthew T. (2000). *The Tibetan Assimilation of Buddhism: Conversion, Contestation, and Memory.* Oxford: Oxford University Press.

Kamata Shigeo 鎌田茂雄 (1971). *Zengen shosenshū tojo* 禪源諸詮集都序 (Prolegomenon to the Collection of Expressions of the Chan Source). *Zen no goroku,* no. 9. Tokyo: Chikuma shobō.

Katz, Steven T. (1978). "Language, Epistemology, and Mysticism." In Katz, ed., *Mysticism and Philosophical Analysis,* pp. 22–74. New York: Oxford University Press.

Kieschnick, John (1997). *The Eminent Monk: Buddhist Ideals in Medieval Chinese Hagiography.* Honolulu: University of Hawai'i Press.

——— (1995). "The Idea of the Monk in Medieval China: Asceticism, Thaumaturgy, and Scholarship in the Biographies of Eminent Monks." Ph.D. diss., Stanford University.

Kim Kugyŏng 金九經 (1935). *Kyokan Lyokdae poppo gi* 校刊歷代法寶記 (A Collated Edition of the *Lidai fabao ji*). Seoul: Kangwŏn ch'ongsŏ.

Kimura, Ryūtoku (1981). "Le dhyāna chinois au Tibet ancien après Mahāyāna." *Journal Asiatique* 269: 183–192.

Kirkland, Russell (2002). "The History of Taoism: A New Outline." *Journal of Chinese Religions* 30: 177–193.

——— (1997–98). "Dimensions of T'ang Taoism: The State of the Field at the End of the Millennium." *T'ang Studies* 15–16: 79–123.

Kitagawa, Joseph M., and Mark D. Cummings, eds. (1989). *Buddhism and Asian History. The Encyclopedia of Religion.* New York: Macmillan.

Kohn, Livia (1991). *Taoist Mystical Philosophy: The Scripture of Western Ascension.* Albany: State University of New York Press.

——— (1987). *Seven Steps to the Tao: Sima Chengzhen's "Zuowang Lun."* Nettetal: Steyler Verlag.

Komazawa daigaku Zenshūshi kenkyūkai 駒沢大学禅宗史研究会, eds. (1978). *Enō kenkyū—enō no denki to shiryō ni kansuru kisoteki kenkyū* 慧能研究一慧能の伝記と資料に関するの基礎的研究 (Huineng Studies—Fundamental Studies of Huineng's Biography and Its Materials). Tokyo: Taishūkan shoten.

Kondō Ryōichi 近藤良一 (1974). "*Rekidai hōbō ki* no shōshahon ni tsuite「歴代宝法記」の諸写本について (Regarding the manuscripts of the *Lidai fabao ji*)." *Indogaku bukkyōgaku kenkyū* 印度学仏教学研究 21(2): 313–318.

——— (1968). "*Hyakujō shingi* no seiritsu to sono genkei 百丈清規の成立とその原型 (The Establishment and Provenance of *Baizhang's Pure Rules*)." *Hokkaidō Komazawa Daigaku kenkyū kiyō* 北海道駒澤大学研究紀要 3: 19–48.

Kuhn, Dieter, and Helga Stahl (1991). *Annotated Bibliography to the* Shike shiliao xinbian 石刻史料新編 *(A New Edition of Historical Materials Carved in Stone).* Heidelberg: Würzburger Sinologische Schriften.

Kuo, Li-ying (1994). *Confession et contrition dans le bouddhisme chinois du Ve au Xe siècle.* Paris: École Française d'Extrême-Orient.

Lai, Whalen (1992). "Chinese Buddhist and Christian Charities: A Comparative History." *Buddhist-Christian Studies* 12: 5–33.

——— (1990). "The Chan-ch'a ching: Religion and Magic in Medieval China." In Buswell, ed., *Chinese Buddhist Apocrypha,* pp. 175–206.

——— (1987a). "Tao-sheng's Theory of Sudden Enlightenment Re-examined." In Gregory, ed., *Sudden and Gradual,* pp. 169–200.

——— (1987b). "The Earliest Folk Buddhist Religion in China: T'i-wei Po-li ching and Its Historical Significance." In Chappell, ed., *Buddhist and Daoist Practice in Medieval Chinese Society,* pp. 11–35.

Lai, Whalen, and Lewis Lancaster, eds. (1983). *Early Ch'an in China and Tibet.* Berkeley Buddhist Studies Series. Berkeley: Asian Humanities Press.

Lamotte, Etienne (1988). *History of Indian Buddhism.* Trans. Sara Webb-Boin. Louvain: Institut Orientaliste de Louvain, from the French original published in 1958.

Lamotte, Etienne, trans. (1944–80). *Le Traité de la Grande Vertu de Sagesse.* 5 vols. Louvain: Institut Orientaliste de Louvain.

Lau, D.C., trans. (1963). *Tao te ching.* London: Penguin Books.

Levering, Miriam (1992). "Lin-chi (Rinzai) Ch'an and Gender: The Rhetoric of Equality and the Rhetoric of Heroism." In Cabezón, ed., *Buddhism, Sexuality, and Gender,* pp. 137–156.

——— (1982). "The Dragon Girl and the Abbess of Mo-shan: Gender and Status in the Ch'an Buddhist Tradition." *Journal of the International Association of Buddhist Studies* 5(1): 19–35.

Lévi, Sylvain, and Edouard Chavannes (1916). "Les seize Arhat protecteurs de la loi." *Journal Asiatique* (July–August): 5–50; (September–October): 189–304.

Li Lincan (1982). *A Study of the Nan-chao and Ta-li Kingdoms in the Light of Art Materials Found in Various Museums.* Taibei: National Palace Museum.

Li Rongxi (1993). *The Biographical Scripture of King Aśoka.* Berkeley: Numata Center for Buddhist Translation and Research.

Li Yuzhen 李玉珍 (1989). *Tangdai de biqiuni* 唐代的比丘尼 (Nuns of the Tang Dynasty). Taibei: Taiwan xuesheng shuju.

Liebenthal, Walter (1956–57). "The World-Conception of Chu Tao-sheng." *Monumenta Nipponica* 12(1–2): 65–104; (3–4): 241–268.

——— (1956). "Notes on the 'Vajrasāmadhi.'" *T'oung Pao* 45(4–5): 347–386.

——— (1955a). "A Biography of Chu Tao-sheng." *Monumenta Nipponica* 11(3): 64–96.

——— (1955b). "Chinese Buddhism During the 4th and 5th Centuries." *Monumenta Nipponica* 11(1): 44–83.

——— (1952). "The Sermon of Shen-hui." *Asia Major* (n.s.) 3(2): 132–155.

——— (1948). *The Book of Chao.* Peking (Beijing): Catholic University Press.

——— (1947). "On the Sanskrit Equivalent of Fo-t'u-teng." *Sino-Indian Studies* 3(1/2): 127–130.

Lieu, Samuel N.C. (1992). *Manichaeism in the Later Roman Empire and Medieval China.* 2d ed., rev. and expanded. Tübingen: J.C.B. Mohr (Paul Siebeck).

Lin, Lu-tche (1981). *Le règne de l'empereur Hiuan-tsong (713–756).* Trans. R. de Rotours. Paris: Collège de France, Institut des Hautes Études Chinoises.

Link, Arthur E. (1960). "Shih Seng-yu and His Writings." *Journal of the American Oriental Society* 80(1): 17–43.

——— (1958). "Biography of Shih Tao-an." *T'oung Pao* 46: 1–48.

Little, Stephen, ed. (2000). *Taoism and the Arts of China.* Chicago: Art Institute of Chicago.

Loewe, Michael, ed. (1993). *Early Chinese Texts: A Bibliographical Guide.* Berkeley: University of California, Society for the Study of Early China and Institute of East Asian Studies.

Lopez, Donald S., Jr. (1995). "Authority and Orality in the Mahāyāna." *Numen* 42: 21–47.

Lopez, Donald S., Jr., ed. (1996). *Religions of China in Practice.* Princeton: Princeton University Press.

———. (1995a). *Buddhism in Practice.* Princeton: Princeton University Press.

———. (1995b). *Curators of the Buddha.* Chicago: University of Chicago Press.

———. (1988). *Buddhist Hermeneutics.* Honolulu: University of Hawai'i Press.

Lynn, Richard John (1994). *The Classic of Changes: A New Translation of the I Ching, as Interpreted by Wang Bi.* New York: Columbia University Press.

Ma Shichang 马世长 (1978). "Guanyu Dunhuang Cangjing dong de jige wenti 关于敦煌藏经洞的几个问题 (Some Questions Concerning the Library Cave at Dunhuang)." *Wenwu* 文物 12: 21–33.

Macdonald, Ariane (1971). "Une lecture des Pelliot Tibetain 1286, 1287, 1038, 1047, and 1290: Essai sur la Formation et l'emploi des mythes politiques dans la religion Royale de le Sron-Bcan Sgam-po." In Macdonald, ed., *Études tibétaines dédiées à la mémoire de Marcelle Lalou,* pp. 190–391. Paris: Adrien Maisonneuve.

Macdonald, Ariane, and Yoshiro Imaeda, eds., vol. 1 (1971) and vol. 2 (1978–79). *Choix de Documents Tibétains.* Paris: Bibliothèque Nationale.

Mair, Victor (1989). *T'ang Transformation Texts: A Study of the Buddhist Contribution to the Rise of Vernacular Fiction and Drama in China.* Cambridge: Harvard-Yenching Institute Monograph Series.

——— (1983a). *Tun-huang Popular Narrative.* Cambridge: Cambridge University Press.

——— (1983b). "The Narrative Revolution in Chinese Literature: Ontological Presuppositions." *CLEAR* 5(1).

——— (1981). "Lay Students and the Making of Written Vernacular Narrative: An Inventory of Tun-huang Manuscripts." *CHINOPERL Papers* 10: 5–96.

Makita Tairyō 牧田諦亮 (1973 & 1975). "Kōsōsen no seiritsu 高僧伝の成立 (The Formation of the *Gaoseng zhuan*)." *Tōhō gakuhō* 東方学報 44: 101–125; 48: 229–259.

Mala, Guilaine, and Ryūtoku Kimura (1988). "Une Traité Tibétain de dhyāna chinois (Chan 禪)." *Bulletin de la Maison Franco-Japonaise*, n.s. 11(1): 1–103.

——— (1981). "Additif à 'L'Introduction au Tibet du bouddhisme sinisé d'après les manuscrits de Touen-huang,' de Paul Demiéville, Bibliographie corrigée et complétée." In Michel Soymié, ed., *Nouvelles contributions aux études sur Touen-houan*, pp. 321–328. Geneva and Paris: Librairie Droz.

Maraldo, John (1986a). "Is There Historical Consciousness Within Ch'an?" *Japanese Journal of Religious Studies* 12(2/3): 141–172.

——— (1986b). "Hermeneutics and Historicity in the Study of Buddhism." *Eastern Buddhist* 19(1): 17–43.

Maspéro, Henri (1911). "Sur la date et l'authenticité du *Fou fa tsang yin yuan tchouan*." In *Mélanges d'Indianism (offerts à S. Lévi par ses élèves)*, pp. 129–149. Paris: E. Leroux.

——— (1910). "Le songe et l'ambassade de l'empereur Ming, étude critique des sources." *Bulletin de l'École Française d'Extrême-Orient* 10: 95–130.

Mather, Richard B. (1979). "K'ou Ch'ien-chih and the Taoist Theocracy at the Northern Wei Court, 425–451." In Holmes H. Welch and Anna Seidel, eds., *Facets of Taoism*, pp. 103–122. New Haven: Yale University Press.

——— (1976). *Shih-shuo Hsin-yü: A New Account of Tales of the World, by Liu I-ch'ing with Commentary by Liu Chün.* Minneapolis: University of Minnesota Press.

Matsuda Yūko (1988). "Chinese Versions of the Buddha's Biography." *Indogaku Bukkyogaku kenkyū* 印度学仏教学研究 37(1): 24–33.

McMullen, David (1988). *State and Scholars in T'ang China.* Cambridge: Cambridge University Press.

——— (1973). "Historical and Literary Theory in the Mid-Eighth Century." In Wright and Twitchett, eds., *Perspectives on the T'ang*, pp. 307–342.

McRae, John (forthcoming). *Zen Evangelist: Shenhui (684–758), Sudden Enlightenment, and the Southern School of Chinese Chan Buddhism.* Honolulu: University of Hawai'i Press.

——— (2002). "Shenhui as Evangelist: Re-envisioning the Identity of a Chinese Buddhist Monk." *Journal of Chinese Religions* 30: 123–148.

——— (2000). "The Antecedents of Encounter Dialogue in Chinese Ch'an Buddhism." In Steven Heine and Dale S. Wright, eds., *The Kōan: Texts and Contexts in Zen Buddhism*, pp. 46–74. New York: Oxford University Press.

——— (1998). "Shen-hui's Vocation on the Ordination Platform and Our Visualization of Medieval Chinese Ch'an Buddhism." *Zenbunka kenkyūjo kiyō* 禅文化研究所紀要 24: 43–66.

——— (1995). "Chinese Religions—The State of the Field, Part II. 'Buddhism.'" *Journal of Asian Studies* 54(2): 354–371.

——— (1994). "Yanagida Seizan's Landmark Works on Chinese Ch'an." *Cahiers d'Extrême-Asie* 7: 51–103.

——— (1992a). "Encounter Dialogue and the Transformation of the Spiritual Path in Chinese Ch'an." In Peter N. Gregory, ed., *Paths to Liberation: The Mārga and Its Transformations in Buddhist Thought,* pp. 339–369. Honolulu: University of Hawai'i Press.

——— (1992b). "Political Implications of a Zen Portrait." In Bernard Hung-Kay Luk, ed., *Contacts Between Culture,* vol. 4, pp. 76–81. Lewiston, ME: Edwin Mellon Press.

——— (1987). "Shen-hui and the Teaching of Sudden Enlightenment in Early Ch'an Buddhism." In Gregory, ed., *Sudden and Gradual,* pp. 227–278.

——— (1986). *The Northern School and the Formation of Early Ch'an Buddhism.* Honolulu: University of Hawai'i Press.

Minn Young-gyu 閔泳珪 (1991). "Shisen kōdan shushūi 四川講壇趣拾遺 (Selections from a Lecture Series on Sichuan)." *Chūgai nippō* 中外日報, July 26 (24509): 1; July 29 (24510): 1; and July 30 (24511): 1–2.

Miyaji Akira 宮治昭 (1989). "Kijiru daiichi yōbu no voruto tenjō kutsu hekiga キジル第一様式のヴォールト天井窟壁画（下）(Murals on Vaulted Ceilings in the Type One Style Kizil Caves (II))." *Bukkyo Geijutsu* 仏教芸術 (Ars Buddhica) 183: 29–60.

Mizuno Kōgen 水野弘元 (1987). *Buddhist Sūtras: Origin, Development, Transmission.* Tokyo: Kōsei.

——— (1981). *Hokkugyō no kenkyū* 法句経の研究 (A Study of the *Dhammapada*). Tokyo: Shunjūsha.

——— (1961). "Gisaku no *Hokkugyō* ni tsuite 偽作の法句経について (Regarding the Apocryphal *Dhammapada*)." *Komazawa daigaku Bukkyōgakubu kenkyū kiyō* 19: 11–33.

Mizuno Seiichi and Nagahiro Toshio (1952–56). *Yun-kang (Unkō sekkutsu): The Buddhist Cave-Temples of the Fifth Century A.D. in North China. Detailed Report of the Archaeological Survey Carried Out by the Mission of the Toho Bunka Kenkyūsho, 1938–1945.* 16 vols., supplement and index. Kyoto: Jinbun kagaku kenkyūjo.

Mollier, Christine (1990). *Un apocalypse taoïste du Ve siècle: le livre des incantations divines des grottes abyssales.* Paris: Collège de France, Institut des Hautes Études Chinoises.

Morrison, Elizabeth (1996). "Contested Visions of the Buddhist Past and the Curious Fate of an Early Medieval Buddhist Text." Seminar paper, Stanford University.

Murcott, Susan (1991). *The First Buddhist Women: Translations and Commentary on the Therigatha.* Berkeley: Parallax Press.

Nagao, Gadjin M. (1991). *Mādhyamika and Yogācāra.* Albany: State University of New York Press.

Nakamura, Hajime (1980). *Indian Buddhism: A Survey with Bibliographical Notes.* Hirakata: Kansai University of Foreign Studies.

Ñāṇamoli, Bhikkhu, and Bhikkhu Bodhi, trans. (1995). *The Middle Length Discourses of the Buddha: A New Translation of the Majjhima Nikāya.* Boston: Wisdom Publications.

Naquin, Susan, and Chün-fang Yü, eds. (1992). *Pilgrims and Sacred Sites in China.* Berkeley: University of California Press.

Nattier, Jan (2003). *A Few Good Men: The Bodhisattva Path According to the Inquiry of Ugra (Ugraparipṛcchā).* Honolulu: University of Hawai'i Press.

——— (1991). *Once Upon a Future Time: Studies in the Buddhist Prophecy of Decline.* Berkeley: Asian Humanities Press.

——— (1988). "The Meanings of the Maitreya Myth: A Typological Analysis." In Alan Sponberg and Helen Hardacre, eds., *Maitreya, the Future Buddha,* pp. 23–47. Cambridge: Cambridge University Press.

Nishiwaki Tsuneki 西脇常記 (1997). "Guanyu Bolin suocang Tulufan shoujipin zhong de Chanji ziliao 關於柏林所藏吐魯番收集品中的禪籍資料 (Regarding Chan Text Materials in the Turfan Collection Stored in Berlin)." Translated into Chinese by Qiu Yunqing 裘雲青. *Suyuyan yanjiu* 4: 136–139.

Nogami Shunjo, ed., vol. 1 (1965) and vol. 2 (1972). *Ancient Copies of Buddhist Scriptures Discovered in the Tun-huang Caves.* Kyoto: Seminar of Oriental Studies in Otani University.

Obata Hironobu 小畠宏允 (1976a). "*Rekidai hōbōki* to kodai Chibetto no Bukkyō「歴代法宝記」と古代チベットの仏教 (The *Lidai fabao ji* and Buddhism in Ancient Tibet)." In *Yanagida Seizan, Shoki no Zenshi II* 初期の禅史 II, pp. 325–337. Tokyo: Chikuma shobō.

——— (1976b). "Pelliot Tib. no. 116 bunken ni mieru sho Zenshi no kenkyū (Pelliot Tib. No. 116 文献にみえる諸禅師の研究) (A Study of the Zen Masters Who Appear in the Document P. Tib. 116)." *Zenbunka kenkyūjo kiyō* 禅文化研究所紀要 8: 33–103.

——— (1974). "Chibetto no Zenshū to 'Rekidai hōbōki' チベットの禅宗と「歴代法宝記」(Tibetan Chan and the *Lidai fabao ji*)." *Zenbunka kenkyūjo kiyō* 禅文化研究所紀要 6: 139–176.

Ochiai Toshinori (1991). *The Manuscripts of Nanatsu-dera. With remarks by Makita Tairyō and Antonino Forte.* Trans. and ed. Silvio Vita. Kyoto: Italian School of East Asian Studies.

Ochō Einichi 横超慧日 (1970). *Hokugi bukkyō no kenkyū* 北魏仏教の研究 (A Study of Buddhism in the Northern Wei). Kyoto: Heirakuji shoten.

——— (1958). *Chūgoku Bukkyō no kenkyū* 中国仏教の研究 (A Study of Chinese Buddhism). Kyoto: Hōzōkan.

——— (1957). "Shaku Dōan no honyakuron 釈道安の翻訳論 (Daoan's discourse on translation)." *Indogaku bukkyōgaku kenkyū* 印度学仏教学研究 5(2): 448–458.

Oda Yoshihisa 小田義久 (1989). "Tonkō Sankaiji no 'Ken issai nyūzōkyō mokuroku' 敦煌三界寺の「見一切入蔵経目録」(The 'Catalogue of Scriptures Checked' of Dunhuang's Sanjie Temple)." *Ryūkoku daigaku ronshū* 龍谷大学論集 (434–435): 555–576.

Okawa Takashi 小川隆 (1987). "Tonkōbon 'Rokuso tankyō' to 'Rekidai hōbōki' 敦煌本「六祖壇経」と「歴代法宝記」(The Dunhuang Editions of the *Platform Sūtra of the Sixth Patriarch* and the *Lidai fabao ji*)." *Shūgaku kenkyū* 宗学研究 28: 175–178.

Okimoto Katsumi 沖本克巳 (1976). "Chibettoyaku *Ninyūshigyōron* ni tsuite チベット訳二入四行について (A Study of the Tibetan Translation of the *Two Entrances and Four Practices*)." *Indogaku bukkyōgaku kenkyū* 印度学仏教学研究 48.

——— (1975). "bSam yas no shūron の宗論 (1)—Pelliot 116 ni tsuite について (The Sectarian Treatises of Samye Monastery (1): Regarding P. Tib. 116)." *Nihon Chibetto gakkai kaihō* 日本西藏学会会報 21: 5–8.

Oldenberg, Herman, trans. (1879). *Vinaya Piṭakam.* London: Williams and Norgate.

Ono Hōdo 大野法道 ([1954] 1963). *Daijō kaikyō no kenkyū* 大乗戒経の研究 (A Study of the Mahāyāna Precepts Scriptures). Tokyo: Sankibō busshorin.

Orzech, Charles D. (1998). *Politics and Transcendent Wisdom: The Scripture for Humane Kings in the Creation of Chinese Buddhism.* University Park: Pennsylvania State University Press.

——— (1996). "The Scripture on Perfect Wisdom for Humane Kings Who Wish to Protect Their States." In Lopez, ed., *Religions of China in Practice,* pp. 372–380.

——— (1989). "Puns on the Humane King: Analogy and Application in an East Asian Apocryphon." *Journal of the American Oriental Society* 109(1): 17–24.

Pan, Yihong (1992). "The Sino-Tibetan Treaties in the Tang Dynasty." *T'oung Pao* 78: 116–161.

Paul, Diana Mary (1979). *Women in Buddhism: Images of the Feminine in Mahāyāna Tradition.* Berkeley: Asian Humanities Press.

——— ([1974] 1980). *The Buddhist Feminine Ideal: Queen Śrīmālā and the Tathāgatagarbha.* Missoula: Scholar's Press.

Pelliot, Paul (1996). *L'inscription nestorienne de Si-ngan-fou.* Edited with supplements by Antonino Forte. Kyoto: Italian School of East Asian Studies; Paris: Collège de France.

——— (1923). "Notes sur quelques artistes des Six Dynasties et des Tang." *T'oung Pao* 22: 253–61.

——— (1920). "Meou-tseu ou les doutes levés." *T'oung Pao* 19: 255–435.

——— (1906). Review article on *Les pays d'Occident d'aupres le Wei lio* by Edouard Chavannes. *Bulletin de l'École Française d'Extrême-Orient* 6: 361–400.

Penkower, Linda (2000). "In the Beginning . . . Guanding 灌頂 (561–632) and the Creation of Early Tiantai." *Journal of the International Association of Buddhist Studies* 23(2): 245–296.

Peterson, Charles A. (1979). "Court and Province in mid- and late T'ang." In Twitchett, ed., *The Cambridge History of China: Vol. 3, Sui and T'ang China, 589–906, Part I,* pp. 464–560.

——— (1973). "The Restoration Completed: Emperor Hsien-tsung and the Provinces." In Wright and Twitchett, eds., *Perspectives on the Tang,* pp. 151–191.

Poceski, Mario (2000). "The Hongzhou School of Chan Buddhism During the Mid-Tang Period." Ph.D. diss., University of California at Los Angeles.

Prebish, Charles S. (1975). *Buddhist Monastic Discipline: The Sanskrit Prātimokṣa Sūtras of the Mahāsāṃghikas and the Mūlasarvāstivādins.* University Park: Pennsylvania State University Press.

Puett, Michael J. (2001). *The Ambivalence of Creation: Debates Concerning Innovation and Artifice in Early China.* Stanford: Stanford University Press.

Pulleyblank, Edwin G. (1976). "The An Lu-shan Rebellion and the Origins of Chronic Militarism in Late T'ang China." In John C. Perry and Bardwell L. Smith, eds., *Essays on T'ang Society,* pp. 32–60. Leiden: Brill.

——— (1955). *The Background of the Rebellion of An Lu-shan.* London: Oxford University Press.

Python, Pierre, trans. (1973). *Vinayaviniścaya-Upāliparipṛcchā.* Paris: Adrien Maisonneuve.

Rabinow, Paul, ed. (1984). *The Foucault Reader.* New York: Pantheon Books.

Rao Zongyi 饒宗頤, ed. (1994). *Dunhuang miaozhenzan jiaolu bing yanjiu* 敦煌邈真讚校錄并研究 (Critical Edition and Study of Dunhuang Portrait-Eulogies). Taibei: Xinwenfeng.

Ray, Reginald A. (1994). *Buddhist Saints in India: A Study in Buddhist Values and Orientations.* Oxford: Oxford University Press.

Rhys Davids, T.W., trans. ([1890] 1992). *The Questions of King Milinda (The Milindapañha by Nāgasena).* 2 vols. Delhi: Motilal Banarsidass.

Robinet, Isabelle (1997). *Taoism: Growth of a Religion.* Trans. Phyllis Brooks. Stanford: Stanford University Press.

Robinson, Richard H. (1978). *Early Madhyamaka in India and China.* New York: Samuel Weiser.

Roccasalvo, Joeseph F. (1980). "The Debate at bSam yas: A Study in Religious Contrast and Correspondence." *Philosophy East and West* 30(4): 505–20.

Rogers, Michael C. (1968). *The Chronicle of Fu Chien: A Case of Exemplar History.* Berkeley: University of California Press.

Rong Xinjiang 榮新江 (forthcoming). "Tangdai FoDao erjiao yanzhong de waidao—Jingjiao tu 唐代佛道二教眼中的外道——景教徒 (Foreign Religions from the Viewpoints of Buddhists and Daoists in the Tang—Christians)."

——— (2002). "Youguan Dunhuangben *Lidai fabao ji* de xin ziliao 有關敦煌本歷代法寶記的新資料 (Concerning New Materials on the Dunhuang Manuscripts of the *Lidai fabao ji*)." *Jiechuang Foxue* 戒幢佛學 2: 94–105.

——— (2001). "*Lidai fabao ji* zhong de Momanni he Mishihe<歷代法寶記>中的末曼尼和彌師訶 (Mani and Messiah in the *Lidai fabao ji*)." In *Zhonggu Zhongguo yu wailai wenming* 中古中國与外來文明 (Medieval China and Foreign Civilizations), pp. 343–385. Beijing: Sanlian shudian.

——— (1999–2000). "The Nature of the Dunhuang Library Cave and the Reasons for Its Sealing." *Cahiers d'Extrême-Asie* 11: 247–275.

——— (1997). "Dunhuang ben Chanzong dengshi canjuan shiyi 敦煌本禪宗燈史殘卷拾遺 (Recovering Remnants of Dunhuang Manuscripts of Chan Sect Lamp Histories)." In *Zhou Shaoliang Xiansheng xinkaijiuzhi qingshou wenji* 周紹良先生欣開九秩慶壽文集, pp. 231–244. Beijing: Zhonghua shuju.

——— (1996). "Dunhuang cangjingdong de xingzhi ji qi fengguan yuanyin 敦煌藏經洞的性質及其封閉原因 (The Nature of the Scriptural Library Cave at Dunhuang and Reasons for Its Sealing)." *Dunhuang Tulufan yanjiu* 敦煌吐魯番研究 2: 23–48.

——— (1994). "Dunhuang miaozhenzan niandai kao 敦煌邈真讚年代考 (A Chronology of Dunhuan Portrait Eulogies)." In Rao, ed., *Dunhuang miaozhenzan jiaolu bing yanjiu*, pp. 353–369.

Ruegg, David Seyfort (1989). *Buddha-nature, Mind, and the Problem of Gradualism in a Comparative Perspective: On the Transmission and Reception of Buddhism in India and Tibet.* London: School of Oriental and African Studies.

Samuels, Jeffrey (1999). "Views of Householders and Lay Disciples in the Sutta Pitaka: A Reconsideration of the Lay/Monastic Opposition." *Religion* 29: 231–241.

Sato, Chisui (1978). "The Character of Yun-kang Buddhism." *The Memoirs of Tōyō Bunkō* 36: 39–83. (Translation of an article that originally appeared in *Tōhō gakuhō* 東方学報 59, 1–2 [1977]: 27–66.)

Satō Tetsuei 佐藤哲英 (1981). *Zoku Tendai daishi no kenkyū: Tendai Chigi o meguru shōmondai* 続天台大師の研究：天台智顗おめぐる諸問題 (Continued Studies of Tiantai Masters: Issues Concerning Tiantai Zhiyi). Kyoto: Hyakkaen.

——— (1963). "Tonkō shutsudo Hōshō oshō nembutsu san 敦煌出土法照和尚念佛讃 (The Venerable Fazhao's Hymn of Buddha Recollection That Was Unearthed at Dunhuang)." In Seiiki bunka kenkyū kai 西域文化研究會, eds., *Rekishi to bijutsu no shomondai* 歷史と美術の諸問題, pp. 196–222. Kyoto: Hōzōkan.

——— (1961). *Tendai daishi no kenkyū: Chigi no chosaku ni kansuru kisoteki kenkyū* 天台大師の研究：智顗の著作に関する基礎的研究 (Studies of Tiantai Masters: Basic Research on Zhiyi's Works). Kyoto: Hyakkaen.

Schaefer, Edward H. (1963). *The Golden Peaches of Samarkand: A Study of T'ang Exotics.* Berkeley: University of California Press.

Schopen, Gregory (2004). *Buddhist Monks and Business Matters: Still More Papers on Monastic Buddhism in India.* Honolulu: University of Hawai'i Press.

——— (1997). *Bones, Stones, and Buddhist Monks.* Honolulu: University of Hawai'i Press.

Schipper, Kristofer M. (1994). "Purity and Strangers: Shifting Boundaries in Medieval Taoism." *T'oung Pao* 80: 61–80.

——— (1985). "Taoist Ritual and Local Cults of the T'ang Dynasty." In Michel Strickmann, ed., *Tantric and Taoist Studies*, vol. 3, pp. 812–34. Brussels: Institut Belge des Hautes Études Chinoises.

——— (1975). *Concordance du Tao Tsang: Titres des ouvrages.* Paris: École Française d'Extrême-Orient.

Schipper, Kristofer M., and Wang Hsiu-huei (1986). "Progressive and Regressive Time Cycles in Taoist Ritual." In J.T. Fraser et al., eds., *Time, Science, and Society in China and the West*, pp. 185–205. Amherst: University of Massachusetts Press.

Scott, David (1995). "Buddhist Responses to Manichaeism: Mahāyāna Reaffirmation of the 'Middle Path.'" *History of Religions* 35(2): 148–162.

Seidel, Anna (2003). "Den'e (Chuanyi 傳衣, Transmission of the Robe)." In Lévi et al., eds., *Dictionnaire Encyclopédique du Bouddhisme d'après les sources chinoises et japonaises,* vol. 8 (edited by Hubert Durt), pp. 1171–1178. Paris: Adrien Maisonneuve.

——— (1984a). "Taoist Messianism." *Numen* 31: 161–174.

——— (1984b). "Le sûtra merveilleux." In Michel Soymié, ed., *Contributions aux études sur Touen-houang, III,* pp. 305–361. Paris: École Française d'Extrême-Orient.

——— (1983). "Imperial Treasures and Taoist Sacraments: Taoist Roots in the Apocrypha." In Michel Strickmann, ed., *Tantric and Taoist Studies,* vol. 2, pp. 291–371. Brussels: Institut Belge des Hautes Études Chinoises.

Sekiguchi Shindai 関口真大 (1969). *Tendai shikan no kenkyū* 天台止観の研究 (A Study of Calming and Contemplation in the Tiantai School). Tokyo: Iwanami shoten.

——— (1957). *Daruma daishi no kenkyū* 達摩大師の研究 (A Study of the Great Master Bodhidharma). Tokyo: Shunjusha.

Seo, Kyung-bo (1969). "A Study of Korean Zen Buddhism Approached Through the *Chodangjip* (祖堂集)." Ph.D. diss., Temple University.

Sharf, Robert H. (2002). *Coming to Terms with Chinese Buddhism: A Reading of the Treasure Store Treatise.* Honolulu: University of Hawaii Press.

——— (1992). "The Idolization of Enlightenment: On the Mummification of Ch'an Masters in Medieval China." *History of Religions* 23(1): 1–31.

——— (1991). "The 'Treasure Store Treatise' (Pao-tsang lun) and the Sinification of Buddhism in Eighth Century China." Ph.D. diss., University of Michigan.

Shi Shuqing 史树青 (1976). "Ribenguo shoucang de Tangdai Yixing deng renhuaxiang 日本国收藏的唐代一行等人画像 (Portraits of [Master] Yixing et al. Stored in Japan)." *Wenwu* 文物 3: 31–35.

Shih, Heng-ching (1992). *The Syncretism of Chan and Pure Land Buddhism.* New York: Peter Lang.

Shiina Kōyū 椎名宏雄 (1980a). "*Hōrinden* itsubun no kenkyū 寳林傳逸文の研究 (A Study of the Missing Sections of the *Baolin zhuan*)." *Komazawa daigaku Bukkyōgakubu ronshu* 11: 234–257.

——— (1980b). "*Hōrinden* makikyū makijū no itsubun" 寳林傳巻九巻十の逸文 (The Missing Text of *Baolin zhuan* Fascicles Nine and Ten)." *Shūgaku kenkyū* 宗学研究 22: 191–198.

Shinohara, Koichi (2000). "The Kasaya Robe of the Past Buddha Kasyapa in the Miraculous Instruction Given to the Vinaya Master Daoxuan (596~667)." *Chung-Hwa Buddhist Journal* 13(2): 299–367.

——— (n.d.). "Imagining the Jetavana in Medieval China: An Exploratory Discussion of Daoxuan's Jetavana Diagram Scripture."

——— (1994). "Biographies of Eminent Monks in a Comparative Perspective: The Function of the Holy in Medieval Chinese Buddhism." *Chung-Hwa Buddhist Journal* 7: 477–500.

——— (1991). "A Source Analysis of the *Ruijing lu* ('Records of Miraculous Scriptures')." *Journal of the International Association of Buddhist Studies* 14(1): 73–154.

——— (1990). "Dao-xuan's Collection of Miracle Stories About 'Supernatural Monks' (*Shen-seng gan-tong lu*): An Analysis of Its Sources." *Chung-Hwa Buddhist Journal* 3: 319–380.

——— (1988). "Two Sources of Chinese Buddhist Biographies: Stupa Inscriptions and Miracle Stories." In Granoff andShinohara, eds., *Monks and Magicians:,* pp. 119–228.

Shinohara Toshio 篠原寿雄 and Tanaka Ryōshō 田中良昭, eds. (1980). *Tonkō Butten to Zen* 敦煌仏典と禅 (The Buddhist Scriptures from Dunhuang and Chan). Kōza Tonkō, no. 8. Tokyo: Daitō shuppansha.

Silk, Jonathan (1994). "The Origins and Early History of the *Mahāratnakūṭa* Tradition of Mahāyāna Buddhism with a Study of the *Ratnarāśisūtra* and Related Materials." Ph.D. diss., University of Michigan.

Siren, Osvald (1956). *Chinese Painting: Leading Masters and Principles,* vol. 3. London: Lund Humphries.

Somers, Robert M. (1986). "Time, Space and Structure in the Consolidation of the T'ang Dynasty (A.D. 617–700)." *Journal of Asian Studies* 45(5): 971–994.

Soper, Alexander (1959). *Literary Evidence for Early Buddhist Art in China.* Ascona, Switzerland: Artibus Asiae.

Sørensen, Henrik H. (2004). "Michel Strickmann on Magical Medicine in Medieval China and Elsewhere." *History of Religions* 43(4): 319–332.

——— (1991). "New Information on the Date of the Third Patriarch Sengcan's Death." *Studies in Central and East Asian Religion* 4: 90–92.

——— (1989). "Observations on the Characteristics of the Chinese Chan Manuscripts from Dunhuang." *Studies in Central and East Asian Religion* 2: 115–139.

Stein, Rolf A. (1979). "Religious Taoism and Popular Religion from the Second to Seventh Centuries." In Holmes H. Welch and Anna Seidel, eds., *Facets of Taoism: Essays in Chinese Religion,* pp. 53–82. New Haven: Yale University Press.

Stevenson, Daniel (1996). "Visions of Mañjuśrī on Mount Wutai." In Lopez, ed., *Religions of China in Practice,* pp. 203–222.

——— (1987). "The T'ien-t'ai Four Forms of Samādhi and Late North-South Dynasties, Sui, and Early T'ang Buddhist Devotionalism." Ph.D. diss., Columbia University.

——— (1986). "The Four Kinds of Samādhi in Early T'ien-t'ai Buddhism." In Gregory, ed., *Traditions of Meditation in Chinese Buddhism,* pp. 45–97.

Strickmann, Michel (2002). *Chinese Magical Medicine.* Stanford: Stanford University Press.

——— (1990). "The *Consecration Sūtra:* A Buddhist Book of Spells." In Buswell, ed., *Chinese Buddhist Apocrypha,* pp. 251–290.

Strong, John (1985). "The Buddhist Avadānists and the Elder Upagupta." In Michel Strickmann, ed., *Tantric and Taoist Studies in Honor of R.A. Stein,* vol. 3, pp. 862–81. Brussels: Institut Belge des Hautes Études Chinoises.

——— (1983). *The Legend of King Aśoka: A Study and Translation of the* Aśokāvadāna. Princeton: Princeton University Press.

——— (1979). "The Legend of the Lion-roarer: A Study of the Buddhist Arhat Piṇḍola Bhāradvāja." *Numen* 26(1): 50–88.

Sullivan, Michael (1979). *The Arts of China.* Rev. ed. Berkeley: University of California Press.

Sutton, Donald S. (1996). "Transmission in Popular Religion: The Jiajiang Festival Troupe of Southern Taiwan." In Meir Shahar and Robert P. Weller, eds., *Unruly Gods: Divinity and Society in China,* pp. 212–249. Honolulu: University of Hawai'i Press.

Suzuki D[aisetsu] T[eitarō] 鈴木大拙貞太郎 (1968–71). *Suzuki Daisetsu Zenshū* 鈴木大拙全集 (Complete Collected Works of D.T. Suzuki). 30 vols. Tokyo: Iwanami shoten.

——— (1953). "Zen: A Reply to Hu Shih." *Philosophy East and West* 3(1): 25–46.

——— (1949). *The Zen Doctrine of No-mind: The Significance of the Sūtra of Hui-neng Wei-lang.* London: Rider and Co.

——— (1932). The *Laṅkāvatāra Sūtra.* London: Routledge and Kegan Paul.

Suzuki D[aisetsu] T[eitarō] 鈴木大拙貞太郎 and Kōda Rentarō 公田連太郎, eds. (1934). *Tonkō shutsudo Kataku Jinne zenji goroku* 敦煌出土荷沢神会禅師語録 (The Discourse Record of Heze Shenhui Found at Dunhuang). Tokyo: Morie shoten.

Suzuki Tetsuo 鈴木哲雄 (1970). "Hotōji Mujū no 'Munen' 保唐無住の無念 (The 'No-Thought' of Bao Tang Wuzhu)." *Indogaku bukkyōgaku kenkyū* 印度学仏教学研究 18(1): 270–273.

Swanson, Paul (1989). *Foundations of T'ien-t'ai Philosophy.* Berkeley: Asian Humanities Press.

Takakusa, Junjiro ([1896] 1966). *A Record of the Buddhist Religion as Practiced in India and the Malay Archipelago (A.D. 671–695).* Delhi: Munshiram Manoharlal.

Takeuchi Kōdō 竹内弘道 (1985). "Shinshutsu no Kataku Jinne tōmei ni tsuite 新出の荷沢神会塔銘について (On the Recently Found Stele Inscription of Heze Shenhui)." *Shūgaku kenkyū* 宗学研究 27: 313–325.

Tanaka, Kenneth K. (1990). *The Dawn of Chinese Pure Land Buddhist Doctrine: Ching-ying Hui-yüan's Commentary on the Visualization Sutra.* Albany: State University of New York Press.

Tanaka, Kenneth K., and Raymond E. Robertson, eds. (1992). "A Ch'an Text from Tun-huang: Implications for Ch'an Influence on Tibetan Buddhism." In Stephen D. Goodman and Ronald M. Davidson, eds., *Tibetan Buddhism: Reason and Revelation,* pp. 57–78. Albany: State University of New York Press.

Tanaka Ryōshō 田中良昭 (2003). *Hōrinden yakuchū* 宝林伝訳注 (An Annotated Translation of the *Baolin zhuan*). Tokyo: Uchiyama shoten.

——— (1998). "'Jinne tōmei' to 'Kōbochinju tōmei' no shutsugen to sono igi「神會塔銘」と「候莫陳壽塔銘」の出現とその意義 (The Discovery and Significance of the Memorial Inscriptions for Shenhui and Houmochen)." *Zenbunka kenkyūjo kiyō* 禅文化研究所紀要 24: 221–236.

——— (1991). "Tonkō zenseki no kenkyū jōkyō to sono mondai ten 敦煌禅籍の研究状況とその問題点 (Some Questions Regarding the State of Dunhuang Chan Bibliographic Research)." *Komazawa daigaku Bukkyōgakubu ronshu* 20: 41–55.

——— (1989). "A Historical Outline of Japanese Research on the Chinese Chan Writings from Dunhuang." *Studies in Central and East Asian Religion* 2: 141–169.

——— (1983). *Tonkō Zenshū bunken no kenkyū* 敦煌禅宗文献の研究 (A Study of Dunhuang Chan Manuscripts). Tokyo: Daitō shuppansha.

——— (1981). "Relations Between the Buddhist Sects in the T'ang Dynasty Through the Ms. P. 3913." *Journal Asiatique* 269: 163–169.

——— (1980). "Zenshū Tōshi no Hatten 禅宗灯史の発展 (The Development of the 'Histories of the Lamp' in the Chan School)." In Shinohara Toshio 篠原寿雄 and Tanaka Ryōshō, eds., *Tonkō Butten to Zen* 敦煌仏典と禅 (The Buddhist Scriptures from Dunhuang and Chan), pp. 99–123. Tokyo: Daitō shuppansha.

——— (1978). "Shoki Zenshū to Dōkyō 初期禅宗と道教 (Early Zen Buddhism and Daoism)." In *Dōkyō Kenkyū ronshū* 道教研究論集 (Collected Essays on Taoist Thought and Culture), pp. 403–428. Tokyo: Kokusho hankō kai.

Tang Yongtong 湯用彤 ([1938] 1991). *Han Wei Liang Jin Nanbei chao Fojiaoshi* 漢魏兩晉南北朝佛教史 (A History of Buddhism in the Han, the Wei, the Two Jins, and the Northern and Southern Dynasties). Shanghai: Shanghai shudian.

Teiser, Stephen (1994). *The Scripture on the Ten Kings and the Making of Purgatory in Medieval Chinese Buddhism.* Honolulu: University of Hawai'i Press.

——— (1988). *The Ghost Festival in Medieval China.* Princeton: Princeton University Press.

——— (1985). "T'ang Buddhist Encyclopedias: A Bibliographical Introduction to Fa-yüan chu-lin and Chu-ching yao-chi." *T'ang Studies* 3: 109–28.

Thompson, Stuart (1988). "Death, Food, and Fertility." In James L. Watson and Evelyn S. Rawski, eds., *Death Ritual in Late Imperial and Modern China*, pp. 71–108. Berkeley: University of California Press.

Tokiwa Daijō 常盤大定 ([1934] 1973). *Hōrinden no kenkyū* 宝林傳の研究 (Research on the *Baolin zhuan*). Tokyo: Kokusho kankōkai.

Tokiwa Gishin 常盤義伸 and Yanagida Seizan 柳田聖山 (1976). *Zekkanron: Eibun yakuchū, genbun kōtei, kokuyaku* 絶観論：英文譯注、原文校定、国譯 (The *Jueguan lun:* English Annotations, Collation of Original Texts, and Japanese Translation). Kyoto: Zenbunka kenkyūjo.

Tokuno, Kyoko (1994). "Byways in Chinese Buddhism: The Book of Trapusa and Indigenous Scriptures." Ph.D. diss., University of California at Berkeley.

Tonami, Mamoru (1988). "Policy Towards the Buddhist Church in the Reign of T'ang Hsüan-tsung." *Acta Asiatica* 55: 27–47.

Trenckner, V., et al., eds. (1888–1925). *Majjhimanikāya.* London: Pali Text Society.

Tsai, Kathryn Ann, trans. (1994). *Lives of the Nuns: Biographies of Chinese Buddhist Nuns from the Fourth to the Sixth Centuries.* Honolulu: University of Hawai'i Press.

Tsukamoto Zenryū 塚本善隆 (1985). *A History of Chinese Buddhism: From Its Introduction to the Death of Hui-yüan.* Trans. Leon Hurvitz. 2 vols. Tokyo: Kodansha, from the Japanese original published in 1979.

——— (1976). *Chūgoku Jōdo kyōshi kenkyū* 中国浄土教史研究 (Research on the History of the Chinese Pure Land School). In *Tsukamoto Zenryū chosakushū* 塚本善隆著作集, vol. 4. Tokyo: Daitō shuppansha.

——— (1959). "Jūju biku kaihon 十誦比丘戒本 (The *Sarvāstivāda Prātimokṣa*)." In *Shodōzenshū* 書道全集, pp. 189–190. Tokyo: Heibonsha.

——— (1957). "The Śramaṇa Superintendent T'an-yao 曇曜 and His Time." Trans. Galen Eugene Sargent from the Japanese original published in 1942. *Monumenta Serica* 16: 363–396.

——— ([1942] 1974). *Hokuchō Bukkyōshi kenkyū* 北朝仏教史研究 (A Study of the History of Buddhism in the Northern Dynasties). Reprinted in *Tsukamoto Zenryū chosakushū* 塚本善隆著作集, vol. 2. Tokyo: Daitō shuppansha.

——— ([1933] 1975). *Tōchūki no jōdokyō* 唐中期の浄土教 (The Pure Land School of the Middle Tang). Kyoto: Hōzōkan.

Tucci, Giuseppe ([1958] 1986). *Minor Buddhist Texts, II.* Delhi: Motilal Banarsidass.

Twitchett, Denis (1992). *The Writing of Official History Under the T'ang.* Cambridge: Cambridge University Press.

——— (1979). "Hsüan-tsung (reign 712–56)." In Twitchett, ed., *The Cambridge History of China: Vol. 3, Sui and T'ang China, 589–906, Part I,* pp. 333–463.

——— (1973). "The Composition of the Tang Ruling Class: New Evidence from Tunhuang." In Wright and Twitchett, eds., *Perspectives on the Tang,* pp. 47–85.

——— (1963). *Financial Administration Under the T'ang Dynasty.* Cambridge: Cambridge University Press.

——— (1956). "Monastic Estates in T'ang China." *Asia Major* (n.s.) (5): 123–46.

Twitchett, Denis, ed. (1979). *The Cambridge History of China: Vol. 3, Sui and T'ang China, 589–906, Part I.* Cambridge: Cambridge University Press.

Ueyama Daishun 上山大峻 (1990). *Tonkō bukkyō no kenkyū* 敦煌仏教の研究 (Research on Dunhuang Buddhism). Kyoto: Hōzōkan.

——— (1981). "Études des manuscrits tibétains de Dunhuang relatifs au bouddhisme de dhyāna. Bilan et perspectives." *Journal Asiatique* 269: 287–293.

——— (1974). "Tonkō shutsudo Chibettobun Zen shiryō no kenkyū 敦煌出土チベット文禅資料の研究 (Studies on Tibetan Texts of Chan Materials Unearthed at Dunhuang)." *Bukkyō bunka kenkyūjo kiyō* 仏教文化研究所紀要 13: 1–10.

Ui Hakuju 宇井伯寿 ([1935, 1941, 1943] 1966). *Zenshūshi kenkyū* 禅宗史研究 (Research on the History of the Zen School). 3 vols. Tokyo: Iwanami shoten.

Uray, G. (1983). "Tibet's Connections with Nestorianism and Manichaeism in the 8th–10th Centuries." *Wiener Studien zur Tibetologie und Buddhismuskunde* 10: 399–429.

Verellen, Franciscus (1994). "A Forgotten T'ang Restoration: The Taoist Dispensation after Huang Ch'ao." *Asia Major* (3rd series) 7(1): 107–153.

——— (1992). "'Evidential Miracles in Support of Taoism': The Inversion of a Buddhist Apologetic Tradition in Late Tang China." *T'oung Pao* 78: 217–263.

——— (1989). *Du Guangting (850–933): taoïste de cour à la fin de la Chine médiévale.* Paris: Collège de France.

Waley, Arthur (1968). "Two Posthumous Articles." *Asia Major* 14: 242–246.

——— (1960). *Ballads and Stories from Tun-huang.* London: George Allen and Unwin.

——— (1931). *A Catalogue of Paintings Recovered from Tun-huang by Sir Aurel Stein, K.C.I.C.* London: British Museum.

Waley, Arthur, trans. (1938). *The Analects of Confucius.* London: George Allen and Unwin.

Wang Bangwei (1994). "Buddhist Nikāyas Through Ancient Chinese Eyes." In Heinz Bechert, ed., *Sanskrit-Wörterbuch der buddhistischen Texte aus den Turfan-Funden.* Göttingden: Vandenhoeck and Ruprecht.

Wang-Toutain, Françoise (1994). "Le bol du Buddha: propagation du bouddhisme et légitimité politique." *Bulletin de l'École Française d'Extrême-Orient* 81: 59–82.

Wang, Yi-t'ung, trans. (1984). *A Record of Buddhist Monasteries in Loyang.* By Yang Hsüan-chih. Princeton: Princeton University Press.

Watanabe Masahide 渡部正英 (1982). "'Rekidai hōbōki' ni tsuite no ichi kōsatsu「歴代法宝記」についての一考察 (An Inquiry Regarding the *Lidai fabao ji*)." *Shūgaku kenkyū* 宗学研究 23: 215–220.

——— (1981). "'Den hōbōki' to 'Rekidai hōbōki' ni tsuite「伝法宝紀」と「歴代法宝記」について (Regarding the *Chuan fabao ji* and the *Lidai fabao ji*)." *Shūgaku kenkyū* 宗学研究 22: 212–216.

Watson, Burton, trans. (1997). *The Vimalakirti Sutra.* New York: Columbia University Press.

———. (1993a). *The Lotus Sutra.* New York: Columbia University Press.

———. (1993b). *The Zen Teachings of Master Lin-chi.* New York: Columbia University Press.

———. (1964). *Chuang Tzu.* New York: Columbia University Press.

Wayman, Alex, and Hideko Wayman, trans. (1974). *The Lion's Roar of Queen Śrīmālā: A Buddhist Scripture on the Tathāgatagarbha Theory.* New York: Columbia University Press.

Wechsler, Howard C. (1985). *Offerings of Jade and Silk: Ritual and Symbol in the Legitimation of the T'ang Dynasty.* New Haven: Yale University Press.

Weinstein, Stanley (1987a). *Buddhism Under the T'ang.* Cambridge: Cambridge University Press.

——— (1987b). "Chinese Buddhist Schools." In Mircea Eliade, ed., *The Encyclopedia of Religion,* pp. 482–487. New York: MacMillan.

——— (1973). "Imperial Patronage in the Formation of T'ang Buddhism." In Wright and Twitchett, eds., *Perspectives on the T'ang,* pp. 265–306.

Welch, Holmes H. (1967). *The Practice of Chinese Buddhism.* Cambridge: Harvard University Press.

——— (1963). "Dharma Scrolls and the Succession of Abbots in Chinese Monasteries." *T'oung Pao* 50(1/3): 93–149.

Whitfield, Roderick (1995). *Dunhuang, Caves of the Singing Sands: Buddhist Art from the Silk Road.* London: Textile and Art Publications.

——— (1982). *Art of Central Asia: The Stein Collection in the British Museum.* 2 vols. Tokyo: Kodansha.

Willemen, Charles, trans. (1978). *The Chinese Udādavarga: A Collection of Important Odes of the Law (Fa Chi Yao Sung Ching).* Brussels: Institut Belge des Hautes Etudes Chinoises.

Wilson, Thomas A. (1995). *Genealogy of the Way: The Construction and Uses of the Confucian Tradition in Late Imperial China.* Stanford: Stanford University Press.

Wright, Arthur (1990). *Studies in Chinese Buddhism.* Ed. Robert M. Somers. New Haven: Yale University Press.

——— (1973). "T'ang T'ai-tsung and Buddhism." In Wright and Twitchett, eds., *Perspectives on the T'ang,* pp. 239–263.

——— (1957). "Seng-jui Alias Hui-rui: A Biographical Bisection in the *Kao-seng Chuan.*" *Sino-Indian Studies* 5(3/4): 272–293.

——— ([1954] 1993). "Biography and Hagiography: Hui-chiao's Lives of Eminent Monks." In *Studies in Chinese Buddhism,* pp. 73–111.

——— ([1948] 1990). "Fo-t'u-teng: A Biography." In *Studies in Chinese Buddhism,* pp. 34–68.

Wright, Arthur, and Denis C. Twitchett, eds. (1973). *Perspectives on the T'ang.* New Haven: Yale University Press.

Wu, Chi-yu (1960). *Pen-tsi king: Livre du terme originel.* Paris: CNRS.

Wu, Pei-yi 吳百益 (1979). "Self-Examination and the Confession of Sins in Traditional China." *Harvard Journal of Asiatic Studies* 39(1): 5–38.

Xiang Chu 項楚, ed. (1991). *Wang Fanzhi shi jiaozhu* 王梵志詩校注 (Annotated Critical Edition of the Poems of Brahmacārin Wang). Shanghai: Shanghai guji.

Xiong, Victor (1996). "Ritual Innovations and Taoism under Tang Xuanzong." *T'oung Pao* 82: 258–316.

Yamaguchi Zuihō 山口瑞鳳 (1984). "Tora o tomonau daijūhachi rakanzu no raireki 虎を伴う第十八羅漢図の来歴 (Tracing the Origins of the Image of the Eighteenth Arhat Accompanied by a Tiger)." *Indō koten kenkyū* 6: 392–422.

——— (1973). "Chibetto Bukkyō to Shiragi no Kin oshō チベット仏教と新羅の金和尚 (The Silla Monk Kim and Tibetan Buddhism)." In Kim Chigyŏn and Ch'ae Inyak, eds., *Shiragi bukkyō kenkyū* 新羅仏教の研究 (Studies in Korean Buddhism), pp. 3–36. Tokyo: Sankibō busshorin.

Yampolsky, Philip B. (1967). *The Platform Sūtra of the Sixth Patriarch.* New York: Columbia University Press.

Yanagida Seizan 柳田聖山 (1988). "Jinne no shōzō 神会の肖像 (The Portrait of Shenhui)." *Zenbunka kenkyūjo kiyō* 禅文化研究所紀要 15: 215–242.

——— (1985). "Goroku no rekishi 語録の歴史 (A History of the 'Recorded Sayings' Genre)." *Tōhō gakuhō* 東方学報 57: 211–663.

——— (1983a). "The Li-Tai Fa-Pao Chi and the Ch'an Doctrine of Sudden Awakening." Trans. Carl Bielefeldt, in Lai and Lancaster, eds., *Early Ch'an in China and Tibet,* pp. 13–49.

——— (1983b). "The 'Recorded Sayings' Texts of Chinese Buddhism." Trans. John McRae, in Lai and Lancaster, eds., *Early Ch'an in China and Tibet,* pp. 13–49.

——— (1981). "*Taishō shinshū daizōkyō* to *Rekidai hōbōki,* oyobi sono shūhen no mondai「大正新修大蔵経」と「歴代宝法記」、およびその周辺の問題 (The *Taishō* and the *Lidai fabao ji,* and Problems Surrounding Them)." In Furuta Shōkin hakase koki kinen kai 古田紹欽博士古稀記念会, ed., *Bukkyō no rekishiteki tenkai ni miru shokeitai* 仏教の歴史的展開に見る諸形態, pp. 371–387. Tokyo: Sōbunsha.

——— (1978). "Shinzoku tōshi no keifu: jo no ichi 新続灯史の系譜：叙の一." *Zengaku kenkyū* 禅学研究 59: 1–39.

———, ed. (1976a). *Shoki no Zenshi II: Rekidai hōbōki* 初期の禅史 II—歴代法宝記 (Early Chan History II: *Lidai fabao ji*). *Zen no goroku,* no. 3. Tokyo: Chikuma shobō.

——— (1976b). "Mujū to Shūmitsu: Tongo shisō no keisei o megutte 無住と宗密—頓悟思想の形成のめぐって (Wuzhu and Zongmi: Concerning the Formation of the Concept of Sudden Awakening)." *Hanazono daigaku kenkyū kiyō* 7: 1–36.

———, ed. (1975a) *Sōzō ichin Hōrinden, Dentō gyokuei shū* 宋蔵遺珍宝林傳、傳燈玉英集. Tokyo: Chūbun shuppansha.

———, ed. (1975b). *Ko Teki zengaku an* 胡適禪學案. Kyoto: Chūbun shuppansha.

——— (1974a). "Zenseki kaidai 禅籍解題 (A Bibliographical Introduction to Zen Works)." In Nishitani Keiji 西谷啓治 and Yanagida Seizan, eds., *Zenke goroku* 禅家語録, no. 2, pp. 445–514. Tokyo: Chikuma shobō.

——— (1974b). *Sodō shū* (Chodangjip) 祖堂集. Kyoto: Chūbun shuppansha.

——— (1972a). "Shishū Chisen zenji sen *Hannya shingyō so* kō 資州智詵禅師撰「般若心経疏」考 (Regarding the 'Commentary to the Prajñāpāramitā Sūtra' of Chan Master Zhishen of Zizhou)." In *Hana samazama: Yamada Mumon rōshi koki kinenshū* 花さまざま：山田無文老師古稀記念集, pp. 145–177. Tokyo: Shunūsha.

——— (1972b). "Tonkō no Zenseki to Yabuki Keiki (1) 敦煌の禅籍と矢吹慶輝 (Dunhuang Zen Bibliography and Yabuki Keiki)." *Sanzō* 三蔵 54: 1–8.

——— (1972c). "The Life of Lin-chi I-hsüan." *Eastern Buddhist* 5: 70–94.

———, ed. (1971) *Shoki no Zenshi I: Ryōga shijiki, Denhōbō ki* 初期の禅史 I—楞伽師資記、伝法宝記 (Early Chan History I: *Lengqie shizi ji, Chuan fabao ji*). *Zen no goroku* 禅の語録, no. 2. Tokyo: Chikuma shobō.

——— (1970). "Daruma Zen to sono haikei 達摩禅とその背景 (Bodhidharma Chan and Its Background)." In Enichi Ochō 横超慧日, ed., *Hokugi bukkyō no kenkyū* 北魏仏教の研究 (A Study of Buddhism in the Northern Wei), pp. 115–77. Kyoto: Heirakuji shoten.

———, ed. (1969a) *Daruma no goroku: Ninyū shigyō roku* 達摩の語録: 二入四行論 (The Recorded Sayings of Bodhidharma: The *Treatise on the Two Entrances and Four Practices*). *Zen no goroku,* no. 1. Tokyo: Chikuma shobō.

——— (1969b). *Mu no tankyū: Chūgoku zen* 無の探求: 中国禅 (An Investigation of Mu: Chinese Zen). In collaboration with Umehara Takeshi 梅原猛. Tokyo: Kadogawa shoten.

——— (1967). *Shoki Zenshū shisho no kenkyū* 初期禅宗史書の研究 (Research on Early Chan Historiographical Texts). Kyoto: Hōzōkan.

——— (1963). "Denhōbōki to sono sakusha 伝法宝紀とその作者 (On the *Chuan fabao ji* and Its Compiler)." *Zengaku kenkyū* 禅学研究 53: 45–71.

——— (1961). "Zenmonkyō ni tsuite 禅門経について (A Textual Study of the *Chanmen jing*)." In *Tsukamoto hakase shoju kinen bukkyō shigaku ronshū* 塚本博士頌寿記念仏教史学論集, pp. 869–882. Kyoto: Tsukamoto hakase juju kinen kai.

Yang Zengwen 楊曾文, ed. (1996). *Shenhui heshang chanhua lu* 神會和尚禪話錄 (Records of the Chan Talks of the Venerable Shenhui). Beijing: Zhonghua shuju.

——— (1993). *Dunhuang xinben liuzu tanjing* 敦煌新本六祖壇經 (A New Manuscript of the *Platform Sūtra* of the Sixth Patriarch). Shanghai: Shanghai guji.

Yang Liansheng (1961). "The Organization of Chinese Official Historiography." In W. G. Beasley and E. G. Pulleyblank, eds., *Historians of China and Japan.* London: Oxford University Press.

Yifa (2003). *The Origins of the Buddhist Monastic Code in China: An Annotated Translation and Study of the* Chanyuan Qinggui. Honolulu: University of Hawai'i Press.

Yoshikawa Tadao 吉川忠夫 (1992). "Hai Kyū den: Tōdai no isshidaifu to bukkyō 裴休傳：唐代の一士大夫と仏教 (The Biography of Pei Xiu: A Tang Official and Buddhism)." *Tōhō gakuhō* 東方学報 64: 115–277.

Yoshioka Gihō 吉岡義豊 (1955). "*Kanpōhonnaiden* seiritsukō 漢法本内傳成立考 (Examination of the Formation of the *Inner Transmission of the Dharma in the Han*)." *Chizan gakuhō* 智山学報 3.

Zeuschner, Robert B. (1976a). "The Hsien Tsung Chi (An Early Ch'an [Zen] Buddhist Text)." *Journal of Chinese Philosophy* 3: 253–268.

——— (1976b). "A Selected Bibliography on Ch'an Buddhism in China." *Journal of Chinese Philosophy* 3: 299–311.

Zhang Guangda and Rong Xinjiang (1998). "A Concise History of the Turfan Oasis and Its Exploration." *Asia Major* (3rd series) 11(2): 13–36.

Zhang Hongxiu 張鴻修 (1995). *Zhongguo Tangmu bihua ji* 中國唐墓壁畫集 (A Collection of China's Tang Dynasty Tomb Murals). Guangzhou: Lingnan Art Publishing House.

Zhang Xihou 張錫厚, ed. (1983). *Wang Fanzhi shi jiaoji* 王梵志詩校輯 (Critical Edition of the Poems of Brahmacarya Wang). Beijing: Zhonghua shuju.

Zheng Binglin 鄭炳林 (1992). *Dunhuang beimingzan jishi* 敦煌碑銘贊輯釋 (An Annotated Compilation of Dunhuang Memorial Inscription Eulogies). Lanzhou: Gansu jiaoyu.

Zürcher, Erik (1982). "Prince Moonlight: Messianism and Eschatology in Early Chinese Buddhism." *T'oung Pao* 68(1/3): 1–75.

——— (1981). "Eschatology and Messianism in Early Chinese Buddhism." In W.L. Idema, ed., *Sinica Leidensia*, pp. 34–56. Leiden: Brill.

——— (1959). *The Buddhist Conquest of China: The Spread and Adaptation of Buddhism in Early Medieval China*. 2 vols. Leiden: Brill.

Index